WORLD PHILOSOPHY

WORLD PHILOSOPHY

Essay-Reviews
of
225 Major Works

4

1896 - 1932

Edited by
FRANK N. MAGILL

Associate Editor
IAN P. McGREAL
Professor of Philosophy
California State University
Sacramento

SALEM PRESS
Englewood Cliffs, N.J.

Library of Congress Catalog Card Number: 82-060268

Complete Set: ISBN 0-89356-325-0
Volume IV: ISBN 0-89356-329-3

First Printing

Some of the material in this work also appears in *Masterpieces of World Philosophy in Summary Form* (1961)

PRINTED IN THE UNITED STATES OF AMERICA

CHRONOLOGICAL LIST OF TITLES
IN VOLUME FOUR

WORLD PHILOSOPHY

WHAT IS ART?

Author: Leo Tolstoy (1828-1910)
Type of work: Aesthetics
First published: 1896

PRINCIPAL IDEAS ADVANCED

Art is the intentional communication of feelings.

The artist uses colors, sounds, words, or other materials to create an object which will provoke in the spectator the feeling the artist himself once had and which he intends to pass on to others.

True art is not only sincere, but infectious; the more widespread the appeal and effectiveness of the work as a means for the communication of feeling, the better the work is as art.

The highest art is that which communicates the feeling of brotherhood and the love for one's neighbor.

Tolstoy, like Plato, believed art too important to be judged in terms of art alone. Since art is capable of making men better or worse, better citizens or worse citizens, better men or worse men, the social and ethical consequences of art must be considered in judgments about art. Tolstoy denied that a work of art can be great but corrupting, artistically good but morally evil.

Tolstoy was sixty-eight when he published *What is Art?* thirty years after the completion of *War and Peace*, nineteen years after the completion of *Anna Karenina*. However, Tolstoy's long-standing concern with the nature and function of art is revealed by "Schoolboys and Art" (1861), an account he wrote of discussions with his pupils thirty-five years prior to publication of *What is Art?*

The answer Tolstoy finally found to the question "What is art?" is very simple. Art is the intentional communication of feelings. In a work of art the artist creates something which calls up, first in the artist and then in others, a feeling experienced by the artist. According to Tolstoy, the creation of a work of art proceeds along the following lines. First, the artist has an experience or feeling, such as fear, joy, grief, anger, hope. He then desires to share this feeling with others, to infect them with it, to give them this same feeling, to make them fearful, joyous, grief-stricken, angry, or hopeful. In order to communicate his feeling to his fellow men he creates a work of art, a story, a song, a poem, a play, a painting. If he is successful, if he has created a genuine work of art, his creation will give him again his original feeling, but—and this is more important—it will give other men this same kind of feeling. Art is essentially a means of communication; it is the most direct and immediate form of communication since the very feeling which led the artist to create his work of art is experienced by his audience. The artist does not merely describe his feeling of joy or grief, nor does he merely reveal or show his feeling of anger or fear; the artist shares his feelings with other men by creating something which makes them feel joy, grief, anger, or fear.

It is not very surprising that Tolstoy rejected as pseudoart much of what is usually accepted as art. Art must originate with an experience or feeling of the artist. Much pseudoart comes from insincerity, or the attempt to create a work of art which does not grow from an actual experience or feeling. The aspiring artist, lacking any feeling which could be conveyed by a genuine work of art, tries to imitate the accepted artists. In his effort to achieve recognition the artist who has nothing to communicate tries to give the public what they want by copying the popular fashions or by following the formulas learned in school. Tolstoy denies that anything created in answer to an external inducement rather than to an inner need can be genuine art.

Nevertheless, sincerity, however necessary, is not sufficient. Even if an aspiring artist is sincere, he may fail in his effort to create a work of art. The attempt to communicate the genuine feeling may be ineffective. An artist is judged not by his feelings but by his creation. Good intentions are not enough. In addition to feeling, a work of art requires adequate form. However, Tolstoy recognizes only one measure of adequate form, infectiousness. A work of art must infect the audience; it must compel the audience to feel what the artist felt. Adequate form requires individuality rather than imitative repetitiousness, brevity rather than bulkiness, clarity rather than obscurity, simplicity of expression rather than complexity of form. The adequate form of a genuine work of art is shown by the universality of its appeal. A genuine work of art does not need an interpreter. A genuine work of art is not restricted to an elite, to the happy few. A genuine work of art directly and immediately creates in other men the feelings of the artist.

Art, then, demands the adequate expression of genuine feeling. However, Tolstoy adds yet a third requirement, not a requirement which determines whether something is art, but a requirement which determines whether something is good art—morally good, worthy of support and encouragement. Tolstoy recognizes that art can be morally corrupting, that art which is good art judged by the sincerity of the artist's feeling and the successful communication of this feeling might still be undesirable. The feeling communicated is also important. If the feeling or the experience which the artist is communicating is evil or perverse or trivial or silly, it is possible for the work of art to be artistically good but morally bad. Tolstoy says that art demands sacrifices not only from the artist but also from other men. The artist is a member of society; his efforts must be supported in many ways by his fellow men. The question of what kind of art is worth the sacrifice demanded is a moral question; Tolstoy's answer to this question is clearly a moral answer. The feelings communicated by a work of art are not relevant when we are trying to decide whether it is a work of art, but they are relevant when we are trying to decide whether it is good, whether it is worthy of support and encouragement.

Tolstoy rejected orthodox Christianity; he was excommunicated by the Synod of the Russian Church in 1901 and after his death in 1910 was interred without Christian burial. Tolstoy attacked Church Christianity as a corruption of the original teaching of Jesus. The brotherhood of man, the golden rule, the turning of the other cheek, love for all men, including those who hate you, are the essential teachings Tolstoy sees in the New Testament but not in the Church. There is a very close connection between Tolstoy's views on art and on religion. Art is the handmaiden of religion. The feelings communicated by the artist to his fellow men by the work of art will in the case of the best art be feelings which unite men, which increase their love for each other. The final judgment on a work of art must be a moral judgment as well as an aesthetic judgment. Tolstoy writes, "The estimation of the value of art (or rather, of the feelings it transmits) depends on men's perception of the meaning of life; depends on what they hold to be the good and evil of life."

The connection between art and religion, the service art is expected to give religion, the consequences for art of Tolstoy's perception of the meaning of life are clearly stated in the closing paragraphs of *What is Art?* "The task for art to accomplish is to make that feeling of brotherhood and love of one's neighbor, now attained only by the best members of society, the customary feeling and instinct of all men. By evoking under imaginary conditions the feeling of brotherhood and love, religious art will train men to experience those same feelings under similar circumstances in actual life; it will lay in the souls of men the rails along which the actions of those whom art thus educates will naturally pass. And universal art, by uniting the most different people in one common feeling by destroying separation, will educate people to union and will show them, not by reason but by life itself, the joy of universal union reaching beyond the bounds set by life."

Tolstoy saw in the art of the Middle Ages an example of true art. In that period religion provided a basis common to the artists and the mass of the people, so that the feelings experienced by the artist could be communicated to the mass of the people. This true art, shared by the whole community, ended when the people who rewarded and directed art lost their religious belief. The universality of the art of the Middle Ages was followed by a split between the art of the upper classes and the masses of the people. The development of an exclusive art, incomprehensible to most men, seriously weakened and almost destroyed art itself. The subject matter of art became impoverished; the only feelings acceptable for communication were pride, discontent, and sexual desire. The artist became a professional, living by his art, creating counterfeits of art rather than genuine works of art. Critics, perverted but self-confident, took away from plain men the valuation of art.

Genuine art, Tolstoy argues, needs no critics. If the work succeeds in transmitting the feeling of the artist, there is nothing for the critic to do. If the work fails to transmit the feeling of the artist, there is nothing the critic can do. The final perverted and perverting consequence Tolstoy ascribes to the reduction of art to an amusement for the upper classes is the establishment of art schools. Tolstoy, a teacher as well as an artist, denies that a school can evoke feeling in a man, or teach him how to manifest his feeling in a way which will transmit his feeling to others. Art schools destroy the capacity to produce real art in those who have the misfortune to enter them; they do nothing more than train imitators of artists, professionals who produce on demand the counterfeits of art which amuse the perverted upper classes, provide the critics with an excuse for their activity, and debase the taste of the masses.

If there is any danger that admiration for the artistic achievements of the author of *War and Peace* and *Anna Karenina* will lead to uncritical acceptance of Tolstoy's theories about the nature and purpose of art, it is more than balanced by the danger that contempt for Tolstoy's critical judgments will lead to uncritical rejection of these theories. It is quite possible that judgments of Tolstoy's point of view as perverse and even stupid (as in F. M. Cornford's introduction to Book IX of Plato's *Republic*) are caused by Tolstoy's judgments on particular works of art rather than by his theories as to the nature and purpose of art. *War and Peace, Anna Karenina,* and in fact all of his own work except the stories, *God Sees the Truth but Waits* and *A Prisoner of the Caucasus,* fall, in Tolstoy's eyes, into the category of bad art. Included with the Psalms, the writings of the Jewish prophets, the *Iliad* and *Odyssey, Don Quixote,* and *The Pickwick Papers* as examples of genuine art are Dickens' *A Christmas Carol, Uncle Tom's Cabin,* and Millet's drawing "The Man with the Hoe." Tolstoy praises as true art Pushkin's short stories and poems, but calls *Boris Godunov* "a cold, brain-spun work" produced under the influence of false criticism. Sophocles, Euripides, Aeschylus, Aristophanes, Dante, Milton, Shakespeare, Goethe, Raphael, Michelangelo, Bach, Beethoven, Wagner—these are among the artists judged and found wanting by Tolstoy. Michelangelo's "Last Judgment" is called absurd; Beethoven's piano sonata in A major, Opus 101 (Hammerclavier) is bad art because it "artificially evoked obscure, almost unhealthy, excitement"; Beethoven's Ninth Symphony is bad art because it neither transmits the highest religious feeling nor unites all men in one common feeling; from *Hamlet* Tolstoy received "that peculiar suffering which is caused by false imitations of works of art." Baudelaire is criticized on two counts: the feelings transmitted are "evil and very base" and these feelings are expressed with "eccentricity and lack of clearness," in fact with "premeditated obscurity." Baudelaire is judged lacking in "naïveté, sincerity, and simplicity," but overflowing with "artificiality, forced originality, and self-assurance."

Tolstoy directs his most detailed and extensive criticism in *What is Art?*

against Wagner's operas. He describes a performance of *Siegfried*. Tolstoy calls this a "model work of counterfeit art so gross as to be even ridiculous." He was unable to sit through the entire performance and "escaped from the theatre with a feeling of repulsion." Tolstoy sees in *Siegfried* almost everything he detests in pseudoart. It would be incomprehensible to a peasant with unperverted taste; it is accepted because fashionable by the "cream of the cultured upper classes"; it requires a great deal of wasted labor; it provides the art critics with an excuse for their activity; and it perverts and destroys the capacity to be infected by genuine art.

It would be a mistake to judge Tolstoy's view on art by the examples he chooses. Tolstoy himself says that he does not attach great importance to his selection since he believes he is among those whose taste has been perverted by false training. Since the examples appear to be chosen to illustrate or explain Tolstoy's theory, they are less important than the theory itself.

Others have agreed that art is the language of emotions, that art expresses or communicates feelings. But the distinctive feature of Tolstoy's theory is his claim that the actual experience is communicated by art. We do not merely recognize that the poem is an expression of grief; we do not merely recognize that the author was moved by an authentic feeling of grief. If the poem is a genuine work of art, we grieve. The connection between art and life cannot be made closer. Tolstoy, like Plato, denies the autonomy of art, the uniqueness of aesthetic experience.—*J.L.*

Pertinent Literature

Jahn, Gary R. "The Aesthetic Theory of Leo Tolstoy's *What is Art?*," in *Journal of Aesthetics and Art Criticism*. XXXIV, no. 1 (Fall, 1975), pp. 59-65.

Gary R. Jahn correctly perceives that Leo Tolstoy's theory of art is built upon a double foundation. On one side is an aesthetic theory by which Tolstoy seeks to demonstrate the difference between art and non-art, and between art in general and art in the narrow sense of the word. On another side is a moral theory developed by Tolstoy to evaluate the quality of admitted works of art. When Tolstoy speaks of "good art" as opposed to "bad art," the terms "good" and "bad" are intended strictly in a moral sense. Although a work judged by Tolstoy as bad art would qualify as genuine art, it would be regarded as having a morally bad effect on its public.

Historically, Tolstoy's moral theory has not been able to withstand the devastating objections leveled by the critics, leading many thinkers to dismiss his theory of art as a whole. Jahn, however, following a path first suggested by Israel Knox, shows that it is possible to reject the moral component of Tolstoy's theory of art and yet retain the aesthetic component. In the present essay Jahn examines three basic assumptions underlying Tolstoy's aesthetic theory, clarifies Tolstoy's terminology, and makes a solid case for the view that Tolstoy's aesthetic theory deserves serious reevaluation.

Tolstoy's first assumption is that art is a form of communication. By "communication" he means both the process of *expression*, whereby an artist's subjective experience is transposed into a form which makes it accessible to others, and the process of *infection*, whereby the perceiver of a work of art actually assimilates and himself experiences what the artist has expressed. That art is a form of communication is an assumption certainly not unique to Tolstoy; and while it may be challenged on various grounds, it does explain why the value of a work of art depends, at least in part, upon an audience.

The second assumption is that what art communicates is most properly described by the term "feeling." It is here that Tolstoy's aesthetic theory differs, in particular, from that of Eugène Véron. Whereas Véron regards art as an intended communication of emotions, Tolstoy maintains that while art includes emotions it may go beyond them as well. Art encompasses a broad range of human experiences, not being limited to emotional states such as anger, fear, sorrow, and happiness. If a relevant distinction needs to be made, it is not between emotions and other feelings, but between *feelings* and *thoughts*.

According to Tolstoy, through speech people communicate thoughts; by art they communicate feelings. By "thoughts" he means anything which is objectively the same for all persons: mathematical calculations, matters of accepted historical fact, observable natural occurrences, and the like. By "feelings" he means any human experience which does not fall into the category of thought. Thus, in addition to emotions, feelings include impressions, sensations, intuitions, and general attitudes—in short, any experience defined by its inherent subjectivity.

The third assumption is that two main categories of art are distinguishable: (1) art in the broad sense, which incorporates all communications of feelings, and (2) art in the narrow sense, which includes only those works that communicate a certain type of feelings—namely, those stemming from the "religious perception" of the artist. Jahn accurately notes that Tolstoy is primarily concerned with the smaller category, what he refers to as "art in the full meaning of the word."

The greatest difficulty in understanding Tolstoy on this latter point is that in *What is Art?* he never adequately defines what he means by "religious preception." Jahn explains that if Tolstoy is using that notion in some religious sense, then the assumption would seem to be arbitrary and without basis. However, by drawing upon one of Tolstoy's later works, "What Is Religion, and Wherein Lies Its Essence?" Jahn goes on to show how Tolstoy defines "religious perception" basically as a person's understanding of himself and of his relation to the universe which surrounds him. Art, in the full meaning of the word, therefore, comes to be envisioned as a communication of those feelings which reflect such traditionally important human concerns as "Who am I?," "Why am I here?," and "How am I related to the world around me?" Interpreted in this way, Tolstoy's third assumption appears to be neither arbitrary nor radically contrary to common sense.

Insofar as Tolstoy's three assumptions are at all reasonable, his aesthetic theory warrants further consideration. Upon reflection it does seem, in one way or another, that art is a form of communication, that its subject matter is all subjective experience, and that in its more definitive sense it pertains to those aspects of human experience which traditionally have been judged as having greatest importance.

Macy, John Albert. "Tolstoi's Moral Theory of Art," in *Tolstoy and the Critics: Literature and Aesthetics*. Edited by Holley Gene Duffield and Manuel Bilsky. Chicago: Scott, Foresman and Company, 1965, pp. 66-78.

This essay originally appeared in *Century Magazine*, Volume LXII (1901), two years after the publication of Leo Tolstoy's *What is Art?* Everyone acknowledges that Tolstoy's theory of art has a moral as well as an aesthetic dimension. John Albert Macy contends that because these two aspects are so interwoven, to separate them even for purposes of criticism or evaluation would be to distort the meaning and intention of Tolstoy's doctrine. According to Macy, Tolstoy's theory of art is necessarily to be understood as a *moral* theory of art. If Tolstoy teaches anything, it is that all art is worthless which leads away from morality. The question is: How satisfactory is Tostoy's view?

Tolstoy defines art as the communication of feeling. Art consists in the artist's calling up in himself a feeling once experienced and conveying this feeling in such a way that others are "infected" by that same feeling and enabled to experience it themselves. Genuine art, then, prevents isolation and effects a common brotherhood of man because the artist and all those to whom his art communicates become partners in a common experience. True art moves away from the personal toward the universal, away from a purely individual consciousness toward a universal consciousness. A key step in Tolstoy's analysis is that the "universal" is represented in any given race and period by the prevailing religious consciousness. Hence the quality of art is measured by the degree to which it communicates this religious consciousness.

To sum up, genuine art is the communication of feeling as a result of the contagiousness or infectiousness which unites artist and spectator in a common experience. The stronger the contagion, the better the art. However, when it comes to describing the content of art, namely, the feelings being communicated, Tolstoy's statements about "good" art and "bad" art are intended strictly in a moral sense. To make good art, the feelings communicated must be good. It fcllows, therefore, that the value or worth of any piece of art ultimately is determined by the moral quality of the art content. To the extent that a culture's morality is manifest by the religious consciousness of the day, it also follows that the best art is that which has as its subject matter the religious consciousness of the time.

Macy draws attention to at least three problems with Tolstoy's theory. The first pertains to Tolstoy's denial that beauty provides a standard for art. Traditionally the value of art has been regarded as the extent to which it awakens and preserves a sense of beauty. Tolstoy, however, views the worth of art strictly as a means to improving the moral quality of life. Thus his final standard for judging art is morality, not beauty. The reason he excludes beauty from the realm of aesthetics is because he likens beauty to pleasure. His argument runs as follows: beauty is only another name for selfish pleasure, or personal preference; there is no common standard of pleasure or beauty, since what I find beautiful is what pleases me, and what you find beautiful is what pleases you; therefore, beauty cannot be a standard for judging art.

Macy points out in rebuttal that Tolstoy fails to consider the many different types of pleasure, and that aesthetic pleasure certainly is not identical with all pleasures. This failure is in itself enough to falsify the equation of beauty with pleasure, but there are even more crucial problems with Tolstoy's account. Tolstoy seems not to understand that individual preferences are fundamentally expressions of personal values which have been generated by subjective emotional and intellectual experiences. Personal preferences reflect value judgments which, like all judgments, have a built-in subjectivity; but to dismiss beauty from the realm of aesthetics just because it involves personal preference would be tantamount to dismissing all thought and experience, since personal preference emanates from thought and experience. Finally, Macy observes that Tolstoy's argument against using beauty as a standard of art works equally well against using morality as a standard, since Tolstoy's own theory is in essence an expression of his own preference, his own sense of value.

A second misconception of Tolstoy is that art is *the means* for expanding religious consciousness and developing community life and brotherhood—in short, for improving the morality of society. It is one thing, says Macy, to demand that art not hinder morality; if art is immoral, we can sympathize with Tolstoy's effort to regenerate art and save morality. But it is something else entirely to expect art to shoulder the burden of sustaining and revitalizing the moral character of society. Tolstoy has mistaken the nature of art when he binds it to the task of morality.

Third, in defining art as the communication of feeling, Tolstoy mistakenly assumes that any human being can experience the expressed feelings of another. When discussing the question of who is qualified to judge what is good art, he remarks that "good art is always intelligible to everyone." More specifically, he contends that the everyday worker, the toiler in the field or factory, is as perfectly capable and truly qualified as anyone to judge the worth of any piece of art. Macy argues that such is plainly not the case. He claims that art cannot infect someone with a feeling which that person has never had before. The capacity for communication of feeling depends on the previous experiences of the spectator. A person with wider experiences has a greater capacity for reexperiencing what the artist expresses. Cultivated people who have seen much, felt much, worked much, and tried much are simply that much more qualified to judge the value of art, because they are more capable of experiencing the feeling which the artist himself experienced. The conclusion which Tolstoy should have reached is that any work of art can mean something different to different people, according to their different temperaments, past experiences, and attitudes toward life.—*R.A.S.*

ADDITIONAL RECOMMENDED READING

Daniels, Charles B. "Tolstoy and Corrupt Art," in *Journal of Aesthetic Education.* VIII, no. 4 (October, 1974), pp. 41-49. Daniels criticizes Tolstoy's theory of art first by showing that on the basis of Tolstoy's view the true test of art is universal understanding (as a result of the communication of feelings by a universally understood sign which is the work of art), then by posing the following dilemma. Either you can agree with Tolstoy, in which case you must condemn nearly all the classical works in the fine arts as aesthetically and morally corrupt; or you can acknowledge that those same classical works are aesthetically worthwhile at least to some people, in which case you must reject Tolstoy's doctrine that aesthetic merit lies in the success with which a work of art fulfills its role as a universal communicative sign. The manner in which Daniels develops this dilemma is most convincing.

Duffield, Holley Gene and Manuel Bilsky, eds. *Tolstoy and the Critics: Literature and Aesthetics.* Chicago: Scott, Foresman and Company, 1965. The book begins with some short selections from the works of Aristotle, Sir Philip Sidney, Eugène Véron, Cleanth Brooks, and M. H. Abrams, thereby providing a framework for understanding Tolstoy's theory of art. Excerpts from Tolstoy's own writings give access to the crucial aspects of his theory. The major portion of the book is a series of essays by eminent philosophers who directly or indirectly defend, attack, and explain Tolstoy's main ideas on art and literature.

Simmons, Ernest J. "What Is Art?," in *Introduction to Tolstoy's Writings.* Chicago: University of Chicago Press, 1968, pp. 118-134. For students and interested readers this essay provides a useful introduction to the central themes of Tolstoy's *What is Art?* Simmons gives added perspective to Tolstoy's theory of art by drawing upon statements from some of Tolstoy's other nonliterary works, including observations on theater, painting, music, and sculpture, as well as literature.

THE WILL TO BELIEVE

Author: William James (1842-1910)
Type of work: Ethics, philosophy of religion
First published: 1897

PRINCIPAL IDEAS ADVANCED

Decisions between hypotheses proposed to our belief are genuine options when they are living (of vital concern to us), forced (no third alternative is possible), and momentous (presenting a unique opportunity of considerable importance).

Whenever a genuine option cannot be settled on intellectual grounds, it is right and necessary to settle it according to our passional inclinations.

The religious option concerning the belief in God is a genuine option which promises most to the person who has the passional need to take the world religiously.

Men possess free wills which are not determined; determinism—the theory that decisions are causally determined—fails to account for the sense of human freedom.

Now a classic, this work takes its title from the first ten separate essays written at different times. Originally presented as lectures to academic clubs, these essays express "a tolerably definite philosophic attitude" which James named *radical empiricism*—an ordinary man's empiricism which takes experience as it comes, "seeing" even matters-of-fact as subject to possible future reinterpretation; yet radical for its rejection of dogmatic monism in the face of the obvious plurality of the things making up the universe. James also wanted to make a case for the right of men to believe some moral and religious postulates for whose certainty the evidence can never fully be on hand. Sympathetic to a wide range of philosophical viewpoints, James sought to give intellectual significance to the role of the emotions in specified contexts. He also criticized the prevailing academic opinion that only scientific methods can produce an adequate understanding of the human condition.

The first four essays ("The Will to Believe," "Is Life Worth Living?," "The Sentiment of Rationality," and "Reflex Action and Theism") are concerned directly with religious problems. Two others ("The Dilemma of Determinism" and "The Moral Philosopher and the Moral Life") also give some attention to religious aspects of ethical problems. A final essay ("What Psychical Research Has Accomplished") defends scholars who inquire into the possibility that mental life may involve phenomena which escape our ordinary scientific criteria. The remaining essays ("Great Men and Their Environment," "The Importance of Individuals," and "On Some Hegelisms") show James's concern to find commonsense facts philosophically interesting; to criticize some unexamined assumptions of rationalism; and to resist the spread of absolutist and totalist theories which swallow up the individual in an "environment," overlook human differences by stressing only similarities, and ignore diversity in emphasizing unity.

Three broad types of subject matter receive treatment in James's book. These are the nature and motives of philosophizing, the justification of religious and moral beliefs, and the nature of the moral enterprise. A common theme also runs through what would otherwise be a collection of unrelated essays. This theme is the problem of the relation of evidence to specific human beliefs. If the book has a positive thesis, it is that men may rightfully hold certain religious, moral, and metaphysical beliefs even when conclusive evidence for their adequacy is absent. James resists the positivistic tendency of his age to assume that scientific methods will prove able to decide all important questions about existence. Similarly, he expresses criticism of any extreme rationalistic reliance on logic as the sole criterion of philosophical adequacy. There are some beliefs which are truths-in-the-making. "And often enough our faith beforehand in an uncertified result *is the only thing that makes the result come true*," he writes. One comes to understand that James is moved to philosophical activity by a desire to justify the rightness of certain beliefs— that God exists, that men possess free will, that moral effort represents a genuinely objective worthiness, that pain and evil cannot justify suicide, and that practical as well as theoretical needs ought to influence one's philosophical outlook.

The book's historical influence partly stems from the nature of the problems addressed by the author. Most of these problems are close to ordinary human experience. James also reassures those thinkers who, unconvinced that a completed metaphysical system is really possible, want to resist making a forced choice between philosophical certainty and philosophical skepticism. Philosophical argument can take place fruitfully somewhere on this side of certainty, according to James. Yet such argument need not lapse into arbitrariness. Logic is a subservient instrument. It is subject to the felt needs of religious, moral, and practical demands. James argues that a qualified moral idealism need not lead to sentimentalism in escaping the twin threats of pessimism and nihilism. Some philosophical viewpoints are relatively more adequate than others even though no one viewpoint can hope to exhaust the whole domain of reality. Such a generous spirit animates James's essays that even critics who are unpersuaded by some of the arguments nevertheless recognize in them the evidences of a rare and gifted philosophical mind.

The book's opening essay is crucial for the broad way it sketches the nature, purposes, and possibilities of philosophizing. Written in 1879, "The Sentiment of Rationality" states convictions which are presupposed in James's more restricted discussions of topics in religious and moral philosophy. A number of basic questions caused James to write this essay. What is the philosophic quest really about? What are the conditions which any philosophy must meet if it is to be accepted? How can one know that the philosophic demand for a peculiar kind of rationality has been satisfactorily met?

Philosophic pursuit of a rational conception of existence marked by universality and extensiveness succeeds whenever a feeling of intellectual "ease, peace, rest" is the result. Any adequate philosophy must satisfy two kinds of human distress. One is theoretical—the intellectual concern to form a general conception of the universe. The other is practical—the moral and religious desire to include men's passional natures in any philosophical consideration of how men are to act and what they should believe.

Two cravings gnaw at the philosopher. Intellectual simplification is always one philosophic need. Simplification requires reduction of the world's numerous details to fewer significant abstractions which stress similarities. Theoretical life would be an impossibility without such abstractions. The other need is the clear demand for recognition of the perceived differences among things. Philosophic rationality results only when each of these competing impulses receives serious consideration. James insists that philosophizing involves a continuous, yet never fully successful, synthesizing of these two cravings—a mark of whose successful handling is the feeling that some original puzzlement no longer proves irritating to the mind. As an activity, philosophizing must involve the whole man. Philosophizing must therefore often give way to hosts of other intellectual quests since its own unique function is to discover a general picture of "the hang of things."

An important conviction operates at this point in James's development. It is that any metaphysical conception must remain open to future possible theoretical anxiety. Man's need of a philosophic view of the nature of things results only in partial and temporary satisfaction. Any instance of the feeling of rationality can itself founder on the shoals of the question about its justifiability. Even if the world *is* a certain way, it *might* yet be otherwise. Thus the worry about "nonentity" arises, named by James "the parent of the philosophic craving in its subtilist and profoundest sense." Through awareness of a possible other state of affairs, men can lose the feeling of rationality once gained. No single logically consistent system can still man's theoretical demands when he is faced by the query: Why just this sort of world and no other? "Every generation will produce its Job, its Hamlet, its Faust, or its Sartor Resartus." Mystical ecstasy can realize the psychological equivalent of the feeling of rationality when logic proves inadequate. Yet "empiricism will be the ultimate philosophy," for even the mysteriousness of existence depends on an irreducible fact about a universe which is dissatisfying to our theoretical demands.

Exclusive concern with the theoretical impulse leads men to skepticism or to a sense of wonder about the universe. One or the other arises when a completed metaphysical system begins to wane. Does the matter end here?

Denying that it does, James argues that now the practical life acquires a heightened rational significance. Practical demands play a role in one's choice of a philosophy when systems exist whose logical methods are equally sound. Men's belief that their wills can influence the future must receive justification in any important philosophical system. Men can adopt that philosophy which most fully satisfies certain moral and aesthetic requirements of human nature.

The better philosophy is always relevant to men's expectations about the future. Yet there is no one, final, "better" philosophy. For example, a philosophy which retains the notion of substance will remain a perennial contender for human acceptance. Similarly, idealism will remain a challenging possibility for thinkers requiring an identification of the universe with our personal selves, materialism for thinkers wanting an escape from selves. James concludes that temperamental differences are important in the quest after the sentiment of rationality. To be humanly acceptable, a philosophy must limit moral skepticism and satisfy men's belief that they "count" in the creation of a future world. According to James, no philosophy can succeed which ignores the practical craving after a world which is partly responsive to men's future expectations, their human faiths, and their commonsense conviction that moral striving genuinely counts for something.

Take the question: Does God exist? James rejects the agnostic argument that one ought never to hold beliefs for which conclusive evidence is lacking. Reasonable persons seek both to avoid error and to attain the maximum amount of truth. Yet there may be questions such that neither "yes" nor "no" replies are justified by existing evidence but to which men may rightfully give an affirmative belief-response. James insists that the matter of God's existence is such a question, as are questions about the importance of the individual, the value of life versus suicide, and the possible existence of human free will. *How* men treat such questions is important. James argues that men may believe certain statements for reasons of the heart when conclusive evidence is lacking and the beliefs help to initiate future discoveries of a practical kind. This thesis forces James to consider the problem of the relation of evidence to belief.

Belief involves a willingness to act on some hypothesis. James insists that any proposition may serve as a hypothesis—though he is not always clear about the form of such a hypothesis. Ordinarily, a proposition like "This litmus paper is blue" is not considered a hypothesis because it lacks a proper hypothetical form. A proposition of the form: "If this litmus paper is put into a given solution, it will turn red," is a hypothesis capable of some testing provided the proper details are supplied. But James had in mind statements of moral and religious belief whose adoption by men might result in bringing about a desired truth. One may help to make another person's attitude friendly towards himself by adopting a believing attitude toward the statement: "X is friendly towards me." Belief in some propositions is a requirement of their future possible verification. According to James, religious beliefs may often be of this kind. Religious beliefs involve one in assenting to statements for which conclusive evidence is absent. James wants to defend the right of men to hold such beliefs if they meet specified conditions. A man has an option to believe certain hypotheses in religion and morals if the hypotheses are living rather than dead, forced rather than avoidable, and momentous rather than trivial.

What makes a hypothesis "living," "forced," and "momentous" is its relation to a thinker's interests. The test here seems to be predominantly psychological and cultural, for an individual's interests are what they are, however caused. James admits that not all men will find the same hypothesis living, forced, and momentous—giving the example of a Christian confronted with the command: "Be a Theosophist or be a Mohammedan." Yet James insists that the God-hypothesis confronts men with a genuine "option," meaning that such an option is living, momentous, and forced. He argues that the agnostic who neither affirms nor denies God's existence has already decided against such an existence. The agnostic decides to give up all hope of winning a possible truth in order to avoid a possible error in a situation for which evidence must in principle be inconclusive. The agnostic's right to disbelieve in this case is no greater than the religious man's right to believe.

A critic may say at this point that James's way of arguing may encourage men to choose their beliefs by an individualistic criterion of psychological comfort—something on the order of the command: "Believe what you need to believe." James warns his readers that he is countering academic people's disregard of the passional aspects in human decision-making and that the right to believe occurs only in a matter which "cannot by its nature be decided on intellectual grounds." James apparently thinks the genuine religious option concerns the *thatness* of God's existence rather than the choice of an existing institutional means for expressing one's decision to believe in God's existence. Yet he does seem to argue, on the other hand, that those who are agnostics choose to treat the God-hypothesis as a dead one. Moral and religious options are such that, if the believer takes an affirmative stance regarding a belief, they promise that the better aspects will win out in the universe and a man will be better off for believing. One might put even the God-hypothesis in a psychological form: "If you believe that God exists, even now you will be benefited." Yet it is not clear that James would wish to regard the force of the central religious hypothesis as purely psychological.

In discussing features of the moral landscape, James once again shows his distrust of intellectual abstractions and generalizations. He is convinced philosophers can never produce an airtight, finished moral system. Nor can moral philosophers dogmatically solve all issues in advance of actual situations. Yet James openly defends two general moral notions. One is that human demands and obligations are coextensive. The second is that men have a right to believe they are free. Any genuinely moral philosopher places his own cherished ideals and norms in the scales of rational judgment even as he realizes that no one standard measure is attainable which will apply to all occasions. The moral philosopher holds no privileged status for deciding concrete instances of conflict in human demands. James insists that the moral philosopher "only knows that if he makes a bad mistake the cries of the wounded will soon inform him of the fact."

James advances the thesis about coextensiveness of demands and obligations in the essay "The Moral Philosopher and the Moral Life." There are no intrinsically "bad" demands, since demands are simply what they are. Without them, there could be no basis of moral life. Here James seeks to give due recognition to biological and psychological facts. He wants an "ethical republic." Terms like "good" and "bad"—whose meanings constitute the metaphysical function of moral philosophizing—refer to objects of feeling and desire. Only "a mind which feels them" can realize moral relations and moral law. James insists that the moral philosopher must "vote for the richer universe"—that which can accommodate the widest possible range of human wants. Yet James fails to make clear how the philosopher may determine what should pass as the richer universe if all demands have equal status in principle. On this issue James seems to appeal to intuition, for he argues that "the nobler thing *tastes* better"—indicating that he recognized that some demands are more appealing than others.

The most suggestive essay concerned with a moral issue is "The Dilemma of Determinism," in which James argues that, though no proof is possible, man does possess free will. This is a unique defense of indeterminism which presupposes a metaphysical position; namely, that the universe is in reality a pluriverse containing objective possibilities of novelty. The problem which concerns him is that of the relation of freedom to chance rather than of freedom to cause. "Chance" is a relative word which tells one nothing about that of which it is predicated. "Its origin is in a certain fashion negative: it escapes, and says, Hands off! coming, when it comes, as a free gift, or not at all." James disliked the contemporary distinction between "hard" and "soft" forms of determinism. The "soft" form of determinism argues that causality is quite compatible with responsible action and ethical judicability. What James wanted to discover is the metaphysical view necessary to determinism. He concluded it is a view which takes possibilities never actualized as mere illusions. James insists that determinism is unable to give adequate account of human feelings about possibility—the feeling that the universe contains genuine choices or alternatives, objectively real risks. Indeterminism insists that future volitions can be ambiguous, and "indeterminate future volitions *do* mean chance."

According to James, determinism results in an unavoidable dilemma. It must lead either to pessimism or to subjectivism. Men share a universe which daily calls for judgments of regret about some things happening in it. But if events are strictly necessitated, they can never be otherwise than what they are. Taken seriously, human regrets suggest that though some feature of the universe could not have been different, yet it would have been better if it were different. This reasoning leads to pessimism. James argues that men can give up pessimism only if they jettison their judgments of regret. Men can perhaps regard regrettable incidents—including the most atrocious murders—as teleological links in a chain leading to some higher good. Murder and treachery then cease to be evils. But a definite price must be paid for such a teleological optimism. The original judgments of regret were themselves necessitated, on the determinist's position. Some other judgments should have existed in their place. "But as they are necessitated, nothing else *can* be in their place." This means that whether men are pessimists or optimists, their judgments are necessitated.

One escape from this pessimism-optimism impasse is to adopt subjectivism. The practical impulse to realize some objective moral good can be subordinated to a theoretical development of an understanding of what is involved in goodness and evil. The facts of the universe can be valued only insofar as they produce consciousness in men. Subjectivism emphasizes the knowledge of good and evil in order to underscore the nature of human involvement. Experience rather than the objective goodness or badness of experience becomes the crucial factor for any moral subjectivism. But the indeterminist must reject subjectivism because it fails to do justice to men's empirical notions of the genuinely *moral* significance of human experiences. In addition, subjectivism leads to mere sentimentality and romanticism.

James concludes that common sense informs men that objective right and wrong involve real limits. Practical reason insists that "conduct, and not sensibility, is the ultimate fact for our recognition." Only indeterminism can make sense out of this practical insistence on objective right and wrong. Yet indeterminism does not argue that Providence is necessarily incompatible with free will. In an example involving chess, James shows how Providence can be like a master chess player who, though knowing the ultimate outcome of the game, must face unpredictable moves by an amateur player. On the other hand, James concludes that indeterminism gives men a special view—"It gives us a pluralistic, restless universe, in which no single point of view can ever take in the whole scene." James concludes that men have a right to be indeterminists and to believe in free will even in the absence of a persuasively final proof.—*W.T.D.*

PERTINENT LITERATURE

Madden, Edward H. "Introduction," in William James's *The Will to Believe and Other Essays in Popular Philosophy*. Edited by Frederick H. Burkhardt. Cambridge, Massachusetts: Harvard University Press, 1979.

This volume, the sixth in a series entitled "The Works of William James," uses modern critical techniques to provide a definitive edition of the collected essays published by William James in 1897. Edward H. Madden's Introduction discusses all ten of them, showing how they advanced James's philosophy and how his critics responded.

Although these articles were prepared for diverse occasions between 1879 and 1896, Madden finds their unifying theme in James's conviction that all intellectual activity is affected by volition and emotion. Thought serves desire and need: willing directs thinking and at times even feeling. Madden notes that James explores these motifs in a free and often breezy style, but not without the care that makes serious philosophy. Thus, the articles are "popular" in the sense that James intended them to deal with fundamental topics that concern us all: for example, good and evil, freedom, and religious faith.

Madden thinks James's essays must be understood in terms of the author's ambivalence toward science. It is true that James himself was a scientist, but he was also skeptical about claims made by some of his scientific colleagues, particularly those who would condemn as illegitimate any beliefs for which sufficient evidence is lacking. According to Madden, James does not deny that one can obtain objective conclusions from critical inquiry, but he does defend a person's right to believe what needs require, if after consulting available evidence the outcome remains inconclusive.

Such a position drew criticism because some philosophers suspected that James's view would close off inquiry, thus legitimating belief without a continuing unbiased search for evidence. Granting that James may not have done full justice to such criticism, Madden does not ascribe this possible oversight to some presumed tendency of James's to believe too much too soon. In fact, Madden asserts, James had the greatest difficulty making up his mind on any issue.

In addition to discussing "The Will to Believe" (1896), Madden calls special attention to "The Dilemma of Determinism" (1884) and "The Moral Philosopher and the Moral Life" (1891), two articles he takes to be among James's most significant. The central concern of the former is whether the future is open or closed, whether possibilities are concretely real or illusory. Putting the issue in this way, Madden believes, was a sound move for James to make in defending human freedom against determinism. Unfortunately, James did not carry the analysis far enough. As Madden sees it, he failed to develop an adequate theory of human agency to go with his open-ended universe. James goes on to defend the reality of a finite God, and Madden finds that possibility intriguing. However, Madden also believes that some of James's early critics were correct: things come out too neatly when James makes divine power both limited enough to excuse God from responsibility for evil and yet sufficient to guarantee the ultimate significance of moral values.

As for "The Moral Philosopher and the Moral Life," Madden states that

James's ethical theory aims at the maximum fulfillment of human desire. James rejects, however, the classical utilitarian emphasis on pleasure and advocates instead a strenuous mood that battles evil sacrificially and heroically. Madden notes John Dewey's attraction to James's conviction that moral theory cannot be fully developed in advance of paying attention to actual desires and circumstances. Nevertheless, Madden also sees problems in James's position. In particular, although James argues that our sense of the good must be constructed and revised in light of actual needs and circumstances, it seems to Madden that James's fundamental and apparently unchangeable commitment to maximize everyone's satisfaction may not be consistent with his empirical orientation.

Smith, John E. *The Spirit of American Philosophy*. New York: Oxford University Press, 1963.

This classic study interprets the philosophies of Charles S. Peirce, Josiah Royce, John Dewey, and Alfred North Whitehead, as well as the thought of William James. Attempting to locate a common American spirit among these varied thinkers, John E. Smith finds it in the belief that thought not only interprets life theoretically but also directs it practically. His chapter on James, subtitled "Purpose, Effort, and the Will to Believe," relates this thesis to James's analysis of human experience.

Smith acknowledges James's thought to be far less simple than a first glance may suggest, but he also indicates that James should have formulated his central tenets with greater rigor. Nevertheless, James's philosophy is distinctively American because it underscores the vitality and variety of experience and accepts the challenge of adventure in an open-ended existence. According to James, everyone has a right, even a duty, to be guided by personal experience. For James, Smith adds, human plans and purposes are dominant forces. We use them to discover and to create a rational world where we can feel at home as much as possible.

A consistent voluntarism, Smith believes, characterizes James's philosophy, but an emphasis on the active elements in thought and feeling is not without difficulty as it is illustrated in James's "will to believe." Although no idea of James's, or of American philosophy generally, is as well known, neither has any concept been so frequently misinterpreted. If the fault does not lie entirely with James, at least some of it does, and Smith sifts the wheat from the chaff.

James's accent on the will left him vulnerable to criticism that it was acceptable for belief to be arbitrary. Thus, Smith agrees that James's second thought—namely, to speak instead of "the right to believe"—would have served him better. A right involves not only what one may do; it usually entails boundaries and responsibilities as well. In fact, Smith asserts, James did limit the right to believe, not perfectly, perhaps, but better than some criticisms imply. Smith notes James's provisions that the will or right to believe should come into play only if one faces an option that is live, forced, and momentous, and only if reason alone cannot give a final verdict. Then he draws out some significant characteristics of the actual situations in which James would think a choice is essential to determine belief.

Some of James's examples do not ring true, Smith argues; but James is on the right track in holding that there are times when belief is a necessary condition for having experience that can provide convincing evidence. Knowing whether God is real or whether it is valid to say that "love never fails," Smith suggests, are two examples where James's account is reliable. Unless we are willing to consider the possiblility that God exists or that love never fails, it is unlikely that we will ever be able to have the experience that could support such beliefs.

James also argues that belief is sometimes crucial for creating facts as well as for discovering them. Belief in oneself or in what another person is going to do is often critical in directing action. James's position does not deny that some situations may involve limits that we cannot control. Still, the will can be decisive in determining what possibilities will become actualized in a particular set of circumstances.

More carefully than James did himself, one must distinguish between cases where belief is necessary to discover facts and where belief is necessary to create them. In addition, one must recognize that such circumstances are not the only ones, although undeniably they are correctly described by James as momentous. Appreciation of these limits, Smith argues, goes far toward making James's analysis intelligible and trustworthy.

Davis, Stephen T. *Faith, Skepticism, and Evidence: An Essay in Religious Epistemology.* Lewisburg, Pennsylvania: Bucknell University Press, 1978.

Stephen T. Davis does not provide an overview of William James's essays as Edward H. Madden's article (see above) has done; nor does he share John E. Smith's concern to detect what is distinctively American in James's thought. Instead, utilizing the logical techniques of analytic philosophy, Davis probes James's essays, particularly "The Will to Believe," to show how those writings clarify the nature of religious faith and the possible justifications for religious belief. He shares Smith's appraisal: If correctly interpreted, James's argument in "The Will to Believe" is sound. Davis goes into the greater detail, however, in applying James's thought to issues concerning evidence and religious belief.

James wonders whether it is ever rational to believe a proposition on other than intellectual grounds. As Davis sees it, in asking whether one is ever intellectually justified in believing a nonevident proposition, James's aim is to defend the rationality of religious belief, at least in certain circumstances, although his argument is not restricted to religion.

Later philosophers have seen an important distinction in "The Will to Believe." James, they argue, did not notice sufficiently that there are two main arguments in the essay. Following Gail Kennedy, Davis refers to them as "the will to believe argument" and "the right to believe argument."

The first holds that faith is sometimes self-verifying. In certain cases one's belief can be a causal factor in that belief's becoming true. For example, if you believe that a particular person likes you, your belief may help to bring about that person's liking you. Or, your belief that you can leap across a chasm can help to bring about your success in doing so.

A second argument, Davis says, focuses on what James calls a genuine option. This part of James's analysis asserts that it is sometimes rational to believe on the basis of passional need rather than on the basis of objective evidence alone. Before defining a genuine option, it is important to note that James limits such cases to those that cannot be decided solely on intellectual grounds. He is interested in propositions whose truth value is unknown and where the available evidence bearing on their truth value is ambiguous.

Davis proceeds to interpret James's understanding that a genuine option must be live, forced, and momentous. In addition to possessing some sense of truth, a live option makes a real and serious appeal. Moreover, if such an option is also forced, it will permit no third alternative. For example, if you say, "Either call my theory true or call it false," the option is avoidable because I can decide not to call your theory anything at all. But if you say, "Either accept this truth or go without it," there is no middle way. If I decide *not* to decide whether to accept that truth or to go without it, I will go without it. Finally, if the option is also momentous, it is unique and cannot be duplicated exactly.

Taking note of James's argument that in the case of a genuine option one has the full intellectual right to believe something on the basis of passional need, Davis next explores James's opinion that "the religious hypothesis" is a genuine option. For James, such a hypothesis entails belief that perfection is eternal, that the best things in the universe are the more eternal things, and that we are better off even now if we believe that perfection is eternal. Understood in this way, Davis asserts with James, religious beliefs are rationally justifiable.

The key to Davis' argument is that the "'liveness' and 'momentousness' criteria" are superfluous for James. If an option is forced and the evidence bearing on it is ambiguous, those conditions are sufficient for James's appraisal to be valid. James's skeptical opponents want suspended judgments in all cases where evidence is ambiguous. But surely, Davis argues, in the case of an option that is both forced and ambiguous, James is correct. If the evidence is ambiguous, one cannot decide what to believe on the basis of evidence. And if the option is forced, one cannot decide to suspend judgment. The only alternative is belief on some basis other than evidence, which is exactly what

James is trying to justify.—*J.K.R.*

ADDITIONAL RECOMMENDED READING

Beard, Robert W. "'The Will To Believe' Revisited," in *Ratio*. VIII, no. 2 (December, 1966), pp. 169-179. This article is an insightful appraisal of James's criteria for "genuine" options.

Clive, Geoffrey. *The Romantic Enlightenment: Ambiguity and Paradox in the Western Mind (1750-1920)*. New York: Meridian Books, 1960. Clive's chapter, "The Breakdown of Empirical Certainty: William James and the Leap," links James's analysis of "the will to believe" to Søren Kierkegaard's existentialism.

Conkin, Paul K. *Puritans and Pragmatists: Eight Eminent American Thinkers*. Bloomington: Indiana University Press, 1976. More than any other major American philosopher, Conkin argues, James exalted the human will, but his voluntarism often left him on shaky philosophical ground.

Kennedy, Gail. "Pragmatism, Pragmaticism, and the Will to Believe—A Reconsideration," in *The Journal of Philosophy*. LV, no. 14 (July, 1958), pp 578-588. Kennedy's essay carefully analyzes a distinction between situations in which beliefs are self-verifying (the *will* to believe) and circumstances in which one is justified in believing more than evidence strictly warrants (the *right* to believe).

Roth, John K. *Freedom and the Moral Life: The Ethics of William James*. Philadelphia: The Westminster Press, 1969. Roth provides an extensive discussion of "The Moral Philosopher and the Moral Life" and accentuates James's emphasis on our freedom to develop meaningful lifestyles of our own choosing.

Roth, Robert J. *American Religious Philosophy*. New York: Harcourt, Brace & World, 1967. In a chapter on "William James and the God of Pragmatism," Roth gives special attention to "The Sentiment of Rationality," "Is Life Worth Living?" and "Reflex Action and Theism," as well as to "The Will to Believe."

Russell, Bertrand. *A History of Western Philosophy*. New York: Simon and Schuster, 1945. Russell says that James's analysis in "The Will to Believe" is a specious defense of religion.

Stroh, Guy W. *American Philosophy from Edwards to Dewey: An Introduction*. Princeton, New Jersey: D. Van Nostrand Company, 1968. *The Will to Believe and Other Essays in Popular Philosophy*, argues Stroh, clearly manifests the humanism in James's philosophy.

Wild, John. *The Radical Empiricism of William James*. Garden City, New York: Doubleday & Company, 1969. Interpreting James's psychology and its similarities to European phenomenology and existentialism, Wild sees James's essays as fundamental expressions of his convictions about the freedom of the mind and the strenuous life.

THE RIDDLE OF THE UNIVERSE

Author: Ernst Heinrich Haeckel (1834-1919)
Type of work: Philosophy of nature
First published: 1899

PRINCIPAL IDEAS ADVANCED

A scientific philosophy must join experience with speculation.

The greatest triumphs of science, including the cellular theory and the theory of evolution, are philosophic achievements.

In a scientific age a monistic philosophy is necessary, one in which matter and spirit are abstractions from a single physical nature, attributes of the universal substance.

Man is distinguishable quantitatively, but not qualitatively, from the lower animals.

Haeckel was one of the leading biologists of the nineteenth century, best known today for his formulation of the "Biogenetic Law": "Ontogenesis is a brief and rapid recapitulation of phylogenesis." That is, the embryo of an animal in its developments passes successively through stages in which it resembles adult forms of its evolutionary ancestors. He was the first German biologist who wholeheartedly supported Darwin's theories, in the popularization of which he did for Germany what Thomas Henry Huxley did for England. In *Die Welträtsel* (literally, "The World-Riddles"), which was an enormously popular book, he attempted to present an overall picture of the universe and man's place therein, in accordance with the new insights of evolutionary theory.

Despite the suggestion of mystery in its title, the work is emphatically not skeptical. As far as Haeckel was concerned, the world-riddles had been solved. In 1880 the eminent physiologist Emil Du Bois-Reymond enumerated seven enigmas: (1) The nature of matter and force, (2) the origin of motion, (3) the origin of life, (4) the (apparently preordained) orderly arrangement of nature, (5) the origin of simple sensation and consciousness, (6) rational thought and the origin of speech, and (7) the question of the freedom of the will. Du Bois-Reymond declared the first, second, and fifth to be utterly "transcendental" and insoluble; the third, fourth, and sixth to be possibly soluble; and he professed ignorance as to which group the seventh belonged. On the contrary, wrote Haeckel, the "transcendental" problems are settled by the monist conception of substance; the third, fourth, and sixth are already "decisively answered by the theory of evolution"; while "the freedom of the will is not an object for critical, scientific inquiry at all, for it is a pure dogma, based on an illusion, and has no real existence."

The nineteenth century, drawing to its close as Haeckel wrote, was the century of science. It saw great advances in chemistry, particularly in the chemistry of carbon; in physics the unity of forces in the entire universe was at last established, as well as the highly important Law of Substance—encompassing the principles of conservation of energy and matter. The greatest discoveries were in biology: the cellular theory and organic evolution. Technical progress in every field was immense.

All this should have effected a revolution in philosophy, but it did not. Because of churchly opposition to enlightenment, in conjunction with the political policies of ignorant and reactionary lawyers, the progress of science has not been equaled in moral and social life. "And from this obvious conflict there have arisen," Haeckel wrote, "not only an uneasy sense of dismemberment and falseness, but even the danger of grave catastrophes in the political and social world." Anthropism, "that powerful and worldwide group of erroneous opinions which opposes the human organism to the whole of the rest of nature, and represents it to be the preordained end of the organic creation, an entity essentially distinct from it, a godlike being," still reigned. It could be overthrown only by a scientific philosophy.

In his scientific philosophy Haeckel intended to join experience with speculation. Plato and Hegel on the one hand, Bacon and Mill on the other, were too one-sided. "The greatest triumphs of modern science—the cellular theory, the dynamic theory of heat, the theory of evolution, and the law of substance—are *philosophic achievements*; not, however, the fruit of pure speculation, but of an antecedent experience of the widest and most searching character."

At the time there were two prevailing kinds of philosophy: dualitic (or supernatural) and monistic. Monism, in the tradition of Spinoza and Goethe, held that "matter cannot exist and be operative without spirit, nor spirit without matter." It was therefore distinct from materialism. (But Haeckel, of course, regarded the classical and nineteenth century materialists as allies against supernaturalism.) A monistic world view was inevitable once the implications of the laws of substance and of evolution had been grasped.

The place of man in nature had to be clearly specified. Haeckel expounded the facts of comparative anatomy to show that man is a vertebrate, a tetrapod, a mammal, a placental, a primate, a catarrhine, and, among the catarrhines, much more closely allied to the anthropoid apes than the latter are to the cynopitheci on the next rung down. He outlined the evolutionary explanation of this classification.

According to Haeckel, if man is continuous physically with the rest of nature, so is he also in soul. For ". . . we consider the *psyche* to be *merely a collective idea of all the psychic functions of protoplasm.* In this sense the 'soul' is merely a physiological abstraction like 'assimilation' or 'generation.'" Psychology is "a section of physiology." In accordance with this conception, Haeckel presented a mass of data (of the sort later emphasized by the behaviorist psychologists) in the attempt to show that gradations of sensibility, spontaneous movement, reflex action, and memory correspond in their complexity to the degrees of organization of the evolutionary scale. Man is not distinguishable qualitatively, only quantitatively, from the lower animals with respect to intelligence, emotions, and even language. Indeed, Haeckel argued, there is a greater difference between Goethe and an Australian than between an Australian and a dog. (We are not told why this alleged fact is not a counter-instance to the correlation of bodily structure and mental ability.)

The Riddle of the Universe states that psychic qualities, like bodily ones, are inherited; they are determined at the moment the sperm cell penetrates the ovum. (But Haeckel agreed with Chevalier de Lamarck that acquired characteristics can to some degree be passed on to descendants; he was aware of, but rejected, August Weismann's theory of the continuity of the germ plasm.) In an individual, "psychic life runs the same evolution—upward progress, full maturity, and downward degeneration—as every other vital activity in his organization."

For Haeckel, the will, as simply one mode of psychic activity, is thoroughly determined by heredity and adaptation. Consequently, there could be no question of exceptions from the iron laws of nature.

Consciousness, which Haeckel distinguished from sensibility, is described as "the central mystery of psychology." Haeckel pointed out that much psychic life—in man as well as in other animals—is unconscious, and that the higher animals are obviously conscious too, as the comparative physiological effects of narcotics, anaesthetics, and hypnotism demonstrate. But where consciousness begins on the scale of animal life is impossible to determine. Perhaps the centralization of the nervous system is a prerequisite. Haeckel did not believe that consciousness is an inherent property of all matter, but he argued that unconscious sensation and will do pertain essentially to matter. In man and the higher animals, at any rate, brain physiology has succeeded in locating the actual seat ("or preferably the organ") of consciousness.

Belief in the immortality of the soul, "that highest point of superstition," is not universal, not occurring in Buddhism, Confucianism, or early Judaism. The "typically Christian idea is thoroughly materialistic and anthropomorphic," being that of the resurrection of the body. The more metaphysical conception, stemming from Plato, really amounts to the theory that the soul is a gas. But if it were (Haeckel observes, with ponderous Teutonic *Witz*), "we could then catch the soul as it is 'breathed out' at the moment of death, condense it, and exhibit it in a bottle as 'immortal fluid' (*fluidum animae immortale*). By a further lowering of temperature and increase of pressure it might be possible to solidify it—to produce 'soul-snow.' The experiment has not yet succeeded." And in any case, he wrote, it would be a dreadful thing if the soul *were* immortal.

So much for man. As for the universe at large, the fundamental principle for its understanding is the law of substance, which "in the ultimate analysis is found to be a necessary consequence of the principle of causality." Taking energy to be the same as Spinoza's "thought," Haeckel declares: "To this profound thought of Spinoza our purified monism returns after a lapse of two hundred years; for us, too, matter (space-filling substance) and energy (moving force) are but two inseparable attributes of the one underlying substance." Matter is of two sorts: the ordinary kind, and ether, "the existence of which as a real element is a *positive fact*, and has been known as such for the last twelve years." The relation of these two is, Haeckel admits, obscure. Perhaps matter is a sort of "condensation" from ether. Empedocles was right, in principle, in making Love a cosmic force; for there is a *"unity of affinity in the whole of nature*, from the simplest chemical process to the most complicated love story."

The universe is a perpetual-motion machine, infinite in extent and duration. Processes within it are cyclic. "Hence the theory of *entropy* is untenable," because if it were true, the universe would have a beginning and end, a state of affairs "untenable in the light of our monistic and consistent theory of the eternal cosmogenetic process. . . ."

Haeckel outlines the history of the earth (in accordance with the nebular hypothesis of Kant and Laplace), of life (though he holds that living creatures must have originated spontaneously at some time, he does not speculate on the details of this), and of man. Teleology, Haeckel observes, has long been banished from the inorganic sciences, which are consequently atheistic. Darwin banished it from biology too. It is not only fruitless but in error ever to regard evolution as a purposive process, as is shown by instances of dysteleology such as the survival of the vermiform appendix. Haeckel put himself in opposition to all "philosophy of history." The phrase "survival of the fittest" carried no moral implications for him. While all processes are rigidly determined, they are at the same time subject to "chance" in the sense of absence of aim or purpose.

The Riddle of the Universe deals with theory of knowledge, but somewhat sketchily. Sensations, synthesized by association in consciousness, produce presentations—"internal pictures of the external objects given us in sensation." By comparison we know that there is a consensus of normal observers. The presentations of normal observers "we call *true*, and we are convinced that their content corresponds to the knowable aspect of things. We *know* that these facts are not imaginary, but real." Skeptical objections that "the brain, or the soul, only perceives a certain condition of the stimulated nerve, and that, consequently, no conclusion can be drawn from the process as to the existence and nature of the stimulating environment" are dismissed by arguing that in the evolutionary process the different sense organs have developed their specificity to various classes of stimuli by adaptation from originally undifferentiated sense cells.

"The presentations which fill up the gaps in our knowledge, or take its place, may be called, in a broad sense, 'faith.'" For Haeckel a conception of knowledge (such as positivism) attempting to dispense with theories and hypotheses is impossible. Religious faith, however, is quite a different thing from scientific hypotheses, since the former is incompatible with the facts of observation.

The remainder of the book is devoted mostly to a polemic against Christianity in general and Roman Catholicism in particular, and to an outline of monist religion and ethics. (In this section occurs the famous description of the God of popular religion as a "gaseous vertebrate.") The world system of the modern scientist is pantheism. Atheism is "only another expression for it, emphasizing its negative aspect, the nonexistence of any supernatural deity." The three goddesses of the monist are truth, beauty, and virtue. Goodness consists in charity and toleration, compassion and assistance. Ethics can be scientific, for science shows that the feeling of duty rests "on the solid ground of *social instinct.*" Egoism and altruism are both natural laws and equally indispensable. The Golden Rule (found in many cultures antedating Christianity) is the supreme principle. While Christ was an admirable man, "the noble prophet and enthusiast, so full of the love of humanity," he was far below the level of classical culture, even though his father was Greek (so Haeckel informs us). Even purified Christianity is ethically objectionable in despising egoism: "'If any man will take away thy coat, let him have thy cloak also,' translated into the terms of modern politics, means: 'When the pious English take from you simple Germans one after another of your new and valuable colonies in Africa, let them have all the rest of your colonies also— or, best of all, give them Germany itself.'" In despising the body Christianity leads to dirtiness; in denying souls to animals it condones cruelty; in despising earthly goods it is inimical to civilization; in deprecating sex it dishonors love and the family. But Haeckel believed that science was on the march and would someday supercede much of Christian dogma. The "free societies" of monists, he predicted, would decorate not with madonnas and crucifixions but with paintings of the beauties of nature, such as the radiolaria, the thalamophora, and the medusae.

Haeckel had the type of mind to which broad outlines are more congenial than fussy details; this was evident even in his biological researches. And though throughout his life he served honorably, even heroically, in the forefront of the battle for freedom of thought and liberal politics against entrenched reaction and bigotry, he was nevertheless tenacious, even vain, of his own opinions, tending always to answer criticism with abuse. In consequence, even the biological sections of *The Riddle of the Universe* present as settled facts many theories which were exploded, or at least qualified, at the time of writing. Outside biology Haeckel had no competence at all, as his ludicrously dogmatic remarks on ether and the law of entropy make painfully clear.

The "monism" that Haeckel served up as the new philosophy is almost too vague for criticism. To say merely that entities so *prima facie* disparate as sensation, will, and life are inherent properties of "one substance" is not to produce a philosophy, much less a "monistic" one, in any but a trivial verbal sense.

The main objection to Haeckel as a philosopher is that he fails to come to grips at all with those problems that are incumbent upon a thinker of his point of view to treat: principally the well-known epistemological objections against identifying consciousness with brain activity. It is not enough just to show, however elaborately, that without a brain there is no thought.

Nevertheless, to show the absolute necessity of the brain itself to thought *is* the indispensable first step to a satisfactory philosophy of mind. And if today we can take it for granted and pass immediately to (perhaps) subtler theorizing, we can do so only because Haeckel (among others) in the nineteenth century transformed into solid fact what from Lucretius to Dietrich von Holbach had been only speculation.

In this and other respects Haeckel deserves some sort of praise or homage for having helped to create the general climate of opinion in which a more satisfactory scientific philosophy can be worked out. That man, including his "soul," *is* a part of nature, and not exempt from scientific study, is now an axiom of educated thought everywhere except in a few citadels of medievalism. It was not so when Haeckel wrote—when Darwin was forbidden to be mentioned in the German schools, and had not even been heard of in Tennessee.

The modern reader may find it quaint that Haeckel argues so solemnly for conclusions that are now commonplace. His boisterous attacks on religion may even be deemed offensive, being contrary to the amiable doctrine that there has never been a war between science and religion. But there was, to paraphrase Galileo; and even those who find it convenient to assume that at any rate the war has been terminated should not be so ungrateful as to refuse Haeckel some gratitude for this happy state of affairs.—*W.I.M.*

PERTINENT LITERATURE

Perry, Ralph B. *Present Philosophical Tendencies.* New York: George Braziller, 1952.

Ralph B. Perry takes Ernst Haeckel's *The Riddle of the Universe* to be the most widely read and the most influential contemporary (1911) defense of materialism. It also, he thinks, provides the best illustration of the problems materialism faces.

Perry reports that Haeckel took two laws—one to the effect that matter is conserved, the other to the effect that energy is conserved—and combined them into one under the name "the law of substance." Haeckel holds that the sum of matter fills, and the sum of force is operative in, all of infinite space. Haeckel, Perry continues, holds that all phenomena whatever are produced by force. Further, the various forces, or energies, of which heat, sound, light, and electricity are examples, are conceived by Haeckel as being particular instances of a single, basic energy.

Analogously, Perry notes, Haeckel held that the various chemically diverse substances are forms or "condensations" of a single, basic matter. Further, Haeckel holds, matter, or substance that fills space, and energy, or force that produces motion, are themselves attributes of a still more basic substance. Force and matter cannot occur or be instantiated separately, and each is to be ascribed to an all-pervasive substance. Part of the significance of this for Haeckel, Perry reports, is that mind-body dualism—the view that a mind is one kind of substance and a body a different kind of substance—is resolved.

What this amounts to, Perry explains, is this. Haeckel identifies spirit with energy or force or activity; conversely, he identifies physical affinity and resistance with (psychological) inclination and aversion. The passion that draws Paris to Helen and the movement which unites two atoms of hydrogen and one atom of oxygen into a molecule of water, Perry quotes Haeckel as claiming, are basically the same.

Holding this sort of identity claim, Perry suggests, involves Haeckel in resurrecting the notion of an indeterminate force-matter which had been postulated some 2,500 years previously; Perry sees it as a revival of hylozoism (the view that the "primary stuff" of the universe is alive) and animism (the view that inanimate objects and natural phenomena have living souls). In different terms, Perry describes it as a "cosmic generalization" of one's experience of emotion or desire.

Nevertheless, Perry adds, for Haeckel one has not reached a knowledge of things as they really are. The perspective described above is descriptive only of what is knowable about things, and Haeckel takes the actual nature of things—the essence or essential properties of the substance of which force and matter are attributes—to be beyond our ken. For Haeckel, then, Perry reports, how things *are*, independent of thought, at least as far as what is primitive is concerned—that by which other things are to be explained but which itself requires no explanation—not only is not known but also in principle cannot be known.

The result of this sort of perspective, then, Perry notes, is not knowledge, but agnosticism. This, Perry apparently thinks, is the inevitable result of Haeckel's procedure or methodology. As Perry explains this methodology, it goes as follows. Such items as weight, mass, force, energy, and the like are "constant ratios of variables." They are mathematical proportions of observable properties. For Haeckel, Perry tells us, each such ratio is viewed as expressing a simple essence whose nature is not revealed to us when we know the ratio in question. Similarly, for Haeckel, knowing Newtonian mechanics gives us mathematical formulae which apply to forces but which give us no insight into the nature of the phenomena which satisfy the formulae, a nature which is for Haeckel qualitative rather than quantitative. (Apparently no observable qualities will do for the purpose of understanding essences or natures, they being too superficial, and such qualities having in any case been left behind in the descent to a primitive substance whose attributes are force and matter.) That there *are* such natures or essences associated with, or presupposed by, constant ratios of variables (or, by implication, that there is one unknowable essence of a substance that underlies the sum of all force-matter) is, Perry insists, something Haeckel simply *assumes*.

Perry is bothered, too, by a certain vagueness in Haeckel's monism. Haeckel intends that his monism be incompatible with the existence of God, the immortality of the soul, and human freedom of choice. This intent is carried through, Perry suggests, by his appealing to whatever residue remains of the scientific meanings of "force" and "energy" (and "matter"). But, Perry reminds us, force and energy do not as such belong to the primitive substance, even insofar as they are conceived as physical attributes.

Perry is making two points here. One is that, given the extraordinarily loose analogies by which Haeckel "reduces" spirit to energy, one could as rationally—no more, but no less, plausibly—"reduce" energy to spirit. To whatever degree "mind" or the mental have any meaning after such a reduction (and the same problem arises here as arose about Haeckel's use of the terms "matter" and "material") one could claim that everything that exists has a mind or is mental. As Perry puts it, one could as reasonably reduce mechanism to freedom, and matter to God (thereby standing Haeckel on his head), as proceed in Haeckel's preferred direction.

Perry's other point is one he makes tellingly by an analogy with mystical, or negative, theology. In such theology, Perry reminds us, God is said to be good and wise, but good and wise in a sense that transcends our comprehension. The net effect is that we are told: (1) "God is good and wise" is true; (2) "Good" and "wise" apply to God, but only in a sense of these terms that transcends our thought. But in the inevitable absence of any explanation of any sense in which these terms *do* apply to God, there is really no difference between (1) and (3): "Good" and "wise" do not apply to God at all. Negative theologians prefer (2) to (3) but this seems to be a preference without a basis in any substantial difference between (2) and (3).

Perry suggests that Haeckel tells us something very similar, not about "good" and "wise" and God but about "force" and "matter" and primitive substance. "Force" and "matter" apply to primitive substance, but in a sense (at best) only vaguely analogous to that in which we understand them. Perry indicates that this is hardly, if at all, distinguishable from our not being able to apply these terms, in any significant sense, to primitive substance at all.

In both cases, that of negative theology and of Haeckel, Perry contends, there *seems* to be a view with some actual content being expressed, because familiar words are used to express it. But it is part of, or at least entailed by, the view itself, in each case, that those very words are to lose their (ordinary) sense (and what sense they do bear is not only not explained, but also said to be necessarily unknown to us). That there is an actual position, possessed of cognitive content, Perry contends, is but an impression created by what Perry calls "verbal suggestion."

Copleston, Frederick. "Non-Dialectical Materialism," in *A History of Philosophy*. Vol. VII. Garden City, New York: Doubleday & Company, 1965.

Frederick Copleston tells us that the nineteenth century saw a collapse of Hegelian absolute idealism. What followed was a nondialectical, non-Marxist materialism, a position alleged to follow from taking science seriously. While, in Copleston's judgment (which seems in this regard to express scholarly consensus), this movement did not include profound philosophical thought, it was influential. Indeed, its lack of profundity, along with the prestige gained from its claim to be based on science and its expression in nontechnical language, was responsible for its influence.

Among the figures prominent in the development and expression of this perspective were such figures as Karl Vogt (1817-1895), Jacob Möleschott (1822-1893), Ludwig Büchner (1824-1899). Vogt was a zoologist famous mainly for having claimed that the brain secretes thought as the liver secretes life. Möleschott, according to Copleston, was a physiologist, physician, and professor who held that force or energy is an essential property of matter and that the existence and order of the world can be explained in purely materialistic terms. He thus rejected any distinction, in terms of types of explanation offered, between the natural sciences and the social sciences, including psychology and history.

Büchner, Copleston notes, wrote the best-known expression of this perspective in his *Force and Matter* (1855). He rejected any philosophy which could not be grasped by the general reader and held matter and force to be identical. Further, Copleston explains, he, like Möleschott, supposed that whatever exists can be explained by appeal to force and matter as principles of explanation. He thus regarded force and matter as that which is given, not requiring explanation, but that in terms of which anything else is explained.

The materialistic perspective, Copleston reminds us, was not unopposed in Germany. Friedrich Albert Lange (1828-1875) published a massive *History of Materialism* (1866) in which he criticized materialism from a Neo-Kantian position. Copleston informs us that Lange viewed materialism insofar as he thought it legitimate, as a methodological, not a metaphysical, principle. Lange suggested that a practicing natural scientist is legitimate in restricting his professional concerns to the existence and properties of physical objects, but not, as scientist (nor, in Lange's view, in any case), in claiming that nothing nonmaterial exists. Further, Lange claimed, consciousness, while presupposed by science because required for scientific experimentation and theorizing, is not analyzable in materialist terms.

Copleston reports that Lange's criticisms (only briefly indicated here) were sufficiently persuasive to lead to a "second wave" of materialist thought which appealed to Darwinism for its rationale. According to Copleston, Haeckel's *The Riddle of the Universe* gave this second wave its most characteristic and popular exposition in Germany.

Ernst Haeckel, Copleston indicates, was a professor of zoology at Jena who published in this field but also wrote books in which he expounded a view which he based on the theory of evolution. Charles Darwin's *On the Origin of Species by Means of Natural Selection* was published in 1859 and *The Descent of Man* in 1871. Between the appearance of these books by Darwin, Haeckel developed a monistic philosophy which he proffered as a substitute for traditional religion and which he thought provided the link between religion and science. The titles of two of his other books—*Monism as Connecting Religion and Science* (1892) and his *God-Nature, Studies in Monistic Religion* (1914)—reflect this perspective.

Copleston offers a summary of *The Riddle of the Universe* along these lines: Haeckel thinks that human reflection has thrown up various problems or riddles, some of which he regards as genuine and others which he regards as spurious. Only one of these, which Haeckel calls "the problem of substance," is in his opinion comprehensive. It is to this problem that Haeckel addresses his monism. Substance, according to Haeckel, has two attributes: force and matter. Haeckel calls the thesis that force and matter are conserved "the comprehensive law of substance" and, taking this thesis to be also the universal law of evolution, he draws the conclusion that the universe is a whole within which (lower-level) natural laws are also always and everywhere the same. Haeckel also concludes that, given this thesis, one can dispense with postulating the Kantian triad of God, freedom, and immortality.

Haeckel rests his ethics, Copleston notes, not on rational grounds along the lines of Kant's categorical imperative, but on social instincts; and he takes as his highest ideal the attainment of harmony between egoism and altruism. Copleston quotes Haeckel to the effect that Herbert Spencer found in the theory of evolution a basis for monistic ethics.

Copleston remarks that Haeckel rejects both "materialism" and "atheism" as appropriate terms for his viewpoint. Haeckel believes every atom of matter has force, hence is active and hence is spiritual as well as material; nevertheless, Copleston notes, Haeckel's view is what would ordinarily be described as materialism. Haeckel describes his view as pantheistic, not atheistic; he apparently views religion, Copleston reports, as a matter of cultivating science, ethics, and aesthetics, and pantheism as a matter of calling the universe "God." Thus, Copleston suggests, Haeckel's pantheism differs from atheism only in that, in Haeckel's view, pantheists express a feeling, or perhaps have an attitude, toward a material universe about whose properties they basically agree with atheists.

Copleston concludes his discussion of nondialectical materialism by noting two developments which, occurring after the publication of *The Riddle of the Universe*, also served to carry on (as well as to clarify) this position. One concerns the publication of *The Overcoming of Scientific Materialism* (1899) by Wilhelm Ostwald (1853-1932). Ostwald was a Nobel Prize winning chemist who was closely identified with Haeckel's views. Copleston indicates that a German Monist Society was founded, under Haeckel's patronage, in 1906, and that Ostwald not only became president but also published *The Monist Century* in 1912. Indeed, Copleston tells us, he resigned his chair of chemistry in 1906 in order to publish on philosophical topics. What, then, was the "overcoming of scientific materialism" about which Ostwald speaks? Nothing more, Copleston records, than the substitution of the concept of energy for that of matter. Energy, Ostwald suggests, can take different forms, including nonconscious and conscious, thus broaching the other development. Regarding this other development, Copleston relates that Richard Avenarius (1843-1896) and Ernst Mach (1838-1916) both sought to develop a notion of pure or uninterpreted experience. Thus Avenarius in a *Critique of Pure Experience* (1888-1890) and Mach in *Contributions to the Analysis of Sensations* (1886) developed the notion of sensations which were alleged to be (compare Ostwald's energy) neither mental nor physical. As Copleston sees, the notion of such a primitive, neutral stuff involves commitment to neither materialism nor idealism.—*K.E.Y.*

ADDITIONAL RECOMMENDED READING

Chadwick, Owen. *The Secularization of the European Mind in the Nineteenth Century*. Cambridge: Cambridge University Press, 1976. The Gifford Lectures for 1973-1974, written in a lively style with a wealth of information.

Edwards, Paul, ed. *The Encyclopedia of Philosophy*. New York: Macmillan Publishing Company and The Free Press, 1967. A brief discussion in Volume Three of Haeckel's views (by Rollo Handy), plus a short bibliography.

Joad, C. E. M. *Guide to Modern Thought*. New York: F. A. Stokes Company, 1933. A popular, critical discussion of the materialism of the nineteenth and early twentieth centuries, plus other influential movements of the period.

——————— . *The Recovery of Belief*. London: Faber and Faber, 1952. A book written for the "educated public," as was *The Riddle of the Universe*, which argues for the sort of perspective against which *The Riddle of the Universe* was written; also concerned with science and religion.

Lange, Friedrich A. *The History of Materialism and Criticism of Its Present Importance*. New York: Arno Press, 1974. A multi-volume history, with critique, of materialist views.

Merz, John T. *A History of European Thought in the Nineteenth Century*. London: Blackwood and Sons, 1907-1914. A comprehensive intellectual history of nineteenth century Europe, arranged topically.

THE WORLD AND THE INDIVIDUAL

Author: Josiah Royce (1855-1916)
Type of work: Metaphysics
First published: Vol. I, 1900; Vol. II, 1901

PRINCIPAL IDEAS ADVANCED

Being can be understood as an absolute system of ideas which embody the fulfillment of purposes.

All knowledge is of matters of experience.

The individual self must be defined in ethical terms by reference to a life plan.

As a free individual each person by his will contributes to the world and to God's will.

Although no perfection is to be found in the temporal world, the Eternal Order is perfect.

Because we are finite, union with the infinite God is realized.

Professor Josiah Royce of Harvard University has proved to be the most durable American proponent of what is, for the most part, an outworn metaphysical creed: Absolute Idealism. *The World and the Individual* is composed of two series of Gifford Lectures delivered before the University of Aberdeen in 1899 and 1900, the first entitled "The Four Historical Conceptions of Being," and the second, "Nature, Man, and the Moral Order." In these lectures Royce developed, with some significant changes, earlier ideas which he had presented in such works as *The Religious Aspects of Philosophy* (1885) and *Studies of Good and Evil* (1898).

A statement of the core of Royce's philosophical position appears in the last lecture of the second volume: "The one lesson of our entire course has thus been the lesson of the unity of finite and of infinite, of temporal dependence and of eternal significance, of the World and all its Individuals, of the One and the Many, of God and Man. Not only in spite, then, of our finite bondage, but because of what it means and implies, we are full of the presence and the freedom of God."

This is a truly revealing statement considered not only as a condensation of Royce's central claim, but also as indicating the characteristic mode of argument which gives Royce's philosophy its individual content and flavor, distinguishing it from other Hegelian idealisms. For what does Royce maintain?—That from man's finitude, God's infinite presence and freedom follow. Royce supposed that the finite, the limited, is conceivable only by comparison with an actual infinitude. It is as if he had argued that man, in virtue of his limitations, suggests the actual unlimited, the Absolute—otherwise, there would be no sense in saying that man is "limited," that he does not come up to the mark. We are reminded of Descartes' argument that knowledge of man's imperfection leads to knowledge of the actuality of God's perfection and, hence, of God's existence.

If we consider the general character of Royce's argument, we can see that it takes the form of the claim that from imperfection, knowledge of perfection follows. Hence, from knowledge of purpose, knowledge of fulfillment follows; from knowledge of error, or of its possibility, knowledge of the actuality of truth follows; from knowledge of the partial, knowledge of the Absolute; from knowledge of the individual, knowledge of the community—and from knowledge of the unfulfilled and finite individual and community, knowledge of the fulfilled, infinite, "Individual of Individuals," God himself, follows.

To appreciate the character of this argument, used by Royce in these several ways, we have only to turn to an earlier essay, "The Possibility of Error." In this essay, a chapter from *The Religious Aspect of Philosophy*, Royce argued that the possibility of error implies the actuality of "an infinite unity of conscious thought to which is present all possible thought." Royce suggested that an error is a thought which aims at being a complete thought in regard to its chosen object, and it is only by comparing the incomplete or inadequate thought with a complete or adequate thought that the incomplete thought can be known to be erroneous. Furthermore, not only could the error not be *known* to be erroneous were there not a complete thought present to a thinker who could compare the complete thought with the erroneous thought, but the error could not even be an error were there not such an actual complete thought and actual, knowing thinker. For how could the idea be incomplete by reference or comparison to *nothing*, or by reference to something other than a thought; no, for an error to be an error, an actual, adequate thought (and thinker) must exist. Since "there must be possible an infinite mass of error," there must be *actual* an infinite, all-knowing thought.

A pragmatist such as William James or Charles Sanders Peirce would say that a belief can be understood to be erroneous *if* what one *would* receive in the way of experience, *were* one to act appropriately, *would* run counter to one's expectations. But the mere *possibility* of a more satisfactory and adequate experience was not enough for Royce. Unless there were *actually* a complete idea, no belief could possibly be erroneous, for no belief could fail to measure up to a complete idea unless there actually were such a complete idea.

In the Preface to *The World and the Individual* Royce writes: "As to the most essential argument regarding the true relations between our finite ideas and the ultimate nature of things, I have never varied, in spirit, from the view maintained in . . . *The Possibility of Error*. . . ." He goes on to refer to a number of books in which the argument was used, and then states that "In the present lectures this argument assumes a decidedly new form. . . ." The argument in its new form is presented in Chapter VII of the first volume of

The World and the Individual, the chapter entitled "The Internal and the External Meaning of Ideas." Here the argument concludes with the fourth (and final) conception of Being considered by Royce: "*What is, or what is real, is as such the complete embodiment, in individual form and in final fulfillment, of the internal meaning of finite ideas.*" The three conceptions of Being which Royce examined and rejected prior to settling upon this final idea were those of realism, mysticism, and critical rationalism. The fourth conception of Being, for all of the novelty of its presentation, is fundamentally that with which readers of Royce's earlier works are familiar; and the argument in its support is, strictly speaking, not a new argument distinguishable from the one to be found in "The Possibility of Error" and *The Conception of God* (1897), but—as Royce himself wrote—the argument in "a decidedly new form."

To understand the argument in its new form a distinction must be drawn, in Royce's terms, between the "internal and external meaning" of ideas. According to Royce, an idea "is as much an instance of will as it is a knowing process"; that is, an idea is a partial fulfillment of the purposive act of desiring to have an adequate conception of something. By the "internal meaning" of an idea Royce meant the "conscious embodiment" of the purpose in the idea. If I try to get a clear idea about someone, then to the extent that my thoughts are directed by that interest and come to have something of the content they would have were I entirely clear in my conception, then to that extent my idea has internal meaning. Unless to some extent I fulfill the purpose of my thought by thinking accurately, I cannot be said to have an object of thought: in thinking about someone, I have to think accurately enough, at least, to identify him as the object of my conception. Internal meaning, then, is a function of, and consequence of, human will and purpose.

But ideas refer beyond themselves to something external, not part of their content. And Royce asks, "How is it possible that an idea, which is an idea essentially and primarily because of the inner purpose that it consciously fulfills by its presence, also possesses a meaning that in any sense appears to go beyond this internal purpose?" The answer is that the external meaning of an idea is the "completely embodied internal meaning of the idea." Or, in other words, a finite thought fulfills itself to some extent by managing to be *about* something; but what the thinker aims at is a more complete and adequate idea, a fuller conception, one that fulfills his purpose in thinking. Yet unless there is such an adequate idea, such an external meaning, then the incomplete thought, the unfulfilled idea, the partial conception, aims at nothing; and if it has no objective, it cannot fail; and if it cannot fail, it cannot be incomplete or partial. Hence, the possibility of unfulfilled internal meanings implies the actuality of external meanings; and the totality of external meanings is God. God is the "Other," the fulfillment of purpose, which alone can be the object of thought. An idea is true to the extent that it "corresponds, even in its vagueness, to its own final and completely individual expression."

Royce built his conception of God in such a manner that God, or that Being which is the absolute fulfillment of all individual wills, "sees the one plan fulfilled through all the manifold lives, the single consciousness winning its purpose by virtue of all the ideas, of all the individual selves, and of all the lives."

Another insight which serves to illuminate Royce's philosophy and his method is the realization that for Royce, "the world is real only as the object of true ideas." This proposition is not peculiar to us because we tend to interpret the word "object" as we choose in order to adjust the claim to our own philosophies. But realize that, for Royce, to be the "object" of an idea is to be that at which the idea aims, its objective; and the objective of the idea (of the thinker) is a completely adequate thought, one that fulfills his original purpose in thinking. Hence, if "the world is real only as the object of true ideas," the world is real only as an absolutely adequate thought, itself an expression of will. The consequence is that God alone is real—but, then, insofar as any individual or any thought fulfills the purpose which has being because of the finite individuals and wills, then just to that extent the finite individual or thought has Being, is part of Being. Thus, unity is achieved despite the variety and finitude of things. The individual contributes to the Being who fulfills the purposes of the individuals.

With the final conception of Being, the first volume of *The World and the Individual* comes to a close. In *Nature, Man, and the Moral Order*, the second volume of these Gifford Lectures, Royce worked out the implications of his conception in order to present an idealistic theory of knowledge, a philosophy of nature, a doctrine about self, a discussion of the human individual, a portrait of the world as "a Moral Order," a study of the problem of evil, and some conclusions concerning the bearing of these matters on natural religion.

Royce's idealistic theory of knowledge is a reaffirmation of his central predisposition to accept as real only that which fulfills the purpose of an individual will. Realists talk about "hard" facts, he writes, but analysis shows that "hard" facts are understandable as facts which enable us "even now to accomplish our will better than we could if we did not acknowledge these facts." A fact is "*that which I ought to recognize* as determining or limiting what I am here consciously to do or to attempt." A distinction is drawn between the ethical Ought, definable by reference to a more rational purpose than our own, and a theoretical Ought, definable by reference to a world of recognized facts which embodies and fulfills purposes. To know, then to apprehend a fact, is to come to have the thought which the present thought would be were its purpose (its internal meaning) fulfilled by further considerations (the external meaning); to know is to think what you *ought* to think relative to the purpose of your thought. Facts are *objective* in that they are "*other than*" the present, incomplete thoughts; our grounds for acknowledging facts are *subjective* in that they are related to our purposes, the intentions of our wills; but the objective and subjective are synthesized by "the essential *Teleological* constitution of the realm of facts . . ."—a teleological constitution which is understood once reality or Being is recognized as absolutely ordered and fulfilling will.

Royce argues that to us who see the reality in a fragmentary fashion, facts appear to be disconnected; but there is, he claims, a linkage of facts which illuminates the particular character of each fact. Analogously, through temporal failures and efforts the reality of eternal fulfillment is won.

To Royce it appears that our wills are such that they cannot be satisfied by the mere addition of content, additional facts; for the full expression of will, other wills are necessary. Finally, fulfillment comes only from a system of wills which is such that Being is a unity, a one out of many, a will (the Individual of Individuals) which is the infinite, eternal embodiment of individual wills which, by their temporal efforts, have contributed to the reality of the whole.

According to Royce, the idea that nature is hopelessly divided between matter and mind is itself the product of a scientific enterprise motivated by social concerns. The fulfillment of that social concern is best served by recognizing the unsatisfactory character of a conception which maintains a diversity in nature, an irreconcilable tension between matter and mind. The conception of the natural world "as directly bound up with the experiences of actually conscious beings" is more in accord with the Fourth Conception of Being which the first series of lectures was designed to advance. The idea of a nonconscious, nonliving, nonwilling reality is unacceptable, for to *be*, to be *real*, is to be the conscious fulfillment of purpose. Thus, if nature is real, nature is the conscious fulfillment of purpose.

The idea of the human self is constructed not by reference to any "Soul-Substance" but, as we might expect, by reference to an "Intent always to remain another than my fellows despite my divinely planned unity with them. . . ." There is no conflict between individual selves and the Divine Will, "for the Divine Will gets expressed in the existence of me the individual only in so far as this Divine Will . . . includes within itself my own will, as one of its own purposes."

In order to justify the claim that reality exhibits a moral order, Royce insists that every evil deed must sometime be "atoned for" or "overruled" by some individual self; in this manner, perfection of the whole is realized. The evil of this world is in its incompleteness, its partial fulfillment of purposes—but since the incomplete, the unfulfilled, make sense only by reference to an actual Absolute, by being incomplete they make Being possible as an ordered whole.

Royce regarded God, or Absolute Being, as a person, that is, as "a conscious being, whose life, temporally viewed, seeks its completion through deeds. . . ." God is the totality of all conscious efforts, but viewed eternally, God is an infinite whole which includes temporal process. Man is also a person, but not absolute; his reality finally consists in God's reality—God and man are one.

Since the self possesses individuality, a uniqueness of purpose, it can be satisfied only by what is Other, by what fulfills that purpose, namely, God. But God is eternal. Consequently, the immortality of self is assured.

One can come to understand, provided he views Royce's arguments with sympathetic tolerance, how if the self is realized only in God, there is a sense in which the self (the individual) and God are one—although viewed from the varying perspectives of time and purpose, they are distinct. But if the self and God are one, then, in the respect in which they are one, they are alike: God's eternity, then, is man's; and this is man's immortality. Although the individual self, in being distinguished from other selves by his peculiar purposive striving, is only partial; yet, in contributing to the reality of the Absolute and in becoming unified with the Absolute, it is itself absolute. The part is equal to the whole, even though, considered otherwise than by reference to the final unity, the part is distinguishable from the whole.

One cannot fail to be persuaded of Royce's moral sincerity and intellectual acumen for *The World and the Individual* is eloquent witness to both. Fantastic as the idealistic image is to the realist who presupposes an unconcerned and unconscious material world as the barren scene of his pointless adventures, it has a certain intellectual charm and moral persuasiveness to one who is willing to sympathize with the interest that leads a man such as Royce to fail to understand how anything could be *real*, could be worthy of the honorific name "being," which did not show itself to be a conscious effort to go beyond the limits of fragmentary knowledge and experience to a recognition of and identity with the whole of such effort. If such a proposition as, "All Being is the fulfillment of purpose," is taken not as a description of the facts of the matter in regard to the kind of world the physicist studies, but as a suggestion that all human effort be directed to the ideal cooperation of all seekers after truth and goodness, *The World and the Individual* comes to be recognizable as a revolutionary manifesto directed to the human spirit—something quite different from the naïve speculative expression of an idealistic philosopher remote from the world of hard facts and hard men.—*I.P.M.*

PERTINENT LITERATURE

Marcel, Gabriel. *Royce's Metaphysics*. Translated by Virginia Ringer and Gordon Ringer. Chicago: Henry Regnery Company, 1956.

In 1956 the existential thinker Gabriel Marcel added a foreword to this study of Josiah Royce, which he had published in French nearly forty years earlier. The great value of Royce's philosophy, he asserted, was that it marked "a kind of transition between absolute idealism and existentialist thought." Most scholars agree that "transitional" is a good term to describe *The World and the Individual*, the massive two-volume work based on Royce's Gifford Lectures of 1899-1900. This book, it is often claimed, belongs to a middle period in the development of his thought. In it one can see Royce advancing ideas originally set forth in *The Religious Aspect of Philosophy* (1885), but the positions that he offers on knowledge, God, and community have not yet achieved the richness and novelty that they would come to possess in *The Problem of Christianity* (1913). Nevertheless, Marcel's appraisal of Royce's thought also fits *The World and the Individual*: ". . . his philosophy is an important landmark in the development of contemporary thought."

Marcel's overview of Royce's metaphysics leads him to concentrate on three aspects of *The World and the Individual*. The first is Royce's theory concerning the relation between an idea and its object. Royce sees, correctly in Marcel's view, that an idea has not only a representational aspect but also volitional and intentional qualities. Marcel concurs that the relation between these "external" and "internal" meanings points toward an inescapable issue— namely, the question of what is the true connection between them.

The author underscores the point that Royce's book attempts to undercut all ultimate forms of dualism. In so doing Royce argues that external meanings are actually a reflection of internal meanings. Indeed, in the final analysis the universe is the manifestation of the purpose and will of an Absolute Knower or God. In this context, Marcel is particularly attracted to Royce's treatment of the ancient problem of "the one and the many" in the Supplementary Essay appended to Volume I of *The World and the Individual*. Although Marcel does not find Royce's treatment completely persuasive, which helps to explain why he sees Royce's philosophy as involved in a transition from absolute idealism to existentialism, he is intrigued by Royce's attempt to fathom what the life of an Absolute Knower might be.

Royce's account of a "self-representative system" tries to show that infinite multiplicity can be grasped without contradiction. The core of his argument, Marcel suggests, is that there really are purposes whose meaning is both logically sound and dependent upon comprehension of an infinite multitude of particulars. Marcel is willing to agree that an actual, graspable infinite is not unthinkable, but he does not believe that such reality squares with "the contingency of finite individuals." He acknowledges that Royce's analysis of time and eternity seeks to clarify how the full meaning of becoming could only be possessed by a form of knowing that can comprehend change as a succession and as a totality. But as Royce attempts to cope with the meaning of individual contingency in this setting, it still seems to Marcel that the all-encompassing Absolute Individual does more to compromise the individuality of other beings than to guarantee it, as Royce promises.

More to Marcel's liking is Royce's differentiation between "description" and "appreciation," a distinction established earlier but elaborated in *The World and the Individual*. He applauds Royce's emphasizing that these two perspectives, far from being separable or ultimately in conflict, are complementary in a way that Royce perceived in especially insightful ways. What Royce calls "the world of description" is dependent upon and even an expression of "the world of appreciation"; the latter level of social understanding and value is a precondition for the objectivity of abstract reflection and scientific research which characterize a descriptive awareness and give us powerful tools to carry out our purposes. Marcel suggests that as Royce emphasizes these diverse aspects of consciousness and reality, he is feeling his way toward a less rigid notion of the Absolute and is at the same time articulating views akin to existential theories that emerged later in the twentieth century.

Smith, John E. *Royce's Social Infinite*. New York: The Liberal Arts Press, 1950.

John E. Smith's book is a good companion for Gabriel Marcel's commentary on *The World and the Individual* because it gives special attention to the problem of community in Josiah Royce's thought. Although Royce's later works—*The Philosophy of Loyalty* (1908), *The Sources of Religious Insight* (1912), and *The Problem of Christianity* (1913)—predominate in Smith's study, the author stresses that *The World and the Individual* is pivotal in the development of Royce's thought about God. This development, Smith argues, moves away from a conviction that the Absolute is an encompassing awareness that grasps all truth simultaneously and reconciles at once every conflict of finite wills.

As Royce revises his earlier position, he emphasizes the point that existence is an actual infinite in the sense of being a well-ordered system or community which has its roots in a form of interpretation that is triadic. Smith agrees with Marcel in believing that the place where Royce breaks much of his new ground is in the Supplementary Essay to the first volume of *The World and the Individual*. More than Marcel, however, Smith stresses that Royce seems to realize now that the Absolute cannot grasp everything immediately—by "appreciation," if you will—but must have a form of awareness that places greater emphasis on mediation, interpretation, and even description.

In Royce's early writings, Smith asserts, the Absolute Self is portrayed as fully actualized truth and goodness, so that the finite progress made by human beings toward knowledge and excellence constitutes no real progress for God. Royce's accent is on the completeness of thought that characterizes the Absolute. Such awareness grasps immediately and intuitively what a finite form of consciousness could comprehend only in a mediated and discursive way. This view carries forward into *The Spirit of Modern Philosophy* (1892). Drawing on the distinction between description and appreciation, it implies that the mode of God's awareness is an eternal appreciation of all existence.

The World and the Individual, Smith believes, does not relinquish Royce's conviction that God is primarily to be understood in terms of wholeness, unity, and inclusiveness of insight. The latter quality, moreover, still entails immediacy and appreciation. But novel elements now begin to appear in Royce's conception of God. System and order become more pronounced as characteristics of God's awareness, thus suggesting that a more mediated and discursive quality may be present in the Absolute's life. These new factors, Smith believes, put Royce on the course that eventually results in a theory that comes to see reality as both an infinite system and a community of interpretation.

These changes enter Royce's view of God, Smith notes, partly in response to Royce's desire to buttress his conviction that the Absolute is not simply a knowing consciousness but also a willing self. As a willing God, Royce's Absolute expresses itself in multiple purposes and activities. The dynamism implied by such an emphasis on will in *The World and the Individual* evidently led Royce to move even further away from a focus on the immediate awareness of all-encompassing thought and toward a theory that would make God's awareness no less thorough but better able to do justice to the moving texture of experience.

Although *The World and the Individual* takes its bearings primarily from epistemological and metaphysical issues, as Royce intensifies his stress on the Absolute-as-Will and on the notion that a dynamic communal conception of existence must be accentuated, elements of his ethic of loyalty can be discerned. While only latent in *The World and the Individual*, Smith implies, this substantive work of Royce's middle period is also an essential step on the way to his mature moral philosophy.

Kuklick, Bruce. *Josiah Royce: An Intellectual Biography*. Indianapolis: Bobbs-Merrill, 1972.

This book, supplemented by the author's *Rise of American Philosophy* (1977), is the most detailed recent study of Josiah Royce. It revolves around three main themes: (1) the centrality of logical problems in Royce's work; (2) the significance of Immanuel Kant in setting many of the issues that concerned him; and (3) the relationship between pragmatism and idealism as these trends developed at Harvard around the turn of the century. Bruce Kuklick's discussion of *The World and the Individual* reflects them all. As it does so, Kuklick also accents Royce's understanding of specifically human existence.

Kuklick underscores Royce's belief that ideas are volitional. Human thought expresses purpose: thus both knowing and willing are not separable affairs and human beings actually participate in the construction of their own world. Kuklick points out that in Royce's view knowing is activity; but this fact leaves us always short of full comprehension even as we may move toward increased understanding. Ultimately the completeness that we seek is found in the Absolute, and Royce's argument in *The World and the Individual* intends to ensure the notion that our finite experience can only have the sense that it actually possesses if the Absolute is real. Kuklick is not convinced by Royce's metaphysical arguments; he is somewhat more impressed by Royce's suggestions about the nature of human consciousness.

According to Kuklick, Royce provides a view of human consciousness not significantly different from the theory of William James. At least in its human form, consciousness is in process, and it is characterized by selective attention. Ideas emerge as possible plans of action. That is, to have an idea means that there is a self prepared to take action so as to fulfill an aim related to the object of the idea. In so doing, the world takes shape through human agency, although not, of course, in accord with just any interpretation that we can muster. We encounter factors of resistance in our experience, and thus a distinction between volition and cognition emerges which Royce prefers to analyze in terms of the internal and external meanings of ideas.

What we seek, Kuklick interprets Royce to say, is a correspondence between internal and external meanings; but the correspondence that we seek is still intelligible only in terms of purpose. An idea can be true only if it corresponds to its referent in the fashion that the idea intends. Herein lies the basis for Royce's claim that he was not less a pragmatist than James. However, Royce added the qualification that his was an "absolute" pragmatism. He did so because he believed that the correspondence we finite selves actually do experience in time can have the validity it clearly does possess only if there is a full correspondence between knowledge and volition. That full correspondence, Royce argues, can exist only if the Absolute is real.

Royce's Absolute involves a union of finite and fragmentary selves. The human individual, Kuklick understands Royce to argue, is aware of the world and itself, but the constraints of time keep the awareness partial and incomplete. Royce turns this existential predicament to the best, however, by interpreting our sense of finitude so that it implies a place for us within something much larger and much more inclusive. Neither James's pragmatism nor the thought of Gabriel Marcel's existential colleagues would be likely to find so near at hand Royce's optimistic assurance that human finitude is transcended by a meaningful Absolute in whose life we participate. Nevertheless, Kuklick's account of *The World and the Individual* helps to show that Royce's reading of human existence is related to other philosophical trends from the recent past, even if its metaphysical resolutions are far removed from them.—*J.K.R.*

ADDITIONAL RECOMMENDED READING

Buranelli, Vincent. *Josiah Royce*. New York: Twayne, 1964. Buranelli accentuates Royce's conviction in *The World and the Individual* that "ideas are like tools. They are there for an end." He sees Royce's "pragmatism" as akin to that of Charles Sanders Peirce.

Cotton, James Harry. *Royce on the Human Self*. Cambridge, Massachusetts: Harvard University Press, 1954. As Cotton spells out Royce's theories of selfhood, he also argues that there is not a sharp break between *The World and the Individual* and *The Problem of Christianity* but "only a seeming one."

Flower, Elizabeth and Murray G. Murphy. "Josiah Royce," in *A History of Philosophy in America*. Vol. II. New York: G. P. Putnam's Sons, 1977, pp. 695-769. The authors cite the second volume of *The World and the Individual* as a "major advance" in Royce's account of "appreciation" and "description" but conclude that he leaves unsettled as many problems as he solves.

Fuss, Peter. *The Moral Philosophy of Josiah Royce*. Cambridge, Massachusetts: Harvard University Press, 1965. *The World and the Individual*, says Fuss, contributes foundational elements that committed Royce to the basically "self-realizationist" moral philosophy elaborated more completely in his later works.

Jarvis, Edward A. *The Conception of God in the Later Royce*. The Hague, The Netherlands: Martinus Nijhoff, 1975. Jarvis provides a detailed analysis of the theological developments in *The World and the Individual*, sharing the view of other commentators that it points a way toward the more adequate perspective of *The Problem of Christianity*.

Roth, John K., ed. *The Philosophy of Josiah Royce*. New York: Thomas Y. Crowell, 1971. The editor suggests that the lasting contributions of Royce's *The World and the Individual* are to be found more in his analysis of finite human experience than in his metaphysical conclusions about the Absolute.

Royce, Josiah. *The Basic Writings of Josiah Royce*. Edited by John J. McDermott. Chicago: University of Chicago Press, 1969. McDermott comments on the "herculean task" Royce set for himself in *The World and the Individual*: nothing less than to provide a complete account of the nature of experience.

Schneider, Herbert W. "Josiah Royce," in *A History of American Philosophy*. New York: Columbia University Press, 1963, pp. 415-424. Schneider sees the Supplementary Essay of *The World and the Individual* as a reworking of Royce's entire philosophy in the light of suggestions about logic that he absorbed from Charles Sanders Peirce.

AESTHETIC

Author: Benedetto Croce (1866-1952)
Type of work: Aesthetics, metaphysics
First published: 1901

PRINCIPAL IDEAS ADVANCED

Art is intuition, and intuition is the expression of impressions.

A sense impression or image becomes an expression, or intuition, when it is clearly known as an image, and when it is unified by the feeling it represents.

The externalization of works of art by the fashioning of physical objects which will serve as stimuli in the reproduction of the intuitions represented is not art.

Art is not concerned with the useful, the moral, or the intellectual.

The fanciful combining of images is not art.

Intuitions are of individuals, not universals.

The theoretical activity of the spirit has two forms: the aesthetic and the logical; the practical activity is composed of the economic and the moral.

The aesthetic values are the beautiful (the expressive) and the ugly; the logical values are the true and the false; the economic values are the useful and the useless; and the moral values are the just and the unjust.

Benedetto Croce's *Aesthetic as Science of Expression and General Linguistic* is the first of three volumes comprising Croce's *Philosophy of the Spirit*; the other two volumes are the *Logic* and the *Philosophy of the Practical.* Croce is generally regarded as an inspired proponent of the idealist strain in philosophy, and the *Aesthetic*, the introduction to his theory, continues to be the work for which he is known; and, it is by his aesthetic theory that he is judged.

The entire thesis of the *Aesthetic* rests on the concept of intuition, and because of the ambiguity of that term, Croce's work has never received the critical attention which is possible for those capable of reading the work in the original Italian. No English term, used without careful qualification, has enough levels of meaning, enough systematic ambiguity, to carry the burden of Croce's central idea. If, in addition, as may very well be the case, one must bring to the reading of the *Aesthetic* a certain tolerance of mind which the prevailing empiricist temper makes difficult, it becomes even more evident that one must resist the temptation to understand Croce all at once; the idea, however deceptively direct its initial expression, must be built with great care, according to Croce's plan.

With this warning in mind, it becomes possible to take certain phrases as initial statements of Croce's position, retaining them as expressions to be illuminated by further discussion and reflection, for otherwise they are practically meaningless. Thus, for Croce, art is intuition, intuition is expression; art is the expression of impressions, and expression is the objectification of feelings by way of representative images. Many negations follow from these affirmations; of them, the most important, for those who would understand Croce, is the denial that the work of art is a physical object.

Croce begins the *Aesthetic* with a careful elaboration of the distinction between intuitive and logical knowledge; it is a distinction which bears some resemblance to Bergson's distinction between intuitive and scientific or conceptual knowledge, but there is a difference. Bergson seemed to be concerned to argue that certain matters cannot be understood analytically or by classes; they must be *felt*, in their internal particularity; to know by *being*: that is intuition. For Croce, the distinction between the object as known from the outside and as realized by itself is not the critical distinction, although it is encompassed by the distinction he does stress; for Croce, intuitive knowledge is the possession of images, but of images clarified by the attention of spirit, freed of all vagueness by the act of apprehension. The idea is remarkable enough to need and deserve amplification, and fortunately there are examples by the use of which Croce's idea of intuition becomes clear.

He asks how a person can be said to have an intuition of a geometrical figure, or of the contour of the island of Sicily, if he cannot draw it. The notion that the artist is skilled in the act of transferring an image from the mind to some physical surface, as if his peculiar gift were in the handling of a pencil or brush, is repudiated by Croce. Unless one possesses a sensation or impression contemplatively, realizing it as an individual image, expression has not taken place; under the influence of sentiment one may suppose that he intuits, but unless he knows an image as an expression, he deceives himself.

To enforce his point, Croce points out that the term "expression" is generally limited to verbal expression, but he uses it to cover nonverbal expressions of line, color, and sound.

Apparently, for Croce, expression is not merely the clear apprehension of an image; the image is expressive of the feeling which it evokes, and it is an expressive of feeling that it becomes full expression or intuition. Thus, in the *Breviary of the Aesthetic* (1913, like the *Aesthetic*, translated by Douglas Ainslie) Croce writes that "what gives coherence and unity to the intuition is feeling: the intuition is really such because it represents a feeling, and can only appear from and upon that." He then goes on to affirm that "Not the idea, but the feeling, is what confers upon art the airy lightness of the symbol: an aspiration enclosed in the circle of a representation—that is art. . . ."

The *Breviary*, which is in many respects a superior expression of Croce's aesthetic theory, is interesting because of the series of denials by which the positive import of Croce's idea is brought out by contrast. To claim that art is intuition, that the artist produces an image which is expressive of feeling, and that he realizes this image in its full individuality, involves the denial that art is a physical fact (for physical facts, according to Croce, *"do not possess reality"*); it also involves the denial of the claim that art is concerned with the useful, with pleasure and pain; it denies that art is a moral act (for art, unlike morality, "is opposed to the practical of any sort"); and, finally, it denies that art is conceptual knowledge (for intuition is unconcerned with the distinction between reality and unreality).

Croce distinguishes between "fancy," which he describes as "the peculiar artistic faculty" and "imagination"; unfortunately, the translation of this passage of the *Breviary* is misleading, for by "imagination" Croce meant the fanciful combination of images, while by "fancy" he meant the production of an image exhibiting unity in variety. The distinction can be grasped by reversing the terms: the mere fanciful handling of images is not art, and the composite image thereby produced is not a work of art; but if the imagination holds on to a sense impression, realizing its presence, taking an interest in it because it serves as the embodiment of feeling, then the image is a work of art.

The esoteric character of Croce's central idea diminishes as one realizes that Croce was concerned to emphasize the artist's ability to see more clearly what others only vaguely sense. "The painter is a painter," he writes in the *Aesthetic*, "because he sees what others only feel or catch a glimpse of, but do not see."

Having argued for the claim that art is intuition, and that intuition is expressive knowledge, Croce considers the critical rejoinder that, although art is intuition, not all intuition is art. He rejects the sophisticated notion that art is the intuition of an intuition—that is, the expression of intuitions. He argues that there is no such process and that what critics have regarded as the expression of expression is, as intuition, the expression of a more complex field of impressions than is ordinarily covered by intuition. He goes on to suggest that the word "art" is often used to call attention to intuitions more extensive in their scope than ordinary intuitions. But from the philosophical point of view—which is concerned with essence and not with quantity—all intuition is art.

If the question arises as to whether content or form is the distinctive aesthetic element in intuition, and by content is meant impressions and by form, expression, then the aesthetic fact, the distinctive aesthetic element, is form.

Because art is the elaboration of impressions, the unifying of impressions into a single, intuited image expressive of feeling, it is a means of liberation for man; the objectification of the passions frees men from their practical influence. The artist is a man of passion who is nevertheless serene; that is because he utilizes sentiment in the intuitive activity, and by that activity he liberates and purifies himself. The paradox of the artist is resolved once it is realized that sensation is passive, but intuition, as the contemplative and creative activity of realizing images as expressive symbols, is active; through activity the artist dominates what would otherwise dominate him.

Art is intuitive knowledge and not conceptual knowledge because knowledge by concepts, according to Croce, is knowledge of the relations of intuitions. Thus, conceptual knowledge depends upon the intuitive, and the latter cannot be reduced to the former. Furthermore, concepts are universals; an intellectual conception is concerned with what is common to a number of things, or intuitions. But intuitions are of particulars; individual images become expressions and serve as works of art. Croce concludes his discussion of this point with the remark that "The intuition gives the world, the phenomenon; the concept gives the noumenon, the Spirit." But this statement is misleading unless we remember that the world presented in intuition is one in which distinctions between actual and possible, true and false, pleasant and unpleasant, and good and bad are irrelevant.

Croce passes from a positive statement of his aesthetic theory to a criticism of rival theories. He considers briefly and in turn the theories that hold art to be an imitation of nature, the representation of universals, the presentation of symbols or allegories, or the portrayal of various forms of life. All such theories commit the fallacy of mistaking the intellectual for the artistic, confusing the concept with the intuition. Once a person concentrates on the *type* of subject matter, the *mode* of treatment, the *style* exhibited, he loses the aesthetic attitude; he has passed on to the scientific or intellectual activity, the exercise of logic, which is concerned with concepts, or universals. "The science of thought (Logic) is that of the concept," he insists, "as that of fancy (Aesthetic) is the science of expression."

As the criticism continues, the outlines of Croce's philosophy of spirit become better defined. The theoretical activity of the spirit has two forms: the aesthetic and the logical; the practical activity also has two forms: the useful or economical, and the moral. "Economy is, as it were, the Aesthetic of practical life; Morality its Logic." Economy is concerned, then, with the individual and his values (just as aesthetic is concerned with the individual intuition and its value), while morality is concerned with the general, with the values of the universal. Nevertheless, the economic will (the practical will) is not the egoistic will; it is possible to conduct oneself practically without being limited to a concern for self. To act morally, one must act economically; but the reverse is not necessarily the case. To conduct oneself economically is to adjust means to ends, but to conduct oneself morally is to adjust means to *ideal* ends, to what the spirit would desire were it rational, aiming at the noumenon, the spirit, of the self. Just as aesthetic is concerned with phenomena, and logic with noumena, so the economic is concerned with the phenomena and morality with the noumena, the ideal.

The beautiful, considered as aesthetic value, is defined by Croce as "*successful expression*," but, realizing that expression which is not successful is not expression, Croce concludes by writing that beauty is expression. Consequently, the ugly is unsuccessful expression, or the failure to achieve expression.

Corresponding to the polar values of beauty and ugliness in the aesthetic are the values of truth and falsity for the intellectual, the useful and the useless for the economic, and the just (or good) and unjust (or evil) for the moral. In every case, the positive value results from the successful development of spiritual activity.

Croce's central criticism of any form of aesthetic hedonism—of any theory which regards art as the production of the pleasurable—is that aesthetic hedonism fails to distinguish between the beautiful, which is the pleasurable as expression, and other sources of pleasure. He scornfully rejects any theory which finds the source of artistic activity in the sexual, in the desire to conquer. He admits that "one often meets in ordinary life poets who adorn themselves with their poetry, like cocks that raise their crests," but he argues that such a man is not a poet, but "a poor devil of a cock or turkey."

For Croce, the physical reproduction of intuitions, the making of physical objects that will stimulate those who experience them to the activity of re-creating the intuitions, is an aid to memory, or a way of preserving intuitions. Physical reproduction is called "externalization," and it is defined as the activity of producing stimuli to aesthetic reproduction.

In ordinary language, the physical objects found on the walls of art museums, the statues of stones or metal that stand in gardens, and other such physical, created objects are works of art; but for Croce only intuitions are works of art; the inner image guides the production of the physical "reproduction," but the physical object is never the aesthetic fact. To confuse the techniques necessary for the externalization of art with the art activity itself is to confuse "Physic" with "Aesthetic." Externalization is a practical activity, while aesthetic is a theoretic activity. Art is thus independent not only of the intellectual, the useful, and the moral; it is independent of the activity of externalization (which is one kind of useful activity). The effort to reproduce the expression by means of the physical object involves the effort to restore the conditions under which the physical object was produced by the artist; works that are to serve as stimuli to expressions are "*historically conditioned.*"

Croce concludes his *Aesthetic* with a chapter in which he explains why he chose to add the words "*and General Linguistic*" to the title *Aesthetic as Science of Expression*. Aesthetic is the science of expression since, for Croce, art is expression (intuition), and aesthetic is the systematic attempt to acquire knowledge about expression. But Croce claims that aesthetic and linguistic are a single science; philosophical linguistic is aesthetic; "Philosophy of language and philosophy of art are the same thing." Aesthetic is the science of general linguistic, then, because language is expression, and aesthetic is the science of expression. The defense of his thesis depends upon Croce's decision to mean by "Linguistic" a rational science, the pure philosophy of speech, and by "speech," any mode of expression.—*I.P.M.*

PERTINENT LITERATURE

Orsini, Gian N. G. *Benedetto Croce: Philosopher of Art and Literary Critic.*
Carbondale: Southern Illinois University Press, 1961.

Benedetto Croce, probably Italy's most cherished and heralded thinker in
the first half of the twentieth century, enjoys an enviable reputation among
those philosophers who study aesthetics, but he remains virtually unknown
to those who do not. This state of affairs is all the more puzzling when one
realizes that Croce made contributions, some original, to almost all of the
traditional areas of philosophy. The fact is that Croce's reputation in his native
country has not been matched elsewhere, and especially not in the English-
speaking world. One of the merits of Gian N. G. Orsini's book is that, apart
from the extensive discussion of Croce's aesthetics, it provides a clear picture
of the philosopher's output during a long working life.

Orsini is first and foremost a literary critic who was motivated by the reading
of Croce's literary aesthetics to examine the formidable system of metaphysics
which underlies all of his work on the philosophy of art. Orsini sets out, then,
to examine critically Croce's doctrines about art in the hope that they will
offer insight of a philosophical nature into the aesthetics of the various arts.
Croce's theories of the nature of art and the nature of art appreciation are
considered to be variations of the general theory of art known as expressionism. Orsini presents Croce's theory and the many changes the theory
underwent from the first publication of the *Aesthetic* in 1901 through the
Breviary of the Aesthetic and *The Essence of Aesthetic*; furthermore, whenever
Croce's theory has been challenged consistently by English-speaking philosophers, Orsini does his best to record the objections and criticisms and to
test Croce's theory against them. This is an absolutely essential aspect in a
commentary on Croce as the latter's theses in the *Aesthetic* are for the most
part presented dogmatically without the support of arguments.

Orsini begins by presenting the basic and controlling tenet of Croce's theory
of art, that all art consists in the production of images of particulars. This is
the process called "intuition," which was defined by Croce as being identical
with expression. One of the criticisms of Croce's aesthetics is that the theory
creates needless ambiguity in the use of the term "intuition." First of all,
"intuition" has been used as a technical term by philosophers to mean sometimes "immediate or instinctive knowledge of a fact" and sometimes "the
immediate apprehension of an object to the mind through the senses." Without complicating the issue, the importance of the different uses of "intuition"
for Croce is that the former meaning refers to a conceptual process by which
philosophical truths are comprehended and which involves meaning, whereas
the latter meaning refers to the apprehension of a particular or of an indi-

vidual. Orsini is adamant that Croce is clear in his use of "intuition" and urges, in Croce's defense, that "intuition" has always had this dual use in the English language. We are to understand, then, that for Croce "intuition" involves the immediate apprehension of a particular—namely, an image. In addition, there is a second charge of ambiguity brought against Croce and his use of "intuition": that he is often unclear as to whether he means the process of intuition, which is universal, or the object of intuition, which is always a particular. Orsini does not really defend Croce against this second charge of ambiguity except to say that the confusion is inherent in the use of the term "intuition" in the English language and that Croce's use of the term to mean either the process of intuiting or the object which is intuited is almost always clear from the context of the discussion. The reader must not think that these are mere linguistic quibbles, for it is the heart of Croce's theory of aesthetics that art is the successful expression of emotion through intuition, a process which involves images, not ideas or thoughts. Orsini does well to concentrate on this aspect of Croce's theory and the objections brought against it.

The most influential as well as the most problematic and controversial aspect of Croce's aesthetics is the theory that all art is fundamentally the expression of emotion. The particulars or individualized images of which knowledge is gained in intuition are merely expressions of emotions and feelings. This is true of all the art forms—poetry, painting, or sculpture— each of which, says Orsini, must be defined as lyrical—that is, as expressive of the artist's emotions. After pointing out that this doctrine of Croce was only fully developed after the *Aesthetic* had been through nine editions, Orsini attempts to expand on Croce's often dogmatic-sounding statements concerning the theory of expression, thereby defending Croce against the quite justified objections which have been raised. One of the most crippling objections to Croce's theory of art is this: the content of all art, indeed, the only possible content of art, is emotion, according to Croce, and successful art is therefore successful expression of emotion. It follows from this, however, that what has not succeeded in finding expression has no existence at all; furthermore, good art becomes just that art which exists—all art that has been created. Orsini's defense of Croce's position here is to argue that the distinction between good and bad art consists in the degree to which the images involved are animated by feeling or are simply mechanical combinations uninformed by the emotional life of the author or artist.

This counterargument only raises another problem for Croce, a problem which Orsini appreciates but to which he fails to give full philosophical due. The problem is how we are to determine the adequacy of the image to the emotion that it is supposed to express; the criterion can only come from the image, for the artist alone knows what his emotion was really like. And if this is the case, then we are back to our original position of having, initially at least, to regard even the most trivial of "artistic" expressions, whether poetical or pictorial, as works of art. What Orsini has to say about this problem amounts to the assertion that we rely on our sense of artistic judgment in evaluating a poem or painting; for example, we know when a poem has overstated the quality of the emotional input of the poet. No doubt we do this, as Orsini says, all the time, but it is not an answer to the *philosophical* problem of producing a criterion for what is to count as a work of art, a criterion which allows us to distinguish between an expression that is not art and an expression which is genuinely artistic. Still, Orsini has identified this difficulty, which is of central importance to Croce's entire theory of the nature of art.

Finally, we come to Orsini's discussion of yet another difficult aspect of Croce's theory of expression. For Croce, in a genuine artistic creation, both the individual, unique image and the emotion associated with it are ultimately one and the same. Orsini attempts to shed some light on this difficult doctrine by suggesting that we understand this to mean that the image and the emotion appear at the same time and in the same act. The act, according to Orsini, is the act of expression, which means that, for Croce, emotion and the expression of emotion are *not* two separate things. The feeling only becomes *a* determinate and unique feeling in its expression. Croce provides a philosophical foundation for this doctrine of the synthesis of image and emotion in the act of expression, but he does not do so in any of the editions of the *Aesthetic*. The important point in Orsini's explanation of the identification of image and emotion is that Croce does not regard the work of art in question as a symbol for the emotion expressed, so that poetry does not "stand for" something else which is not poetry. The image and the emotion are inseparable, and thus the work of art—a poem, for example—stands for itself. The externalization of emotion and image in expression is, says Orsini, less like using language to be understood and is more like, as in the case of a poet and his thought, giving the poet's thought a body from which it can never afterwards be separated. This is expressionism in one of its most extreme forms, and Croce, along with Robin George Collingwood, has been one of its strongest advocates in this century.

De Gennaro, Angelo A. *The Philosophy of Benedetto Croce*. New York: Greenwood Press, 1968.

The purpose of Angelo A. De Gennaro's book is to make American scholars more aware of the thought and work of Benedetto Croce. The author has therefore attempted to produce an essay which will serve both as a useful and much-needed introduction to Croce's work and as an easily accessible analysis of the problems of Croce's main themes. These are admirable goals, as there has always been the suspicion that the reason for Croce's relative obscurity in Britain and America is that he presented his thought in a style and philosophical manner which was incomprehensible to many Anglo-American philosophers and scholars.

Although this book does not deal exclusively with Croce's aesthetics, those chapters which do not are nevertheless valuable for the analysis and discussion they provide of topics which bear directly on the *Aesthetic* and the related works on the theory of art.

De Gennaro tells us that the problem of the nature of art and art appreciation was the one problem with which Croce was concerned throughout his working life; and within the context of this problematic issue, the question of the role and nature of intuition was the most important. De Gennaro argues that Croce's theory of art as intuition and, subsequently, of art as expression, deserves to be given the status of a genuine discovery, for at the time it was first formulated—the early years of the twentieth century—the dominant theories concerning the nature of art were all anathema to Croce's way of thinking. During this period, art was thought to be intimately connected with one or another of the following: naturalism, hedonism, morality, or philosophy. De Gennaro brings in the work of Émile Zola, Gabriele D'Annunzio, and Giovanni Verga as representatives of these opposing theories of the nature of art. Indeed, Croce went out of his way to criticize the proponents of naturalism for whom art was identical to the art-product and who thus made art a physical or material thing. Because art is a theoretical rather than a practical act, art can never be associated with conceptions of pleasure-producing objects or objects the purpose of which is to induce a specific kind of moral action. Both of these are practical activities which lie entirely outside the artistic process—namely, expression. To equate art with a good dinner or an act of the will is to misunderstand that the driving force in an artistic temperament is feeling.

A similar error, says De Gennaro, is committed by those who insist that art is a conceptual process of some sort. If art involved the use of concepts or ideas, the particularity of each work of art—a particularity derived from the uniqueness of the artist's feeling and image—would be inexplicable, for concepts are universal whereas intuitions are particulars. This is roughly the criterion Croce uses in distinguishing art from any other activity, such as philosophy or science. Art and the appreciation of art are forms of nonconceptual knowledge involving intuition and particulars, not concepts and universals. If one asks, as one ought to at this point, how a novel can be a work of art when it involves the rather obvious use of concepts, Croce's response is that the novel considered as a whole presents an intuition even though the parts taken separately have conceptual import.

De Gennaro does not press this objection or possible exception to Croce's theory of art as intuition, but one can see that Croce is hard put to maintain that art and art appreciation are forms of knowledge while also maintaining that art is a sensuous, not an intellectual medium. But this is exactly what he has to maintain, and indeed, does maintain, in order to derive the consequences, so important for his theory of aesthetics, that what art says or provides knowledge of cannot be said or known in another way, since this would contradict the assumption that art does not involve conception, but intuition.

The second, highly important, aspect of Croce's theory of aesthetics which De Gennaro focuses upon is the assertion that a mental state (intuition or feeling) and its expression are not two separate phenomena but rather two aspects of a single process. De Gennaro exemplifies this by referring to the problem of form (expression) and content (intuition or feeling). In light of Croce's doctrine of intuition as expression, a doctrine which De Gennaro regards as profound and original, there is no difference between form and content. The true artist, who must be able to feel deeply, will produce work which expresses itself with deep feeling, or, what amounts to the same thing now, in good form. One of the controversial consequences of this assertion by Croce is that classification of the arts is impossible. The important thing is the artist's feeling, not whether the artist creates an epic, a tragedy, or a statue. The translation of poetry, for example, is declared by Croce to be an impossibility, for if poetry is the expression of feeling, then one poetical world cannot be compared with another. In an attempt to make this extreme doctrine more acceptable, De Gennaro explains that, for Croce, language is neither imitative of nature nor an external object, but a form of spirituality. As such, every man speaks according to his own language, individuality, and background. Art is thus the manifestation of the spirit, and the spirit of the individual artist will be expressed in a way which is pertinent to the uniqueness of that individual.

To summarize and expand slightly on De Gennaro's commentary on this aspect of Croce's theory: when it is said that a work of art expresses a particular feeling, the work of art is identified with the feeling. Any attempt to offer a generalized description of a work of art, according to which we might say that one work of art seemed to express the same feeling as another work of art, would not be a description of the unique quality of *this* or *that* particular work of art. Thus, each work of art is, so to speak, an expression of its own autonomous world, and no work of art can be replaced by any other with the intention of producing, upon those wishing to appreciate that work of art, the same aesthetic experience.

The conclusion, De Gennaro points out, remains problematic: no work of art can be considered as a means to the production of anything which is identifiable apart from it. What De Gennaro actually says is that the theory remains "in conflict," by which he means that art, for Croce, exists for its own sake only.—*J.P.D.*

ADDITIONAL RECOMMENDED READING

Brown, Merle E. *Neo-Idealistic Aesthetics*. Detroit: Wayne State University Press, 1966. A study of the development of the movement called "Neo-Idealistic Aesthetics" by the author. The movement begins with the early writings of Croce and ends with the aesthetics of Robin George Collingwood. A good discussion and criticism of Croce's distinction between art and "conventional" forms of knowledge. Brown offers a Hegelian (dialectical) interpretation of Croce's aesthetics.

Palmer, L. M. and H. S. Harris, eds. *Thought, Action and Intuition as a Symposium on the Philosophy of Benedetto Croce*. Hildesheim, Germany: George Olms, 1975. The best collection of articles in English on Croce's work, including a substantial section on his aesthetics. There are contributions from philosophers, historians of ideas, and scholars. Critically and philosophically, this collection is essential for English readers of Croce.

Scruton, Roger. *Art and Imagination*. New York: Harper & Row Publishers, 1974. An excellent contemporary work in aesthetic theory which attempts to give an empiricist account of aesthetic experience. In doing so, the author has a number of enlightening remarks to make about idealist aesthetics, including Croce's. Challenges Croce's fundamental points in a lively and philosophically rewarding way.

Seerveld, Calvin G. *Benedetto Croce's Earlier Aesthetic Theories and Literary Criticism: A Critical Philosophical Look at the Development During His Rationalistic Years*. Kampen, The Netherlands: J. H. Kok, 1958. A lively monograph on Croce's aesthetics up to 1915 with detailed discussion of the changes in his idea of art as intuition and expression. A good account of Croce's shift towards idealism.

AN INTRODUCTION TO METAPHYSICS

Author: Henri Bergson (1859-1941)
Type of work: Epistemology
First published: 1903

PRINCIPAL IDEAS ADVANCED

Metaphysics is the science which uses intuition.

Intuition is a kind of intellectual sympathy by which one understands an object by placing oneself within it.

Intuitive knowledge is superior to analytic knowledge for intuitive knowledge is both absolute and perfect, while analytic knowledge is relative and imperfect.

Science depends on symbols and employs the analytic method; consequently, science deals with classes rather than with individual objects; it can grasp time, motion, change, and the self only by reducing the fluid to the static.

Intuition, on the other hand, reveals reality as a changing, restless flux—a kind of creative mobility that can never be understood by the use of static concepts.

This famous essay first appeared in the *Revue de Metaphysique et de Morale* in January, 1903. Published in book form in 1912, it has been translated into many languages and constitutes what many philosophers consider to be the best introduction to Bergson's philosophy. Strictly speaking, the title is misleading. The book is not an introduction to metaphysics but rather an introduction to the *method* of metaphysics: *intuition.* While there is a close relation between Bergson's view of the world and his conception of the intuitive method, the emphasis in this book is predominantly on the latter. Metaphysics, in fact, is *defined* by Bergson as the science which uses intuition.

Neither the term "intuition" nor the conception of a direct and immediate way of knowing objects was original with Bergson. A number of rationalists had used the word to describe the awareness of certain basic notions which exhibit a kind of transparency as to their truth and are commonly spoken of as "self-evident." The mystic has often described the culmination of his mystic experience, in which he sees God face to face, as an intuitive experience. Many philosophers have recognized, as Bergson did, the need for a direct, as well as an indirect, way of knowing and have variously characterized intuition as "acquaintance," "sensation," "introspection," "instinct," "feeling." To Bergson goes the credit for extracting what is common to all of these conceptions of immediacy and for portraying the intuitive method in a clear and forceful manner by means of a wide range of vivid examples.

Intuition is defined by Bergson as "the kind of intellectual sympathy by which one places oneself within an object in order to coincide with what is unique in it and consequently inexpressible." In contrast, the method of analysis attempts to grasp the object by portraying the features which it possesses in common with other things. Analysis, therefore, always sees an object partially—from a certain perspective—rather than in its individuality and in terms of its peculiar properties. Intuition gives us what the object is in itself; analysis provides only the shell or the husk.

Of all the metaphors which Bergson uses to contrast the method of intuition with that of analysis, the spatial one is perhaps the most frequent. Consider the contrast between entering into an object and moving around it. Because of spatial perspective an object appears different from various points of observation—larger or smaller, of different shapes, sometimes of varying colors. To identify the object with any one of these appearances would be a mistake. All such knowledge is relative and partial. But the object has a true character of its own; otherwise it would not be capable of exhibiting itself in these many ways. We could not determine this character merely from the many appearances, for there would be an infinity of such manifestations, and we could not create the object by merely adding them together. But if we can intuitively grasp the object by "entering into it" we can see its essential nature and we can then predict what the various perspectives will be. This knowledge does not depend on a point of view, nor does it use any symbols. Hence it is *absolute* rather than *relative*.

Bergson illustrated the difference between intuition and analysis by examining the two methods by which we come to know a character whose adventures are portrayed in a novel. After the author has portrayed the hero through his speech and behavior we feel that we understand him. But this knowledge is superficial and unreliable unless we can succeed at some time in identifying ourself with him, unless we *become* the hero and experience his feelings and drives. Once we have done this we can see that his speech and behavior flow naturally from his personality; we are able, having seen him from the inside or absolutely, to account for his actions relative to varying situations. Having grasped his unique nature we are able to recognize what he has in common with other people—what may be known of him through descriptions, symbols, and analysis.

Intuitive knowledge, according to Bergson, is not only absolute but *perfect*, whereas analytic knowledge is *imperfect*. Try to ascertain what the inner meaning of a poem would be by examining its translations into all possible languages, each with its own shade of meaning, and each correcting the other. The individual translations would be only symbolic representations and could never add up to the true meaning of the poem; they would all be imperfect because partial, and even their sum could not give the intended meaning.

Analysis and intuition are the respective methods of positive science and metaphysics. Science works with symbols—words, numbers, diagrams, graphs. It makes comparisons between forms and reduces complex forms to simple ones; it deals with *classes* of things, not with the *individual objects*.

Metaphysics, on the other hand, attempts to grasp the world without any expression, translation, picture, model, or symbolic device. It is the study which claims to dispense with symbols.

From the many illustrations which Bergson gives of the contrast between the intuitive and the analytic methods three may be selected for special emphasis. These are to be found in our knowledge of the *self*, of *duration*, and of *motion*.

According to Bergson, as I first look at myself I see three things: a series of perceptions of the external world, a group of memories which adhere to the perceptions, and a crowd of motor habits or urges. But as I examine these elements more carefully they seem to recede from my true self, which begins to take on the character of the center of a sphere with the perceptions, memories, and tendencies radiating outward toward the surface. The self which I discover here is not like any flux that I know, since the successive stages merge into one another, each retaining something of what has just passed and each giving a hint of what is still to come. It is not like a series of discrete elements but more like the unrolling of a coil or the rolling up of a thread on a ball. Or it can be compared to a spectrum of colors, with insensible gradations from one hue to the next. But none of these metaphors is quite adequate. The spectrum, for example, is something which is ready made, while the self is a living, growing, developing being, with retentions of what has taken place in its past existence and expectations of what is to come. The inner life of the self has variety, continuity, and unity—yet it is not merely the synthesis of these, for they are themselves abstract and static concepts, while the self is characterized by mobility.

Both empiricists and rationalists miss the real self, for they try to find it in its *manifestations*, which they mistake for its *parts*, not realizing that these are really *partial expressions* of a *total impression* obtained through intuition. The empiricist can find in the personality nothing but a series of psychical events, which he calls "states of the ego." But the ego eludes him because he has only a very confused notion of what it is that he is looking for; he is seeking an intuition but he is using in this search the method of analysis, which is the very negation of it. However closely the states are joined, and however thoroughly the intervals are explored, the ego escapes. We might as well conclude that the *Iliad* has no meaning because we fail to find it in between the letters of which it is composed.

Rationalism is no more successful. It, too, begins with the psychical states. But it realizes that the unity of the personality cannot lie merely in the series of percepts, images, and feelings. Hence, it concludes that the self must be something purely negative—the absence of all determination, form without content, a void in which shadows move. Small wonder that the rationalist finds it hard to distinguish Peter from Paul; if the ego itself is devoid of determination, the individual self must be also. Thus the empiricist tries to construct the unity of the self by filling in the gaps between the states by still other states, while the rationalist tries to find the unity in an empty form. The empiricist reduces the string of beads to the unstrung beads; the rationalist to the unbeaded string; *both* lose the reality with which they began. What is needed is a new empiricism which will define the self through an intuitive examination of the self. This definition can hardly produce a concept at all, since it will apply to only one object. But certainly no concept of the self can be reached by taking sides with empiricism or with rationalism. Only from an intuition of the self in its uniqueness can we descend with equal ease to both philosophical schools.

Bergson offers the idea of duration as another illustration of what happens when we try to understand the world through analysis. From one point of view duration is *multiplicity*; it consists of elements which, unlike other elements, encroach on one another and fuse. If we try to "solidify" duration by adding together all of its parts we fail; we find that we get not the mobility of the duration but the "frozen memory of the duration." From another point of view duration is *unity*. But it is a moving, changing, and living unity, not at all like the abstract and empty form which pure unity demands. Shall we then try to get duration by combining multiplicity and unity? But no sort of mental chemistry will permit this; we cannot get from either of them or from their synthesis the simple intuition of duration. If, however, we start with the intuition, then we can easily see how it is unity and multiplicity, and many other things besides. Unity and multiplicity are only standpoints from which we may consider duration, not parts which constitute it.

Here again Bergson shows the error in trying to understand the world through analysis. Movement can be considered as a series of potential stopping-points; these are points through which the moving object passes, its positions at various times during its motion. Now suppose there were an infinite number of such potential stoppages. Would there be motion? Obviously not. If the object were judged to be *at rest* at each of these positions, no sum of them—finite or infinite—would constitute motion. If the object were judged to be *in motion* at each of these positions, then we should not really have analyzed motion; we should only have broken up a long motion into a series of shorter ones. Passage is movement, and stoppage is immobility, and the two have nothing in common. We try to get mobility from stoppages to infinity, and then, when this fails to give us what we want, we add a mysterious "passage from one stoppage to another." The trouble is, of course, that we have supposed rest to be clearer than motion, and the latter to be definable from the former by way of addition. What we should recognize is that mobility is simple and clear, and that rest is merely the limit of the process of slackening movement. Given an intuition of motion, rest becomes easily understood; without this intuition the motion can never be grasped, whether approached from rest or from any of the other points of view which constitute notes of the total impression.

Through the intuition of movement we can know it *absolutely* rather than *relatively*. Here again Bergson uses the spatial "inside" and "outside" distinction to sharpen the contrast between the two methods of knowing. When we know motion absolutely we insert ourselves into the object by an act of imagination. When we know it relatively we see it only as a function of coordinate systems or points of reference, or as dependent on our own motion or rest with reference to it. The only way really to understand motion is to move. Motion has an interior (something like states of mind), and when we intuit motion we sympathize with this inner nature. We no longer view the motion from outside, remaining where we are, but from within, where the movement really is.

Bergson admits that there are certain difficulties in accepting the intuitive method. Two of these may be mentioned.

One difficulty is that the adoption of the intuitive method requires a change in our ordinary habits of thinking. When we try to understand an object we customarily pass from the concept to the thing, rather than the reverse. Now concepts are abstractions and generalizations; they portray only what is common to objects, not what is peculiar to them. If, then, we try to capture an object by putting concepts together we are doomed to failure. For a concept can only circumscribe around an object a circle, which is too large and does not fit exactly. Realizing this in the case of any one concept, we add another concept, which is also too large but which partially overlaps the previous circle and thus cuts down the area within which the object is to be found. Then we continue the process to infinity, confidently believing that we shall finally reach an area so small that it will contain *only* the object, will characterize it uniquely, and thus will coincide with it. But while the area does coincide with the *properties* it does not coincide with the *object*; the identity of the properties and the object can be grasped only if we start with the object, not if we start with its properties. If we know the thing we can understand its properties, for from a unity we can proceed to the various ways of viewing that unity; but once the unity has been divided into many symbolic expressions, it can never be restored. There will ever remain a gap between the object which is a unique member of a class and the class of which the object is the only member. To avoid this predicament we have only to reverse the usual methods of thinking. Instead of starting with concepts and trying to get objects we should start with intuitively grasped objects and then proceed to symbolize their aspects and properties. Only in this way can inconsistent concepts be harmonized, and only in this way can concepts be molded to fit their objects.

A second difficulty in accepting the intuitive method is that it seems to displace science and render all of its conclusions worthless. But Bergson cautions against this inference on the grounds that both science and the analytic method have an important practical role to play. To illustrate, let us return to the concept of *motion*. We saw that motion cannot be grasped in its essence by thinking of it as an infinite series of positions occupied by the moving object. But now suppose we wish to stop a moving object—as we might well wish to do for certain practical reasons. It will then be very important for us to know where the object is at this precise moment. Science, by the analytic method, can provide us with this information. Indeed, the need for this kind of information accounts for the exactness and precision of science, for its well-defined concepts, and for the method of inductive generalization which it so effectively employs. Through the centuries increased emphasis on the techniques of logic has brought about great improvement in the scientific method. This, in turn, has increased our control over the world. But we do not thereby penetrate deeper into the heart of nature. We can use nature better; we can see better how it will behave toward us and how we should behave toward it, but we do not have the intellectual sympathy which is identical with true understanding. Every concept is a *practical* question which we put to reality. Reality replies in the affirmative or in the negative. But in doing so it hides its true identity.

What sort of a world is it that is revealed by intuition? For an answer to this question we must go to Bergson's other works. Here he states only a few conclusions which can be drawn. Reality is external, but it can be directly experienced by mind. It is characterized primarily by such words as *tendency*, *mobility*, *change*, *flux*. It is a world *being made* rather than a world *ready-made*. It is better understood as a "longing after the restlessness of life" than as a "settling down into an easy intelligibility," as a world of Soul than as a world of Idea.

In this way Bergson tells us about intuition. His success in this attempt, however, leads us to wonder. Has he not in the achievement of his goal destroyed the very thesis of his book; namely, that the true nature of intuition cannot be communicated by means of abstract, general, or simple ideas? For hs has used ideas to communicate successfully the nature of intuition. Perhaps his reply would be that he has not really analyzed intuition. What he has done is to select illustrations of intuition so skillfully that we have been able in each case to identify ourselves with intuition and thus to receive an intuition of intuition.—*A.C.B.*

Pertinent Literature

Goudge, Thomas A. "Introduction," in Henri Bergson's *An Introduction to Metaphysics*. Translated by T. E. Hulme. Indianapolis: Bobbs-Merrill, 1949.

Henri Bergson's first major works, *Time and Free Will* (1889) and *Matter and Memory* (1897), revealed their author's strikingly original turn of mind and left his audience with high expectations of things to come. Thomas A. Goudge, who has also written a helpful article on Bergson for *The Encyclopedia of Philosophy* (New York: Macmillan Publishing Company, 1967), judges that *An Introduction to Metaphysics* did nothing to discourage those hopes; indeed, he ranks this essay as a pivotal one in Bergson's career. It carried forward themes from the earlier pair of books and also pointed the way toward two other important volumes, *Creative Evolution* (1907) and *The Two Sources of Morality and Religion* (1932).

Metaphysics seeks to understand the nature of existence itself. If such understanding is to occur, Bergson thought, one needs to clarify how it can be found. Thus, Goudge explains, Bergson's *An Introduction to Metaphysics* begins by distinguishing two fundamentally different ways of knowing. Intellect, naturally oriented toward practical concerns, provides one route. Breaking things up into discrete units that can be measured and enumerated, it gives us the power we associate with science. Bergson argued, however, that this approach also obscures our understanding of being itself, for intellect objectifies reality in order to organize it for human purposes. The knowledge intellect achieves is relative. What Bergson wanted instead, Goudge asserts, is absolute knowledge of existence. Therefore, *An Introduction to Metaphysics* claimed that an immediate, nonconceptual form of awareness—intuition— provides what is needed to reveal metaphysical truth.

One major set of tasks for Bergson's *An Introduction to Metaphysics*, Goudge states, was to clarify further what this intuitive form of knowing entails and to ascertain where to start in obtaining such awareness. Thus, Goudge writes, Bergson denied that there is some special faculty or non-natural source that gives us what is required. Nor did he interpret intuition merely as emotion or feeling that comes without effort. Intuition necessitates disciplined concentration, Bergson emphasized. We have to go beyond ordinary concerns with action and immerse ourselves in the indivisible current of consciousness. Thus, special attention directed at the individual person's immediate experience of self is the starting point for metaphysics.

If our self-apprehension is clear, Bergson contended, we encounter the becoming of personality through time. Indeed, we experience, as Goudge puts it, "a ceaselessly changing process." In his view, Bergson's greatest originality emerged when he went on to say that the inner experience of the self actually gives us intuitive knowledge of absolute reality, which is revealed to be a constantly changing and novel flowing of activity.

Bergson used the term "duration" to convey many of reality's chief qualities. Goudge unpacks Bergson's understanding of that idea by suggesting that, in addition to using the term to point out heterogeneous and irreversible becoming, Bergson intended "duration" to express his belief that being's vitality is characterized by freedom and unpredictability. In fact, Goudge notes, Bergson was doubtful that being's dynamism could ever be fully grasped by images or concepts. Only through direct intuition can one begin to approach it adequately. Goudge goes on to remark that Bergson was fundamentally mystical and not very sympathetic to the detail of logic. Hence, unsolved problems abound in his metaphysics. Nevertheless, Goudge affirms that Bergson portrayed the temporality of existence and thereby life's novelty and perpetual uniqueness more vividly than any other philosopher.

Jones, W. T. "Kant to Wittgenstein and Sartre," in *A History of Western Philosophy*. Vol. IV. New York: Harcourt, Brace & World, 1969.

In a chapter on "Three Philosophies of Process," W. T. Jones compares Henri Bergson's outlook with those of John Dewey and Alfred North Whitehead. All three of these philosophers, Jones contends, inherited and continued the tradition of tackling classical questions about the nature of reality. Their responses to those issues, however, were critical and innovative. In particular, Jones argues, these philosophers of evolution accentuated how change and development are present throughout existence.

Of this trio, Whitehead and Bergson were the more metaphysical, and between the two of them, Bergson was the more romantic. Jones makes that appraisal because *An Introduction to Metaphysics* attacks the adequacy of conceptual knowledge. Indeed it holds that intellect falsifies the continuity of existence by organizing experience discursively. In contrast, Jones points out, Bergson favored intuition, which he regarded as providng direct access to the nature of reality. Jones describes how Bergson started with the self in undertaking his search for metaphysical truth; but he underscores the fact that Bergson did not stop at that point. By going further, Bergson's efforts produced some of his most profound difficulties as well as some of his richest insights.

As Bergson looked within, Jones explains, he discovered the experience of change itself. More specifically, Bergson spoke of "duration," the term he employed to signify how the self revealed by intuition continuously unfolds in new experiences that incorporate the past as they move always into the future.

Bergson's thought was decisively influenced by previous evolutionary theories, but his originality appeared in the conviction that the self reveals a vast cosmic energy, which pours itself out in endless vibrancy and variety. This energy Bergson took to be reality itself. Jones doubts, however, that Bergson's entry into the self, even if his intuition about its qualities was correct, would make it possible for him to speak with confidence about anything more than himself. Bergson also saw this dilemma and tried to transcend it. Nevertheless, Jones thinks that Bergson remained in a trap. He never showed satisfactorily that no difference exists between appearance and reality, between "the process (experienced in intuition) and the things processing (the material and bodily structures experienced in sense perception and studied in science)." Thus, Jones concludes, Bergson's view was intriguing speculation, but it could not claim to be demonstrated truth.

An additional unresolved dilemma, Jones asserts, swirled around Bergson's use of language. Bergson was forever concerned that the mind's ordinary conceptual patterns would intrude, leaving metaphysics captive to rigid and inadequate categories. On the other hand, if Bergson were actually to carry out his metaphysical enterprise, he would need somehow to describe reality in general terms. Although Bergson aimed to find what he called "supple, mobile, and almost fluid representations" to solve this problem without distortion, the result, Jones argues, was a slippery reliance on metaphor, which imposed limitations that Bergson failed to recognize sufficiently. He employed metaphors as arguments, states the author, but when challenged about their adequacy in that regard, Bergson would back off and hold that they were not to be taken literally. Jones concludes that Bergson's ambivalence, if not antipathy, toward the conceptual adequacy of reason was yet another factor that made it exceedingly difficult and perhaps even impossible for him to offer convincing evidence that his metaphysical speculation was true. Jones believes that *An Introduction to Metaphysics* cuts an instructive middle way between an overconfident rationalism and a positivistic rejection of metaphysics, but he finds that Bergson's own antirationalism left him wide of the target he hoped to hit.

Copleston, Frederick C. *A History of Philosophy*. Vol. IX. Garden City, New York: Doubleday Image Books, 1977.

Frederick C. Copleston concurs with W. T. Jones in the view that reliance on metaphorical language compromised the precision of Henri Bergson's thought, but he also shares Thomas A. Goudge's appreciation for the French philosopher. Although Bergson never aspired to construct a comprehensive metaphysical system, Copleston explains, "a more or less unified world-outlook emerges from his successive writings." That outlook, implies the author, contains considerble trustworthy insight.

Bergson's distinction between intuition and intelligence meant not only that metaphysics and science have different methods and subject matters, but also that metaphysics reveals the true nature of reality in ways that science never can. At the heart of this belief, Copleston stresses, is Bergson's desire to be as faithful as possible to the concreteness and immediacy of experience, which he takes to be our most fundamental point of encounter with being itself. Scientific intelligence abstracts from these immediate encounters. If it serves practical ends by doing so, its static concepts distance us from awareness of the surging vitality disclosed when we intuit our participation in the original impetus for life—an "*élan vital*," as Bergson called it—whose inexhaustible becoming empowers everything and makes all existence an evolutionary process.

Few thinkers were more critical of the intellect's power to conceptualize reality as it is in itself, and yet Bergson evidently went on to articulate the metaphysical truth that he found revealed by intuition. At this juncture, Copleston commiserates with those who question Bergson's consistency. Wanting to ensure that Bergson's position is not misrepresented, however, Copleston notes that Bergson never intended his linguistic descriptions to be metaphysically sufficient by themselves. Reflection and articulation are essential to convey intuition's content and to draw out its significance, but the results of such reflection and articulation will never be adequate unless one shares the intuition from which they are drawn and to which they point. To assess Bergson's acccounts only at the level of theoretical formulation, Copleston suggests, would be to miss their point. For Bergson, the function of such accounts is largely to direct us toward the intuitive awareness upon which metaphysical truth depends.

Although Bergson believed that prolonged intuition would produce philosophical agreement, he also recognized that such insight and consensus rarely emerge in practice. Bergson certainly defended his own views as better than those of others, but Copleston emphasizes that he never proclaimed them to be definitively demonstrated truths. Bergson's approach, thinks Copleston, was more to sketch a portrait of what experience showed, arguing to defend his vision as he went along but not without recognition that his account was tentative and speculative. Indeed, Copleston asserts, the broad strokes of Bergson's philosophical brush account for his greatest influence. If his outlook on reality has been eclipsed recently by analytic and existential perspectives, nevertheless Bergson's nonmechanistic view of life had liberating effects. It cannot be maintained that a Bergsonian school of philosophy resulted; but Copleston concludes that Bergson's wide, if not easily definable, influence stimulated diverse and significant thinkers such as William James and Pierre Teilhard de Chardin.—*J.K.R.*

ADDITIONAL RECOMMENDED READING

Alexander, Ian W. *Bergson: Philosopher of Reflection*. London: Bowes & Bowes, 1957. By viewing reality as a vital process, Alexander argues, Bergson exerted extensive influence, especially on Continental philosophy.

Bocheński, I. M. *Contemporary European Philosophy*. Translated by Donald Nicholl and Karl Aschenbrenner. Berkeley: University of California Press, 1956. This book identifies Bergson as the most important and original proponent of what Bocheński calls "life-philosophy."

Čapek, Milič. *Bergson and Modern Physics: A Reinterpretation and Re-Evaluation*. Dordrecht, The Netherlands: D. Reidel, 1971. The author analyzes three aspects of Bergson's philosophy: his biologically oriented epistemology, the meaning of "intuition," and the relation between Bergson's theory of matter and those of contemporary physicists.

Gallagher, Idella J. *Morality in Evolution: The Moral Philosophy of Henri Bergson*. The Hague, The Netherlands: Martinus Nijhoff, 1970. At the foundation of Bergson's moral philosophy, the author suggests, was Bergson's broad conception of experience and its emphasis on intuition's power to disclose reality in ways unknown and unknowable to intellect.

Maritain, Jacques. *Bergsonian Philosophy and Thomism*. Translated by Mabelle L. Andison and J. Gordon Andison. New York: The Philosophical Library, 1955. Although not uncritical of Bergson, Maritain regards Bergson's metaphysics as "one of the most profound, most penetrating, and most audacious of our time."

Marsak, Leonard M., ed. *French Philosophers from Descartes to Sartre*. New York: Meridian Books, 1961. The editor underscores how *An Introduction to Metaphysics* reflects Bergson's concern to rescue human experience from the crippling effects of scientific determinism.

Pilkington, A. E. *Bergson and His Influence: A Reassessment*. Cambridge: Cambridge University Press, 1976. In addition to exploring relationships between Bergson and four of his contemporaries—Charles Péguy, Marcel Proust, Paul Valéry, and Julien Benda—the author also links Bergson's thinking to that of Edmund Husserl and Jean-Paul Sartre.

Smith, Colin. *Contemporary French Philosophy: A Study in Norms and Values*. London: Methuen, 1964. Focusing on Bergson's contributions to ethics, Smith interprets Bergson as part of a French philosophical tradition that stresses the complementarity between knowing and acting.

Starkie, Enid. "Bergson and Literature," in *The Bergsonian Heritage*. Edited by Thomas Hanna. New York: Columbia University Press, 1962. According to Starkie, Bergson wanted *An Introduction to Metaphysics* to bridge the gap between science and metaphysics, which he regarded as the greatest problem facing modern philosophy.

PRINCIPIA ETHICA

Author: George Edward Moore (1873-1958)
Type of work: Ethics
First published: 1903

PRINCIPAL IDEAS ADVANCED

The adjective "good" names an indefinable, unanalyzable, simple, unique property.

The term "naturalistic fallacy" is applied to any theory which attempts a definition of good, for if good is simple, it has no parts to be distinguished by definition.

Sometimes the value of a whole is not simply the sum of the values of its parts. [The Principle of Organic Unities.]

One's duty, in any particular situation, is to do that action which will cause more good than any possible alternative.

The ideal good is a state of consciousness in which are combined the pleasures of aesthetic contemplation and the pleasures of admiring generous qualities in other persons.

That G. E. Moore's *Principia Ethica* has attained the status of a modern classic is amply attested by the number of references made to its central concepts and arguments. Moore's central contention is that the adjective "good" refers to a simple, unique, and unanalyzable property. He claims that propositions containing value terms and ethical predicates are meaningful and can be found to be either true or false, even though the word "good" names an indefinable property knowable only by intuition or immediate insight. Moore also argues that the truth of propositions predicating intrinsic goodness—that is, that something is good on its own account, quite without reference to its value as a means—must likewise be seen immediately and without proof. The term "naturalistic fallacy" is proposed to name the error of mistaking some property other than goodness for goodness itself. Any definition of "good" would involve reference to something having distinguishable aspects or parts—hence, not simple; but since goodness is simple, any such definition would be false, an instance of the naturalistic fallacy.

The failure of previous systems of ethics, Moore alleges, is attributable to their imprecise formulations of the questions peculiar to ethics. His objective is to discover and lay down those basic principles according to which any scientific ethical investigation must proceed. Ethics should be concerned with two basic questions: "What kinds of things ought to exist for their own sakes?"—which presupposes knowledge of good—and "What kinds of actions ought we to perform?"

The first task of ethics, then, is to determine what "good" means. The only relevant type of definition is not a verbal definition but one which describes the real nature of what is denoted by stating the parts constituting the whole referent. But in this sense of "definition," "good" cannot be defined. It is a simple notion, not complex. The word "good," like "yellow," refers to an object of thought which is indefinable because it is one of many similarly ultimate terms presupposed by those complex ones which can be defined. True, one can give verbal equivalents of these notions; for example, yellow can be described in terms of light vibrations of certain frequencies—as the physicist might describe it—but light waves are obviously not identical with yellow *as experienced*. One either knows yellow in his experience or he does not, for there is no substitute for the visual experience. Likewise, while there are other adjectives, such as "valuable," which can be substituted for "good," the property itself must be recognized in an act of direct insight.

With respect to the notion of good (as a *property* indicated by the adjective—not as a substantive, "a good" or "the good"), and to propositions predicating intrinsic goodness, Moore is an intuitionist. Such propositions are simply self-evident; proof is neither possible nor relevant. But in other respects Moore rejects intuitionism; he denies that such propositions are true *because* they are known by intuition. Holding that this, like any other way of cognizing, may be mistaken, he also denies that propositions in answer to the second basic question—concerning what *ought* to be done—can be known intuitively, since it is a question of means involving intricate causal relations and variable conditions and circumstances. Judgments about intrinsic goodness are true universally if true at all, but in order to know what we ought to do, that is, to know that any given action is the best, we would have to know that the anticipated effects are always produced and that the totality of these reflect a balance of good superior to that of any alternatives. Such judgments can be only probable, never certain. Thus, both types of ethical judgment presuppose the notion of good, but in ways not always clearly distinguished. The situation is complicated because various combinations of intrinsic and instrumental value and disvalue or indifference may occur. Obligatory acts may have no intrinsic value at all, and acts which are impossible and thus not obligatory may have great intrinsic goodness.

But things having this simple, unique quality of goodness also have other properties, and this fact has misled philosophers into what Moore terms "the naturalistic fallacy." To take any other property, such as "pleasant" or "desired," no matter how uniformly associated with good, as *definitive* of "good," is to make this error. These other properties exist in space and time, and hence are in nature; on the other hand, good is nonnatural; it belongs to that class of objects and properties which are not included in the subject matter of the natural sciences. Thus, when someone insists that "good" *means* "pleasant," or in the substantive sense, "pleasure," he is defining good in terms of a natural object or property; that this is fallacious may be seen by substituting for the meaningful question, "Is pleasure good?" the question implied by such a definition: "Is pleasure pleasant?" Clearly we do not mean the latter, Moore insists, or anything like it, and can by direct inspection see what we do mean— we are asking whether pleasure is qualified by an unanalyzable and unique property.

That we can have this notion of good before our minds shows that "good" is not meaningless. The idea that it names a complex which might be analyzed variously must be rejected because we can always ask about any proposed definition of good as complex, "Is X good?" and see that the subject and predicate were not identical. For example, suppose "good" were defined as "that which we desire to desire." While we might plausibly think that "Is A good?" means "Is A that which we desire to desire?" we can again ask the intelligible question, "Is it good to desire to desire A?" But substituting the proposed definition yields the absurdly complicated question, "Is the desire to desire A one of the things which we desire to desire?" Again, obviously this is not what we mean, and direct inspection reveals the difference between the notions of good and desiring to desire. The only remaining alternative is that "good" is indefinable; it must be clear, however, that this condition applies only to what is meant by the adjective "good," not to "*the* good"; were the latter incapable of definition and description, ethics would be pointless.

Moore calls attention to another source of great confusion, the neglect of what he calls the "principle of organic unities." This is the paradoxical but most important truth that things good, bad, and indifferent in various degrees and relationships may constitute a whole in which value of whole and parts are not regularly proportionate. Thus, it is possible for a whole made up of indifferent or even bad parts to be good, or for one containing only good parts to be indifferent or bad, and in less extreme cases, for parts of only moderate worth to constitute wholes of great value. Crime with punishment may make a whole better than one of these two evils without the other; awareness of something beautiful has great intrinsic goodness, but the beautiful object by itself has relatively little value, and consciousness may sometimes be indifferent or bad. The relationship of part to whole is not that of means to end, since the latter consists of separable terms, and upon removal of a means the same intrinsic value may remain in the end, which situation does not obtain for part and whole. Failure to understand the principle of organic unities causes erroneous estimation of the value of a whole as equal to that of the parts.

The foregoing principles and distinctions form the core of Moore's ethics and underlie both his criticism of other views and the final elaboration of his own. He argues that naturalistic theories which identify good with natural properties must either restrict the sense of "nature" if they define "good" in terms of the natural, since in other respects the evil is just as "natural" as the good, or else must select some special feature of nature for this purpose, as does Herbert Spencer in describing the better as the more evolved. In any case the naturalistic fallacy occurs. Hedonism, the view that "pleasure *alone* is good as an end. . . ," is by far the most common form of ethical naturalism, and it receives more detailed treatment. Hedonism is initially plausible, Moore concedes; it is difficult to distinguish being pleased by something from approving it, but we do sometimes disapprove the enjoyable, which shows that the predicate of a judgment of approbation is not synonymous with "pleasant." But most hedonists have fallen into the naturalistic fallacy. John Stuart Mill furnishes a classic example when he asserts that nothing but pleasure or happiness and the avoidance of pain are desirable as ends, and then equates "desirable" with "desired." Actually Mill later describes other things as desired, such as virtue, money, or health; thus, he either contradicts his earlier statements or makes false ones in attempting to show that such things as virtue or money are parts of happiness. He thus obliterates his own distinction—and one upon which Moore insists—between means and ends.

Moore writes that of the hedonists only Henry Sidgwick recognized that "good" is unanalyzable and that the hedonistic doctrine that pleasure is the sole good as an end must rest on intuition or be self-evident. Moore here freely admits what others might regard as a serious limitation in the intuitionist method—that Sidgwick's and his own intuitions conflict and that neither is able to prove hedonism true or false. But this is disturbing primarily because of the disagreement rather than the lack of proof, Moore adds, since ultimate principles are necessarily incapable of demonstration. The best we can do is to be as clear as possible concerning what such intuited principles mean and how they relate to other beliefs we already hold; only thus can we convince an opponent of error. Mill had rejected Jeremy Bentham's view that the only measures of value in pleasure are quantitative, and he had suggested that there are differences in kind; we learn these by consulting competent judges and discovering their preferences. But if pleasure is really the only desirable end, differences in quality are irrelevant; thus, Sidgwick reverted to the simpler form of hedonism, but specified that the ultimate end is related essentially to human existence. Moore submits reasons for rejecting Sidgwick's intuitions. The first objection is that it is obvious that the most beautiful world imaginable would be preferable to the most ugly even if no human beings at all were there to contemplate either. It follows that things separable from human existence can be intrinsically good. But pleasure cannot be good apart from human experience; it is clear that pleasure of which no one was conscious would not be an end for its own sake. Consciousness must be a *part* of the end, and the hedonistic principle is thus seen to be false: it is not pleasure alone but pleasure together with consciousness that is intrinsically good.

The importance of this conclusion lies in the method used to achieve it—that of completely isolating the proposed good and estimating its value apart from all related objects—for the same method shows that consciousness of pleasure is not the only good. Surely no one would think that a world consisting of nothing but consciousness of pleasure would be as good as one including other existents, and even if these were not intrinsically valuable, the latter world could be better as an organic unity. Similar methods of analysis refute other forms of hedonism—egoistic and utilitarian; Moore concludes that, at best, pleasure would be a criterion of good were pleasure and the good always concomitant, but he regards this as very doubtful and supposes that there is no criterion of good at all.

The chief remaining type of ethics Moore criticizes is what he calls "metaphysical ethics" positing some proposition about a supersensible reality as the basis for ethical principles. He admits that the metaphysicians are right in thinking that some things that *are* are not natural objects, but wrong in concluding that therefore whatever does not exist in nature must exist elsewhere. As noted above, things like truth, universals, numbers, and goodness do not exist at all. But metaphysical ethicists such as the Stoics, Spinoza, and Kant have tried to infer what is good from what is ultimately real and thus have committed a variant of the naturalistic fallacy, for whether the reality involved is natural or supernatural is irrelevant. To the second basic ethical question, "What kind of actions ought we to perform?" a supersensible reality might be relevant, but typical metaphysical systems have no bearing on practice. For example, if the sole good pertains to an eternal, perfect, Absolute Being, there is no way by which human action can enhance the goodness of this situation.

Perhaps the metaphysical ethicists have thus erred through failing to notice the ambiguity of the question, "What is good?" which may refer either to good things or to goodness itself; this ambiguity accounts for the inconsistency between such propositions as that the only true reality is eternal and that its future realization is good, when what is meant is that something like—but not identical with—such a reality would be good. But in this case it becomes clear that it is fallacious to define good as constituted by this reality. While "X is good" is verbally similar to other propositions in which both subject and predicate stand for existents, it is actually radically different; of any two existents so related we may still ask, "Is this whole good?" which again shows the uniqueness of the value predicate.

Because of Moore's precise analytical method, the details of his criticism of other positions cannot be treated adequately here, but they are in principle germane to the lines suggested above, as is also his account of practical ethics. It is essential to remember that in answering the question as to what we ought to do once we know intuitively what things are good as ends, a different method must come into use. Since practical ethical judgments assert causal relations between actions and good or bad effects, the empirical method affording probability, never certainty, is indicated. Thus, Moore differs from traditional intuitionists both in his definition of "right" and in his account of how it is known. Right is not to be distinguished from the genuinely useful, and duty is "that action, which will cause more good to exist in the Universe than any possible alternative." In practice our knowledge of right and duty is most limited, so we must consider as duties those acts which will *usually* yield better results than any others. Such limitations do not excuse individuals from following the general rules, but when the latter are lacking or irrelevant, attention should be redirected to the much neglected intrinsic values of the foreseeable effects. It follows, of course, that virtue, like duty, is a means rather than an end, contrary to the views of some Christian writers and even of Kant, who hold inconsistently that either virtue or good will is the sole good, but that it can be rewarded by something better.

It remains to state Moore's conception of "*the* good" or the ideal. He notes that he will try to describe the ideal merely as that which is intrinsically good in a high degree, not the best conceivable or the best possible. Its general description follows: "The best ideal we can construct will be that state of things which contains the greatest number of things having positive value, and which contains nothing evil or indifferent—*provided* that the presence of none of these goods, or the absence of things evil or indifferent, seems to diminish the value of the whole." The method of discovering both the intrinsically valuable and its degrees of value is that previously mentioned: the method of isolation. It will show that "By far the most valuable things, which we know or can imagine, are certain states of consciousness, which may be roughly described as the pleasures of human intercourse and the enjoyment of beautiful objects." Moore stresses the point that it is these wholes, rather than any constituents, which are the ideal ends.

In aesthetic appreciation there are cognition of the object's beautiful qualities and also an appropriate emotion, but neither of these elements has great value in itself compared to that of the whole, and to have a positive emotion toward a really ugly object constitutes a whole which is evil. Beauty is thus not a matter of feeling: "the beautiful should be *defined* as that of which the admiring contemplation is good in itself," and whether an object has true beauty "depends upon the *objective* question whether the whole in question is or is not truly good, and does not depend upon the question whether it would or would not excite particular feelings in particular persons." Subjectivistic definitions of beauty commit the naturalistic fallacy, but it should be noted that beauty can be defined as it is above, thus leaving only one unanalyzable value term, "good." Consideration of the cognitive element in aesthetic appreciation shows that knowledge adds intrinsic value; aside from the value of true belief as a means or that of the actual existence of the object, it is simply and clearly better to know it truly rather than merely to imagine it. Thus appreciation of a real but inferior object is better than that of a superior but imaginary one.

The second and greater good consists of the pleasures of personal affection. All the elements of the best aesthetic enjoyments plus the great intrinsic good of the object are present here. Part of the object consists of the mental qualities of the person for whom affection is felt, though these must be appropriately expressed in the bodily features and behavior. Since "Admirable mental qualities . . . consist very largely in an emotional contemplation of beautiful objects . . . the appreciation of them will consist essentially in the contemplation of such contemplation. It is true that the most valuable appreciation of persons appears to be that which consists in the appreciation of their appreciation of other persons . . . therefore, we may admit that the appreciation of a person's attitude toward other persons . . . is far the most valuable good we know. . . ." From these assertions it follows that the ideal, contrary to tradition, must include material properties, since both appreciation of beauty and of persons requires corporeal expression of the valuable qualities.

Since the emotions appropriate to both beautiful objects and to persons are so widely varied, the totality of intrinsic goods is most complex, but Moore is confident that "a reflective judgment will in the main decide correctly . . ." both what things are positive goods and the major differences in relative values. But this is possible only by exact distinction of the objects of value judgment, followed by direct intuition of the presence, absence, or degree of the unique property, good.

Twentieth century students of ethics have benefited immeasurably from Moore's attempt to be clear and precise in the analysis of ethical principles and from his redirection of attention to the really basic questions. Some critics cannot accept certain major conclusions concerning the indefinability of "good," its presence to intuition, its objective status, and the consequent treatment of the "naturalistic fallacy," but even the nature and the extent of the disagreement he has aroused testify to Moore's stature as a philosopher of ethics.—*M.E.*

PERTINENT LITERATURE
Schilpp, Paul A., ed. *The Philosophy of G. E. Moore* (The Library of Living Philosophers). Vol. IV. London: Cambridge University Press, 1968.

Each volume of The Library of Living Philosophers contains not only articles written for that volume critically examining the works of a philosopher but also the philosopher's replies to those critics. The points George Edward Moore selects for rejoinder are those he regards as most important; nearly a third of his "Reply to My Critics" is on ethics, and most of that is on his *Principia Ethica*. Contributors to the Paul A. Schilpp volume who deal with *Principia Ethica* include C. D. Broad, Charles L. Stevenson, William K. Frankena, H. J. Paton, and Abraham Edel. Here we can only sample the exchanges of views rather than give comprehensive coverage to this admirable volume.

Broad focuses on two questions: What is the distinction between a "natural" and a "non-natural" characteristic? and, what, if any, is the connection between the doctrines that "good" is simple and unanalyzable and that it is nonnatural? Failing to find clear and detailed answers, Broad sets out to supply the basis for an explanation. He posits nonethical "good-making" characteristics, whose presence may make the object possessing them intrinsically good. But if "good" is a simple quality present in the intrinsically good thing, not definable at all, it will hence not be definable in natural terms; thus there is indeed a connection between the claim that "good" names a simple quality and the claim that it names a nonnatural quality.

On Moore's hypotheses, some important features follow. *If* good is a characteristic, it *is* nonnatural; one accepting this is committed to believing that there are *a priori* notions, of which goodness is one; and because of the necessary connection between the natural good-making characteristics of an object and its nonnatural goodness, judgments of its goodness are *synthetic a priori* judgments (necessarily true, although not true by definition). The alternatives for those unwilling to accept these implications are that either goodness is a natural characteristic or that the connections between good-making characteristics and the goodness that they determine is only contingent, not necessary.

Stevenson exhibits some of Moore's arguments in such a way as to show that Moore's affirmations are compatible with that sort of naturalistic view that regards emotive meaning as the meaning of "typically ethical" expressions. Thus Moore cannot hold up his intuition of goodness as a nonnatural quality as the only alternative to existing, defective naturalisms. Alleging that Moore has confined himself systematically to cognitive meanings as the substance of typically ethical utterances, Stevenson suggests, Moore has shut himself off from an alternative preferable to declaring "good" indefinable.

Frankena investigates the relation of "good" (or "value") to obligation. This principle of Moore, on the strength of which he is often called a utilitarian but not a hedonistic utilitarian, is that the act which an agent ought to do is always the one that promotes the most possible intrinsic good in the universe. Frankena analyzes Moore's conception of "good" at some length, concluding that if good is simple, as Moore insists, then it does not have external relations to moral agents; it does not suffice as a basis of judgments of what is right and therefore of what ought to be done; hence its presence cannot compel an act by a moral agent. Thus, goodness has no obligatoriness and is not normative. And if not, then there is no reason to call it indefinable or nonnatural.

Paton asks whether the goodness of a thing might not vary with varying circumstances. Moore's later description of good as "worth having for its own sake" seems to assume a relation to a mind or self. Paton does not see that it is proven in *Principia Ethica*, or follows from the view that goodness is simple and unanalyzable, that good does not vary. He himself finds that the only thing good in all circumstances, not varying according to those circumstances, is, as Immanuel Kant suggested, a good will. Otherwise there are cases of good objects whose goodness depends on relations to other, variable things.

Paton also explores the relation of good to will. Is it the case that to be good is to be willed in a certain way (say, rationally), or is it the case that to be willed in a certain way is to be good? While Moore regards such a relation to be only empirical, he has not ruled out by argument the possibility that there might be a necessary reciprocal connection. Paton would call for exploration of the possibility that a thing to be good must satisfy some desire, will, or need. Acknowledging this possibility, he says, still need not commit the naturalistic fallacy.

Edel makes a thorough examination of Moore's entire ethic, treating it as a logical system and extracting and arranging its terms, definitions, postulates, and rules for the formation of ethical statements and procedures for interpretation and for determining the truth and falsity of ethical statements within the logical structure. Edel essays to discover whether any values are expressed in the structure itself or by its adoption. Screening out considerations of instrumental values while preservng intrinsic value, Moore's postulates (Edel finds) require the absolute constancy of value. From this foundation flow several consequences that make the logical structure a vehicle for (in Edel's terms, not Moore's) several broad values. These consequences are that the doctrine encourages contemplative vision rather than practical problem-solving in ethical matters; the only possible type of interpretation of value relations is intuitive; the ultimate function of ethics becomes an aesthetic experience of contemplating conceived worlds and intuiting their intrinsic good; duties are little explained, but the difficulty of knowing them becomes impressive; existing conventional moralities, even when practiced in the face of rational criticism of their provisions, are greatly supported, while innovation in action is strongly discouraged; yet bold speculation and openness to newly conceived values may elevate the human spirit despite its bonds to mundane morality.

Now it is Moore's turn. In reply to both Broad and Frankena on the relation of "good" and "ought," Moore essays to give more information about the meaning of "good." He introduces the comparative form "better," and offers a sense of "better" of which "good" is the positive degree. Examples: "This world is better than any other possible world would have been," and (in paraphrase) "If there were two worlds, neither containing any pleasure but one containing more pain than the other, the other would be better." Thus it would be true of a "good" world that it is a world whose existence is better than if no world exists at all. Yet Moore refuses to *define* "good" in terms of this sense of "better"; he wishes only to *exhibit* this sense to us.

Moore finds Stevenson persuasive, but decides he has reasons to remain with his early view that "good" is indeed a characteristic. He plies Frankena with a great number of queries as to Frankena's meanings, and challenges Frankena's step from the view that statements of the presence of value do not include and are not identical with statements about obligation, to the view that such statements are not normative. Moore in fact disputes virtually all of Frankena's points, with the exception of the point that since "good" is simple it cannot be defined in terms of obligation.

As for Paton, Moore now concedes that the proposition that there exists a state of affairs which is good entails the proposition that some experience does exist—in other words, that good must be related to mind. In elaborating one of Paton's examples, Moore gives an instance of the good which underscores his insistence that an object be seen on the whole before being judged as to goodness. In the case given, he places the good in the motive rather than in the carrying out of the act. He asserts that the whole combination would have been equally good, intrinsically, no matter what the circumstances under which it occurred.

Moore disclaims understanding Edel's essay sufficiently to reply. Edel has undertaken the impossible task of searching for structure where no structure existed or was intended, and in doing so has produced a fantastic misrepresentation of Moore's doctrines.

White, Alan R. "Ethics," in *G. E. Moore: A Critical Exposition.* Oxford, Basil Blackwell, 1958.

Alan R. White treats George Edward Moore principally as a founding spirit of the British analytical movement in contemporary philosophy. Setting forth Moore's conceptions of analysis as processes of inspection, division, and distinction, White finds that as early as 1903, in *Principia Ethica*, Moore was already applying these methods to ethical investigations.

Defining the field of ethics by the question "What is good?" Moore is interested in "good" only in one sense—ethical, simple, and indefinable— known only by intuition. Yet Moore does not claim that an ethical truth is true *because* it is known by intuition; thus he is not a traditional intuitionist. Moore mentions many other senses of "good." White objects that these are not the many meanings of one ambiguous term, but rather that "good" has one meaning only, its valuative meaning, and that these variations are differences in the applicability of that meaning under differing circumstances.

White protests again that Moore does not actually stick to the view that good (goodness) is unanalyzable, but actually analyzes good by the method of distinguishing it from other notions.

White finds the naturalistic fallacy to be the equating of *any* two notions or terms that are actually distinct. He shows clearly the close relation of this conception to the "open question" method, upon which Moore depends to reveal the fallacy—that is, to show that any naturalistic notion is not the same as "good."

White claims that Moore confused meaning with naming, taking the meaning of any word to be that thing—either physical or mental—that it names, and, upon being unable to find a physical meaning for "good," arrogated it to the status of a property that had a mental, although objective, meaning. He did not consider any third possible thing that could comprise its meaning. This explains many of the criticisms of "good" as a character, simple, indefinable, and independent. It also helps to explain why Moore is almost persuaded by Stevenson that he should heed emotive meaning, where he might find the sort of meaning he could not more clearly exhibit in the sphere of cognitive meaning. Moore need not insist that propositions about good are true or false, in the sense of a correspondence theory of truth, for ordinary language—which ought to be Moore's standard—has many other well-established usages.

In examining Moore's conception of the "intrinsically good," White commends the substitute expression "if quite alone" for "intrinsically." It best expresses Moore's intended meaning, and makes evident the relation of intrinsic goodness to the test by isolation for anything alleged to be intrinsically good. Actually, White suggests, the phrase "intrinsically good" does not convey one particular sense of "good," but rather signals a particular type of reason for applying the word. It expresses the claim that for *this* good object, the claimant discerns ultimate good, beyond which there is no further ground, hence no further explanation. Basically, White concludes, Moore is trying to show us that all the various reasons to apply "good" correctly rest upon these ultimate judgments, expressed in the application of "good" without a reason.—*J.T.G.*

ADDITIONAL RECOMMENDED READING

Broad, C. D. "Is 'Goodness' a Name of a Simple Non-Natural Quality?," in *Proceedings of the Aristotelian Society*. N.S. XXXIV (1934), pp. 249-268. A careful discussion of the issue raised by Moore's contention that goodness is simple and unanalyzable.

Frankena, W. K. "The Naturalistic Fallacy," in *Mind*. XLVIII, no. 192 (October, 1939), pp. 464-477. A penetrating and influential statement.

Hudson, W. D., ed. *New Studies in Ethics*. Vol. II. New York: St. Martin's Press, 1974. Chapter by J. N. Findlay on "Moore, Rashdall and Ross," and chapter by G. J. Warnock on "Intuitionism." Two careful critiques of Moore's ethics.

Jones, E. E. C. "Mr. Moore on Hedonism," in *The International Journal of*

Ethics. XVI (July, 1906), pp. 429-464. Concentrates on the degree to which Moore's view approaches a hedonistic utilitarianism.

Lewy, Casimir. *G. E. Moore on the Naturalistic Fallacy*. Oxford: Oxford University Press, 1965. Another thoughtful analytic examination of the "fallacy" named by Moore.

THE LIFE OF REASON

Author: George Santayana (1863-1952)
Type of work: Metaphysics, philosophy of history
First published: 1905-1906

PRINCIPAL IDEAS ADVANCED

The philosophy of history is an interpretation of man's past in the light of his ideal development.

The life of reason, which gives meaning to history, is the unity given to existence by a mind in love with the good.

By the use of reason man distinguishes between spirit and nature, and comes to understand his own wants and how to satisfy them.

Instinct which originally showed itself only in animal impulses takes on ideal dimensions and leads man into service for society and God.

Finally, in art, which is the imposing of form on matter, but most of all in science, which puts the claims of reason to the test of fact, the life of reason reaches its ideal consummation.

In his autobiography, Santayana says that *The Life of Reason* had its origin in a course which he gave at Harvard University entitled "Philosophy of History." It drew heavily from Plato and Aristotle, but also from Bacon, Locke, Montesquieu, and Taine. We may add Schopenhauer (who was the subject of Santayana's PhD dissertation), and his professor William James, whose biologically oriented psychology left a strong impression on Santayana.

For Santayana, the philosophy of history implies no providential plan of creation or redemption but is simply "retrospective politics"; that is to say, an interpretation of man's past in the light of his ideal development. It is the science of history which deals with events inferred from evidence and explained in terms of causal law. But not content with a mere knowledge of what has happened, man has a strong propensity toward trying to find meaning in events as if history were shaped to some human purpose. Admittedly, it is not; still, the exercise is profitable, for it is one of the ways in which we discover what goals we wish to pursue in the future. The failures and successes of our forebears, as their acts will appear when measured by our ideals, can help us to appraise our standards, as well as to enlighten us with respect to how far they can be attained. But it can serve its function only if we remember that it is ideal history—an abstract from reality made to illustrate a chosen theme—rather than a description of actual tendencies observable in the world.

The theme which Santayana selects as giving meaning to history is the rise and development of reason. Unlike his idealistic counterparts, who think of nature as the product and embodiment of reason, he conceives reason as a latecomer on the evolutionary scene and very much dependent upon what has gone before. This is not to say that there is no order in nature prior to the dawn of consciousness in man. Santayana's contention, on the contrary, is that reason, which is too often thought of in the abstract, schoolmasterly fashion, is in reality an extension of the order already achieved in organized matter. In its earliest phase, it is nothing more than instinct which has grown conscious of its purposes and representative of its conditions. For in the dark laboratories of nature, life has already solved the hardest problems, leaving to its strange child, reason, nothing to do at first but amuse itself with the images which drift through the mind while the body goes about its accustomed business. We can scarcely call it reason until, distinguishing these mental states from objects, reason gradually sees what the parent organism is about, what it runs from, what it pursues, and how it manages each new eventuality. Then it begins to play its role. Where instinct is dependent on present cues, reason can summon thoughts from afar, suggest short cuts, and balance likelihoods. Often its well-meant suggestions lead to destruction; but, on the other hand, its occasionally fruitful counsels tend to perpetuate themselves in habits and customs, as a shelter of branches which, devised for one night's protection, remains standing and becomes a rudimentary home. It is in this way that reason, an adjunct of life, comes to have a "life" of its own.

Reason, by this accounting, is the servant of will or interest. It is these that determine what is good. Santayana calls the Life of Reason the unity inherent in all existence.

Santayana traces reason's career through five phases. He devotes one book to each.

Reason in Common Sense may be regarded as introducing the other books. It outlines the origins of the two realms, nature and spirit, whose fortunes are followed through the rest of the work. Out of an originally chaotic experience, man learns to distinguish first the stable, predictable realm of nature. Regularity and order are present there; and things occurring repeatedly can be identified and their habits noted. But in a great part of experience, images come and go in no discernible pattern, and combine in innumerable ways. This remainder we come to designate as spirit: it is the seat of poetry and dreams, and later of philosophy and mathematics.

Human progress may be viewed as the gradual untangling of these two realms. The rich garment of sight and sound under which nature appears to our senses conceals its structure and beguiles man into supposing that trees and rivers have spirits and pursue purposes not unlike his own. It is practical experience—fishing and agriculture—that gradually teaches him otherwise, enabling him to strip off irrelevant qualities, and discern the mechanical process underneath. Not surprisingly, he is sometimes reluctant to leave behind the more congenial picture of poetry and myth. But insofar as he becomes aware of his advantage, he learns to prefer things to ideas, and to subordinate thinking to the arts of living.

Almost as difficult as discerning nature is the task of deciding what is good. Before consciousness awakened, instinct guided the body toward the satisfaction of genuine, if partial, needs. But when ideas appeared, impulse was diverted, and moral perplexity began. False gods arose, which exist only in imagination, and these must be set aside in favor of ideas which live up to their promises. And there is the further problem of subordinating the claims of competing goods under a common ideal. Reason has not to go beyond human nature to discover the truth and order of values. By understanding man's wants and the limits of his existence, it points him toward his highest fulfillment, that is, his happiness—than which he has no other end.

Viewed in these larger aspects, the rational life is sanity, maturity, common sense. It justifies itself against romanticism, mysticism, and all otherworldliness which betoken a failure to distinguish between ideal and real, or a misguided flight from nature to the world of dreams.

Reason in Society follows the course of man's ideal attachments from the passionate love of a man for a maid to the fancies of a man of taste and finally to the devotions of a saint. The instincts which unite the sexes, bind parents and offspring, and draw the lonely from their isolation into tribes and cities, when illuminated with the flame of consciousness, take on ideal dimensions and give rise to love, loyalty, and faith. It is the mark of love to combine impulse and representation; and no one who has truly loved can be entirely deaf to the voice of reason or indifferent to the liberal life toward which it calls.

Santayana groups societies into three classes. The first, which he calls *natural* societies, includes not merely the family, but economic and political groups. In these, association is more instinctive than voluntary: but they serve reason well when the regimen that they prescribe becomes the means of fashioning strong, reliant individuals who, without disloyalty to their origins, form *free* societies based on mutual attachments and common interests. Such persons, in possession of their own wills, may go further and create *ideal* societies, which is what we do when, forsaking the company of men, we make beauty or truth our companion.

In its social expressions, perhaps more than anywhere else, reason has to draw the fine line between crude fact and irresponsible fancy. Somewhere between the shrewd materialism of Sancho and the lofty madness of Don Quixote, there is a way of living which incorporates the ideal in the actual, whether in love or in politics. Therein lies the liberal or free life for man.

Reason in Religion develops the view, which is perhaps as characteristic of Comte as it is of Hegel, that religion is a half-way station on the road from irresponsible fancy to verifiable truth. It is neither to be rejected out of hand as imbecile and superstitious, nor rationalized and allegorized until it agrees with science. In the story of human progress it fulfills a civilizing function, but under serious disabilities: for although it pursues the same goal as reason, it relies upon imagination instead of logic and experiment. On the positive side, its occasional profound insights into moral reality have spurred mankind to needed reforms; but this gain is offset by its stubborn adherence to an anthropomorphic view of nature which closes the way to systematic advance.

A lifelong student of the religions of the West, Santayana illuminates his theme with detailed criticisms of the major traditions. The Hebrew religion gets high marks for its wholesome emphasis upon morals, but is censured for its dogmatic and intolerant spirit. The Christian gospel, which dramatizes man's efforts to transcend his nature, is an important step toward the goal of freedom; but it needs to be blended with pagan ritual if man is not to lose sight of his moral dimensions. Along the Mediterranean shores, such a paganized Christianity developed. But it remained strange to its converts in the northern forests. Gothic art, philosophy, and chivalry are, by contrast, a barbarized Christianity, and have as their proper motif the native religion of the Teutons. This it was that, coming of age, threw off the world-denying gospel and emerged in its proper sublimation, first as Protestantism, then as romanticism and Absolute Egotism. Less mature, and further divorced from reality than Catholicism, Gothic Christianity lingers on in various idealisms—moral, political, philosophical—obscuring the path of reason.

Reason in Art is broadly conceived to include every activity which "humanizes and rationalizes objects." For Santayana, with his classical bias, artistic activity consists in imposing form upon matter. Like religion, art is preoccupied with imagination; but its concern is more wholesome because, instead of mistaking fancies for facts, it fashions facts according to its ideal preferences. Thus, each genuinely artistic achievement is a step forward toward the goal of rational living.

Man's earliest constructions must have been clumsy and unprepossessing, not even rivaling the spontaneous products of nature. Compared, for example, with the prancing of a stallion, the movements of a savage in his dance are crude and ridiculous. But when art frees the dance from the excitement of war or courtship, and makes the intention its study, a new form of discipline and social control appears which purges the soul. So man tames his own spirit and gladdens it with sights and sounds.

The advance of civilization is not always friendly to free creation. Customs, acquiring almost the force of instincts, stifle invention; and products have a way of enslaving their producers. A society which looks upon art as truancy from business condemns the artist to vagrancy and robs his genius of its normal incentive. It has entered a post-rational phase because it has lost touch with man's genuine needs. Art is no mere pleasurable accessory to life. Man is engaged in liberal and humane enterprise in the measure that, transcending his animal needs and vulgar ambition, he becomes the master of the conditions of his existence, visits on them his kind of perfection, and renders their tragic aspects endurable by clothing them in intelligible and regular forms.

Reason in Science brings the Life of Reason to its *logical* conclusion; for, as Santayana defines science, it is the consummation of the rational ideal in the light of which the other phases of human life have been interpreted and alongside which they have been judged. Insofar as the standard has been presupposed all along, this final volume is somewhat anticlimactic. What saves it from this lot is the feeling of contemporaneousness that goes with the word "science," together with the belief (characteristic of the period in which the work appeared) that mankind has *actually* entered the scientific era for which all previous history was but the prelude. Science, says Santayana, is practically a new thing: only twice in history has it appeared—for three hundred years in Greece and for a comparable time in the modern West. Art and religion have had their day—nothing more is to be expected from them. They bow before the new techniques of measurement and verification. The fruits of science, however, have scarcely begun to appear; and the morrow is sure to bring many surprises.

Santayana's purpose, however, was not primarily to trumpet the dawn of a new day. Optimism with respect to the future was never one of his characteristics. But he was concerned to defend tough-minded naturalism against tender-minded idealism and against all kinds of compromise. Perhaps we might say that his trumpet blast is an effort to frighten off the enemies of science who, he thought, would yet have their way.

To this end, he stresses the sharp distinction between the realm of nature and the realm of spirit. There is a science corresponding to each of these which, using classic terms, he designates respectively as *physics* and *dialectic*.

The ideal expression of physics is mechanics, because the laws governing the behavior of matter are there made perfectly intelligible. But mechanics is exceptional, true only in the gross. The forms and repetitions of nature are never simple and never perfect. Nevertheless, all knowledge which has to do with facts must adopt a mechanical principle of explanation. This is true, Santayana insists, even in the sciences that treat of man—notably history and psychology. There are no special "historical forces," such as idealists are wont to suppose: historical causation breaks up into miscellaneous natural processes and minute particular causes. Similarly, there are no "moral causes," such as biographers and literary psychologists presume: the part of psychology which is a science is physiological and belongs to the biology of man.

As physics comprehends all sciences of fact, dialectic includes all sciences of idea. Its perfect expression is mathematics, which makes possible the deductive elaboration of hypotheses in physics. But another branch of dialectics elaborates the relationship between conflicting human purposes or ideals. Socrates, who pioneered in its development, first established rational ethics. Purely a normative science, it sheds great light on human undertakings, and is presupposed in any study (such as the present one) which attempts to deal intelligently with problems of good and evil. But it is limited to ideas, and cannot take the place of observation and experiment in questions that have to do with existence.

As between questions of fact and questions of purpose, the latter are by far the more fateful, since it is within their domain to decide whether the Life of Reason is to be pursued. Here Santayana considers at length the subject of post-rational ethics and religion. The age of the Greeks passed. In mathematics, physics, and medicine, knowledge continued to progress; but meanwhile a sense of world-weariness descended upon men's minds, causing them to turn their backs on worldly enterprise and seek consolation in pleasure or compensation in ecstasy, or to deaden disappointment by asceticism and obedience. The humanism of Socrates gave place to Stoicism, Epicureanism, Skepticism, and to a revival of pagan cults, all founded on personal or metaphysical despair. In Christianity a similar experience of disillusion forced the imagination to take wings and seek its hope beyond the clouds.

In Santayana's judgment these post-rational systems are not to be condemned. They witness to the fact that life is older and more persistent than reason and knows how to fall back on more primitive solutions to its problems when its bolder experiments fail. And, even in retreat, they hold on to certain conquests of reason, which they fortify and furnish in rare fashion. So, true sages can flourish and true civilizations can develop in retrogressive times, and supernaturalism can nourish a rational and humane wisdom.

This, however, is not to admit that the post-rational systems are an advance over the rational even in the solution of man's spiritual enigmas. And when the same despair breeds arbitrary substitutes for physical science, it is time to cry alarm. Santayana's final chapter, "The Validity of Science," is devoted to criticisms of science, particularly from theologians and transcendental philosophers. The former wish to combine scientific explanation with relics of myth, and so preserve a sanction over moral and political behavior. What the latter seek is less clear. Their attack consists in showing (what was never in doubt) that the findings of science are relative; such philosophers, apparently, aim at freeing their minds of intelligible notions so that they can swim in the void of the vegetative and digestive stage of consciousness.

Science is not beyond criticism. A healthy skepticism respecting the claims of reason is ever in order. It is an integral part of science to review its findings, and purge itself of arbitrariness and bad faith. For its whole aim is to free the mind from caprice by bringing it under the control of objective principles. Santayana quotes Heraclitus' saying, "Men asleep live each in his own world, but when awake they live in the same world together." Religion and art are too much like dreaming; when man brings his dreams under the control of the real world, on the one hand, and the principle of contradiction, on the other, he passes from mere faith and aspiration to knowledge and expectation.—*J. F*

PERTINENT LITERATURE

Kirkwood, M. M. *Santayana: Saint of the Imagination*. Toronto: University of Toronto Press, 1961.

M. M. Kirkwood has designed her book in order to realize two purposes: (1) to portray the man George Santayana by complementing his own auto-biographical account with materials drawn from his letters, and (2) to explicate the significant strands in his philosophical thought. Her major thesis is summed up in the subtitle of her book—that Santayana was a "saint of the imagina-tion." On the philosophical level, she holds that for Santayana the naturalist it is imagination which, with its creative power, lifts man above the other animals and unleashes his creative capacity to create culture as it unfolds in the institutions of art, religion, and science, and which also enables him to live the spiritual life absorbed in the contemplation of essences. On the bio-graphical level, she sketches the imaginative life of Santayana the man and attempts to show the continuity of his career. She depicts Santayana as more a poet than a philosopher, but always as a person who was constant in his naturalist convictions, courageous and sincere about his religious feelings, and unremittingly creative until the end.

Chapters 9 and 10 are devoted to the exegesis of *The Life of Reason*, as it appeared in the first edition in 1905 and 1906, published in five volumes. The general title of both chapters reveals the author's line of interpretation: "The Imagination Producing a Philosophy."

Chapter 9 treats *Reason in Common Sense* and *Reason in Society*. Kirkwood canvasses Santayana's definitions of reason as she expounds the epistemology and theory of values contained in *Reason in Common Sense*; she seeks to trace and elucidate his descriptions of the office of reason in the creation of human culture—an office conspicuous in the quest for harmony of human impulses among themselves and also with the natural environment. In her exposition of *Reason in Society* she pauses to remark that, since the book is replete with remarkable judgments of humane wisdom together with direct, practical applications, it is more interesting than its more profoundly philo-sophical antecedent.

Chapter 10 takes up *Reason in Religion*, *Reason in Art*, and *Reason in Science*. Kirkwood observes that Santayana may have been influenced by his parents to regard religions as artificial and fictitious, but that he nevertheless experienced deep religious feelings which he would not gainsay. Although Santayana's naturalistic convictions repudiated the supernatural, he persisted in the appreciation of the value of religion as fundamental to human civili-zation, locating its validity not in the facts it alleges but in the ideal values it posits, values manifest in the religious virtues of piety, spirituality, and charity.

Kirkwood finds *Reason in Art* a less striking volume than *Reason in Religion*;

but in her brief exposition she associates its themes with the argument of Santayana's earlier work, *The Sense of Beauty*. She rounds out her treatment of *The Life of Reason* with a discussion of the final volume, *Reason in Science*. Here she focuses on Santayana's moral philosophy, attending to his tripartite division of prerational morality, rational ethics, and postrational morality, and delineating his preference for rational ethics.

Methodologically, Kirkwood stays close to the text, summarizing each volume of *The Life of Reason* and interspersing her summary with numerous quotations from Santayana. These are selected to underscore the role of the imagination, which is twofold: (1) imagination as Santayana's own faculty enabling him to create, and (2) imagination as a special agency in human culture. Religion may serve to illustrate her theme. Santayana as a naturalist did not believe in religion as a doctrinal creed stating truths about existence. Disbelief in Santayana's case, however, did not seduce him to discount the imaginative power of religion as a vessel of beauty and a vehicle of moral significance.

In Chapter 14, Kirkwood considers the abridged, one-volume edition of *The Life of Reason*, which appeared in 1954. Following the account of its publication reported by Daniel Cory, she relates that the aged philosopher worked over the Triton edition with a red crayon while his literary secretary, Cory, assisted him. She esteems the one-volume edition as the occasion for the philosopher to complete his task by remaking an early, basic work in order to round out his thought. While Chapter 14 does not mention every revision, it outlines the major differences between the earlier and later editions and calls attention to the most significant changes and deletions. Particularly noteworthy is that in the 1954 edition Santayana dropped the term "mechanism" and its derivatives in numerous passages and substituted the terms "materialism" and "naturalism" and their derivatives.

Munitz, Milton K. *The Moral Philosophy of Santayana*. New York: Humanities Press, 1958.

Milton K. Munitz regards George Santayana as primarily a moral philosopher who sought to understand the conditions of life and to estimate its possible goods. He finds two strands running through Santayana's thought which contribute to both its strengths and weaknesses: naturalism and eclecticism. The naturalism draws upon traditional views of man, knowledge, and nature associated with the Greeks, particularly with Aristotle; it portrays man as a being in nature whose impulses and desires point to ideals or goals as their satisfactory fulfillment; it is realistic in the theory of knowledge; and it proposes the ideal of a good life which, grounded in nature, embraces both the theoretical and practical functions of man. The eclecticism, on the other hand, introduces doctrines which are incompatible with the naturalism—a

Platonic doctrine of essence, an epistemological dualism characteristic of British empiricism with its implication of skepticism, and a theory of spirituality which is otherworldly. The eclecticism is alleged to split Santayana's thought into an untenable metaphysical, epistemological, and moral dualism. Munitz clearly favors the naturalistic strand in Santayana's thought, and criticizes or reinterprets the eclectic factors along consistently formulated naturalistic lines.

This compact book is divided into three parts: (1) naturalism and dualism, (2) the life of reason, and (3) the spiritual life. It is the second part which concentrates on *The Life of Reason*, although comments which illuminate this work appear in other chapters. In Chapter 1, for example, Munitz distinguishes three stages in the development of Santayana's thought. The first is otherworldly and pessimistic; the second is naturalistic and humanistic; and the third reverts to the outlook of the first. It evinces, to use Santayana's term, a "post-rational" mind—one disappointed in the ability to attain natural happiness and seeking solace in mystical self-absorption.

According to Munitz, *The Life of Reason* belongs to the second stage; it is the best expression of Santayana's humanism and naturalism. In Chapter 2 Munitz concentrates on this masterpiece. He opens with an attempt to ascertain the meanings of "the life of reason." He locates its roots in Santayana's famous statement that "everything ideal has a natural basis and everything natural an ideal development." This principle is traced in its various ramifications through the historical progress of mankind; it is also delineated in the possible ideal not yet attained, in personal ethics and in social morality, in concrete particular values and in general principles. The life of reason, based on nature, involves, on the one hand, the acceptance of the specific natural conditions of life, values stemming from fundamental natural impulses, and, on the other, the operation of intelligence which finds the means to satisfy fundamental impulses and desires and, further, criticizes them in order to transform them into a harmony—among themselves and with external reality. Since, therefore, the ideal emerges within a natural process as the desired or desirable terminus or goal, it is no transcendent entity but a practical function.

Unfortunately, according to Munitz's interpretation, Santayana strayed from his naturalism and humanism. Taking off from themes to be found in his earliest works but also present in *The Life of Reason*, he propounded a doctrine of spirit and of spirituality which proposes escape from natural life to purely mystical and aesthetic contemplation of essences. Hence Munitz charges that Santayana's later works undermined the naturalism and humanism of his middle period. Untenable dualisms result: essence is separated from existence and mind from its objects; and the natural ideal of the good as happiness consisting in the harmonious satisfaction of desires is replaced with the mystical ideal of absorbing the individual in the passive contemplation of pure essences.

Singer, Beth J. *The Rational Society: A Critical Study of Santayana's Social Thought*. Cleveland: The Press of Case Western Reserve University, 1970.

This critical study of George Santayana's social and political philosophy covers *The Life of Reason*, in particular *Reason in Society*, and *Dominations and Powers*. Beth J. Singer, unlike Milton K. Munitz, finds Santayana's later thought continuous with the earlier and stresses its persistent naturalism. By naturalism she means a materialist interpretation of reality, extended to morality, society, and politics. Whereas Singer acknowledges that there are ambiguities in Santayana's materialism, she discounts them and emphasizes instead the constancy of his advocacy of epiphenomenalism as the key to his steadfast naturalism. For epiphenomenalism restricts causation to the physical order, so that mind, reason, and its ideals, although they are natural effects of physical causes, have no causal efficacy. Of course she does not deny the difference between Santayana's social and political philosophy in *The Life of Reason* and that in the later *Dominations and Powers*. The difference, however, consists in his abandonment of the moral ideal of inclusive harmony, best represented in Greek rational ethics, which he upheld in *The Life of Reason*, for a kind of moral relativism. When Santayana wrote *The Life of Reason*, he used the ideal of Greek rational ethics to judge other moral ideals, but subsequently he became disillusioned about the practicality of any ideal service as a standard to evaluate other ideals.

While comments on *The Life of Reason* are strewn throughout this compact volume, Chapters 4 through 6 are particularly germane to an understanding of this masterpiece. It is in Chapter 6, "Moral Idealism and Moral Rationality," that Singer presents her thesis that the change in Santayana's moral philosophy assumes a form different from that alleged by Munitz. Santayana is not embroiled in a contradiction between naturalism and eclecticism, but he did revise his concept of moral rationality. He ceased to identify spirituality, attended by moral idealism, with the life of reason. Still he retained them together not as successive and mutually exclusive stages of life, but rather as two complementary dimensions. Nevertheless, Singer's interpretation concedes that, because of the epiphenomenalism (which is indeed the essential element of Santayana's naturalism), it is difficult to explain how reason could be practical.

Chapter 4, "Natural Society," is an exposition and critical interpretation of Santayana's classification of the three stages of society presented in *Reason in Society*: the natural, the free, and the ideal. Natural society is the outgrowth of natural needs: individuals associate for the sake of nutrition, reproduction, and governance. In the discussion of natural society Santayana's antipathy for liberalism and democracy surfaces, as does his preference for a hierarchical social order dominated by a natural aristocracy. Free society in Santayana's sense is an association of persons by affinity rather than necessity—by devotion to common goals or interests; it occurs despite separation in space and time. Ideal society is composed of those vast institutionalized systems of symbols which make up civilization—art, religion, and science.

In Chapter 5, "Biology and Civilization," Singer scrutinizes Santayana's conception of race and his view of its role in the history of civilization. Santayana held that biology undergirds morality, society, and civilization. He even went so far as to claim that races, defined as kinds of individuals molded by breeding and selection, shape the characters of the individuals they embrace and actually determine their destinies. Espousing this doctrine of race in *Reason in Society*, Santayana divided the white race (or people) from the black, and he praised Jews, Greeks, Romans, and the English for their superiority. The doctrine of race survives and is reinforced in the later work, where Santayana grounded morality on race. Critical of Santayana's racism, Singer remarks that Santayana confused the transmission of social custom with biological heredity and erroneously equated national character with pedigree.—*A.J.R.*

ADDITIONAL RECOMMENDED READING

Howgate, George W. *George Santayana.* New York: A. S. Barnes & Company, 1961. First published in 1938, this is an early exposition and interpretation of Santayana's moral philosophy in *The Life of Reason* with stress on the Spanish and individualistic features.

Lachs, John, "Santayana's Moral Philosophy," in *The Journal of Philosophy.* LXI, no. 1 (January 2, 1964), pp. 44-61. A systematic but sympathetic treatment of Santayana's ethics which draws upon other works in addition to *The Life of Reason.*

Moore, A. W. Reviews of *The Life of Reason*, Vols. I-IV, in *The Journal of Philosophy.* III, no. 7 (March 29, 1906), pp. 211-221; and Vol. V, in *The Journal of Philosophy.* III, no. 17 (August 16, 1906), pp. 469-471. Book reviews by a distinguished member of the "Chicago School" of pragmatists who criticized Santayana sharply for making reason impotent rather than efficacious in human life and culture.

Reck, Andrew J. "Realism in Santayana's *Life of Reason*," in *The Monist.* LI, no. 2 (April, 1967), pp. 238-266. An examination of the realisms, epistemological and metaphysical.

Sprigge, Timothy L. S. *Santayana: An Examination of His Philosophy.* London: Routledge & Kegan Paul, 1974. A critical formulation and appraisal of Santayana's materialism and ethical theory in *The Life of Reason.*

Vivas, Eliseo. "From *The Life of Reason* to *The Last Puritan*," in *The Philosophy of George Santayana* (The Library of Living Philosophers). Edited by Paul A. Schilpp. La Salle, Illinois: Open Court, 1940, pp. 315-350.

CREATIVE EVOLUTION

Author: Henri Bergson (1859-1941)
Type of work: Metaphysics
First published: 1906

PRINCIPAL IDEAS ADVANCED

The attempt to understand the self by analyzing it in terms of static concepts must fail to reveal the dynamic, changing character of the self.

There is an interesting force that shows itself in living things, an élan vital that has endured through the ages, accounting for the creative evolution of life and of instinct and intelligence in living things.

Instinct is limited in that although it grasps the fluid nature of living things, it is limited to the individual; but intellect is limited in that although it constructs general truths, it imposes upon life the static character of concepts.

But by the capacity of intuition, a disinterested and self-conscious instinct, a kind of knowledge is made possible which is superior to that provided by either instinct or intellect working separately.

At the time of his death in 1941, in the France dominated by the Nazis, Bergson was a relatively forgotten man, forgotten by the cultivated public and given little attention by the professional philiosopher. Yet in the first two decades of this century he was lionized by the former and respected and often received enthusiastically by the latter. His fame was made by his immensely popular *Creative Evolution*. In this book he engages in metaphysical speculation on the grand scale, projecting his views back into the remote past and forward into the future. He speculates about matters that are difficult to speak about and impossible to verify in any of the traditionally accepted ways. Indeed, he mounts a concerted attack on traditional philosophic assumptions and techniques, insisting in particular that the dominant mechanistic and materialistic approach can lead only to a gross misrepresentation of reality. The chief villain here is intellect itself, for it can operate only through the use of concepts, and concepts are fixed, static categories that cannot contain fluid reality. There was a strong strain of anti-intellectualism in Bergson.

These basic views are expressed first in his discussion of the self. Perhaps the most noteworthy feature of our own inner life is the unceasing change that occurs there, the unceasing flow of thoughts, feelings, perceptions, and volitions. It is quite natural to think of this change as a succession of states in which each state holds the stage for a while before it is followed by its successor. Pursuing this analysis, we are led to think of the states themselves as internally static and changeless, for change is just the replacement of one state by another. Similarly, we are led to think of time as a succession of moments within which temporal change does not occur. Having cut the self into a collection of independent and static atoms of experience, we then wonder how this collection can constitute a unified, dynamic self, but we solve this difficulty by postulating the existence of an unexperienced mental substance that supports them, holds them together, and accounts for the manner of their succession.

We have gone astray, Bergson says, because we have tried to describe the dynamic, pulsating self by using concepts that inevitably impose their foreign rigidity upon it. Change in the self is not a process in which unchanging blocks are successively cast into and out of existence. Rather, it is a continuous process occurring in a self in which "states" (if we must use this term) are not units demarcated by sharp lines, but are at most centers of intensity trailing off indefinitely within the unbroken fabric of experience. Because it is growing, the self is changing in a direction that cannot be reversed, the past accumulating around the present as snow accumulates around a rolling snowball. To be such a changing thing is to be a self, and to experience such irreversible change is to have a history. This dynamic snowballing time, this time that counts, is real time or "duration," as Bergson calls it to distinguish it from the conceptualized, static, essentially reversible time of the mathematician. Memory is not the recalling of experiences that have long departed, but is the past living on in the present, affecting our present behavior. Consequently, in the self there is no exact repetition of past patterns, and novelty is the rule. Man is free, for in using the past he creates the future. We can discover all this for ourselves if we attend to our own inner life and are not misled by the concepts intellect would like to impose. Duration is not to be thought about; it is to be experienced, for only experience can reveal it to us.

Compared with the self, physical objects do not grow and change, they do not have memories, they do nothing new, they do not have histories, and they do not endure, for time makes no difference to them. The planets revolve as they always have, and they will continue to do so, except insofar as they are subject to changing external forces. The static concepts of mathematics and physics apply quite appropriately to them because they lend themselves to description in just such terms. These differences between physical objects and the living self indicate the presence of something in the latter that is not in the former, some dynamic element that makes the difference between the accumulative, purposeful, creative behavior of the one and the passive, repetitious, monotonous existence of the other. If we turn to biological phenomena and especially to the evolution of living things, we will discover overwhelming evidence in support of this thesis. One of the main examples is that of the evolution of the eye. Both the complex arrangement of otherwise useless components and the long history of increasingly complex sensory organs cannot be explained plausibly unless we assume some sort of integrating force that is moving in a definite direction.

Bergson cites the biological evidence that supports the fact of evolution, but we are not concerned with the fact itself as much as we are with what it presupposes. Darwin's theory of the survival of the fittest is all right as far as it goes, but it does not explain why mutations should occur in the first place or why many of them survive when they have no immediate survival value.

Bergson rejects three theories before he offers his own. First, he says that no mechanistic or materialistic account will do, for such an account forces the dynamic processes of life into the straitjacket of physical concepts and, in insisting that the future is determined completely by the past, repudiates the duration, freedom, and creation that are evident in the realm of living things. Second, Bergson rejects any finalistic view that describes the world as being attracted or directed toward some future goal, some end it cannot avoid, for such a view replaces one form of determinism by another. Finally, he repudiates the vitalism that was current in the biology of his day, for the postulation of a vital principle whose function is restricted to explaining the organization of parts and drives within the individual does not explain the fact of evolution.

Bergson's own view is a sort of cosmic vitalism in which the vital principle or *élan vital*, as he calls it, is life itself as it has endured through the ages, and evolution is the history of the effort of life to free itself from the domination of matter and to achieve self-consciousness. Beginning as the dimmest spark distinguishing the living from the dead, thrusting itself out in various directions, the *élan vital* has tried one by one the experiments represented by the divergent branches of the evolutionary tree. Many of the resultant forms have long ago been rejected as unsuitable, and others have been allowed to stagnate as the *élan* has continuously diverted its energies into the more promising ones. It pushed out into the vegetable and animal kingdoms and found that the latter allowed it greater scope. It discovered that the storage and explosive release of energy lead to freedom, that motion and consciousness are better than a sedentary torpor, that defense through high mobility and dexterity is better than that of armor, and so on through a host of minor and major alternatives. The most significant dichotomy of all has been that between the arthropods which have developed through the various insect forms to culminate in the hymenoptera, and the vertebrates which have diversified but culminated in man. This dichotomy is significant because the culminating species embody the best solutions the *élan* has yet found in its long struggle to emancipate itself from the matter that drags it down, the solutions represented by instinct and intelligence.

Both instinct and intelligence emerged as instruments for manipulating matter. Intellect fulfills this function through its ability to apprehend problems and to produce the mechanical devices needed to solve them. In fact, according to Bergson, intelligence is the faculty of making objects—such as tools to make tools—and of varying the manufacture at will. Arising from the animal's hesitation in a dilemma, intelligence expresses itself in thought rather than in action; developing the technique of language, it can operate when the original stimulus is no longer present; becoming aware of this subjective process it develops self-consciousness; concentrating on relations and forms, it frees itself from matter and develops the ability to generalize; and finally, using these resources and indulging its aroused curiosity, it turns from practical to theoretical matters. Instinct, too, operates through the use of tools, but the tools in this case are integral parts of the body, tools designed for a specific use and limited to that use. The instinctive reactions of the insect are sure and precise, but their scope is both limited and invariant. Instincts are released directly in action and function unconsciously. Yet they do involve an important kind of knowledge—not knowledge *about*, but an unconscious empathy with their object.

Both intellect and instinct have their advantages as well as their disadvantages. Among the great advantages of intellect are its consciousness and its ability to discover general truths, but it has disadvantages stemming from its inability to grasp things except through forms that are suggested to it by the object but crystallized into sharply defined concepts by itself. Thus, it is limited in two respects; it can grasp only the external form of a thing, and it cannot avoid seeing in the thing the static nature of the concept through which it is seen. Instinct has the advantage of grasping the fluid nature of living things, but it is limited to the individual and has not attained consciousness.

The production of instinct and intelligence is an experiment in which the *élan* has been articulating divergent but complementary tendencies that have lain dormant in it from the beginning. Through the resultant clarification it is readying itself to combine the desirable features of each in a new capacity that will transcend both. This new capacity already appears fleetingly in man. It is the capacity of intuition, a capacity that may be described briefly as instinct that has become disinterested and self-conscious. Artists to a greater extent, and most men to a lesser, are able to place themselves in a sort of divining sympathy with things and with other people. Intuition manifests itself in situations in which men are not dominated by disinterested thought—in the crises of life where problems press in and drastic action is required, and in moments of intense joy, sadness, or commiseration. In such cases and for a brief time we know our own inner being and that of others in a much more intimate fashion than we do when we sit in our studies and describe ourselves. Life then becomes aware of itself, of duration, and of the world, not through the distorting mediation of concepts, but directly and immediately. Man in his present state cannot maintain such insight for long, but if the *élan* is successful it will develop beings who can. What the nature of that intuition will be, and whether the *élan* will attain its goal of complete self-consciousness and complete dominance over matter, we cannot tell. We cannot tell for we are manifestations of the *élan*, and it does not know. It is striving less blindly than it did in past ages, but still, it does not know.

In the first half of his book, when he pits the *élan* against matter, it appears as if Bergson were maintaining that the world is composed of two radically different and independent principles. But in the latter half he makes it clear that he does not maintain such a metaphysical dualism. The distinction he has made between the *élan* and matter shares the defect of all distinctions made by the intellect—it is overdrawn. On the one hand the physical world around us is not quite as static and inert as it appears in the enclosed systems of the physicist, for if we regard it over long periods and great expanses we will find that it does not repeat itself quite as monotonously as we sometimes think it does. On the other hand, the self is not a continuously creative, pure-burning center of energy, for it can lapse into periods of lethargy during which it approaches the status of a physical thing. This is not to deny that there is a big difference between *élan* and matter, but it is to deny that the difference is an absolute one. It has the signs of being a difference in degree rather than one in kind.

If we retrace our steps in time we will find that the difference was even less long ago. Did the first organic things differ radically from the inorganic compounds from which they arose? Did not their emergence presuppose some prior creative activity? Indeed, Bergson speculates, life and matter stem from a common inarticulated source that contained neither as we know them, even though it did contain the tendencies from which they have evolved. Feeling dimly a need for creation, the primal substance began to stir, and gathering strength erratically but gradually, it generated life and matter by processes that are the inverse of each other.

Sometimes Bergson writes as if the quickening in the original indeterminate source has led to its articulation into parts that vary in their vitality, the less vital lapsing into relatively passive matter that resists the efforts of the more vital to move it or to move through it. At other times he writes as if the resistance to life stems from life itself. It is pictured as a frail element that overextends itself, that depletes itself, and that lapses into lethargy before it can gather itself together for another spurt. Matter is tired life. If the *élan* is a flowing current, then matter is a congealing of it. If the *élan* is a cosmic tension, then extension is the interruption or disappearance of that tension.

Bergson expresses himself in two particularly vivid metaphors. The first is that of a vessel of steam from which live jets escape, travel through space, lose their energy, condense into water and fall, only to provide a cooling medium that saps the energy of the jets that in penetrating it try to carry it with them in their upward thrust. Thus, through the ages, both life and matter have come from an inexhaustible reservoir, generated by processes that are the inverse of each other, and having inverse effects upon each other. The other, and perhaps better, metaphor is that in which the emerging *élan* is likened to a series of skyrockets. Imagine an original skyrocket that rises, slows down, and bursts, scattering its exhausted fragments through the sky. Imagine also that as it bursts it releases a number of rockets that gather speed and mount upwards in various directions through the debris. Some of these, retarded by their own weight and slowed by the resisting ashes of their predecessors, will simply fizzle out, doomed to do no more than scatter debris yet higher in the sky. But, in a final burst, some will release still others that will probe the upper reaches before they too die, barrenly or fruitfully. In this fashion the original urge to life has climbed through the ages, fighting its own lethargy, thrusting through or by the static remnants of its past endeavors, gathering strength to go off in new directions, sometimes succeeding and sometimes failing in its attempt to attain higher levels of consciousness.

Bergson's reliance on vivid metaphors of this sort accounts in part for the immediate impact the book had, but it also gives rise to some of the more severe criticism leveled at him. Metaphors are suggestive, but they are not accurate. Time and the self may both be like a rolling snowball rather than like a series of beads on a string; matter may be like congealing jelly or life like a river seeking the easiest path through the constraining land, and the *élan* may be like steam or skyrockets, but such suggestions should be followed by hard-headed, nonmetaphorical analyses. Although Bergson was often a good critic of others' speculations, the exposition of his own doctrine remains both ambiguous and vague. The concepts of duration, matter, *élan vital*, and intuition are never entirely clarified, and different images of them are not really reconciled. Furthermore, the distinction between epistemological and metaphysical considerations is not maintained, particularly in the discussion of matter where it is often unclear whether the villain is our concept of matter or matter itself. His criticism of the mathematician's account of space and time is based on an inadequate knowledge of the mathematics of the continuum, for apparently he believed all series must be discrete series. Finally, his attacks on the extent and accuracy of intellectual knowledge, and in particular his assumptions that the intellect must distort and that it is the blind captive of its own distortion, seem too extreme.

Perhaps Bergson would reply that although the intellect is capable of giving us knowledge of a sort, better knowledge may be achieved by intuition. Perhaps he would defend his use of metaphors in this way also, arguing that in using them he deliberately intends to lead us away from conceptual analysis, which must fail, toward intuition which alone can succeed. Intuition, duration, the self, or the *élan* cannot accurately be described simply because they are indescribable; he can only point to the sort of experience in which they are immediately known, and urge us to discover them for ourselves.—*L.M.*

PERTINENT LITERATURE

Chevalier, Jacques. *Henri Bergson.* Translated by Lilian A. Clare. New

York: Macmillan Publishing Company, 1928.

In his book *Henri Bergson*, Jacques Chevalier seeks to defend Henri Bergson's philosophy from those who would understand it as a type of antiintellectualism, pure intuitionism, radical indeterminism, or idealism. Chevalier admits that all of these elements are, to some extent, involved in Bergson's philosophy, but he contends that the thrust of Bergson's thought is much more balanced and realistic. In Chevalier's opinion, Bergson's philosophy is the most adequate philosophy of its time.

Chevalier begins his book with a study of the intellectual milieu of France toward the end of the eighteenth century and then proceeds to give an account of Bergson's life and the development of his thought. According to Chevalier, there were a number of factors in Bergson's environment which led him to champion intuition, freedom, and duration, as opposed to intellectualism (the doctrine that all knowledge is conceptual), determinism (the doctrine that everything that happens could not have happened otherwise), and mechanism (the doctrine that "life" is simply a complex machine). Bergson did not wholly reject intellectualism, determinism, and mechanism. Rather, he maintained that, in addition to conceptual knowledge, there is direct knowledge; in addition to some things being determined, other things are free; and in addition to there being mechanistic aspects of life, there are spiritual aspects.

Chevalier maintains that Bergson's philosophy is realistic in both its method and its doctrines. Bergson's method is realistic in that it begins with what is given in experience and also in that it builds upon information obtained through scientific experiments. According to Chevalier, Bergson's realistic method is his greatest contribution to philosophy.

Moreover, Chevalier is convinced that the substance of Bergson's philosophy—the content of his doctrines—is realistic. At the heart of Bergson's philosophy stands his doctrine of knowledge, his epistemology. Unlike Immanuel Kant and those who followed him, Bergson maintains that it is possible to know things as they are in fact. Kant taught that what is known is shaped by universal categories of understanding, and therefore it is not possible to know things as they are in themselves, but only as they appear. Bergson, on the other hand, holds that through intuition it is possible to know things in themselves.

In Chevalier's final section, "The Trend of Bergsonian Thought: God and Man's Destiny. The Metaphysical Revival," the religious dimensions of Bergson's philosophy are considered. In Chevalier's estimation, one can discern an implicit doctrine of God in Bergson's works *Time and Free Will*, *Matter and Memory*, and *Creative Evolution*. In these works, Bergson implies the existence of a God who is characterized by personality—or, rather, superpersonality—freedom, and creativity. Bergson is neither a monist nor a pantheist; he believes that God created the world and is active in the world, but is not identical with the world.

In the first part of this century Bergson's philosophy was very controversial. A few persons, most notably George Santayana and Bertrand Russell, were highly critical of it; but a great many others were extremely impressed by it and considered themselves "Bergsonians." Jacques Chevalier's book, *Henri Bergson*, stands as a classic work in the tradition of the Bergsonians.

Gunter, Pete A. "The Heuristic Force of *Creative Evolution*," in *The Southwestern Journal of Philosophy*. I, no. 3 (Fall, 1970), pp. 111-118.

Scientists and philosophers have generally agreed that Bergson's understanding of biological matters is unscientific. In his article "The Heuristic Force of *Creative Evolution*," Pete A. Gunter argues that this is not the case. A careful study of Bergson's most famous work, *Creative Evolution*, Gunter contends, reveals that Bergson's vitalism is not unscientific and that, in fact, it is capable of explaining certain scientifically accepted facts and of leading the way to the discovery of new facts. Gunter develops his argument around four aspects of Bergson's thought: his concept of matter and life, his treatment of physics and biology, his concept of intuition and its relevance to the natural sciences, and his concept of biological time.

Gunter's first point is that Bergson's understanding of matter and life is not dualistic. The apparent dualism between Newtonian atoms and vital impulses disappears when one recognizes that, according to Bergson, matter and life are both characterized by dynamic movement. Gunter maintains that Bergson judges there to be a "natural contrast" between living organisms and nonliving matter, but that this natural contrast falls short of a metaphysical dualism.

Gunter's second concern is to show that, for Bergson, physics and biology are similar disciplines. Although there are passages in *Creative Evolution* which suggest that physics is precise and scientific while biology is not and never can be, this is not Bergson's position. Precision is more difficult to achieve in biology than in physics because living things are more dynamic than are nonliving things; nevertheless, both sciences approximate real objects and both sciences are subject to certain limitations.

The third issue with which Gunter deals is Bergson's concept of intuition and its relevance to the natural sciences. Bergson maintains that intuition plays a role in all scientific explanations. Apart from intuition there simply are no explanations. This is not to say that all branches of science are equally dependent upon intuition or that intuition alone is sufficient. According to Gunter, Bergson maintains that the amount of intuition that is required for explaining a fact depends upon the amount of life in the fact to be explained; that intuition may be checked against information obtained according to scientific methodology. When properly understood, then, Bergson's appeal to intuition in the life sciences is not unscientific.

Gunter's fourth concern is to discuss Bergson's concept of biological time as the internal pace of an organism. Unlike physical or clock time, biological time is not comprised of equal units; instead, it accelerates in the developmental stages of an organism and decelerates in the decaying stages. Gunter cites various studies dealing with "biological clocks" which appear to support Bergson's theory of biological time.

In Gunter's estimation, Bergson's understanding of biological events is still relevant and deserves careful consideration by members of the scientific community. Gunter's thesis is well argued.

Santayana, George. *Winds of Doctrine: Studies in Contemporary Opinion.* New York: Charles Scribner's Sons, 1913.

Included in his work *Winds of Doctrine* is George Santayana's celebrated and unsympathetic critique of Henri Bergson's evolutionary philosophy. Santayana recognizes Bergson as the most representative and remarkable philosopher of the period just preceding World War I, yet he takes issue with virtually every aspect of Bergson's philosophy. He strongly opposes Bergson's evolutionary understanding of reality, introspective method, anthropomorphic tendencies, mysticism, and assessment of science and reason.

Santayana raises two important objections to Bergson's evolutionary understanding of reality: he objects to Bergson's phychophysical dualism and his conclusion that human beings are the final stage of evolution. Santayana believes that Bergson undercuts his own evolutionary theory on both accounts. A truly evolutionary position would not be dualistic: it would explain life in terms of matter. By contending that life is not a natural expression of material being but rather is the natural expression of a "life force" which is nonmaterial, Bergson's philosophy is less evolutionary than it could be. Bergson's evolutionary position is further undermined by his assumption that human beings are the final product of evolution. A truly evolutionary philosophy would hold that the process which has led up to human beings will continue beyond human beings. An evolutionary process cannot have final ends. In Santayana's estimation, Bergson's evolutionary position is internally inconsistent.

According to Santayana, Bergson's notion that evolution culminates in human beings is tied to his introspective method and his anthropomorphic tendencies. Bergson "turns inward"—becomes introspective—because he is afraid to look outward. He is afraid of space, mechanism, necessity, death, reason, and the discoveries of science. In Santayana's words, Bergson suffers from "cosmic agoraphobia." Bergson escapes these fears by turning inward and by concluding that this inner world is finally the most real world, that everything actual must resemble it in some fashion. Bergson's "metaphysics," then, is simply a projection of his personal psychology onto the world at large.

According to Santayana, Bergson spoils his psychology by pretending that it is a metaphysics.

Santayana recognizes the attractiveness of Bergson's philosophy. It would be nice if evolution were simply a process to create human beings and if everything actual resembled our inner selves. It also would be nice if scientific discipline were unnecessary and if the truth concerning anything could be obtained through careful introspection, as Bergson contends. But is this actually the case? Is there any reason to think that Bergson is correct? Santayana firmly believes that there is not, that Bergson's philosophy is almost entirely specious.

Santayana's essay raises many important objections to Bergson's philosophy. One need not accept his judgment of Bergson's thought, but one must deal with the issues he has raised.—*M.F.*

ADDITIONAL RECOMMENDED READING

Carr, Herbert Weldon. *The Philosophy of Change: A Study of the Fundamental Principle of the Philosophy of Bergson*. London: Macmillan and Company, 1914. A sympathetic and careful study of Bergson's major philosophical doctrines.

Gunter, Pete A. *Henri Bergson: A Bibliography*. Bowling Green, Ohio: Philosophy Documentation Center, 1974. This work contains an introduction which includes a biographical sketch; a list of works by Bergson; and a complete list of works published about Bergson.

Hanna, Thomas, ed. *The Bergsonian Heritage*. New York: Columbia University Press, 1962. *The Bergsonian Heritage* is a collection of three essays and seven short papers dealing with the importance of Bergson's thought. The essays are: "What Bergson Means to Us Today," by Edouard Morot-Sir; "Bergson Among Theologians," by Jaroslav Pelikan; and "Bergson and Literature," by Enid Starkie.

Lindsay, Alexander D. *The Philosophy of Bergson*. London: J. M. Dent & Sons, 1911. Lindsay's thesis is that Bergson's thought is best understood by comparison with Kant's. Like Kant, Bergson was interested in resolving the antinomies found in uncritical thought by reassessing the limits of philosophy and by establishing a new method.

Maritain, Jacques. *Bergsonian Philosophy and Thomism*. Translated by Mabelle L. Andison in collaboration with J. Gordon Andison. New York: Philosophical Library, 1955. This is a translation of *La Philosophie Bergsonienne*, which was first published in 1914. The book presents an explication of Bergson's thought and a critical examination of his major doctrines. As the English title indicates, Maritain draws upon Thomistic philosophy in his critique of Bergsonian doctrines.

Vandel, Albert. "L'Importance de *L'Evolution créatrice* dans la genèse de la pensée moderne," in *Revue de Théologie et de Philosophie*. IX, no. 2 (1960), pp. 85-108. Vandel traces the history of evolutionary theory since Jean Baptiste Lamarck. He also discusses Bergson's contribution to evolutionary theory and the influence of Bergson's thought on F. Leenhardt, G. Mercier, and Pierre Teilhard de Chardin. Unfortunately, this article has not been translated into English.

THE NATURE OF TRUTH

Author: Harold Henry Joachim (1868-1938)
Type of work: Epistemology
First published: 1906

Principal Ideas Advanced

An idea is true if it fits in with other ideas to form a coherent whole.

To conceive something clearly and logically involves more than recognizing logical relationships; it involves achieving a coherency in one's judgments that goes beyond abstraction to material considerations.

Error is the distortion that results from a partial view of things; truth is the ideal of achieving a structure of judgments that fits the totality of all experience.

Joachim's short treatise, *The Nature of Truth*, has come to be regarded as the classical statement of the coherence theory of truth. The book is modest in size (180 pages), sticks closely to the point, and is written in that lucid style which often graces the writings of British philosophers. It is a work that philosophers can read with ease and profit.

Joachim divides the work into four chapters as follows: (1) Truth as Correspondence, (2) Truth as a Quality of Independent Entities, (3) Truth as Coherence (with a section on The Coherence-Notion of Truth, and a section on Degrees of Truth), and (4) The Negative Element and Error. The first two chapters are statements and criticisms of alternative views which prepare the way for the positive statement of the coherence theory in Chapter III. In the last chapter Joachim further supports the coherence theory by arguing that the problem of error cannot be accounted for as satisfactorily within the alternative theories as it can within the coherence theory.

Joachim begins by considering the view that correspondence means that *for a mind* two "factors" (Joachim's word) correspond in their structures and purposes. This is a very general and abstract conception of correspondence, and it applies to such things as portraits and photographs as well as to descriptions in words. The fundamental notion involved is that of copying. A portrait or a photograph or a description is faithful if it conveys, as a whole, the same sense of purpose or significance as does the original of which it is a copy, and if it is such a faithful copy we say it is *true*. But, Joachim argues, the concern with a *whole* having a purpose or significance indicates that the faithfulness of the copy is a symptom rather than the fundamental characteristic of truth. It is the systematic coherence of the whole that makes it a faithful copy (if it is), and therefore the important element in the truthfulness of the copy is its coherence.

From this abstract version of the correspondence theory, Joachim moves on to consider the correspondence that supposedly holds between a judgment and the referent of the judgment—the fact to which it refers. Here he rests his case on the claim that both the judgment and the referent of the judgment are finally mental. Both the judgment and its referent are elements in "experience," and experience for Joachim, as for all idealists, is finally mental. The correspondence is a correspondence (or identity) of structure between two kinds of experience. However, Joachim balks at abstracting a structure or form in such a way as to neglect the matter or material which exhibits the structure. At stake here is the doctrine of internal relations, to which we must shortly turn for a more detailed discussion. The point can be made here, however, that Joachim refuses to compare the form of the judgment with the form of the experienced fact. Thus, both the judgment and the experienced fact which is the referent of judgment remain embedded in experience. Experience, furthermore, is a totality containing the judgment and the experienced fact as elements. Both have significance, for Joachim at any rate, within this wider context of experience, and if they are abstracted from the concreteness of experience they lose their significance. Experience, finally, is the coherent whole which gives significance to both the judgment and its referent. Again, coherence seems to be the key to truth.

In his second chapter, "Truth as a Quality of Independent Entities," Joachim states and rejects what he understands to be the position taken by G. E. Moore and the early Bertrand Russell, the Russell of *The Principles of Mathematics* (1903). Two assertions are the object of Joachim's concern here: (1) There are simple facts which can be experienced or apprehended without being affected in any way by this experiencing or apprehending. (2) There are logical entities, called "propositions," which are the proper subjects of the predicates "true" and "false." Joachim disagrees with both assertions. With regard to the first assertion—namely, that there are facts which are unaffected by men's experiencing of them—Joachim points out that there is certainly a difference between a complex which is a fact, but which is not an *experienced* fact, and a complex which is a fact, but which is also experienced. This line of reasoning, of course, would not distress either Russell or Moore in the least. But Joachim seems to believe that this difference implies that experiencing a fact somehow changes the fact. However, to say this is to misrepresent Joachim (and other idealists as well), for he does not admit that there are any such things as unexperienced facts. To be a fact is to be experienced—in this regard Joachim stands in the same position as did Berkeley.

Part of what is involved in Joachim's rejection of the view that experiencing facts does not change them is the parallel case regarding judgments as opposed to propositions. Just as there are no unexperienced facts for an idealist, so there are no "propositions," whereby "proposition" is meant the content of a judgment considered as apart from the assertion of it by some person. These propositions are the "independent entities" which the chapter heading refers to. Russell, Joachim claims, regards truth and falsity as predicates of independent logical entities called propositions. If there are propositions which can be considered in abstraction from their being asserted by some person, and if there are facts which can be apprehended without that apprehension changing them, then there are two "factors" which can be examined in order to see whether or not they correspond. For a coherence view to stand, then, it is important to reject this possibility decisively. Joachim tries to do this by arguing that it makes no more sense to talk about facts which are not experienced than to talk about propositions which are not asserted by someone. Here it becomes obvious that the earlier inclusion in the statement of the correspondence view of the words "for a mind" is crucial for Joachim. Facts are all *experienced* facts, and propositions are all *asserted* propositions (that is, judgments). But the premise Joachim offers—namely, that we always deal with experienced facts and asserted propositions—does not support his conclusion—namely, that we cannot speak of facts and propositions in abstraction from some mind which experiences the facts and asserts the propositions.

The inference just mentioned rests, for Joachim, on the doctrine of internal relations. We should look at this doctrine before proceeding. It is not elaborated by Joachim in *The Nature of Truth*, but he admits that he is assuming it, and it provides the background and real motivation for the rejection of Russell's position.

Essentially the doctrine of internal relations is a denial, a denial that relations are real entities having any status or meaning apart from the situations in which they are exemplified. There is a certain plausibility in this view. It seems, *prima facie*, that we come to speak of relations as a result of interpreting our experience. We may, for example, come into a room and have a complex, but unitary, experience which includes seeing a dog under the table, smelling the fragrance of a vase of flowers, hearing the radio playing a popular song, and so forth. Our unreflective apprehension of the room may be such that these elements are not distinguished, but rather are experienced as an undifferentiated totality. However, in interpreting our experience, we analyze and describe and classify the unity into a multiplicity of things having qualities and standing in relations. Joachim takes the usual idealist view that in moving from the unitary experience of such a totality to the reflective interpretation of it we abstract from the real. Therefore, although it is true that we must talk of relations (and qualities and terms as well, because they are similar to relations in this respect) in describing our experience, these relations are abstractions, and hence they are unreal—partially unreal at best, perhaps totally unreal. Certainly they do not have status as independent entities. When we say that "the dog is under the table," we are abstracting from the unity of our experience, and if we go further and think about the relation of "being under" by itself and apart from its exemplifications, we have performed still another act of abstraction. But these abstractions have taken us out of the immediacy and concreteness and unity of the experience itself, and they have given us instead something formal and unreal.

Nevertheless, idealists such as Joachim make a concession to the fact that we do use relations in describing our experience. Our knowledge structure, according to idealists, is constructed out of immediate experience by means of judgments, judgments which do assert relations. Thus, in spite of our recognition of the undifferentiated totality as something without relations (so says the idealist), our knowledge construction out of this experience does contain judgments which assert relations. To this extent, relations do have a status and function. Still, relations, if they are regarded as something independent of their concrete manifestations in experience, are abstractions out of experience and are thus not genuinely real. The proof of this is that there is no way of compounding the concreteness of our experience out of the judgments asserting relations (or qualities). We cannot synthesize our experience out of the descriptions or judgments we make; to do so would give us a mere aggregate of formal characteristics and not concrete experience. We simply cannot achieve the individuality and uniqueness of experience by compounding judgments. Nevertheless, we are forced to use relations, so our best course is to recognize that we have abstracted and are therefore speaking of the only partially real.

Thus, the doctrine of internal relations really consists of two assertions: (1) Relations are not independently real, and they have no significance apart from the situations in which we judge them to be present. (2) Relations are arrived at by abstracting from concrete experience and thus, although necessary in judgment, they have only a partial and derivative reality. It is this doctrine that lies behind Joachim's rejection of the Moore and Russell position. The doctrine of internal relations rests on the conviction that abstraction from the immediacy of experience is falsification, but certainly the independent facts and propositions of Russell are abstractions from experience; therefore, such independent facts and propositions must be rejected by Joachim.

In his third chapter Joachim takes up the positive exposition of the coherence theory. The doctrine of internal relations also provides a fine background for this theory, for, as we shall see, the coherence theory is really one way of expressing the doctrine of internal relations and its implications.

Joachim offers as an abbreviated formulation of the coherence theory the following: "Anything is true which can be conceived." He continues by explaining what he means by the term "conceive." He points out that he does not mean "image" or "imagine." What he does mean by "conceive" is "think out clearly and logically." But here it is important to bear in mind the distrust of abstraction which we saw manifested in the doctrine of internal relations. For most contemporary philosophers, "to think out clearly and logically" suggests drawing the implications of a set of statements. To do so would be possible also in the case of false statements or fictional statements, and there is even a sense in which a set of truth functions or propositional functions could be elaborated deductively. We would say that we are thinking out clearly and logically the implications of "All men are mortal" and "X is a man" if we draw the conclusion that "X is mortal," yet it might be false that all men are mortal, and it certainly is neither true nor false that X is a man. We seem to have something less than truth in this case. But for Joachim we are not able to think something out clearly and logically if we abstract in such a manner from the fullness and concreteness of immediate experience. Thus, the coherence theory reveals again the usual idealist rejection of any kind of formalism. It is this rejection which scuttles the misunderstanding of the coherence theory which takes it to be the view that whatever is logically consistent is true. It is not uncommon to hear that the coherence theory is refuted by the fact of alternative geometries, each logically consistent, but incompatible with the others. If Euclidean geometry is true (so this argument goes), then non-Euclidean geometries are false, since they are inconsistent with Euclidean geometry. Thus, we would have something consistent but false, and the coherence theory is therefore false. But this identification of "coherence" with "consistency" is rejected explicitly by Joachim. He states that whatever is true will certainly be consistent, but he denies that bare consistency is a sufficient condition for truth. Consistency is a formal characteristic; coherence is a richer notion which includes material considerations as well.

But let us turn to giving a positive account of coherence. It does seem to make sense to say that the totality of our experience is some sort of system. For one thing, our experience seems to be temporally organized; our memories refer to past events, our expectations have a future reference. There also seem to be repeatable elements in our experience; every twenty-four hours I go to sleep, eat food, and drink water. At regular intervals I go to work and return home again. But within *my* experience, at any rate, certain other possibilities are not genuine. I cannot, for instance, play first base on a major league baseball team. To say that yesterday I hit a home run for the Giants in their game with the Braves simply does not fit in with the rest of my experience. Thus, by the time I fill in *all* the elements of my experience, certain possibilities are ruled out, while others are unmistakably included. As I proceed to interpret the totality of my experience by making the judgments that comprise my knowledge structure, I come closer and closer to reflecting the richness and fullness of this totality. The goal I strive for is a complete recasting of my experience in a set of judgments. The nearer I come to achieving this complete account of my experience in a system of judgments, the nearer I approach truth.

This endeavor to reach truth as the reconstruction of the totality of my experience leads naturally to some other features of the coherence theory. It is quite consistent with saying that the more complete my structure of judgments, the nearer I approach truth, to say also that truth is properly reserved as a predicate for the total structure of judgments. Truth, for Joachim, is not a predicate of particular propositions or judgments; it is rather a predicate of the total system of judgments. Furthermore, absolute truth is an unrealizable goal. The best I can ever come up with is partial and incomplete truth. Nor is this all, for there is a sense in which I might say that a certain specific judgment which I now make is partially true because it occupies a place in the total structure of judgments which I have developed as of this date. But as the days and years go by I will be adding to this structure of judgments, making it more adequate and more complete. But if I retain the original judgment in the wider and more adequate structure, it becomes more and more true. As the knowledge structure expands and comes closer to completion, any given judgment in it becomes more true. Joachim points out that a simple mathematical relation, such as 3 squared equals 9, is truer for the skilled mathematician than it is for the boy in grade school who has just committed it to memory. Truth, on this view, admits of degrees.

What "think out clearly and logically" comes to, then, is this: We must see the judgments as elements in a rational structure which is constantly being enlarged and therefore is approaching ever closer to a complete account of the totality of our experience. Truth is the ideal of the complete faithfulness of such a structure of judgments to the totality of experience.

The last section of Joachim's book deals with the problem of error. He points out that the correspondence theory is unable to handle the matter of error as adequately as the coherence theory. Essentially, the coherence theory of error is that error represents a partial truth which is superseded as the system of judgments becomes more complete. I may make a judgment now that the moon is made of green cheese, and this may cohere with the limited set of judgments I now have. However, as I fill in the gaps in my structure of judgments, I recognize that the judgment that the moon is made of green cheese does not cohere with the remainder of my judgments. I therefore replace this judgment with one which fits in better with the other judgments I have made. Error is thus a kind of stage we go through on the way to fuller truth. Error is the distortion that results from a partial view.

It has been fashionable in recent decades to smile indulgently at the foolishness of idealism generally and the coherence theory of truth specifically. It seems fair to say, however, that recent philosophizing about the relation between meaning and use probably has raised questions that suggest a reexamination of what the great idealists such as Joachim had to say about truth as coherence. For certainly it can be said that before a statement's truth value can be determined, its meaning must be understood. But if meaning is related to use, and use is related to a context in which terms and statements occur, then some of the points raised by the coherence theorists seem to have relevance again. If the coherence theory can enlighten some comtemporary philosophical disputes, then a classic statement of it, such as Joachim's *The Nature of Truth*, deserves careful study once again.—*R.E.L.*

PERTINENT LITERATURE

Moore, G. E. "External and Internal Relations," in *Proceedings of the Aristotelian Society*. XX (1919-1920), pp. 40-62.

G. E. Moore quotes Harold Henry Joachim's *The Nature of Truth* to the effect that "no relations are purely external," that "all relations qualify or modify or make a difference to the terms between which they hold," and that "no terms are independent of any of the relations in which they stand to other terms." He finds similar remarks in F. H. Bradley's *Appearance and Reality* and devotes his essay to discussing the meaning and truth value of the claim Joachim and Bradley both make.

Moore finds it no easy matter to say exactly what that claim is, and he focuses on a proposition which he takes to be at least part of what they affirm. One thing, he suggests, which they do *not* mean is that the fact expressed by, say, "Edward VII is the father of George V" is simply composed of these things: Edward, George, and the relation of fatherhood. One might advance Moore's point by saying that the fact thus expressed is not properly represented by saying that three things—George, Edward, Fatherhood—exist. For if we represent these by *G*, *E*, and *F*, respectively, that all three exist can be represented equally well by: (i) *G*, *E*, *F*; (ii) *G*, *F*, *E*; (iii) *F*, *G*, *E*, or (iv) *E*, *F*, *G*. But only (iv) represents Edward's bearing the relation *being father of* to George. Moore claims, then, that while it is true that no state of affairs comprising one thing being related to another is properly represented simply by saying that the related items plus the relation exists, this fact is not sufficient to support Joachim's and Bradley's point.

A second proposition Moore thinks important to distinguish from the claim Joachim and Bradley share is the claim that a thing is modified or changed by every relationship it has to anything else. This, Moore suggests, is false, since things which do not change (Moore perhaps has in mind abstract entities and/or transitory entities which exist only for a moment) stand in relations to other things. (Moore might also argue that if I am stationary in New York while identical twins in Los Angeles exchange seats at a dinner party, my spatial relationships to these twins change, but it seems false that therefore I am changed.) Thus, "modify" must be taken in some nonliteral sense.

What then, in part, does Joachim mean, at least according to Moore? If *A* is the father of *B*, then *being father of B* is a *relational property A* has. It is, Moore suggests, *relational properties* with which Joachim's claim is concerned, not *relations* such as *fatherhood*. Further, Moore suggests, when Joachim and others say that relational properties "modify" what has them, they mean not merely that these things do have these properties, but also something like this: if A has relational property P, then the proposition *Any-thing that does not have P is not A* is a necessary truth. The alleged necessary truth is not the whole conditional statement *If A has P, then anything not having P is not A*, which one would hardly care to deny; it is, rather, that the *consequent* of the conditional statement (what follows "then") is supposed to be a necessary truth, provided only that the antecedent (what comes between "if" and "then") is true.

Still further, Moore continues, the idea is not merely that if *A has P* is true, it then *follows* that *Anything not having P is not A* is necessarily true. Joachim and others, Moore believes, have something further in mind. By "is not A" or "is different from A," they mean not merely "numerically different" but also "qualitatively different." Two marbles which differed only in their spa-tiotemporal properties would be numerically but not qualitatively different. Joachim and others, in Moore's opinion, are contending that if A has relational property P, then it is not merely true but also a necessary truth that anything not having P is not merely numerically but also qualitatively different.

Moore summarizes all this by saying that where A is an object and P a relational property, Joachim and others claim that: (1) if A has P, then (it is a necessary truth that) anything not having P is qualitatively different from A; (2) if A has P, then it follows from this that (it is a necessary truth that) anything that does not have P is numerically different from A. Moore takes both (1) and (2) to be false and spends the remainder of his essay arguing to this effect.

Consider, Moore suggests, a visual image "before one's mind's eye," as the phrase goes. Suppose one is seeing, in this sense, a large, red circle against a white background. Then consider, say, the left half of that circle. It is true that the left half of that circle has the relational property *being the left half of a circle* and the quality *being red*. It is true that any visual circle which does not contain the particular left half in question is not the circle I am seeing. It does not follow that any visual circle which does not contain the particular left half in question is qualitatively different from—does not share in *being red* or is not exactly the same shade of red as—the circle I am seeing. And since this is so, Moore argues, (1) is false. Part, then, of what Joachim and others contend, Moore argues, is mistaken. Moore thinks the same goes for (2).

Here, Moore is careful to distinguish between (2), which he takes to be false, and a different but similar proposition, which he takes to be true, namely: (3) If A has P at time *t*, then anything which does not have P at *t* is different from A. Surely (3) is true, and indeed a necessary truth. But this is not what (2) says, and Moore apparently thinks that if one avoids confusing (2) with (3), one can see that (2) is false. What (2) says can be put in this way: *A is P* entails *Necessarily, if x does not have P then x is distinct from A*, which in turn entails *Necessarily, A is P*. This, or something much like it, seems to Moore to be the idealistic view. In that view, every relational property a thing has, it has necessarily. If *A* is *B*'s father, then if *A* had not fathered *B*, *A* would not have been himself. And, in the case of many relational properties, Moore suggests, this is plainly false. Its falsity is plain, Moore holds, from a commonsense perspective and also from several other arguments which Moore offers.

Russell, Bertrand. *My Philosophical Development*. New York: Simon and Schuster, 1959.

Harold Henry Joachim was Professor of Logic from 1919 to 1935 at Oxford University. An idealist, he held that no proposition is wholly true. A proposition, he held, is true insofar as it leads to a knowledge of the system of propositions to which, he assumes, it necessarily belongs, but is false insofar as it expresses that system incompletely and so imperfectly. Thus he finds it impossible ultimately to distinguish between incomplete knowledge and error. In 1907, Bertrand Russell read, to the Aristotelian Society, a paper on Joachim's *The Nature of Truth*, a long section of which Russell included in his intellectual biography.

Russell finds a particular proposition basic to Joachim's views, a proposition he calls the *axiom of internal relations*. It can be expressed as "every relation is grounded in the natures of the related terms." Given this axiom, Russell explains, it follows that each thing will have its nature which exhibits its relation to everything else, distributively considered, and to the whole which is comprised of everything whatever. Suppose, then, that the nature of just one thing were to be fully and entirely understood. Then the nature of everything else, and of the whole, would be fully and entirely understood, and conversely. So it follows from the axiom that nothing is known unless everything is known, or that if anything is known, then everything is, a view which Russell calls "the monistic theory of truth."

Russell asks whether there are any reasons for accepting the axiom of internal relations and finds two (or, perhaps, he says, two ways of stating one). The first is the principle of sufficient reason, according to which, if a proposition is true, there must be some reason why it is true rather than false (or, if some state of affairs obtains, there must be some reason why it obtains, rather than not obtaining). To this, Russell responds as follows. The principle of sufficient reason cannot simply mean that, for any proposition *P*, some other proposition *Q* can be found which is true and entails it. For while 4 + 4 = 8 is true and entails 2 + 2 = 4, it would be absurd to explain the truth of the latter by reference to the truth of the former. The idea of the principle is that the proposition which provides the reason for the truth of the other be simpler, less complex, than the one whose truth it explains. But the simpler, or less complex, a proposition is, the less true it is, according to the idealistic doctrine of Joachim. Further, it seems false that (in a noncircular and justificatory fashion) every true proposition can be derived from some other.

The other reason, Russell says, is this: if A and B are related to one another in a certain way, then were they not so related, they would not be A and B; so it must be essential to them that they are so related. To this line of reasoning, Russell replies to this effect. It is true that if A and B are related in way R, then *A and B are not related by R* is false, and (in one sense) a false statement implies anything, including that A and B are not A and B. But that fact is of no help to the idealist. It is also true, Russell notes, that if A and B are related in way R, then any pair of things not related in way R is numerically distinct (but not therefore qualitatively distinct) from A and B. (Further, *A and B are related in way R* does not entail *Being related in way R is essential to A and B* or *Necessarily, A and B are related in way R*.) None of this, Russell suggests, in fact provides any reason for thinking the axiom to be true.

The other question to ask, Russell notes, is whether there are any reasons to reject the axiom. Russell thinks there are. One argument he offers goes as follows. A relation R is asymmetrical if *A has R to B* entails *B does not have R to A*. *Being larger than* is an asymmetrical relation. Suppose A is larger than B. One can try to express this by saying that A has volume X and B has volume Y, but then one must add that X is larger than Y. Sooner or later, Russell says, barring infinite regress, "we come to a relation not reducible to the adjectives of the related terms." Another way of saying this is that, barring infinite regress, we come to a relationship between A and B which is not simply a matter of A's having one nonrelational quality and B's having another nonrelational quality, but is also a matter of those qualities being related in a particular way. The same argument, Russell notes (referring us to a fuller statement in the *Principles of Mathematics*, Sections 212-216), can be given using any asymmetrical relation as an example.

Another argument, which Russell describes as "more searching," goes like this. What Joachim means by the "nature" of a term (an object in a relation to some other object) must either be such that the nature of an object is identical with the object, or such that it is not. Suppose they are different. Then each must be related in some way to the other, and this relation, without endless regress, cannot be reduced to something that is not a relation. So, if one puts the connection between an object and its nature in a way consistent with the axiom, one must suppose that an object and its nature are identical. Then, Russell continues, every true proposition which ascribes a predicate to a subject is analytic or tautological, since an object is its whole nature of which that predicate is a part. But then the question arises as to what makes various predicates to be predicates of a single subject.

Russell presses the objection hard. If the nature of an object is to be made up of its predicates, and to be the same as the object itself, then it seems that no proper analysis can be given of objects. For we cannot say that a set of predicates belongs to a single subject only if they cohere in a certain way, since that would, Russell notes, base predication on a certain relationship rather than, as the view under discussion requires, reducing all relations to predications.

Indeed, Russell, in ways still more abstract, argues that things are worse still, for (as Russell plausibly argues) if the axiom is true, there can be only one thing. There also can be only one proposition which attributes a predicate to a subject, and it is itself not quite true, as it suggests that this subject and this predicate are distinct, which (given the axiom) they are not.

Russell thinks, then, that there is no reason to accept, and very good reason to reject, Joachim's view of truth and the axiom on which, he contends, that view rests.—*K.E.Y.*

ADDITIONAL RECOMMENDED READING

Blanshard, Brand. *The Nature of Thought*. Norwich: Jarrold and Sons, 1939. Wide-ranging studies in logic and psychology, with references to Joachim.

Ewing, A. C. *Idealism: A Critical Survey*. London: Methuen, 1934. A discussion of the main themes of idealism, with discussions of Joachim's views.

Joachim, H. H. Descartes' *Rules for the Direction of the Mind*. Edited by E. E. Harris. Bury, England: East Midland Publishing Company, 1957. An example of Joachim's interest and expertise in early modern philosophy.

——————— . *A Study of the Ethics of Spinoza*. Oxford: Clarendon Press, 1901. Further work by Joachim in early modern philosophy.

Johnson, W. E. *Logic*. Cambridge: Cambridge University Press, 1921-1924. A discussion of topics in logic and metaphysics, including many themes of interest to Joachim.

Taylor, A. E. *Elements of Metaphysics*. London: Methuen, 1903. An exposition of a perspective in metaphysics with similarities to Joachim's, written before Taylor adopted the views expressed in *The Faith of a Moralist*.

PRAGMATISM

Author: William James (1842-1910)
Type of work: Epistemology, philosophy of philosophy
First published: 1907

PRINCIPAL IDEAS ADVANCED
Pragmatism is both a philosophical method and a theory of truth.
As a method, it resolves metaphysical disputes by asking for the practical consequences of alternative resolutions.
Once a distinction of practice is made, theoretical difficulties disappear.
As a theory of truth, Pragmatism claims that ideas are true insofar as they are satisfactory; to be satisfactory, ideas must be consistent with other ideas, conformable to facts, and subject to the practical tests of experience.

Occasionally a book succeeds in giving influential expression to an attitude and a set of principles which eventually make up a historically important philosophical movement. This is the case with William James's *Pragmatism.* Borrowing the term from his philosophical contemporary, Charles S. Peirce (1839-1914), James attempts in a series of published lectures to popularize and defend "a number of tendencies that hitherto have lacked a collective name." Pragmatism came to dominate the American intellectual scene for more than two decades as well as to gain recognition as a uniquely American philosophical position. To this historical phenomenon of the pragmatic movement James's book still serves as a sympathetic if sometimes polemical introduction. Its eight related essays discuss the origin and meaning of Pragmatism as well as suggest how the pragmatic method can be applied to troublingly perennial problems in metaphysics and religion. The contents give evidence of James's belief that philosophizing, as a technical concern, must always involve consequences for the life of common sense and common men.

Given the question: Can a philosopher settle all philosophical disputes disinterestedly?—James replies in the negative. The point here is not that philosophers ought to ignore claims of logic and evidence. Rather, the point is that philosophical "clashes" involve more than logic and evidence. James insists that no philosopher can wholly "sink the fact of his temperament," however responsibly he seeks to give "impersonal reasons only for his conclusions." A philosophical attitude necessarily becomes colored by a man's temperament. In "The Dilemma in Philosophy," which opens *Pragmatism,* James argues that a fundamental opposition in temperament has marked the history of thought—that between rationalism and empiricism. The rationalist values "abstract and eternal principles"; the empiricist, "facts in all their crude variety." Aware that so hard and fast a distinction can serve only a rough-and-ready use, James suggests that clusters of traits tend to distinguish the rationalist from the empiricist. Rationalists are "tender-minded," "intellectualistic," "idealistic," "optimistic," "religious," "free-willist," "monistic," "dogmatical." Empiricists are "tough-minded," "sensationalistic," "materialistic," "pessimistic," "irreligious," "fatalistic," "pluralistic," "skeptical."

This rule of thumb distinction between two attitudes James applies to his view of the existing philosophical situation. This situation is one in which even children "are almost born scientific." Positivism and scientific materialism tend to dominate the scene, favoring the empirically minded outlook. Yet men also seek to preserve an element of religiousness. James insists that a philosophical dilemma arises which is unacceptable to his contemporaries: adopt a positivistic respect for empirical facts which ignores religion or keep a religiousness which is insufficiently empirical. James will settle for neither alternative. He asserts that "in this blessed year of our Lord 1906" the common man as philosopher demands facts, science, and religion. The ordinary man cannot find what he needs in the philosophical country store. Materialists explain phenomena by a "nothing but" account of higher forms in terms of lower, while religious thinkers provide a choice between an empty transcendentalist idealism (whose Absolute has no necessary relation to any concretely existing thing) and traditional theism (whose compromising nature lacks prestige and vital fighting powers). Rationalist elements in idealism and theism emphasize refinement and escape from the concrete realities of ordinary, everyday life. The result is that for the common man's plight "Empiricist writers give him a materialism, rationalists give him something religious, but to that religion 'actual things are blank.'"

For this dramatically staged intellectual predicament James has a philosophical hero ready in the wings. It is "the oddly-named thing pragmatism." Pragmatism is offered as a philosophy which can salvage the religious values of rationalism without perverting man's many-sided awareness of facts. It can also take account of the way temperamental demands inevitably affect foundations of philosophical systems. What James promises for his generation is a kind of philosophical synthesis which locates personal ways of seeing things squarely in the heart of philosophical subject-matter. What this involves he describes in two essays: "What Pragmatism Means" and "Pragmatism's Conception of Truth."

Pragmatism is both a method and a theory of truth. The method can be used by men holding widely different philosophical persuasions. Its function is chiefly that of settling metaphysical disputes which seriously disturb men. Metaphysical arguments involve "notions" about which one can always ask whether the notions lead to any practical consequences. Such notions must be shown to make a difference in human conduct if they are to prove meaningful. Two Jamesian examples can illustrate what is meant here. One example concerns an argument about whether, if a man circles a tree around whose trunk a squirrel is also moving, one can say the man "goes round" the squirrel.

James shows how the answer depends on what is meant by "round." Mean by "going round" that the man is in successive places to north, east, south, and west of the squirrel, then he does go round the animal. Mean, on the other hand, that the man is behind, then to the right of, then in front of, and then to the left of the squirrel, then the man may not actually go round the squirrel—since the animal may move simultaneously with the man's movements. James concludes that an argument of this kind, if analyzed, turns out to be a verbal one.

Another example illustrates how the pragmatic method is compatible with many possible results. James asks his readers to view the method as being like a corridor in a hotel, whose doors open into many rooms which contain thinkers involved in a variety of intellectual pursuits. These pursuits may be metaphysical, religious, or scientific. Metaphysically, one room may harbor a man working out an idealistic system, while another may shelter a thinker attempting to show that metaphysics is an impossibility. James insists that the pragmatic method is neutral regarding the kinds of thought going on in the rooms. Nevertheless, he insists that as a theory of truth Pragmatism favors the nominalist's preference for particulars, the Utilitarian's stress on what is useful, and the positivist's dislike of metaphysical speculations and merely verbal solutions of problems. James believes men wanting to employ words like "God," "Matter," "the Absolute," "Reason," and "Energy" should use the pragmatic method in seeking to show how such notions can have practical effects.

As an instrumentalist theory of truth, Pragmatism views sharp distinctions between logic and psychology with great suspicion. Ideas are instruments which help to dispel doubt when inherited bodies of opinion no longer produce intellectual ease. Belief means the cessation of doubting. But what makes a belief true? James asserts that an idea is true if it permits the believer to attain "satisfactory relations with other parts of our experience." This genetic conception of truth—influenced by Darwinian biology—sees ideas as true for specified situations, always in principle subject to change and reevaluation. Some critics interpret James's emphasis on the contextual truth of an idea as meaning a man may believe whatever happens to make him comfortable. James rejects any wish-fulfilling conception of pragmatic truth. He states conditions which any idea must satisfy to qualify as workable. These conditions are quite conservative: Ideas must prove consistent with other ideas (including old ones) conformable to existing facts, and subject to experiential corroboration and validation.

James is mostly critical of rationalistic metaphysical ideas leading to no observable differences in domains of human conduct. He rejects claims about *the* Truth. Nevertheless he will consider even theological ideas as possibly true as long as their proponents can show them to affect some actual person's behavior. "Truth lives, in fact, for the most part on a credit system." Truth concerns matters of fact, abstract things and their relations, and the relations of an idea to the entire body of one's other beliefs. Ideas unable to conform to men's factual knowledge simply cannot have what James calls "cash-value."

James's relevant essays about truth sometimes raise questions which they do not satisfactorily answer. Some critics accuse him of advocating a subjectivist theory of truth. Elsewhere, James defends his views by suggesting two kinds of criteria for testing the meaning of any sentence. First, a sentence has meaning if it leads to observable consequences in experience. Second, a sentence is meaningful if someone's belief in it leads to behavioral consequences. James seems to employ the first view when he writes about scientific and factual knowledge. He uses the second view when discussing certain moral and religious beliefs. It is the second view which worries some critics, who think that—if taken literally—it can justify as true any psychologically helpful belief.

The bulk of the remaining essays in *Pragmatism* seek to illustrate how the pragmatic method and theory of truth may be applied to specific problems. These are predominantly philosophical rather than scientific problems. In "Some Metaphysical Problems" and "The One and the Many" he applies the generous theory of meaning to such problems as the meaning of substance, the relative values of materialism and spiritualism, the problem of evil, the debate about freedom of the will, and the merits of monism and pluralism as cosmological notions. "Pragmatism and Common Sense" discusses three kinds of knowledge whose truth-claims are perennial. "Pragmatism and Humanism" and "Pragmatism and Religion" indicate how Pragmatism can mediate in disputes among hard-headed empiricists and abstract rationalists.

Taking the traditional puzzles about substance, design in nature, and free will, James argues that such metaphysical issues often lead to no genuine consequences for action if treated in solely intellectual terms. "In every *genuine* metaphysical dispute some practical issue, however conjectural and remote, is involved." Metaphysical arguments thus concern something other than what seems the case. Influenced by the thing-attribute aspect of grammar, men worry about substance because they suppose a *something* must support the external and psychological objects of our perceivable world beyond what these objects are experienced *as*. James asks us to imagine that a material or spiritual substance undergoes change without altering our perceptions of its supposed attributes. In such a case our perception of the properties would be the same as before. It follows that the notion of substance as standing for something beyond perceived qualities of objects can add nothing to our actual knowledge of the things in the world. Only in the Catholic claims about the Eucharist can the notion of substance have any practical use—a religious one. Similarly, arguments whether God or matter best explains the origin and development of the universe are unimportant so far as the observable facts go. Only one's expectations about the future can make the theist-materialist issue important. The pragmatic method leads to a slight "edge" for theism, according to James, since the belief in God "guarantees an ideal order that shall be permanently preserved." *What* the world is like, even if God created it, remains a matter for patient scientific labors to discover. The theistic conception of the world's origin permits men a kind of enjoyment which materialism excludes. Morally, theism is preferable since it refuses to take human disasters as the absolutely final word, while materialism denies the eternity of the moral order.

The question whether there is design in the world is also pointless if raised with scientific intent. The design issue is really a religious one. It is not open to purely rational solution. The significant aspects of the issue concern *what* that design may be, as well as *what* the nature of any possible designer. James applies a similar treatment to the determinism versus free will controversy. For him, this is an out-and-out metaphysical issue rather than interesting solely in relation to the discussion of moral judicability. To decide in favor of free will means to accept a faith that the universe can be improved through human effort. James calls this faith in improvability "meliorism." In turn, such a belief requires rejection of any absolute monistic conception of the cosmos. It requires belief in the notion that reality is a multiverse. The universe is neither simply one nor an absolute randomness. It is a pluriverse which contains specific kinds of unity as well as directly experienced "gaps." It is not *now* an absolute unity in light of our experience, but men may hope for such a completed unity as a possible future cosmic event.

James insists on the misleading nature of traditional metaphysical disputes. Metaphysical arguments seem to concern problems which human intellect can solve if only that intellect "gets them right." Yet, they are really practical problems. They are significant only when found to express hidden religious and moral issues. The pragmatist favors a decision for free will, belief in God's existence, faith in an increasing unity in a pluralistic universe, and hope that elements of design exist as grounds for one's belief in meliorism. Faith may rightfully decide when human reason proves insufficient. The reason is that such faith expresses confidence in the promise of the future and results in beneficial consequences for our present living.

James rejects metaphysical monism for moral and religious reasons. Monism implies a certain completedness about the universe even now. This completedness requires the denial of free will and, if God exists, of a worthwhile God. Nevertheless, James's pluralism includes the view that many kinds of unity compose the universe. Intellect aims neither at variety nor unity, but at totality. The world contains important unities but is not a total unity. Some parts of the world are continuous with others, as in spacetime; practical continuities appear (as in the notion of physical gravity); and there are systems of influence and noninfluence which indicate existence of causal unities. Furthermore, there are generic unities (kinds), unities of social purpose, and aesthetic unities. These are experienced. Yet, James says, we never experience "a universe pure and simple." Pragmatism therefore insists on a world as containing just as many continuities *and* disjunctions as experience shows to exist.

The only ultimate unity may be an absolute knower of the system. Even the system may not always be considered to be a necessary unity, since the world may exist as eternally incomplete—actually subject to addition and loss. Our knowledge of such a world grows slowly, through scientific criticism, common sense, and philosophic criticism. No one can demonstrate conclusively which, if any, of these ways of knowing is the truest. Common sense builds up customary ways of organizing the materials of experience. It uses such concepts as thing, same or different, kinds, minds, bodies, one time, one space, subjects and attributes, causal influences, the fancied, the real. Scientific criticism adds more sophisticated notions, like "atoms" and "ether," say, casting some doubt on the adequacy of commonsense concepts. The philosophical stage gives no knowledge quite comparable to the other two. Philosophical criticism does not make possible description of details of nature. Our decisions about which philosophical views to adopt must turn on practical rather than theoretical criteria. On the other hand, choice between common sense and scientific notions will rest on existence of kinds of corroboration which, in principle, will always be lacking in the cases of competing philosophical claims.

The essays in *Pragmatism* express a loosely stated yet consistent philosophical viewpoint. Through them runs the excitement of discovery that, if only the pragmatic method be adopted, many old and perplexing issues can be translated into practical ones. James seems eager to help men discover the metaphysical views which will conform to their experienced needs. On the other hand, he wants to insist on binding tests when the pragmatist handles common sense and science. He is less insistent on such tests in religious and moral domains. His major thesis is that "all true processes must lead to the fact of directly verifying sensible experience *somewhere*, which somebody's ideas have copied." His generosity remains attractive even to some critics who reject his philosophical conclusions.—*W.T.D.*

PERTINENT LITERATURE

Thayer, H. S., ed. "Introduction," in William James's *Pragmatism.* Cambridge, Massachusetts: Harvard University Press, 1975.

In his Introduction to this volume, which is the first in a recent series of critical editions of the writings of William James, H. S. Thayer notes that the publication of *Pragmatism: A New Name for Some Old Ways of Thinking* (1907) unleashed a storm of controversy. Disputes about the merits of the work still swirl. Thayer sorts out the issues by setting James's book within the context of his full philosophical career.

For nearly thirty years prior to the appearance of *Pragmatism*, writes Thayer, James had explored the problems and themes that would culminate in his pragmatic theories of meaning and truth. Early on, James became convinced that knowing is an activity in which human emotions and practical concerns play a governing part. We cannot make reality conform completely to the heart's desire, but human aims are significant. Inquiry functions in their service. By 1885, Thayer believes, James was already advancing a view that would locate the truth of propositions in their ability to lead us successfully toward obtaining fulfillment of the practical expectations they entail.

Humanistic concerns are salient in James's book, and Thayer claims that one of its major goals was to explore how pragmatism might clarify religious problems. In themselves these aims would not have been sufficient to provoke the debate that *Pragmatism* has caused, but those objectives were linked to James's unique theory of truth, which said more than enough to set philosophical nerves on edge. Thayer contends, however, that much of the ensuing conflict has been due to misunderstandings that can be largely corrected by keeping three points in mind.

The first is that James's own statements about truth do not all fit together easily because, by his own admission, the theory was never formulated completely. Indeed, Thayer's second point is that James probably chose unwisely in calling his suggestions about truth a *theory* at all. For James intended to give no exhaustive account or definition of truth, asserts Thayer, but rather to elucidate what other theories had neglected or failed to explain. Third, James sought in particular to make more intelligible the traditional position that true propositions "agree" with reality.

Elaborating on his third point, Thayer explains that such agreement is found when ideas guide human activity into satisfactory adjustments to reality. What James wanted to provide, Thayer emphasizes, is a critical and intersystematic interpretation of what those relationships entail. Consistency, coherence, and simplicity, along with the pressure of stubborn fact and the weight of everyday experience, all exert their influence in James's account.

Thayer does not deny that James also believed that our judgments about truth and reality rightly include some relativity. Not only do people carve existence up in different ways, depending on their needs and interests, but also basic beliefs, religious ones for example, may be true for some persons and false for others. Contrary to the usual criticisms, Thayer argues, James's handling of these aspects of experience was neither a logical muddle nor a defense of capricious subjectivism. James took with utmost seriousness the fact that truth depends on objective relations, but such relations are often formed in a decisive way by the drives, projects, and expectations of individuals. Consequently those relations may differ, and as they do so, the resulting truth also varies.

No doubt, says Thayer, problems remain in James's account of truth. Two instances are James's tendencies to identify the true with the useful and to equate truth and verification. Even in these cases, however, Thayer's interpretation remains sympathetic, for he implies that patient and detailed reconstruction may save James's ideas from error without giving up their intended meanings. Thayer does not provide that reconstruction here, but he concludes that *Pragmatism* is an extraordinary philosophical statement because of James's unflagging concern to address "the real perplexities, the uncertainties and resurgent hopes that permeate ordinary human experience."

White, Morton. *Science and Sentiment in America: Philosophical Thought from Jonathan Edwards to John Dewey.* New York: Oxford University Press, 1972.

The most intriguing dimensions in the history of American philosophy, Morton White suggests, are the responses American thinkers have made to challenging developments in modern science. William James provides a case in point, for he came to philosophy by way of physiology and psychology and was well equipped to appreciate the power and value of scientific method. Nevertheless, that recognition did not lead James to champion science over every other form of human experience. In fact, James's background in the sciences moved him to warn against reductive tendencies in scientific theory. Thus, White notes, James's *Principles of Psychology* (1890) and his essays in *The Will to Believe* (1896) defend the rightful authority of sentiment or feeling to determine moral, religious, and metaphysical beliefs.

According to White, James's early writings advocated not a dualism but a "trialism" where the fixation of belief is concerned. James held that, in addition to cases where beliefs are properly determined by individual feeling that goes beyond public empirical evidence or the insight of pure reason, there are areas where belief is and should be formed only by the two latter elements. White finds places in *Pragmatism* where this "trialism" persists, but he is most fascinated by a more radical thesis that James was exploring in 1907, namely, that *all* beliefs are colored by personal sentiment. The provocative claim that intellect, will, taste, and passion mix and mingle in all human knowledge prompts White to subtitle his chapter on William James: "Pragmatism and the Whole Man."

A "holistic" theory of knowledge is what White sees James developing in *Pragmatism.* He argues, moreover, that James's position culminated a struggle that had gone on in American philosophy for more than 150 years, initiated when Jonathan Edwards tried to locate a distinctive base for religious knowledge by appealing to a "Sense of the Heart." The core of James's holistic epistemology, White contends, exists where James argues that the process of arriving at a belief, or of finding a belief to be true, involves an appraisal that involves our whole stock of opinions. Human beliefs and challenges to them are continually being weighed in relation to one another. Equilibrium depends on the ability of the total stock of beliefs to accommodate emotional desires, needs for consistency, aims to anticipate experience, and aesthetic yearnings for elegant explanation. Thus, White interprets James to say, the truth of scientific theories, far from being imposed upon us, now takes on qualities similar to that of religious or moral convictions. Human opinion is uncoerced by experience not only in the latter realms but in the former as well. In meeting or failing to meet James's holistic conditions, scientific theories, too, fall under James's pragmatic theory of truth.

The crux of the matter, White asserts, is James's emphasis that beliefs are never tested in isolation but always as parts of a stock of opinions. The stock of opinions is not absolutely fixed, but neither is it totally malleable. Experience entrenches some beliefs much more firmly than others. To gain status as a personal or a public belief, either a new claim will have to be one that can be accommodated to existing beliefs or it will require older beliefs to be revised or scrapped. What distinguishes James's pragmatic theory of truth, White contends, is that he developed his notion of coherence so that our existing stock of beliefs may be challenged, and rightly so, not only by logical inconsistency or stubborn fact but also by unsatisfied desire. Nor did James think that any elements in the stock of beliefs could be deemed immune from these diverse challenges. If new beliefs had to battle their way to acceptance against previously established views, James also held that metaphysical beliefs and even convictions about physical realities or logical principles might be subject to alteration or abandonment if they came into conflict with facts or feelings of sufficient authority.

The major contribution of James's *Pragmatism*, White infers, is the insight that the whole person appraises opinion by appeal to many different factors. Sentiment can always be one of them. As never before, White observes, James gave feeling and immediate experience a central role in American philosophy, so much so that he "represented the triumph of Romanticism in American thought."

Wild, John. *The Radical Empiricism of William James*. Garden City, New York: Doubleday & Company, 1969.

John Wild's book has done more than any other to relate the philosophy of William James to the insights of European phenomenology and existentialism. Differing from many interpreters of James's thought, Wild gives primary attention to *The Principles of Psychology*; but far from ignoring James's *Pragmatism* and its sequel *The Meaning of Truth* (1909), he finds that their major theses are defensible provided one corrects the excesses that left James open to legitimate criticism.

When Wild refers to James's "radical empiricism," he has in mind his lifelong concern to describe and clarify human experiences as they are actually lived through. Distrusting systems of thought constructed by reason alone, James placed a premium on open empirical investigation. Wild sees James's pragmatic theories of meaning and truth as part and parcel of that priority. For example, Wild points out, James understood that neither sense perception nor rational conceptualization grasps reality completely. Existence always shows itself to have further depths and relations that are presently unknown, and thus investigation must continue if our knowledge is to advance. That investigation requires perception and conceptual analysis to work in tandem. The former is clarified only when the light of conceptual analysis is shed upon it, but the adequacy of concepts and theories is validated only when they lead to fulfilled expectations in concrete experience.

James, says Wild, shared the existential insight that there is no necessary connection between meaning and being. What that insight meant for James, Wild explains, is that truth is not a property that every proposition possesses or lacks automatically. James saw that truth exists only if a match between a meaning and an actually existing reality turns up somewhere in experience. Admittedly we do at times speak of truth as eternal and complete. No human person, however, encounters any verification that is absolutely final. Complete knowledge and absolute truth, James held, are best regarded as regulative ideals. The strength of such proposals, Wild finds, is that James's remarks about truth were firmly based in descriptions of what actually occurs as we seek knowledge and inquire after truth.

Nevertheless, Wild does not believe that James kept everything in focus as well as could be desired. Preoccupied with moral and religious issues, James was correct to think that there is no corroboration within human experience apart from activities that men and women perform; but Wild thinks that James should have placed greater stress on the role that facts play in validating most empirical judgments.

Wild anticipates White's proposition that James's earlier writings made sharper distinctions among the different kinds of belief that confront us. He agrees, too, that *Pragmatism* tends to blur those distinctions in favor of an increased authoritative role for feeling and sentiment; but on the whole Wild has less sympathy for James at this juncture than does Morton White. On the other hand, Wild joins both White and H. S. Thayer in holding that indictments of "subjectivism" commonly brought against James usually rest on misinterpretations. James did not believe, Wild argues, that a belief is ever sufficiently justified merely if one feels satisfied by it. Critical testing that brings a belief into coherent relationships with life's many dimensions is always required. That conviction, Wild maintains, is further evidence of James's desire to develop a philosophy that is constantly in touch with the lived experience of individuals and groups.—*J.K.R.*

ADDITIONAL RECOMMENDED READING

Allen, Gay Wilson. *William James: A Biography*. New York: The Viking Press, 1967. This study of James's life cites four major elements in his philosophy—pluralism, radical empiricism, tychism, and theism—and underscores how James's *Pragmatism* interprets the universe as one of flux and change.

Ayer, A. J. *The Origins of Pragmatism: Studies in the Philosophy of Charles Sanders Peirce and William James*. San Francisco: Freeman, Cooper & Company, 1968. This noted British philosopher argues that James's concern to find a place for religious belief, without compromising empirical evidence or sound intellectual standards, is a chief motivation behind *Pragmatism*, which contains a consistent and even tenable view of truth if James's theory is properly interpreted.

Dooley, Patrick K. *Pragmatism as Humanism*. Chicago: Nelson-Hall, 1974. The pivotal ingredient in James's thought, and the key for understanding *Pragmatism*, the author suggests, is his distinctively humanistic outlook.

Earle, William James. "William James," in *The Encyclopedia of Philosophy*. New York: Macmillan Publishing Company, 1967. Earle sees James's *Pragmatism* as an exploration of what it means to believe and in particular what it means in actual experience to find ideas true or false.

Flower, Elizabeth and Murray G. Murphy. *A History of Philosophy in America*. 2 vols. New York: G. P. Putnam's Sons, 1977. Flower and Murphy suggest that James's *Pragmatism* can still alert us to the subtlety and richness of experience, the purposeful quality of thought, and the active character of knowing.

James, William. *The Writings of William James: A Comprehensive Edition*. Edited by John J. McDermott. New York: Random House, 1967. McDermott sees James's *Pragmatism* as an epistemological elaboration of themes and principles set forth earlier in *The Principles of Psychology*.

Morris, Charles. *The Pragmatic Movement in American Philosophy*. New York: George Braziller, 1970. While James extended pragmatism beyond the parameters of C. S. Peirce's outlook, Morris argues that the two thinkers ended up with highly similar theories of meaning.

Rorty, Amelie, ed. *Pragmatic Philosophy*. Garden City, New York: Doubleday/Anchor Books, 1966. In her comments in this anthology, the editor judges James's writings, including *Pragmatism*, to be engaging but not always precise and rigorous.

Roth, John K. *American Dreams: Meditations on Life in the United States*. San Francisco: Chandler and Sharp, 1976. The author discusses James's pragmatic outlook in the context of James's meliorism, a middle position between an optimism that sees progress as inevitable and a pessimism that finds gloom and doom ahead.

THE MEANING OF TRUTH

Author: William James (1842-1910)
Type of work: Epistemology
First published: 1909

PRINCIPAL IDEAS ADVANCED

An idea is true if it works; truth happens to an idea; the true is whatever is expedient in the way of thinking.

In answer to the objection that such a theory makes truth a function of attitude so that truth has nothing to do with reality, the critics are reminded that knowledge depends on immediate, perceptual experiences (brute facts) and on the satisfactory use of concepts.

A concept (proposition) is true if it is such that, if acted upon, what one would receive perceptually is what one expects; in this sense, a true proposition satisfies an expectation.

No idea is satisfactory unless it works in such a way as actually to put the person who counts on the idea into a harmonious relationship with reality.

Although satisfaction is subjective, it can be a sign of objective truth.

In 1908 William James published his famous volume *Pragmatism*, in which he exposited the pragmatic theory of truth. His views were immediately attacked by a great many philosophers in the United States, England, France, and Germany. James felt that the criticisms were mainly due to a misunderstanding of the views presented in his book and in the writings of his fellow pragmatists. He, therefore, gathered together a group of his articles and papers, dating back to 1884, which he hoped would clarify the pragmatic theory. In addition, he joined to these a series of answers he had previously published against specific objections, plus a few new replies to the most recent criticisms. This collection was published under the title of *The Meaning of Truth* and constitutes the most complete explanation of James's theory of truth.

The general types of objections that James tries to answer are that the pragmatic theory of truth is entirely subjective, and that the pragmatic theory denies that truth has anything to do with reality. In *Pragmatism*, James had presented his famous formulation of the theory—truth is that which works; it is something that happens to an idea. The truth of an idea is the process of verifying it. What is true is what is expedient "in the way of our thinking," just as what is right is only what is expedient in our behavior.

Critics immediately pointed out that if an idea's truth depends merely on its satisfying someone's needs or wishes, then truth is a function of attitude and condition and has nothing to do with reality. In fact, the critics argued, an idea could actually be false in terms of reality, and yet true pragmatically for somebody. Choosing some of James's examples, especially from his *Will to Believe* (1897), opponents pointed out that if somebody believed that God exists, and this belief worked for him and satisfied him, then the belief would be true according to pragmatism, even though it is possible that it is false in fact.

James sought to respond to all of his critics by showing them what he had already said about the psychology of gaining true knowledge, about the reality of what we know, about the objectivity of what we know, and about misunderstandings of the pragmatic method and theory. The first few essays in *The Meaning of Truth*, "The Function of Cognition" (1884), "The Tigers in India" (1895), "Humanism and Truth" (1904), "The Relation Between the Knower and Known" (1904), "The Essence of Humanism" (1905), "A Word More About Truth" (1907), and "Professor Pratt on Truth" (1907), all stress the contention that the pragmatic psychological explanation of truth requires that truths deal with reality and that they must, from their very character, be objective.

The opponents, according to James, all hold to a view that in the knowing process there are three elements: the knower, the object that is known, and a third entity called "the knowing." An idea or belief is true, by this theory, if what is known corresponds to the actual object that is known. This theory creates an "epistemological gulf" between the knower and what he is trying to know. In some mysterious way, James points out, the knower has to leap over this gulf, by means of the process labeled "knowing," and get from his own beliefs and ideas to the objective state of affairs in order to ascertain whether he possesses true knowledge. Various theories of knowledge have been presented to try to explain how the leap takes place. But, James insists, to the extent that these theories ever succeed in illuminating the mysterious process, they turn out to offer portions of the pragmatic account, and they show that a psychological understanding of what occurs in knowing is, in fact, what knowing is.

Knowing consists, in James's account, either of a direct, immediate awareness, such as knowing that this paper is white, or of a conceptual knowledge in which a concept, such as "tigers in India," is connected and employed, in the context of immediate experience which the world supplies, with satisfactory results.

An immediate experience is not a datum which the mind sees and then tries to relate to something "out there." Instead, for James, it is a "brute fact," and the mental content and the perceived object are one and the same thing. It is only later, in terms of other theories we work out, that we develop two different ways of describing this one fact, that the paper is in the mind, or that the mind is "around" the paper. The rock bottom of our world is the experiencing of brute facts. According to James's theory of radical empiricism, these facts occur, they are the basic data of which we are aware (awareness of them, is, itself, a brute fact), and they occur together with their relations to one another as part of the "given" experiences. (Here, James rejects the classical empirical theory of David Hume and John Stuart Mill, which holds that experience consists of atomic, individual data that are completely separate and distinct.)

These immediate, perceptual experiences are "real" and "objective." What such a proposition meant for James is that in the actual context of life, these experiences provide a hard-core residuum which we cannot alter or ignore and hence must accept. The claim that these experiences are "real" in some further transexperiential sense James finds difficult to fathom, since, as far as he can see, any attempt that might be made to explain what is real about experience, or how it might be determined that an experience is real, would have to appeal to our direct, psychological acquaintance with the "reality" of brute facts.

Conceptual experience, knowledge of facts not immediately or directly given in experience, is known, and is known to be true, by its relationship to the context of perceptual experience. A proposition makes sense and is true by reference to a sequence of perceptions and a sequence of actions which, if followed out, would terminate in harmonious and satisfactory experience. In the example that James analyzes, that of the "tigers of India," this concept points to others, to actions which we might or do perform, and to the context of our experiences, both "real" and "ideal." In terms of our expectations, we would be dissatisfied (surprised) if shown a picture of a jaguar and told it was an Indian tiger. But we would be satisfied if we went to India, or thought of going to India, and perceived, or thought of perceiving, a certain striped animal which was usually called a tiger. The concept, then, of "tigers in India" works harmoniously and satisfactorily within the context of our other experiences, whereas other concepts do not work as well and hence are rejected as untrue. Conceptual experience grows and changes as the experience of harmonious and satisfactory relations between experiences grows and develops. Thus, in keeping with James's doctrine in *Pragmatism*, truth is something that happens to an idea. An idea can become more or less true as it is employed in relation to other experiences. An idea which does not seem to be harmonious or satisfactory in relation to other experiences may become more harmonious as experience changes and grows.

Throughout the essays, James tries to make the notions of "working," "satisfactory," and "harmonious" clearer, since much of what he claims is his opponents' misunderstanding of pragmatism stems from their misinterpretations of these terms. The terms cannot be precisely defined, for there are so many different ways in which ideas may work satisfactorily or harmoniously in our experience. But, in general, in view of the account offered about the psychology of "knowing," ideas can work harmoniously and satisfactorily only insofar as they conform to "reality." Since reality consists of the perceptual and conceptual experiences that we have, an idea that did not conform to, or fit in with, reality, would not be harmonious with the context of our experiences. Hence, ideas work not because we want them to, but because their working is conditioned by the "real" world of our experience.

Further, James insists in several of the essays, working is not merely a practical matter, and satisfaction is not merely a pleasant personal feeling. The terminology employed in *Pragmatism* may have led critics to conceive of an idea as "working" only in terms of physical actions occurring and succeeding in their aim. But, James explains, working is a complex process involving the solving not only of practical problems, but of theoretical ones as well, plus the overall satisfaction that we can gain only by having our conceptual and immediately experienced world form a consistent and harmonious whole. As human beings, we seek and demand more than mere practical or utilitarian satisfaction. We are unable to accept perceptual or conceptual experiences which conflict with others that we have had, or which conflict with concepts or theories that have worked in the past. Whenever we seem to be faced with such discrepancies, we seek other immediate and conceptual experiences in order to overcome the difficulties, so that our entire world of experience and thought will form a harmonious whole. Then, and only then, will our ideas work satisfactorily.

Some of the statements of the pragmatic theory, including some of James's early ones, make it appear that the feeling of satisfaction involved in having a consistent perceptual and intellectual world is a purely subjective and psychological matter. "The sentiment of rationality," as James labels it, is a feeling that normal, reasonable people have when everything they believe and perceive fits together. In *The Meaning of Truth*, James stresses the point that this sentiment of satisfaction is, in fact, actually achieved only through uniting one's conceptual and perceptual experience consistently into one harmonious world. The satisfaction involved may be subjective and psychological, but it requires theoretical effort and logical consistency.

In the eighth essay of *The Meaning of Truth*, "The Pragmatist Account of Truth and Its Misunderstanders" (1908), James reviews his answer to his critics regarding the relation of pragmatic truth to "reality," "objectivity," and "consistency." The opponents have insisted that since, according to the pragmatists, the truth of beliefs consists in their giving satisfaction, and since satisfaction is a subjective condition, then the subject receiving satisfaction can manufacture his own truths when he likes, depending only on what satisfies him, and having nothing to do with "reality" or "objectivity." But, James points out, human beings are so constituted that the kinds of satisfactions they actually do find in their beliefs occur as a result of believing that there are independent physical realities, that there are other minds, that there have been past events, and that there are eternal logical relations. And, "Above all we find *consistency* satisfactory, consistency between the present idea and the entire rest of our mental equipment, including the whole order of our sensations, and that of our intuitions of likeness and difference, and our whole stock of previously acquired truths." The pragmatist, James asserts, treats his satisfactions as possibly true guides to reality, and not as guides that are true solely for him. The critics appear to suppose that because "satisfaction" is a subjective feeling it therefore cannot indicate objective truth, while the pragmatist contends that since this feeling is, in fact, our final way for deciding what is, and what is not, objectively true, the feeling of satisfaction is interwoven with "reality" and yields "objective truth."

But the critics object again, pointing out that it is a notorious fact that erroneous views and beliefs are often quite satisfactory to the person who holds them. Hence, the satisfactory feeling cannot suffice to guarantee the objective truth of a belief, its relation to reality. James replies that the pragmatist has said only that the feelings of satisfaction are indispensable for "truth-building." He has not claimed that the feelings themselves are sufficient. The critic criticizes the pragmatic theory by considering feelings of satisfaction out of the actual contexts in which truth-satisfactions occur coincident to our being led to direct experience of reality. If only the feelings took place, we would not actually be completely satisfied, because something, the awareness of immediate reality, would be missing. Therefore, James contends, given the situations in which truth-satisfactions are felt by human beings, the subjective and even solipsistic problems that the critics of pragmatism raise are not really relevant, since one does not and would not feel satisfied unless what one believed led to an awareness of reality—that is, to future experiences of a sort one anticipated.

The remaining seven essays deal with various forms of the same objections that had come up in books and articles that had just appeared in the United States, England, France, and Germany against James's formulation of the pragmatic theory of truth. Though interesting points occur in these essays, they deal, for the most part, with restatements of James's reasons for denying the subjectivist charges of his critics and with reassertions of his contention that the pragmatic theory is realistic and objective. From the present-day perspective, the most interesting of these essays is the one dealing with the objections raised by the English philosopher Bertrand Russell.

In the essay "Two English Critics," James deals with criticisms of pragmatism that Russell had presented in his article, "Transatlantic Truth," that had appeared in the *Albany Review* in 1908. Russell argued that according to the pragmatists a true proposition is one such that believing it is worthwhile. If this be the case, he claimed, anyone who believes that a proposition is true must already have ascertained that its consequences are, in actual fact, good. And, in many instances, it is obviously much more difficult to settle the question of whether the consequences are good than whether the original proposition is true. Hence, the pragmatic test cannot really be applied to tell if any given proposition is true.

James replies that Russell has made the pragmatic theory appear silly by taking the notion of "good consequences" as a sign or criterion of a proposition's truth. Instead, James contends, the potential consequences are the "lurking" motives for the making of truth-claims, though they may also, occasionally, serve as measures or marks of truth. The consequences are not the *logical* premises for beliefs, although they do give intelligible practical meaning to calling a belief true or false. The consequences are the *psychological* reasons for our asserting beliefs and the psychological cues for our acting upon our beliefs.

Russell's attack continues, contending that it follows from the pragmatic definition of "truth," that a proposition can be true even though what it asserts is false. A proposition is true if it works, for the pragmatists, and "it works" means that "it is useful to believe it." Hence, by substituting definitions for the terms defined, one comes to the conclusion that to assert that a proposition such as "Other people exist" is true, means that it is useful to believe that other people exist, even if, in fact, they do not.

James rejects Russell's criticism by insisting that it results from "vicious" abstractions. Russell has abstracted the pragmatic terms from the context in which they occur and has juggled definitions to come to his conclusion. "But may not real terms . . . have accidents not expressed in their definitions?" James asks. Beliefs, James insists, have their objective content, as well as their truth. For this reason, when somebody believes that other people exist, both the consequences and the so-called objective content are involved in his belief. In effect, James denies that the nature of truth can be examined abstractly, in terms of definitions. Instead, it must be examined in the context of the real situations in which it occurs.

The fifteen essays that comprise *The Meaning of Truth*, though extremely repetitious, contain an important exposition of James's pragmatic theory. The work also presents one of the best discussions, from the pragmatic side, of the standard objections that have been and still are being raised to James's theory. In view of more recent considerations of pragmatism, the essays are most intriguing in showing how James tried to establish that his theory does not rest on the purely subjective. Whether one is convinced or not, one is impressed by James's attempt to grapple with the fundamental points raised by his critics.—*R.H.P.*

PERTINENT LITERATURE

Ross, Ralph, ed. "Introduction," in William James's *The Meaning of Truth: A Sequel to "Pragmatism"*. Ann Arbor: University of Michigan Press, 1970.

Another person's thought cannot be understood unless one approaches it sympathetically. That principle was one of William James's basic convictions, and Ralph Ross uses it to guide his discussion of *The Meaning of Truth* (1909). Sympathetic analysis need not be the same as acceptance, but Ross surmises that James had something genuinely new and important to say. Observing how James complained repeatedly that his critics had misrepresented him, Ross gives accurate interpretation top priority.

In *The Meaning of Truth*, James brought together "all the work of my pen that bears directly on the truth-question." The initial essay, "The Function of Cognition," was originally printed as early as 1885. Others had appeared subsequently, and only a few of the papers were published for the first time. Ross finds the collection repetitious, but he also judges the papers to reveal growth in James's thinking and to vindicate James's appraisal that discussion of the pragmatic theory of truth would "mark a turning point in the history of epistemology."

Ross argues that James used *The Meaning of Truth* mainly to justify what was most readily justifiable in *Pragmatism*. Thus, James elaborated what he meant in using terms such as "expedient" and "satisfactory" to define "truth." If the true is the expedient or the satisfactory, as James had said, he did not mean that the expedient is merely what anyone takes to be useful or that the satisfactory is simply any psychic gratification at all. Instead, Ross testifies, James intended the expedient to point out "a means fitted to an end" and "satisfactory" to designate the gratification resulting when thought achieves consistency, tested results, and insight empowering exploration of new questions.

By responding to the easier issues, claims Ross, James failed to say enough about some of the boldest propositions set forth in *Pragmatism*. One instance is James's belief that "truth *happens* to an idea. It *becomes* true, is *made* true to events." Critics jumped on this assertion because James seemed to blur a crucial distinction between (1) the truth of an idea and (2) our discovery that an idea is true. The latter can *happen*, James's critics agreed, but such a happening does not constitute an idea's truth. An idea, in fact, already is true or false before one discovers which case holds. Ross insists, however, that James was driving for an insight that went deeper than his critics realized.

Truth, Ross takes James to say, is about experience. There may well be realities beyond experience, but knowledge and therefore truth are not outside of it. Thus, Ross suggests, James argued that an idea has truth only insofar as it guides us through a process culminating in experience that fulfills expectations that the idea has led one to possess. In this way, experience makes ideas true. To think of them simply as *being* true, without *becoming* true, abstracts from the actual process of experience, which leads us not to some antecedent transexperiential reality but to experienced reality that has existence only as experience itself unfolds. The author does not anticipate objections that might be brought against his interpretation of James on this issue, but clearly Ross implies that he finds more merit in James's position than the scorn it has received would allow.

Moore, Edward C. *American Pragmatism: Peirce, James and Dewey*. New York: Columbia University Press, 1961.

Claiming that pragmatism is America's unique contribution to Western philosophy, Edward C. Moore begins his study by stressing that pragmatism also spawned intense feelings pro and con. If the intensity of such debates has cooled recently, the interpretation of William James's philosophy remains a delicate matter; for Moore contends that James's pragmatism lacks philosophical precedents.

James's pragmatism follows naturally from his radical empiricism, Moore believes, and the author refers to *The Meaning of Truth* in clarifying what that empiricism involved. Its essence, writes Moore, is contained in James's postulate that "the only things that shall be debatable among philosophers shall be things definable in terms drawn from experience." Moore interprets that passage to mean that an object is what it is "known-as," to use James's word; and what the object is "known-as" depends on actually experienced relations between the object and one who encounters it. James referred to these experienced relationships as "practical consequences," a choice of terms that Moore finds unfortunate because it fueled the mistaken impression that James denigrated the theoretical dimensions of experience. Instead, Moore argues, James wanted only to put reasonable checks on speculation by insisting that the meaning of theories depends upon their ability to lead us into experience at the level of sensation and feeling.

We use concepts to interpret experience, and Moore suggests that James's empiricism entails that their meaning consists of nothing more or less than all of the sensations that may be expected from, and all of the reactions we must prepare toward, the object intended by the idea. James's intriguing theory of truth emerged when he brought this pragmatic theory of meaning to bear on the meaning of the term "truth" itself.

According to Moore, James often found references to truth deceptively abstract because they overlooked how human knowing is an activity. Knowing requires us to pursue a line of thought, to go through a series of actions, and to experience the results of doing both. James accepted the traditional formula that true ideas agree with reality. More than most philosophers, however, he emphasized how this use of "agree" could not be meaningful unless it took seriously how our knowledge entails action.

Assuming that the idea of an object involves expected sensations and anticipated reactions, James could naturally call an idea a plan or a guide for activity. Thus, to know whether a particular idea is true, we would have to follow the guidance of the idea and see whether we are led as expected and required to react as anticipated. Only to the extent that we are, Moore underscores, would James say that our idea is true. This "fit" between idea and reality, James holds in *The Meaning of Truth*, is the agreement between them. That agreement, in turn, is truth itself, at least insofar as one can make the meaning of truth intelligible within the boundaries of James's radical empiricism.

A corollary of this analysis, Moore points out, is James's emphasis that truth is in the making, not something eternally fixed and final. In this respect, Moore concludes, James's pragmatism is a worthy option between an irrational skepticism and a dogmatic absolutism. As it affirms the possibility of genuine knowledge, James's pragmatism also rightly recognizes that our experience is a fallible venture seeking to find and even to create the agreement between ideas and facts wherein truth lives, moves, and has its being.

Smith, John E. *Purpose and Thought: The Meaning of Pragmatism*. New Haven, Connecticut: Yale University Press, 1978.

John E. Smith recounts William James's scenario about what often happens to a new philosophical view. First, said James, the outlook is branded unintelligible, outrageous, or both. Later the theory may be called understandable, but it will be labeled obvious or trivial. Finally, having become more familiar with the position, the initial opponents will claim that they created it. Smith thinks pragmatism experienced this fate, and thus he believes that the time is ripe to look at pragmatism's meaning afresh.

Arguing that James overestimated how easy everything would be if people only consulted experience and resisted the lure of abstract conceptualization, Smith takes his bearings from a middle ground. It gives full credence neither to claims that reduce all criticisms of pragmatism to misinterpretations of its teachings nor to charges that pragmatism is little more than a particularly seductive relativism. Desiring to concentrate on the pragmatists' fundamental hypotheses rather than on the historical development of pragmatism, Smith aims to recover what they actually said about their own questions and concerns.

Smith notes A. J. Ayer's claim in *The Origins of Pragmatism* (1968) that the roots of pragmatism trace back to ancient Greece and specifically to Protagoras' teachings that "man is the measure of all things." If that citation contrasts with Edward C. Moore's earlier estimates of pragmatism's uniqueness and originality, Smith's allusions to *The Meaning of Truth* concur with Moore's in starting with the connections between James's pragmatism and his radical empiricism. In particular, Smith stresses James's "most distinctive metaphysical thesis," which is that the universe exhibits a continuity that necessitates no transcendental ego or Absolute to hold things together. Coupling this thesis with James's belief that we experience conjunctive relations and that the only matters debatable are those drawn from experience, Smith infers that James is committed to interpret truth as involving a process that takes us from a judgment to the state of affairs about which the judgment makes a claim.

Explanations about how that process works and how it actually defines the meaning of truth led James into many difficulties. Some were deserved because on occasion, as James himself admitted, his language was imprecise and ambiguous. Hoping that *The Meaning of Truth* would reduce the vagueness, James continued to insist, Smith observes, that one must distinguish between truth and reality. "Realities," said James, "are not *true*, they *are*; and beliefs are true *of* them." Smith takes this proposition to mean that James, his moral "idealism" notwithstanding, should not be viewed as a philosophical idealist in disguise; and he also implies that James's distinction between truth and reality lends credibility to his claim that pragmatism was indeed "a new name for some old ways of thinking."

James, Smith contends, was less a maverick than some appraisals assume. Although discontented with traditional formulations about how truth consists of agreement or correspondence between ideas and realities, James still operated within a classical conception of the nature of truth. His novel contribution, Smith finds, was to argue that correspondence cannot be adequately interpreted as a fixed and unchanging relation. It must encompass the activity of inquiry and the tracking of consequences. Thus, Smith proposes that James's theory of truth be described as one of "dynamic correspondence."— *J.K.R.*

ADDITIONAL RECOMMENDED READING

Commager, Henry Steele. *The American Mind: An Interpretation of American Thought and Character Since the 1880's*. New Haven, Connecticut: Yale University Press, 1950. Commager describes James's pragmatism as a practical outlook, individualistic and helpful, which epitomizes the most authentic American thought.

Copleston, Frederick. *A History of Philosophy*. Vol. VIII, Part II. Garden City, New York: Doubleday/Anchor Books, 1967. Warning how important it is not to caricature James's theory of truth, Copleston nevertheless finds that pragmatism is subject to serious criticism owing to James's opinion that "satisfaction" is a basic element in truth.

Eames, S. Morris. "The Meaning of Truth in William James," in *The Philosophy of William James*. Edited by Walter Robert Corti. Hamburg: Felix Meiner, 1976. Because James left us no finished theory of truth, says Eames, the legacy of his thought is the need to keep searching for an adequate view that does justice to new developments in science and logic.

Kuklick, Bruce. *The Rise of American Philosophy: Cambridge, Massachusetts 1860-1930*. New Haven, Connecticut: Yale University Press, 1977. *The Meaning of Truth*, Kuklick contends, is especially significant because it underscores James's close relations to the Kantian tradition.

Reck, Andrew J. *Introduction to William James: An Essay and Selected Texts*. Bloomington: Indiana University Press, 1967. Although his pragmatic theory of truth does not command the allegiance of most contemporary philosophers, Reck affirms that James's radical empiricism has gained new respect.

Schneider, Herbert W. *A History of American Philosophy*. New York: Columbia University Press, 1963. Schneider's puckish judgment is that James's theory of truth, which interpreted truth in terms of "satisfaction," had a hard time satisfying anyone but James himself.

Stroh, Guy W. *American Philosophy from Edwards to Dewey: An Introduction*. Princeton, New Jersey: D. Van Nostrand Company, 1968. Stroh stresses James's insistence in *The Meaning of Truth* that one cannot spell out what truth is without explaining how truth is obtained.

Thayer, H. S. *Meaning and Action: A Critical History of Pragmatism*. Indianapolis: Bobbs-Merrill, 1968. Noting that James was through and through a moralist, Thayer calls attention to James's view that truth is not a category different from goodness but rather one type of goodness.

Wilshire, Bruce, ed. *William James: The Essential Writings*. New York: Harper Torchbooks, 1971. An adequate understanding of James's theory of truth, Wilshire asserts, cannot be obtained unless one takes account of James's psychology and metaphysics.

THE PRINCIPLE OF INDIVIDUALITY AND VALUE

Author: Bernard Bosanquet (1848-1923)
Type of work: Metaphysics, philosophy of value
First published: 1912

PRINCIPAL IDEAS ADVANCED

An individual is not a mere particular, nor is he a personality finding supreme value in experience; an individual is a whole organized from mutually supplementing parts.

The world process is moving in the direction of greater integration of its parts.

The principle of individuality, when viewed in terms of ideas, is the principle of harmony, cooperation, and noncontradiction.

Purpose is secondary to individuality; to understand the world, one must understand it not in terms of purpose but on the principle of individuality.

Value depends on order and harmony; a life acquires value when it contributes to the realization of a larger whole.

The Absolute may be an individual in whom all selves are brought together in a single thought.

In this, his first series of Gifford Lectures, Bernard Bosanquet dealt with the perennial metaphysical problem of how the world can be one and at the same time many. In his day there were pluralists, who denied that the world is one, and monists, who denied that it is many. In between were dualists, who held that mind, *élan vital*, or some such unifying principle is engaged in eternal struggle against matter and chance. Bosanquet, maintaining that the world is an integral whole, pointed out that it is the characteristic of a whole to bring diverse elements together into a higher unity.

The term "individual," as employed by Bosanquet, is a synonym for "whole." He carefully distinguished his use of the word from other meanings that the word has. Some philosophers have made it synonymous with "particular," in accordance with the logic of classes and members. Useful as the familiar scheme of universal and particular is for many purposes, Bosanquet complained that because it proceeds by abstraction, it leads away from rather than toward ultimate truth. For example, the notion "man" is arrived at by leaving out such characteristics as height, color, musical ability, and the like in order to find those characteristics that are common to all members of the class. When a concrete human being is thought of simply as a particular instance of the class man—as he is likely to be viewed by scientists—everything that makes him an individual is left out. Bosanquet said that it is a misuse of language to call the particular an individual.

Other philosophers have used the term "individual" to stand for human personality in its unique, idiosyncratic aspect. The nineteenth century, with its democratic and romantic sentiments, may be said to have discovered "personality." Every human being, regardless of his status, was said to have infinite value, not so much in his identification with the image of eternity as in virtue of the supreme value attached to each man's "experience." Several schools of thought proclaimed the primacy of consciousness, and declared that novelty is the highest good. Under their influence, the term "individual" came to stand for the fresh, the spontaneous, the original; they did not hesitate to affirm that the only thing of value in the whole universe is the immediate, unrepeatable experience of conscious beings; and that, if there is a God, he must resemble man in these respects.

Bosanquet rejected this account of individuality no less firmly than the other. He maintained that empirical consciousness has so little coherence it is fatuous to think of it as one in any sense. A healthy man has unity when viewed as a physical organism; and when viewed as a moral and spiritual being he has the measure of unity which good habits and knowledge impart to his behavior. But there is no comparable unity in the consciousness of man, which is a tumbling chaos of sensations and fancies. When here and there our experience achieves unity, this comes from the order of the world which is experienced, not from man's fleeting awareness.

True individuals, Bosanquet held, are everywhere around us. A flower is an example; so is a family, a poem, or a machine. Wherever parts fit together in a larger complex and differences mutually supplement each other to form wholes, there the principle of individuality is found. Mostly, said Bosanquet, we are not conscious of it, because, like the air we breathe or the light by which we see, it is too obvious. We become conscious of this principle of individuality chiefly in those situations where we had not expected to find it, as, for example, when through the artist's eye we see a wood where we thought there were only trees, or through the sociologists' investigations we discover that a crowd is something more than the men and women who make it up.

Bosanquet was an idealist, but only in the sense that Plato was, for whom "ideas" were the real determinations of things and not the contents of man's mind, as philosophers since Descartes have so often affirmed. He was an "objective" idealist because he held that the relations which determine things do not depend on anyone's awareness of them. To make clear his affiliations, he made bold to say that his philosophy was "materialism or externalism with a difference."

Although many idealists in his day felt it necessary to decry the naturalistic account of evolution which explained the origin of species in mechanistic terms, Bosanquet rather welcomed the stringent impersonalism of the Darwinian world view. He said that the sciences proceed by abstraction; hence, they leave out much that is important, but this does not mean that their account is false. After all, a mechanism is an individual in which the parts function only because they are mutually adapted to each other. Bosanquet's chief complaint against naturalism was that it misconstrued the principle of the uniformity of nature. He said that the less reflective advocates of mechanism and materialism wrongly supposed this principle to mean that the future will resemble the past, whereas philosophers such as J. S. Mill understood quite well that such resemblance as occurs in nature is a result of the interconnection of its parts. The law of gravity is a good example because it explicitly mentions the mutual attraction of bodies and specifies that it is proportional to the masses and their distance apart. Natural selection is another example: it affirms that those organisms which are suited to their environment tend to survive in the struggle for existence.

Evolution was not essential to Bosanquet's view of the world, inasmuch as his fundamental outlook was one he shared with such nonevolutionists as Plato and Spinoza. But on the basis of scientific evidence he accepted evolution and worked it into his account of the world. In his view, the world-process is moving in the direction of greater integration of its parts. On the lower levels, determination is almost entirely mechanical. Even in living organisms, adaptation is mostly repetitious and associative. But as we follow the process to higher planes, we find more freedom of adaptation and a more explicit determination of the parts by the organism as a whole.

Another aspect of naturalism that vexed many idealist philosophers was the view that mind or consciousness merely reflects bodily behavior and has no power to originate or modify behavior. Against this view, commonly called epiphenomenalism, they advanced the view called interactionism, which contends that mind has an independent existence and is both acted upon by body and acts on it. Here, again, Bosanquet leaned toward the naturalist position. He argued that a man can do nothing merely by entertaining a purpose in his mind. For example, it is easy to propose a charitable undertaking; but carrying it out depends upon skills and habits which require a lifetime to develop and are no part of consciousness at all, having their locus as nearly as we can tell in the brain and nervous system. He did not deny that "higher" mental processes distinguish the conduct of men from that of lower creatures; but he maintained that consciousness is not the working part of these higher processes.

This is not to say that he regarded consciousness as playing an unimportant part in the life of man or its emergence as insignificant in the evolution of the world. On the contrary, in its role of spectator, mind has a value of its own. Here the unconscious unities and adaptations of the world appear on a new plane: they are understood, appreciated, enjoyed. In a manner reminiscent of Spinoza, Bosanquet held that there are two ways of viewing the world. If it is viewed as external, it appears to be a texture of conflicting forces seeking to resolve their oppositions in the most economical fashion. If it is viewed from within, it takes the appearance, rather, of conflicting ideas which are seeking logical resolution. Bosanquet's logic, of course, was not the logic of linear inference which Spinoza learned from Descartes, but Hegel's dialectics, which supposes that initial antinomies are reconciled in a higher synthesis. The evolution of the species and the history of man have causal explanations, but they can also be viewed as the working out of the logical principle of noncontradiction. Things can be different, Bosanquet insisted, without being contradictory. Colors, for example, may clash or they may harmonize. The principle of individuality which, viewed in external terms, yields the notion of an organism (a self-maintaining machine), when viewed in terms of ideas is the principle of harmony, cooperation, and noncontradiction.

Bosanquet rejected the view, popular among opponents of naturalism, that the world can be understood in terms of purpose. Purpose, he argued, is always secondary to individuality. Finite wholes, which are never entirely self-sufficient, have wants; and behavior designed to satisfy these wants, by adapting means to the desired end, is what is meant by purpose. Such adaptation, however, is not to be confused with the adjustment of parts within a whole. To achieve a purpose means to remove differences, for, when the want is satisfied, both ends and means cease to exist. It is the mark of an individual, however, that it does not abolish differences but reconciles them in a higher unity. The sentimental novel exemplifies the purposive standpoint: when the lovers are united, after overcoming many obstacles, the novel must end. Greek tragedy exemplifies the principle of individuality: conflicts find their resolution in a transformation of the will of the protagonist. Bosanquet did not deny that there is purpose in the world, on the preconscious as well as on the conscious plane. But he did deny that the notion of purpose has any value for understanding evolution or history, or the destiny of man, or the world as a whole. The reason at work everywhere about us, he said, is not intelligible in terms of means and ends; it is intelligible only on the principle of individuality.

Bosanquet reasoned about value in a similar way. The ordinary nineteenth century understanding of value made it equivalent to satisfaction. But satisfactions, like purposes, exist only in finite individuals, so that to equate value with the satisfaction of wants makes it quite a minor thing. And if, as was commonly maintained, it is not the satisfaction as such that is good but the consciousness which a man has of the satisfaction, it is more minor still. For Bosanquet, not the satisfaction of a purpose but the harmony of a whole is what has value, and the more comprehensive the whole, the greater the value. He maintained, with Plato (*Republic*, Book IV), that society has more value than any of its members, and that the value of personal life and effort derives from the function a man fulfills in the greater whole. Thus, the housewife, the worker, the soldier, the statesman become valuable as they perform the duties of their respective stations.

Bosanquet accepted the dictum of T. H. Green (*Prolegomena to Ethics*,

1883) that there is no value where there is no consciousness; but he urged that consciousness is not valuable by itself—the value lies in that of which we become conscious, and only secondarily, in the quality of mind which is able to appreciate values. These considerations led Bosanquet to set aside the usual moralistic and hedonistic interpretations of man's existence and put in their place an aesthetic one. Appreciation of the order and harmony of the world, whether in terms of science or art or philosophy, was, in his view, the thing for which consciousness is properly suited. Getting pleasure is a function of a healthy constitution; good morals a function of mental hygiene and social discipline. One does not have to take thought about them. Moreover, they hold only limited opportunities for self-realization. Man deepens and integrates his conscious life only as he progresses toward understanding and appreciating the world. By learning to think coherently, improving his judgment, cultivating his taste, he achieves the fullness and freedom which are the prerogative only of conscious selves or souls.

Bosanquet criticized the view that creative excellence in art lies in novelty or in so-called originality. Rather, he said, it consists in the artist's penetration of reality which permits him to reveal treasures beyond the scope of the average mind. In his view, the vision of the artist is closely related to the theory of the scientist: both are expressions of the "logic which lays bare the heart and structure of things, and in doing so purifies and intensifies the feeling which current appearances are too confused and contradictory to evoke."

This vision, Bosanquet said, is impersonal and can be shared. Not everybody shares it equally because of differences in mind due to training and native genius. Moreover, physical circumstances, such as fatigue or illness, limit one's mental power. But the value is there, however completely or partially the empirical consciousness manages to lay hold on it. That what is primary is the object of vision rather than the consciousness which possesses it appears when we observe that our most satisfactory experiences are those in which self-consciousness moves into the penumbra and leaves us aware only of the truth.

The emphasis which modern men have put on self-consciousness and personality favors a pluralistic view of mind. It suggests that minds rise like so many pillars, each isolated from the others. Bosanquet proposed, as a more likely figure, that we think of human minds as ocean waves, some rising to greater heights than others but otherwise occupying the same space. He said that social experience is like a single mind in several bodies—the child, the worker, the statesman each being conscious of the same whole in varying degrees. Finite minds, he said (borrowing an expression from Hegel), are "copulas"; and he added, "Every self is the representative center of an external world." Nature becomes alive in it; the experiences of other selves are shared. In this way each mind "expands from its place in nature to a more or less wide and deep participation in the Absolute."

About the Absolute, Bosanquet was not very specific. In affirming it, he signified his conviction that the world is a whole, that is, a meaningful system. According to Bosanquet, there is nothing strange or extreme in such a view: all meaningful activity, whether devotion to duty or the search for truth, presupposes it. But is the Absolute a mind? Is the Whole conscious of what takes place within it? Bosanquet supposes that it is, not as finite selves are conscious when, as finite, they have the sense of being other than what they know, but in a manner suggested to us by those rare moments in which we come near to losing ourselves in our vision of the world. Such high awareness, said Bosanquet, such "perfect union of the mind and nature" as is exemplified in Dante's great poem, distantly figures a complete experience in which all nature, all selves, are brought together in a single thought. Such, it may be, is the Absolute.—*J.F.*

PERTINENT LITERATURE

Pringle-Pattison, A. Seth. *The Idea of God in the Light of Recent Philosophy: Gifford Lectures for 1912, 1913 at Aberdeen*. New York: Oxford University Press, 1920.

Although Bernard Bosanquet was not primarily a philosopher of religion, the main impact of his Gifford Lectures was on men who, like A. Seth Pringle-Pattison, approached philosophy from its theological side and were trying to redraw the lines of battle between religious philosophy and scientific naturalism. In place of the old theism, with its preexisting God, they were exploring a new "process theology," which treated God as coeternal with his creation. By this means they could claim affinity to what Pringle-Pattison calls "the higher naturalism," which allowed for stages in the evolutionary process. Bosanquet's contribution to this line of thought lay primarily in the favorable treatment which he accorded to organic evolution and in the importance which he attached to the continuity between man's physical and his mental constitution. Pringle-Pattison quotes from the lecture "The Bodily Basis of Mind," in which Bosanquet had said that the soul is "essentially connected with or even founded upon its environment . . . out of which it brings a principle of unity."

Philosophers who were interested in religion and ethics had shied away from the Absolute idealism of F. H. Bradley and Bosanquet and, looking more in the direction of Hermann Lotze and Immanuel Kant than toward Georg Wilhelm Friedrich Hegel, had developed what they called Personal idealism. In an earlier work, *Hegelianism and Personality* (1887), Pringle-Pattison had led in this protest. But in the present work he makes a notable effort to reunite the two camps; and, while Bosanquet is only one of the "recent" philosophers dealt with in the book, his recent lectures receive special attention because, as the author says, ". . . along with the large amount of general agreement, there was a difference of emphasis, to say the least, in our ways of holding the Idealist creed."

As a speculative thinker, Pringle-Pattison was drawn to the doctrine that reality is an organic whole. Correct philosophy could mean only tracing out the structures discernible in the whole; and he found the concrete, empirical manner in which Bosanquet traced these structures in his Gifford Lectures, mounting from the lower and less stable to the more perfect and harmonious, far more persuasive than the abstract reasoning to be found in Bradley's *Appearance and Reality*. Bradley had characterized the Absolute in negative terms, but Bosanquet's principle of inclusiveness and harmony made it possible to think of it in terms drawn from moral and aesthetic life. Pursuing this line, Pringle-Pattison concludes that the Absolute is properly thought of as personal. And the second half of the book explains how it is possible to trace out the teleological principle in the universe by which the Absolute creates finite selves in order to realize its own latent capacities for love and suffering.

Because the Gifford lectureship is oriented toward religion, Bosanquet had touched on theological issues. One such was the question whether it makes sense to speak of a creator creating creators: Bosanquet concluded that this is a contradiction. Another question was whether it is possible to think of the universe as having a purpose: again, he concluded that it is not. Even though he was willing to say, with John Keats, that the world is a vale of soul-making, he qualified this as being true only from a finite standpoint. Soul-making presupposes something out of which souls are made and carries the implication that they survive earthly existence, neither of which propositions Bosanquet would agree to. His view, as the author points out, was that what primarily has value is not the particular center of consciousness but "the contribution which the particular center—representative of certain elements in the whole—brings to the whole in which it is a member." In other words, for Bosanquet the formal distinctness of finite selves is due to impotence, what is of value in a self being the content which it has in common with many selves. In the Absolute, the finites blend and are resolved. Pringle-Pattison refers to the passage in which Bosanquet speaks of two persons working together in such a way that A's failings counteract B's, and says, "If A and B could be shaken up in a bag together they would make a perfect man." That, according to Bosanquet, is an intimation of how the material of finite selves is redistributed and readjusted in the Absolute.

To all of this Pringle-Pattison raises the kind of objection which personalists and pragmatists (and later, existentialists) always raise against speculative philosophy. "The too exclusive monism of the system," he says, "depends on a defective idea of what is meant by a self or by the fact of individuation in general." He reminds us that the philosophical claim here involved had earlier been enunciated by Bosanquet in his *Logic*, where it is stated that all finite individuals reduce to "connections of content within the real individual to which they belong." In other words, for Bosanquet, finite things do not exist in the mode of subject but only in the mode of predicate or universal. But, says Pringle-Pattison, "no number of abstract universals flocking together can give you the concretely existing individual." The unity which constitutes a self, he explains, is not the unity which an object has for a spectator but the very different kind of unity which a subject has for itself. The creation of "beings who are really selves," possessing a measure of "apartness" so that they can act freely with respect to the whole of which they are members, is, he says, "the main miracle of the universe." That we are unable to understand it he finds not surprising.

McTaggart, J. Ellis. Review of Bernard Bosanquet's *The Principle of Individuality and Value*, in *Mind*. N. S. XXI, no. 83 (July, 1912), pp. 416-427.

J. Ellis McTaggart writes about Bernard Bosanquet's lectures in the same way one imagines him commenting on writings by his Cambridge students. That he could assume these patronizing airs was owing to the fact that he had himself thoroughly explored Hegelian logic and was the exponent of another brand of idealism even more remote from the view of the man in the street than was the brand that he was criticizing. For example, when Bosanquet points to "the general trueness and being of whole provinces of advanced experience, such as religion, or morality, or the world of beauty and of science" and says that these furnish higher evidence than does the abstract principle of noncontradiction, McTaggart observes that this contention is probably unsound but that Bosanquet's arguments deserve careful consideration. This comes from a man who in his own work made a point of never weakening a proof by introducing an appeal to experience.

It is certainly the Cambridge don who, almost automatically, writes "Standard of what?" when Bosanquet says that we should "take for our standard what man recognizes as value when his life is fullest and his soul at the highest reach," and notes that in any case we would need another standard by which to know when our lives are fullest. But the criticism goes deeper. Bosanquet, he says, is everywhere inclined to underestimate the degree to which men differ, speaking as he often does of "the claims of the obvious" and "the reasonable faith of resolute and open-minded men." Honest thinkers have disagreed on every philosophical question. None of the beliefs which are appealed to is self-evident or generally admitted. They all need to be proved; and if they can be proved, most of the philosophies of the past will be disproved.

The lecture entitled "The Concrete Universal" is singled out as the most important of the series because here we learn what Bosanquet understands by individuality. McTaggart complains, however, that it contains two accounts: according to one, the world is described as a system of members each of which contributes to the unity of the whole; according to the other, the identity of the whole is represented as subordinating diversity to itself so that identity and difference are distinguished only as points of view. Although the two are presented as being identical, the second, says McTaggart, goes much further than the first. Here he drops the matter; but readers of *Mind* who had read nothing by McTaggart would have heard that McTaggart denied that wholes have any existence over and above that of the members of which they are constituted, and that his favorite example was a college or other close-knit society, members of which exist only by virtue of their relation with one another and with the whole.

Two further points are made in connection with Bosanquet's theory of individuality. McTaggart notes that while he sometimes speaks of "wholes" and "systems," his favorite term is "world," so that we are told that "the true embodiment of the logical universal takes the shape of a world whose members are worlds." This, says McTaggart, can only mean that the series of worlds within worlds is endless, and he finds unsatisfactory a note in which Bosanquet denies that this must be the case. The objection is of interest chiefly in view of McTaggart's own contention that nothing is simple and that everything is infinitely divisible. A second complaint is that, in his discussion of individuality, Bosanquet has not sufficiently explained the unity which determines which collections are and which are not systems. The unities of art are appealed to by Bosanquet. But McTaggart professes himself unable to understand why Salisbury Cathedral, for example, would be less a unity if a gasometer were substituted for its present tower. He was not just being perverse: it was a principle with him that groups can be formed of any substances. He was thinking in terms of logic (theory of sets) rather than in terms of aesthetic experience.

Of the lecture "The Bodily Basis of Mind," McTaggart remarks that almost the whole could have been written by a complete materialist. Bosanquet's right to call himself an idealist, says McTaggart, depends on whether, in calling finite selves "individuals," he is saying anything more than a materialist would be saying who called them an aggregate. According to McTaggart, Bosanquet, in denying that man has ultimate value, seems to be saying that man is no more important than any other part of the universe. That scarcely qualifies him as an idealist for McTaggart, to whom it is "self-evident that every conscious self has any ultimate value," and that nothing which is not a conscious self has any "ultimate value." McTaggart, whose idealism had affinities with the doctrines of Gottfried Wilhelm Leibniz and of George Berkeley, held that the concept of matter is self-contradictory; and, noting Bosanquet's objections to Pan-Psychism, he remarks that, although he does not think that Pan-Psychism has been proved, neither can he see that it has been disproved.

In this provocative fashion, McTaggart states and criticizes the chief thesis of each lecture. But perhaps his main criticism is the one he makes at the beginning. Bosanquet had intimated in his Preface that there was not much left for a philosopher to do and that his task was to bring home certain conclusions and not to invent "new theoretical conceptions." McTaggart is unable to agree. Even if one admits, as he is inclined to do, that "some form of idealism is true," it is clear that that form has not yet been put forward. Existing forms all exhibit difficulties and require fundamental modifications. Hence, he submits that "the invention of theoretical conceptions" is just what the times require.—*J.F.*

ADDITIONAL RECOMMENDED READING

Acton, H. B. "Bosanquet, Bernard," in *The Encyclopedia of Philosophy*. Edited by Paul Edwards. Vol. I. New York: Macmillan Publishing Company, 1967, pp. 347-350. *The Principle of Individuality and Value* is treated under metaphysics.

Bosanquet, Bernard, *et al.* "Do Finite Individuals Possess a Substantive or an Adjectival Mode of Being?," in *Proceedings of the Aristotelian Society*. N. S. XVIII (1917-1918), pp. 479-581. A full exchange between Bosanquet and Pringle-Pattison on the question of whether the world exists for the development of finite selves.

Foster, Michael B. "The Concrete Universal: Cook Wilson and Bosanquet," in *Mind*. N. S. XL, no. 157 (January, 1931), pp. 1-22. Shows how this logical term was used by Bosanquet and others.

Haldar, Hiralal. "Bernard Bosanquet," in *Neo-Hegelianism*. London: Heath Cranton, 1927, pp. 257-295. A popular exposition of Bosanquet's metaphysics and political philosophy by an Indian philosopher.

Metz, Rudolf. "Bernard Bosanquet," in *A Hundred Years of British Philosophy*. London: George Allen & Unwin, 1938, pp. 345-359. Best brief account of Bosanquet's philosophy. There are comparable articles on McTaggart and Pringle-Pattison.

Rogers, Arthur Kenyon. "Absolute Idealism," in *English and American Philosophy Since 1800: A Critical Survey*. New York: Macmillan Publishing Company, 1922. The eighteen pages devoted to Bosanquet are comparative and critical rather than expository.

IDEAS: GENERAL INTRODUCTION TO PURE PHENOMENOLOGY

Author: Edmund Husserl (1859-1938)
Type of work: Metaphysics, epistemology
First published: 1913

PRINCIPAL IDEAS ADVANCED

Natural sciences are, by nature, dogmatic; the phenomenologist must undertake a critical study of the conditions under which knowledge is possible.

To distinguish within experience that which experiences from that which is experienced, one must suspend natural beliefs; this suspension of belief is made possible by a method of bracketing by which we talk not about trees and selves as items external to experience but of the "trees" and the "perceptions" of experience.

Noema, that which is perceived, is dependent upon noesis, the perceiving; but noema has the kind of being peculiar to essences.

The absolute forms of essences which owe their actuality in consciousness to acts of perceiving are Eideia, eternal possibilities of quality, related to other Eideia by external relations.

The term "phenomenology," as it is used by Husserl and his disciples, designates first of all a principle of philosophical and scientific method. The usual method of natural science proceeds from a body of accepted truth and seeks to extend its conquest of the unknown by putting questions to nature and compelling it to answer. The phenomenological method adopts a softer approach. Setting aside all presuppositions and suppressing hypotheses, it seeks to devise techniques of observation, description, and classification which will permit it to disclose structures and connections in nature which do not yield to experimental techniques. It has been widely fruitful in psychology and the social sciences, as well as in epistemology and value-theory.

Husserl, in his *Logical Studies* (1900-1901), did much to advance general phenomenological studies. But he had in view a specifically philosophical application of the technique which many of his associates did not completely grasp, or failed to share. *Ideas* was written with a view to clearing up the distinction between phenomenological psychology, which he regarded as a legitimate, but secondary, science, and phenomenological philosophy, which, he was prepared to maintain, is the foundation of all science. When a sociologist or psychologist conducts a phenomenological investigation, he puts aside all the usual theories and assumptions which have governed research in that field: but he cannot rid himself of all presuppositions (such as, for example, the belief in the existence of the external world, the constancy of nature). As Plato saw, every science must proceed upon some assumptions—

except philosophy. To fulfill its promise, the phenomenological approach must bring us at last to an absolutely presuppositionless science. Pure phenomenology, or phenomenological philosophy, is, in Husserl's opinion, precisely that. (It has long been the aspiration of philosophers to make their science an absolute one, one that rids itself of all presuppositions and stands with open countenance before pure Being. Husserl stands in this tradition.)

Phenomenology is not to be confused with "phenomenalism," a name sometimes given to extreme forms of empiricism, such as that of Ernst Mach, which maintains that nothing is real except sense-data. In fact, this is one of the misconceptions which phenomenology is designed to overcome. If the empiricists are right, the unity and order which we are accustomed to find in the world are not given in experience but put there by the activity of the mind. Genetic psychology, which seeks to explain the origin of our various mental habits and responses, would therefore hold the key to understanding our whole view of the world. A good example is J. S. Mill, who in his *A System of Logic* (1843) undertook to explain the force of syllogistic reasoning in terms of associationist psychology. Other positivists and pragmatists have attempted to give a psychological theory of knowledge and of valuation. Husserl argued, however, that the empiricists were wrong, that they did not come to their conviction about the absence of order and intelligibility in the pure data of experience by examining what is given there, but had it as an Idol of the Theater (to use Francis Bacon's term). It follows that they have misconceived the task of psychology in supposing that it can discover in the mind laws which give rise to the meaning of the world, and that it is incumbent upon us to set about developing new accounts of logic, knowledge-theory, aesthetics, and ethics which stand on their own evidence. In place of *psychologism* (a misconceived psychology or science of the soul) what is needed, if justice is to be done to experience, is *phenomenology* (science of phenomena, or appearances).

Husserl takes his place, then, in the forefront of those twentieth century philosophers who have sought to reaffirm the autonomy of various philosophical disciplines over against psychology. He was equally concerned to turn back the tide of the popular-scientific view of the world which he called naturalism. The particular sciences, by nature, are dogmatic. That is to say, they proceed without examining the conditions under which knowledge is possible. This is not to be held against them. But when anyone attempts to build a natural philosophy on the findings of the sciences, his uncritical procedure opens the way to skepticism, because the categories in terms of which we grasp natural events are unsuited to take account of conscious events, including the pursuit of scientific truth. It seems innocent enough to explain consciousness in terms of natural causes until we recollect that matter and the laws which govern its behavior are themselves part of our experience. This, according to Husserl, is the point at which the philosopher must step in. His primary task, in fact, will be to distinguish within experience the part that experiences from the part that is experienced.

There are many overtones of Descartes in Husserl's writings. The former philosopher, in order to escape from the ambiguities and uncertainties of our ordinary, natural experience, developed a method of doubting. By bringing under question the whole phenomenal world, he laid bare a world of logical forms which he could not doubt. Husserl adopts a similar method. He talks of "suspending" our natural beliefs, including the fundamental conviction of every healthy mind that there is a world "out there," that there are other selves, and so on. We are asked to "alter" this natural standpoint, to "disconnect" our beliefs about causation and motion, to "put them out of action." This is, of course, only a methodological procedure, in order to help us overcome our animal bias and make it possible for us to take a coolly intellectual view of things. Greek philosophy used the term *epochē* to indicate the suspense of judgment. Husserl presses this term into his service.

To make his meaning clear, he uses the example of looking with pleasure into a garden where an apple tree is blossoming. From the natural standpoint, the tree is something that has transcendent reality in space and time, and the joy of perceiving it has reality in the psyche of a human being. But Descartes has reminded us that perceptions are sometimes hallucinations. We pass, therefore, from the natural to the phenomenological standpoint, bracketing the claims of both the knower and the known to natural being. This leaves us with "a nexus of exotic experiences of perception and pleasure valuation." We can now speak of the content and structure of the situation without any reference to external existence. Nothing is really taken away from the experience, but it is all there in a new manner. In order to indicate this, the use of quotation marks is helpful. We can now speak of "tree," "plant," "material thing," "blossoming," "white," "sweet," and so forth, and be sure that we are talking only about things that belong to the essence of our experience. Similarly, at the opposite pole, we can distinguish "perceiving," "attending," "enjoying," and other ego-acts. These each have their special characters, and repay analysis.

Husserl was at one time a student of Franz Brentano (1838-1917), who had said that what distinguishes mental acts from nonmental acts is that the former invariably refer to something other than themselves. Drawing from the scholastics, he said that they are "intentional." Husserl makes constant use of this discovery. To designate the ego-acts, which are not limited to cognition but include as well various attitudes such as doubting and supposing, as well as volitions and feelings, he uses the Greek word *noesis* (literally, a perceiving). To designate the corresponding objects, for instance, "tree," "fruitful," "charming," he uses the corresponding word *noema* (literally, that which is perceived). An important part of the analysis of consciousness consists in tracing the relation between these. In each case, the *noesis* is real and fundamental, but *noema* is dependent and, strictly speaking, unreal. In our example, "the perceiving of the tree" is actual and constitutive of "the tree perceived." But conversely, though it does not have reality, *noema* has being, which is lacking to *noesis*: that is to say, it is composed entirely of essences, which are eternally what they are and stand in necessary or *a priori* relations with each other. The same thing is true of volition and other modes. "The valuing of the tree" is a *noesis*. It has the same reality as "the perceiving of the tree." Correspondingly, "the value of the tree" is a *noema*. It does not have reality, but it has the same kind of essential being as the structure and properties have which make up the object of cognition. The value-characters likewise take their place in an *a priori* system together with other values.

As long as our interest, as philosophers, is directed primarily toward the life of the mind, we shall be chiefly interested in exploring the various *noeses*. Husserl's delineation of these is subtle and perceptive, and goes a long way toward persuading the reader of the necessity of this descriptive groundwork, although as is sometimes true of the drawings of a microscopist we may have difficulty in recognizing in it the familiar features of the mind. His account of "meaning," for example, should be studied by those who are interested in semantics, and his analysis of "sentiment" and "volition" provides an instructive approach to the question of the relation between emotions and values. One thing is common to all *noeses*, according to Husserl: all are at bottom *thetic*, or postulational; Husserl speaks of them as *doxa* (Plato's word for "opinion"). This does not imply that some of our *noeses* are not characterized by "certainty," just as others are characterized by a "sense of likelihood" or "doubt." But in any case, it is what we commonly call a "moral certainty." The conviction is a mode of the "perceiving" rather than a function of anything lying in the "perceived."

But in the present work Husserl does not consider mental acts *per se*. He studies them because they provide the key to the various grades and types of objects which make up the *noemata*; for, corresponding to "perception" there is the realm of "colors," "shapes," and "sizes"; and corresponding to "perceptual enjoyment" there are "dainty" pink and "gloriously" scented. These qualities owe their actuality in consciousness to the *noeses*; but they are part of an order of being which is absolute and independent. Husserl calls all such absolute forms or essences *Eideia*, to avoid the ambiguities of such words as Ideas and Essences. They are eternal possibilities, each perfectly definite and distinct from every other, but also linked with every other in a system of eternal relations. Thus, "pink," "white," "green" are species under the genus "color"; and "color" itself stands in a hierarchy of perceptual "qualities." A similar hierarchical structure embraces the *noema* of value.

Husserl, who began his philosophical studies as a logician, was preeminently interested in the grammar of meaning. He claims that, on a very abstract level, all *noema* exemplify universal relations which can be formulated in a

Mathesis Universalis such as Leibniz conceived. But the theorizing logician does not do justice to the wealth of formal relations which lie before the phenomenologist. "Its field is the analysis of the *a priori* shown forth in *immediate* intuition, the fixing of immediately transparent essence and essential connexions and their descriptive cognition in the systematic union of all strata in pure transcendental consciousness." It begins by distinguishing various regional ontologies—of which the "formal region" exploited by the logician is only one. "Material regions" are numerous. The region of the physical *Thing* will serve as an example. The question presents itself as follows: "How are we to describe systematically the *noeses* and *noemata* which belong to the unity of the intuitionally presenting Thing-consciousness?" Leaving aside the *noetic* factor, the problem is to analyze the essential connections by which "appearances" present themselves as "one and the same thing." The analysis discloses that a mere *res extensa* is conceivable apart from the idea of a *res materialis* and a *res temporalis*. Yet as a matter of fact, a thing as presented to "us humans" involves all three of these. So, there are "strata" and "formations" constituting the thing. And it is necessary to analyze each of these unities in turn. The problem of "presentation in space" has here to be faced. Although, according to Husserl, its meaning has never yet been completely grasped, it now appears in clear light—namely by "the phenomenological analysis of the *essential* nature of all the noematic (and noetic) phenomena, wherein space exhibits itself intuitionally and as the unity of appearances."

In the present volume, as is proper in an introduction, Husserl is able only to indicate the direction which the investigation must take. And one must look to his other works, and those of his disciples, to see the analyses carried out in detail. While Husserl worked chiefly in the field of epistemology, his disciples carried the method into axiology and philosophical anthropology (Max Scheler), aesthetics (Theodor Lipps), sociology (Karl Mannheim), comparative religion (Rudolph Otto), and ethics (Nicolai Hartmann), not to mention the "existentialism" of Martin Heidegger and Jean-Paul Sartre. For the ordinary reader, these developments are more interesting and fruitful than pure phenomenology. But that is because it is difficult for most people to exercise themselves about the sheer possibility of knowledge. Husserl's significance, as a philosopher, is that, like Descartes and Kant, he appeared at a time when the foundations of science were themselves threatened, and irrationalism, skepticism, and nihilism threatened the very nerve of Western civilization. He sought to revive knowledge, to make possible once again a rational view of the world and of the human enterprise. He was conscious of being the continuer of a long tradition, and with some reluctance admitted to falling under the classification of idealist. He most resembles Kant, and his work can be summed up as the search for the transcendental conditions which make "meaning" (scientific, ethical, aesthetic, religious) possible.
—J.F.

PERTINENT LITERATURE
Kohák, Erazim V. *Idea and Experience: Edmund Husserl's Project of Phenomenology* in *IDEAS I.* Chicago: University of Chicago Press, 1978.

Phenomenology is at once a concrete philosophy of experience and a formal method of inquiry founded upon radical reflexivity. During the past fifty years phenomenology has become the dominant philosophical force in Western Europe, while in England and America it has had a profound impact through its applications in psychology, sociology, and the other human sciences. The name most commonly associated with phenomenology as it is known today is Edmund Husserl. Yet it is not easy to penetrate his philosophy, or even to describe what he means by phenomenology. Because of the magnitude and complexity of his work, together with a technical terminology which is often obscure and bewildering, understanding Husserl can be at times nearly impossible. For this reason Erazim Kohák's commentary is most welcome. He cuts through Husserlian verbiage and carefully presents Husserl's ideas using ordinary language, thus opening the doors to Husserlian phenomenology for those who are not scholars in the field.

Kohák guides the reader through the first nine chapters of Husserl's influential *Ideas: General Introduction to Pure Phenomenology.* The aim is to retrieve and elaborate the simple, basic insight crucial to all of Husserl's work—namely, that *to know means to see.* For Husserl, the primordial starting point of all knowledge, the ultimate source of the validity of all rational assertions, is not speculation, not pure reason, but a kind of direct "seeing," an experiential awareness which people sometimes acknowledge with the startling exclamation, "Oh, *now I see!*" In a sense, Husserl's phenomenology evolves as an anatomy of *direct seeing.*

Kohák's presentation is unique in that he actually utilizes the method of phenomenology in his study of phenomenology. Much has been written concerning the so-called "phenomenological method." Husserl, in fact, many times refers to his own work as a study of method. Kohák, however, rightly points out the mistake in thinking of phenomenology's "method" as a special set of techniques or procedures. More accurately, what is intended by the term "method" is a certain stance or perspective, a manner of orientation. As a descriptive science of human experience, phenomenology proposes a fundamental cognitive reorientation; and the goal, as in any science, is to promote *seeing and grasping clearly.* In a similar manner, by approaching Husserl from a phenomenological perspective, Kohák's goal is to enable the reader to "grasp" more clearly the main features of Husserl's philosophy, or way of philosophizing.

The subject matter of phenomenology is lived experience; the task is a scrupulous examination and clarification of what and how we actually experience in our most ordinary daily living. Husserl's slogan "Back to the things themselves" means "Back to experience." Any answers to our questions are to be found in experience itself: if not there, then nowhere. The trouble is that as we live it, experience is highly elusive, and as it is represented by poets, scientists, and philosophers it seems to change from account to account. Too often our descriptions do not faithfully record our experience as actually lived. Kohák gives the example of marriage. As lived, marriage is a *way of being*; it is a mode of existence for two people. Yet when the "facts" of the marriage are being described—the living arrangements, the rights and obligations, who cooks and who washes dishes, who earns the money—the lived reality of *being married* seems to evaporate. We need a special focus, a special perspective on experience to see it as it is lived. Husserl would say we need a rigorous, radically reflexive, phenomenological perspective.

Phenomenological seeing requires effort, just as does ordinary seeing. We frequently see indistinctly and unclearly, and accordingly we need to look again, carefully, painstakingly, directing our focus until the object emerges clearly. This is also the case in phenomenological reflection, where the "object" we are looking for is our own experience as actually lived. Pure experience, however, cannot be grasped by any ordinary means of attentiveness. What is required, according to Husserl, is a radical shift in viewpoint and a suspension of what he calls the "natural standpoint."

The natural standpoint is the conventional, habitual, commonsense point of view evident in ordinary, everyday experience. The most pervasive feature of the natural standpoint is the attitude that there exists a real world "out there," constantly there to be seen, touched, and heard, a world not subjectively invented but objectively given. From the natural standpoint, the objects of our world are encountered as spatially and temporally ordered, all things exhibiting an identity, a history, and a causal origin. From the natural, customary point of view, the world is experienced as a shared world, an intersubjective world, a world which is there for all of us and to which all of us belong.

The problem with the natural standpoint, according to Husserl, is that in a subtle way it turns the subject away from lived experience. As lived, reality is the *experiencing of* an object. From the natural standpoint, reality is *the object*; the experiencing is purely incidental to it. But if we are to achieve knowledge of reality, we must "see" reality as it is given, as actually lived—or, as Husserl puts it, we must look at it "in brackets."

Phenomenological bracketing, or *epoché*, is a methodological suspension of the natural standpoint, a shift away from the habitual stance we assume toward the world, and a shift toward pure, unadulterated experience in its brute givenness. Using Kohák's illustration, bracketing is a "switching off," as when we switch off an electric lamp. The lamp is still there, but now as one of the objects in the room, not as that which illuminates everything else. In suspending the natural standpoint, the phenomenologist in a sense is "switching off the world." *Epoché* does not imply denying or canceling out the world. The world, like the lamp, is still there, but no longer as that which illuminates or explains experience. On the contrary, it becomes a datum to be explained. Phenomenological bracketing allows us to "grasp" the reality of the world *as experience* or, in Husserl's terminology, *as phenomenon*.

Once the need and justification for bracketing is clearly seen, it will require no further explanation. Yet, as Kohák acutely recognizes, seeing is rarely accomplished at a glance. So to further help the reader to understand the idea of *epoché*, he goes on to consider possible applications of bracketing in areas such as theology, sociology, and physics. The main point which comes out of his discussion is that knowing is seeing, and that sometimes seeing can be achieved only through a radical shift in focus.

In other chapters of the book Kohák explicates Husserl's ideas on experience and intersubjectivity, reflection, intentionality, transcendental subjectivity, and the relation of phenomenology to empiricism and idealism. At each step of the way his commentary is lucid, straightforward, and insightful. As a whole, this book deserves to be ranked as one of the finest introductions to Husserl's phenomenology.

Natanson, Maurice A. *Edmund Husserl: Philosopher of Infinite Tasks*. Evanston, Illinois: Northwestern University Press, 1973.

The basic principle of phenomenology is the intentionality of consciousness, the idea that all consciousness is consciousness *of something*. In itself this is not too astounding. But the emphasis which Edmund Husserl brings to bear upon this principle is that the objects of consciousness—that is, the *intentional objects*—must be understood as part of the unified structure of consciousness itself. This is due to the fact that the intentional object is endowed with *meaning*. In his book on Husserl, Maurice Natanson provides a fine exposition of the meaning and implications of the principle of intentionality.

When it is said that consciousness is intentional, one of the important things meant is that consciousness by its very nature *directs* itself toward its object. The principle signifies that between consciousness and its object there is an essential relationship which can be described metaphorically as "aiming toward." Any given experience, for example, seeing a tree, involves even at the most elementary level a sense of direction such that I see *this* rather than *that*. Insofar as I am seeing something (some object), it is correct to say that I am *directed toward* the object I am conscious of—in this case, the tree.

Husserl distinguishes between the intentional object, in his words, the "noema," or object *as meant*, and the real, or "transcendent," object. After agreeing that consciousness is necessarily *of something*, the question arises as to what can be said about this "of something."

Husserl asks us to suppose that we are looking at a blossoming apple tree in the garden. From the natural standpoint—that is, from the ordinary, every-day way of looking at things—the apple tree is something that exists in the reality of space. Real relations are thought of as subsisting between us and the real tree. Husserl refers to our "real" tree as a transcendent object, insofar as its existence is conceived as being completely independent of our perceptual experience. Now the ordinary person firmly believes, and rightly so, that when we speak about objects of consciousness we are referring at least some-times to actual entities like the apple tree. But if we go on to identify our "intentional object" as being the real apple tree, a difficult problem arises with regard to the possibility of hallucination.

Under conditions like those described above, it is not contradictory to suppose that the so-called perception may be in fact a mere hallucination, in which case the "perceived" object—the apple tree which is believed to stand before us—does not actually exist. But how can one be said to "perceive" an apple tree if no apple tree actually exists? Husserl resolves the apparent perplexity by carefully distinguishing between the real object (which may or may not actually exist) and the objective *meaning* of the perceptual act, the latter being the intentional correlate of consciousness. Real tree or not, the intentional structure of the perceptual experience remains intact, such that there is a consciousness of "this apple tree in bloom." To speak of the inten-tional object, in other words, is to speak of the *sense* or *meaning* of the perceptual experience.

Natanson illustrates how at the base of all perception is perceptual *meaning*. By its very nature the act of consciousness harbors within itself a meaning of some sort, and this meaning is the intentional (noematic) element present in all determinate modes of concrete consciousness. Thus the internal structure of consciousness is fundamentally the relationship between consciousness and its objective meaning: a relationship which sees consciousness always directed toward, reaching toward, or groping for a meaningful content.

In one of the most illuminating sections of his book, Natanson demonstrates how intentionality makes it possible for us to experience sameness, and thus to enjoy a world of familiar, repeatable, and expectable events. An intentional object is not something which appears and disappears with a given act of consciousness, but something which remains identical through different modes of consciousness and moments in time. Although conditions under which I perceive something may vary considerably, the identity of the intentional object is unaffected. In the apple tree *as meant*, we have something which can be thought of as the same throughout an indefinite number of presentative acts. Natanson gives the following illustration. Suppose I am on a bus and casually glance at the face of the woman sitting across from me. I see her face, now from the front, now in profile. As the bus goes through a tunnel, the light changes, her face looks different—yet it is the same face. Changes in light, vantage point, or time do not affect the identity of the object *as meant*. I may close my eyes and reopen them, I may turn my head and then look back again, and still the intentional object remains invariant. The prize of intentionality, stresses Natanson, is identity.

The principle of intentionality is only one aspect of Husserl's phenomenology. Other important topics which Natanson addresses include Husserl's phenomenological method, bracketing and the suspension of the natural standpoint, the concept of *Lebenswelt* (life-world), and the manner in which phenomenology provides a critique of traditional philosophy and a foundation for the human sciences.—*R.A.S.*

ADDITIONAL RECOMMENDED READING

Elliston, Frederick and Peter McCormick, eds. *Husserl: Expositions and Appraisals*. Notre Dame, Indiana: University of Notre Dame Press, 1977. Both in title and content, this work joins exegesis and criticism. The essays are grouped into three parts, dealing respectively with general philosophical themes in Husserl, specific phenomenological concepts and methodological considerations, and comparisons and contrasts with other major figures and traditions in contemporary philosophy. Of the twenty-three articles included, eleven are published for the first time.

Kockelmans, Joseph J. *A First Introduction to Husserl's Phenomenology*. Pittsburgh: Duquesne University Press, 1967. This book succeeds in giving a relatively clear and concise overall picture of the main themes and topics in Husserl's philosophy.

Kolakowski, Leszek. *Husserl and the Search for Certitude*. New Haven, Connecticut: Yale University Press, 1975. The book, which is a set of three lectures delivered at Yale University, takes as its point of departure Husserl's quest for the absolutely unquestionable foundation of knowledge. Kolakowski argues that Husserl's attempt to attain epistemological certitude not only failed but was bound to fail.

Ricoeur, Paul. *Husserl: An Analysis of His Phenomenology*. Translated by Edward G. Ballard and Lester E. Embree. Evanston, Illinois: Northwestern University Press, 1967. Ricoeur ranks as one of the giants in the phenomenological movement. This collection of nine individual essays provides a unified interpretation of the most influential elements of Husserl's phenomenology, along with creating a link in the development of Ricoeur's own existential phenomenology.

Sokolowski, Robert. *Husserlian Meditations: How Words Present Things*. Evanston, Illinois: Northwestern University Press, 1974. A philosophical commentary on the work of Edmund Husserl. Sokolowski conjoins interpretation with criticism as he investigates Husserl's doctrines for the purpose of advancing truthfulness. The chapters on internal time-consciousness and the phenomenological reduction (viewed as a move from mundane experience to genuine philosophical reflection) are especially fruitful.

ART

Author: Clive Bell (1881-1964)
Type of work: Aesthetics, philosophy of art
First published: 1914; second edition, 1949

PRINCIPAL IDEAS ADVANCED

What distinguishes art from what is not art is significant form.

Works of art provoke a distinctive emotion, the aesthetic emotion.

The quality common and peculiar to works of art, a quality that accounts for their provoking the aesthetic emotion, is significant form.

Significant form in art moves us profoundly because it expresses the aesthetic emotion of the artist.

The aesthetic emotion is the response of a person to the recognition of pure form, the ultimate reality.

Art becomes decadent and finally dies when the love of imitation and skill overcomes the love of pure form, of things-in-themselves.

In the Preface to the original edition of *Art*, Clive Bell announces his intention to develop a complete theory of visual art. He concedes that his book is a simplification, but he nevertheless suggests that his generalization about the nature of art is true, coherent, and comprehensible. He acknowledges the value of numerous conversations with Roger Fry, and he hints that some of his views may have been tempered somewhat by criticisms advanced by Fry, but it is clear from Bell's Preface that he supposes himself to have discovered the key to aesthetics; and it is apparent to anyone who reads his book that, according to Bell, what distinguishes fine art from what is not art is significant form.

In 1948 Bell contributed to a new edition of his book, and in the Preface to the new edition, he writes that were he to revise *Art* so as to bring it into line with his present views (in 1948) he would have to write a new book. But he argues that there is some value in allowing the book to stand as a record of what he and persons like himself were thinking in the years just before World War I.

The truth of the matter is that whatever the failings of *Art* as a philosophical attempt to clarify the domain of art, and whatever the differences between what Bell thought in 1913 and what he thought in 1948, the idea of what he called "Significant Form" has invaded aesthetics and secured for itself a permanent place in the field of candidates for serious reflection. Many critics (such as Curt John Ducasse) have received the idea of significant form with scorn, arguing that Bell never explained what set off the kind of form he wrote about from forms in nature that have been found to be aesthetically appealing. And, to be fair to the critics, it does seem as if Bell suggests that somehow the artist makes a difference to form that distinguishes the form in art from any form to be found in nature. But it is possible that Bell meant, at least in part, that artistic form, as conditioned by the artistic imagination, is a clear sign of that imagination and hence of the artist; consequently, one takes artistic form as something to be grasped and appreciated as the product of some artist's effort to affect aesthetic experience through the creation of form; the form is a sign of artistic effort and accordingly invites the attempt to make sense of it as an expressive vehicle.

Bell begins his work sardonically with the observation that if it is improbable that "more nonsense has been written about aesthetics than about anything else," it is only because not enough has been written in aesthetics. Any theory of aesthetics worth serious critical attention, Bell writes, requires both artistic sensibility and the capacity to think clearly. Unfortunately, Bell comments, those who appreciate art are hardly competent to think about it, while those who are able to reason and analyze are unlikely to grasp the sense of art.

Bell regards the starting point of aesthetics as "the personal experience of a peculiar emotion." Works of art provoke what Bell calls the "aesthetic emotion," and the central problem of art is that of determining what it is that gives rise to the aesthetic emotion. If it can be discovered what quality, common and peculiar to works of art, provokes the aesthetic emotion, then the problem of getting at the nature of art will be resolved, Bell contends.

The quality common to all works of art, to all objects that provoke the aesthetic emotions, Bell claims, is *significant form*. In such works as the windows at Chartres, a Persian bowl, Chinese rugs, and the paintings of Paul Cézanne, "certain forms and relations of forms" stir the aesthetic emotions. Such relations and combinations of lines and colors that reveal themselves as aesthetically moving are what Bell calls "significant form."

Bell considers the objection that his theory makes aesthetics a purely subjective matter, in that the theory rests upon the personal experience of a distinctive emotion. But, Bell contends, since there is no way of recognizing a work of art other than by the feeling one has from it, no system of aesthetics can be founded on objective truth. Nevertheless, aesthetics can have general validity. Differences of opinion as to what works are works of art can be explained by reference to differences of opinion as to the presence or absence of significant form.

As to the question concerning the causes of our being moved by works of art, Bell replies that it is no business of aesthetics to explain why significant form moves us; it is enough, he contends, if we recognize that a distinctive aesthetic emotion is provoked by the significant form of the work of art. However, as having a bearing on the relation of art to life, the question is relevant, and Bell's answer (given later, in Chapter III, "The Metaphysical Hypothesis") is that significant form moves us because it expresses the emotion of the maker of the work. (The further implications of this response will be noted later in this account of Bell's views.)

Bell considers the objection that his theory of significant form appears to dismiss color as having aesthetic value. He argues that the distinction between form and color is "unreal" in that there is no such thing as a colorless line or space. Significant form in visual art *is* the form of certain combinations of lines and colors; consequently, form and color are inextricably related.

Since natural objects—such as butterflies and flowers—may be beautiful, and since such objects do not provoke the aesthetic emotion, Bell prefers not to identify the significant form of art as "beauty"—and for the same reason he denies that natural objects have significant form (except insofar as, when seen by the artist as embodying pure form, they can be experienced as a manifestation of "God in everything, of the universal in the particular, of the all-pervading rhythm"). There are common uses of the term "beautiful," Bell reports, that are not at all relevant to the discussion of aesthetics—such as when one speaks of "beautiful huntin'," and even when one speaks of a woman as "beautiful," it is more likely that one means that she is sexually desirable than that she stirs any aesthetic emotion.

The hypothesis that works of art move us aesthetically because they have significant form (significant form being the form that moves us aesthetically—that is, that provokes the distinctive aesthetic emotion) has the merit of explaining things, Bell contends. The theory explains why it is that certain descriptive paintings, no matter how skilled, may excite our admiration without moving us aesthetically: they lack significant form. Descriptive (representative) paintings may convey information and in their realistic detail amuse us, Bell writes, but they cannot occasion "aesthetic rapture."

Bell contends that his theory also explains why it is that most persons who care for art are moved most of all by primitive art. The untutored artist is unconcerned with accurate representation, Bell argues; in the works of primitive artists there is "sublimely impressive form" because such works show an absence of representation and "technical swagger." (In a footnote Bell remarks that exact representation is not bad but aesthetically indifferent, and he concedes that a "perfectly represented form may be significant.").

The appreciation of art depends not only on a sense of form and color, Bell writes, but also on the knowledge of three-dimensional space. He concedes that to interpret a painting as three-dimensional is to take it as to that degree representational, but such representation is sometimes necessary as contributing to the appreciation of three-dimensional form. The form, not the representation that makes form evident, is what is important in art. Bell concludes that the representation of three-dimensional space is "neither irrelevant nor essential" to art but that all other forms of representation are irrelevant. An artist who relies on representation is "too feeble," too weak in his aesthetic emotions, and too defective in his sensibilities to be able to create significant form without relying upon subject matter, Bell contends.

It is because of significant form that great art is universal and eternal in its appeal, Bell maintains. To appreciate significant form no particular cultural background is needed. If a work has significant form, it has "the power to provoke aesthetic emotion in anyone capable of feeling it."

Bell claims that his aesthetic theory illuminates the history of art. The primitive is unable to create the kinds of illusions a skillful representational painter can produce, but since he has an intense desire to express the sense of form, the works he produces are appealing and meaningful to anyone able to apprehend form. But art becomes decadent, Bell contends; the demand by "the gross herd" for "speaking likenesses" is joined with the demand by "the choicer spirits" for exhibitions of cleverness and skill. The result is work that is deficient in significant form. Bell refers to the "tedious portraiture of Holland" and to the "Gothic juggling in stone and glass" as examples of the effects of the demands for illusions and exhibitions of representational skill. "Before the late noon of the Renaissance art was almost extinct," Bell writes; but he argues that the Post-Impressionist revival returned art to its finest principles. He particularly admires Cézanne for his emphasis on significant form, as made evident in his paintings. The greatest painters, Bell writes, are those who defy the prevailing interests and practices and concentrate on significant form: Nicolas Poussin, Claude Lorrain, El Greco, Jean-Baptiste Siméon Chardin, Jean Auguste Dominique Ingres, Pierre Auguste Renoir, Giotto, and Paul Cézanne (among others). The bulk of artists, however, are "virtuosi and dunces."

Bell distinguishes between technique and the capacity to create significant form. Post-Impressionism brought about a return to art not because of new techniques but because of the revival of the only kind of interest that makes art possible: the interest in significant form.

The "metaphysical hypothesis" that Bell presents is designed to account for the power of significant form—or, one might say, for the significance of the kind of form art makes evident. He argues that form as created by artists is aesthetically moving because it expresses the emotion of its creator—and the emotion of the artist is distinctive and moving because it is a response to the recognition of "pure form." Bell identifies the formal significance of material things with their significance considered as ends in themselves. When objects are considered not as utilitarian objects and not in their relations to human interests but simply as objects, they are then being considered "formally," Bell maintains; and such form is the "essential reality" of things and hence an aspect of "the universal in the particular, of the all-pervading rhythm"—in fact, "of the God in everything. . . ."

The pure form that provokes the peculiar emotions felt by artists, emotions conveyed to the public through expression in works of art, need not come from material objects, Bell points out; the forms may be found in recollections or in the products of imaginative effort. Whatever the source of the artist's emotion, the emotion determines the form of the work by which the emotion is expressed. Hence, Bell argues, it is futile to go to a gallery looking for expressions of the aesthetic emotion; one must look for significant form, and upon finding it one will be in a position to understand that what makes significant form moving is precisely what moved the artist who created it.

Part I of Bell's book, "What is Art?," provides the bulk of Bell's philosophical message; but Part II, "Art and Life," is also philosophically relevant in that it relates Bell's aesthetic (and "metaphysical") theory of art to religion, history, and ethics.

Artists are not practical, Bell contends; that is, artists *qua* artists do not identify and label things according to their uses, for they see things as means to the aesthetic emotion, as forms to be recognized and appreciated. Through the discovery of form one recognizes things as ends in themselves. Speaking of artists, Bell writes, ". . . because they *perceive* things as 'ends,' things *become* for them 'means' to ecstasy."

Since religion is concerned with spiritual, emotionally significant matters, religion may be allied with art, Bell suggests. Like the artist, the mystic finds the physical universe to be a means to ecstasy. Bell finds it credible that both religion and art express "the individual's sense of the emotional significance of the universe. . . ."

Because both art and religion are concerned to discover and enjoy the ultimate reality of things, and because the discovery of reality is a spiritual discovery and art a manifestation of man's spiritual state, the great ages of religion tend to be the great ages of art, Bell argues. Accordingly, he maintains, the history of art is also a spiritual history. What Bell recommends and practices, then, is not the making of aesthetic judgments by reference to history but the understanding of history—spiritual history, the only important kind—in the light of aesthetic judgments. (In Part III, "The Christian Slope," Bell attempts to show that art rises or declines according to the degree to which the spiritual concern for ultimate reality is dominant and triumphant over the interest in what is merely useful or clever.)

Under the chapter title "Art and Ethics" Bell considers the question, "What is the moral justification of art?" The question is whether art is good in itself or a means to good (or, one might add, no good at all). As to the meaning of "good," Bell expresses his agreement with G. E. Moore's view that the term "good" refers to a simple and consequently unanalyzable property. Nevertheless, Bell asserts, everyone knows perfectly well what is meant by "good."

Bell attempts to dispose of the philosophical claim that pleasure is the only thing good in itself by calling attention to John Stuart Mill's contention that some pleasures are superior in quality to others. If pleasure is the sole good, Bell argues, then what would make some pleasures better than others? (Bell fails to recognize the possibility that Mill used the term "pleasure" not for experience of a certain unique quality but for any experience of any quality that has value *qua* experience.) Bell also rejects the view that the term "good" means "pleasurable" or "pleasure." Although it is perhaps a truism to say that pleasure is good, it cannot be conceded that everything good is either pleasure or pleasurable.

However, Bell accepts Moore's contention that only states of mind can be good as ends (and he notes with satisfaction Moore's rejection of his former claim that beauty is also good in itself). Consequently, Bell holds that the moral justification of any particular kind of human activity is determined by discovering whether the activity is a means to good states of mind. It is immediately apparent that art is morally justifiable, Bell concludes, because art delights the mind through the revelation of significant form.

To determine that something is a work of art and to treat it as such is to make a momentous moral judgment and to foster the end that gives value to action, Bell insists. He argues that art is the most powerful and dependable means to spiritual exaltation, and he contends that once a work is taken to be a work of art there is nothing to be gained by considering it in any way other than as a work of art. There is no conflict between moral value and aesthetic value because artistic worth—the power of a work of art that significant form provides—so affects human states of minds that no better means to what is good as an end can be conceived.

After his discussion of "The Christian Slope" in Part III, Bell devotes Part IV to praise of Cézanne as the artist primarily responsible, through his devotion to form, for the resurgence of art in the Post-Impressionist period. The triumph over those who delight in imitation and skill was made possible, Bell writes, through the return to an emphasis on significant form.

In Part V, "The Future," Bell argues that society harms and depresses art when conventional culture blinds people to significant form and when middle-class values so affect parents who would cultivate their children as to make it unlikely that even children with original sensibilities will come to appreciate and be enraptured by art. The best thing society can do for art, Bell insists, is to provide freedom for the artists; society need not reward artists, for artists find the quality of life that art makes possible reward enough. Bell concludes that art is a religion and that, practically speaking, it serves human beings better than the religion of humanity.—*I.P.M.*

PERTINENT LITERATURE

Ducasse, Curt John. "Significant Form," in *The Philosophy of Art.* New York: Dover Publications, 1966, p. 309.

In the second edition of his influential work in aesthetics, *The Philosophy of Art* (originally published in 1929 and reviewed in this work as one of the main entries), Curt John Ducasse includes as appendixes his scathing criticism of Clive Bell's conception of "significant form" and an essay, "Some Questions in Aesthetics," in which he replies to criticisms of the first edition of his book.

Ducasse begins his comment on Bell with the sardonic remark that the term "Significant Form" had "gained a certain vogue among persons whose interest in aesthetics does not take them beyond the outskirts of the subject." Ducasse reports that Bell presumed himself to have discovered an unusual kind of aesthetic value, but Ducasse contends that the term "significant form" is given no meaning by Bell. Ducasse compares Bell's introduction of significant form to Mark Twain's published account of a petrified man whose thumb was against his nose and the fingers spread out (although the description was disguised by being presented piecemeal in a supposedly scientific account). Nobody caught on to Twain's joke, Ducasse reports, and the article was published all over the world; similarly, nobody has caught on to Bell's joke, and Bell (Ducasse writes) must be suffering from an "ingrowing joke" he can hardly afford to acknowledge.

Bell's introduction of the term "significant form" was in response to the question "What quality is shared by all objects that provoke our aesthetic emotions?" But, Ducasse points out, when the question is asked what significant form is, the answer Bell gives is that significant form is that which moves us aesthetically. Thus, Ducasse concludes, the term "significant form" is like the mathematician's "X"—simply a name for what the author is looking for. The task of discovering what kind of form "significant" form is becomes more difficult, Ducasse contends, when Bell declares that the distinction between form and color is "an unreal one." By making the term "form" mean also "content," Ducasse declares, Bell robs the term "significant form" of any meaning whatsoever.

Ducasse points out that Bell distinguishes between the beauty of nature and aesthetic (artistic) beauty. In fact, Bell suggests that what calls forth the aesthetic emotion *not* be called beautiful. (Ducasse scornfully rejects Bell's suggestion that when a woman is called beautiful all that is meant is that she has sex appeal.)

When Bell moves into metaphysics, it appears from Ducasse's criticism that things get worse instead of better. Bell purports to explain why it is that "significant form" (whatever it may be) moves persons aesthetically: it is "because it expresses the emotion of its creator." Ducasse comments (with mock enthusiasm) that for a moment there appears to be some hope that Bell is saying something meaningful: there is the suggestion in what he says of Leo Tolstoy and Benedetto Croce. But, Ducasse remarks critically, if significant form in art moves us aesthetically because it expresses the emotion of its creator, how can the artist, at least, receive the aesthetic emotion from nature? Here Bell provides a metaphysical theme (thereby enticing the unwary into his trap, Ducasse remarks)—namely, that nature provides the aesthetic emotion because of the significance of things-in-themselves, a significance that is,

Bell writes, "the significance of Reality."

Ducasse is unabashedly scornful: "I submit that in thus embodying the most arrant nonsense in such marvellously impressive language, and with never even a sly wink, Mr. Bell has crowned himself king of the wags." And he takes Bell to task for misusing some of Arthur Schopenhauer's key ideas. Ducasse contends that Bell is left with the idea that only works of art have significant form and that significant form is acquired by a work when it expresses the emotion of its maker. But Bell never explains how significant form differs from form that is not significant nor does he explain how a work acquires significant form as a result of expressing its creator's emotions.

In opposition to Bell, Ducasse argues that works of art could not be media of emotional communication were it not that objects give us emotions naturally. Yet it certainly does not follow that if an object naturally moves us, there is a mind behind the object that is expressing itself by way of that object. Ducasse's conclusion is that Bell uses the term "Significant Form" as "a clever catchword for putting a real aesthetic problem out of the way in a painless and humane fashion."

Bywater, William G., Jr. *Clive Bell's Eye*. Detroit: Wayne State University Press, 1975.

Clive Bell's Eye is, in a way, three books in one. Part I (to be reviewed here), itself entitled "Clive Bell's Eye," is an essay (of more than a hundred pages) by William G. Bywater, Jr., on Clive Bell's philosophy of art and, in particular, on the idea of significant form. Part II, "Clive Bell's Work After *Art*," consists of eleven articles written by Bell between 1919 and 1950. (This section is prefaced by comments written by Bywater in which he relates the content of the articles to the ideas presented in *Art*. This introductory material by Bywater will also be reviewed briefly in what follows). Part III is "A Checklist of the Published Writings of Clive Bell" prepared by Donald A. Laing. This volume is, then, a particularly valuable resource for anyone interested in Bell's ideas—especially since there is a paucity of critical commentary on Bell's aesthetics.

In his essay on Bell, Bywater concentrates on his idea of art criticism, his theory of significant form, his metaphysical hypothesis and "Bell's movement toward . . . a humanistic formalism." Bywater refers in the first section of his essay—"The Nature of Criticism"—to Arnold Isenberg's distinction between *normative* criticism, which requires a norm as a basis for value judgment, and *non-normative* criticism, which avoids judgment in order to concentrate on the effort to provide directions for the perception of art. Many people suppose that Bell's emphasis on art as the embodiment of significant form entails his taking a normative approach to criticism. Bywater argues, however, that Bell's approach to criticism is audience-oriented in that Bell conceives of the critic as a guide who helps the audience to perceive works of art; the critic shows the audience what parts of a work of art combine to produce significant form. Thus, the critic does not (according to Bell, as represented by Bywater) judge that a work is good because it has significant form; the work's having significant form is a condition of its being a work of art, but the critic's task is to show the work and allow the audience to discover the significant form.

For Bell, Bywater claims, the proposition that "art is significant form" is a definition. The definition purports to call attention to a quality common to all that we call fine art; and it claims, in effect, that this quality can be found at the level of perception and feeling. As presented and defended, Bywater suggests, the definition also provides the basis for an effort to establish a community of valuation. Furthermore, Bell's theory can be understood to provide a basis for recommendations on how to look at particular works of art and on how to view the history of art. By concentrating on art as significant form, by seeing art as the presentation of form, one tends to discourage the appetite for representational features and to encourage modes of perception that fasten on the formal aspects of art.

Bywater then refers to the kind of argument used by William E. Kennick and Morris Weitz, who have maintained that any effort to discover a quality common to works of art is futile because the term "art" has no essential conditions for its employment. Bywater points out that the failure of many philosophers to discover a common quality in no way requires the conclusion that there is no such quality and that the logic of "art" is so complex that no summary statement can encompass it. Because Bell did not presuppose the impossibility of discovering a common quality, he was prepared to find one if it were there—and he considered that he had done so with the discovery of significant form.

The discussion of significant form is enhanced by the use of copious illustrations of works that would conventionally be described as "works of art." An appreciation of the details and direction of Bywater's comments depends on close attention to his text and to the illustrations. However, a hint of his approach to the problem of illuminating Bell's idea of significant form can be gained by attending to his remarks about Paul Cézanne, who was, from Bell's point of view, "one of the greatest artists the world has known," as Bywater reports. According to the author, "Bell is able to say that the work of Cézanne, and the others, possesses significant form because the space in these works is organized in such a way as to achieve a sense of depth in a work while still maintaining a dynamic relationship between foreground and background planes, which flattens the entire work." What is necessary in achieving significant form is not that the problem of connecting depth to surface be solved, Bywater comments, but that each segment of a work stand in dynamic relationship with all the other segments.

Bywater argues that although it is understandable that many critics of Bell have called Bell's aesthetics formalistic, there are good reasons for rejecting that description. In the first place, Bell did not oppose objective or representative art; all that he required is that, as Bywater writes, "the representational be fused with the design." (However, it is the form that counts, of course.) In the second place, the standard formalist downplays the role of the spectator and argues that form is an objective, not a subjective, feature of the work. But for Bell, the aesthetic emotion is central; only when aesthetic form moves can significant form and, hence, aesthetic quality be recognized. Finally, Bell's position differs from the standard formalist position in that the conventional formalist believes there are paradigms or formulas for producing or appraising form in art, while Bell argues that there are no such paradigms or formulas.

It is impossible to summarize through the use of verbal descriptions Bell's conception of significant form, Bywater contends. To know significant form one must find it in art. Hence, although one can *say* that "a painting possesses significant form when the forces it contains are balanced, controlled *vis à vis* the two-dimensional picture plane," to *know* significant form one must experience "the tensions controlled in a painting."

Despite Bell's emphasis on significant form as the essence of art, he attempted to relate art to life. The first such effort consisted in his relating art to the aesthetic emotion; and emotions, of course, are the emotions of living persons. The second and major effort consisted in an appeal to what Bell calls his "metaphysical hypothesis," with which Bywater deals in the third part of his lengthy essay. Bell ventures the metaphysical suggestion that significant form is moving because it reveals an ultimate reality that can reveal itself only through form. The ultimate reality of things is revealed when they are seen not as means but as ends—and they are seen as ends only when seen in their formal aspects.

Bywater concludes, after a lengthy discussion of the relationships of Bell's metaphysical hypothesis to his aesthetic position, that Bell's attempt to combine the two theories fails: ". . . Bell's position is incoherent in the long run." Bywater then attempts to develop the outlines of a coherent humanistic formalism.

Bywater appears to interpret Bell's significant form as aesthetic form, and although Bywater emphasizes the dynamic relationships in a work of art—so that there is no danger that one will confuse form with static design—there remains the question of whether he has succeeded in getting at the heart of the mystery and, hence, the appeal of Bell's faith in *significant* form—that is, form that is not merely appealing (to those sensitive enough to be drawn to it) but is also a *sign* of something the implicit presence of which enhances the form by which it is known. Bywater suggests including the creator of art, the artist, within the "community of feeling which has the art work as its focus. . . ." Perhaps, then, it is the artist who is signified by the form of his creation and gives to aesthetic form in art its distinctive power and value. But Bywater appears to focus on the "guiding emotion" of the artist as an animating feature of art, one that Bell tended to ignore. Significant form is, then, a sign of the artist's emotion. But would such a sign be especially moving and significant (important) on that account? One would like to see Bywater explore the possibility that significant form is moving not only because it signifies the resolution of an aesthetic problem but also because it is a sign of the human capacity, the artist's power, to be creative in the resolution of problems. A theory to the effect that significant form is significant and moving because it proves the creative power and triumph of the human being, the artist, might very well reconcile Bell's aesthetic and metaphysical hypotheses.—*I.P.M.*

ADDITIONAL RECOMMENDED READING

Beardsley, Monroe C. *Aesthetics: Problems in the Philosophy of Criticism.* New York: Harcourt, Brace and World, 1958. Beardsley discusses the idea of significant form, but Bywater calls his account "simplistic."

Bell, Clive. *Civilization* and *Old Friends*. Chicago: University of Chicago Press, 1974. Two volumes collected into one. Essays on the Bloomsbury group. Includes an essay on Roger Fry and some discussion of aesthetic theory.

Kennick, William E. "Does Traditional Aesthetics Rest on a Mistake?," in *Mind*. LXVII, no. 267 (July, 1958), pp. 317-334. An interesting defense of the proposition that the search for a definition of art is futile.

Weitz, Morris. "The Role of Theory in Aesthetics," in *Problems in Aesthetics*. Edited by Morris Weitz. New York: Macmillan Publishing Company, 1959. Another argument against the possibility of defining art, but at the same time a positive account of the role of aesthetic theory.

OUR KNOWLEDGE OF THE EXTERNAL WORLD

Author: Bertrand Russell (1872-1970)
Type of work: Epistemology, metaphysics
First published: 1914 (Lowell Lectures, Boston, March and April, 1914)

PRINCIPAL IDEAS ADVANCED
The method of logical analysis makes the resolution of philosophical problems possible by defining the limits of scientific philosophy so as to exclude speculative metaphysics.

We can account for our knowledge of the external world by realizing, through logical analysis, that the world as we know it is a construction from the data given in sense experience; an individual's "private world" is the class of all data within his perspective, and a perceived object is the class of all aspects to be found in all the perspectives which include the object.

The conception of permanent things can be constructed by reference to appearances if points are defined by reference to enclosure series of spaces, and if time is defined by reference to classes of events simultaneous with each other.

Zeno's paradoxes of motion can be resolved by use of the mathematical theory of continuity.

The significance of this book lies in the fact that it proposed a new method for philosophizing. While the method suggested was not strictly novel (it had been previously used by such mathematical logicians as George Boole, Giuseppe Peano, and Gottlob Frege), it was modified by Russell and transferred from mathematical to philosophical subject matter. Russell called it the "logical-analytic" method or the method of "logical-atomism." Since the publication of these lectures the method has been taken over and radically modified and broadened by a large school of philosophers who call themselves "analysts" and who constitute an important group in the modern philosophical world.

The analytic method, as Russell formulated it, is less ambitious than that of classical philosophy in that it does not claim to determine the nature of reality or the universe as a whole. What it does is both less speculative and less sweeping, but more scientific. It uses the techniques of modern logic and modern mathematics, and employs such concepts as *class*, *relation*, and *order* for the purpose of clarifying and solving some of the perennial problems of philosophy which have not yet yielded to satisfactory solution. There are many such problems, but Russell here considers those concerned with the nature of the external world, with how the world of physics is related to the world of our ordinary sense experience, and with what is meant by space, time, continuity, infinity, and causation. The book consists of illustrations of the application of the logical-analytic method to these problems for the purpose of showing its fruitfulness. Russell insists that his results are to be taken as tentative and incomplete, but he believes that if any modification in his method is found necessary, this will be discovered by the use of the very method which he is advocating.

The philosophies of two typical representatives of the classical school— F. H. Bradley and Henri Bergson—are first examined in order to show the errors which these men made. Bradley found the world of everyday life to be full of contradictions, and he concluded that it must be a world of Appearance only, not of Reality. His error lay in his attempt to determine the character of the world by pure reasoning rather than by going to experience and examining what he found. Bergson believed that Reality is characterized fundamentally by growth and change; he then concluded that logic, mathematics, and physics are too static to represent such a world and that a special method called "intuition" must be employed. His mistake was twofold: (1) He supposed that because life is marked by change and evolution the universe as a whole must be so described; he failed to realize that philosophy is general and does not draw conclusions on the basis of any of the special sciences. (2) His emphasis on life suggests that he believed philosophy to be concerned with problems of human destiny. But such is not the case; philosophy is concerned with knowledge for its own sake, not with making men happier.

One reason why the logical-analytic method was not more widely employed earlier, according to Russell, is that it was new and only gradually replaced some of the earlier and erroneous conceptions of logic. The traditional (syllogistic) logic had been quite generally abandoned as inadequate. The inductive logic of Bacon and Mill had been shown to be unsatisfactory because it cannot really show why we believe in such uniformities as that the sun will rise every morning. Our belief in universal causation cannot be *a priori*, since it is very complicated when formulated precisely; nor can it be a postulate, for then it would be incapable of justifying any inference; nor can it be proved inductively without assuming the very principle which one is trying to prove. Russell claims that Hegel made the mistake of confusing logic with metaphysics, and that only mathematical logic provides the tool by which we may hope to solve philosophical problems.

Mathematical logic is both a branch of mathematics and a logic which is specially applicable to mathematics. Its main feature is its formal character, its independence of all specific subject matter. Looked at formally, it can be said to be concerned with propositions. The main types of propositions are *atomic* propositions, such as "Socrates is a man"; *molecular* propositions, which are atomic propositions unless connected by *and, if, or, unless*; and *general* propositions, such as "All men are mortal." In addition, there must be *some* knowledge of general truths which is not derived from empirical evidence. For example, if we are to *know* that all men are mortal we must also know that the men we have examined are all the men there are. This we can never derive from experience, since empirical evidence gives us only particular truths. Thus, there are certain general truths which, if they are known, must be either self-evident or inferred from other general truths.

It is obvious that one of the oldest problems of philosophy is the problem concerning our knowledge of the external world. In applying the logical-analytical method to this problem Russell finds that what we have to begin with (something which is always vague, complex, and inexact) is knowledge of two kinds: (1) Our acquaintance with the particular objects of everyday life—furniture, houses, people, and so on; and (2) our knowledge of the laws of logic. These may be called "hard" data since doubt in such cases, while it *could* occur, normally would not, and if it did, would probably be considered pathological. Most of us would be willing to add to these data certain facts of memory, some introspective facts, spatial and temporal relations, and facts of comparison, such as the likeness or unlikeness of two shades of color.

But Russell argues that certain very common beliefs probably should be excluded from our data. One is the belief that objects persist when we are not perceiving them. Another is the belief in the existence of other minds and of things outside our experience which are revealed by history and geography. These should be called "soft" data, since they can be doubted and are actually derived from our belief in hard data. The problem, then, is to determine whether the existence of anything other than our own hard data can be inferred from these data.

In formulating the question by asking whether we can know of the existence of anything independent of ourselves, Russell finds that the terms "independent" and "ourselves" are too vague to determine whatever solution we happen to be seeking. What we *can* show, however, is that the appearances of an object—its color, shape, and size—change as we move toward it or away from it, or around it. Russell calls these appearances "sense-data," and he then defines a "private world" as an object seen from a certain perspective. If we move around an object we shall discover that the sense-data change and that correlated with these changes are the bodily sensations associated with our movements. Then, if we assume the existence of other minds, we can correlate their private worlds and perspectives with ours and define an object as the *class* of all of its perspectives. This is much safer than inferring a *thing* which exhibits itself in these perspectives. The *perspectives* are certainly real and constitute hard data; the thing is an inference and may be mistaken. A class is merely a logical construction, and we have thus substituted a logical construction for an inferred entity. This explanation fits the facts, has no empirical evidence against it, and is free from logical contradictions. Russell thus regarded himself as having solved the problem of how we know an external world.

Another philosophical problem that yields to Rusell when his logical-analytic method is applied to it is that of the relation between the world of physics and the world of sense-data. According to physics, the world consists of material bodies, located in space and time and having a high degree of rigidity and permanence. While the bodies themselves may change, they are made up of particles which are themselves unchanging and indestructible. On the other hand, the world of sense-data for any one of us comes and goes; even such permanent things as mountains become data for us only when we see them; they are not known with certainty to exist at other moments. The problem of "getting these worlds together" involves the attempt to construct things, a single space, and a single time out of the fleeting data of experience.

Permanent things can be constructed if we can find some way of connecting what we commonly call "appearances of the same thing." While some sort of continuity among appearances is necessary, it is not sufficient to define a thing. What is needed in addition is that the appearances of a *single* thing obey certain physical laws which the appearances of *different* things do not.

In much the same way the dimensionless points (no one has ever seen a perfect point) of physics must be constructed out of the surfaces and volumes of our sensory experience. Using the fact that spaces can be observed to enclose other spaces (like Chinese boxes), Russell constructs "enclosure-series" which can be called "point-producers" because points can be defined by means of them. Russell does not, however, define a point as the lower limit of an enclosure-series, for there may be no such limit. Instead he defines it as the series itself; thus, a point is a logical entity constructed out of the immediate data of experience.

It can now be seen how Russell derives the concept of durationless instants of time. Events of our experience are not instantaneous; they occupy a finite time. Furthermore, different events may overlap in time since one event may begin before the other, but there may be a common time during which they both occur. If we restrict ourselves to the time which is common to more and more overlapping events we shall get durations which are shorter and shorter. Then we can define an instant of time as the class of all events which are simultaneous with one another. To state accurately when an event happens, we need only to specify the class of events which defines the instant of its happening.

Russell reminds us that since the days of Zeno philosophers have wondered about the problem of permanence and change, and especially about the apparent paradox of motion. Some motions, such as that of the second hand on a watch, seem to be continuous since we can actually *see* the movement; other motions, such as that of the hour hand, seem to be discontinuous because we can observe only a broken series of positions. Russell's solution to this apparent contradiction in the nature of motion lies in the mathematical theory of continuity.

Continuity is regarded as, first, a property of a series of elements, of terms arranged in an order, such as numbers arranged in order of magnitude. Second, a continuous series must in every case be "compact," which means that no two terms are consecutive and that between any two terms there is always another. If space is thought of as being made up of a continuous series of points, and time as a similar series of instants, then motion will consist of a correlation between a series of different points in space and a series of different instants in time. But Russell cautions us that we must not say that a body moves from one point in space to the next, for if the series is truly compact there is no next point in space, no next instant in time. This takes care of the difficulty we experience in thinking of a continuous motion as consisting of a very rapid series of jumps from one position to another.

Bergson argued that motion is simple, indivisible, and not validly analyzable into a series of states. In replying to him Russell argues that on grounds of physiology, psychology, and logic there is no incompatibility between the mathematical theory of continuity and the evidence of the senses. From physiology we learn that sensations do not cease instantaneously but gradually die away. Thus when we see a rapid motion we do not perceive it as a series of jerks because each sensation blends into its successor. From psychology we learn that there are actually cases of sense-data which form compact series. If a blindfolded person is holding a weight and to this a small additional weight is added, he may not observe the added weight if it is small enough. And if still another weight is added he may still not notice it. But if both weights had been added at once, he might have detected the difference. This proves that weights form a continuous series. Finally, on grounds of logic, Bergson must be mistaken. For if analysis always falsifies, there could never be two facts concerning the same thing, and this would make motion, which depends on the distinction between earlier and later, impossible.

After a discussion of Kant's conception of infinity, Russell turns to an analysis of Zeno's famous paradoxes. Zeno had four arguments designed to show the impossiblity of motion—all based on his theory of the infinite divisibility of space and time. His first argument was designed to prove that a runner cannot get to the end of a race course, for if space is infinitely divisible, he will have to cover an infinite number of points in a finite time, and this is impossible. According to Russell, Zeno's error came from thinking that the points must be covered "one by one." This would, apparently, require an infinitely long time, for the series has infinitely many elements. But the series actually has a limit of 1, and this specifies the instant when the runner will complete the race.

Zeno's second argument attempts to show that Achilles can never overtake the tortoise if he gives it a head start, for by the time Achilles reaches the point where the tortoise was at any given time, the tortoise will always be slightly ahead. Achilles must then make up this distance, but again the tortoise will be slightly in advance. Achilles gets always closer to the tortoise but never is able to pass him. Russell claims that Zeno's error here is the same as in the previous case—an infinity of instants does not necessitate an infinitely long time.

Zeno's third argument begins with the claim that whatever occupies a space equal to itself must be at rest. An arrow in flight always occupies a space equal to itself; hence, it cannot move. Here Zeno supposes that the arrow could not move through an instant because this would require that an instant have parts, and this cannot be. But Russell points out that the mathematical theory of infinity has shown that since there are no consecutive points or instants, an instant *can* have parts. When this is realized Zeno's difficulty disappears.

Zeno's last argument attempts to prove that "half the time may be equal to double the time." This is illustrated by a column of soldiers passing another column at rest and a third column marching in the opposite direction. In the first case the soldiers pass only half as many soldiers as in the second case, yet these actions both take place during the same time. The error again disappears for Russell with the recognition that there is no "fastest" motion which requires that slow motion have intervals for rest interspersed.

According to Russell's analysis, infinite numbers differ from finite numbers in two ways: (1) Infinite numbers are *reflexive*, while finite numbers are not, and (2) finite numbers are *inductive*, while infinite numbers are not. A number is reflexive when it is not increased by adding 1 to it. Thus the number of members in the class 0, 1, 2, 3 . . . n is the same as the number in the class 1, 2, 3, 4 . . . n plus 1. Even more surprising, the number of even numbers is equal to the total number of numbers (even and odd). It is therefore possible in the case of infinite numbers for a part of a class to equal the whole class.

Infinite numbers are also noninductive. Inductive numbers possess a certain property which can be called "hereditary." This is like the property of being named "Jones," which, if it applies to a man, also applies to all of his male descendants. Every property which belongs to 0 and is hereditary belongs to all of the natural numbers, and we can define the natural numbers as those which are inductive. To all such numbers proof by mathematical induction applies.

Philosophers have tried to define numbers, but without much success. Russel refers to the mathematician Frege, who recognized that numbers are neither physical nor mental but logical—that is, numbers are properties of general terms or general descriptions and thus are applicable to classes, not to things. The author asks: "When do two classes have the same number of members?" and answers "When a one-to-one correlation can be set up between them." This applies both to finite classes which can be counted and to infinite classes which cannot. As an example, Russell refers to monogamous countries where the number of husbands is the same as the number of wives, though we may not know how many of both there are because the relation of marriage is a correlating relation. The number of a class can then be defined as the class of all classes which are similar to it—that is, which have a one-to-one correlation with it. Note that number is not a *property* of a class but is a *class of classes*. This is a valid conception even if classes are considered to be fictions, for there is a method for translating statements in which classes occur to statements in which they do not.

Russell's final application of the logical-analytic method is to the problem of causation and free will. Causation is a complicated relation that must be described by a carefully worded formula: "Whenever things occur in certain relations to each other (among which their time-relations must be included), then a thing having a fixed relation to these things will occur at a date fixed relatively to their dates." The evidence for causation in the past is the observation of repeated uniformities, together with knowledge of the fact that where there appears to be an exception to such uniformities we can always find wider ones which will include both the successes and failures. The only guarantee we could have that such a causal law would continue to hold in the future would be some sort of *a priori* principle. The law of causality is therefore an *ideal* law, possibly true, but not known to be true.

Determinism can be demonstrated, Russell believes, only if we can show that human actions are theoretically predictable from a sufficient number of antecedents. This we cannot do, he claims. In the great majority of cases, volitions probably have causes, but the only evidence for this is the fact of repeated instances. Furthermore, since causes do not *compel* their effects the will is free in the sense that our volitions are the results of our desires, and we are not forced to will something which we would rather not will.—*A.C.B.*

PERTINENT LITERATURE

Schilpp, Paul A., ed. *The Philosophy of Bertrand Russell* (The Library of Living Philosophers). Evanston, Illinois: The Library of Living Philosophers, 1946.

Perhaps no single contribution to the literature of commentaries has been more fruitful than Paul A. Schilpp's The Library of Living Philosophers. Each volume contains not only a set of critical essays written by persons who are themselves distinguished philosophers, but also a carefully composed reply by the philosopher whose work is subjected to examination. This particular volume is supplemented by a bibiliography of Bertrand Russell's work to 1945.

W. T. Stace's essay "Russell's Neutral Monism"; Albert Einstein's "Remarks on Bertrand Russell's Theory of Knowledge" (printed in both German and English); Andrew Paul Ushenko's "Russell's Critique of Empiricism"; and Roderick M. Chisholm's "Russell on the Foundations of Empirical Knowledge" all have something to do with the ideas in Russell's *Our Knowledge of the External World*, even when the critics are primarily concerned with other works by Russell.

Stace refers repeatedly to *Our Knowledge of the External World* in considering Russell's neutral monism. Stace explains at the outset of his essay that by neutral monism he understands the view that mind and matter are constructed, as he says, "out of the same 'stuff.'" The difference between the mental and the physical, insofar as it can be made out, is a difference in relations, not in what is related. The task for the neutral monist, then, according to Stace, is that of determining what the neutral (neither matter nor mind basically) stuff is, what matter is, and what mind is. According to Stace, neutral monism hopes to get rid of psychophysical dualism and to provide empiricism with directly perceivable data. Stace argues that Russell's *The Analysis of Mind* (1921) deals with neutral monism's account of the mental; *Our Knowledge of the External World* applies neutral monism to the problem of matter. (In his reply, Russell comments that he wishes Stace had also considered Russell's *Analysis of Matter*.)

Stace acknowledges that in 1914, when *Our Knowledge of the External World* appeared, Russell was not yet a neutral monist. But the work is significant in that a phenomonalistic theory of matter appeared there, later to be supplemented by the view of mind expressed in *The Analysis of Mind*. In the *Problems of Philosophy*, on the other hand, a work that appeared in 1912, Russell expressed views that revealed him as a psychophysical dualist: matter is one sort of thing, mind another. The physical object was described as the cause of sense-data in that the sense-data, the given received in perception, were the appearances of the object. The move to neutral monism consisted in striking out the physical object as that which appears, although unknown; the physical object is now conceived in terms of sense-data, as a set of data, each member of which occupies the space it has in perception. Public space becomes simply a construct of what is common to private spaces.

In the second edition of *Our Knowledge of the External World* in 1928, according to Stace, Russell struck out references in which a distinction was made between sensations and sense-data, thereby converting the book to an expression of neutral monism. The sense-data considered as aspects of a thing constitute the physical object; the sense-data at any point in space constitute a perspective. When one adds to the perspective an organism and mnemonic causation (memory connections), one has the mind. So runs neutral monism, according to Stace.

Stace's criticism of Russell's neutral monism is directed toward three theories—the theory of neutral stuff, of matter, and of mind. In the account of Russell's conception of neutral stuff as sensations or "things similar to sensations," Stace notes, first of all, that Russell's neutral monism is not pure. In *The Analysis of Mind* Russell argued that the "American realists" (New Realists) were only partly right in regarding all "stuff" as neutral; mental images are only subjective, while unperceived occurrences are purely physical.

Stace does not regard Russell's partial neutral monism as a fault.

Russell's theory of matter has three objectives, Stace writes: to eliminate psychophysical dualism, to explain matter solely by reference to verifiables consisting of sense appearances, and to resolve the problem of the relativity of sensation.

Stace concludes that Russell cannot eliminate dualism if his theory is only partially a neutral monism; he cannot explain matter solely by reference to verifiables of a kind exemplified by sensations, because he persists (as perhaps he should) in regarding physical events as in some way "generative," giving rise to sensations but not themselves of the sensation type. As for the problem of the relativity of sensation: Russell, as he himself admits, has difficulty with it; but he appears to resolve it by regarding the "place" of data to be the place where they are given (in the head of a perceiver) so that there are as many places as there are observers or possible observers. (The thing is where the lines of data-places converge.)

The problem of mind for Russell is the problem of explaining mind without reference to consciousness—only to neutral entities. Stace rejects the suggestion that monism is somehow superior to dualism; what is important is what is the case. His second objection to Russell's theory of mind is that it depends on the assumption of a unique relation which would not itself be reducible to "sensations" of the neutral kind; such a relation would be purely subjective. Third, Russell's theory denies introspection; how, then, is the relation which makes data subjective or mental known? There is no answer. Finally, according to Stace, Russell cannot explain how general ideas are formed from particular data.

In his reply to Stace's article, Russell concedes that he has abandoned some of the views expressed in *Our Knowledge of the External World* and *The Analysis of Mind*. He argues for a wider sense of "verifiables" than that having to do solely with sensations; he continues to argue for unperceived aspects as constituents of light waves or sound waves, and he argues that sensations are causally linked to physical objects.

Jager, Ronald. "Atomism: Theories of Knowledge," in *The Development of Bertrand Russell's Philosophy*. New York: Humanities Press, 1972.

Ronald Jager's book accomplishes what its title suggests: it traces the development of Bertrand Russell's thought. Ideas follow one another not simply chronologically but logically and generically, as a matter of intellectual development. By far the most intriguing drama exhibited in the ingenious course of Russell's thought is the drama of his struggle to justify the idea of neutral entities, sense-data that would be present in sensation but exist unperceived as aspects of physical objects. Jager calls attention to an essay published in 1914, "The Relation of Sense Data to Physics" (*Scientia*, no. 4; reprinted in

Mysticism and Logic, 1918, Chapter VIII), in which Russell proposes giving the name "sensibilia" to objects that have the same status as sense-data but are not necessarily data to any mind. The *sensibile* becomes a sense-datum by entering into the relation of acquaintance; that is, a *sensibile* as known is a sense-datum; a sense-datum out of mind is a *sensibile*.

Jager reports that Russell persistently claimed that sense-data are physical; *Our Knowledge of the External World* is one place in which he did so. Thus, according to Russell, sense-data are "constituents of the actual world," and accordingly are, at least in part, the "subject matter of physics." Sometimes, however, as in *Mysticism and Logic*, he speaks of the possibility of defining the objects of physics as "functions" of sense-data (but not, apparently, of sense-data as "functions" of physical objects). In any case, Jager writes, Russell had a great deal of difficulty answering such questions as to the causes of sense-data or as to why it makes more sense to describe them as "physical" than as "mental." He does consider whether sense-data can exist unperceived, and his answers vary. Russell argued that there is no reason why they could not; but he was not sure whether after perception they disappeared or resumed status as *sensibilia*.

The question of the status of sense-data after perception gives rise to other troublesome questions: Can they change color, appear to different sense organs, have back sides, have unperceived qualities, and so forth? Jager suggests that these questions do not appear to be empirical issues; no further examination of sense-data would help in the answering of such questions. (Jager does not suggest, however, that the problem is linguistic, a matter of deciding what to mean by "sense datum," although he does speak of the difficulty as "conceptual." At least part of the difficulty stems, it appears, from Russell's not deciding how to use the term; and it seems likely that he used it in different ways on different occasions.)

Russell's primary concern, Jager points out, is not with the conception of sense-data but with the relation of sense-data to physics and with the relation of sense-data to the particulars of logical atomism, the basic elements of reference. Because of the ambiguity of the term "sense datum" and because of Russell's persistence in regarding conceptual problems as empirical, his theory acquired an influential strength: the difficulties were glossed over, the appeal of common sense was strong, and there was the technical appeal of logical construction.

Our Knowledge of the External World, Jager writes, offers a "synoptic" account of how the logical construction might proceed. The problem is whether one can know anything about the external world, the world (if there is one) beyond the private world, the world of immediate experience. Jager gives an account of Russell's reconstruction of a penny in terms of sense-data. The place of the penny is the intersection point of all its appearances from all possible perspectives. Each "aspect" or datum is a member of two classes:

the class of aspects constituting the thing, and the class of aspects constituting a given perspective. Russell indicated how from data, analysis, and propositions arranged in deductive chains, one forms premises for a body of knowledge. His theory gave rise to his logical atomism and, later, to the tenets of the logical positivists. In his 1918 lectures, "The Philosophy of Logical Atomism," Russell developed his ideas into a provocative and influential doctrine.—*I.P.M.*

ADDITIONAL RECOMMENDED READING

Pears, D. F., ed. *Bertrand Russell: A Collection of Critical Essays.* Garden City, New York: Anchor Books, 1972. An excellent collection, including essays by W. V. O. Quine, A. J. Ayer, Jaakko Hintikka, Anthony Quinton, Grover Maxwell, C. A. Fritz, Rudolf Carnap, Kurt Gödel, and C. S. Chihara; with a bibliography of Russell's writings by H. Ruja.

Schilpp, Paul A., ed. *The Philosophy of Bertrand Russell* (The Library of Living Philosophers). Evanston, Illinois: The Library of Living Philosophers, 1946. Mentioned yet again because of its excellent bibliography.

THREE LECTURES ON AESTHETIC

Author: Bernard Bosanquet (1848-1923)
Type of work: Aesthetics
First published: 1915 (Delivered at University College, London, 1914)

PRINCIPAL IDEAS ADVANCED

Aesthetic experience is distinguishable from other experience in that it is pleasant, stable, relevant, and common.

The aesthetic experience is contemplative, not practical; it is organizational, and both personal and general.

The aesthetic response is a response to form and substance in an appearance, requiring the imagination, and resulting in the pleasant awareness of a feeling embodied in the appearance.

The most satisfying aesthetic experience is realized when the artist forms his work in harmony with the character of his medium.

In its proper sense, beauty is what is common to artistic products insofar as they are excellent; beauty may be easy or difficult; difficult beauty is characterized by intricacy, tension, and width—that is, it is complex, provokes heightened feelings, and demands breadth of interest.

For Bosanquet there is a significant difference between the philosophy of art and art criticism, art instruction, or the psychology of art. The critic distinguishes good from bad works of art, while the teacher of techniques is concerned with ways of producing beauty. The psychologist explains in terms of causes the feeling of pleasure associated with the work of art. The philosopher's function is to take the facts discovered by others, select those that are relevant, and expand them into ideas which are exhaustive and self-consistent.

According to the philosopher's method, what is an aesthetic experience as Bosanquet explains it? In its simplest form it is a feeling of pleasure distinguished from other pleasant feelings by being *stable*, *relevant*, and *common*.

The aesthetic experience is *stable* in the sense that it is not satiable. We do not satisfy the need for aesthetic feeling in the way that we satisfy the need for food. We may become physically tired at a museum, but we do not tire of responding to aesthetic objects.

The aesthetic response is to the whole object as sufficient in itself; it is *relevant*. We may receive pleasure from hearing a dinner bell, but it is likely to be in anticipation of dinner, not in the sound of the bell itself.

The aesthetic feeling is *common* because it can be shared and is increased by sharing. It is a product of education. "To like and dislike rightly is the goal of all culture worth the name."

Since the aesthetic experience is a response to an object, it has other characteristics which help to explain it. First, it is *contemplative*. It does not try to alter or use the object. Second, it is *organizational*. To Bosanquet this property of the aesthetic response to the object was of great importance. Through it, he was able to relate the aesthetic experience to the individual who has the feeling and beyond the individual to a type of experience. Thus the aesthetic experience is both personal and general. The individual has his experience of the art object, but his experience can be described so that others can have the experience too. From this property of organization, the value of the aesthetic experience arises.

The object is valued for what it is in itself. One can use an object or have information about it without responding to it aesthetically. One may know its history, market value, cause, and location, for example. The aesthetic experience is a response to what is there, to what the object is in itself, and not to some relation the object has to other things or other people.

Since the aesthetic response is not to some aspect of the object but to its inner organization, it may be described as a response to form. Form is not merely technical form in the sense of sonnet form, not merely shape in the geometric sense. It is the combination of these forms with matter of such a sort that form and matter become one object. The response to form and substance as one is the aesthetic response.

The aesthetic object is an appearance, not a real thing. A poem about love is not love; the painting of a house cannot be lived in. As an appearance, the aesthetic object can be known, but not known about. We know about a painting when we know its history, how it was painted, and by whom. This knowledge is a response to the painting as object, but it is not an aesthetic response to the painting as appearance. Bosanquet writes, "Great objects of art contain myriads of elements of form on different levels, knit together in more and more complex systems, till the feeling which they demand is such as to occupy the whole powers of the greatest mind, and more than these if they were to be had."

Because we do not regard the aesthetic object as something to be understood or manipulated, because our response is to the appearance rather than to the reality, it is a response that requires the use of the imagination. Imagination is the mind considering possibilities. Its use in practical concerns is limited to the consideration of real possibilities. In aesthetic matters this restriction does not apply; there is no need for agreement with reality. The aesthetic use of imagination has for its end satisfaction through feeling. Although in its practical use the imagination is limited, in its aesthetic use it is set free.

In short, the aesthetic experience is defined by Bosanquet as "the pleasant awareness of a feeling embodied in an appearance presented to imagination." The critic to be a good critic must first be a spectator. He must have the aesthtic feeling and then reflect on it. A good critic is one who leads others to an aesthetic experience of an object. His reflection on his aesthetic feeling, his judgment of how it is furthered by the form of the object, his judgment of where the object fails to give aesthetic satisfaction, should furnish the raw material for his critical pronouncements.

Bosanquet contends that the aesthetic experience can best be understood by considering simple rather than complex examples. He cites as examples easy melodies and dance steps, geometric figures such as the circle and the cube, decorations on the entablatures of some buildings. Each object considered has formal elements and contains the three characteristics of aesthetic objects: stability, relevance, and community. It is important to notice that none of these patterns is representational. Representation introduces a new factor because the thing represented carries the spectator beyond mere pattern to association and toward the problem of the beauty of nature. Poems about events, statues of individuals, pictures of familiar objects bring to aesthetic appreciation the test of facts. But there is the danger of subordinating aesthetic quality to knowledge; that is, of turning an aesthetic object into a representation of facts. However, we cannot and should not ignore factual content. It too is a medium of expression and has aesthetic value. Much of the significance of the work of art may lie in its factual content. Green trees remind us of summer and bare trees of winter, smiles denote happiness and tears sorrow. We have learned these symbols through experience and this knowledge is essential to aesthetic appreciation. The representational work of art is always more than mere pattern in the sense that repeated curves form a pattern, but it is a pattern in the sense that it represents a type or norm. In Bosanquet's words, "Man's mind possesses a magic by which it can extract the soul of the actual thing or event, and confer it on any medium which is convenient to him, the wall of a cave, or a plate of gold, or a scrap of paper."

Since, according to Bosanquet, the artist reproduces the object as type in a different medium, his aesthetic theory would have to be modified to accommodate developments in the fine arts since the appearance of *Three Lectures on Aesthetics*. Nonrepresentational painting could not be dealt with in terms of Bosanquet's theory as he has stated it. He says, for example, that representation "introduces an enormously larger and deeper world than the world of non-representative pattern-designing." Much of modern art is not pattern-designing, but neither is it representational. It would have to be for Bosanquet like music, which does not represent objects but represents emotions. The beauty of nature presents a similar problem. We must somehow regard it as we would a work of art, as an appearance which we love or admire, not simply as a series of objects to be understood or used. Nature as beautiful is nature as expressive rather than as the content of a rational construction.

How are the arts to be classified? There are different arts and their classification should reveal the roots of the aesthetic experience—that is, of beauty.

Bosanquet begins with the fact that different artists may take the same subject and treat it in different mediums and in different ways. This difference in treatment is due in large part to the demands of the medium. The properties of a medium lead the artist to do certain things that another medium would not lead him to do. There is a triadic relation here, a triple interaction of the subject, the artist, and the medium. Clay leads the artist in a different direction from wrought iron, and stone in still another way. Bosanquet says in summary of this point, "The feeling for the medium, the sense of what can rightly be done in it only or better than in anything else, and the charm and fascination of doing it so—these, I take it, are the real clue to the fundamental question of aesthetics, which is 'how feeling and its body are created adequate to one another.'"

Bosanquet is concerned to show that his theory applies to folk arts as well as to fine arts. He was influenced here by Ruskin, Pater, and Morris; and all in turn influenced John Dewey.

The artist idealizes nature. What does this mean for Bosanquet? It does not mean that the artist creates the abstract, general type. He does not paint or describe a tree which is somehow a summary of what all trees have in common. He paints a tree which is particular and individual, but which expresses its ideal type through its individuality. Bosanquet was a philosophical idealist, and it is a part of his theory that the individual can express his place in the total scheme of reality without losing his individuality.

The artist's experience is the source of his subject matter. Some event in the external world, either an objective or subjective happening, is felt in its relations to other events. Through these relations the event takes on a magnitude and importance which are its significance and which are expressed through some medium. The artistic medium communicates just as language communicates. A superb use of medium is like the happy choice of words to express an idea; the idea is enhanced through the choice of words. Subject, artist, and medium are common characteristics of all the arts, and it is through these properties that "all good art is one."

In consequence, the word *beauty* is used in two senses. In one, it refers to what is common to all artistic activity insofar as it produces excellence. In the other sense, it refers to what most people find aesthetically pleasing.

The first sense, which for Bosanquet is the more correct one, includes art that to ordinary people seems strange, grotesque, or awesome. Certain types of art at a given time will be appreciated only by the aesthetically educated. Beauty in this first and wider sense is of two sorts, difficult beauty and easy beauty. Easy beauty—the simple tune, the rose, the beautiful face—is pleasing to everyone; nevertheless, it can be beauty of the highest type.

Difficult beauty, Bosanquet argues, contains three elements which explain its difficulty. These are *intricacy,*, *tension*, and *width*. *Intricacy* is the property that many objects have of being analyzable into component parts. A painting may be seen as telling a story, as a juxtaposition of shapes, as a relation of colors and so on. Full appreciation depends on the ability of the spectator to see these elements as related in a harmony. *Tension* is the capacity to provoke heightened feeling which we often associate with tragedy, but which is within the capacity of every art form. It elicits a response to art that many people would prefer to avoid, a complete identification of the individual with the full impact of the work of art. The third dimension of difficult art is *width*, the power of satisfying a wide range of interests. Many people fail to respond to some forms of art, for example to the comic when it makes ridiculous something that they hold dear. But if the spectator has a wide range of interests, he can respond to comedy and to the other demands that the variety of the arts make; he must shift his mood to respond to the mood of the work of art.

Bosanquet's distinction between easy and difficult beauty is not a sharp one, nor was it intended to be. One and the same work of art may be both when seen by the ordinary person and by the connoisseur. His purpose was to extend the meaning of beauty to include all aesthetic excellence and to allow what he considered to be an adequate distinction between the beautiful and the ugly.

What many persons regard as ugly is whatever they are incapable of appreciating. To experience aesthetic pleasure from an object is to repsond to its beauty, but to fail to feel this pleasure is not to prove that the object has no real aesthetic quality. True ugliness is a property of an object that no normal imagination could see as beautiful however sensitive this imagination might be. An object expresses beauty, but it cannot express ugliness. To be ugly is to have properties which frustrate the expression of beauty. We expect to receive an aesthetic response from the object, but its properties prevent and nullify our expectation. We find ugliness in insincere art, in art where beauty is attempted and the attempt fails. Thus, for Bosanquet, nature is never ugly, because it lacks conscious intent. Again we see an effect of philosophical idealism. The ugly is an inconsistency in the concept and execution of the aesthetic object. The artist first imagines and then expresses so as to communicate feeling. Aesthetic feelings have their source in every experience of living, but the artist relates his experience to other possibilities of experience, and in this relation is beauty. Beauty is the source of aesthetic pleasure for the artist and for the spectator.—*J. Co.*

PERTINENT LITERATURE

Pepper, Stephen C. *The Work of Art.* Bloomington: Indiana University Press, 1955.

Although Bernard Bosanquet's *Three Lectures on Aesthetic* is often cited as an example of aesthetic theory from a philosophical idealist, few critics have concentrated on the particular features of his philosophy of art and beauty. His contributions to aesthetic theory are more often acknowledged or alluded to than criticized. Stephen Pepper's interest in Bosanquet stems from Pepper's concern to develop the notion of "funding," a term devised by John Dewey to refer to the fusion of past experiences in a present aesthetic experience. The aesthetic object, Pepper argues, is not best understood as a single object but as "a little nest of related objects." He then refers to "a famous passage" from Bosanquet's *Three Lectures on Aesthetic* in which Bosanquet argues that the "appearance" that is the aesthetic object will not be recognized as an expression of feeling unless it is satisfactory as pattern and expressive through its concrete character. The pattern and the concrete character succeed in embodying feeling when they do because of other experiences which contribute to the aesthetic experience. Thus, according to Bosanquet, one interprets the Discobolos through one's experience of human bodies; an abstract pattern acquires significance by being related, in experience, to "the realm of nature and man. . . ."

In commenting on this passage, Pepper remarks that both George Santayana and Bosanquet attempted to make clear the power of "funding" to bring related matters from past experience to bear on the aesthetic perception of a work of art. Pepper's interest is in explaining how an adequate perception of a work of art considered as a complex object is possible, and he maintains that funding is a significant part of the process.

Pepper distinguishes three closely interrelated aesthetic objects, all combining as a "nest of objects" to become the work of art for the perceiver: the physical object contemplated, the immediate perceptual object, and the object of criticism. According to Pepper, the physical vehicle is the source of perceptual stimulation (a painting, for example, is the source of the experience of perceiving the painting); the "object of criticism" is "some sort of synthesis or evaluative goal of the sequence of perceptual immediacies." One makes sense of a sequence of perceptions and thereby generates an object of criticism not by simply funding all perceptions but by recognizing the aesthetic relevancy of the perceptions funded. Aesthetic relevancy must be made out by a contemplator competent to develop an intuitive sense of a perceptual whole.

The object of criticism, Pepper argues, is an "objectively defined ideal" in that no particular funded perception is identifiable with it. Thus, the object of criticism (what one might call the work of art "proper") is described by Pepper as a dispositional property of the physical vehicle: the physical work of art is such that if contemplated by a competent perceiver, it yields a "funded system of relevant perceptions." Such a funded system is the object of criticism, the third in the nest of objects that is the work of art.

In the remainder of his book Pepper considers whether a judgment of beauty can be true (his answer is yes, in that a work of art can have the capacity to satisfy certain consummatory norms), the dynamics of a masterpiece (involving reference to "natural norms of human response"), the "control object" (the vehicle of aesthetic contemplation), a reply to extreme relativists, and the concept of fusion in Dewey's aesthetics. These various topics are unified by Pepper's theme that the controlling quality of a work of art is "the fusion of the relevant details in the object of criticism."

Tomas, Vincent, Douglas Morgan, and Monroe Beardsley. "The Concept of Expression in Art," in *Artistic Expression*. Edited by John Hospers. New York: Appleton-Century-Crofts, 1971.

John Hospers' anthology of philosophical articles in aesthetics would be useful as background material in the study of aesthetics itself or in the critical examination of any particular philosophical aesthetic theory. The six essays on the expressive *process* and the nine essays on the expressive *product*, however, are particularly relevant in the consideration of Bernard Bosanquet's aesthetics since Bosanquet regarded the work of art as the embodiment in appearance of a feeling—in short, as an expression of feeling. Even nature, for Bosanquet, acquires beauty insofar as it is expressive.

Although most of the essays thus bear on a study of Bosanquet, an article (or, more accurately, a composite of articles) by Vincent Tomas, Douglas Morgan, and Monroe Beardsley, entitled "The Concept of Expression in Art," is more directly related to Bosanquet's work (to which reference is made) than are the others.

Tomas begins his essay with a reference to Leo Tolstoy, George Santayana, Bosanquet, Curt John Ducasse, Louis Arnaud Reid, and John Dewey as philosophers who have maintained that art is expression. Tomas points out that these philosophers distinguish between "expression" as the artistic *process*, as the artistic *product*, and as an *aesthetic object*; that is, Tomas suggests, these philosophers write of artistic expression, objective expression, and aesthetic expression. Tomas' thesis is that aesthetic expression is basic and that what he calls the "two terms theory" of aesthetic expression is mistaken. Since artistic expression is defined by reference to the artistic product and the product, in turn, by reference to the aesthetic expression, if we want to be clear about the aesthetic expression, he maintains, we must recognize that the "expressive thing" and the "thing expressed" are but one thing, not two.

Artistic expression, according to Tomas, is the consciously controlled process consisting in the objectification of feeling; the product of such a process is an objective expression of feeling in that it has the capacity, under certain circumstances, of causing an aesthetic contemplator to have the feeling. (The artist's activity is *not* expressive in this second sense: one would not, by contemplating the artistic process, be caused to have the feeling being embodied.) Tomas points out that the class of expressive things is not coextensive with the class of works of art. The countryside is objectively expressive in that it is able to provoke feelings in observers, but it is not on that account a work of art.

In his discussion of aesthetic expression Tomas refers to Santayana's claim that we find in aesthetic expression two terms: the expressive "thing" (a word, an image) and the "thing" expressed, some thought or emotion. Santayana contended, further, that aesthetic expression requires the union of these two terms; the second must be "incorporated" in the first. Tomas argues that when music expresses sadness, the music and the sadness are apprehended as one thing. The music as expression does not *represent* the sadness, as a sign might; it "presents" the sadness. He cites with approval Dewey's comment that the expressive object does not "lead" to an experience but constitutes one.

The ambiguity of the so-called two terms is then discussed by Tomas. He refers to Bosanquet's remark that the central problem of the aesthetic attitude is how a feeling can be introduced into an object. Tomas also refers to the question as put by Louis Arnaud Reid in his *A Study in Aesthetics* (1915): "How does body, a nonmental object, come to 'embody' or 'express,' for our aesthetic imagination, values which it does not literally contain?" Tomas contends that this problem considered by Santayana, Bosanquet, and Reid, among others, is a "pseudo-problem." The problem is a pseudoproblem, Tomas argues, because it rests on the false assumption that the value or feeling expressed is not literally in the aesthetic "body." Tomas quotes Reid as writing, "The 'joy' expressed in music is not *literally* in the succession of sounds."

Tomas' defense of his position is undertaken by his first of all arguing that the "expressive thing" is not a physical thing or event; what is expressive is the content of perceptual experience, what Tomas calls "qualities." Tomas then criticizes the view that a distinction can be made between the aesthetic "surface," made up of sense qualities, and the feeling import. He rejects the view that there are two terms of aesthetic expression—the "expressive thing," which is a set of sense qualities presented in consciousness, and that which is expressed, the feeling import, which is merely "suggested." According to Tomas, both the expressive thing (the music, say) and the thing expressed (the sadness of the music) are presented; both appear in aesthetic contemplation. Furthermore, there is a sense in which both are subjective in that both are present in contemplation and the feeling is in the expressive thing: the sadness is in the music. Also, there is a sense in which both are objective in that the aesthetic surface (the expressive thing) and the feeling are features of the phenomenological content that has become the object of aesthetic contemplation and is distinguished from the subject who contemplates. Hence, he concludes that the "aesthetically expressive object is one thing, not a fusion of two": the music and the sadness are one thing.

In criticism of Tomas' view, Douglas N. Morgan argues (on the basis of a series of careful distinctions) that Tomas' view, if analytic (about the phenomenal object) is true but theoretically unimportant; if Tomas' view is empirical (as to the location of the sadness of music, for example), there is little evidential support, if any. Monroe Beardsley, however, tends to support Tomas' view and to agree with Tomas' claim that the word "express" is used in various ways that give rise to pseudoproblems. These three philosophical responses to the question asked by Bosanquet (and others) of "how a feeling can be got into an object" are well worth careful examination for anyone interested in appraising a view, such as Bosanquet's, that art is the expression of feeling.—*I.P.M.*

ADDITIONAL RECOMMENDED READING
Ducasse, Curt John. *The Philosophy of Art.* New York: Dover Publications, 1966. A revised and enlarged edition of Ducasse's work first published in 1929. Ducasse argues that art is the objective expression of emotion.

Hospers, John, ed. *Artistic Expression.* New York: Appelton-Century-Crofts, 1971. An anthology of philosophical essays on art and expression; includes articles by Leo Tolstoy, Benedetto Croce, R. G. Collingwood, John Hospers, John Dewey, C. J. Ducasse, Edmund Gurney, George Santayana, Wassily Kandinsky, Charles Hartshorne, Rudolf Arnheim, O. K. Bouwsma, Vincent Tomas, Douglas Morgan, Monroe Beardsley, and Guy Sircello.

Santayana, George. *The Sense of Beauty.* New York: Charles Scribner's Sons, 1896. Santayana argues that beauty is pleasure objectified.

THE IDEA OF THE HOLY

Author: Rudolf Otto (1869-1937)
Type of work: Philosphy of religion
First published: 1917

PRINCIPAL IDEAS ADVANCED

Holiness is the quality unique to religious experience; the presence of the numinous, that which is holy, is universally experienced as a kind of fearful awe in the presence of the mysterious.

The numen, the divine, must be known through the religious feeling; but the feeling itself cannot be described.

In the presence of the holy the human being is aware of his own nothingness, and with the feeling of creature-consciousness he becomes aware of the wholly other, that which overpowers while it charms.

The absolute distinction between numen and creature is overcome by God's grace.

The nineteenth century was marked by a permeation of almost every field by the "scientific methodology" as the one valid method for analysis and interpretation. It appeared that religion, with its suprasensible object, its competing theologies, its prescientific world view, its emotionalism, and its origins in "superstition," was incompatible with this scientific epoch. In this situation, two possibilities were open—either that science admit the possibility of a universal "nonrational" mode of experience, and thus the possibility of religion as a legitimate human enterprise, or that it insist uncompromisingly on a narrow empiricism, reducing religion to some nonreligious common denominator. Until the last several decades, the latter option was largely chosen.

Anthropologists such as James George Frazer and Émile Durkheim, and psychologists such as Freud, interpreted religion in purely naturalistic terms, as a primitive mentality or immature projection. Philosophers such as Hegel saw it as a symbolic or mythological version of what philosophy better understood logically and conceptually. Such attacks tended to discredit religion as a *sui generis*, unique, and *bona fide* mode of experience, apprehension, and expression.

One of the problems indigenous to a study of religion encouraged such naturalistic reductions—the near impossibility of generalizing concerning the content of religion. To almost any definition of religion offered, there are recognized religions which prove the exception. When one recalls the atheistic branches of Hinduism, the "ritualless" religion of the Quakers, the "nonmoral" aspects of fertility religions, the antitheological sects in Protestantism, as well as the claims of communism and "the democratic way of life" to religious devotion, one can see how seemingly unmanageable, indeed questionable, is the inclusive entity called religion.

Within the realm of religion itself, however, there had been a continuing attempt from the time of Kant's collapse of the theistic arguments to defend the legitimacy of religion philosophically from a post-Kantian perspective. Kant himself had prepared such a defense when in the second *Critique* he held God, immortality, and freedom to be legitimate postulates from the sense of duty, and in the third *Critique* he saw in the experience of beauty and sublimity a nonrational indication of suprasensible purposiveness in the universe. Where strict reason ended in antinomies, unique *sui generis* experiences, universal to the human species, provided entry into the realm of the noumenon.

It was Friedrich Schleiermacher (1768-1834) who saw the possibilities for religion here, writing *On Religion; Speeches to Its Cultured Despisers* (1799). Drawing from his own pietist heritage, he rejected religion as dogma, belief, metaphysics, ethics, or a combination of these. Religion is a unique experience belonging to the realm of "feeling" (Gefühl) or "affection." This primal feeling is of a "deeper unity with the whole," a sense of "absolute dependence" upon the Infinite and Eternal; from this sense of utter contingency morality flows as action and doctrine as reflection. Schleiermacher used this understanding as a foundation for interpreting Christianity in *The Christian Faith* (1821-1822), and this classic marked the beginning of liberal Protestant theology. Because this work overshadowed his *Speeches*, few recognized the importance of the latter for the emerging discipline of philosophy of religion.

During the past several decades, there have been increasing attempts by many anthropologists and sociologists to restore religion to integrity. Descriptive, nonvaluational studies of cultures have been rejected in favor of a cultural analysis and interpretation in terms of "cultural universals." Bronislaw Malinowski, for example, understands religion in terms of his "functional anthropology" as the universal and necessary response of man to the crises or mysteries of existence such as birth and death. Psychologists such as Carl Jung, Gordon Allport, and Erich Fromm see religion as a necessary component of harmonic psychic realization. Perhaps the best philosophic attempt in this endeavor, however, is Rudolf Otto's classic work, *The Idea of the Holy*. He stands solidly with Buber, Bergson, Tillich, and perhaps James, in the Kantian approach of Schleiermacher. His is no mere reduction or critique of religion, but an exposition of the universal experience called "religious," carefully documented from anthropology, psychology, and philosophy. It is a monumental apology for "religious experience" as a unique, legitimate, and necessary dimension of human existence.

Otto's work is misunderstood if seen, as some have, as an irrational approach to religion; rather, it is a rational analysis of the suprarational aspects uniquely characterizing the experience of the Divine. As he says, "This book, recognizing the profound import of the non-rational for metaphysic, makes a serious attempt to analyse all the more exactly the *feeling* which remains where the *concept* fails, and to introduce a terminology which is not any the more loose or indeterminate for having necessarily to make use of symbols." Otto clearly insists upon the necessity of reason, operating through analogy, in predicating attributes of the Divine. But even the most ardent rational theologians confess that such concepts do not comprehend God's deepest essence, which requires comprehension of a different sort. In forgetting this, Otto claims, orthodox Christians have most often given a one-sided, rationalistic interpretation of God. This has misled most thinkers into failing to see that of all human experience, the religious is "unmistakably specific and unique, peculiar to itself."

"Holiness" is that quality which Otto finds unique to the religious feeling. But since this term has come to mean "moral goodness," he has coined the word "numinous" to designate its original sense. This ingredient cannot be strictly defined, for as a feeling it must be evoked to be known. As a result, Otto's presuppositions are radical—since the religious cannot be reduced to anything but itself, only the person who can recall "a moment of deeply-felt religious experience" is in a position to understand religion, its uniqueness and its validity. Only with this common datum before the reader will Otto suggest continuing.

Schleiermacher's similar attempt to isolate this religious feeling, exhibiting it as "the feeling of absolute dependence," Otto finds inadequate on two counts. First, Schleiermacher's terminology is prone to subjectivism, failing to indicate the qualitative distinction between the religious awareness and analogous experiences between finite creatures. Otto finds the term "creature-consciousness" far more expressive of Schleiermacher's essential meaning— the "emotion of a creature, submerged and overwhelmed by its own nothingness in contrast to that which is supreme above all creatures." But more importantly, Schleiermacher inferred the fact of God from an experience exhibited as self-consciousness. To this Otto strenuously objects, for "creature-feeling" arises only when something "numinous" which is objective and external to the self is experienced as being present.

Otto's investigation indicates that the presence of the numinous is universally experienced as the "mysterium tremendum." This mysterious object can thus be "known" only by analyzing human feelings when in its presence. Otto's chosen term, "tremor," suggests fear, but his meaning is closer to "dread," "being aghast," or perhaps best, "awe." In primitive religions this element is evinced by "daemonic dread"; we still preserve something analogous in the terms "ghostly," "uncanny," or "supernatural." Old Testament references to divine wrath, jealousy, and anger are all reflections of this quality.

The second ingredient is that of "overpoweringness," "absolute unapproachability," or "majesty." From this awareness of one's nothingness emerges religious humility. Together these qualities produce the feeling of "creature-consciousness." The final ingredient is "urgency," the "energy" of the numinous object, the awareness of the numen as active, living, and willing. As analogies, Otto warns, these symbolic expressions of feeling dare not be taken for rational concepts; they are pointers and not containers of unique religious feeling. This idea is basic for Otto—we can *feel* the special character of the numen while being incapable of adequate conceptualization.

The more difficult aspect of Otto's designation to analyze is "mysterium." Otto's best alternative symbol is "the wholly other," that which is utterly beyond and yet elicits overwhelming astonishment. Here we perceive the basic religious polarity. Not only is there the quality of awe, overpowering-ness, that which "repels," but uniquely intertwined with it is that of fasci-nation. This is the Dionysiac element in all religions, the charm, the entrancement, the allurement, indeed, the intoxication, from which the ra-tional qualities of love, mercy, pity, and comfort emerge. Otto's imagination strains here for the precise word; he settles for "grace." It is ironic to Otto that previous analyses have usually not recognized this unique polarity, for without it worship cannot be understood. Dread alone can create only a worship of expiation and propitiation; man's yearning for the numinous object *for its own sake* would be totally inexplicable. Such analyses cannot deal with the intense fascination which is the mystical "moment," the experience of conversion, salvation, redemption. In this basic tension rests the awareness that God is not simply ground of all that can be thought, but is himself subject on his own account.

Otto not only draws from primitive and traditional religions for documen-tation but also uses analogous feelings from other realms for the sake of clarity. Above all it is Kant's analysis of the sublime which he finds best, for the sublime is likewise beyond adequate conceptualization and exhibits the same dual character. From such feelings, Otto attempts to show that while one feeling can give rise to a similar one, feelings themselves do not change. For example, moral obligation does not evolve from constraint by custom; these are qualitatively distinct. The idea of "ought" can arise only because there is an *a priori* potentially within man. Other feelings may arouse the moral sense, but they are not its explanation or cause. The same, Otto con-cludes, is true of the numinous feeling—it is *sui generis* and *a priori*, and is not derived from any other, although it may be stimulated.

Although the nonrational numinous feeling is the source of all religion, it is not its totality. As Kant showed Otto, nonrational data is schematized by rational concepts; in the same way a permanent connection is established between religious feeling and analogous feelings through the internal necessity of reason. The higher religions mark the most developed schematization of the universal numinous feeling.

Otto's most suggestive illustration of this view comes from music. At its base is a nonrational feeling, the wholly other aspect of which is schematized by reason according to more commonplace experiences; this schematization can be only partly successful, for its origin is an ever-mysterious, *sui generis* feeling. Here Otto makes an important point which others, like Buber, blur— the nonrational of music and the nonrational of the numinous dare not be confounded, for "each is something in its own right, independently of the other."

Man's response to the numinous is, on the one hand, the concomitant of creature-consciousness—the awareness of uncleanness, of sin, not from consciousness of any definite moral fault, but from a general "disvaluation" in the presence of the holy. On the other hand, there is the feeling of appreciation and praise of the numen in comparison. The holy thus possesses value in two senses: first, appreciation is the awareness of subjective value for the individual; second, the sense of awe is an awareness of objective value which claims homage. So understood, it appears that moral transgression is neither the source of man's search for redemption nor an adequate penetration into the feeling of the God-man relation. What is needed in the presence of the numen is atonement, a covering of nothing in particular but a freeing of the creature from profaneness, a rendering numinous of the approacher himself. The paradox of religion is that the absolute distinction between numen and creatures is overcome by God's admission of the creature into his presence— this is the meaning of grace for Otto.

There are two movements operating in the evolution of religion from its universal basis to its plethora of forms and manifestations. The first is a process totally within the nonrational sphere whereby primitive dread becomes worship and daemonic power becomes divine power. The second, which is subsidiary, is the process of rationalization and moralization on the basis of the primary numinous consciousness. It is this latter which has been traditionally called "the history of salvation." It is here that the holy is completed and filled, for it becomes likewise the good. One of Otto's basic concerns is to exhibit the dogmas of rational theology as simply conceptual attempts to clarify different aspects of this base feeling. Note, for example, one of his typical conclusions—"predestination we have found to be nothing but the intensified 'creature-feeling' in conceptual expression, and to be altogether rooted in the numinous consciousness."

It is helpful here to place Otto's psychological analysis within a philosophic whole. His work is best seen as the development of a fourth Kantian *Critique*. Throughout he is obedient to the Kantian analysis of reason and the process of knowing. What he is intent on exhibiting is the "objective" datum of the numinous as well as an *a priori* category of the holy within man. Thereby the fact of religious experience is preserved, its universality guaranteed, and the transcendent mystery of the Divine affirmed, while human symbols and concepts of the numinous are given a status commensurate with other modes of human apprehension. All Kantian categories have sense impression as their occasion, but never as their source; so it is with Otto's *a priori* of the holy, that predisposition of the human spirit which differs from both pure and practical reason. This distinction he sees Kant as having made in the *Critique of Judgment* (1790), defending there not "aesthetic" in the sense of "beautiful," but a separate "faculty of judgment based upon feeling of whatever sort from that of the understanding, from discursive, conceptual thought and inference." Religion, being grounded in feeling, shares this "objective validity, universality and necessity" exhibited by Kant.

Otto's "proof" of this is twofold: the introspectivve analysis that we have described, and his assumption of the general correctness of the Kantian *Critiques*. What must be seen is the radical difference between a universal potentiality (*a priori*) and a universal possession. The obvious lack of the latter, Otto maintains, has wrongly been seen as a disproof of the former; but maturation of the religious *a priori* has taken a large part of history, commensurate with the time required for the pure and practical realms. This *a priori* nature of the religious Otto applies to its nonrational and rational aspects, and to the inward, necessary interrelation of the two. As long as the numinous experience and its rational schematization occur in vital dialogue, they are true to both the numinous and the human spirit; in fact, this harmony Otto sees as the best criterion of the relative ranks of religion. Conceptualization, although always imperfect (for the experiential ground is ever wholly other), is possible, for the inborn capacity of each man may be aroused to a feeling of the numinous through the rational analogies of another. Schematization both reveals and communicates the feeling that is at its roots nonrational.

What Otto is intent on eliminating is the perennial distinction between general and special revelation, natural and historic religion. History and the individual are always in interrelation, the former providing the stimuli for the development of the *a priori* dispositions of the latter, the latter being thereby attuned to specific portions of history as manifestations of the holy. For Otto, they operate together or not at all.

Otto's work is not the only attempt of this sort; in fact, similar attempts, most of which have emerged from a clearly Christian context, have established the liberal wing of Protestant theology. On the one hand, most of these have failed to do justice to the claims of orthodoxy, and, on the other, they have not sufficiently escaped the narrowly apologetic predilections of that tradition to do justice to the general religious phenomenon. Otto's work more successfully escapes these limitations and comes as one of the best contemporary attempts to restore religion to the status of a *sui generis*, unique, and valid mode of experience and relations to reality.—*W.P.J.*

PERTINENT LITERATURE
Campbell, C. A. *On Selfhood and Godhood*. London: George Allen & Unwin, 1957.

A classic in its own right, *On Selfhood and Godhood* is an expanded version of the 1953-1954 and 1954-1955 Gifford Lectures presented by C. A. Campbell at the University of St. Andrews. The overall theme of the lecture series is the sphere of natural theology; that is, the related issues of whether knowledge of God, his nature, and his relationship to the world is possible. Campbell takes this complex of issues as being summarized by the question: Is religion true and, if it is, in what sense is it true?

In order to deal properly with the question, Campbell claims that he must first establish that the self is real, for without the existence of a substantial self the central religious claim that the soul exists and is immortal cannot be supported. Establishing that the self exists takes up the entire first set of lectures. In the course of his argument Campbell also sets forth his influential libertarian defense of free will. It is the second set of lectures, however, which is of most interest to the student of Rudolf Otto's thought. It is there that Campbell examines in detail Otto's doctrine of religious experience and finds it to be essential for establishing the objective validity of religion. Campbell's lectures, in addition, point out the limitations of Otto's approach to the issue of whether the numinous can have objective validity, and put forth an independent argument to establish this further end.

Even the first parts of the second lecture series, in which Otto is not directly dealt with, provide an important contribution for understanding Otto's thought. Campbell first argues that theism, as it is ordinarily understood, is the logical culmination of man's religious beliefs. The discussion thus narrowed, he then asks the question: Is rational theism self-contradictory? He interprets rational theism as the position that the attributes assigned to the theistic God have a literal meaning; and, based upon that interpretation, he argues that any being that is perfect cannot in any literal sense be assigned such attributes as thinking and willing. Willing, for example, implies a defect in the present situation and the envisioning of an improved future state of affairs. This in turn, however, implies that if God wills in a literal sense the previous state of affairs, it points to a deficiency in him. The God of literal theism must therefore ultimately be imbued with mystery, and once this is granted, one seems to be committed to the claim that his characteristics must be interpreted in a symbolic fashion.

Campbell thus argues that the true strength of a position such as Otto's is the recognition of the distinct overplus of meaning which is associated with the Holy. Otto's position in this regard is limited, however, by his inability to move beyond the strong claim for the nature of religious experience (a psychological claim) to an epistemological justification of that claim. According to Campbell, Otto correctly perceives that the suprarational is actually the source of the rational understanding of God, but he fails to provide an adequate argument for the objective validity of that source. Otto's Kantian use of the schema shows that the conceptual characteristics have their basis in an initial emotional encounter with the numinous. Introspection shows that this experience has subjective validity in that the religious experience is radically different from any other for the subject. In relation to the nature of the source of the experience, however, Campbell argues that the autonomy of the religious experience is not demonstrated. It is, for example, on the objective level very similar to certain kinds of dream experiences. Thus, to establish the objective validity of religion, a different sort of argument from one based on the *a priori* nature of religious experiences is necessary.

The concluding lectures attempt to show that the argument can be established on the basis of a parallel to the type of metaphysical argument used to make claims about that which is ultimately real and on the basis of the moral argument for the existence of God as the source of an objectively valid morality. For the student of Otto, the important insight here is that Campbell rejects the notion of the *a priori* as it is employed by Otto and shows an alternative way to obtain the same conclusion.

According to Campbell, none of this is significant, however, without the foundation of Otto's account of the religious experience. Campbell's work thus has a twofold value for the student of Otto: it clarifies the distinction which needs to be made between the psychological and the epistemological issues in *The Idea of the Holy*, and it demonstrates why Otto's account of the religious experience is so vital for any adequate understanding of the philosophy of religion.

Davidson, Robert F. *Rudolf Otto's Interpretation of Religion*. Princeton, New Jersey: Princeton University Press, 1947.

Robert F. Davidson's book is a comprehensive and systematic study of Rudolf Otto's thought, the first to appear in English and still the most complete exposition of Otto's philosophy of religion. Through a far-reaching examination it demonstrates that Otto's *The Idea of the Holy* represents a creative synthesis of all the major trends in modern German theology. Davidson argues that Otto's major contribution to the synthesis is his emphasis on the concept of religious autonomy. It is the idea of religious autonomy which gives Otto's mature position unity and originality and which points to the ultimate deficiency in his analysis. In the concluding chapters of the book Davidson therefore moves beyond Otto, but he does so always from a sympathetic perspective. His approach is concerned to show how Otto's writings can be made more complete and consistent, given that Otto himself was not interested in providing a systematic philosophy of religion.

Otto's main aim was to provide an understanding of the concrete religious experience, using an approach which can best be described as phenomenological; that is, he looked at the phenomenon of religion as it presents itself to the experiencing subject. In doing so he called on a wide range of theological literature and descriptions of the religious experience from diverse cultural contexts. Davidson begins his examination of the background which shaped Otto's thinking with Martin Luther's breakthrough to an emphasis on faith, which showed that purely rational and conceptual knowledge must of necessity be incomplete in the realm of religion. From there he traces the notion of religious autonomy as it developed in the Romanticism of Friedrich Schleiermacher and in the modified Kantianism of Albrecht Ritschl. In the context of influences on Otto's thought he devotes an entire chapter to the idealism of Jacob Fries, who attempted to free religion from the moral imperative which Immanuel Kant had established in *Critique of Pure Reason*.

It is Fries, Davidson argues, who established the immediate background for both Otto's major contribution to theology and his major metaphysical difficulty. Fries had argued that only religious insight can bridge the gap between the phenomenal and the noumenal realms, thereby giving religious experience an apparent priority over other forms of experience. Otto believed, however, that Fries had not gone far enough because the autonomy established in this way was still on the level of reason and therefore lacked a peculiarly religious character. The autonomous religious categories of a sense of sanctity, an awareness of sin, and the recognition that salvation is assured, Otto believed, can only find their expression in the completely emotional quality which the experience of the numinous provides. This immediate apprehension transcends a limited rational understanding, being encompassed only by a special and unique faculty which Otto called divination. Otto argued for the validity of this category on the basis of an adaptation from Kant's interpretation of knowledge. The experience of the numinous is, he claimed, *a priori*; that is, it provides an objective claim to the truth of that knowledge independent of the specific forms of experience. He then linked this numinous insight to the rational/moral side of God through a process of analogy or schematization.

Davidson finds Otto's adaptation of the Kantian concepts of the *a priori* and schematism utterly confused. He argues that this connection cannot be made on a Kantian foundation once the complete severing of the numinous from the rational side of the Holy has been granted. In the concluding chapters he therefore presents what might be termed a doctrine of "modified autonomy" based on Otto's original insight. The categories of the numinous must be seen as functioning as a binding force in the very genesis of rational values. In this way, he claims, the superiority and consequent autonomy of the religious categories can be retained, while at the same time they are explicitly related to the rational side of experience. Contrary to Otto, he thus argues that the moral element is present in the religious experience from the start. What needs to be established is not a separation of the Kantian connection between morality and religion, but rather a reevaluation to determine which element has priority in the relationship. Davidson, given his interpretation of the centrality of religious autonomy in Otto's thought, is thus willing to modify Otto's claim regarding the complete disjunction of the religious and the moral in order to retain the metaphysical coherency of the position as a whole.

Reeder, John P., Jr. "The Relation of the Moral and the Numinous in Otto's Notion of the Holy," in *Religion and Morality*. Edited by Gene Outka and John P. Reeder, Jr. Garden City, New York: Anchor Books, 1973.

In a volume which raises the issue of the relationship between religion and morality, the essay by John P. Reeder, Jr., on Rudolf Otto's thought has a prominent place, because in Otto's work some of the major difficulties associated with the issue come to the fore. Reeder's overall claim is that Otto's attempt to make the numinous the ground and the source of the moral is bound to fail, primarily because of the fact that it necessitates conceptualization of that which by its very nature is not conceptualizable. Reeder thus rejects on principle the general thesis put forth by Robert F. Davidson in his commentary on Otto's *The Idea of the Holy*.

Otto had seen the Holy as consisting of two elements or aspects, the numinous and the rational/moral. The question at issue for Reeder is how these two aspects can be related and what resultant claims are possible about man's moral obligations based on God's will. Can man ever know what these obligations are? Can there be any obligations at all? In Otto's attempt to answer the questions, Reeder finds a permanent dilemma. It seems that if God has a dual nature, both numinous and rational, then man cannot know what God's will is, since the immediate numinous experience which is given priority by Otto does not relate man to God's moral injunctions. If, on the other hand, God has only one nature which is in some sense subject to predication, then Otto must explain how this is possible when the numinous has been characterized as eluding all conceptualizations.

It is clear that by means of this procedure Reeder emphasizes an inherent ambiguity in Otto's thought. When Otto wrote of the numinous experience his account, being linked to an insight by the subject, was able to make use of immediate feelings and intuitions. When, however, he spoke of the numinous as an objective referent, a subjective account was no longer adequate. He therefore turned to Immanuel Kant's notion of schematization, which linked pure concepts to the objects of experience. According to Reeder, however, a radically different problem faced Kant, and therefore Otto's application ultimately failed. Kant wanted to relate formal *a priori* categories to the experience of the world. The schemata were a way to make that experience intelligible. Otto, on the other hand, had to show that the rational and the numinous are linked objectively in one idea, the idea of the Holy. For Kant the issue was thus one of application, while for Otto it was one of coordination. Kant's procedure thus cannot by itself justify the assumed co-ordination. Ultimately, Otto thus had to resort to the claim that the link was a self-evident, *a priori* one, utilizing another adaptation from Kant. Again, however, the transfer cannot work, according to Reeder, since the use of the *a priori* is for Kant a way of interpreting the world conceptually, while the numinous, which must be an essential aspect of the *a priori* recognition, escapes all conceptualization.

Reeder's thesis might thus be summarized as the claim that application of Kant's categories is illegitimate in all cases when they are applied to the nonconceptual. The numinous aspect of the Holy, however, is by definition nonconceptual. Therefore the Holy cannot be analyzed using Kantian categories, and Otto's claim reduces to an unjustified, and probably unjustifiable, assertion. The only possible escape is to give the conceptual priority, and Reeder finds some indication of this in Otto's later work *Freedom and Necessity*. This shift in priorities, however, necessitates rejection of the complete autonomy of the numinous, which Reeder finds to be irreconcilable with Otto's intentions in *The Idea of the Holy.—H.C.L.*

ADDITIONAL RECOMMENDED READING

Benz, Ernst, ed. *Rudolf Otto's Bedeutung für die Religionswissenschaft und die Theologie Heute.* Leiden, The Netherlands: E. J. Brill, 1971. A series of essays on Otto's thought in honor of his one-hundredth birthday.

Diamond, Malcolm L. *Contemporary Philosophy and Religious Thought.* New York: McGraw-Hill Book Company, 1974. The section on Otto in this excellent introduction to the philosophy of religion summarizes some of the main criticisms of Otto's thought.

Moore, John M. *Theories of Religious Experience with Special Reference to James, Otto, and Bergson.* New York: Round Table Press, 1938. An early epistemological critique of Otto's thought.

Otto, Rudolf. *Religious Essays: A Supplement to 'The Idea of the Holy'.* Translated by Brian Dunn. London: Oxford University Press, 1931. A set of essays clarifying the main ideas in Otto's earlier work.

Paton, Herbert J. *The Modern Predicament.* London: George Allen & Unwin, 1955. In a short section on Otto, the famous Kant scholar points out some major difficulties in Otto's appropriation of Kant.

Turner, Harold W. *Rudolf Otto, 'The Idea of the Holy': A Guide for Students.* Aberdeen: Aberdeen Peoples Press, 1974. A short chapter-by-chapter commentary, intended specifically for the student.

INTRODUCTION TO MATHEMATICAL PHILOSOPHY

Author: Bertrand Russell (1872-1970)
Type of work: Philosophy of mathematics
First published: 1919

PRINCIPAL IDEAS ADVANCED
Mathematics can be shown to be a logical development of certain basic ideas; mathematics can be reduced to logic.

The number of a class is the class of all those classes which are similar to it. (Classes are similar when their members can be put into a one-to-one relation with each other.)

A relation is symmetrical when if one thing has the relation to another, the other has the same relation to it; a relation is transitive when if one thing has the relation to a second, and the second has the same relation to a third, the first has the relation to the third. (Other relations are defined.)

An infinite cardinal number satisfies the equation, n *equals* n *plus* 1. *(An infinite collection has parts which have as many terms as the infinite collection itself.)*

By distinguishing between types of entities it is possible to avoid paradoxes which have perplexed philosophers for centuries.

Mathematical truths are a priori *and have nothing to do with facts about the world; they are logical tautologies.*

Bertrand Russell wrote three books on mathematical philosophy: *Principles of Mathematics* (1903); *Principa Mathematica* (with A. N. Whitehead, 1910-1913); and *Introduction to Mathematical Philosophy.* The last of these is substantially a condensation and simplification of the second, which is a large three-volume work (with a contemplated fourth volume which never appeared), expressed almost wholly in specially devised symbols and containing formal proofs showing that mathematics can be "reduced" to logic. Since these proofs are somewhat formidable for one not versed in mathematics and not having an aptitude for mathematical symbolism, Russell attempted in the present book to acquaint the reader with the main results of the earlier study in a language which, while necessarily technical, does not require either the understanding of formal proofs or the ability to manipulate abstract symbols.

The general thesis of the book is that we can start with the familiar portions of mathematics, say, such a statement as "2 plus 2 equals 4," and go either "up" into higher mathematics, leading to the consideration of fractions, real numbers, complex numbers, infinite numbers, integration, and differentiation, or "down" into lower mathematics, leading through analysis to notions of greater abstractness and greater logical simplicity. The latter route, which is the approach adopted primarily in recent mathematics, and consequently less familiar to nonmathematicians, asks not what can be defined and deduced when we assume that 2 plus 2 equals 4 but what more general ideas and principles can be found in terms of which 2 plus 2 equals 4 can be defined and deduced. In other words, the most obvious and easy things in mathematics do not come logically at the beginning, but somewhere in the middle, just as the bodies which are easiest to see are neither those which are very near nor those which are very far, but those which are at a "moderate" distance. The easiest conceptions to grasp in mathematics are neither the complex and intricate ideas nor the logically simple and abstract ideas, but the common-sense notions involved in the whole numbers.

The reason why such a study can be called "mathematical *philosophy*" is to be found in the fact that although many of the notions considered in this type of investigation—*number, class, relation, order, continuity, infinity*—have been traditionally examined by philosophers, without (according to Russell) very much success, interesting results can be obtained when the methods of speculative philosophers are replaced by the more refined and precise methods of the mathematicians and logicians. In order to stress his point Russell frequently argues that these newer conceptions render the traditional philosophical problems insoluble, or perhaps meaningless.

(Because of the fact that the book is already a condensation of a much larger work, no systematic survey of its contents is possible without reducing the work to a series of more or less meaningless definitions and postulates. The attempt will be made, therefore, in what follows, not to cover the book in its entirety but to extract certain typical problems and show how Russell formulates them and solves them.)

Perhaps the best example of Russell's mathematical philosophy is his definition, following Giuseppe Peano, of the notion of the natural numbers. One could hardly imagine a concept which would seem clearer to the ordinary man than that exemplified by the series:

0, 1, 2, 3, . . . *n, n* plus 1 . . . Yet Peano shows that though this notion is familiar it is not understood. It can be reduced, in fact, to three primitive ideas and five primitive propositions. The notion involved in the use of "primitive" must first be explained.

Since all terms that are defined are defined only by means of other terms, we must accept some terms as initially clear in order to have a starting point for our definitions. This procedure does not require that these latter terms be *incapable* of definition, for we might have stopped too soon and we might be able to define them if we go further. On the other hand, there *may be* certain terms which are logically simple in the sense that they cannot be analyzed into any other terms. The decision between these two possibilities is not important for logic; all that is needed is the knowledge that since human powers are finite, definitions must always begin with some terms which are at least undefined at the moment, though perhaps not permanently.

Primitive *propositions* have the same status. Whenever we prove propositions to be true, we do so by reducing them to other propositions, which must themselves be proved by reducing them to still other propositions. Ultimate proof, therefore, presumably cannot be achieved unless we assume certain propositions to be self-evident. But mathematicians have quite generally abandoned the notion of "self-evidence" since it seems to rest on psychological rather than on logical considerations, and permits truth to vary from individual to individual. However, they have granted that there must be in any formal system certain propositions, unusally called "postulates," which are unproved *within the system*, though they may be provable by going to still more basic postulates *outside the system*.

Peano's three primitive ideas are "0," "number," and "successor." These ideas can be illustrated, though not defined, in terms of the natural numbers. For example, by "successor" he means the relation which holds between 1 and 0 when we say that 1 is the successor of 0, and between 1 and 2 when we say that 2 is the successor of 1.

Peano's five primitive propositions are:

(1) 0 is a number.

(2) The successor of any number is a number.

(3) No two numbers have the same successor.

(4) 0 is not the successor of any number.

(5) Any property which belongs to 0, and also to the successor of every number which has the property, belongs to all the numbers.

Several remarks about this definition of "number" are in order. In the first place, the five primitive propositions enable us to extend the series indefinitely, since by (2) a number *always* has a successor, and by (3) no new successor obtained can be one of the previous numbers, and by (4) zero can occur only as the first member of the series. Postulate (5) is the familiar principle of mathematical induction which enables us to prove that a certain theorem which is true of 0, and when true of 0 is true of 1, and so on, must be true of all numbers.

In the second place, Peano's system, while it is exemplified by the natural numbers, does not apply to them uniquely. In fact, it proves to be an *abstract* system in the sense that it need have no interpretation at all, or it may have a variety of different interpretations. For example the series,

$$0, 2, 4, 6, 8, \ldots$$
$$1, \tfrac{1}{2}, \tfrac{1}{4}, \tfrac{1}{8}, \ldots$$

would exemplify Peano's axioms, though in such instances the notions "0," "number," and "successor" would take on different meanings. Indeed, the biblical series,

$$\text{Adam, Cain, Enoch, Irad} \ldots$$

would constitute an exemplification of his axioms provided the notion of "successor" is properly defined, and that there are certain hereditary properties which are always transmitted to the male offspring. Any series which possesses the properties defined by the postulates is called a "progression," and there are obviously very many instances of progressions in the world.

In the third place, all traditional pure mathematics may be shown to contain only propositions about the natural numbers. This indicates the fundamental importance of what Peano succeeded in doing.

Finally, since Peano's axioms do not guarantee that there will be anything in the world which exemplifies them, and since we want our numbers to be such as can be used for the purpose of counting common objects, we should supplement Peano's work by making it into a theory of arithmetic. This was done by another mathematician, named Gottlob Frege. It requires the introduction of the notion of "class." A class may be defined in two ways: by enumerating its members—say, Brown, Jones, and Robinson—or by mentioning a defining property, as when we speak of "inhabitants of London." The former is called "extensional," the latter "intensional." The latter is more fundamental, since extension can always be reduced to intension, but intension often cannot, even theoretically, be reduced to extension. This is important for the definition of numbers, for numbers themselves form an infinite collection and cannot be enumerated. Furthermore, it is probably true (though this cannot be demonstrated) that there is an infinite number of collections in the world—for example, an infinite number of pairs. Finally, we wish to define "number" in such a way as to permit the existence of infinite numbers as well as finite ones, and this requires that we be able to speak of the terms in an infinite collection by means of a property which is common to all its members and peculiar to them.

Proceeding in this way, Russell shows how it is possible to demonstrate when two classes "have the same number"—that is, exhibit a property in terms of which their number could be defined. This can be done by showing that the classes are "similar," where "similarity" is defined in terms of having a one-to-one relation to each other. For example, in countries where neither polygamy nor polyandry is permitted, the relation "spouse of" constitutes a relation on the basis of which the class of married men can be shown to be similar to the class of married women. The use of this criterion does not require that we be able to *count* either class, and we can know that the number of married men is the same as the number of married women without knowing the number of either. The notion of similarity is therefore logically more simple than the notion of counting, though not necessarily more familiar. If we now make a bundle of all pairs, of all trios, and of all quartets, and then extend this to a bundle of all classes that have only one member (unit classes), and to a bundle of all classes that have no members (null classes), we could then go on to say that by "2" we mean the property which is common to all pairs, by "3" we mean the property which is common to all trios, and so on. However, Russell does not choose to do so because he is afraid that if we suppose some property in nature which we call "twoness" we may be unconsciously creating a metaphysical entity whose existence is debatable. Of the class of couples we can be sure, but of the metaphysical 2 we cannot. Therefore, he defines the number "2" simply as the *class* of all couples, not as the *property* which they all possess. And, more generally, *the number of a class is the class of all those classes which are similar to it.* This definition sounds odd, but it is precise and indubitable and can be shown to apply to the world in such a way as to make arithmetic possible.

Another idea which Russell examines is that of "relation." There are many different kinds of relations, each having its own properties and uses. For example, certain relations are *symmetrical*. A relation, R, holding between a and b is symmetrical if when aRb, then bRa. For example, the relation "spouse of" is symmetrical but the relation "father of" is asymmetrical. Certain relations are *transitive*. A relation, R, is transitive if when aRb and bRc, then aRc. For example, the relation "ancestor of" is transitive, but the relation "father of" is intransitive. Certain relations are *connected*. A relation, R, is connected with regard to a class of objects a,b,c,d . . . if taking *any* two terms from the class, say, a and c, then either aRc or cRa. Thus, if I take any two integers, one is smaller and the other is greater, but this is not true of complex numbers; if I take any two *moments* of time, one must be earlier than the other, but of two *events* in time this is not the case since they may be simultaneous.

On the basis of this discussion of the concept of "relation" Russell shows how we can define "order." In a sense "to order" means "to arrange," and all orders, therefore, are as arbitrary as are arrangements. But when we say that we are ordering the natural numbers, we are really looking for certain relations between them, which themselves generate a certain arrangement. "We can no more 'arrange' the natural numbers than we can the starry heavens; but just as we may notice among the fixed stars either their order of brightness or their distribution in the sky, so there are various relations among numbers which may be observed, and which give rise to various different orders among numbers, all equally legitimate." Ordering, therefore, is an operation which is performed on a class when we discover a relation which holds among its members and which has certain characteristics. The notion of *progression*, which was mentioned earlier, is a special case of a class which is ordered on the basis of a relation which is asymmetrical, transitive, and connected.

The notion of "infinity," which has puzzled philosophers since the days of the Greeks, can easily be defined. There are many different kinds and levels of infinite numbers, and only the simplest, the infinite cardinal numbers, are examined. Russell points out that what he had previously called the "natural" numbers can also be called the "inductive" numbers, such usage indicating merely that we are naming the numbers in terms of Peano's fifth postulate rather than in terms of something else. The principle of mathematical induction can be crudely stated in the form, "what can be inferred from next to next can be inferred from first to last."

Suppose that we now take under consideration the collection of the inductive numbers themselves. This collection cannot itself have as its number one of the inductive numbers, for if we suppose n to be any inductive number, the inclusion of zero in our collection compels us to say that the number of such a collection will be n plus 1. Hence, the number of inductive numbers is a new number, which is different from all of them and is not possessed of all inductive properties. This number is called an "infinite cardinal number" and its unusual character is shown in the fact that it satisfies the equation, n equals n plus 1. A class possessing such characteristics is called a *"reflexive"* class (one which is similar to a proper part of itself) and the number of such a class is a reflexive cardinal number. A still more surprising characteristic of an infinite cardinal number is that it satisfies the equation, n equals $2n$. For example, the number of *even* inductive numbers is the same as the number of *all* inductive numbers, both odd and even. Leibniz used this fact to prove that infinite numbers are impossible, but modern mathematical logicians use it only to show that the commonly accepted belief that the whole is greater than one of its parts is really not true and is based on an unperceived vagueness in some of its terms.

Granting the existence of infinite numbers (Russell limits himself to lower-order infinites, that is, infinite cardinals) an interesting question arises: Does there exist in the world a class the number of whose members is infinite? An affirmative answer to this question *appears* to be demonstrable. Assume that the number of individuals (the meaning of the term "individual" is left undefined for the moment) is some finite number, say n. Now there are mathematical truths which inform us, first, that, given a class of n members there are 2^n ways of selecting some of its members (including the extreme cases where we select all or none), and, second, that 2^n is always greater than n. If we now start with a class of n members, then add to this the class of classes that may be formed from n, namely, 2^n, then add the class of classes of classes that may be formed from this, namely, 2^{2n}, and so on, we shall have a total whose number is the infinite cardinal. Hence, the number of "things" in the world is infinite.

Russell confesses that he formerly believed this to be a valid proof. But he now rejects it because it involves what has come to be called the "confusion of types." The fallacy consists in the formation of "impure" classes. If there are n *individuals* in the world, and 2^n *classes* of individuals, we cannot form a new class whose number is n plus 2^n. Classes are logical constructions, not things, and the two "types" cannot be combined. Plato argued that since the number 1 has being, but is not identical with being, 1 plus being equals 2; then 1 plus 2 equals 3; and so on; hence the world is infinite. Two mathematicians, Bernard Bolzano and Richard Dedekind, argued that because ideas of things are "things," and because there is an idea of every thing, the class of "things" is a reflexive class (since it is similar to a part of itself) and its number must be infinite. Russell tries to show not only that these "proofs" have an air of hocus-pocus about them, but also that unless we prevent this confusion of types we shall be able to prove all sorts of self-contradictory statements—for example, that if a class is a member of itself, it is not a member of itself. One way to avoid both the feeling of uneasiness and the paradoxes is to define the word "individual" as referring to an entity of a certain "type," the word "class" as referring to an entity of another type, the word "relation" as referring to an entity of still another type, and so on.

The problem which Russell here formulates has given rise in recent literature to the distinction between languages and metalanguages, a metalanguage being a language which talks about a language. It then becomes important not to confuse these two "types" of language because absurdities and paradoxes may develop if we do.

In conclusion, Russell returns to the general question concerning the nature of mathematical philosophy and its relations to logic and empirical knowledge. Mathematics, formerly defined as the science of quantity, can no longer be so defined. Many branches of geometry have nothing to do with quantity, and even arithmetic, which is commonly thought to deal with numbers, concerns itself rather with the more basis ideas of one-to-one relations and similarity between classes. The generalization of the notion of order also means that mathematics is no longer particularly concerned with the number series.

What, then, is this new study which starts with mathematics and ends with discussions of classes, relations, and series? It may be called indifferently either "logic" or "mathematics"; the choice of name is not important. But its *characteristics* should be clarified.

In the first place, it does not deal with particular things or particular properties. It tells us that 1 plus 1 equals 2 but not that Socrates and Plato are two. A world in which there are no individuals would still be a world in which one and one are two. Traditional logic which tells us "All men are mortal and Socrates is a man" implies that "Socrates is mortal." But it does not tell us that all men *are* mortal or that Socrates really *is* a man. Thus the validity of a syllogism is independent of the truth or falsity of its premises. We try to express this by representing the *form* of the syllogism, independent of its *content*. We say, "No matter what values x and A and B may have, if all A's are B's and x is an A, then x is a B." We realize that the argument is valid for all individuals without the necessity for demonstrating it for Socrates and Plato and all the rest of the individuals, and it is valid for cats and four-legged creatures without demonstrating it for each particular cat. We can say that the "form" of a proposition is that which remains unchanged when every constituent of the proposition is replaced by another. The proposition "Socrates is earlier than Aristotle" has the same form as "Napoleon is greater than Wellington." In every language there are certain words whose function is merely to indicate form. These are called "logical constants." For example, the word "is" in the proposition "Socrates is human" is a logical constant. In pure mathematics the only constants which occur are logical constants. In this sense, therefore, logic and mathematics are one.

But in the second place, both mathematics and logic deal with propositions of a peculiar sort, quite different from those which are commonly called "empirical." They may be called "tautologies," though Russell confesses that he does not know how to define this term. (One of Russell's students, Ludwig Wittgenstein, later did define the term.) They are propositions which we seem to be able to know without any appeal to experience; for example, we know that the syllogism about Socrates is valid merely be examining the argument in its abstract form, not by appealing to experience. But this is merely a fact about the way in which we know such propositions, not about the propositions themselves. Russell admits that this analysis brings him to the very frontier of knowledge, that he cannot give a more precise definition of logical truths. He feels that these propositions are in some sense *a priori* and that they can be said to be analytic, providing we adopt a new meaning for this term. But he feels that he cannot define them in spite of being quite familiar with the kind of property which he is trying to define. He ends by apologizing for his inability to make the subject matter of the book clear without the use of technical words, but he expresses the hope that readers will not hesitate to acquire the mastery which is necessary for such understanding.—*A.C.B.*

PERTINENT LITERATURE

Strawson, Peter F. "On Referring," in *Mind*. LIX, no. 235 (July, 1950), pp. 320-344.

In Chapter 16 on "Descriptions" in *Introduction to Mathematical Philosophy*, Bertrand Russell offered his famous theory of (definite) descriptions. Peter F. Strawson's "On Referring" is a detailed (if also controversial) critique of Russell's widely accepted theory.

Strawson explains Russell's theory in these terms. Although there is currently no French king, the sentence "The king of France is wise" apparently is significant or meaningful or not nonsense. One question Russell's theory was intended to answer is: How can this sentence be meaningful when there is no king of France? To put the query generally: How can a sentence of the form "The X is Y" be meaningful when there is nothing to which "the X" refers?

One answer, Strawson notes, is given by the following argument: Suppose we use S to refer to the sentence "The king of France is wise." "The king of France" is the subject of S. So if S is a significant sentence, it is a sentence about the king of France. If, however, there is not in any sense a king of France, S is not about anything (including the king of France). Now S is significant. So there must, in some sense or other, be a king of France.

Another argument to the same intent, Strawson notes, goes as follows: S is significant. A significant sentence is either true or false, so S is either true or false. S is true if the king of France is wise, and S is false if the king of France is not wise. The king of France is wise or not wise, however, only if in some sense there is such a being. So, in some sense, there is a king of France.

Strawson reminds us that Russell, not surprisingly, is not persuaded by either of these arguments, nor does he accept—any more than does Strawson himself—the peculiar conclusion which they share. Still, Strawson continues, Russell's reasons for rejecting these arguments are more interesting than the sheer fact that he does reject them. Russell offers an analysis of S which is intended to preserve S's significance without falling prey to any such conclusion as these arguments proffer.

What this Russellian analysis amounts to, Strawson explains, goes as follows: One who asserts S is asserting: (1) There is a king of France; (2) there is not more than one king of France; (3) there is nothing which is king of France and not wise. Strawson suggests that Russell arrived at this analysis of S by inquiring as to what conditions there are under which S will be true; these, (1)-(3) are intended to capture. Strawson grants that (1)-(3) state *necessary* conditions of S's being true.

Further, Strawson continues, one can see how, on this analysis, S will turn out to be meaningful or significant even though its subject term does not meet with referential success. For, on Russell's view, if there is nothing to which "the king of France" refers, then (1) is false. If (1) is false, S is false; and if S is false, then S is meaningful or significant. *Being false* is as much a modality of *being meaningful* as is *being true*.

Still further, Strawson notes, one who offers a Russellian analysis of S will be in a good position to reject the arguments noted above. Why? Strawson is not detailed in his exposition of this, but the answer is clear enough. Russell's analysis allows for referential failure to establish meaningfulness as nicely as does referential success. If one says "The A is B" and there is no A, then what one says is false, since "the A" (so to speak) attempts to denote something but does not. By cutting the connection between significance and referential success, Russell cuts the nerve of both of the arguments noted above, each of which requires that significance and referential success be necessarily connected.

For all its plausibility and popularity among philosophers, Strawson contends, Russell's analysis is faulty. In explaining why he thinks this, he distinguishes between *a sentence*, a *use* of a sentence, and an *utterance* of a sentence. S is a sentence. If John uttered S during the reign of Louis XIV, Jean uttered

S during the reign of Louis XV, and Joseph uttered S yesterday, then not only do we have three utterances of S, but, since we also have three uses of S, there is no problem about these utterances having different truth values. Thus if Louis XIV was wise and Louis XV foolish, John will have uttered a truth and Jean will have uttered a falsehood. If John and Mary utter S simultaneously, each will have used the same sentence; in such a case, there is one use but two utterances, and each utterance will have the same truth value as the other.

More carefully, Strawson contends that, strictly speaking, sentences themselves are neither true nor false, but we use sentences to express true or false propositions. Further, he suggests, *a sentence* is not about some person, but a particular *use* of a sentence determines who it is (in that use) about. (Given John's use, S was about Louis XIV; given Jean's use, S was about Louis XV.)

Given this set of distinctions, Strawson believes that we can see what is correct and what is incorrect in Russell's theory of descriptions. Russell, Strawson believes, is correct in contending that S is significant and that one now uttering S makes a true assertion only if there is now exactly one person who is king of France and wise. Strawson adds, however, that Russell was wrong in thinking that anyone who now uttered S would be making a true or a false assertion.

Rather, Strawson claims, the truth or falsity of S simply would not arise, because there is no king of France. The view, then, is that if one says "The X is A" when there is no X, what one says is neither true nor false. Strawson asserts, then, that S is significant, although no present use of S will succeed in making an assertion that is false (or an assertion that is true). The reason S is nevertheless significant or meaningful, Strawson tells us, is that S could be used, in certain circumstances, to say something true or false. Thus Strawson believes he has offered a theory which shares with Russell's the advantage of rejecting the viewpoint expressed in the two arguments mentioned earlier, and accounts better for the puzzlement he thinks we would and should feel were we to hear someone now utter S seriously.

Strawson's rather complex essay considers these (and other) matters in more detail, and Russell replied to Strawson in a lively chapter of *My Philosophical Development* entitled "Mr. Strawson on Referring," to which the reader is referred for further discussion of these issues.

Reichenbach, Hans. "Bertrand Russell's Logic," in *The Philosophy of Bertrand Russell*. Edited by Paul A. Schilpp. New York: Harper & Row Publishers, 1963.

Hans Reichenbach, having begun by expressing his appreciation for the clarity of and his essential agreement with the content of Bertrand Russell's views, offers an exposition of some of Russell's fundamental views in logic.

The first phase of modern logic, Reichenbach declares, began with the work of George Boole. It included the work of Augustus de Morgan, Charles Sanders Peirce, Giuseppe Peano, Georg Cantor, Gottlob Frege, and Arthur Schröder. The second phase, he informs us, is to be dated from Russell's logical works. He adds that there are several reasons for this: various technical improvements that Russell introduced, the creation in his work of a symbolic logic claiming to include all of mathematics, a "skillfully chosen notation," and a brilliant writing style.

Reichenbach turns, then, to technical improvements. One of these is the concept of a *propositional function*. (A propositional function—for example, *X is blue*—is an expression containing one or more constituents having no determined value, such that when they are given a determined value—as in, *My cat is blue*—turn out to be either true or false.) Russell included in this notion not only a view of grammatical predicates as defining classes but also a view of relations as defining classes. Russell used this notion, Reichenbach reminds us, in his theory of descriptional functions (according to which *The friendly fool paid the bill* becomes *There is an x such that x is friendly and x is a fool and x paid the bill, and for any y, if y is friendly, a fool, and paid the bill, then y is the same as x*). Relational predicates (such as, *is smaller than Mary*, as in *John is smaller than Mary*, which could be partially symbolized as *There is an x and a y such that x is John and y is Mary and x is smaller than y*) also can appear in such descriptions, thus giving Russell's analysis of descriptions great generality.

Another technical improvement, Reichenbach notes, is Russell's use of material implication. This logical relation, long known and realized to have somewhat peculiar consequences, and previously shown not to lead to mistaken results, was first used by Russell, Reichenbach reports, to develop a whole system of logic.

Material implication can be defined as follows. Let "p" and "q" be sentence-variables, or "stand-ins" for declarative sentences. One can define "material implication"—usually symbolized by "⊃"—by stating the conditions under which "p⊃q" will be true. This is done by saying that "p⊃q" will be true unless "p" is true and "q" is false. More strictly, a statement of material implication constructed by replacing "p" by a declarative sentence and replacing "q" by a declarative sentence will be true unless the sentence that replaces "p" expresses a truth and the sentence that replaces "q" expresses a falsehood. As Reichenbach notes, this produces the surprising result that the sentence *"Snow is black" materially implies "Sugar is green"* is true, since *Snow is black* is false and only material implications of the pattern *truth-materially-implies-falsehood* are false. Reichenbach hints, however, that what is important is that one will not get the result of true premises leading to a false conclusion if one constructs one's system of logic in such a way that premises-to-conclusion derivations are constructed by use of implication; no argument-form or argument-structure will be sanctioned as valid if an argument of that form or structure can have true premises and a false conclusion.

Reichenbach explains that Russell's rationale for using material implication was to develop a logic which was extensional, or whose predicates were construed extensionally, although Russell realized he was taking but one step in this direction. (The *extension* of the predicate *red* is all the things that are red.)

Russell, Reichenbach adds, claims to have shown that mathematics is part of logic. The argument for this thesis, he notes, comes in two steps. The first comes in terms of defining the positive integers, using only purely logical concepts, including the operators *all* and *there is*. The second step consists in showing that the whole of mathematics (in an appropriate sense of "reducible") is reducible to the concept of natural number. Reichenbach compares Russell's achievement in this regard, which he regards only as an *in principle* reduction of mathematics to logic, to the achievement of Niels Bohr's theory of the atom in unifying physics and chemistry (also only in principle).

Reichenbach discusses the first step of Russell's reduction. He explains that Russell, using Cantor's notion of similarity of classes, defines *two classes, A and B, have the same number (of members)* as *it is possible to establish a one-to-one correspondence between the elements in A and the elements in B*. Suppose *A* contains Alvin, Albert, and Alan, and *B* contains Bill, Bob, and Bert; then *A* and *B* have the same number. Further, Reichenbach explains, the class of all classes having the same number of members as *A*, or as *B*, constitutes the number *3*. Thus, Reichenbach notes, Russell regards a number as a class of classes. A statement saying that something has a number-property is thus translatable without remainder into a statement saying that this thing is a member of a particular (second-order) class, or class of classes.

This definition of number, Reichenbach remarks, results from an application of a principle Russell made into a cornerstone of logic; namely, the *principle of abstraction*. The usual notion of abstraction involved considering some property shared by various items, Reichenbach notes; but for this Russell substitutes the notion of a class which is comprised by all the objects that have some particular relation to one another. This substitution, Reichenbach emphasizes, again substitutes extensionality for intensionality.

Rather than trying to define the term "green," according to Russell, one can point to a green item *A* and say that something is green if it is the same color as *A*. The idea is that "green" has no meaning besides that given it by this procedure; it has no intension. The denial that there is any meaning other than that given the term "green" by the procedure indicated, Reichenbach claims, is a standard example of the use of Ockham's razor.

This is also true, Reichenbach continues, of Russell's definition of number. For example, one could point to, say, Alvin, Albert, and Alan, and then stipulate that it is the number of this particular (and any like-numbered) class which we shall call "three." Here, too, the approach is extensional, and any meaning or "intension" not provided to "three" by this procedure is cut away by another application of Ockham's razor.

Reichenbach adds that Russell also provides a purely logical way of defining a number, one which does not involve ostensive definition or reference to some particular class of objects. The definition of "one," for example, in English (and leaving aside the logical notation) runs: "a class F has the number 1 if the class has a member such that if anything is the member of this class then it is identical with this member." This sort of formal definition eliminates empirical reference from the definition of a number. In all of this, Reichenbach makes clear his basic agreement with Russell's perspective.

Reichenbach provides still further discussion of Russell's much-debated "reduction" of mathematics to logic, as well as other topics, to which (along with Russell's reply to Reichenbach) the reader is referred.—*K.E.Y.*

ADDITIONAL RECOMMENDED READING

Copi, Irving M. and James A. Gould, eds. *Contemporary Readings in Logical Theory*. New York: Macmillan Publishing Company, 1967. An excellent collection of contemporary essays on various topics in logic and philosophy and philosophy of logic.

Kneale, William and Martha Kneale. *The Development of Logic*. London: Oxford University Press, 1967. A history of logic from Greek times through Russell and beyond.

Prior, A. N. *Formal Logic*. Oxford: Clarendon Press, 1962. A discussion of contemporary logic, with some historical sections, which includes many references to Russell and a presentation of the system he and Whitehead developed.

Russell, Bertrand. *The Principles of Mathematics*. Cambridge: Cambridge University Press, 1903. Russell's first book-length essay in mathematics and philosophy.

Russell, Bertrand and Alfred North Whitehead. *Principia Mathematica*. Cambridge: Cambridge University Press, Vol. I, 1910; Vol. II, 1912; Vol. III, 1913. The *magnum opus* of twentieth century logic, which revolutionized the field.

SPACE, TIME, AND DEITY

Author: Samuel Alexander (1859-1938)
Type of work: Metaphysics
First published: 1920 (Gifford Lectures, Glasgow, 1916-1918)

PRINCIPAL IDEAS ADVANCED

Philosophy attempts to identify the generic and specific features of whatever exists.

The ultimate reality is space-time; matter is composed of motions which, in turn, are made up of point-instants.

The categories of being are fundamental properties of space-time; the major categories are identity, existence, relation, and order.

Matter, life, and consciousness are as real as the universal features of reality; they are emergent qualities of the space-time reality.

Deity is the highest order of being, the principle of evolution, the mind of the world.

Samuel Alexander belonged to the generation of English philosophers which found itself in revolt aginst the neo-Hegelianism of Bradley and Bosanquet. His philosophy shares most of the characteristics of the realism of that period: its conviction that experience can be analyzed into elements which are directly intuited; its insistence that the mental act is a different thing from the object known; and its inclination to account for the order of nature in nonspiritual terms. He went further than many realists in the role which he accorded to the natural sciences in philosophy; and further than most in his optimism respecting the possibilities of an all-inclusive system.

Philosophy, as Alexander understood it, differs from science not so much in method as in content. It has for its subject matter the pervasive aspects of things. In other words, it deals with those features of the world which recur over and over and in a wide variety of contexts. It has to identify these features, but also must discover their interrelations. The undertaking is recognizably Aristotelian, particularly in the contention—basic to Alexander's construction—that nature forms a pyramid, with general features at its base which permeate everything in nature, and successively more special features characterizing those which occur at higher levels. Thus, motion is an extremely basic character; matter is more special; life is more special still. And in each case, the higher presupposes the lower.

Space, Time, and Deity is Alexander's comprehensive work. Many philosophers tell us what they think philosophy should be, then apologize for offering us a mere sketch or sample. Alexander provides us with a finished work which is in many respects a masterpiece. The broad outline is implemented in a manner which shows sound knowledge both of the history of

Western philosophy and of the revolutionary developments of contemporary science. Perhaps it does so completely what it sets out to do that nothing remains for the reader but to put it on a shelf and explore new avenues.

In Alexander's system, the ultimate reality from which all things are engendered is space-time. This preeminently modern conception was no doubt suggested to him by the developments of mathematical physics; but it owes at least as much to Bergson's intuition of time as duration. And Alexander, who was first and last an empiricist, although he did not venture to teach physicists their business, thought it important not to confuse geometrical constructions with the world of experience which, as a philosopher, he was bound to describe. For the common conception of a three-dimensional space moving like a column through fourth-dimensional time, he substituted the image of molecules of gas moving inside a closed container. The value of this figure is that it preserves the notion of a space made up of points successively occupied by instants of time. Such is the nature of the world we experience. Its ultimate constituents are events which, besides their location in space, also have a past and a future. What we call matter, Alexander maintained, is composed of many motions, just as motions are made up of events or point-instants.

A prominent feature of Alexander's book is his discussion of the *categories*. These are viewed by him as fundamental determinations of being. They are not to be confused with *qualities*, which in his system are variable and accidental, because the categories are universal and constitutive. They are *a priori* in the sense that they are known in advance to apply to every existing thing. But they are genuine features of reality and not mere dispositions of the mind, as Kant had held. For this reason, Alexander did not pretend to deduce them by any necessity, logical or mechanical. The realists held that the business of the philosopher is not to explain everything but to describe what he finds. And Alexander's procedure was to disclose one after another of the traditional categories of philosophy as fundamental properties of space-time itself.

Thus, *identity* and *diversity* (the first two categories) need not be regarded as peculiarities of man's intellect nor as archetypal forms which determine the limits of all being, but as primary characteristics of the point-instant. Time exhibits sameness as duration; it exhibits difference as succession. Similarly, space exhibits unity as being a continuum, diversity as being composed of parts. The inseparability of space-time is bound up with these features. Alexander argued that space is what gives time its unity and that time is what gives space diversity; otherwise time would be a mere succession and space would be blank unity.

Being or *existence* is simply another name for identity of place and time. Alexander rejected the notion of neutral being supposedly embracing entities which transcend sense experience. But he did not on that account deny that *universals* are real. On the contrary, he maintained that they are patterns or habits which determine actual events. They are a kind of identity as between different particular happenings. Thus, they exist, have their own efficacy, and may be apprehended directly by minds. A distinction is made between universals and *particulars* and *individuals*.

Relations express the continuity of space-time. Alexander resisted a physicalism which would reduce all relations to those of space and time, but he held that in the last analysis all relations do depend upon spatiotemporal ones. A relation is a connection in virtue of which two terms enter into a whole. A simple example is an interval of space or of time. A more complex one is the relation of a king to his subjects. In this example, where a set of acts and passions constitute the total situation, the relation is not directly a feature of space and time; but the acts and passions of men are themselves complex patterns of space-time events.

Order is a separate and a major category of its own; identity, existence, and relation complete the class of major categories.

Substance, Alexander maintained, is a relation between the spatial and temporal elements in a definite volume of space-time. It is no "brute senseless somewhat" (Berkeley) which serves as a support for qualities, but the spatial contour within which a particular set of qualities exists. A portion of space-time is a substance in virtue of being the seat of motion, though the motion be as simple as the flight of an electron. Empty space is included in substance at the molecular or atomic level—supposing these to be miniature planetary orbits. But it is not part of the substance on a macroscopic scale. The holes of a sponge, to cite Alexander's example, are not part of the substance of the sponge.

Causality (here treated as a category) is a relation between substances. It spells out the implications of Alexander's fundamental hypothesis that space-time is a continuous system in which every event is related to one which precedes it and to one which follows. The popular notion of causality distinguishes between things and events, which the present view does not. A thing is already a complex of motions, and it becomes a cause when one or more of its constituent motions is continued in a different motion. Alexander greatly simplified a notoriously difficult issue. For him, all causality is *a tergo*: the cause must be adjacent to the effect in space, and immediately prior in time. He rejected the suggestion of Ernst Mach and the positivists that the notion of causality has been rendered obsolete by the progress made by science in the use of mathematical descriptions. For Alexander, a mathematical description, to be relevant, must describe something. If formulae mean anything, they assert a reciprocal determination of two motions, which is what is here understood as causality. *Reciprocity* is a separate, but related, category. *Quantity, intensity, whole, parts, number*, and *motion* complete the categories.

The description of space-time and of the categories takes up the entire first volume of the work. Although the matter is abstract, the method is comparatively simple and straightforward. Categories apply equally to all existents, from a simple motion to a thought. Once the nature of space-time is grasped, the delineation of the particular categories is merely a matter of detail. It is otherwise when we come, in the second volume, to consider *quality*. For one of Alexander's main tenets, which he shared with Moore, Russell, and the American neorealists, was that emprical objects have real and independent existence. Other naturalists and materialists have held that the categories are sufficient to account for all actual determinations of being. In attempting to maintain that matter, secondary qualities, life, and consciousness are just as real as the universal features of the world, Alexander was confronted with a challenging task. The problem was to conceive of the relation between quality and its spatiotemporal or categorical ground—how, in other words, certain spatiotemporal complexes are correlated with such empirical facts as materiality, vitality, entelechy, and knowledge—ultimately also, with goodness, beauty, and truth.

The method, therefore, in this part can no longer be simple description and analysis. Since what is sought is the correlation between quality and its categorical ground, Alexander looked for an unambiguous instance of this correlation, and proceeded by analogy to apply it through the length and breadth of the world. The instance which he chose as a paradigm is the correlation between *mind* and the *nervous system*. This connection, because it is uniquely open to our inspection, is suited as none other to unlock the mystery. On the basis of the findings of neurology he argued that the mind is something new in life but that it is not a separate entity. There is but one process which, viewed in the context with nutrition, respiration, elimination, is vital; but viewed in its unique aspects (as meaningful) it is of a different order. This theory suggests that when a neural process has a specific complexity, intensity, and connection with other processes and structures, it takes on new characters so that, without ceasing to be vital, it becomes mental.

With this instance before him, Alexander proceeded to generalize. Happily, he could draw upon the work of Lloyd Morgan, the biologist, who had introduced the distinction between additive and *emergent* qualities. Some combinations in nature are purely quantitative, such as molecular weights. But others give rise to qualitative changes, such as the properties of water, which could never be predicted from the properties of hydrogen and oxygen. Alexander cites the famous lines from Robert Browning's poem *Abt Vogler*, which tells the story of a musician who out of three sounds framed, not a fourth sound but—a star! This is what happens in the higher vertebrates when *mind* emerges; and, Alexander suggests, it is our best clue to what happens when certain motions give rise to chemical *matter*, and certain chemical combinations give rise to *life*. The novelty is not something added—Alexander repudiated "vitalism" just as he repudiated "animism." Life is basically chemical, but it is a specific grade of matter which manifests properties that defy description in chemical terms. The same is true of matter: it is motion, and from one point of view "nothing but motion"; still, it has properties (hardness, color, special affinities) which other motions do not have and which, if we were committed to a reductionist logic, must be regarded as "unreal" because they are not categorical.

It is in connection with his discussion of mind and the neural system that Alexander treats the problem of *knowledge*. He regards it as erroneous to suppose, with many modern philosophers, that epistemology is the foundation of metaphysics. Rather, it is a chapter of metaphysics, a special case of the way in which a finite thing, on any level of being, is in rapport with its environment. Any two things which are connected, as mind is with the object of cognition, in the same space-time, interact causally, not only according to their spatial relations but also according to their special natures. The latter introduce a selective factor, particularly important in accounting for perception. A table is differently affected by the wall and by the fireplace; in a similar manner, the optic nerve reacts to some qualities and not to others.

But neural activity as such is not cognition, which comes into being only on the level of consciousness. And it is here that we meet the characteristic epistemological problem: whether the objects of the mind's perception are qualities of the thing or the activity of the brain itself. Alexander maintained that they are both, but in different respects. To make his idea clear he introduced two new terms which have gained a certain currency. The mind's awareness of the neural activity he called *enjoyment*; its awareness of the qualities of the thing perceived he called *contemplation*. The object of perception is not the modification of the nervous system, but the process of knowing is. And it is by living through or enjoying the latter that the mind confronts or contemplates the thing. Alexander saw a similarity between this account and the doctrine of Spinoza, who stated that the mind is the "idea of the body." He also believed that it got at the truth which G. E. Moore elucidated in his "Refutation of Idealism."

Cognition can be understood as analogous to other natural processes, but judgment, necessary to the resolution of value problems, is unique in that it is always a *social* phenomenon. Thus, instead of involving merely the mind and its object, judgment also involves a *norm*; and this norm, Alexander argued, comes into being only through social intercourse. A man who grew apart from society might form a judgment and later correct it in the interest of efficiency. His mistake would be misadventure, not an error. Only when he found his judgment disagreeing with the judgment of another would he become aware that judgments have a reality of their own. This would put him, for the first time, in the position to distinguish between the judgment and the thing judged, between truth (or error) and reality (or illusion). The same holds true of goodness and beauty, which outside a social context would be no more than volitions arising out of pleasurable anticipations. They take their place as values when judged in accordance with a standard which arises as a result of a meeting of minds.

This is the part of Alexander's philosophy which seems to most students to represent a departure from the strict realist standpoint. He has abandoned the view that values exist in things and has denied that they are given instantly in experience. His realism has, in fact, given place to a naturalistic metaphysics which permits him to "explain" values as real, in the sense that a "whole situation," consisting of knower and known, is real. Values, says Alexander, are not objective in the way secondary qualities are, nor subjective in the way pains and pleasures are. Subject and object mutually determine each other in an organic whole. He reminds us of objective idealism when he goes on to argue that "coherence" is the only criterion, not only of truth but also of goodness and beauty, and he appeals to the larger experience of society to decide what is coherent. But the biological emphasis is never far away. One of his contentions is that knowledge (and *a fortiori* the other values) is fundamentally an expression of will, for "judging is the speculative side of volition, and what is willed in willing is the proposition or object judged." In fact, his account of truth bears many resemblances to pragmatism. He agrees that the test of truth is that it works, but he denies that this is all that can be said about it. It works, he adds, because it is determined by the nature of reality.

But we must return to the broad outlines of Alexander's theory, and in particular to the notion of *deity* with which, in Book IV, he brings his system to its completion. Two main features have been noted so far. The first is that everything in the world is made up of motions, more or less complex; the second is that a particular combination of motions has qualities which are inseparable from it. The former was worked out by Alexander in terms of point-instants and the categories which make up the space-time continuum; the latter, in terms of the theory of emergent characters. The one is *a priori*; the other empirical. But this distinction, important as it is, is not an absolute one. What is lacking so far is the notion of *evolution*, according to which emergence is built into the very stuff of the world itself—the point-instant. Mere points would be static. The point-instant is dynamic. Its spacial component corresponds to the body; it is the "matter" of which the world is formed. Its temporal component corresponds to the mind; it is the "form" which generates qualities in space. Creativity and development are, in this sense, built into the nature of the world.

This is about as far as Alexander is willing to go in the direction of traditional theology. The religious impulse demands for its object a being which is higher than man. But philosophy wants a principle of explanation which is relevant to the world of its experience. If we combine these two, we arrive at the conception of a universe engendering within itself ever higher orders of being, with deity as the one beyond the human mind. If time is designated as the "mind of Space," deity can be described as the "mind of the whole world." But this would be merely figurative, since deity is nowhere actualized. A stricter account would be to say that God is the "infinite world with its nisus toward deity."

Alexander distinguishes between *deity*—which is a quality higher than but analogous to matter, life, and mind—and *God*, which he defines as "a being which possesses deity." Man has *faith* in God, based upon his *experience* of deity. This latter is a veridical experience and not mere imagination. Deity does not now exist, but as the next order to evolve, it is experienced as future; and in Alexander's system, past and future are just as real as the present. Alexander argues for the autonomy of the religious sentiment through which deity is apprehended. It is a specific kind of consciousness, not reducible to the apprehension of value. For although the religious emotion is likely to be communal, and the God of faith is ordinarily thought of as on the side of the good, the religious emotion is a unique "hungering and thirsting after" the totality of being in its striving toward deity.

When he approached the problem of religion exclusively in terms of "religious experience," Alexander was in step with the liberal theology of that day. And presumably his own strong empirical bias prevented him from postulating God as a creative agent, in the way that Lloyd Morgan and A. N. Whitehead were to do. This is the more remarkable because several times Alexander points to lacunae in his own system (for example, the existence of emergent qualities) which, on the "principle of sufficient reason" solicit the service of a First Mover. But Alexander declines the gambit. "As being the whole universe," says he, "God is creative, but his distinctive character of deity is not creative but created." As for the mystery of empirical being, he prefers to accept it "with the 'natural piety' of the investigator. It admits no explanation."—*J.F.*

PERTINENT LITERATURE

McCarthy, John W. *The Naturalism of Samuel Alexander.* New York: King's Crown Press, 1948.

John W. McCarthy was attracted to the study of Samuel Alexander because, unlike the specialists in philosophy, the British thinker offered a comprehensive analysis of experience which takes account of religion, art, and morality within the framework of science. The basis of the system, according to McCarthy, is naturalism. Despite McCarthy's avowed appreciation of Alexander's achievement in understanding and ordering all facets and kinds of experience, he nevertheless criticizes the philosopher for assuming without explanation certain concepts and procedures which underlie and unify the system, such as, for example, the use of the principle of analogy.

In Chapter I McCarthy presents the basic notions of Alexander's system. Paramount in this interpretation is the principle of an evolving hierarchy. Four levels are distinguished and charted: (1) Being, (2) Value, (3) Knowing, and (4) Purpose; and these levels and their subdivisions are correlated with one another. McCarthy analyzes the levels of Being into Structure and Quality and shows that, in an ascending order, these levels embrace: (1) Space-Time (motion) with Space the structural aspect and Time the qualitative aspect; (2) materiality, with matter the structural aspect and secondary qualities the qualitative aspect; (3) animals and plants, with organism described as a physicochemical process displaying the structural aspect and life the qualitative aspect; (4) man, with body the structural aspect and mind the qualitative aspect; and (5) God, with the whole world, called his body, exhibiting the structural aspect and deity the qualitative aspect. McCarthy also sketches the levels of value in an ascending order and correlates them with the levels of Being. The levels of value are: (1) the atomic values, (2) the physicochemical values, (3) the life values of plants and animals, (4) human values, continuous with the values of life, but crowned with the values of art, truth, and goodness, and (5) the values of God.

McCarthy then takes up the levels of knowing and finds correlations between its levels and the others in all instances except the highest levels, which pertain to God and his values. Thus at the lowest level of knowing fall the needs things have of one another, so that it corresponds to the two lowest levels of being and value. The level of knowing which then comes into view has to do with stimulus and response and instinctive behavior, a level correlated with levels (3) of being and value, while the highest level of knowing subsumes practical knowing and contemplation; it corresponds to the levels of Man and of Human Values. Finally, McCarthy surveys the levels of Purpose, correlating these, too, with all but the highest levels of Being and Value—God and his values. Thus at the lowest level of Purpose appears the adaptation of a being to its environment, and this activity correlates with the three lower levels of Being, Value, and Knowing. Purpose at its highest level is evident in intelligent functioning, which involves reflection upon and employment of means in regard to ends; at its highest level, then, Purpose corresponds to the fourth levels of Being, Value, and Knowing, which represent man, human values, and practical knowledge and contemplation, respectively.

McCarthy pursues his interpretation of Alexander's philosophy in the ensuing chapters which touch upon the entire compass of human experience: Chapter II on art, beauty, and aesthetics; Chapter III on goodness; Chapter IV on truth; Chapter V on the tertiary qualities; Chapter VI on value; and Chapter VII on religion.

A major yet tacit feature of Alexander's system, McCarthy argues, is the use of analogy, and he endeavors to make this principle explicit in order to assess the strengths and weakness of the system. Two instances which McCarthy explicates are noteworthy. From the discovery of the mind-body relationship at the human level of being, Alexander derived a metaphysical formula which he then extended to the subhuman levels of being, and also, above man, to God. Similarly, from the consideration of human values, Alexander proceeded to apply his findings not only to inorganic and nonhuman organic levels of being but also to God.

McCarthy detects the unifying theme in Alexander's naturalism in biological concepts. These concepts inter-link Alexander's naturalistic metaphysics and his theory of value, rendering his philosophy more coherent than less sympathetic commentators, such as Milton Konvitz, allow. According to McCarthy, the central unifying biological concept in Alexander's system is the concept of nisus (which, incidentally, Alexander probably borrowed from Benedictus de Spinoza but revised). Palpable in impulses and instincts at any level of life, nisus is defined as the tendency in each thing to move to the next higher level of being, drawing the lower levels along with it. Running through the levels of being in an ascending order, nisus is the creative force in the universe which accounts for materiality, secondary qualities, life, mind, the human values, and deity, all these spun out of primordial space-time. The cosmic nisus is construed to be, in the final analysis, tantamount to the urge of the entire universe toward deity.

Brettschneider, Bertram D. *The Philosophy of Samuel Alexander: Idealism in "Space, Time, and Deity."* New York: Humanities Press, 1964.

This book is both an exposition of Samuel Alexander's philosophy in *Space, Time, and Deity* and a critical examination of the extensive commentary it has inspired. Bertram D. Brettschneider notes that Alexander explicitly affiliated his philosophical project with the realistic movement which included such famous thinkers as Bertrand Russell and G. E. Moore, and which flourished in Britain and America during the first quarter of the twentieth century. The realists, as Brettschneider points out, discarded the traditional problems of systematic philosophy and imitated the formal and empirical sciences, directing their investigations into technical specialized topics and eschewing speculation in favor of analysis and criticism. By contrast, Alexander endeavored to construct a comprehensive philosophical system. Although professedly based on realistic foundations, Alexander's system, according to Brettschneider, is in fact sustained by the philosophical presuppositions of objective or absolute idealism. Espoused by T. H. Green, F. H. Bradley, and Bernard Bosanquet, this idealism is the philosophy against which the realists rose in revolt. Like the idealists, and unlike the realists, Alexander approached the traditional metaphysical questions which are at the core of systematic philosophy. He deemed the epistemological relation of mind to its object to be a minor segment of the vast field of metaphysics, and he strove to penetrate the ultimate nature of existence, unraveling the universal and necessary characters of all things, the fundamental categories which are genuinely *a priori*.

Brettschneider's articulation of his thesis that absolute idealism undergirds Alexander's systematic philosophy follows the development of the argument presented in *Space, Time, and Deity*. In Chapter I he treats Alexander's contention that Space-Time is the ultimate stuff, or substance, which makes up the universe. In Chapter II he discusses the categories, such as identity and diversity, existence, universality, relation, causality, substance; and he construes these categories to be both *a priori* and objective, the basic universally pervasive properties or determinations of space-time. In Chapter III he examines Alexander's theory of emergent evolution and deals with the qualities which allegedly emerge from primordial space-time—qualities which indicate distinct levels of existence: motions, purely physical matter, matter enriched with secondary qualities, life, and mind. In Chapter IV he explores mind, Alexander's highest level of finite existence, and shows its relation to the rest of the cosmology. Brettschneider devotes Chapter V to a consideration of Alexander's theory of value and Chapter VI to Alexander's conceptions of God and deity.

Brettschneider's commentary on the views of Alexander's critics is extensive and probing. In Chapter I, for example, he presents and evaluates the criticisms of Rudolf Metz, G. F. Stout, Bosanquet, C. D. Broad, Dawes Hicks, Alfred P. Stiernotte, and John Laird; and he compares Alexander's conceptions with related conceptions of Edmund Husserl, Plato, Russell, Henri Bergson, and Bradley. This genre of philosophical criticism permeates Brettschneider's densely compact book. Consequently, all the major and some of the minor comments on Alexander's thought are elucidated, evaluated, and sublated in the unfolding argument that his philosophy, despite its realist professions, is essentially an expression of absolute idealism.

Hence, for Brettschneider, Alexander's construal of finite individuals as modifications of space-time is equated with the idealist formula that finite individuals are adjectival modes of the Absolute. Further, relations, which Alexander grounds in space-time, are interpreted to be, not external as the realists hold, but internal as the idealists claim. Also, in his treatment of truth, beauty, and goodness, Alexander approached values by means of holistic conceptions upheld by the idealists, culminating in his advocacy of the principle of coherence as the nature of value and as a pervasive character of the universe. Among the idealist philosophers, it is Bradley whose doctrines are deemed by Brettschneider to have been unconsciously presupposed by Alexander. Nevertheless, in conclusion, Brettschneider observes that the thesis that Alexander's system rests on absolute idealist foundations must be qualified in the light not only of Alexander's emphatic advocacy of realism in regard to epistemology and value theory but also to his vehement denial of any absolutes.

Stiernotte, Alfred P. *God and Space-Time: Deity in the Philosophy of Samuel Alexander*. Foreword by Henry Nelson Wieman. New York: Philosophical Library, 1954.

Alfred P. Stiernotte maintains, in the first place, that Samuel Alexander relates the ethical and religious aspirations of man to the universe in a close-knit system which contains a philosophy of religion that rivals the older theologies and idealisms in respect to comprehensiveness and adequacy. He concentrates on the conceptions of God and of deity, presenting Alexander's justification for these conceptions and examining the objections that have been raised against them. Stiernotte contends, in the second place, that the deity of Alexander is accessible to contemporary religious conceptions and experiences, displaying affinities with the empirical and realistic theologies as well as the process theologies developing in twentieth century America. The book is divided into two parts: Part I is mainly expository, and Part II is critical and evaluative.

Part I has four chapters. The first expounds Alexander's realism; it treats the epistemology, the doctrines of space-time and the categories, and the theory of emergent evolution, including the distinct levels of existence. Insisting upon the primacy of relativity and temporal process in Alexander's system, Stiernotte denies that the totality of space-time is akin to the Absolute of idealism. The second chapter treats Alexander's conceptions of God and of deity. Thus God is viewed as having body, identified with the whole of space-time, and a mind. Deity is the mind of God, an emergent quality which arises in successive stages of the evolutionary process and which is manifest in the cosmic nisus rather than as a completed accomplishment. Deity in relation to religious consciousness is the topic of the third chapter. Here Stiernotte uncovers the ground of Alexander's doctrine of religious sentiment or feeling in Reality. Religious emotion, fueled by the nisus of space-time which penetrates man and all finite existents, establishes an intimate connection with God represented as possessing deity. Since God is the body of the cosmos pictured as the whole of space-time, and deity is his emergent quality, Stiernotte concludes that Alexander's system reconciles the claim of pantheism that God is immanent in the world with the tenet of theism that God transcends the world. Nevertheless, Stiernotte faults Alexander for lacking a personal conception of God and for pluralizing deity into an infinity of finite existents. Thus criticism invades the exposition, continuing in the fourth chapter, where Stiernotte discusses deity and value, probing the alleged subjectivism of Alexander's theory of value, his treatment of the problem of evil, and the question of immortality.

Part II reiterates some of the critical themes which surfaced in Part I, and it, too, unfolds in four chapters. The first examines Alexander's system as a whole; the second concentrates on nisus in regard to the metaphysical relationship of God and deity; and the third focuses on deity, value, and person. Surveying the cosmology of space-time as a whole, Stiernotte defends Alexander against his major critics, showing how the system agrees with the findings of contemporary science; that, indeed, it is especially consonant with process philosophy. On the doctrine of nisus, however, Stiernotte finds in favor of those critics, such as G. Dawes Hicks and John Laird, who scored against the obscurity of the conception of deity as a quality to emerge in the future from an ongoing temporal process out of which numerous other qualities have also evolved. Moreover, since Alexander regarded deity as fragmented in the "mind" portions of existents higher than man, Stiernotte underscores the bizarre polytheistic implication of this theology. He also underscores vacillation on Alexander's part between the conception of deity as the creative nisus immanent in the temporal process and the conception of deity as the climactic emerging quality. Further, Stiernotte tightens his earlier strictures that Alexander's theory of value is undermined by an incipient subjectivism; and he reiterates Alexander's neglect of the person, stressing that, in fact, persons are the crowning achievements of evolution. In the concluding chapter, after discarding such indefensible components of Alexander's philosophy as those criticized above, Stiernotte lists and elucidates what he deems to be the lasting worthwhile elements of Alexander's system: (1) the primacy of metaphysics, (2) the realism, (3) the reality of time, (4) the recognition of religious experience as a distinctive response of the whole human personality, and (5) the conception of God as nisus, which he compares to Henri Bergson's *élan vital*, Jan Christiaan Smuts's holism, and Alfred North Whitehead's doctrine of creativity.—*A.J.R.*

ADDITIONAL RECOMMENDED READING

Broad, C. D. *The Mind and Its Place in Nature*. London: Kegan Paul, Trench, Trubner & Company, 1925, pp. 648-650. A passing criticism of Alexander's theory of the status of mind as a form of Emergent Neutralism by a famous Cambridge analytic philosopher.

Dasgupta, Sudhir Ranjan. *A Study of Alexander's Space, Time, and Deity*. Serampore: Hooghly, 1965. An exposition and interpretation of Alexander's philosophy as a compromise between realism and idealism.

Hicks, G. Dawes. Review of Samuel Alexander's *Space, Time, and Deity*, in *The Hibbert Journal*. XIX, no. 3 (April, 1921), pp. 573-581. A review by an influential British critical realist who charged that Alexander's theory of the emergence of qualities from space-time is indefensible.

Konvitz, Milton R. *On the Nature of Value: The Philosophy of Samuel Alexander*. New York: King's Crown Press, 1946. An original essay on the metaphysics and theory of value which takes off from a sympathetic yet critical interpretation of Alexander's system.

Murphy, Arthur E. "Alexander's Metaphysic of Space-Time," in *The Monist*. XXXVII, nos. 3 and 4 (July and October, 1927), pp. 357-358 and 624-644. A penetrating critical study by a leading American philosopher who argued that Alexander's system is embroiled in a major contradiction between absolutist and relativist conceptions of space-time.

Reck, Andrew J. *Speculative Philosophy*. Albuquerque: University of New Mexico Press, 1972, pp. 207-219. An examination of Alexander's system as a kind of process philosophy.

TRACTATUS LOGICO-PHILOSOPHICUS

Author: Ludwig Wittgenstein (1889-1951)
Type of work: Logic, philosophy of philosophy
First published: 1921

PRINCIPAL IDEAS ADVANCED

The world is made up of atomic facts; atomic facts are facts which are incapable of analysis into more elemental facts.

Propositions are logical pictures of (possible) facts; what is common to a proposition and the fact it pictures is logical structure.

A proposition does not express *the form of a possible fact; it* shows *it.*

To give the general form of proposition is to give the essence of all description and of the world; any proposition whatsoever can be formed by drawing from the class of elementary propositions and using various logical operations.

Philosophy is a process of clarification; the propositions of natural science are meaningful, but the attempt to say something meaningful in ethics, aesthetics, or metaphysics is bound to fail, for any such attempt involves the impossible task of talking about the world from the outside.

This is an unusual book, both in content and in style. In content it is about logic, though the author finds the chance in discussing this subject to say much about the theory of signs, epistemology, metaphysics, and philosophy in general. Furthermore, in talking about logic Wittgenstein indicates that there are many things which we cannot say about logic, not because we do not know them, or even because we do know them but cannot find words by which to express them, but because they are literally *inexpressible* by means of *any* language. Consequently we must remain silent about them.

In style the book is also strange. The sentences (or sometimes groups of sentences) are all numbered in accordance with a plan. For example, a certain sentence has the number 3; this follows sentences 1 and 2 in the order of the natural numbers. But between 2 and 3 are sentences numbered, for example, 2.0122 and 2.151. Sentence 2.0122 is a statement referring to statement 2. Statement 2.151 follows statement 2.1 and is a comment on it; but 2.1, in turn, is another comment on 2, and follows it. All statements are in this way arranged in a unique, linear order based on the decimal notation, and the reader is able to determine by the number attached to each sentence what *general* topic is being considered, what *special* aspect of this general subject is involved, and so on, sometimes to the fourth level of specialization.

Furthermore, because of the unusual meanings associated with many of the terms employed by the author, the editor has chosen to publish on facing pages the original German text and its parallel English translation. This permits the reader who is familiar with German to improve his understanding of the text by checking with the original German and in many cases to detect fine shades of meaning which might otherwise have escaped him. In a book where such common words as "fact," "object," "meaning," and "truth" occur in great abundance and are employed with somewhat unusual connotations, the parallel translation is of great help. The book also contains a valuable introduction, written by Bertrand Russell, which both summarizes the text and criticizes it on some important points.

For convenience of discussion it will be well to combine Wittgenstein's discussion of Proposition 1 and the remarks on it, with Proposition 2 and all of the remarks contained in Propositions numbered 2.0. Proposition 1 states that the world is everything that is the case; Proposition 2 asserts that what is the case, the fact, is the existence of atomic facts. The world, then, is made up of atomic facts and is constituted by them. Atomic facts are facts which are incapable of analysis into more elemental facts. This does not mean that atomic facts cannot be analyzed, but only that they cannot be analyzed into other atomic facts. An atomic fact is itself a combination of objects (entities, things), each of whose essence lies in its being a constituent of an atomic fact. But the objects which are elements of atomic facts cannot themselves be analyzed, since they form the substance of the world. If we take advantage of the illustration of an atomic fact which Russell gives in his introduction (Wittgenstein does not give illustrations of atomic facts), we may say that it is what is asserted by the proposition "Socrates is wise." This contains two objects, *Socrates* and *wise*, each of which, in its own unique way, unites with the other to form the atomic fact. Traditional philosophy would call these objects "substances" and "qualities." Wittgenstein states that however different from the real world an imaginary world might be, it must have something, its form, in common with the real world. Since the form is given by the objects, we may presume Wittgenstein to be saying that any imaginable world would have to contain substances and qualities, however these might differ from those in our real world. The world is the totality of atomic facts; it also determines the nonexistence of atomic facts, for the nonexistence of an atomic fact is a kind of fact. Reality, therefore, is the totality of atomic facts plus the fact that these are *all* the atomic facts.

Beginning with Proposition 2.1, continuing more or less explicitly through Proposition 4, and extending implicitly through the rest of the book, Wittgenstein examines what is meant by saying that a proposition is a picture of a fact. He describes this picturing relation variously as "modeling," "standing for," "representing," "corresponding with," "depicting," and "projecting." We should note, first, that a proposition is itself a fact. By this is not meant the propositional sign which expresses the fact, though Wittgenstein admits that propositions can be expressed perceptibly through the senses, but rather the *sense* of the proposition. The point is, of course, that the proposition is a *logical* picture of the fact, not a *visual* one or an *audible* one. He says that it represents the fact in "logical space"—a metaphor which he uses repeatedly throughout the book. Its representative character lies in its form or structure, which means a coordination of the elements in the picture with the objects in the fact, and an identity of logical form exhibited by both the picture and the fact. Thus the proposition "Socrates is wise" pictures the fact of Socrates' wisdom because "Socrates" represents Socrates, and "wise" represents wisdom, and the form exhibited by "Socrates" and "wise" in the propositional relation is the same as that exhibited by Socrates and wisdom in the fact. That this is a logical form rather than a spatial form is to be seen in the fact that while the sentence "Socrates is wise" has a spatial order of its elements, neither the *meaning* of the sentence nor the *fact* asserted by the sentence is spatial; what is common to the meaning and the fact is a logical structure.

More precisely, the proposition does not strictly represent the fact, but rather the *possibility* of the fact, the possibility of the existence and nonexistence of atomic facts. A proposition whose expression mentions a complex is not nonsense if this complex fails to exist, but simply false. A proposition represents what it represents independently of its truth or falsity, through its form of representation, through its *sense*. Furthermore, by virtue of the identity of form which runs through various facts, the picture represents every reality whose form it has; thus "Socrates is wise" also pictures the fact that Plato is human.

"The logical picture of the facts is the thought" (Proposition 3). To say that an atomic fact is thinkable means that we can imagine it. And if it is thinkable it must also be logical, for anything which is "unlogical" could not be expressed at all. Language cannot express anything which "contradicts logic" any more than a spatial figure can represent anything which contradicts the laws of space, or can represent the spatial coordinates of a point which does not exist.

The sign through which thoughts are expressed is the propositional sign. Both the proposition and the propositional sign are facts. In the propositional sign the elements (the words) are combined in a definite way so that the objects of the thoughts correspond to the elements of the propositional sign. The simple signs used in propositional signs are called "names." Objects can only be named and spoken about; they cannot be asserted. Names cannot be further analyzed; they are primitive signs. They have meanings only in the context of propositions.

A propositional expression presupposes the forms of all propositions that it expresses, and thus it may be said to characterize a form and a content; the form is constant, and everything else is variable. If every constituent part of a proposition is changed into a variable, the logical form (the logical prototype) remains. Thus, to use an example which Russell gives elsewhere, if we change the proposition "Socrates drank hemlock" into the proposition "Coleridge ate opium," the form of the proposition, "ARB," remains. This may be called a "propositional variable."

In the language of everyday life the same word often signifies in two different ways, and different words signify in the same way. For example, the verb "to be" appears sometimes as the sign of equality, sometimes as the expression of existence, sometimes as an intransitive verb, and sometimes as a sign of identity. Words of this kind are the cause of some of the most fundamental confusions in thought, especially in philosophical thought. The only way to avoid these difficulties is to invent a special symbolism—a symbolism which obeys the rules of *logical* grammar (logical syntax). Such rules follow of themselves if we know only how every sign signifies. Bertrand Russell and the mathematician, Gottlob Frege, have invented such logical symbolisms, but even these do not exclude the possibility of error.

The great advantage of a logical language is that it calls our attention to formal properties of objects and facts. This is not because propositions express the form of facts, but because they "show it" and do not state it. No proposition is capable of representing its form of representation, for this would require something which is impossible—the picture would have to place itself outside its form of representation. "The proposition *shows* how things stand, *if* it is true." The existence of a structure in a possible state of affairs is not *expressed by* the proposition which presents the state of affairs; it is *shown in* the proposition by means of its structure. The identity of form which is exhibited by the proposition and by the fact accounts for the representation of the fact by the proposition, but this does not give the proposition a *formal property* of representing the fact. It would be as meaningless to ascribe a formal property to a proposition as to deny it of the proposition. And it would be equally meaningless to assert that one form has a certain property and another form has a different property, for this assumes that there is sense in asserting that either form has either property. We do not ascribe properties to forms nor do we ascribe forms to propositions or states of affairs. In this respect formal concepts differ from proper concepts. The proper concept "man" can be expressed by a propositional function, for example, "x is a man"; but the formal concept "object" cannot be expressed by "x is an object." In this expression "x" is a sign of the pseudo-concept *object*, and to say that a rose is an object (thing, entity) is to utter nonsense. The same holds true of such words as "complex," "fact," "function," and "number," which should be represented in symbolism by variables, not by proper concepts. Recognizing these as variables shows the absurdity of making such statements as "There are objects" (supposedly patterned after "There are books") or "There is only one 1" (which according to Wittgenstein is as absurd as it would be to say "2 plus 2 is at 3 o'clock equal to 4"). To summarize, then, the great advantage of a precise logical symbolism is that it prevents us from talking nonsense. The correct use of the symbols, as was said above, follows immediately if we know how every sign signifies.

A further consequence of the notion that "object" is a pseudoconcept is the impossibility of finding some "property" which all "objects" possess. We have already seen that atomic facts are complex and contain objects as elements of a certain structure. These objects are unanalyzable. Consequently, to name a certain atomic fact is to presuppose the truth of a certain atomic proposition, namely, the proposition asserting the relatedness of the constituents of the complex; and this, in turn, presupposes the naming of the constituents (object) themselves. But now, according to Wittgenstein, since the concept "object" is a pseudoconcept, there is no way by which we can describe the totality of things that can be named. This means that we cannot say anything about the totality of what there is in the world. There is no property, such as self-identity, which all objects possess. To say that if all objects were exactly alike they would be identical, and there could be only one object in the world, is to assert not a logical truth, but an accidental characteristic of the world. Consequently, we cannot use self-identity as a property by which we can "locate" an object. Instead, we signify objects by means of letters, and different objects by different letters.

The simplest proposition, the elementary proposition, asserts the existence of an atomic fact. Such a proposition is a concatenation of names and is incapable of analysis into further propositions. Now it is an important thesis of Wittgenstein that all propositions are truth-functions of elementary propositions and can be built up from them. (An elementary proposition is a truth-function of itself.) Truth-functions are obtained in the following way: Suppose all elementary propositions were given. Each of these could be either true or false. Therefore a proposition containing three elementary propositions p, q, r could have a truth-function T,T,F, or T,F,T, and there would be eight such possible truth-functions; in case there were four elementary propositions there would be sixteen truth-functions. Starting with any group of elementary propositions the truth-functions formed from them may be arranged in a series.

Of the propositions, two kinds are particularly important. One of them, called a "tautology," is a type of proposition which is true for all the truth-possibilities of the elementary propositions. The other, called a "contradiction," is a proposition which is false for all the truth-possibilities of the elementary propositions. The truth of a tautology is *certain*; the truth of a contradiction is *impossible*; the truth of all other propositions is *possible*. Here we have the serial arrangement of propositions which forms the basis for a theory of probability. An example of a tautology is "It is either raining or it is not raining"; this is always true regardless of whether the p and the *not-p* which it contains are true or false. A tautology, therefore, "says nothing" about the world, for it is true of all possible states of affairs. An example of a contradiction is "It is both raining and it is not raining"; this is false regardless of whether the p and the *not-p* which it contains are true or false. A contradiction therefore also "says nothing" about the world, for it is false for all possible states of affairs. Tautologies and contradictions are without sense. "Contradiction is the external limit of the propositions, tautology their substanceless center."

Logical operations are those which produce propositions from other propositions. For example, "denial" (not), "logical addition" (either-or), "logical multiplication" (and) are all logical operations. Thus, operations do not assert anything; the *result* of an operation, a proposition, does assert something; and what it asserts depends upon the elementary propositions on which it is based. We can thus express the general form of all propositions; this is a propositional variable whose values would be all possible propositions. Wittgenstein states this form in abstract symbols; it means, according to Russell's statement in the *Introduction*, "whatever can be obtained by taking any selection of atomic propositions, negating them all, then taking any selection of the set of propositions now obtained, together with any of the originals—and so on indefinitely."

We saw above that language cannot express anything that contradicts logic. Wittgenstein now resumes the discussion of this topic and points out that we cannot say what we cannot think. We cannot say that there is *this* in the world but there is not *that*, for such a statement would imply that logic can exclude certain possibilities from the world; but in such a case logic would have to "get outside the limits of the world"; that is, it would have to consider these limits from both within and without the world. However, logic cannot go beyond itself; "logic fills the world: the limits of the world are also its limits." This principle also has applications for solipsism. Solipsism is correct, but cannot be asserted; it can only be "shown." The subject who knows is the limit of the world; he does not belong to it. The best example of this theory is the field of vision: there is nothing *in the field of sight* that permits us to conclude that it is seen by an eye.

Reality, for Wittgenstein, proves to be very loose-knit. No atomic fact contradicts any atomic fact, and no atomic fact can be inferred from an atomic fact. There is no causal nexus in nature, and belief that there is such a thing is superstition. Induction is a process of assuming the simplest law that can be made to describe the regularities of nature. But there is no necessity in this process. The only necessity is a *logical* necessity, and the only impossibility is a *logical* impossibility; and these presumably do not exist in the world.

The *sense* of the world lies outside the world. If there were *value* it would have to "lie outside all happenings and being-so. For all happenings and being-so is accidental." As a consequence, ethics and aesthetics cannot be expressed, and are transcendental.

What, then, is philosophy? It seems to have two tasks. One is to show that every proposition is a picture of a fact. This cannot be *said*, for no proposition can say anything about itself. That a proposition has, for example, the subject-predicate form cannot be said in a proposition, and that a proposition has the form "*p* or *q*" cannot be said in a proposition. Nor can it be said how a proposition pictures reality. A sentence has no *apparent* pictorial character. But neither does a musical score, or a phonograph record; and neither does a pattern of sound waves obviously picture the sound themselves. Yet all of these stand to that which they represent in a relation which can be seen in the similarity of structure holding between them and the facts. There is a "law of projection" which enables us to translate the picture into the fact, though this *law* cannot be stated. And since the law cannot be stated, we should not try to do so. Wittgenstein therefore concludes with proposition 7, "Whereof one cannot speak, thereof one must be silent."

But there *is* another task for philosophy. Philosophy is not a theory, like one of the natural sciences, ending in a series of conclusions which can be called "philosophical propositions." It is an activity, a process of clarification, in which we try to delimit thoughts which are obscure and confused. If philosophy finds that the *answers* to its questions cannot be expressed, it should realize that its *questions* have not been properly expressed, for "if a question can be put at all, then it *can* also be answered." To doubt where there are no questions is absurd. To insist that the problems of life have not been touched by the sciences, and yet to be unable to formulate these problems which remain in a language which is clear enough to permit an answer is really to say that there is no problem left. This is precisely what Wittgenstein says. "The solution of the problem of life is seen in the vanishing of this problem." The right method of philosophy is to turn all of the things which can be said over to the scientists, who will *say* them, and then when anyone asks a metaphysical question, to point out to him that his question is meaningless. Philosophy will then "see the world rightly."—*A.C.B.*

PERTINENT LITERATURE

Ramsey, Frank P. "Critical Notice of Ludwig Wittgenstein's *Tractatus Logico-Philosophicus*," in *Mind*. XXXII, no. 128 (October, 1923), pp. 465-478.

Frank P. Ramsey's "Critical Notice" remains the best short introduction to Ludwig Wittgenstein's *Tractatus*. He begins by noting that the "attractive epigrammatic flavor" of the book may detract from Wittgenstein's explanations of his technical terms and theories, but that the Introduction to the book written by Bertrand Russell and printed with it may partly make up for the deficiency of its discursive style. However, Ramsey was also among the first—Wittgenstein himself evidently *was* the first—to call attention to the fact that there are serious errors in Russell's Introduction. The most important of these is that Russell evidently thought that Wittgenstein's investigation of symbolism was directed at discovering "the conditions that would have to be fulfilled by a logically perfect language." This is certainly false; Ramsey attributes the error to a too quick generalization from the few passages in which

Wittgenstein *is* concerned with a logically perfect and not just any language, "e.g., the discussion of 'logical syntax' in 3.325ff." (All decimal references herein refer to the numbered passages of the *Tractatus*.) He goes on to argue that many other passages, notably 4.002ff, indicate that the *Tractatus'* doctrines are intended to apply to ordinary, natural languages and indeed to language as such. Ramsey does appear to agree with Russell in supposing that the book's fundamental thesis is that "in order that a certain sentence should assert a certain fact there must, however the language may be constructed, be something in common between the structure of the sentence and the structure of the fact." Since this thesis depends on Wittgenstein's notions of a "picture" and its "form of representation," Ramsey addresses most of the balance of his review to a critical examination of them.

According to the *Tractatus*, all meaningful sentences are used to represent facts pictorially. However, a picture itself is a fact, "the fact that its elements are combined in a definite way." The elements of the picture are coordinated with the constituents of the fact which it pictures, and "These co-ordinations constitute the representing relation which makes the picture a picture." In Ramsey's interpretation, "a picture represents that certain objects are combined in a certain way" means "the elements of the picture are combined in that way, and are co-ordinated with the objects by representing relation which belongs to the picture." Ramsey argues that Wittgenstein's use of "form of representation" is ambiguous between: (1) "the (possibility of the) way in which the elements of the picture are combined"; and (2) "the possibility that the things [that is, the constituents of the fact pictured] are so combined with one another as are the elements of the picture." He then points out that, according to the first interpretation, Wittgenstein would be saying only that the picture is itself a fact; and his claim "that we cannot represent or speak about the logical form of representation" would amount to "no more than that we cannot talk about what makes a fact a fact, nor ultimately about facts at all, because every statement apparently about facts is really about their constituents." Ramsey is certainly correct both in suggesting that Wittgenstein believed these doctrines when he wrote the *Tractatus* and also in his further claim that Wittgenstein intended a good deal more than this by his claim that "the picture has the form of representation in common with the pictured." This is brought out by Wittgenstein's second use of "form of representation" noted above, for, as Ramsey points out, it implies "that the things with which its [the picture's] elements are co-ordinated by the representing relation are of such types that they *can* be combined in the same way as the elements of the picture." Ramsey sees this as Wittgenstein's principal reason for the important claim that "the picture contains the possibility of the state of affairs which it represents" [2.203]. (This doctrine is central to the *Tractatus* for it is the book's explanation of the fact that we are able to produce and to understand novel sentences, ones—such as the present sentence—with which we have never before been acquainted.)

Next, Ramsey introduces C. S. Peirce's distinction between type and token in order to clarify Wittgenstein's use of the word "proposition." This sentence begins with a token of the word "this"; all the tokens of that word may be grouped together—on the basis of physical similarity and conventions associating certain noises with certain shapes—into a single type, the word "this." According to Ramsey, Wittgenstein uses the term "propositional sign" for reference to what we would ordinarily call a "sentence" in order to make clear that he is talking about sentences—not in the sense in which they have "the same nature as the words of which they are composed," but rather as tokens of propositions whose "instances consist of all propositional sign tokens which have in common, not a certain physical appearance, but a certain *sense*."

This brings Ramsey to one of the most important theses of the *Tractatus*: namely, that "a thought is a type whose tokens have in common a certain sense, and include the tokens of the corresponding propositions." (As Max Black and others have noted, "here if anywhere we can see the beginning of the 'linguistic turn' in modern [analytic] philosophy," for the *Tractatus* was the first work to systematically argue that all discussion of thought can be replaced with discussion of propositions expressed by propositional sign tokens which picture facts in exactly the same way, share precisely the same pictorial relationship to facts, as thoughts.) As Ramsey points out, Wittgenstein thus reduces the analysis of judgment to the question "What is it for a proposition token to have a certain sense"? Ramsey paraphrases Wittgenstein's answer to this question as "a proposition token is a logical picture; and so its sense should be given by the definition of the sense of a picture; accordingly the sense of a proposition is that the things meant by [that is, referred to by] its elements are combined with one another in the same way as are the elements themselves, that is, logically." (This corresponds to the second use of "form of representation" attributed to Wittgenstein by Ramsey and noted above.)

Ramsey notes that Wittgenstein's definition is not a complete definition in two respects. First, it applies only to elementary proposition tokens, for only such proposition tokens can have *all* their elements correlated with objects, there being no "objects" to correlate with logical constants such as "any," "all," "if," "and," "or," and "not," according to the *Tractatus*. Moreover, because of the redundancy and enormous complexity of ordinary (natural) languages, there are even words in some apparently noncomplex proposition tokens which seem to fail to have "objects" correlated with them. For example, in "a connects b with c," the names "a," "b," and "c" may be correlated with the objects a, b, and c respectively, but it is not clear that there is any "object" to be correlated with ". . .connects . . . with. . . ." Setting aside this latter problem on the Tractarian grounds that a completely analyzed noncomplex proposition token of any language—whether ideally constructed or colloquial—must reduce to simple signs (names) each of which refers to an object, Ramsey notes that one aim of the *Tractatus* theory of truth-functions is to show that there are no "objects" to be correlated with logical constants in truth-functionally complex proposition tokens. This the *Tractatus* attempts to accomplish as follows: an elementary thought or proposition token "p" says that p is the case; such a thought or proposition token is true if p is the case (in other words if its sense agrees with reality; that is, the possible state of affairs it represents is the actual one), and it is false if p is not the case. When a truth-functionally complex proposition is built up using elementary propositions, its truth value is determined by the truth values of its elementary propositions. In a given truth-functionally complex proposition, there will be 2^n combinations of the truth values of its elementary components, and correspondingly 2^n possibilities of existence and nonexistence of the atomic facts whose possibility they picture. The logical constants used in its construction do not themselves refer to "objects" (as do the names out of which the elementary proposition tokens themselves are constituted). Instead, the logical constants determine a unique truth value for each of the truth value combinations of the complex's elementary components, and correspondingly picture the possibility of a (complex) fact. Unlike Gottlob Frege, Wittgenstein does not suppose that propositions refer to abstract entities—"The True" and "The False." Instead, in Wittgenstein's view, the proposition (complex or elementary) is true if the fact it represents exists, and false otherwise. From a Tractarian point of view, the "problem of defining truth" is dissolved once we understand the way in which propositions picture facts. (Chapter 2 of G. E. M. Anscombe's *Introduction to Wittgenstein's* Tractatus uses a game analogy to clarify Wittgenstein's elimination of the abstract, Fregean truth values; see additional readings.)

Next, Ramsey turns to the two extreme cases to which this analysis leads. If the proposition disagrees with all truth possibilities, it is contradictory; and, if it agrees with them all, it is tautologous. In either case, the proposition does *not* say anything—about how the world is, about what is the case. Ramsey acknowledges that Wittgenstein's discovery of the tautologous nature of (many of) the propositions of logic was a remarkable achievement, but he argues that it is doubtful that Wittgenstein's analysis is adequate. First, outside the context of an ideally constructed language, the Tractarian theory does not yield a unique analysis even for propositions which are only truth-functionally complex. Second, in the case of proposition tokens which express propositional attitudes—that is, attitudes towards propositions—Wittgenstein's reduction of, for example, "A asserts 'p'" to "'p' says that p" can at most amount to an analysis of "A asserts 'p' using a certain logical notation." (Wittgenstein presumably would not have seen this as a problem at the time that he wrote the *Tractatus*, for—whatever logical notation or language someone might use in asserting, thinking, or believing "p"—the proposition expressed would have the same logical form and sense because it would picture the same fact.) Third, and more importantly, the *Tractatus* fails to take account of the relation between the person who has a propositional attitude and the proposition toward which he or she has that attitude: for example, A's believing "p and q" may just amount to A's believing "p" and also believing "q"; but A's believing "p or q" is not the same as A's believing "p" or A's believing "q," for A may believe "p" while believing "not-q." Moreover, A believes "not-p" is clearly not the same as its not being the case that A believes "p," for in the former case A believes "p" is false while in the latter case A may have no belief whatever as to the truth value of "p." (Considerations such as these may have been instrumental in Wittgenstein's eventual rejection of the *Tractatus'* view of propositions.)

The balance of Ramsey's "Critical Notice" is devoted to the following: a criticism of Wittgenstein's remarks on the mystical, a criticism in which Ramsey traces the pseudopropositions which Wittgenstein calls attempts to express the mystical to mundane consequences of our linguistic practice; a remarkably incisive discussion of Wittgenstein's treatment of identity; a discussion of his treatment of necessity and possibility; an examination of the *Tractatus'* account of philosophy, in which Ramsey argues that philosophical activity may result in philosophical propositions even if the Tractarian view is correct; and a very brief account of Wittgenstein's general view of the world. One of the most startling conclusions of the *Tractatus*, of course, was that there are no philosophical propositions as such: according to 6.54, although the "propositions" in the *Tractatus* "serve as elucidations . . . anyone who understands me eventually recognizes them as nonsensical, when he has used them—as steps—to climb up beyond them. (He must, so to speak, throw away the ladder after he has climbed up it.)" Ramsey seems to have misunderstood the *Tractatus* on this point for he evidently thought that a substantial analysis of "'p' is significant" is consistent with the Tractarian view, whereas one of its major theses is that it is not possible to *say* what the significance of a proposition is. This thesis presumably follows from other more basic theses of the *Tractatus*—for example, that the sense of any (significant) proposition is (nothing but) the fact whose possibility it pictures.

Ramsey acknowledges that the *Tractatus* includes "remarks, always interesting, sometimes extremely penetrating, on many other subjects, such as the Theory of Types, Ancestral Relations, Probability, the Philosophy of Physics, and Ethics," but he does not include a review or criticism of Wittgenstein's remarks on these topics.

Black, Max. *A Companion to Wittgenstein's* Tractatus. Ithaca, New York: Cornell University Press, 1964.

After a brief general introduction, very helpful comments on Bertrand Russell's Introduction, and a comparison of Ludwig Wittgenstein's problems with Russell's philosophy, Max Black provides a passage-by-passage commentary. Each "installment" of *Tractatus Logico-Philosophicus* is introduced by a brief statement which is followed by line-by-line comments on its sentences. These include explications of difficult terms and explanations of how remarks in that "installment" are related to earlier drafts of the *Tractatus* as well as to many of Wittgenstein's other works. Black also cross-references related parts of the *Tractatus* and provides pithy paraphrases of troublesome passages. These are often complemented by exegetical and critical essays in which Black excavates the *Tractatus'* foundations.

Black argues that the central motif of the *Tractatus* is its treatment of "the essence of logic," and that Wittgenstein's examination of logic and mathematics is not "merely peripheral," as Erik Stenius had maintained in his *Wittgenstein's Tractatus: A Critical Exposition of Its Main Lines of Thought*. Also, Black shows that G. E. M. Anscombe is far off the mark in the first edition of her *Introduction*, which takes the "principal theme" of the *Tractatus* to be the relation of thought to reality; for he shows that its main thrust is to turn this theme into the more promising problem of the relation of language to reality. He notes that Wittgenstein's investigations began with those which occur later in the *Tractatus*—on logic, language, mathematics and probability, science, ethics, and the self. In the final conception, logic, language, and the world are "virtually inseparable," for "the ontology of the 'Tractatus' is a striking combination of an atomistic conception of the universe as an aggregate of mutually independent atomic facts, and an organic conception of logical form—or, what comes to the same, 'logical space.'" As a metaphysical text, it has few peers. Wittgenstein's conception of the world as an aggregate of facts, not of things "sets him off sharply from Aristotle, Spinoza, Descartes—indeed from any of the 'classical philosophers' who come readily to mind, the earlier Russell not excluded," Black writes; for Wittgenstein's conception of *the possibility of language*, led him to reject "the traditional conception of the universe as something that can be referred to by a name."

Wittgenstein's investigation of the possibility of language, *any* language *as such*, resulted in the Tractarian "picture theory" of propositional meaning. He thought that this in turn revealed ("showed" but did not "say" what *is*) the necessary ontological structure of reality. This metaphysics dovetailed neatly with his Viennese *fin de siècle* speculations about God, the self, will, and life and death, as well as with the accounts of science, ethics, and the mystical which then seemed most plausible to him, while "simultaneously" explaining why nothing comparable to scientific knowledge about these matters had been produced by aeons of philosophical thought and writing. Black helpfully comments on much of this; but his treatment in LXXX-LXXXIII of Wittgenstein's remarks on science, causation, induction, and the laws of nature is essential for understanding his commitment to science over meta-physics, given the difficulty of analyzing the principles and laws of science into truth-functional compounds of elementary propositions which picture states of affairs—a task required by the "picture theory" of propositional meaning.

Equally important is Black's explication in II-IV of Wittgenstein's argument for the necessary existence of "objects as the substance of the world." In brief, Black reads the *Tractatus* as limited to an ontology of atomic facts into which the world divides and simple objects which are their substance. Objects (*Gegenständen*) contrast with atomic facts (*Sachverhalten*). Objects are sim-ple; they necessarily exist; they are symbolized by names which "show" some-thing; and they are mutually dependent. Atomic facts are complex; their existence is merely contingent; they are depicted by full sentences which "say" something; and they are mutually independent. Black notes that the *Tractatus* takes internal (logical) properties and relations to be "essentially different from" external (material) properties and relations. This is one of its major contributions to contemporary philosophy. The former are grammatical fea-tures required in order for propositions to express their sense. The latter are (nothing but) combinations of objects. An object is "spatial," "temporal," or "colored" if its form is such that it can be combined with other objects in spatial, temporal, or colored configurations. Thus, material properties and relations are not ontologically ultimate elements which inhere in objects. This is crucially important as shown by Black in LXXXV, "The Incompatibility of Colors." While writing the *Tractatus* and in the years immediately following, Wittgenstein was puzzled by the fact that "This [point in my visual field] is red" and "This [the same point] is blue" appear to exclude one another, or even to be inconsistent; whereas elementary propositions are mutually in-dependent, as are the atomic facts which they depict. Wittgenstein at first believed that such propositions—appearances notwithstanding—were com-plex rather than elementary, and that analysis of them would show that their incompatibility does not involve any mutual dependence between either el-ementary propositions or the atomic facts which they depict. Failure to analyze away their evident incompatibility started Wittgenstein on the investigations which eventuated in his later repudiation of the *Tractatus*.

On Black's reading, Wittgenstein's consignment of philosophy to silence in the concluding remarks of the *Tractatus* is hyperbolic. In LXL Black suggests (in effect) that Wittgenstein may have been confused by the two Tractarian ways in which a proposition can fail to make sense—failing to picture facts at all (*sinnlos*) versus, as it were, "picturing" illusory "metaphysical facts" (*unsinnig*). It seems unlikely that Wittgenstein himself could have been so confused about so fundamental a feature of the *Tractatus*. So, his remarks in 6.53-7 can probably be given a better reading. (In this regard see Russell's Introduction to the *Tractatus*.)—R.L.S.

ADDITIONAL RECOMMENDED READING

Anscombe, G. E. M. *An Introduction to Wittgenstein's* Tractatus. New York: Harper & Row Publishers, 1959. This is an excellent short book-length introduction which was written primarily for students. It especially emphasizes the ways in which the *Tractatus* grew out of the prior works of Frege and Russell. It includes a somewhat useful glossary of Tractarian terms and symbols.

Copi, Irving M. and Robert W. Beard, eds. *Essays on Wittgenstein's* Tractatus. New York: Hafner Press, 1973. There are a number of anthologies of articles on the *Tractatus*. The Copi/Beard collection is notable not only for including perhaps the best selection of Tractarian expositions and critiques but also for an excellent bibliography and for a very useful index of references to the *Tractatus* in the anthology's contents.

Janik, Allan and Stephen Toulmin. *Wittgenstein's Vienna*. New York: Simon and Schuster, 1973. This is an excellent piece of cultural history which excavates the intellectual roots of the *Tractatus*.

Kripke, Saul A. "Naming and Necessity," in *Semantics of Natural Language*. Edited by D. Davidson and G. Harman. Dordrecht/Boston: D. Reidel, 1972, pp. 253-355. The referential theory of the relation between language and reality presented by Kripke is in certain ways like that of the *Tractatus*. However, Kripke's relata are different from Wittgenstein's for he takes ordinary things and the theoretical entities of science to be what are named by designators. His view of necessity and possibility is very different from that of the *Tractatus*. "Naming and Necessity" is especially interesting as a Russellian treatment of the problems posed by seeing language as a representation of reality.

Musil, Robert. *The Man Without Qualities*. Translated by E. Wilkins and E. Kaiser. London: Secker & Warburg, 1960. The first volume of this novel was published in German in 1930. Musil was not able to complete it before his death; however, he published the second volume in 1932, and material which Musil had prepared toward a third volume was published posthumously. The first three volumes of the English translation include the parts which Musil himself completed; a fourth volume includes the unfinished conclusion of the work and some unfinished chapters. Unlike the other works cited in this review of literature pertinent to the *Tractatus*, Musil's book is neither a treatise of technical philosophy nor of cultural history, but rather a fictional work informed by the Tractarian view of the world. The story setting is the preparations in 1913 for a national celebration of the Austrian Emperor's jubilee aimed at imbuing the entire world with the lofty spirit of "our grand old Austrian culture." It encompasses only one year in time, and was to end with the beginning of World War I, but Musil's two thousand completed pages plus about twenty unfinished chapters—some of which exist in as many as twenty versions—are like an ever-expanding total picture of one year's events. The reader is left with a mystical sense that everything that did happen in 1914 and since might somehow be undone by the force of the alternate reality pictured by Musil. This perhaps differs from Wittgenstein's sense of the mystical, as in 6.44: "It is not *how* things are in the world that is mystical, but *that* it exists." Nevertheless, Musil was taken with the *Tractatus*, and *The Man Without Qualities* is an expression of the mystical in the sense of 6.45: "To view the world *sub specie aeterni* is to view it as a whole—a limited whole. Feeling the world as a limited whole—it is this that is the mystical." Musil's work is in the sense of 6.522 a struggle against the limits of our language. That is, it is an attempt to say what can only be felt—that the world is not everything, that there is something outside it, its "sense" or "meaning."

Rorty, Richard. *Philosophy and the Mirror of Nature*. Princeton, New Jersey: Princeton University Press, 1979. This is not a commentary on the *Tractatus*; it is a criticism, largely based on Wittgenstein's *Philosophical Investigations* (see below), of any view according to which nature or reality is mirrored by thought, mind, language, or logic. For the student of the *Tractatus*, the principal interest of Rorty's book is that it makes explicit some of the assumptions and presuppositions of the philosophical tradition out of which the *Tractatus* emerged.

Stenius, Erik. *Wittgenstein's* Tractatus: *A Critical Exposition of Its Main Lines of Thought*. Ithaca, New York: Cornell University Press, 1960. Although this is an interesting and provocative book, it is hardly an exposition of the *Tractatus*. Its primary contribution is that of placing Wittgenstein in the Kantian rather than the British Empiricist wing of Western philosophy.

Wittgenstein, Ludwig. *Notebooks, 1914-1916*. Edited by G. H. von Wright and G. E. M. Anscombe. Oxford: Blackwell, 1961. The *Tractatus* is to a great extent a distillation of material in the *Notebooks*. In many cases, however, the *Notebooks* represent a more tentative stage in Wittgenstein's thinking than do the fully developed views of the *Tractatus*.

——————. *Philosophical Investigations*. Translated by G. E. M. Anscombe. New York: Macmillan Publishing Company, 1953. Wittgenstein is unique among philosophers for having produced two great classics of which the second is the definitive critique of the first. The German edition of this book is printed together with the German text of the *Tractatus*. Wittgenstein suggests in the Preface to the *Investigations* that it should be read together with the *Tractatus* in order to be properly understood. Whereas the *Tractatus* focused on our use of language to refer to things and thereby picture facts, the *Investigations* focuses on other uses of language and sees the *Tractatus* as a typical result of the philosopher's craving for generality.

HUMAN NATURE AND CONDUCT

Author: John Dewey (1859-1952)
Type of work: Ethics
First published: 1922

PRINCIPAL IDEAS ADVANCED

Moralities of the past were deficient in that they were based on arbitrary rules rather than on a scientific understanding of human nature as formed within a social environment.

Human nature is continuous with the rest of nature; ethics is thus allied with physics and biology, and with sociology, law, and economics.

Vices and virtues are habits developed during the interaction of the human organism and the social environment.

Morals are ways of action invented to meet specific situations; reactions to them become habits and acquire prescriptive character.

Education must enable the organism to modify its behavior in the face of novelty.

Reflection upon conduct has as its objective the satisfying resolution of a problem arising from the incompatibility of various impulses.

In the Preface to *Human Nature and Conduct: An Introduction to Social Psychology* Dewey says that his book "sets forth a belief that an understanding of habit and of different types of habit is the key to social psychology while the operation of impulse and intelligence gives the key to individualized mental activity. But they are secondary to habit so that the mind can be understood in the concrete only as a system of beliefs, desires and purposes which are formed in the interaction of biological aptitudes with a social environment."

Thus, to understand ourselves and others in terms of Dewey's theory, we must study human nature and the social institutions in which it functions. Both forces work to shape the individual. Morality is the interaction between the two.

Dewey criticizes the morality of the past as being based largely on arbitrary rules rather than on a scientific understanding of human beings. The few have given and administered rules which the many have obeyed with reluctance, if at all.

Such morality is largely restrictive, concerned with what should not be done. Many people conform, but others circumvent the morality in their practice, while giving lip service to it or by having a theory which avoids it. The romantic device of the glorification of impulse as opposed to knowledge is such a theory. Those who attempt to live by a morality divorced from an adequate theory of human nature inhabit a world in which the ideal and the real are sharply separated. They must renounce one world or live uneasily in a world split in two.

It is Dewey's contention that only knowledge can solve moral problems and that only scientific method holds promise of providing knowledge. The moral life operates in an environmental setting that is both natural and social. Human nature is continuous with the rest of nature, and as a result ethics is allied with physics and biology. Since the activities of one person are continuous with those of others, ethics is allied with such social sciences as sociology, law, and economics. Even the past is not irrelevant. We can study history to understand the present as derived from the past and to help us determine the structure of the future.

The moral acts of a person are closely related to his habits. Habits are compared by Dewey to psychological functions. Both require the cooperation of the organism and its environment. Vices and virtues are not private possessions of a person; they are the result of the interaction of human nature and environment. "All virtues and vices are habits which incorporate objective forces." They can be studied and understood and, as such, can serve as the basis of moral discussion.

Everyone is familiar with bad habits. They are tendencies to action which somehow command us but which we usually have acquired without conscious intent. Since they command, they are will in a clear sense of this word. Since they are demanding, and determine what we regard as significant and what as trivial, they are the self if we are to understand that concept.

Dewey uses this view to replace the belief that will is a separate faculty which, if exercised, can achieve whatever the individual wishes to achieve. A person with a bad habit is not simply failing to do the right thing; he has formed a habit of doing the wrong thing. Habits cannot be dismissed by a simple effort of will any more than rain can be brought on by a simple act of dancing. As one must understand the conditions that cause drought and bring rain, so one must understand the objective conditions which cause and continue habit.

Neither reason nor will can be separated from habit. What one reasons about, what one decides upon, how one acts on decisions is determined by the relation of the human organism to an environment.

Many people have thought that social institutions are the result of individual habits. The contrary is true for Dewey. They are the source of information about habits, in the sense that the individual must acquire habits that conform with those of his social group. This explains the meaning of such terms as group mind, collective mind, and crowd mind. They can mean nothing more than "a custom brought at some point to explicit, emphatic consciousness, emotional or intellectual." Dewey adds, "In short, the primary facts of social psychology center about collective habit, custom."

One might expect that democracy would encourage individuality, but democracy as we live it seems, on the contrary, to encourage conformity. Conformity is due to the unfavorable influence of past custom as it affects beliefs, emotions, and purposes. An education tied to the past "becomes the art of taking advantage of the helplessness of the young; the forming of habits becomes a guarantee of the hedges of custom." But habit is not necessarily conservative. It is any ability formed through past experience. One can acquire the habit to seek new solutions to new problems as easily as the habit to attempt to solve all problems in old ways. Dewey does not describe habit as simply a way of acting; it is also a way of thinking, because thinking requires energy and energy is organized by habit.

Dewey's view of habit places him in opposition to a central contention of the great majority of moralists. They have held that ethical decisions can or must be made by the intellect, unencumbered by nonrational dispositions such as habits or customs. Morality involves relating a set of ideal laws to particular situations and deciding on a course of action which resolves the situation and is in accord with these laws. What classical moralists do not account for, Dewey contends, is the source of ideal laws. Such laws do not suddenly appear, fully formulated, carrying with them their own demand for obedience. On the contrary, they grow like language from incoherent mutterings to complex systems of communication, requiring adherence to rules which are a product of after-the-fact reflection and which acquire a prescriptive character. Morals are ways of acting invented to meet specific situations. When these situations are repeated, the reaction to them becomes a habit and acquires a prescriptive character. Morality refers to social institutions to which we must defer if we are to live. But deference is not implicit obedience. Indeed, implicit obedience to any rule of action is impossible. The rule is derived from the environment, and conditions change. In a completely static world, rules might forever remain the same; but our world is not static, and new rules arise from inevitable change.

We must distinguish between impulses and habits. All human beings love, hate, desire, and avoid; and these impulses have been embodied in social institutions. But what variety there is in these institutions! Different societies utilize the same impulses in many ways: the communism of the South Sea islanders, the pacifism of the Chinese (these are Dewey's examples), the militarism of the ancient Persians, the variety of class morality in almost every society.

The infant is largely potentiality. It is born in an adult environment which provides channels for its impulses; indeed, without these channels the impulses have no meaning, because while an activity stems from the impulse, the nature of the activity comes from the social environment. This environment may be intensely tight, narrow, and restrictive or it may be loose, wide, and tolerant. Dewey advocates the latter sort. He says: "With the dawn of the idea of progressive betterment and an interest in new uses of impulses, there has grown up some consciousness of the extent to which a future new society of changed purposes and desires may be created by a deliberate human treatment of the impulses of youth. This is the meaning of education; for a truly humane education consists in an intelligent direction of native activities in the light of the possibilities and necessities of the social situation."

Dewey describes insistence on conformity as training, not education. Education, properly speaking, must enable the organism to modify its behavior in the face of novelty, rather than to withdraw timidly. Dewey says again and again and in article after article that no old set of habits will ever be adequate to meet new situations. One fact about the future we can be sure of is that it will contain novelty. Old rules sometimes meet new situations but only because the old rules are vague.

By defining human nature as this combination of impulses and social conditioning, Dewey is able to claim that human nature can be changed. As social conditions change, new ways must be devised to meet the change; old impulses are directed into new channels and a new human nature is formed. Indeed, the very words we use to describe human nature—selfishness, greed, altruism, generosity—are social terms and have no meaning apart from our interaction with the environment. A person acts with regard to the consequences of his acts, and a part of these consequences is what others will think of the act.

Instincts provide the motive for action but do not determine the character of the action. To attribute all business activity to the acquisitive instinct is an oversimplification, tending to obscure the study of business enterprise. Another case in point is pleasure. The moral literature of the world is full of tirades branding pleasure as evil. Certainly some excesses of pleasure do harm; but pleasure is as necessary to the human organism as work, which is often taken as its opposite. It is through art and play that new and fresh meanings are added to the usual activities of life. Both have a moral function. Both bring into use the imagination which often finds no part to play in our mundane activities. Both heighten and broaden the meaning of our ordinary concerns. Art and play release energy in a constructive way.

The constructive release of energy is in the direction of meeting new situations by modifying old ways of action. The alternatives are frozen custom or unbridled revolution. What Dewey wants is conscious, reflective reconstruction of society. We must act, but we must act constructively, guided by intelligence.

What, then, is the place of intelligence in conduct? Dewey has already discussed habits. They are related to intelligence in two ways. The first is restrictive. Habits confine intelligence to the problem at hand; but if this were its only function, the goal of intelligence would be mindless action. Intelligence offers the solution; habit takes over and repeats the solution again and again. But habit is not only restrictive. In its second function it presents alternatives.

The more numerous our habits, the greater are the possibilities of action. In explaining this second function of habit, Dewey says that we "know how by means of our habits." This means that through habits of inquiry we recognize the novelty in a situation and marshal our previous experience by means of the channels of habit to meet it. This focus of habits on a problem and the solution which results is an essential function of intelligence. Unless we have habits of inquiry, there is no approach to the problem. We must learn until it becomes habit that problems can be recognized and that to solve them we must recollect, observe, and plan.

Some psychologists believe that intelligence and moral conscience are separate faculties which are unconditioned by experience but which operate on the subject matter of experience when it falls within their realm. Dewey does not share this view. For him, both develop in the human organism as the organism develops. The organism grows in height, learns to swim, evinces a desire for knowledge, accepts, and rejects. Every habit is an impulse. The child learns something, likes what he learns, and then wants to learn more. That he may want to learn more is no more mysterious than that he may want to swim better or that he may want to act morally.

To act morally is to act in the best or wisest way. Such a course of action requires deliberation. To deliberate is to examine with the mind the possible courses of action and their consequences. The possible courses of action which are considered are the result of habit. The choice of one course rather than others simply means that "some habit or some combination of elements of habits and impulse finds a way fully open. Then energy is released. The mind is made up, composed, unified." Deliberation is always the search for a way to act, not an end in itself.

Dewey disagrees with the Utilitarians. Their theory, he believes, is that the intellect calculates the consequences of various courses of action and then chooses the one that will result in the most pleasure. His first objection to this theory is that it depends on the misapprehension that reason leads directly to action. On the contrary, habit furnishes the force of action, not reason nor yet the anticipation of feelings. Secondly, there is the difficulty of predicting future pleasures. Future pleasures depend on our bodily state at some future moment and on the environment of that state. Both of these are independent of present action. "Things sweet in anticipation are bitter in actual taste, things we now turn from in aversion are welcome at another moment in our career." What makes utilitarianism seem plausible to its advocates is their assumption that the organism and its surroundings will remain constant through time. They project the present into the future.

"There is seen to be but one issue involved in all reflection upon conduct: The rectifying of present troubles, the harmonizing of present incompatibilities by projecting a course of action which gathers into itself the meaning of them all." In this sentence Dewey summarizes his ethical theory as he formulated it in *Human Nature and Conduct*. Good means the unity that the organism experiences in an action which harmonizes incompatibilities. A moral act is the solution to a problem. Moral aims are not expressed in precepts that exist outside action but they are consequences or natural effects of action. Men like some consequences and attempt to achieve them again. In this attempt at realization, consequences function as ends. An end is a dream in which present conflict is ended; the environment is corrected; and the future is seen in terms of a concrete course of action. The dream of fixed ends at which all action should aim is another expression of men's hope for certainty in action. That this hope is vain is the subject of another of Dewey's books, *The Quest for Certainty* (1929).

The function of intelligence is to foresee the future insofar as this can be done by means of principles and criteria of judgment. These principles are like habits. When they become fixed and are regarded as changeless, they can restrict action. However, it must be remembered, Dewey warns, that these principles were derived originally from concrete situations and that they deserve the deference due to any generalization that results from experience. They are hypotheses with which to experiment and whose use is to forecast the consequences of action.

What part does desire play in moral judgment? Most theories evaluate desire in terms of its object. But reflection shows that a desire can have a variety of objects. Psychologically, desire drives the organism forward. It gives activity to life. The projected object of the desire and the attained object never agree, however close they may approach one another. Desire acting without will misses its object because action is not controlled. Desire acting with intelligence, Dewey concludes, is led toward its object.

No person who acts can control the future; his control is limited to the present. He may die before his goal is reached or he may no longer desire it as a goal. Neither can he provide all contingencies. If he attempts to do so, he will never act at all. He must act in the present. A new house may be a future goal, but it has to be built in some present if it is to be lived in. Future goals are attained by learning through action in the present. Dewey applies these ideas to education. "If education were conducted as a process of the fullest utilization of present resources, liberating and guiding capacities that are now urgent, it goes without saying that the lives of the young would be much richer in meaning than they are now." This principle can also be applied to modern industrial production. The worker confronted with article after article that he will never use soon loses the interest that might motivate him to make his work efficient. His work seems senseless.

For Dewey, the scope of morals extends to all cases in which there are alternative possibilities of action. The word "conduct" covers every act that is judged better or worse. Morality is not to be severed from other life activities. Every type of conduct incorporates value and gives for good or bad a meaning of life.

Any doctrine of moral conduct which replaces adherence to precepts with a naturalistic theory must explain the fact of freedom. Whatever happens in accord with a law of nature is not free; and if morality is not somehow separated as different in kind from natural facts, moral actions will not be free and men will have become automatons. Dewey must meet this problem. To do so, he defines the person acting freely as having three characteristics: (1) the ability to plan and act in accord with the plan; (2) the capacity to vary plans to meet new conditions; and (3) the conviction that desire and choice are a significant factor in action. The capacity to plan presupposes intelligence, and so intelligence is a precondition to freedom. There are two sorts of freedom, freedom-to and freedom-from. Freedom-from is necessary but restrictive. It must leave room for freedom to act, which requires desire, deliberation, and choice.

For Dewey, we live in a social world. We are conditioned by education, tradition, and environment. The materials on which our intelligence operates come from the community life of which we are a part. Morals are social, and the school as well as other social institutions have a responsibility towards them. The knowledge of how to fulfill moral responsibility must come from the social sciences. Just as a castaway on an uninhabited island has no moral problems, so morality is a natural outgrowth of social living. The question, "Why be moral?" has no meaning in a social context. The moral situation is a part of the social environment in which everyone lives, changing and dynamic, but always present, always presenting its obligations. Morals are actualities. In moral acts we express our awareness of the ties that bind every man to every other.—*J. Co.*

PERTINENT LITERATURE

Geiger, George R. *John Dewey in Perspective.* New York: Oxford University Press, 1958.

Although George R. Geiger (of Antioch College) in his Preface to *John Dewey in Perspective* writes that "to correct the sometimes narrow and occasionally vulgar interpretation of his philosophy there will be deliberate emphasis on the consummatory and esthetic aspects of Dewey's philosophy of experience," he is not suggesting that the work is a study of Dewey's aesthetics; the point is that critics have tended to stress the instrumental aspect of John Dewey's philosophy, while Geiger wants to show the sense of Dewey's concern with the instrumental by calling attention to his emphasis on the quality of experience, the consummatory aspect of experience as an undergoing.

This emphasis is pertinent in the consideration of Dewey's ethics. If one is lulled into presuming that Dewey emphasized morality as a matter of habits, and habits as fixed practices that may or may not survive critical examination, then one can hardly be expected to find Dewey's ethics helpful in the understanding and appraisal of morality and moralities. If, however, a study of human nature reveals no common interest and hence no universal end of conduct, only a variety of interests and objectives, changing with circumstances, and if, further, inquiry yields information by which plans of effective action can be put together, the satisfaction of which in turn yields consummatory experiences of a quality such that the term "enjoyment" applies, then morality can be seen to be most desirable when it incorporates, in the form of habits, practices which inquiry and judgment have encouraged.

Geiger begins his examination of Dewey by making clear Dewey's account of experience. Experience is not to be thought of as a purely subjective matter; as Dewey has often insisted, experience is a doing and an undergoing, an interaction of organism and environment. Since experience is *of* nature, *of* things, and is the interaction of highly developed creatures and the environment, then, as Dewey writes in *Experience and Nature* (1925), "esthetic and moral experience reveals traits of real things as truly as does intellectual experience. . . ." Again, in a pertinent passage from Dewey (quoted by Geiger), Dewey writes that "reverie and desire are pertinent for a philosophic theory of the true nature of things. . . ."

Dewey's point appears to be that our understanding of things and events is most useful, most relevant to our lives, when it is an understanding that involves acting upon and being affected by the world around us; a vital aspect of a complex experience that cannot be grasped by simply attempting to add together discrete phases of the experience is missed if one fails to recognize the suffering and enjoyment of persons. At the same time, the picture is incomplete and false if one supposes that experience is simply subjective, simply pain and pleasure, and ignores the dynamic situation that obtains when creature and environment interact, or, as Geiger suggests, "transact." (Geiger mentions that Dewey in his ninetieth year admitted that the word "experience" was bound to be misinterpreted. One wonders, though, whether a technical terminology would have provoked more discerning attention from Dewey's readers.)

An experience is unified, transactional, and closes with a consummatory phase, according to Dewey. The "esthetic" is a vital part of the complete experience; it has to do with the immediately enjoyed possession of meaning; it is an undergoing of the organism in a transaction that finally makes sense because of that undergoing. Both art and morality would be not only pointless but also impossible without this feature of consummatory experience, what in a broad sense Dewey terms the "esthetic."

In his account of values (as George points out in Chapter 3), Dewey persisted in breaking down the walls between "the immediate and the reflective in human experience." The point is not that there is no difference between what one likes and what, after inquiry and reflection, one would choose; the point is that "values," as distinguished from objects of passing appetite, are discovered in the course of experience; reflection enables us, on the basis of experience, to learn the relationships that obtain between persons and what they act upon and are affected by: such knowledge is the knowledge of values. Dewey has no sympathy for talk about absolute ends, ends-in-themselves, goods out of context, universal goods, and so forth. The knowledge of values is knowledge of what specific processes yield and how the outcome of activity relates to interests that develop in the course of experience.

Geiger makes it clear that Dewey endorses intelligent choice—choice based on what is discovered in experience—in preference to arbitrary choice. But Dewey was not thereby inclined to argue that reflection is an absolute, universal, necessary good. Reflection is useful; it is a process by which meaningful and satisfying experience becomes possible. Goods are specific, and they relate to individual persons in concrete situations; accordingly, it is misleading to talk of reflection (or of pleasure) as an "ultimate value" unless by doing so one succeeds in emphasizing that which is finally useful or satisfying to someone.

In Chapter 6, "Values and Inquiry," Geiger challenges the fashionable dogma that there is an unbridgeable gap between facts and values. Just as Dewey went to great lengths to challenge dichotomies (such as subjective-objective, means-ends, action-contemplation, reality-appearance) that cannot survive critical inquiry, so he labored to make clear the continuity involved in facts and values. There is, of course, no question that scientific inquiry may be *about* values; as Geiger points out, anthropology, sociology, and psychology, among other sciences, take as at least part of their subject matter the values that have been professed and the reasons that have been given and the judgments that have been made.

Dewey's point, Geiger emphasizes, is that there may be inquiry *into* values; one can come to value-conclusions in the course of inquiry; some values withstand the challenge of experiential inquiry, while others do not; values have to do with the resolution of problems, the adaptation of means to ends, the securing of enjoyments that emerge in the course of experience reflectively controlled.

Geiger's entire discussion is clear, insightful, and positive. His book closes with an endorsement of Dewey's philosophy as one that unites human beings and nature, makes humane judgment possible and sensible, and shows the meaning (the consummatory point) of applying intelligent inquiry to the resolution of problems.

Hook, Sidney, ed. *John Dewey: Philosopher of Science and Freedom.* New York: The Dial Press, 1950.

John Dewey: Philosopher of Science and Freedom is what its editor, Sidney Hook, calls a "symposium," a collection of articles written in commemoration of John Dewey's entering the tenth decade of his life. Hook states in his Preface that two themes dealt with in Dewey's work account for the vitality and relevancy of his philosophy: his emphasis on scientific method and its implications for the human generation of meaning, and his concern for human freedom and free societies and for making clear the conditions of freedom. Both of these themes are discernible within Dewey's ethics, and, as it happens, Hook's contribution to the symposium is an examination of some features of Dewey's ethics: "The Desirable and Emotive in Dewey's Ethics."

Hook begins his essay by pointing to two causes of what he describes as the "sterility" of most discussions of value: namely, the study of human values has not been sufficiently empirical, and too many philosophers have begun their inquiry with definitions and problems of analysis.

Concentrating at the outset on problems of definition leads to sterility, Hook contends, because the appeal in such inquiry is to the common usage of terms, and in particular to the common usage of terms in English. Usage, however, can change overnight, Hook insists, and, even worse, there is no dependable connection between ethical behavior and rules of good linguistic usage. Accordingly, Hook argues, any credible ethics will be empirical; it will involve paying attention to value facts and to relevant human behavior.

Hook contends that an empirical fact of great importance for ethics is the fact that questions about values arise in problematic situations. This fact should control subsequent discussion. When habitual responses do not permit the free flow of experience, or when such responses are challenged by others and one gropes for justificatory reasons, the procedures undertaken to resolve these problematic situations serve, in effect, as the data of inquiry. Moral situations are problematic when satisfaction is to be achieved only through inquiry and resultant decision. In the course of inquiry objectives are set and a specific course of action is determined upon from a set of alternative courses of action.

Moral deliberation begins, Hook maintains, with the funded memory of goods and ends to which one is already committed; such goods and ends include values (such as friendship and art) and general rules (such as honesty and truthfulness). The moral problem is one that requires for its resolution a choice between incompatible alternatives—not, he insists, the application of a universal rule to a concrete case. Further, the moral problem requires the resolution of the conflict of ends by a choice that determines (or redetermines) the character of the agent. (Presumably, in deciding upon ends, one considers the consequences of doing so in the various alternatives, and one chooses: the kind of person you are is made out by discovering what you chose and why you chose it.)

Hook continues his analysis of moral problematic situations by calling attention to the fact (what he presumes to be a fact) that any moral decision is final and valid at the place and time it is made (that is, the moral decision does not presume to be eternally prescriptive, nor does it leave itself open for the kind of challenge that consists in calling for futher reasons; that the end is decided upon and that the means are judged to be satisfactory is the end of the matter on that occasion).

Finally, every moral decision, according to Dewey (as Hook reports it), expresses an attitude, a special concern or urgency, and hence has a kind of "quasi-imperative" force. Hook quotes Dewey (in *Ethics*, Second Edition, 1932) as writing, "A moral judgment, however intellectual it may be, must at least be colored with feeling if it is to influence behavior."

It becomes clear that in Dewey's ethics, attitudes, emotive states, and feelings—although necessary to value and to the resolution of moral problems—are not sufficient; it is what one chooses while reflectively considering the results of relevant inquiry that determines values and ends for the one who decides.

Hook offers a careful criticism of views presented by Charles Stevenson and Morton G. White, views that call into question certain aspects of Dewey's ethics. In his rejoinder, Hook emphasizes Dewey's view of moral judgments as problem-solving decisions based on inquiry into causes and consequences of action, the whole making sense as related to the attitudes, interests, and decisions of the person conducting the inquiry. Hence, Dewey does not deny the importance of calling attention to emotive factors, as Stevenson does; but Dewey also succeeds in showing how problematic situations of the kind that relate to human conduct can be resolved through inquiry and intelligence by reference to what is in fact desired or in fact decided upon.—*I.P.M.*

ADDITIONAL RECOMMENDED READING

Boydston, Jo Ann and Kathleen Poulos. *Checklist of Writings About John Dewey, 1887-1977.* Carbondale: Southern Illinois University Press, 1974 and 1978. Covers both published and unpublished studies *about* Dewey's work.

Dewey, John and James Hayden Tufts. *Ethics.* New York: Henry Holt and Company, 1908 and 1932. Dewey wrote Part II and Chapters XX and XXI of Part III.

Morgenbesser, Sidney, ed. *Dewey and His Critics.* New York: The Journal of Philosophy, 1977. A collection of noteworthy articles about Dewey's views, originally published in *The Journal of Philosophy*, and selected for republication by Morgenbesser. Many eminent philosophers are represented.

Schilpp, Paul A., ed. *The Philosophy of John Dewey.* New York: Tudor Publishing Company, 1939 and 1951. Another in the extremely valuable series *The Library of Living Philosophers*, this volume contains the usual features: a biography (by his daughter, Jane M. Dewey, based on material furnished by John Dewey), descriptive and critical essays (by, among others, Bertrand Russell, George Santayana, Hans Reichenbach, John Herman Randall, Jr., Stephen C. Pepper, Alfred North Whitehead, and Henry W. Stuart—who wrote on Dewey's ethical theory), "The Philosopher Replies" (almost one hundred pages of closely reasoned responses to the critical essays), and a bibliography (1882-1950).

Thomas, Milton Halsey. *John Dewey: A Centennial Bibliography*. Chicago: University of Chicago Press, 1962. A careful and thorough index to Dewey's writings.

PHILOSOPHICAL STUDIES

Author: George Edward Moore (1873-1958)
Type of work: Philosophy of philosophy (with examples)
First published: 1922

PRINCIPAL IDEAS ADVANCED

If the language by the use of which philosophical problems and theories are formulated is clarified, the problems often disappear.

There is usually some good reason why the language of common sense is insisted upon, and philosophers would do well to take common sense seriously.

For example, the idealist argues that to be (to exist) is to be perceived, but he fails to distinguish between the awareness of something, on the one hand, and the content of awareness, on the other.

Again, the pragmatists claim that true ideas are simply ideas which work; but this claim is ambiguous, and by a clarification of language it can be shown to what extent it is true and to what extent false.

G. E. Moore was one of the first of a group of philosophers who have since come to be known as the "ordinary language philosophers" or the "Oxford analysts." Moore himself was at Cambridge, closely associated with Russell and Wittgenstein. These three and certain of their followers are sometimes called, by contrast, the "Cambridge analysts," though the distinction between the schools is a fine one and hard to specify. What the analysts have in common is an interest in approaching philosophical problems from the point of view of the language in which they are expressed. The philosophical task, therefore, is characterized by a painstaking analysis of the *formulations* of its problems and the *statements* of its conclusions. Analysis often takes the form of a word-by-word study of a philosophical assertion in the attempt to eliminate vagueness and ambiguity and thus prevent the philosopher from wasting his time by trying to solve pseudoproblems that lead him unconsciously into absurdities and paradoxes. When clarification has been achieved, what were thought to be genuine problems often disappear completely.

This method is well illustrated in the present book. But there is another method which Moore, in contrast to some of the other analysts, considers to be equally important. This is the appeal to "common sense" as a basis for solving philosophical problems. Moore is convinced that there is usually some important sense in which the ordinary man is right when he insists that tables exist, that other people have being when we are not observing them, and that time is real. Therefore, we have only to determine what this sense is in order to refute those philosophers who argue that tables are "mere ideas," or that other people have only apparent being, or that time is unreal. The determination of this meaning requires a careful analysis of language in order to ascertain what is meant by such assertions. But it also provides, after the analysis, a criterion by which the assertions may be judged to be true or false. Thus it permits problems not only to be clarified but also to be solved, because it is based on the assumption that men could not possibly be deceived in these fundamental beliefs.

Philosophical Studies consists of a collection of essays, most of them published previously in periodicals, and all of them illustrating Moore's approach to certain philosophical problems. They fall into two general classes: (1) *problems*, such as to whether there is an external world, whether there are intrinsic values, and whether our feeling of obligation is purely subjective; (2) *claims of certain philosophers* (William James, David Hume, F. H. Bradley) which seem contrary to common sense and which therefore can be shown to be wrong by a careful analysis of the language in which they are expressed.

The first such problem that Moore examines is that of *idealism*. Idealism attempts to prove that the universe is spiritual. One method used for such proof is to argue from the premise that *esse* is *percipi*—to be is to be perceived. To refute this statement would not disprove idealism but it would destroy one of its main arguments. Therefore if it can be shown that *esse* is not *percipi*, the idealistic position is considerably weakened.

This can be done, Moore argues, by distinguishing in any perception the *awareness* from the *content of the awareness*. A sensation of blue differs from a sensation of green in that there are different contents, but a sensation of blue resembles a sensation of green in that they are both cases of awareness. Since the awareness and the content always exist together—for we never have an awareness without a content or a content without an awareness—philosophers have tended to confuse the two and have not realized that we can distinguish the awareness from the blue in the same way that we can distinguish the blue from the green. The awareness is something very elusive, and when we try to focus our attention on it, it seems to vanish. But when we finally discover it, we can see that it has a unique relation to the blue which we express by saying that it is *of* the blue. Now the awareness is obviously mental, but there is no reason whatsoever for concluding that the blue must also be mental. This argument provides no ground for concluding that the blue is not mental, but it removes the ground for concluding that it is. Hence it destroys idealism by destroying one of the strongest reasons for believing it.

Moore now turns to a certain belief which is generally held not only by the ordinary man but also by most philosophers. This belief really has two parts which are interconnected. (1) Something other than ourselves and what we directly perceive exists. (2) Among the thing other than ourselves and what we directly perceive are persons who have thoughts and feelings similar to our own. The first belief involves certain ambiguities, which the second does not; consequently, Moore decides to examine only the latter.

Certain preliminary points must first be clarified. To ask why we believe this statement is not to imply that we should not believe it; we may believe it without grounds, or on the basis of grounds quite different from those which are commonly accepted. Furthermore, we are not asking how we come to believe in the existence of other people, for there may be many things which cause us to believe this, though they may not be grounds for the belief. Moreover, to ask for reasons is to ask for *good* reasons—reasons which are actually believed and such that we would not believe in the existence of other people unless they were true. (Reasons of this kind may be hard to find since philosophers are often in disagreement as to what *good* reasons are.) Finally, when we ask for reasons for this belief we do not mean reasons which will conclusively demonstrate that other people exist; all that we can hope for is that our belief can be established with a certain degree of probability. Since we have the belief, it is likely that there are other people who have thoughts and feelings similar to ours.

The kind of reason which could support such a belief, Moore claims, must have two properties. In the first place, it must be some sort of *generalization*. A generalization has the form, "When A exists, B generally exists also." In this particular case the generalization would be: "When we hear certain words, someone besides ourselves generally has the thoughts which constitute the meanings of those words." The relation in this case is not such that we can say that A *intrinsically* points to B, but merely that, given A, there is a reasonable probability, based on actual occurrences, that B will occur also. In the second place, the evidence for the generalization must itself be obtained through perception. But in making this knowledge rest on perception we must not be confused as to the meaning of this word. In one sense we may be said to perceive the thoughts of others when we interpret what they are saying; in another sense the generalization may be said to rest on the perceptions which other people have had. Both of these meanings of "perception" are excluded in this context.

Moore states that when we set up these requirements concerning the kind of reason which would support our belief in the existence of other people we realize that there can be no such reason. We can show only that certain of our perceptions are connected with certain other of our perceptions, not that certain of them are connected with the existence of other people. This does not mean that we cannot prove the existence of other people but only that we cannot prove it by this method.

If we look again at the kind of reason which would prove conclusively the existence of other persons, we can see that all of us actually perceive two different kinds of "things": "sense-contents," such as patterns of colors and shapes, and perceptions themselves. For example, we can perceive *a blue color* but we can also perceive our *perception* of a blue color. When Berkeley said that *to be* is *to be perceived* he evidently meant that for a sense-content to exist it must be perceived, not that for a perception to exist it must be perceived. But if perceptions can exist without being perceived, why cannot sense-contents also exist without being perceived? Certainly there is nothing self-contradictory in the possibility.

This, then, provides Moore with the proof which he requires. He notes that a certain sense-content (his hand suddenly catching hold of his foot in a particular way) is preceded by another sense-content (a particular feeling of pain). Now if he perceives a similar movement in another person he can infer that this individual has similar feelings (which Moore himself cannot perceive but which stand in the same relation to the other person's movements that Moore's do to his own movement). Such arguments establish the likely existence of others who have feelings similar to those of the observer. The belief is grounded on the assumptions that sense-contents can exist without being perceived, and that analogous relations between sense-contents provide a basis for inference from sense-contents that *are* perceived to sense-contents which *are not* actually perceived.

Moore now offers an illustration of the effectiveness of the analytic method when it is applied critically to the views of another philosopher. He examines the claims of William James in his book, *Pragmatism: A New Name for Old Ways of Thinking* (1907). James claims to establish three things: (1) There is some connection between truth and utility, that is, true ideas are those that "work." (2) Truth is in some sense mutable, rather than static. (3) "To an unascertainable extent our truths are man-made."

Moore's scrutiny of James's arguments shows that there is ambiguity in what he says. According to one interpretation James seems to be trying to prove certain things which are really commonplace and would be accepted by everyone. Among these are the following: most true beliefs are useful and most useful beliefs are true; since the world changes, a given statement may be true at one time and false at another; truth, in the sense of our beliefs, does depend on us both because it depends on our mental history and because we change the world and thus make our beliefs in this altered world true.

But Moore insists that James probably intends to assert something in addition to these truisms, and these further assertions are, according to Moore, quite obviously false. For example: *All true beliefs are useful.* Moore refutes this claim by taking the belief that two plus two equals four, which is obviously true, and then showing that it might be useless—and, indeed, might even get in the way of our solving a problem on which it has no bearing. *All useful beliefs are true.* This is refuted by lies which "work." *Utility is the only property which all true beliefs have in common.* Moore shows that this proposition reduces to an absurdity. For it would require that if on a certain occasion belief in the existence of something were useful, that belief would have to be true even if the thing did not exist. A final example: *Whenever the existence of a belief depends on us the truth of that belief also depends on us.* This statement is ridiculous, for while it may be true that my *belief* that a shower will fall depends on me, the *truth* of that belief does not depend on me, for I do not make the shower fall.

Moore then turns from James to Hume. Hume tries to define the limits of human understanding by examining a certain kind of belief which we all seem to have. This is one concerning "matters of fact" which we have never observed but which are based on past experience; for example, the belief that the sun will rise tomorrow. The results of Hume's analysis, Moore shows, are inconsistent with one another. At one point Hume says that a proposition expressing such a belief can be known, even to the extent of leaving no room for doubt or opposition. At another point he asserts that it cannot be established, since we can never experience external objects directly and cannot therefore know that they exist. In still another place he denies that we can ever know that one fact is causally related with another and consequently that we can ever use past experience as a basis for anticipating future experience. In support of the second and third views Hume uses two arguments—both, according to Moore, invalid. (1) When Hume asserts that we cannot know about external objects he contradicts himself, for he implies that we *do* know that men cannot have this kind of knowledge; but this kind of knowledge *is* knowledge of external objects; namely, knowledge about men and what they can and cannot know. (2) When Hume asserts that from the knowledge that two facts have been causally conjoined in the past we cannot know that they will be causally connected in the future, he is making an unjustifiable assumption—the assumption that because we cannot *prove* a certain statement by means of a certain argument, we cannot *know* that statement to be true. Moore believes that we know many things which do not follow logically from anything else we know, and thus that we *can* know that facts will be causally conjoined in the future even though this latter proposition is not based on what Hume presumes it to be based.

In proceeding to an examination of the problem of perception Moore insists that we need to refine our vocabulary. We must invent a term which will describe what is common to images, dream objects, hallucinations, after-images, and sensations proper. Let us call these all "sensibles." We must then answer two questions: How are sensibles related to our minds? How are sensibles related to physical objects?

In order to answer the first question we must invent another term. We shall say that sensibles are "directly apprehended" by our minds. Attempts to show that sensibles can have any other relation to our minds have been unsuccessful. Furthermore, attempts to show that sensibles cannot exist *unless* they are directly apprehended have also failed. Berkeley claimed that an unapprehended sensible is self-contradictory. But this is clearly not the case. Others have claimed that we have *a priori* knowledge that sensibles must always be apprehended. This, again, is simply not true.

The second question can be answered only if we assume that there are some beliefs of which we can be quite certain, though we may not know exactly how to interpret them. Such beliefs would be illustrated by saying that when I look at two coins of different size I am *really* seeing two coins, that they are *really* circular even though I see them as elliptical, that the coins *have* an inside (though I don't see it), that the upper side of one of the coins is *really* larger than that of the other, and that both coins *continue* to *exist* even when I shut my eyes. We must now add to this belief two others, which are equally certain. (1) The upper side of the coin which I am said to *see* is not simply identical with the visual sensible which I directly apprehend in seeing it. (2) My knowledge of the coins is based on the apprehension of sensibles. The simplest interpretation of these three beliefs is to say that when I really see the coins I mean that *if* I were to move my body in certain ways I should directly apprehend certain *other* sensibles—for example, certain tactual ones. According to Moore this is what we mean when we say that we *really* perceive the coins.

The assertion of F. H. Bradley that time is unreal provides another challenge for Moore in his role as an analytic philosopher. Careful study of Bradley's attempts to prove this philosophical proposition shows that he apparently thinks of the word "time" as having different meanings in different contexts, and that he presumably is using the word "real" in two different senses. He seems to be saying that time exists but is unreal. But if he is using "time" and "real" in their ordinary senses he would seem to be denying that there are any facts of the kind expressed by saying that something happens before something else, or that something happened in the past. To say that time is unreal in this sense is plainly false, for there *are* happenings of these kinds.

How, then, can his error be explained? Simply in terms of a confusion.

He believes (correctly) that time could be unreal even though we do think about time, just as unicorns could be unreal even though we think about them. But he also believes (incorrectly) that because we do think about time there is such a thing as time. From these two premises (one true and the other false) he correctly infers that the statement, "Time is unreal," must be consistent with the statement, "There is such a thing as time." But he is unsuccessful in showing just *how* these statements can be consistent.

In Moore's essay entitled "Some Judgments of Perception," he returns to the question of the status of "sensibles." The problem is not to determine whether we can ever truly make such assertions as "That is an inkstand"— for we continually make such statements and believe them—but what we *mean* when we make them. Certainly two things which we mean are that the inkstand can be selected from surrounding objects and designated as *the* object which we are perceiving, and that if there is an inkstand it is not given to us in any way independently of any sensibles (sense-data). But to say that the inkstand is dependent on sense-data is not to say that it is dependent in the way in which one object is called to mind by another through associative ties.

The problem is to explain what this relation of dependence *is*. Many philosophers would say that the presented object (the sense-datum) is only a *part* of the *surface* of the inkstand. For we can detect that a presented object sometimes changes, and yet this observation apparently provides no basis for concluding that the surface of the object changes. The reason we have to say that it only *apparently* provides no basis is that we can never be sure that the presented object *does* change perceptibly. This has commonly been assumed, but it may not be true. Perhaps it only *seems* to change. Possibly the sense-datum which I see when I look at a tree a mile off is not *really* smaller than the one which I see when I look at it from a distance of only a hundred yards; perhaps it is only *apparently* smaller. If this is true, then we shall have to admit a special, ultimate, not further analyzable, kind of relation expressed by saying that *x seems* blue or *y seems* circular. This kind of relation would have to be sharply distinguished from that expressed in *x is perceived to be* blue or *y is judged to be* circular. Since there seems to be no reason why there could not be such an ultimate relation, Moore concludes that its existence is at least a possibility.

The controversy as to whether value is subjective or objective, Moore says, should be settled by translating it into the problem of whether value is intrinsic or extrinsic. If value is intrinsic it must be objective, but the converse does not hold. When we say that a thing is intrinsically valuable we mean two things: (1) that if it possesses this value at one time, or in one set of circumstances, or to a certain degree, it *must* possess it at another time, and in other circumstances, and to the same degree; and (2) that anything *exactly like* the thing in question *must* possess the value and to the same degree. These statements are not to be understood as using "must" in the sense that there is nothing which is intrinsically valuable and which lacks these characteristics, nor in the sense that an effect must follow its cause. What is meant is that there *could be* nothing which is intrinsically valuable and which lacks these properties, and that a thing which is intrinsically valuable *would have to have* these characteristics even in a universe whose causal laws would be quite different from ours. We can then say that intrinsic predicates and intrinsic values depend on the intrinsic natures of the things which possess them. But yellowness, which is an intrinsic *predicate, describes* the thing which possesses it, while beauty, which is an intrinsic *value, does not describe* its object.

Moore now returns to his examination of the views of other philosophers. F. H. Bradley asserts that all relations are "internal" to the terms related, meaning by this that they all *affect*, and pass into, the being of their terms. Moore believes this statement to be false if applied to *all* relations. He thinks that there are some relations which are internal and some which are external. In order to show the source of Bradley's error he attempts, first, to clear up an equivocation in the logical expression "follows from," and, second, to reveal an ambiguity in the meaning of the word "internal."

The commonly accepted notion of "follows from" is that which is used by Whitehead and Russell in *Principia Mathematica*. This is called "material implication" and is defined by saying that when P materially implies Q it is not the case that P is true and Q is false. The other meaning of "follows from" can be called "entailment" and is defined by saying that when P entails Q, Q can be inferred from P, or Q is deducible from P. The important distinction is that in entailment the relation exhibits a kind of necessity which is not present in the case of material implication.

Now, says Moore, let us define a relational property as a property which a term possesses by virtue of its relation to something else. For example, a man possesses fatherhood because he has the relation of "father" to someone. If we then gather together all relational properties, there are two things which we may assert about them. (1) All relational properties are such that the possession by *x* of the relational property P *entails* that the absence of this property in the case of *y* *materially implies* that *y* is other than *x*. (2) All relational properties are such that the possession by *x* of the relational property P *materially implies* that the absence of this property in the case of *y* *entails* that *y* is other than *x*. These are two ways of stating that if a thing which has a relational property did not have it, the thing would be different. Those who believe in the internality of all relations believe not only that both (1) and (2) are true, but that (2) follows from (1). Neither of these, according to Moore, is correct. (1) is not true of *all* relations, but only of *some*; those of which it is true are internal; those of which it is false are external. Hence, there are some relations which are internal and some which are external. Furthermore, (2) does not follow from (1), as can be seen if we express (1) as

  p entails (*q* materially implies *r*)

and (2) as

  p materially implies (*q* entails *r*).

The following example will show that (2) does not follow from (1):

Let *p* equal All the books on this shelf are blue.

Let *q* equal My copy of the *Principles of Mathematics* is a book on this shelf.

Let *r* equal My copy of the *Principles of Mathematics* is blue.

If we substitute these statements in (1) and (2) above we can readily see that (1) is true, while (2) is false. Hence, Moore concludes, (2) cannot follow from (1).

Finally Moore examines moral philosophy. This commonly deals with two ideas, the first of which—the idea of *obligation*—is really a moral idea, and the second of which—the idea of the *good*—is commonly talked about by moral philosophers but is not properly a moral idea at all. When we talk about *obligation* we discover that there are two kinds of rules: rules of *duty*, which tell us what we ought to *do*, and *ideal* rules, which concern our inner life and tell us what we ought to *be*. When we talk about the *good* we may mean something such as Aristotle had in mind when he defined the good life as the active exercise of mental excellence.

With regard to both of these ideas, Moore says, certain philosophers have claimed that all we mean to say when we assert that a certain action ought to have been done or that a certain state is better than another, is that some person has a tendency to have a certain feeling towards the action or the state. This view makes moral philosophy and ethics mere departments of psychology, and the strange consequence of the view is that no two people can ever argue about whether an act is wrong or not wrong, for the word "wrong" (since it deals with the speaker's feelings) will mean one thing for one speaker and another for another, just as the pronoun "I" means something different to each person who utters it. Hence there can really be no such thing as a difference of opinion on moral matters. Moore believes this conclusion to be absurd, since people *do* differ in opinion on moral matters. We must conclude, then, that ethics is more than psychology, though Moore admits that he has some difficulty in stating just what this additional element is.
—*A.C.B.*

PERTINENT LITERATURE

Ayer, A. J. *Russell and Moore: The Analytical Heritage.* London: Macmillan and Company, 1971.

The names of G. E. Moore and Bertrand Russell are always linked in discussing the history of twentieth century British philosophy, and that is for an important reason. Not only did they come into philosophy together as undergraduates at Cambridge in the late 1890's, but also their joint activities overturned one philosophical tradition and established another (at least one) in its place. When they came to the study of philosophy the reigning philosophical view in Britain was idealism. Both of them in the way that most learners in a discipline do, imbibed the prevailing orthodoxy. However, their adherence was short-lived, and by about 1903 they had, as a result of a complex but joint interaction, succeeded in rejecting the idealist views. Their success was even greater: not only did they shed idealism from themselves but in so doing they also undermined it so as to produce a new orthodoxy in

British philosophy. In fact, they began the new developments in the course of rejecting the idealist tradition.

Philosophical Studies is a collection of Moore's essays published in the early part of his career. Without doubt the most important paper in that collection, historically speaking, is "The Refutation of Idealism." It is in that essay (from 1903) that Moore launched the attack on idealism which played a major role not only in rejecting the past but also in developing a new line of philosophical thought. A. J. Ayer thus spends a good deal of time examining that essay.

Moore's procedure in his essay is to hold that the idealist conclusion that the universe is somehow mental or spiritual rests upon an argument which assumes a certain principle which Moore holds to be unjustifiable. That principle is George Berkeley's: *esse est percipi*; that is, to be is to be perceived (or to be experienced). Moore (typically) then carefully considers how this principle is to be understood. He concludes that the principle rests on a confusion resulting from the failure to make a crucial distinction, and he thereupon emphasizes the distinction between *awareness* and the *content* of awareness.

Ayer does not think that Moore's reading of the principle is correct. He proceeds to develop what is, in some ways, a very different interpretation, but one which still allows Moore's criticism to be relevant. According to Ayer, the idealist principle begins with a consideration of, for example, pains, where for a pain to be (to exist) is for it to be felt, to be experienced. The second move the idealist makes is to assimilate all perceptible qualities (for example, blueness) to such things as headaches, so that to be perceptible is to be experienced. Lastly, the idealist argues that a thing is nothing but a collection of perceptible qualities; hence, to be a thing is to be experienced, perceived.

The next step for Moore (and for Ayer) is, having given the principle a certain interpretation, to subject it to criticism. Ayer says that he would attack the argument at the third stage, where objects are said to be comprised of perceptual qualities. But Moore chooses to make a more ambitious move (more ambitious at least in Ayer's eyes): that of taking on the second stage of the idealist argument for the principle. Moore, that is, critically scrutinizes the assimilation of qualities such as green and hardness to such things as headaches and tickles.

Moore's objection to that move is that "experiencing something" has two components—experiencing (or perceiving or being conscious of) and that which we experience (perceive, are conscious of). Moore concludes that if there are those two components, then *what* we experience can exist independently of our experience of it: blue can exist when not perceived. Hence, to be is *not* to be perceived. To be is one thing; to be perceived is quite another.

The entire question of whether Moore has refuted idealism hinges upon whether his objection is valid. Ayer, for one, does not think that it really works. The crux of the matter concerns the status of such things as headaches and pains in general. Experiencing a headache does not (according to Ayer) enable us to infer that the headache can exist independently of the experience. How can Moore think that such qualities as blue, sweet, and so forth are any different? To be consistent, Moore would have to say that there can be unfelt pains and tickles.

In short, we do make a distinction between headaches and blue—we are committed to saying that headaches *cannot* exist independently of our experience of them, while at the same time we are committed to saying that blueness *can* exist without being experienced. The idealist challenges the distinction and tries to assimilate sensible qualities to headaches. All that Moore's argument does is to *insist* that there is a crucial distinction between a thing's being blue and its being perceived. It goes no way, as it stands, toward showing that something is wrong with the idealist's assimilation. (Here we can see why Moore is a defender of common sense—if the distinction is held to be a piece of common sense, then Moore simply insists that common sense is correct as opposed to the philosopher, here the idealist.)

Even if Moore's argument against the *esse est percipi* thesis fails, as Ayer and others have maintained, and even if he did not succeed in refuting idealism, it is nevertheless true that he thought he had succeeded in such a refutation. That meant that Moore was free to move on to some further philosophical position. The position which his argument supports is realism. His argument commits him to the belief that perceptible qualities exist independently of our perception of them; and that belief led him (and Russell) first to the idea that even such abstract entities as numbers exist independently of human thought and eventually to an entire system of realism.

White, Alan R. *G. E. Moore: A Critical Exposition*. Oxford: Basil Blackwell, 1969.

Along with problems in moral philosophy and philosophical method, the topic of perception occupied G. E. Moore during his long philosophically active life. All these topics are discussed by Moore in the papers collected as *Philosophical Studies*. Yet probably the greatest number of those papers deal, in one way or another, with the topic of perception.

On that subject, however, the papers do not provide a unified view. The reasons for this are clear: the essays were written over a period of fifteen years during the early stages of Moore's professional life; his ideas on perception, as on much else, were just developing during that period. One crucial development came about halfway through the writings on perception gathered in *Philosophical Studies*. In 1920 he gave a series of lectures later published as *Some Main Problems of Philosophy*. In those lectures, when dealing with perception, he introduced the term which was to be central to his later work on perception (and also central to debates on that topic for the next fifty years). This was the term "sense-datum." Of course it was not only a piece of terminology which was introduced: but also along with that came a conception and defense of sense-data, together with a philosophical account of the workings of perception which involved the notion of a sense-datum. (The student of the *Philosophical Studies* should notice how Moore's ideas developed from the pre-1910 papers—"The Refutation of Idealism," and "The Nature and Reality of Objects of Perception,"—to the later essays on perception collected there: "Sense-Data," and "Some Judgments of Perception.")

Moore came to adopt the position that in perception (let us, like Moore, use visual perception as the paradigm of all the senses) what we, in the most important sense, see is something he called a "sense-datum." The problems then facing Moore were concerned with how these things, sense-data, are related to the things we otherwise think and say we see; for example pencils, cows, and such. For us, though, the prior question is why Moore held to the idea that it is, strictly speaking, sense-data we perceive and not physical objects.

Alan R. White, in his examination of Moore's ideas on perception, argues that Moore did not rest his case for the existence of sense-data on just one line of argument but had *six* different ways of supporting the claim. To grasp the nature of Moorean sense-data and to understand why he held that there were such things requires being acquainted with those six methods of arguing for them.

One major source of the idea of a sense-datum certainly was not original with Moore. It rests upon the possibility of asking what some person *actually* saw (perceived) rather than about what he said he saw. For example, Jones says, "I saw Smith take the money," and the defense attorney says, "Now what you actually saw in the darkened room was a man about Smith's size wearing a coat like Smith's. . . ." Moore wants to say that in *all* cases of perception there is something that we actually perceive, see (colors and shapes), and something else we say we see (a cow). A sense-datum will be that which we actually see. Notice that we can go on to ask how what we actually saw (colors and shapes) is related to what was there (was it Smith or merely someone who looked like him?). That is Moore's problem of how sense-data are related to other objects of perception (at least on this line of argument that is how the further problem arises).

While that line (what White calls "The Method of Restriction" from the fact that it emphasizes a restriction on our talk about what we see) was not original with Moore, his second technique for introducing sense-data ("The Method of Selection") is uniquely Moorean. Moore believes that by looking at, for example, one's hand and reflecting a bit one can discover, locate something in one's visual field, which is not one's hand (or whatever) and yet which stands in some relation to one's hand. That something which is discoverable is said by Moore to be a sense-datum. Now this line has perplexed most philosophers—the instructions for picking out sense-data are perplexing. To pursue the matter further would be to go far afield here; it is best to consult White's discussion.

Two of the ways Moore uses to establish the existence of sense-data, ways White calls "The Method of the Ultimate Subject" and "The Linguistic Method," are very much alike. The second line of argument begins with the claim that things always *look* a certain way to a perceiver. Our visual access to a thing is necessarily through how it looks to us. Moore holds that the "look" of a thing is a sense-datum. And, so the Ultimate Subject argument goes, even if we say "I see a table," ultimately we are talking about what appears to be a table, about the look of a table, about a sense-datum. Then the philosophical question for Moore is how the "look" of a table is related to a table.

Lastly, Moore employs two arguments to show that there are sense-data which are concerned with abnormal sensory experiences. Moore analyzes perception into two parts. Perception is an experience of something; so there is the *experience* and what it is of, the *object* of the experience. But sometimes people have the perceptual experience of, say, a cow when there are no cows present (during hallucinations, for example). Moore insists that even then there is something which we do experience—namely, a sense-datum (a cowish sense-datum, the "look" of a cow). The final argument ("The Method of After-Images") is a special case along that line: Moore recommends that we stare at a light, then close our eyes. He insists that we can be said to *see* something—namely, an after-image—and the after-image is a sense-datum.

Problems about the existence and nature of sense-data and their relation to commonly recognized objects of perception have occupied the center of philosophical discussions of perception since Moore introduced the notion into twentieth century philosophy. Undoubtedly the weight of philosophical opinion has swung against Moore and against the existence of sense-data. It is in that context that the final section of White's essay is interesting. In "The Legitimacy of Sense-Data," White defends a version of sense-data. Still, as he well knows, his version would not have been acceptable to Moore. But the philosophy of perception has moved on, and White is able to find virtues in Moore's work where other contemporary critics can see none.—*M.R.*

ADDITIONAL RECOMMENDED READING

Ambrose, Alice and Morris Lazerowitz, eds. *G. E. Moore: Essays in Retrospect*. London: George Allen & Unwin, 1970. Perhaps the best anthology of Moore's writings.

Klemke, E. D. *The Epistemology of G. E. Moore*. Evanston, Illinois: Northwestern University Press, 1969. The only study devoted exclusively to Moore's epistemological ideas.

Schilpp, Paul A., ed. *The Philosophy of G. E. Moore* (The Library of Living
   Philosophers). Evanston, Illinois: Northwestern University Press, 1942. The
   paper by C. J. Ducasse is especially relevant to *Philosophical Studies*; see
   also Moore's reply at the end of the book.

THE PHILOSOPHY OF SYMBOLIC FORMS

Author: Ernst Cassirer (1874-1945)
Type of work: Epistemology, philosophy of culture
First published: 1923-1929

PRINCIPAL IDEAS ADVANCED

The mind creates symbols to interpret the data of experience; to understand knowledge and the significance of science it is necessary to understand the function of symbolic forms in explanations.

Forms of cognition are affected by language and myth; language, myth, and science are all forms of human expression.

Experience begins with the immediacy of feelings; but as living creatures respond in accordance with their needs, certain items in their experience take on sign and symbol functions.

In the phase which follows, the distinction between self and nonself becomes fixed, the flux of sensations is recognized and ordered into things by the use of names, and space and time are conceived.

Philosophy becomes the criticism of language, and religion becomes the criticism of myth.

Ernst Cassirer was one of the few men with sufficient breadth of scholarship to undertake the task of synthesizing the findings of twentieth century science. He wrote authoritatively on the history of ideas and on the methodology of the sciences, as well as on literature, politics, and primitive culture. *The Philosophy of Symbolic Forms* is his masterwork, in which he attempts to give a systematic view of the entire range of human achievement.

Thoroughly at home in the fields of biology and physics, Cassirer nevertheless turned his back on the more unusual type of synthesis (for example, A. N. Whitehead's *Process and Reality*, 1929) which takes nature as ultimate and seeks to interpret man in terms of cosmic evolution. For Cassirer, modern science is more interesting for what it reveals to us about the mind of the scientist than for the information it discloses to us about an alleged material universe. In his synthesis, science is viewed as a cultural phenomenon, the most advanced condition of mind since its emergence from preconscious animal existence. His survey is primarily a philosophy of culture. It traces the evolution of mind rather than the evolution of nature, and indeed gives nature a place among the contents of mind. In short, Cassirer's synthesis is in the idealistic rather than in the realistic tradition.

Cassirer's philosophical lineage is easily traced. He was a member of a group known as the Marburg school (after the university where it flourished), which was dedicated to bringing up to date the philosophy of Immanuel Kant. Kant had never completely broken with the belief that reality is prior to and independent of our knowledge of it. The Marburg group considered this belief inconsistent with Kant's own principles, and carried through the thesis that nothing is real except what is given in experience. They employed Kant's "transcendental method" and sought, by the analysis of perceptions, judgments, and arguments, to uncover the structure of the intellect which makes knowledge possible.

Although Cassirer always worked in this tradition, he went well beyond others of the group in an important respect. It has been characteristic of the successors of Kant to be preeminently concerned with epistemology, or the theory of knowledge. Cassirer came to believe that knowledge is only one aspect of the mind's activity, and he argued that if we are to understand our experience, either our immediate perceptions or our scientific hypotheses, we must familiarize ourselves with the development of language and with mythical thought as well as with the processes of sensation, perception, and judgment. According to Cassirer, language, myth, and knowledge are three distinct but overlapping frontiers on which the human spirit has advanced in its effort to bring under its power the chaos of organic feelings. Forms of perception, such as space, time, and number, together with concepts such as substance, attribute, and causality, all have their origins in primitive symbols, images, and acts. Not only our knowledge of the world, but our consciousness of ourselves as well, presupposes the unfolding and articulation of these "forms"; and such order and intelligibility as we find in our experience is, in actuality, the order which consciousness in its long development has itself created.

In this modified form, the Kantian thesis is no longer dependent on a merely theoretical deduction. As Cassirer has stated it, it is an empirical hypothesis, to be verified by reference to the findings of students in the fields of linguistics and of cultural anthropology. There is, in the three volumes of *The Philosophy of Symbolic Forms* (*Language*; *Mythical Thought*; and *The Phenomenology of Knowledge*), a minimum of the kind of abstruse reasoning which characterizes the *Critique of Pure Reason*. Instead, the author offers us a compendium of modern knowledge in the three fields.

Cassirer first developed the notion of symbolic forms in connection with his studies in the methodology of the sciences (*Substance and Function*, 1910). He maintained that the ordinary view of knowledge, according to which scientific concepts and laws reproduce the actuality of things experienceable by the senses, is disproved by the developments of modern physics. He agreed with those mathematicians and scientists who said that mathematical symbols and such physical concepts as mass, energy, and the atom are not empirical facts in the same sense that light, heat, and electricity are, but are instruments of the intellect which make it possible for us to correlate and order these more immediate aspects of our experience. The problem for the philosopher, according to Cassirer, is to explore the connection between the scientific explanation and the data which it illuminates. Both the range and the precision of the exact sciences derive from the purely formal character of their constructions. How, then, can we account for the agreement between the theories and our actual experience?

Kant's approach seemed to point to the answer. The mind does, indeed, create new symbols to interpret the data of its experience. But in so doing it only carries further the same activity in which it has been engaging since the dawn of consciousness. All our experience has its structure in virtue of the creativity of the mind. An example is the perception of things in space. The vital feelings of earliest men did not include the notion of three-dimensional or any other variety of space. Even among so-called primitive peoples today, a mythical view of space prevails which lacks the universal, homogeneous character that space has for us. Space, in other words, is a symbolic form by which evolving consciousness imposes unity upon the manifold of concrete intuition. And though the higher geometries seem quite to transcend intuition, still they carry with them something of our common spatial representation. Thus, it is not altogether surprising that they have proved useful for correlating new fields of experimental data.

The exact sciences bring knowledge to its highest perfection and provide a capital instance of the role of symbols. A philosopher with fewer universal interests than Cassirer might have stopped with this insight. But the fact that forms of cognition are intertwined with those of language and myth suggested to him the answer to another long-standing problem of philosophy; namely, that of the relation between man's quest for knowledge and his concern for religion, morality, and art. At this point, the philosophy of symbolic forms ceased to be merely a philosophy of science and was projected into a philosophy of culture, in which language and mythology would be treated not simply as stages on the way to knowledge, but as divergent and independent, though supplementary, ways in which man has raised himself above the animals and become the monarch of all he surveys.

Cassirer went considerably beyond Kant, somewhat in the manner of Hegel. He spoke of his philosophy as a phenomenology of spirit in the manner of Hegel, to whose *Phenomenology of the Spirit* (1807) he often refers. For both Cassirer and Hegel history is the story of man's emerging awareness of himself and of his growing freedom and autonomy. They differed in that Hegel conceived the essence of spirit to be reason, from which he concluded that all aspects of culture were related to one another in a logical fashion and found their consummation in pure knowledge. For Cassirer, in step with the pragmatic temper of his time, reason took its place as one function among others. Hence, he did not follow the dialectical part of Hegel's philosophy, or suppose that there is any rational or logically necessary connection between language, myth, and science. As a result, he was less tempted than Hegel to sacrifice the autonomy of art, religion, morality, and other aspects of experience to any one master science, and he remained closer to the position of Kant.

Nevertheless, according to Cassirer, there is a fundamental unity running through all modes of experience. Language, myth, and science are all forms of expression; and governing the internal development of each of these is a kind of law of three stages, which Cassirer claimed as the high point of his philosophy. In a way, it too is a kind of dialectic although much less rigid than Hegel's.

As Cassirer viewed it, the first phase in the development of any branch of experience is characterized by *immediacy*, when consciousness has not yet distinguished clearly between subject and object. The symbol by means of which consciousness succeeds in arresting a portion of the flux is as much a feeling as it is something felt. It has not yet become a medium by which the self responds to the environment, because at this level the vital adjustment is so spontaneous and automatic that no distinction is made between one and the other.

Cassirer drew upon the findings of biology and of animal and infant psychology to reinforce the evidences of cultural anthropology in these matters. He was impressed by the view that each animal species lives in a world of its own which is schematized for it in accordance with its particular organic needs. "Function" determines "form"—that is to say, the form under which the world appears to any living creature. The difference between a sign and a symbol, according to Cassirer, is that the former stands in a one-to-one relationship with the thing signified, whereas the latter has achieved a more universal reference. In terms of function, the sign is an immediate stimulus to the organism and normally leads to a specific response, but the symbol breaks the receptor-effector arc and either waylays consciousness or sends it along a detoured route. In either case, a radical innovation has taken place. A particular feeling no longer merely exists—it has become freighted with meaning.

With this change, Cassirer argues, consciousness is on the way to becoming self-conscious. Still, in the first phase, as has been indicated, a large measure of immediacy remains. Gesture, for example, is partly an expression of feeling, partly an imitative act, and partly a conventional designation of, say, consent. So, presumably, was earliest speech. Such must also have been the condition when myth arose, which has for its province the realm of imagination. The hunter, for example, no longer merely recognized his prey: its image took on magical powers for him; but, as the totemic structure of earlier societies suggests, this occurred without a clear distinction being made between the hunter and the hunted. Knowledge, as distinct from language and myth, is rooted in sensation and properly emerges as the mind gradually discriminates between the external and internal senses and between sense contents and affective tones. In contrast with the usual empiricist account of experience, Cassirer held that sensations are not given as discrete elements of experience, but are abstracted by the mind from a congeries of emotions and feelings.

They are, thus, early symbolic forms and are peculiarly immediate, especially those which, like smell and touch, can be identified, even by the sophisticated mind, either with the self or with the object.

Once it has begun the use of symbols, consciousness evolves by a kind of necessity. Since symbols by their very nature introduce a break into the immediacy of the vital activity, it is inevitable that the break will compound itself. The second phase in this development is characterized by *mediacy*. At this stage, the distinction between the self and the nonself becomes fixed. According to Cassirer, the knowledge of objects precedes the knowledge of the self: only after consciousness has succeeded in dividing and ordering the world of things is it possible for it to form any notion of an inner, subjective realm. This is achieved in large measure through the fixation that language and myth make possible. The flux of sensations is ordered into things endowed with independent, substantial existence: this is largely the function of naming. Space and time, which have their origin in mythical imagination, also contribute to the ordering and differentiation of the world. No sharp distinction is made, however, between fact and fancy: mythical images are reified as well as sensible ones.

It was a happy moment in the history of mind when the symbol could be identified with the thing which it symbolized, a kind of honeymoon between life and spirit. But it could not last. With the discovery of the role of mind in creating symbols and the role of symbols in determining any world-representation, man necessarily entered a third level of consciousness. This took place, as far as language is concerned, at the beginning of philosophy, when the magical connection between the thing and its name was dissolved and man's attention directed to the ideal and functional character of speech. A similar process took place in the world of myth. According to Cassirer, religion developed from mythology when the distinction became clear between the sensible image and that which the image reveals—opening therewith a new dimension in which the norms of myth and magic were no longer valid. It is in the realm of knowledge that man has been slowest to recognize the creative activity of the intellect and the symbolic elements in truth. The Pythagorean-Galilean revolution, which overthrew the world of sense perception, only strengthened the conviction that the intelligible aspects of the world are real and eternal. Only the most modern developments prepare us to accept the ideality of space and time and the functional origin of our concepts of causality and law.

The dialectical movement within the symbol-using consciousness served as the unifying principle for Cassirer's system. Because it is purely formal it enabled him to view experiences of the most diverse kinds as all manifestations of the same fundamental activity. He maintained that this is the basic difference between a critical philosophy, such as his own, and the traditional metaphysical systems which raise one or another objective content of experience to the level of a first principle. The philosophy of symbolic forms does not, like that of Hegel, start with rational necessity, much less, like that of Marx, with material necessity. For Cassirer, rational necessity is itself purely formal: when mind works with logical concepts, it must, to achieve its purpose, follow the connections that are entailed in symbols of this kind. The same thing is true of physical necessity; the kind of order which the mind has imposed on the physical world includes causality. A defect of all metaphysical explanation, according to Cassirer, is that, beginning with an abstract concept of unity, it is compelled to explain all multiplicity, and hence also all knowledge, as illusory. He claimed as the singular merit of his philosophy the fact that it does not suppress any kind of experience. Myth is just as legitimate as mathematics, and aesthetic feeling is not inferior to scientific fact. They merely lie along different axes, and they may represent earlier or later moments in the evolution of form. But one variety of experience is intrinsically no more valuable than another.

On the other hand, though all experiences are, in a sense, equal, they do, on this hypothesis, fit into one another to make up a meaningful universe. And this, according to Cassirer, is something that most empirical and positivist philosophies have not been able to encompass. The mistake he found in these philosophies is their initial claim that experience is composed of discrete sensations and feelings. According to his critical analysis, such is not the case. The least sense content we are capable of discriminating is part of a performed whole. If this fact is admitted, it resolves the difficulty which has always defeated empiricism's efforts to explain how independent parts can come together to form meaningful unities; how, for example, five separate sounds can form a musical theme or an intelligible sentence. For Cassirer, who has as his starting-point not the contents of the mind but the form of the mind as it expresses itself, the musical theme or the intelligible sentence is given first; and on accurate analysis the structure of the whole is found to be implicit in any of the parts.

Like Kant, Cassirer left his system open. He did not claim that its analysis is able to reduce experience entirely to intelligible components. At the lower end, sense contents always remain as a limit, in spite of the fact that any feeling or content taken up into consciousness is already touched with meaning. At times he was not averse to speaking of the lower limits as life, and he showed some sympathy with Henri Bergson's philosophy. But he regarded as futile all mystical attempts to know this prime condition by direct intuition; and any attempt to inquire about it in terms of higher symbols, such as those employed by biology or sociology, would, on his view, be self-defeating. The most that he claimed for his system was that it provided a morphology of consciousness in the act of expressing itself.

His system was also open in the direction of intellect. While he recognized the need for consciousness to become ever more aware of its own creativity, he did not venture to suggest that the consummation was yet in sight, or indeed that there ever would be a condition of perfectly self-contained consciousness. In this respect, the philosophy of symbolic forms invites contrast with Hegel's philosophy of spirit. The latter was governed by a logical *a priori*, which, when it had once disclosed itself, left nothing further to discover. Thus, Hegel's works all bear the impress of finality. But the *a priori* element in Cassirer's system is multiform and complex. Spirit develops in many directions, each of which manifests its own pattern. All that can be said with assurance is that there is always a tendency toward greater freedom of spirit and form, and away from subservience to matter and sense. For Cassirer, a world of pure form and intelligibility is unthinkable. Symbolic forms range along a scale, some dominantly sensible, others dominantly intelligible; but no form, no object which consciousness can entertain, can be completely without its sensible, existential component, any more than it can be without the structural, intelligible part which gives it meaning.

Cassirer's attempt to account for the evolution of culture without reference to natural events (to such matters as climate, geography, economics, and politics) has brought criticism, much as Hegel's system provoked reaction among some of his followers. But Cassirer did not deny that other things besides consciousness influence man's development—he only maintained that any attempt to know them involves us in the use of a symbolic system which may or may not give a valid account of what comes to pass. With good reason, his philosophy has been hailed as a humanist answer to culturologists and economic determinists who subject man to natural laws. If Cassirer is right, nature holds no domination over man other than that which man thinks it holds. At a certain stage of his intellectual development, he is likely to attribute to objects a reality and independence which they do not possess, and submit himself to their bondage. His hope lies in the fact that, sooner or later, he is bound to throw off this yoke of dogmatism and myth. When he does, and becomes fully aware of the creative uses of symbols, new vistas will open before him. This is not to say that life may not perish before the goal is realized or that, unsettled by advancing knowledge and the loss of earlier certitudes, man may not destroy himself. Two works written by Cassirer in exile from his native Germany during World War II (*An Essay on Man*, 1944, and *The Myth of the State*, 1946) represent civilization as a fragile bark, afloat on stormy deeps, which we must make a positive effort to save. His tone, however, remained hopeful, much like that of the eighteenth century Enlightenment, whose heir he was.—*J.F.*

PERTINENT LITERATURE

Hamburg, Carl H. "Cassirer's Conception of Philosophy," in *The Philosophy of Ernst Cassirer*. Edited by Paul A. Schilpp. Evanston, Illinois: The Library of Living Philosophers, 1949, pp. 73-120.

Ernst Cassirer's philosophy is not metaphysics in the usual sense, because Cassirer agreed with Immanuel Kant that one can investigate only the structure of knowledge, not that of Being. On the other hand, he broadened the scope of philosophy beyond what is usually recognized as knowledge to include art, myth, religion, and indeed every form of experience. Hence his philosophy is not epistemology either. It could, Carl H. Hamburg maintains, be called metaphysics of experience; but he defers to Cassirer's preference, which was to view it as a philosophy of culture.

Cassirer pointed out that historically the goal which philosophers have aimed at has been to find principles sufficiently general to take account of all domains of experience while admitting of modifications necessary to accommodate the specific characters of each. The failure of philosophers to achieve this goal he attributes to the antinomal character of the culture-concept—namely, the tendency of philosophers to take one domain of culture (whether science, religion, morality, or art) as ultimate and impose its categories on other domains. Cassirer's hope was that his symbol-concept, arrived at as a result of his study in different domains, might provide the unifying principle needed to fulfill the "culture mission" of philosophy, while avoiding the cultural imperialism which has produced the different dogmatic systems.

Much of Hamburg's article is devoted to making clear what Cassirer meant by his symbol-concept. Cassirer's concern, he points out, was entirely different from that of most philosophers interested in sign-analysis. In ordinary semantics, signs are taken as representing objects for an interpreter who has understanding of both signs and referents. Cassirer was engaged in what might be called metasemantics, because he took it on himself to explain how the interpreter comes to apprehend the sign, the thing signified, and the relation between them. In Cassirer's philosophy, the interpreter is human consciousness; the symbol relation is the perspective within which the world is viewed; symbols are, in Cassirer's words, "*organs* of reality, since it is solely by their agency that anything becomes an object." This means, according to Hamburg, that an object can have meaning only in reference to the pervasive symbolic-relation types of space, time, cause, and number which "constitute" objectivity, and only as it is apprehended in a particular cultural context, whether artistic, mythical, commonsense, or scientific.

The question remains: What precisely did Cassirer mean by saying that the forms through which we experience reality are symbols? In *Substance and Function*, Cassirer had brought Kant up to date by showing that modern scientific knowledge rests not on innate forms of intuition but on systems of conventional signs. It was a new inspiration, however, which led him, in 1917, to propound the thesis that all experience comes to us through symbols. This thesis entailed broadening the symbol-concept to cover all phenomena that exhibit "sense in the senses," to use his favored expression, "and in which something sensuous is *represented* as a particular embodiment of a sense or meaning."

According to Cassirer, the symbol-concept appears in three modal forms: expression, intuition, and conception. The expressive or evaluative mode, present in myth, art, awareness of another's person, and so forth, is characterized by the immediacy with which sensuous elements combine with feelings and emotion: colors and sounds are directly experienced as gloomy or cheerful, as fearful or reassuring. The intuitive mode is more developed than the expressive, in that what is experienced in this way ceases to be merely a qualitative presence and becomes a cue representing something else. Relatively constant elements of experience are singled out from the flux of sensation to form a world of spatiotemporal things-with-properties. This way of seeing or intuiting reality yields the commonsense world of the civilized adult. The third mode is that of conception or theorization. Rules, functions, and laws are employed as means of understanding what has already been experienced. The sciences and philosophy view the world in this way. Cassirer's symbol-function is, of course, an instance of conceptualization, an attempt to find one symbol embracing all symbols.

It has been objected against Cassirer that the symbol-relation does not properly lend itself to the analysis of our evaluative and perceptive experience because these are immediate, whereas symbolism implies a distinction between the sign and its meaning. Cassirer's first response to this objection was always to point out that his theory did not originate in speculation but was an attempt to coordinate results achieved by specialists in various fields who were already employing the mediating function of symbols in their work. He also appealed to psychological experiments dealing with colors and sounds which established the difference between what is sensed (the sign) and what is perceived (the meaning).

Hamburg cites an example that helps to establish the independence of two symbol-moments and also illustrates the symbol-function at work. A line drawing is, to begin with, a simple perceptive experience; but it may "come alive" as an aesthetic form or as a religious symbol or as a mathematical function. In addition, it may be read as a sign of something beyond itself, as indicating the style of a certain period, or as diagraming some natural process. The sensuous impression remains the same: what it "means" varies with the context in which it is viewed.

Langer, Susanne K. "On Cassirer's Theory of Language and Myth," in *The Philosophy of Ernst Cassirer*. Edited by Paul A. Schilpp. Evanston, Illinois: The Library of Living Philosophers, 1949, pp. 381-400.

For Susanne K. Langer, the philosophy of symbolic forms is important because it provides a conceptual framework within which a new synthesis of twentieth century knowledge is made possible. At the beginning of the century, while exciting new discoveries were being made in the sciences, academic philosophy was in a dead period, arguing old issues from the same old standpoints. Ernst Cassirer's greatness appears from the fact that, although remaining faithful to the tradition in which he had been nurtured, he was less interested in defending what Langer regards as decadent metaphysics than in resolving current problems.

The assumption of neo-Kantian idealism, that man's mind constructs the external world, Cassirer did not question. His masterstroke was to recognize the importance of symbolization in determining the forms which the mind brings to bear on what is given through the senses. Immanuel Kant's transcendental or critical method had shown that the forms of intuition and the categories of understanding must be contributed by the mind, but it had shed no light on the question of how these *a priori* constituents arise. Recognizing the close connection between conceptualization and expression (or symbolization), Cassirer was able to answer that question. As Langer sees it, Cassirer advanced as far beyond Kant's Copernican Revolution as Sir Isaac Newton advanced beyond Copernicus. He turned what had been a speculative theory of epistemology into an anthropological hypothesis. Prior to Cassirer, philosophy of mind had been divorced from the scientific study of mental phenomena. Cassirer began with the Kantian doctrine that mind is constitutive of the external world, but by making symbol-formation the fundamental principle of the mind's activity, he made his metaphysics meet the test of fact, drawing on the findings of ethnology, linguistics, art history, and psychology.

Using myth to designate man's early conceptualization of his environment, Cassirer maintained that language is the twin of myth, holding that neither could have developed in isolation. Langer devotes the greater part of her article to expounding Cassirer's insights into the so-called primitive mind. There is, she points out, an ambiguity in what we call experience: like all animals, man undergoes experiences; but only man can have experience, and this is possible to him by virtue of his power of image-making. Symbolic activity begins with imagination, by means of which man endows a part of his experience with the content of the whole. An image is a representation charged with all the expectations that are contained in the complex of which it is a part. Mimicry, gesture, and vocal expression reinforce the image. Language in particular takes on the meaning which the total experience has for man and enables him to respond in suitable ways. The mythical view of the world has a structure of its own, and language articulates this. Of particular interest for understanding the history of the mind is the naming function, by which aspects of experience are hypostatized, and the syntactical function, by which things thus constituted are supposed to possess properties, and to act and be acted upon.

What Cassirer learned from studies in primitive thought found confirmation from studies in clinical psychology, particularly from reports dealing with brain damage. Cases are cited by Cassirer in which the power of abstraction was lost so that the patient was reduced to speaking in metaphors. In other cases, the power of imagination was impaired to the point that, although the patient responded as an animal to the sight of food and drink, he was unable to recognize them by name. Of particular interest to students of language are cases in which the patient recognized the adjectival connotations of names without being able to use names to designate things, thereby confirming the Kantian (or Humean) supposition that what is given is uncomposed sense-data which the normal mind composes into objects.

Although Cassirer interested himself in the detail of psychiatric findings, he did not explore work in dynamic psychology, which, according to Langer, would have provided even more remarkable support for his thesis. Langer attributes this neglect to the deep antipathy which Cassirer felt toward the vitalist assumptions undergirding philosophies of the unconscious, with their tendency to regard man's cultural achievements as by-products of blind activity-drives, whereas for Cassirer they constitute the highest realization of the human spirit. Langer takes it on herself, therefore, to show that, particularly in respect of symbolic behavior, the parallel between Cassirer and Sigmund Freud is very close. In both Cassirer's mythic mode and Freud's mental mechanisms, intense feeling finds expression in symbols, whether images or things, that combine numerous, often conflicting, meanings. To make her case, Langer devotes two pages to quotations from Cassirer to which Freud could, she thinks, subscribe.

One final benefit Langer believes can be derived from Cassirer's theory of language and myth. At the time of her writing the main issue dividing philosophers concerned the place of mind in nature. Philosophers of spirit, who exalted man's rationality, were in retreat before philosophers of life, who raised instinct and passion over reason, even to the point of maintaining that reason is opposed to nature. Indeed, by showing the irrational origins of rational thought, Cassirer might have seemed to be defecting to the irrationalists. In Langer's opinion, however, such was not the case; instead, she sees in his philosophy the possibilities of *rapprochement*. Language is recognized as natural to man, but in its syntactic function, language is the basis for rational thought, and ultimately for everything that distinguishes civilization from barbarism.—*J.F.*

Additional Recommended Reading

Hamburg, Carl H. *Symbol and Reality; Studies in the Philosophy of Ernst Cassirer.* The Hague, The Netherlands: Martinus Nijhoff, 1956. An expansion of Hamburg's article, with particular reference to semiotics.

Hendel, Charles. "Introduction," in *The Philosophy of Symbolic Forms.* Vol. I. New Haven, Connecticut: Yale University Press, 1953, pp. 1-65. Relates Cassirer to his neo-Kantian background.

Langer, Susanne K. *Philosophy in a New Key: A Study in the Symbolism of Reason, Rite, and Art*. Cambridge, Massachusetts: Harvard University Press, 1942. A well-known textbook which fits the philosophy of symbolic forms into a naturalistic framework.

Verene, Donald Phillip, ed. *Symbol, Myth, and Culture: Essays and Lectures of Ernst Cassirer, 1935-1945*. New Haven, Connecticut: Yale University Press, 1979. See the editor's "Introduction" for an up-to-date account of Cassirer's achievement.

I AND THOU

Author: Martin Buber (1878-1965)
Type of work: Theology, epistemology
First published: 1923

PRINCIPAL IDEAS ADVANCED

There is no independent "I" but only the I existing and known in objective relation to something other than itself, an "It," or as encountered by and encompassed by the other, the "Thou."

Just as music can be studied analytically by reference to its notes, verses, and bars, or encountered and experienced in such a manner that it is known not by its parts but as a unity, so the I can relate itself analytically to something other, "It," or it can encounter the other, "Thou," so as to form a living unity.

The "Thou" stands as judge over the "It," but as a judge with the form and creative power for the transformation of "It."

Each encountered "Thou" reveals the nature of all reality, but finally the living center of every "Thou" is seen to be the eternal "Thou."

The eternal "Thou" is never known objectively, but certitude comes through the domain of action.

Since its first appearance in German in 1923, this slender volume has become one of the epoch-making works of our time. Not only does it place within one cover the best thinking of one of the greatest Jewish minds in centuries, but also, more than any other single volume, it has helped to mold contemporary theology. For example, ironically the neoorthodox tradition in recent Protestantism has appropriated in rather wholesale manner Buber's "I-Thou encounter," the "Eternal Subject," and other features. Although such men reinterpret these points from a radical Protestant context, others, such as Tillich, have developed systems that are in fundamental agreement with Buber's fuller understanding. Perhaps at no other point do liberal and orthodox Christian thinkers find so rich a place of meeting.

For Judaism, on the other hand, Buber's writings have been a new leaven. It is not true, as some have maintained, that Buber is a rebel from basic Judaism, that he is simply a Jew by birth and an existentialist by conviction. Rather, Buber is a mortar for the rich heritage of Judaism, some of it long neglected, and certain insights of contemporary thinking. No other writer has so shaken Judaism from its parochialism and applied it so relevantly to the problems and concerns of contemporary man.

Buber's writing is often rhapsodic in quality, frustrating the searcher for clear and distinct ideas; his key work has been aptly called a "philosophical-religious poem." Yet this is as it should be, for Buber is no system builder, but the imparter of a way of life. At its center is a unique type of relation, one universally available and yet almost universally neglected. His task is not so much one of detailed and logical exposition, but one of evoking, eliciting, educing this relation which is its own proof.

Quite early, Buber's youthful mastery of Jewish thought, life, and devotion came into tension with European intellectualism, especially the thought of Kant and Nietzsche. Buber's tentative resolution was that of mysticism, particularly as developed by the post-medieval Christian mystics. But a sense of rootlessness drew him back toward Judaism, first in the form of emerging Zionism, not so much as a political movement as a cultural renaissance. Here, in the venerable roots of Jewish religioculture, Buber found an alternative to man's modern plight of overcommercialism and superintellectualism. But it was in *Hasidim* that his answer became crystalized. This pietist conservative Jewish movement, emerging in eighteenth century Poland, moved him to withdraw from active life for five years of intensive study. The teachings stressed not monastic withdrawal, but joyous life in communities of this world, worshiping in every practical activity.

At this same time Buber encountered translations of Søren Kierkegaard's work. Kierkegaard's insistence on total involvement and absolute commitment, on the priority of subjective thinking, on truth as existential or lived truth, and his stress on the centrality of the individual—all of these elements made immediate contact with Buber's newfound religious devotion. The resulting tension of existentialism and *Hasidim* was creative for Buber. The emphasis of *Hasidim* on the warmth of comunity tempered the cold stress of Kierkegaard on the lonely and anxious individual; the latter's pessimism concerning man was largely dissolved by the general Jewish confidence in man's God-given potential. On the other hand, the existentialist stress on authentic existence grounded in the totally free and responsible decision of the self transformed Buber's earlier concern with mystic absorption and the illusory nature of the commonplace world. In personal experiences resulting from man's seeking him out for help, Buber learned the utter necessity of religion as a this-worldly faith, as a total devotion transforming every aspect of common life together. The unique "I-Thou" was no longer understood as a state of the absorbed individual in unity with an Absolute, but as a permeating relationship with all life—a lived experience, not of loss, but of transformation and fulfillment in reciprocity. With this key awareness, Buber's religious philosophy was fully formed, and it emerged in his greatest writing, *I and Thou.*

Quite clearly, this work is an essay in epistemology; it is epistemology, however, not simply in the traditional sense of understanding the nature and ascertainable truth of commonsense perception, but in the sense of exploring in sweeping fashion the possible "modes" or types of "knowing." It is Buber's thesis that strict empiricism is only one of several kinds of relation with reality, and that a life founded upon this mode alone is anemic to the core. Although he refuses to argue the point, Buber assumes that the plurality of modes corresponds with dimensions within reality itself. Such a contention stands within a time-honored tradition, whether it be Plato's distinction between sense impression and *noesis* or more recently Teilhard de Chardin's distinction between the "inner" and "outer" aspects of all things. Such a distinction, Buber holds, cannot be logically argued, for logic is simply the instrument of one of these modes and does not apply to others. Verification is thus intrinsic to the mode itself; it is self-verifying and requires no further "proof."

Buber's key affirmation is this—"To man the world is twofold, in accordance with his twofold attitude." This overarching attitude is expressed in every language by the words indicating "I," "It," and "Thou." "It" and "Thou" do not signify different things, Buber insists, but two different relations possible between the same self and the same "object." This is an interesting contention, first developed in detail by Kiekegaard, for in general parlance the ground for such distinction is usually held to be within the object itself. Underlying Buber's position here is a radical rejection of Descartes' famed "*Cogito, ergo sum.*" There is no such thing as an independent "I" which, internally certain of its own existence, then moves externally to God and the world. Rather, there is no I in itself but only the I existing and known in these two basic ways.

The "I-It" relation is the realm of objectivity, the realm of "experience," which is generally understood as perceiving, imagining, willing, feeling, and thinking. It includes all activities of the "I" in which there is an object, a "thing," whose existence depends on being bounded by other "things." Here one experiences and extracts knowledge concerning the "surface of things." Above all, the "I-It" experience is unilateral; in it the "I" alone is active, and the object perceived has no concern in the matter, nor is it affected by the experience.

This experience, as well as the "I-Thou," occurs in regard to three spheres—our life with nature, with men, and with intelligible forms. For example, to use Buber's most difficult illustration, in an "I-It" experience with a tree, I may look at it, examine its structure and functions, classify it, formalize the laws of its operation, see it in terms of its numerical components or control and shape it by activity. But not only may I experience the tree but I may enter into relationship with it—this is the mode of "I-Thou." Here I am "encountered" by the tree; I become bound to it, for it seizes me with "the power of exclusiveness." Although this relation is totally different in kind from the "I-It" experience, it is not strictly different in "content." In it one does not have to reject or forget the content of objective knowledge; rather, all of the above enumerated components become indivisibly united in the event which is this relation—"Everything belonging to the tree is in this: its form and structure, its colours and chemical composition, its intercourse with the elements and with the stars, are all present in a single whole."

While objective knowledge is always of the past, the relation of the "I-Thou" is always present, a "filled present." Above all, characteristic of this relation is its mutuality. Yet we cannot say that in this relation the tree exhibits a soul, or a consciousness, for of this we can have no experience. The relation is undifferentiated, and to inquire of its constitutive parts is to disintegrate what is known only as an indivisible whole. Such a wholeness is all-consuming and absolute—a "He" encountered as a "Thou" is a "whole in himself" and "fills the heavens." What Buber means is not that the "He" alone is existent but rather that this relation is such that "all else lives in *his* light."

To one not naturally inclined to Buber's way of thinking, the best available illustrations, as Buber's own examples clearly indicate, are from the arts. In fact, Buber maintains that the "I-Thou" relation is the true source of art. Music can be analyzed in terms of notes, verses, and bars; this is the realm of the "I-It." This same music, however, may be encountered in a living relation in which each component is included, yet experienced not as parts but as an inseparable unity. In artistic creativity, a form which is not an offspring of the artist encounters him and demands effective power. This calls for sacrifice and risk—risk, for endless possibility must be ended by form; sacrifice, because the work consumes the artist with a claim which permits no rest. Buber's interpretation of this artistic form is helpful in understanding the "content" of the "I-Thou" encounter. Says Buber, "I can neither experience nor describe the form which meets me, but only body it forth."

Here we begin to see Buber's transition from the exclusive relation of the "I-Thou" to the inclusive, concerned life which Buber espouses, in contrast to the mystic. The "I-Thou" is consummated in activity, activity which inevitably partakes of the "I-It" experience, but activity which is redeemed, for in being the creative and transforming ground of activity, the "I-Thou" relation is exhibited in its fullness. This creative tension of "It" and "Thou" in the practical life is exemplified in such contrasts as those between organization and community, control and mutuality, and individuals and persons. The "Thou" stands as judge over the "It," but a judge with the form and creative power for its transformation. In existential living the fathomless dimension of the "Thou" is creatively incarnated, as it were, into the commonplace world of the "It." As an "It," the created object will be scrutinized with all the instruments of "objectivity," but as a living embodiment of a "Thou" it has the capacity to lift its perceiver from the commonplace to the all-pervasive dimension of the Thou in which all things fundamentally participate. As Buber continually insists, such relation is not simply subjective, for then it could have no mutuality: "To produce is to draw forth, to invent is to find, to shape is to discover." This relation of "I-Thou" is subjectivity and objectivity in a totality which transcends the "I-It" quality of either in isolation.

We begin to see here that Buber is passing inevitably from the field of epistemology to that of metaphysics. If it be true that the relationship of "I-

Thou" is a valid mode of apprehending reality, a relationship grounded in the very nature of reality, a further question is unavoidable—what is the relation of "Thou" to "Thou," each of which is apprehended as *the* totality and as *the* illuminator of the whole? It is Buber's answer to this question which distinguishes him from aesthetic philosophers such as Santayana, Jordan, and Bosanquet, and marks him as a religious philosopher. He begins by perceiving love as the unique quality of the "I-Thou" relation, love as a "metaphysical and metapsychical fact." This is the nature of the relationship between "Thou" and "Thou," and the "I" as it participates in that which is the constituting relation of all. At this central point Buber comes intriguingly close to Christianity. "Love is responsibility of an I for a *Thou*. In this lies the likeness . . . of all who love, from the smallest to the greatest and from the blessedly protected man . . . to him who is all his life nailed to the cross of the world, and who ventures to bring himself to the dreadful point—to love *all men*." Or again, the "I-Thou" relation is one in which man "calls his *Thou* Father in such a way that he himself is simply Son. . . ." There can never be hatred of a "Thou"; hatred can be only against a part of a being. The "Thou," the whole, can only be loved, for this is the very nature of the mutual relation.

Since each encountered "Thou" reveals the inmost nature of all reality, we see that everything can appear as a "Thou." This is so because in the "I" is an "inborn Thou," an *a priori* of relation. We see this, Buber affirms, as the child's fundamental guide to action from the instinct to make contact by touch and name, to its blossoming in tenderness and love, and its perfection in creativity. All of these emerge from the "I's" inherent longing for the "Thou." Throughout life "I-Thou" encounters continue, but they are not ordered, for they are only "a sign of the world-order." Increasingly one sees this to be so, for every "Thou" inevitably becomes an "It"; but man cannot rest content with only a momentary "I-Thou" relation. The inborn "Thou" can be consummated only in a direct relation with the "Thou" which cannot become "It." All lesser "Thou's" whet the soul for the relation which is abiding, for which all others are mere foreshadows. Through them the "I" sees that the "Thou's" are such only because they possess a "living Centre," that "the extended lines of relations meet in the eternal Thou."

Witness to this is exhibited for Buber even in the practical realm. Men can live in mutual relation only when they first take their stand in mutual relation with a living Center. A great culture rests on an original, relational event from which a special conception of the cosmos emerges. Loss of this center reduces a culture to the impotence of a mere "It." Likewise, marriage is consummated by a couple's mutual revealing of the "Thou" to each other; only thereby do they participate in the "Thou" which is the unifying ground in which mutual relations in all realms are possible. Whatever name one gives to this "Thou," if he really has "Thou" in mind, despite his illusions, he addresses the true "Thou" which cannot be limited by another. Even though he regards himself as an atheist, he stands in a relation which gathers up and includes all others.

This meeting of the "Thou" is a matter both of choosing and being chosen. One can prepare, yet since all preparations remain in the realm of "It," the step from that realm is not man's doing. Thus the word "encounter" is the only one appropriate. Epistemologically, the particular encounters are prior; metaphysically, the Central Thou is eternally prior. Through the former we are addressed by the latter; ours is the response. It is here that we reach the apex of Buber's position—"In the relation with God unconditional exclusiveness and unconditional inclusiveness are one." This relation means neither the loss of world nor "I," but a giving up of self-asserting instinct by regarding all in the love relation of the "Thou." The world of "It" cannot be dispensed with, nor is it evil; it becomes demonic only when the motivating drive is not the will to be related but, for example, in economics is the will to profit, or, in politics, the will to power. Buber's ethic can be clearly stated—man participating in awareness of the Thou "serves the truth which, though higher than reason, yet does not repudiate it. . . . He does in communal life precisely what is done in personal life by the man who knows himself incapable of realising the *Thou* in its purity, yet daily confirms its truth in the *It*, in accordance with what is right and filling for the day, drawing—disclosing—the boundary line anew each day." Such a life is characterized by action filled with meaning and joy, and possessions radiating with "awe and sacrificial power." These are the truths of primitive man, encountering with wonder the immediacy of life, but now purified of superstition and fitted for civilized community. To hallow life is to encounter the living God; to encounter this "Thou" is to hallow life—this is the paradox which best summarizes Buber's thought.

It is in this relation that Buber sees true theology resting. Its basis is not dogma, a content once and for all delivered. It is a compulsion received as something to be done; its confirmation is its product in the world and the singleness of life lived in obedience to it. This is the meaning of revelation, revelation which is eternal and ever available. It must be completed in theology, in objectification, but the abiding sin of religion is to substitute the objectification for the relation, to make the Church of God into a god of the church, to make the Scripture of God into a god of the scripture. The mystery at the foundation of theology cannot be dispelled, yet language can point in the right direction. For Buber the affirmations "God *and* the world" or "God *in* the world" are still in the "I-It" realm; but the declaration "the world in the Thou" points to the true relation. With hesitation, Buber attempts to say more, drawing heavily upon the artistic analogy. The God-man relation is characterized by the polarity of creatureliness and creativity, of being totally dependent upon God and yet totally free. For Buber this tension can only mean that while we need God in order to exist, God needs us for the very meaning of life. That is, "there is a becoming of the God that is"—herein is the eternal purpose of our existence. Mutual fulfillment, which is the "I-Thou" relation, must mean, in the final account, that we are co-creators with God in cosmic fulfillment.

Such declarations will raise immediate questions for the logical philosopher. Is this absolute idealism, pantheism, panpsychism, or process philosophy? In what sense is this the theistic world view of traditional Judaism, centered in the God of providence and history? Buber's refusal to be of any help here shows the degree to which he is not a philosophic system-builder but an existentialist and, above all, a religious thinker. The problem for him is not so much to know as it is to act in lived awareness of the omnipresent "Thou."

But at least this much can be said. In Buber we have the general Kantian position taken to a religious conclusion. The realm of the "Thou" is the realm of the noumenon; here is to be found no causality but the assurance of freedom. The realm of "It" is the phenomenal realm, the realm of necessity, causality, and the objectification of all according to finite categories. But for Buber the noumenal is more than a postulate or an inference. Similar to Kant's impact of the moral imperative and the encounter of beauty and sublimity in the *Critique of Judgment*, the noumenon is encountered through the total self. And finally, as in Kant, the eternal "Thou" is never known objectively, but certitude of it comes centrally through the domain of action. —*W.P.J.*

PERTINENT LITERATURE

Friedman, Maurice S. *Martin Buber: The Life of Dialogue.* Chicago: The University of Chicago Press, 1976.

Maurice S. Friedman is unquestionably the most influential interpreter of Martin Buber's thought. His numerous articles on Buber have not only helped to give prominence to Buber's ideas but have also, to a large extent, given rise to a dominant interpretation of his philosophy. The core of this interpretation can be found in *Martin Buber: The Life of Dialogue*, which Buber himself has called the definitive interpretation of his work.

Friedman's major concern is to disclose a concealed unity in Buber's writings, a philosophic unity which transcends even Buber's own explicit self-understanding. The mystical, existential, and dialogical phases of Buber's philosophizing are seen by Friedman to be thematically unified by the problem of evil. Not only does this interpretation enable Friedman to give coherence to the philosophic dimension of Buber's thought, but it also allows him to integrate the religious dimension which was so influential for all of Buber's insights. This can already be seen in the first, or mystical, phase of Buber's reflections on the nature of the transcendent. The mystic, of course, aims at complete and undifferentiated unity with the ground of life. Correspondingly, evil is then the state of being in which the subject is separated from the transcendent. Even during this phase, however, Buber developed a fundamentally affirmative aspect of his thinking: namely, the belief that redemption is always possible. The basic theme in this spiritual tension between unity and separation is that evil can never gain complete dominance—an insight which was to guide Buber throughout his life. Still in keeping with his Judaic background, in the existential phase of his life Buber saw good as commitment by the whole person and evil as a directionless, purposeless wandering based on a lack of decision. In this phase the object of one's self-realization does not matter; what is considered important is the nature of one's involvement.

The real correspondence between the philosophic and Judaic elements in Buber's thinking came to the fore only in his dialogical writings. There the emphasis was on the meeting between man and God in the I-Thou relationship. One might therefore assume that the I-Thou relationship is the good and the I-It the evil. Friedman shows, however, that it is not solely the one relationship which is good, but rather the proper balance of the two. Buber recognized that no one could live permanently in the I-Thou, for reversion to the mode of I-It is a necessary moment of the dialogue. Thus it is only when the I-It predominates to the exclusion of the I-Thou that it is evil. This dialogical view also shows that God or spirit is not that which is good in itself; it is so only in relation to the world. The emphasis pointed to by Friedman is thus one of balance between a variety of tensions. The meaning of life is revealed only by the pulsating between the Thou and the It. Thus it is the impulse to evil, the domination of the It, which contains in it the very possibility of the good. A fundamental reversal seems always to be promised by the unwavering Thou, which puts an outside limit on the movement away from good.

Through his interpretation of evil Friedman brings to light the deeper meaning of dialogue, which cannot be restricted to an understanding of the I-Thou relationship itself. He sees this confirmed in Buber's later writings, where there is an increasing emphasis on understanding evil as significant in itself, rather than simply as a negative reflection of something else. In his view, Buber's work thus began to flesh out a true philosophical anthropology, one which considered the wholeness of man, rather than only a special moment in his life. Both extremes of existence are rejected. To talk about leading a life of dialogue ultimately means not simply relation, but a dynamic relation which swings between the Thou and the It. It is this fuller understanding which, according to Friedman, is Buber's ultimate solution to the problem of evil and which designates the fundamental reality of man's existence. The very notion of evil is essential to good. What redeems man's existence is thus the fact that even the negative elements of it are essential for a complete, positive life.

Schaeder, Grete. *The Hebrew Humanism of Martin Buber.* Translated by
Noah J. Jacobs. Detroit: Wayne State University Press, 1973.

Noah J. Jacobs' translation of a work originally published in German in
1966 is the most comprehensive study of the totality of Martin Buber's life
and thought in print. It provides not simply an understanding of Buber's
philosophy, but also comprehensively covers the cultural context and the
intellectual influences which had major significance for his thought. Rather
than being simply an intellectual biography or philosophic analysis, this work
should be considered to be an important contribution to intellectual history.
A wide-ranging discussion of Immanuel Kant, Friedrich Wilhelm Nietzsche,
Wilhelm Dilthey, Georg Simmel, and Martin Heidegger, among many others,
gives the interpretation of Buber's thought a significant contextual validity.

Grete Schaeder finds a twofold emphasis in Buber's work, an emphasis
which results both in incompleteness from a purely philosophical or theological perspective and in Buber's major insight—the recognition of the fundamental significance which must be given to the sphere of the Between.
Although, according to Schaeder, the religious dimension always formed a
backdrop to Buber's reflections, in the writings before *I and Thou* the major
concern was always the impact of the religious or secular experiences on man's
life. It is the effects on the future conduct of man which give a personal
revelation by God their significance. The experience of the mystery has a
profound renewing effect, which, however, is not explicable in terms of conceptual understanding. In the first part of *I and Thou* Buber traced the experience back to a submerged primal form of being which is present in all
men. In describing the effects on man he attempted to formulate a philosophical anthropology, but given the fundamental mystery at the source of
the experience, he in fact lacked a secure ontological foundation for the
analysis. The emphasis on the personal aspect of the revelation brought with
it an irreducible subjective element. Schaeder grants, however, that given
Buber's explicit concern with the concrete life of man this lack of foundation
is what must be expected.

Seen from the other, the theological, perspective the undemonstrability of
that which is experienced in revelation is a hindrance as well. The revelation
of the eternal Thou is seen at the same time as uniquely personal and yet
transcultural. Buber was convinced that the eternal Thou functioned as the
backdrop in every relationship, but that the transcendent as such could not
be experienced. He was thus again driven to the subjective dimension.

Given the incompleteness or lack of objectivity of the preceding two perspectives, Schaeder argues that the focus for Buber naturally moved to the
Between, to the "meeting" of the two dimensions. Neither man nor God can
ultimately be understood as a singularity; both must be seen in the context
of their communion in history. This meeting surpasses or precedes rational

philosophizing and moves back to an existence within an attitudinal framework. Buber in this regard was more concerned with life as it is lived than
with philosophizing about it. Ultimately, then, understanding of the I-Thou
dialogue must occur on a symbolic or mystical plane. The meeting of God
and man is a mystery and must remain so; but it is also a certainty that
provides its own confirmation through the effects which it has on man. The
notion of the I-Thou in itself indicates that in the last phase of his thought
Buber recognized that it is man as he lives, as opposed to God, who provides
that more fundamental understanding of himself that must surpass any philosophical anthropology.

Wood, Robert E. *Martin Buber's Ontology: An Analysis of I and Thou.*
Evanston, Illinois: Northwestern University Press, 1969.

Along with other commentators on Martin Buber's thought, Robert E.
Wood recognizes that Buber's primary concern was to provide a description
of the I-Thou experience, to bear witness to a fundamental truth which he
had experienced in his own life. Such an approach of necessity left unexplored
many of the philosophic presuppositions which underpin the experience itself.
In *Martin Buber's Ontology* Wood aims to explore the ontological foundations
of Buber's thought through an explication of the notion of Presence as it binds
together the subject and object in the sphere of the Between. While Wood's
analysis is a good beginning in this direction, he makes it plain that the totality
of such a task requires more than can be found in his book.

Within the context of Buber's entire corpus, his central concern was one
of emphasizing the notion of unity. In varying combinations the theme of the
unity of God, the world, and man is explored through the mystical, existential,
and dialogical phases of his thinking. The mystical phase emphasizes primarily
the question derived from Meister Eckhart of how the unity of God could be
reconciled with the multiplicity of creation. Buber was here striving for unity
beyond distinction. Because of his concurrent immersion in *Hasidism*, however, he also recognized that the unification had to end and a return to life
be undertaken. This in turn led to the existential phase in which a genuine
"I" existing in the world was Buber's goal. Man returns to a higher unity
within himself where the totality of self is sufficient. In this phase the eternal
Thou is not recognized as a necessity; experience of the other only draws one
back into subjectivity.

In 1914, however, a key event occurred in the life of Buber which halted
his drive toward subjectivism. A friend sought him out for advice which Buber
felt he could not give. Shortly afterward the friend was killed in the war.
Buber then recognized that his earlier way of thinking had to be transcended
as a means for understanding man's condition in the world; the beginnings
of his dialogical thinking were generated.

After following Buber's philosophic progress through its development, Wood undertakes a section-by-section analysis of *I and Thou* with the aim of bringing out the ontological import of the main themes discussed by Buber. According to Wood, through his experiental emphasis Buber overcame the limitations of either straightforward subjectivisim or objectivisim. In the "Between" the subject and object are united, but in an ontological sense it is this very Between which first of all lets the subject and object arise. Ontologically, then, the Between has priority and contains a surplus of meaning which would remain even should those elements be removed. However, given Buber's religious orientation, the Between is not pure Between; it is formulated only against the background of the transcendent, which provides the essential unity and which for Buber cannot be explicated but only experienced in the mode of the I-Thou. Inevitably this experiental immediacy degenerates and becomes conceptual, meaning that I-It relationships take the place of the I-Thou relationship.

It is Wood's basic thesis that the experiental unity can be grounded on a metaphysical foundation. The important point to notice in this regard is that such a metaphysics must be a historical, temporal one—that is, one which contains a dialectical recognition of the interplay between the two different modes of I-Thou and I-It. In this metaphysics the transcendent forms the absolute horizon which can be interpreted ontologically even though not as the absolute mystery which it is. Wood is searching for a philosophic completion of Buber's most important insight. The ground itself, he believes, can ultimately be explicated in terms of the relationships which arise from it. Even though Wood does not complete the required metaphysical investigation to achieve that end, he thus outlines an important direction of inquiry for the study of Buber's thought.—*H.C.L.*

ADDITIONAL RECOMMENDED READING

Cohen, Arthur A. *Martin Buber*. London: Bowes and Bowes, 1957. A short introduction which concentrates on the basic themes in Buber's thought, especially the pursuit of the holy.

Diamond, Malcolm L. *Martin Buber: Jewish Existentialist*. New York: Oxford University Press, 1960. Diamond's work links the Jewish and the philosophical elements in Buber's thought.

Hodes, Aubrey. *Martin Buber: An Intimate Portrait*. New York: Viking Press, 1971. This work provides a biographic insight into Buber's life and thought by a close associate.

Kohanski, Alexander. *An Analytical Interpretation of Martin Buber's "I and Thou"*. New York: Barron's Educational Series, 1975. A section-by-section discussion of *I and Thou* intended for the nonspecialist.

Moore, Donald J. *Martin Buber: Prophet of Religious Secularism*. Philadelphia: The Jewish Publication Society of America, 1974. Excellent discussion of the Jewish-Christian dialogue opened up by Buber's works.

Schilpp, Paul A. and Maurice Friedman, eds. *The Philosophy of Martin Buber*
(The Library of Living Philosophers). La Salle, Illinois: Open Court, 1967.
This volume contains thirty essays on Buber's thought and Buber's "Replies
to My Critics." Noteworthy articles include those by Charles Hartshorne,
Helmut Kuhn, Emmanuel Levinas, Gabriel Marcel, and Jean Wahl.

THE MEANING OF MEANING

Authors: C. K. Ogden (1889-1957) and I. A. Richards (1893-1979)
Type of work: Philosophy of language; theory of signs
First published: 1923

Principal Ideas Advanced

A science of symbolism aiming at the discovery of the influences of language upon thought is needed to clear up misconceptions about language and free those who would inquire into language from the tyranny of language itself.

The theoretical problem of the study of language is to determine the relationships among mental processes, symbols, and referents.

Thinking is the interpretation of signs; interpretation is a psychological reaction that can be studied inductively.

There are six canons of symbolization: singularity, definition, expansion, actuality, compatibility, and individuality; by the use of these canons a set of symbols can be well-organized.

Words have evocative (emotive) functions as well as symbolization functions; by this distinction of function, poetry can be distinguished from scientific writings.

Much of the emphasis upon the importance of attending to the uses of language, distinguishing the functions of language, and freeing oneself from the idea that each descriptive term has a clearly definable meaning—an emphasis that characterizes contemporary analytic philosophy—was anticipated by C. K. Ogden and I. A. Richards in their influential study *The Meaning of Meaning*, subtitled *A Study of the Influence of Language Upon Thought and of the Science of Symbolism.* Ogden and Richards' book was published in 1923; Charles W. Morris' *Signs, Language, and Behavior* (a philosophical preface to semiotic, the theory of signs) was published in 1946; between these two publications came philosophical essays, mostly articles, in which a new sophistication about the use of language became evident. In the work of such philosophers as John Wisdom, Gilbert Ryle, John Austin and, of course, Ludwig Wittgenstein, much of it published in the 1930's and 1940's, one finds a radical departure from the misleading traditional view that words are labels or the names of essences—or the even more troublesome view that words have nothing to do with thinking or with what is thought about. The kinds of distinctions Ogden and Richards called for—distinctions in the use of language, in the functions of language, in levels of language—and the recognition of the great variety of language and its resistance to definitive and dogmatic accounting may be found enunciated as theory and confirmed by practice in contemporary analytic philosophy. Whether the emphasis is on the ordinary use of language or on the persuasive or "therapeutic" use of language, what the new sophistication in philosophy involves is an awareness of language as a tool, something to be used in various ways, having various kinds of effects on various kinds of persons in various situations.

Ogden and Richards begin by arguing that the study of language and, in particular, the study of the relation of language to thought and to what thought is about, has been either neglected or mismanaged by those whose studies have something to do with language—philosophers, philologists, semanticists, and ethnologists. The authors use the term "Symbolism" as the name for a scientific study of language in its relations to thought: "Symbolism is the study of the part played in human affairs by language and symbols of all kinds, and especially of their influence on Thought." The authors contend that the easy assumptions that everyone knows what meaning is, or, on the other hand, that no one can know, can be dispelled once the problem of language is approached scientifically.

The account of language and meaning is confined in this work to a study of the relations of the use of words to thoughts and to the things to which the words refer in reflective speech "uncomplicated by emotional, diplomatic, or other disturbances. . . ." According to the authors, the symbolism one uses in speaking is caused partly by the sort of reference being made and partly by such social and psychological factors as the speaker's purpose, the intended effect of the remarks on the persons spoken to, and the speaker's attitudes.

The relation of the symbol to the "referent," the thing referred to, is indirect in that the symbol causes thought, and the thought, in turn, refers to the thing. A symbol does not directly "stand for" a referent, although it is ordinarily supposed that somehow it does, since the symbol *does* refer to the referent—but, the authors emphasize, it does so only by the causal effect on thought of the symbol's being used and the resultant act of referring in thought by which a thing becomes a referent.

Language is often treacherous, Ogden and Richards declare (in fact, it works its treachery upon those who attempt to study language, if they do not do so scientifically). It is helpful, of course, to frame clear-cut definitions; but to do so systematically one must have an adequate theory of definition, and such a theory follows a theory of signs. What the theory of signs teaches is that there is no such thing as *the* meaning of a word, no such thing as the ultimate, revelatory definition.

The primitive, "magical" idea about the relation of words to things is that words somehow naturally belong to things; that to know the word for a thing is somehow to acquire power over the thing or gain access to its inner nature; that if one releases one's name one thereby diminishes the power of self-defense. Superstitions about names will persist, the authors contend, until and unless the study of language becomes scientific—based on systematic observation, providing information by which one gains control.

The traditional approach to the problem of meaning has been not by way of a theory of signs—advocated by the authors—but through introspection.

The assumption has been that a person knows what he means when he says something; all he has to do is think about it. When one adds to this simplistic view the misleading claims of some philosophers, any hope of understanding language and meaning disappears. The most damage done by philosophers stems from their insistence that the relation between a mind and its objects is unique—whether it be the relation between the mind and postulated unique subsistences called "propositions" or between the mind and unique entities called "concepts," "universals," or "properties" (and, they add, "essences"). Ogden and Richards, of course, deny that the relation between thought and its objects, or the symbol (sign) and its user or interpreter, is unique; the relations are accessible to scientific inquiry, and the sooner such inquiry is undertaken the better.

All experience is either enjoyed or interpreted, Ogden and Richards contend, but even what is enjoyed tends to be interpreted. Interpretation, then, is at the center of the use and reception of signs. The effects of signs depend in part on the past history of the person affected by their use; expectations are called up by stimuli similar to those operative in the past. Without the recurrence of types of stimuli, the authors write, "no prediction, no inductive generalization, no knowledge or probable opinion as to what is not immediately given, would be possible."

Truth and falsity can be understood by reference to expectations in contexts linking stimuli and response. If a match is scraped, one expects a flame (because of past experience); the belief that "There will now be a flame" is true if, in the context of scraping, a flame occurs. A sensation provokes an expectation; an expectation is satisfied by another sensation.

The consideration of perception as involving what Ogden and Richards call a "sign-chain" is introduced by a reference to the sign-theory content in H. L. F. von Helmholtz's account of perception. Helmholtz regarded sensations as signs of physical objects, but he insisted that sensations are not pictures of those objects and that the qualities of sensations are not the qualities of objects. The object causes a sensation; the sensation becomes a sign of the object. The sign is interpreted as signifying something other than itself.

The authors state that so-called "direct apprehension" is attributable to a modification of sense organs that in turn effects a modification of the nervous system.

As for knowledge, whether it be perceptual knowledge or knowledge of another kind, a statement that makes a reference is true if the set of referents referred to hangs together in the way stated. We cannot discover "the *what* of referents," Ogden and Richards write; "We can only discover the *how*." Since metaphysicians vainly seek to get at the *what* of things, instead of considering how we are affected by things and, consequently, what the relations are among signs and hence how, in a sense, the causes of sensations—

physical objects—"hang together," no knowledge is possible for them.

Ogden and Richards attribute the persistence of perceptual puzzles (such as, "This same stick which I see in the water is both straight and bent") to the persistence of "bad symbolization." Were it not for ambiguities springing from the confused use of signs, there would be no puzzles. The various senses of the word "see" correspond to various sign-situations that change as the techniques and purposes of investigation change. Hence, whether or in what sense in a situation we "see" a table or wood or cells or atoms or electrons depends on the kind of sign-situation involved; puzzles (of the kind that amuse philosophers) arise from a confusion of sign-situations.

Every system of symbols involves certain regulative presumptions or "canons," Ogden and Richards next point out. They call logicians to task for neglecting to identify the implicit canons of communication. The authors thereupon set forth six of the most important canons: (1) "One Symbol stands for one and only one Referent"; (2) "Symbols which can be substituted one for another symbolize the same reference"; (3) "The referent of a contracted symbol is the referent of that symbol expanded"; (4) "A symbol refers to what it is actually used to refer to; not necessarily to what it ought in good usage, or is intended by an interpreter, or is intended by the user to refer to"; (5) "No complex symbol may contain constituent symbols which claim the same 'place'"; and (6) "All possible referents together form an order, such that every referent has one place only in that order."

To speak of the "place" of a symbol (linguistic sign) is to talk of its function in a complex system of signs; the "place" of a referent is its location in the order of referents. In the case of a false assertion, one can say either that the speaker believes the referent to be in a "place" in which it is not or that the speaker believes himself to be referring to a referent other than the one to which he actually refers.

The six canons specified (Singularity, Expansion, Definition, Actuality, Compatabililty, and Individuality) determine the right use of language in reasoning; symbolic levels can be distinguished and interpretation can be ordered. "These Canons control the System of Symbols known as Prose," the authors contend (emotive language is subject to different sorts of control).

Ogden and Richards suggest as a preliminary classification of methods of definition ("definition routes") eight "simple" routes and two complex routes. The first is a matter of naming something by indicating it while using the term; the authors call this mode of definition "Symbolization." The second involves the use of a demonstrative such as "this" and a claim of similarity; for example, the term "orange" is defined by pointing out some object of orange color and stating "Anything like this in respect of color can be signified by the use of the symbol 'orange.'" This second definition route is called "Similarity."

Other simple definition routes involve reference to (3) Spatial Relations,

(4) Temporal Relations, (5) Causation: Physical (example: the term "thunder" refers to what is caused by certain electrical disturbances), (6) Causation: Psychological (example: the symbol "the unconscious" refers to whatever causes dreams, psychoses, and so forth), (7) Causation: Psycho-physical ("A perception of orange" is "the effect in consciousness of certain vibrations falling on the retina"), and (8) "Being the Object of a Mental State" (the authors refer to desiring, willing, feeling, and referring as examples of what the term "mental state" refers to, and they define "piteous things" as "those towards which we feel pity," and "good things" as "those which we approve of approving."

There is also the possibility of combining simple routes by the method called "Common Complex Relations." (Ogden and Richards give as an example "utility," analyzable into numbers 7 and 8.)

As a practical benefit, the category of "Legal Relations" is provided to complete the list; legal relations, such as "belonging to" and "evidence of," are also complex relations, analyzable by simple definitions.

The authors suggest that in mediating rival views, it is best to assume that the disputants are using terms in different ways; the opposite assumption is more likely to cause trouble.

Such terms as "beauty" and "truth" (as well as "meaning," of course) are not so much single words, Ogden and Richards write, as they are "superficially indistinguishable yet utterly discrepant symbols."

The beginning of the defining process must be the collection of numerous and varied uses of the term to be defined. As a list grows, one becomes aware of distinctions and relations of meaning; the longer the list, the more likely the result will be responsible.

Three devices of controversialists—three argumentative tricks—are mentioned by the authors: The *Phonetic Subterfuge* consists in treating words that sound alike as if their expansions (the spelling out of meanings) were analogous. (John Stuart Mill's comparing "desirable" to "visible" is mentioned—although the authors blame the language, not Mill, and suggest that "desirable" can be defined by the use of the phrase "can be desired" provided that one adds "by a mind of a certain organization.")

The *Hypostatic Subterfuge* consists in hypostatizing contractions—that is, regarding abstractions as factual referents in the world. The authors give as examples such terms as "Liberty," "Democracy," and "Religion."

The *Utraquistic Subterfuge* consists in using a term that has two different but related referents—such as the term "perception," that may refer either to what is perceived or to the perceiving of it—as if it had a single referent. (The ambiguity involved is sometimes called the "process-product" ambiguity—as in such terms as "art" and "science.")

The cure for these linguistic diseases, the authors repeat, is the use of the canons of definition.

Ogden and Richards undertake to illustrate the procedure of definition by considering the question of the meaning of beauty. The term "beauty," the authors contend, has been used and defined in various ways, according to the interests and purposes of those using the term. They sketch out sixteen definitions, not to show that definers differ in their proposals but to make it evident that speakers have meant and emphasized different features of situations through their uses of the term "beauty." (As examples: "Anything is beautiful which causes pleasure," "Anything is beautiful which heightens vitality," and "Anything is beautiful which is the work of genius.")

It is understandable that those who use the term "beauty" as if it had but one use and kind of referent confuse both themselves and others; the problem is compounded when no distinction is made between the symbolic and emotive uses of the word "beauty." (The emotive uses account for the claim by some philosophers that the term "beauty" is indefinable.)

Applying the same procedure of distinguishing uses to the problem of defining the term "meaning," the authors come up with sixteen definitions (some of them involving alternatives). Examples abstracted from the list follow: *Meaning* is: "the other words annexed to a word in the dictionary," "an essence," "emotion aroused by anything," "that which is actually related to a sign by a chosen relation," "what anything suggests," "that to which an interpreter refers (or believes himself to be referring, or believes the user to be referring)."

Some of the uses of language are more troublesome than others in that they are more likely to give rise to misunderstandings. But whatever the use, definition in accordance with the canons will make communication more effective.

The authors conclude by once again urging the development of a scientific study of signs and symbols—a science they call "Symbolism." They remind the reader that although the present discussion has concentrated on symbolization, it is important to proceed to study the evocative aspects of language. Such a science, concentrating on the influence of language on thought, would be extremely helpful in ridding education and discussion in general of linguistic confusions: ". . . when . . . the Phantoms due to linguistic misconception have been removed, the way is open to more fruitful methods of Interpretation and to an Art of Conversation by which the communicants can enjoy something more than the customary stones and scorpions."—*I.P.M.*

PERTINENT LITERATURE

Morris, Charles. *Writings on the General Theory of Signs*. The Hague, The Netherlands: Mouton, 1971.

This volume contains Charles Morris' *Foundations of the Theory of Signs* (1938), *Signs, Language, and Behavior* (1946; see elsewhere in this work the discussion of Morris' *Signs, Language, and Behavior* and of pertinent literature relating to it), and a summary chapter on signs from *Signification and Significance* (1964), together with a number of related articles.

Morris acknowledges the role played by *The Meaning of Meaning* in the development of his ideas about signs and meaning; he writes that he had "been helped to identify the contours of a general theory of signs by *The Meaning of Meaning. . . .*" The *Foundations of the Theory of Signs* begins with the proposition that men are the "dominant sign-using animals." Morris announces his intention to develop the outlines of a science of signs, a theoretical structure to unify the results stemming from various kinds of investigations into the functioning of signs.

Semiotic as the science of signs is both a science and an instrument of the sciences, Morris writes. Semiotic is an instrument of the sciences because every science uses signs. Morris uses the term *semiosis* for the process in which something functions as a sign. He distinguishes the following components in the process: the *sign vehicle*, the *designatum* (what is designated by the use of the sign), the *interpreter* of the sign, and the *interpretant*, the taking-account-of the *designatum*. Accordingly, something is a sign of a designatum to the degree that the interpreter by way of the interpretant takes account of the designatum.

Morris devotes separate chapters to *syntactics*, the study of the logicogrammatical structure of language; *semantics*, the study of the relation of signs to their designata and the objects they denote; and *pragmatics*, the study of the relation of signs to their users.

In Chapter VI, "The Unity of Semiotic," Morris comments on the term "meaning." He asks whether the term "meaning" is a semiotical term, and in response he calls attention to the fact that he has deliberately avoided using the term "meaning." He contends that it is best to avoid using the term, partly because it can be dispensed with and partly because there tends to be a great deal of confusion engendered by its use. In a discussion of the "meaning of 'meaning,'" he writes, the term "meaning" variously refers to designata, to denotata, to the interpretant, to the implications of a term, to semiosis itself, or to significance or value.

In *Signs, Language, and Behavior* Morris refers to attempts that have been made to devise some simple classification of sign uses, and he mentions the influential effect of C. K. Ogden and I. A. Richards' distinction between referential and emotive uses. In line with that distinction, mentioned in *The Meaning of Meaning*, "Pollock distinguishes the referential and the evocative uses of signs; [C. A.] Mace the referential and expressive; [Hans] Reichenbach the cognitive and the instrumental; [Herbert] Feigl the informational and the non-cognitive; [Charles] Stevenson the cognitive and the dynamic." Morris then sets forth what he regards as the four primary sign usages: the *informative*, the *valuative*, the *incitive*, and the *systemic* uses of signs; that is, signs are used "to inform the organism about something, to aid in its preferential selection of objects, to incite response-sequences of some behavior family, and to organize sign-produced behavior (interpretants) into a determinate whole."

In Chapter III, "Modes of Signifying," Morris describes *The Meaning of Meaning* as a pioneer effort to distinguish the signification of signs in scientific discourse from the kind of signification to be found in nonscientific discourse. Morris' interest is in finding behavioral criteria for the fundamental distinction involved. He mentions Ogden and Richards' definition of "emotive" terms as terms used "to express or excite feelings and attitudes." The four main functions distinguished by Ogden and Richards are "symbolization of reference," "expression of attitude to listener," "expression of attitude to referent," and "promotion of effects intended." Morris notes that the term "express" was not defined by Ogden and Richards, and he attempts to get at the criteria of expressiveness by analyzing a passage (in *The Meaning of Meaning*, 5th edition, pp. 223-224) in which the authors contend that words symbolizing a reference may also be signs of "emotions, attitudes, moods, the temper, interest or set of the mind in which the references occur." Morris' conclusion from the account given by Ogden and Richards as to how such signs are produced is that a sign is "emotive" whenever "someone takes the fact of its production as itself a sign of some state of the producer which often accompanies the production of the sign." But Morris points out that any sign may be so understood, and hence the account is too broad.

The truth criterion also fails, Morris contends. One cannot determine whether a sign is emotive simply by asking, of an expression, whether it is true or false (the point being that if it is neither, it is emotive), for the term "true" itself is sometimes used referentially, sometimes emotively. Morris accordingly rejects the attempt to explain emotive signs by reference to expressiveness and the uses of signs. He then proceeds to develop objectively determinable criteria for distinguishing modes of signifying.

Black, Max. *The Labyrinth of Language*. New York: Frederick A. Praeger Publishers, 1968.

Max Black of Cornell University takes as his subject matter a number of important philosophical questions about language. He begins by characterizing human beings as "talkers"; he contends that there are no primitive languages (for every language, even that of the African Bushman and the Australian aborigine, has an elaborate vocabulary and a complex grammar); he calls attention to the variety and unity of language; he emphasizes speech (as opposed to writing) as the primary object of linguistic investigation; he notes the development in the study of language consisting in a recognition of language as involving more than simply the communication of ideas; he writes of the perception of speech, of learning how to talk, of speech as the transmission of messages, of speech as the expression of meaning, and of linguistic systems.

As a philosopher, Black is of course concerned with explicating the nature and course of language. He deals with the relation of grammar to thought and with the various uses of language; he writes of linguistic abuses and reform; and finally (in Chapter 7) he deals with "The Meanings of Meaning."

Black's first reference to C. K. Ogden and I. A. Richards' *The Meaning of Meaning* is to the authors' "Canon of Singularity" (prescribed for a satisfactory symbolism), the proposition that "One symbol stands for one and only one Referent." Black's critical response is that the principle of "one word, one meaning" need not be followed in normal conversation. (Black points out that the word "man" has various meanings, depending on the context.) Accordingly, Black suggests a modification of the principle— namely, that each word should have a unique meaning *in context*. Black then suggests that when a word in context has no meaning, or its meaning is unclear, the case is one of "semantic anemia"; if a word has two or more meanings, the case is one of "contextual ambiguity."

Black's Chapter 7, on "The Meanings of Meaning," shows even in its title the influence of Ogden and Richards (for, after all, Ogden and Richards concluded, after exploring the "meaning of meaning," that the term "meaning" has many meanings). Black states the problem of the chapter as that of answering the questions "What is a meaning?" and "What kinds of things are meanings?"

The idea of meaning as "the thing-intended" is first of all discussed by Black. One supposes that the word "Paris" stands for the city of Paris: it is as simple as that. Black calls this theory of meaning the "bearer-theory," for it regards a thing meant as the bearer of the symbol that means it. Black points out, however, that there are difficulties with this view. If the meaning of the term "Paris" is to be identified with the city of Paris and the population of Paris is constantly increasing, is the population of the *meaning* of the term constantly increasing? Something is wrong with the theory, Black suggests.

The *indirectness* of meaning relations—the fact that terms have meaning because of human intentions and purposes—counts against any view that identifies meanings with things in the world. Hence, it is not surprising that many writers—and here Black cites Ogden and Richards—insist on the triadic character of meaning: a *sign* means *something* to *someone*. The recognition of the indirect character of the meaning relation tempts many writers, Black notes, to identify meaning with something within the speaker, something mental—ideas or concepts in the mind.

The difficulty with identifying meaning as something within the mind of the user of language—an image of some sort or a "conception"—is that scientific investigators are unable to verify the presence of any such mediating meanings, subjective entities standing between words and the world. Accordingly, as Morris suggests in *Signs, Language, and Behavior*, the idea of an "idea" in the mind is not useful, for it provides no criteria for the identification of the presence of such a feature of the speech situation; one must use biological terms if what is said is to be scientifically meaningful. Black concedes that mentalist theories of meaning are not entirely without merit despite the problem of verifiability; such theories do point to the critical role of word-users in the genesis of language. But the "ideas" are, he writes, "no better than idle ghosts."

Causal theories of meaning are next considered by Black. He concentrates on what he calls "psychological theories of meaning," theories that have been advanced by behavioristically oriented psychologists. Ivan Pavlov's experiments with dogs encouraged an account of signs by reference to stimuli, responses, and conditioning. An effort was then made to identify some aspect of a responding animal (said to have been stimulated by a "sign") as the "meaning" of the "sign" (a crude effort being the identification of the dog's salivation with the "meaning" of the sign-stimulus).

A more complex theory advanced by Ogden and Richards is then discussed by Black: namely, the theory that repeated observations of causal sequences cause "engrams" in the brain that are later stimulated by observation of a causal event and produce a "modified cerebral event" similar to the original response occasioned by observation of the effect. The "engram" theory is vulnerable to many objections of the kinds already made against mentalist theories and crude versions of behavioral theories, Black contends, and he refers the reader to Chapter 8 in his book *Languages and Philosophy* (1949), in which he subjects Ogden and Richards' "engram" theory to detailed criticism.

Black concludes his book with an account of a logical pitfall in the construction of theories of meaning. The tendency in theory construction is to presume that words *designate something* and that what they designate is the meaning. But the whole idea that words stand for *things* will not survive critical examination (descriptions of the things simply do not fit the "meanings" of terms).

Since the term "mean" has so many meanings, the only way of studying language and avoiding the pitfalls of theory-construction, Black suggests, is to concentrate on examining the *uses* of words; then, instead of attempting to tie the word to something for which the word in its use "stands," one can *show* another how a word is used. Such an exhibition of use would be more clarifying than any attempt to devise some static equation relating word to object meant.—*I.P.M.*

ADDITIONAL RECOMMENDED READING

Alexander, Hubert G. *Language and Thinking: A Philosophical Introduction.* Princeton, New Jersey: Van Nostrand, 1966. Chapter IV, "Meaning," presents a careful account of the meanings of "meaning." Some references to *The Meaning of Meaning*.

Black, Max, ed. *The Importance of Language*. Englewood Cliffs, New Jersey: Prentice-Hall, 1962. A lively set of philosophical articles on language, including "Words and Their Meanings," by Aldous Huxley, and "The Theory of Meaning," by Gilbert Ryle. Other contributions are by Samuel Butler, C. S. Lewis, Owen Barfield, Bronislaw Malinowski, Alan S. C. Ross, Friedrich Waismann, and W. B. Gallie.

Christensen, Niels Egmont. *On the Nature of Meanings: A Philosophical Analysis*. Copenhagen: Munksgaard, 1961. Christensen presents a theory of meaning, a critical consideration of alternative theories, and a discussion of the relations of theory of meaning to linguistics and epistemology. Some discussion of *The Meaning of Meaning*.

Parkinson, G. H. R., ed. *The Theory of Meaning*. London: Oxford University Press, 1968. An anthology of journal articles by such philosophers as Isaiah Berlin, Friedrich Waismann, P. F. Strawson, and Gilbert Ryle.

THE MIND AND ITS PLACE IN NATURE

Author: Charles Dunbar Broad (1887-1971)
Type of work: Metaphysics, philosophy of mind, epistemology
First published: 1925 (Tarner Lectures, Trinity College, Cambridge, 1923)

PRINCIPAL IDEAS ADVANCED
Of the three theories advanced to account for differences in material objects—vitalism, the theory of emergence, and mechanism—the emergence theory is the most satisfactory: new wholes are formed in nature the behavior of which could never have been predicted from knowledge of the parts.

The mind-body problem (What are the relations between body and mind?) has been made difficult by confusion concerning the meanings of "mind" and "body"; but the solution probably is that mind affects body, and body affects mind.

There must be a center of consciousness which is more than a mere ordering of sense-data, but this center may be nothing more than a mass of bodily feelings.

Memory traces are neither purely mental nor purely physiological; they are psychic factors.

C. D. Broad shares the realist standpoint of his Cambridge colleagues, G. E. Moore and Bertrand Russell, and his work combines the former's meticulous habits of analysis with the latter's respect for the findings of the particular sciences. The present volume deals with the problems which confronted the new realism when it had passed beyond its early polemic phase and was faced with the task of formulating the details of its own position. It is a patient, at times wearisome, ransacking of modern knowledge for clues as to the ultimate constitution of the world. From an overall point of view it presents a single, sustained inquiry into the place of mind in nature, concluding in favor of a kind of emergent materialism. But the argument takes second place to the definition and analysis of problems which arise along the way, so that the work may be profitably consulted in a topical manner.

Among the questions dealt with are those pertaining to mechanism and vitalism, mind and body, perception and matter, the unconscious, and the evidence of man's survival of bodily death. Broad makes no claim to give original solutions to these problems. His method, which is more memorable than his conclusions, is to bring the widest possible range of hypotheses under investigation. Some of these he eliminates on the grounds of linguistic confusion and logical inconsistency, others for want of empirical evidence, until only two or three are left. Of these, he observes with diffidence that the evidence slightly favors one above the others.

Broad holds the particular sciences in high regard and believes that our understanding of the world is entirely dependent upon them. But in Broad's view the construction of a philosophy of nature is hampered by the failure of scientists to check their hypotheses with the findings of men in other fields of investigation. Thus, physicists have too long undertaken to give an account of matter without attending to the findings of biologists; similarly, epistemologists have traditionally discussed mind only in the context of knowledge and have neglected its relations to man's bodily life. Broad sees it as the function of the philosopher to take the lead in helping overcome this departmentalism. By formulating precisely what presuppositions and consequences a given explanatory theory entails, the philosopher seeks to help the scientific worker to see the limits of his evidence and thus to save him from committing himself to a more general hypothesis which, although suited to his purposes, may be rendered dubious by findings in another field. The philosopher must often take it upon himself to bring up alternative possibilities which experimenters have neglected, and to focus evidence upon them from widely separate sources. But the test of rival hypotheses is always the available evidence; and where this is inconclusive, the philosopher must be content to leave his questions unanswered.

Since many of the difficulties which are encountered in explaining "the mind and its place in nature" stem directly from widespread preconceptions about unity, substance, and causation, Broad begins his book by considering these matters at what he calls "the level of enlightened common sense."

The argument between *monists* and *pluralists* he finds confused by the failure on both sides to make clear whether their claims apply to substance, differentiating attributes, or specific forms. Spinoza, for example, claimed that there is one substance, but he supposed that there are many differentiating attributes, whereas Leibniz held that there is but one differentiating attribute but many substances. In our day, according to Broad, there is no serious question of our being anything other than substantial pluralists: what is in dispute is whether there is more than one specific form of being.

The issue between the vitalists and mechanists in biology is illustrative. "Are the apparently different kinds of material objects irreducibly different?" As Broad defines it, mechanism, when strictly interpreted, includes four related assumptions: one kind of stuff, one intrinsic quality, one kind of change, and one fundamental law of change. These assumptions provided an adequate framework for Galilean physics, but they have never been quite satisfactory for chemistry or biology, or for recent physics. When a modern scientist claims that he is a mechanist, he uses the term in a modified sense. According to Broad, there are three possible ways of accounting for apparent differences in the behavior of physical bodies: *vitalism* holds that they are due to a peculiar component, a soul or "entelechy"; *emergence* denies a peculiar component but maintains that new "wholes" are formed in nature the behavior of which could never have been predicted from a knowledge of their component parts:

and *mechanism*, denying both of these contentions, holds that there is never anything in the behavior of the "whole" that is not determined by the parts and, in principle, deducible from a knowledge of them. Of these three hypotheses, Broad finds vitalism the weakest, both because of its obscurity and because of its nonverifiability. It was plausible only so long as it was thought to be the sole alternative to mechanism. Mechanism has in its favor the tidiness which it enables us to bring into our view of the world: since it seems highly probable that living cells are composed of chemical atoms, and that atoms are composed of electrified particles, one has only to suppose that these obey the same elementary laws and that they are compounded according to a single law to open up the possibility of a purely theoretical deduction of the behavior of any body from a knowledge of the number and arrangement of the atoms. But in our present state of knowledge, the facts suggest that there is less unity in the world than is postulated under his ideal. All the sciences present instances of wholes which are not intelligible in terms of their elements. For example, vectors cannot any longer be treated as sums in the ordinary sense of the word; organic compounds composed of identical elements in identical proportions are found to manifest distinct characteristics depending on the structure of the molecule; and, most obvious of all, the data of consciousness—colors, smells—have no intelligible relation to the physical vibrations or chemical changes which we take to be their causes. Such considerations weigh in favor of an emergent theory of nature, according to which each level of phenomena must be dealt within terms of laws peculiar to itself. Broad believes that vitalism arose because of real defects in the mechanistic explanation of biological facts, and that the emergent theory corrects the errors of mechanism with minimum loss to the ideal of unity, order, and law. While continuing to hold to one differentiating attribute, its proponents are pluralists when it comes to the question of special forms, which, they hold, are not illusory.

It is useless to ask whether mental facts are reducible to material or are to be treated as existing in their own right until one has considered what, in the light of current knowledge, these terms can signify. Broad reviews at some length the traditional debate over the *mind-body* question, but expresses grave doubts as to whether the debate serves any useful purpose. The arguments, he says, have been incredibly bad, making it difficult to see how they have imposed on so many learned men. If anything can be concluded from them, it would be in favor of the theory of twofold interaction, rather than of psychophysical parallelism or epiphenomenalism—mind and body reflecting each other's activities. But in Broad's opinion, the notions "body" and "mind" are so badly in need of clarification that it is doubtful whether the notion of interaction is suitable to describe the relation between them. The bulk of the book, therefore, is devoted to investigating the notion of mind in its various contexts.

We can get at it most directly by considering the mind in the *knowledge* situation. Broad enters the contemporary epistemological controversy and devotes separate chapters to perception, memory, introspection, and our knowledge of other minds. Especially important for understanding the constitution of the mind are such questions as: What is the status of sense-data? Are they components of the perceiving mind? Or are they in some way distributed between mind and the physical object? Broad leans away from those theories which regard *sensa* (that is, sense images) as independent of mind and which interpret perception as a selective relation between two physical regions. The difficulty of accounting for illusion on these grounds causes him to favor the view that sensa are peculiarly related to the mind. On this theory, which is closer to critical realism than to neorealism, a distinction must be maintained between the epistemological object and the physical object. The former is made up of sensa—color, size, shape—together with a mass of bodily feelings and quasibeliefs. The physical object is otherwise determined: extension and geometrical properties actually do characterize it, but they are never more than analogous to the size and figure which, as sensa, are present to mind.

But Broad's problem, in this book, is not primarily to give a theory of knowledge. Rather, it is to single out the elements in the knowledge processes which must be described as mental, and to ask whether these mental events presuppose a single substantive mind. Against the neorealists, Broad holds that there must be a center of consciousness which is more than a mere ordering of sense-data in a field; but he leaves open, at this point, the question of whether the center need be conceived as a pure ego and develops the alternate possibility that it is no more than "a mass of bodily feelings." The latter, he believes, is sufficient to account for our conviction that there is a continuing, abiding self which is present as the knower in every cognitive act, particularly if it is allowed that the feelings are "causally dependent on the traces left by past experience."

It is the question as to the nature of these "traces" that opens up the whole problem of *The Unconscious*, to which Broad devotes the third part of his book. His analysis of this ambiguous notion is worthy of being consulted for its own sake. He is not without appreciation for the clinical insights of the psychoanalysts and for the light they have shed upon the existence and activity of traces and groups of traces which are inaccessible to introspection. But he is not so ready to grant the claim that these hidden factors are mental. Two theories balance out about equally at this stage of the investigation: the memory traces which seem called for to explain normal memory as well as aberrant behavior can be interpreted as mental; but they can also be viewed as purely physiological. The fact is, we know nothing about them in detail, and we can predict nothing on one hypothesis that we could not equally well predict on the other; but considerations of simplicity would favor the latter account.

Here we have a further instance of Broad's rule that one must leave open
the choice between rival hypotheses until other fields are heard from. If
epistemology and abnormal psychology are inconclusive, it remains to consider evidence for human *survival* of bodily death. If the mind or any part
of it persists beyond the death of the body, this is important evidence against
the physiological explanation of memory traces.

The traditional arguments for immortality, including the one based on moral
worth, Broad regards as specious. He is more impressed by the evidence
collected by The Society for Psychical Research, particularly accounts of
séances which disclose information presumably unknown to any but deceased
persons. But granting the facts, it is another thing to conclude that the whole
mind survives. The low intellectual and moral quality of the alleged messages
weighs against the view that anything comparable to a pure ego survives.
Broad thinks that it is sufficient to postulate the persistence for a longer or
shorter time after death of a "psychic factor," which is "not itself a mind, but
it may carry modifications due to experiences which happened to John Jones
while he was alive." This gives us a third hypothesis by means of which to
account for the memory traces; they are neither mental nor physiological, but
peculiarly psychic. In the normal personality, on this view, the psychic factor
combines with neural processes to form the mind. In abnormal conditions,
it may be temporarily divorced from the brain, and may (as in the case of
multiple-personalities) organize itself into two or more selves which alter-
nately unite with the same brain. In the entranced medium, shreds and
snatches of psychic stuff come into temporary union with an otherwise vacant
brain and form a "little temporary 'mind'" or "mindkin."

In a final chapter, entitled "Status and Prospects of Mind in Nature," Broad
formulates seventeen types of theory combining the various alternatives which
he has turned up along the way. All of the principal historical positions, from
pure materialism to pure mentalism, appear in this classification, along with
some that are of purely theoretical interest. The extreme positions find little
to recommend them—neither behaviorism, according to which mind is an
illusion, nor mentalism (wrongly called "idealism"), which regards matter
with the same disdain. The various intermediate types are necessarily more
or less sophisticated, since they have to combine "mentality" and "materiality"
in one system. Three of these alone stand up under the crossfire of Broad's
examination. The first is Samuel Alexander's theory in *Space, Time and Deity*
(1920), which Broad calls "Emergent Neutralism." On this theory, the ultimate reality is neither mind nor matter, both of these being emergent characteristics. The second is Bertrand Russell's theory in *Analysis of Mind* (1921),
which Broad calls "Mentalistic Neutralism." It resembles Berkeley's theory
in regarding matter as delusive, but rejects Berkeley's mentalism and takes
mind as no more than a field of neutral sensa. Broad, while he can find no

conclusive reason for rejecting either of these, finds more reason to favor a third theory, which he calls "Emergent Materialism." On this view, reality is thought of as being truly material, and mind as an emergent characteristic depending upon the nervous system. Such a theory is sufficient to account for normal mental activity such as knowing, willing, feeling. The memory traces can be regarded simply as neural patterns, and the notion of unconscious mental states dismissed. But the view can be modified, as we have seen, to take account of abnormal and supernormal phenomena by recognizing, in addition to the neural factor, a distinct psychic factor with its own traits and dispositions. Such a modification of the view can be accomplished, Broad thinks, without abandoning the foundation of materialism, by allowing that the psychic stuff is itself an emergent, and that conscious mind is a compound of neural and psychic factors.

In a brief concluding section, Broad indulges in some speculative flights entitled "The Prospects of Mind in the World." Since mind, as we understand it, exists only in connection with the brain and nervous system, we cannot conceive that it is active in the evolution of the universe or of the human race. The claim of mentalists—that the world is the unfolding of a Cosmic Mind— Broad rejects in favor of the cosmology of modern physics, which conceives of the universe as composed of different systems, some in process of running down and others, presumably, winding up. His rejection of the Cosmic Mind of the mentalists does not rule out Theism, which, he says, is as compatible with materialism as it is with mentalism. But he has nothing to say in its favor, and he concludes with the humanistic refrain, that the prospects are good for man to modify the world favorably by the exercise of his own mental capacities—in the use of which he has barely made a start.—*J.F.*

PERTINENT LITERATURE
Lean, Martin. *Sense Perception and Matter: A Critical Analysis of C. D. Broad's Theory of Perception.* New York: Humanities Press, 1953.

Among the strange views which have been defended by philosophers is the view that man cannot know with certainty that a material world, or world of physical objects, exists. This problem arises when philosophers consider certain problems concerning the nature of perception. In his study *The Mind and Its Place in Nature*, C. D. Broad examines perception and concludes, as many other philosophers have done, that it is not possible to know with certainty (although he believes one can know that it is highly probable) that a material world exists outside the minds of conscious beings.

Martin Lean considers skepticism about the material world bizarre. The problems which philosophers have seen concerning the nature of perception and our knowledge of the material world, Lean labels pseudoproblems— unsubstantial problems which arise from linguistic confusions. The perplexities which worry Broad and other philosophers can be eliminated, Lean maintains, by taking the claims and arguments of these philosophers and rephrasing them in familiar language. To understand perception, it is necessary only to gather together obvious, commonsense facts about perception and supplement them with certain scientific discoveries and explanations. Lean believes that we do know with certainty that a material world exists.

Lean devotes the whole of his book *Sense Perception and Matter* to presenting a detailed critique of Broad's account of perception. He views Broad's account of perception as representative of an approach to the subject which is shared by John Locke, George Berkeley, David Hume, G. E. Moore, Bertrand Russell, and other philosophers. It is this approach which gives birth to the "problem" of knowing the existence of the material world.

Early in his book Lean argues that it is not possible that there are no material objects (so any doubt raised about their existence must be unnecessary). The term "material object," like the names for individual material objects ("table," "book," "noodle"), is learned within ordinary experience and is useful when applied in everyday experience. For this reason, it is not possible that the term "material object" may be found to be inapplicable to everyday experience. Unlike the word "unicorn," the term "material object" was designed to be used for referring to an existing phenomenon, so there must be at least *some* things which the term names, Lean reasons. Like any of the "proofs" of Zeno, an argument which attempts to show that material objects do not exist must be, Lean says, mere sophistry.

As Lean interprets him, Broad believes that the meaning of the expression "material object" is not fully exhausted by elements within experience but refers to a substance which serves as a hypothesis to explain the correlation and interrelationship between different experiences. To this view Lean objects that the concept of a material object could explain nothing unless we were fully acquainted in experience with the type of entity we are hypothesizing. An explanation of a phenomenon can be successful only to the extent that we are familiar with the sort of thing which we are introducing to explain the phenomenon. To speak of a material object as a mere *hypothesis* is to imply that something is lacking in our knowledge of material objects. But on the contrary, Lean replies, it is just because our familiarity with physical objects is so ideal that we are able, by comparison, to speak of *other ideas* as mere hypotheses.

One reason which Broad gives for saying that it is *possible* that there are no material objects is his claim that there is no intrinsic difference between hallucinations and those experiences which we consider nonillusory. There are no features in the experiences themselves by which genuine perceptions might be distinguished from illusory ones. Lean responds that "delusive" is a relative term and thus is meaningful only if there are at least some situations to which it is not applicable; it is meaningful only if some situations are not "delusive." Although Lean admits that hallucinations do not necessarily differ intrinsically from nondelusive experiences, the proof that an experience is nonillusory is found not in the intrinsic features of the experience but in a person's succeeding perceptions, in his perceptions from other senses, and in other people's perceptions. Hallucinations necessarily do not admit of such corroboration.

Broad, like many philosophers before him, believes that the fact that our senses present us with inconsistent perceptual appearances is a further problem for the belief that we are directly aware of material objects. The problem is that the color, size, and shape which an object appears to have vary according to the circumstances in which the object is perceived. A lawn may look light green when viewed under the midday sun but dark green when viewed in the early evening; a blade of grass looks big when viewed from very close up but tiny when viewed from a distance. Similar variations occur when any of the things that are considered material objects is viewed under varying conditions. Broad and other philosophers see this as a difficulty for someone who maintains that there is a single unchanging material object—an object with a single color and size—that one is directly aware of in the different cases. Lean responds that a true color, size, or shape can easily be distinguished from the various colors, sizes, and shapes which an object may appear to have. We all make such distinctions frequently. The true properties of a material object are, he writes, those which are perceived when the object is carefully inspected under normal conditions (under ordinary daylight, for example). The explanation of these variations in perceptions, Lean writes, may be found in the accounts which scientists give of the behavior of light rays and the makeup of the human eye.

Blanshard, Brand. "A Verdict on Epiphenomenalism," in *Current Philosophical Issues*. Edited by Frederick Dommeyer. Springfield, Illinois: Charles C. Thomas, 1966.

In *The Mind and Its Place in Nature*, C. D. Broad takes the position that epiphenomenalism is the most reasonable view on the relation of mind to body. Epiphenomenalism, or what Broad calls "emergent materialism," is the view that mental events (emotions, thoughts, perceptions, and so forth) are mere by-products, mere accompanying "echoes," of events in the physical world. According to this view, a mental event is fully determined by neurological events and does not itself have any causal influence on physical or mental activity. Broad believes that the available scientific evidence supports this interpretation of the relation of mind to body. The view allows one to hold that the actions of people and animals ultimately can be fully explained by reference to the laws of physics and chemistry. The position has many followers among scientists but few among philosophers.

Brand Blanshard is unsympathetic to epiphenomenalism. Although he admits that brain states may influence human thought—the vividness, the sequence or the consistency of thought, for example—he rejects the epiphenomenalist claim that mental events have no power to influence actions or mental events. Neurological activity is at most a necessary but not a sufficient condition for our mental activities and our subsequent actions, Blanshard believes. In reply to the epiphenomenalist, Blanshard argues that purpose or teleology, which Blanshard assumes is exclusively a mental phenomenon, has a central role in explaining human thought and action. The epiphenomenalist is, Blanshard believes, committed to holding that mental activity and human behavior can be fully explained without reference to purpose.

When a person *reasons*, Blanshard argues, the order in which his thoughts follow one another is determined by the person's purpose or goal in thinking. The direction which thoughts take is determined, at least in part, by recommendations from logic and reason. The order in which thoughts follow one another cannot be explained entirely by reference to mechanical laws. The fact that some thoughts are logically irrelevant has a role in explaining the direction which someone's thoughts take. A reference to logical relevance and validity must be central in the explanation. A fact's being *evidence* in favor of a belief may influence thought processes. When thoughts move from premise to conclusion they may follow a track of logical necessity. Logical relevance is a norm which thoughts follow; it is not, Blanshard writes, a property of inert atoms or molecules. When a person adds numbers, the logical relations between the numbers and the person's awareness of these relations influence the direction which his thoughts take, Blanshard writes.

How does an epiphenomenalist account for reasoning?, Blanshard asks. He must hold that the ordering of our thoughts is wholly determined by brain events and that brain events are to be explained by the laws of physics and chemistry. With laws in physics there neither is nor can be purpose or teleology, Blanshard insists. The idea that a thought may be guided by some principle of logical necessity has no place in a wholly mechanistic explanation. Because of his commitment to explaining mental activity entirely by reference to mechanical laws, the epiphenomenalist is unable to assign any role to such nonmaterial, abstract categories as "relevance," "validity," "evidence," or "logical necessity." He is unable to assign such logical features any role in influencing thought activity. Epiphenomenalism is refuted by the fact that thought processes are subject to rationality and purpose.

In maintaining that mental processes are determined entirely by neurological events the epiphenomenalist ignores the fact that the epistemological object—the object of thought—influences the direction which thoughts take. When a person is frightened after seeing lightning strike the tree across the street, his fear is caused by his awareness of the lightning and not simply by some brain process of which he is unaware, Blanshard explains. When someone is thinking about a square with diagonals and he realizes that the intersecting lines must form four triangles of equal size and shape, the nature of the object of thought, and not only the person's brain activity, influences the direction which his thoughts take.

Thought and action are influenced by judgments concerning what ought to be done. They are influenced by considerations of aesthetic relevance, aesthetic necessity, and moral relevance, as well as by those of logical necessity. In short, mental activity and human action are influenced by various normative considerations, and this cannot be satisfactorily explained within a wholly mechanistic framework. Normative relations are not physical relations; they can influence thought processes only because the mind is goal-directed. Mental activity is a struggle to make the potential actual, a struggle directed by normative considerations.

Our intimate familiarity with our own thinking shows us that logic is not powerless over thought as the epiphenomenalist is committed to believing it is, Blanshard adds. It would be absurd, he reasons, to ignore these obvious facts of introspection in favor of some mechanistic account of brain activity whose details are not nearly as well known. Our introspection enables us to be more certain of the influence of logic and other normative considerations on our thoughts than we can be of any nonpurposive molecular brain activity which may accompany our thoughts.—*I.G.*

ADDITIONAL RECOMMENDED READING

Kneale, William C. "Broad on Mental Events and Epiphenomenalism," in *The Philosophy of C. D. Broad* (The Library of Living Philosophers). Edited by Paul A. Schilpp. New York: Tudor Press, 1959, pp. 437-455. Kneale explains Broad's views on the nature of mental events and defends them from possible objections.

Lachs, John. "Epiphenomenalism and the Notion of Cause," in *The Journal of Philosophy.* LX (1963), pp. 141-146. A sympathetic discussion of epiphenomenalism.

Marc-Wogau, Konrad. "On C. D. Broad's Theory of Sensa," in *The Philosophy of C. D. Broad* (The Library of Living Philosophers). Edited by Paul A. Schilpp. New York: Tudor Press, 1959, pp. 487-509. The author criticizes Broad's contention that "sensa" or "sense data" cannot be parts of physical objects.

Russell, L. J. Review of Martin Leans' *Sense Perception and Matter*, in *Philosophy.* XXXI (1956), pp. 175-178. A good defense against Lean's criticisms of Broad's analysis of perception.

ETHICS

Author: Nicolai Hartmann (1882-1950)
Type of work: Ethics
First published: 1926

PRINCIPAL IDEAS ADVANCED

Ideal principles influence real things; values and obligations have autonomous being in the realm of essence, but provide human beings with the foundations of morality.

Valuational insights are possible to men of moral genius who discern new value complexes.

There is a determinate order among values; although values are relative to persons, they have objective status.

Moral values are realized by seeking to secure such nonmoral values as intelligence, health, and equality.

The three principal branches of the good are the noble, richness of experience, and purity.

Moral law can bind the will without determining it because the will operates under the influence of moral obligation, on a plane between the physical and the ideal.

People who suppose that reading a book about ethics should make one a better person will find that Hartmann's work on the subject (especially Volume Two) fully meets their expectations. Broadly conceived, it has something of the character of Aristotle's *Nicomachean Ethics* in that it discusses actual goods, including human virtues, in a manner that enhances our appreciation of them; but it also resembles Kant's *Metaphysics of Morals* (1785) in the way it elaborates the conditions which make morality possible. One may say that it combines the formal ethics of Kant ("duty for duty's sake") and the material ethics of Aristotle ("the good life"), taking from the former the concept of obligation and uniting it in a novel way with the latter's appreciation for concrete value.

According to Hartmann, a new exigency confronts ethics, one which Nietzsche first made plain. Formerly, it was supposed that man knows what is good and what is evil, so that practical ethics need be concerned only with means for realizing self-evident goals, and theoretical ethics only with fitting moral phenomena into one's larger world view. In the present crisis, however, as Nietzsche showed, no goals are any longer self-evident, and we must inquire what is good and what is evil. Nietzsche's attempts to answer this question were, in Hartmann's opinion, sadly incomplete. Intoxicated by the view which opened before him, Nietzsche thought that he had comprehended in a glance the whole realm of values, failing to see that he had entered upon "a field for intellectual work of a new kind." Moreover, his celebrated demand for "the revaluation of all values," with its implicit relativism, contradicted his claims elsewhere to have discovered positive goods. Nevertheless, according to Hartmann, our debt to him is immeasurable. He marks the turning point between backward-looking and forward-looking (Promethean) ethics.

It is clear that under Nietzsche's inspiration Hartmann was grappling with difficulties of the same order as exercised Martin Heidegger and the Existentialists. Man, by virtue of his powers of thinking, is a problem to himself. The rift which thought introduces into his soul sets him ever apart from other animals and confronts him with the ceaseless problem of deciding what sort of being he shall become. According to Hartmann, the first and fundamental question is: "What ought we to do?" This is the practical question, and it has become urgent in our day because Western culture no longer provides a convincing answer. But we cannot answer it until we have answered a second theoretical question: "What is valuable in life and in the world?" This is the question to which philosophical ethics must address itself. Hartmann was not swayed by the skeptical demur that there is no answer, nor by the subjectivist claim that any answer must be an expression of man's will. He believed, on the contrary, that an analysis of moral phenomena discloses the principles which we need to make moral decisions and at the same time sheds light upon the nature of man and his place in the world.

Hartmann's preoccupation with the *problems* of human life is seen in his method. He did not take it as the goal of philosophy to solve problems, for he was reconciled to the possibility that reality may not be completely intelligible. In his view, philosophical progress consists in learning to distinguish between what we know and what we do not know, and again, between what is knowable and what is not. Problems serve as instruments or probes for exploring the conditions of our existence. Certain key problems, which he designated by the Greek word *aporiae*, by the very stubbornness with which they resist our systematizing efforts, keep us alert to disparate kinds of being.

Besides his *Ethics*, Hartmann wrote important systematic works in epistemology and metaphysics, in which he defended a realistic theory of knowledge and a pluralistic theory of being. There are, as he conceived being, many kinds or grades of it, each with its own categories and principles. These seemed to him to be arranged in strata, so that the categories of the lower grades of being continue to operate on higher levels, where, however, they are supplemented by new principles. As a result of his probings, he distinguished the following grades of reality: the spatial outer world, which is subdivided into the inorganic and the organic, and the nonspatial inner world, which is subdivided into the psychic and the spiritual. These make up the real world; in addition, there is the realm of the possible, which has its own claims to being and is ruled by its own principles of determination.

Hartmann's philosophy is materialistic in the same sense as that of George

Santayana and that of Samuel Alexander. He rejected the personalist argument of Max Scheler, which would make the material world dependent for its existence and order on spirit. Accordingly, he saw no basis for the contention that there is a teleology in nature or that everything in nature is governed by reason. Nevertheless, his *aporetic* forced him to maintain that, in some way not comprehensible to us, ideal entities do manifest themselves in the actual world; besides the categories and laws which belong to matter and mind, there are purely ideal principles, such as those of geometry, which influence real things. Similarly, values and obligations, which have autonomous being in the realm of essence, invade time and space, where they provide a framework for our experience of things as good and bad.

Hartmann ran against the whole tendency of modern philosophy in grounding his ethics in his ontology. But the fact that he was compelled to "return to Plato" was not due to any failure on his part to understand what contemporary thought had to offer. It was, rather, due to his judgment that modern schools (idealism, naturalism, and positivism) have all failed to do justice to the actuality of ethics, being misled by their presuppositions. Although initially a member of the Marburg school (neo-Kantian; see, for example, Ernst Cassirer), he became impressed by the phenomenological movement (Edmund Husserl, Max Scheler), which was especially dedicated to the task of rescuing the data of experience from the distortions imposed upon it by theories and hypotheses. Much of Hartmann's *Ethics* is phenomenological research—a painstaking description of morality in all its dimensions. But in Hartmann's view, phenomenology was not enough. Practiced consistently, in accordance with the purpose of its founder, Husserl, it left one the prisoner of his own consciousness, a consequence which, to Hartmann, seemed to contradict the evidence of experience itself. The phenomenology of morals disclosed *aporiae* or problems; and the implications of these led Hartmann to affirm the existence of autonomous values, of conscience, and of free will.

One of the problems which intrigues ethical thinkers is that which commonly goes by the name of cultural relativism. It arises not only in connection with the existence of competing moral systems, but also from the fact that the ethos of any culture undergoes more or less continuous change. Hartmann insisted that this is a real problem. It is not solved by maintaining that values and norms are merely an expression of social needs, because they claim to be much more: we evaluate cultures. On the other hand, to set up one's own scheme of values (say, Utilitarianism) as scientifically founded, then judge all others by its standards, merely raises the problem anew in a comic way. Hartmann met the difficulty by distinguishing, somewhat as Henri Bergson was to do in *Two Sources of Morality and Religion* (1932), between conventional norms, which are mediated by tradition and fixed by language, and valuational insights, which are immediate and vivid, but difficult to hold and to transmit. Hartmann compared the valuational consciousness to a searchlight moving unpredictably over the realm of values. At a given moment it singles out a particular complex, which it esteems and seeks to realize. Thus it happens that values shift within a culture, so that frequently the values to which it gives lip service have in fact been supplanted by others which have no official sanction and, perhaps, not even names. Rival ethical systems are understood in a similar way, particularly those which can be traced to religious and ethical founders: a prophetic spirit makes "valuational discoveries" which his genius impresses upon the consciousness of a people at a critical moment. Their validity and universal appeal rest upon the fact that they are discoveries of a high order; but no value complex can possibly include more than a segment of the possible—hence, the diversity of moral systems. It is the story of the blind men and the elephant over again.

Another fundamental problem of ethics is the conflict between value and obligation. As has been recognized since the time of Socrates, man never wills anything except what has value; on the other hand, whenever we make a moral choice, we express the conviction that some courses of action are superior to others. According to Hartmann, the problem is at the basis of the argument between the two traditional parties in the history of moral philosophy: eudaemonism (emphasizing the pursuit of value) and formalism (emphasizing obedience to law). Each party claims to have solved the problem. But if, instead of trying to solve it, we keep the problem alive in both its aspects, the matter is more complicated than either party is willing to recognize although not entirely unintelligible.

First, there is a determinate order among values themselves, on the ideal plane, what Hartmann called a "scale of values." Here, particularly, Hartmann was carrying out the program of the phenomenological school. There is, he believed, an ideal "valuational space" in which values are arranged according to categorical principles of opposition, of subordination, and of dependence. A hint of Hartmann's procedure in this part may be conveyed if we mention the conflict, widely recognized in the history of mankind, between the value of comprehensiveness and that of individuality. Here the opposition is relative (both are good) and not modal (as between pleasure and pain); but the relation is extremely complex and paradoxical. Individuality is bound up with personality, including man's characteristic functions as both subject and object of intentional acts, and his peculiar capacity for discerning and bearing values. Comprehensiveness, when applied to humanity, involves community, and in this way incorporates individuality; but as a whole, the community is also an individual that, although lacking personal characteristics, is the bearer of values on a grander scale. The community is the subject of far-seeing enterprises that are out of the question for a single mortal, and therefore, it is able to make possible many individual values (for example cooperation, devotion, and sacrifice) which otherwise would not exist. According to Hartmann, these relations are purely *a priori*. They hold for the ethical consciousness, quite apart from their actualization in history, just as mathematical reasoning holds whether it is or is not exemplified in space and time.

But this is only part of the answer. An ideal value is only a possibility. The ethical problem has to do with actual values, which have their locus in existing things and are (or may be) the objects of choice. The problem for the analyst is to do justice to the natural and subjective side of goods without losing the autonomy and objectivity which distinguish values from physical properties and from feelings. Hartmann declared that values "exist" only in the world and only for consciousness. And in this sense he spoke of them as relative. A good dinner or a good deed is such only by reference to the situation and only for a person who contemplates its merit. But Hartmann found these considerations no grounds for the relativistic constructions which some (for example, Nietzsche) had placed upon the matter. The same thing that has been said about values might be said about the measurements of surveying or the laws of psychology—they "exist" only in particular media and for trained minds. But this does not mean that they are without objective significance. So, according to Hartmann, the relatedness of values to things and to minds does not warrant our reducing them, after the fashion of naturalism, to lower categories of existence, or, after the fashion of psychologism, to mental attitudes. Our appraisal has as little to do with determining them as the astronomer's measurements have to do with determining the position of the stars.

Hartmann's analysis of values reveals a basic distinction between those that belong to the subject and those that belong to the object. The former are the specifically moral values, dealing with the character, habits, dispositions, and acts of persons. There are personal positive and negative values which are not moral. As an object, man has various kinds of worth to society and to other individuals; moreover, different traits and capacities, both natural and acquired, have conditional value for him as subject. Intelligence and health are nonmoral values which inhere in persons. Justice and courage are moral values.

It is one of the paradoxes of ethics that moral values are not properly to be sought after. They "ride on the back of" situational values, to use the expression which Hartmann borrowed from Max Scheler. The intention of a man's acts always has to do with values in the world about him. Thus, to the question "How can I be just?" the answer is, "Respect the equal rights of all men." Here the value sought is not justice, but equality; but justice comes into being when a man acts in such a way as to respect men's equal claims.

An unusual feature in a book on theoretical ethics is Hartmann's detailed classification and exposition of particular moral values. The first section deals with moral values in *general*, and devotes a chapter to each of the following:

the good, the noble, richness of experience, and purity. These form, as it were, a trunk (the good) and three main branches. One can be a good man in different ways—but if he is noble, it must be at the expense of richness of experience and of purity. Hartmann thought that there might be other branches: history has had a great deal to do with determining our moral insight, so that inevitably there are gaps in our understanding of values. This is particularly apparent as we move on to consider *special* moral values, which Hartmann placed in three loose groups. The first includes the values of ancient Greece, with special attention to Aristotle's account. The second group begins with brotherly love and includes the cluster of values which historically grew up in the early Christian community: truthfulness, trustworthiness, humility, and others. A third group is necessary to acknowledge values which "have become accessible to our modern perception," but which were not prominent in other times—the love of the remote, radiant virtue, the value of personality, and personal love. Of these, the first two are due to Nietzche, whom Hartmann esteemed as a modern prophet, both because of Nietzsche's rare insight into values and because of his ability to give definition to what had hitherto never had a name.

A third major problem which Hartmann considered is the freedom of the will. Not surprisingly, he took as his starting point Kant's famous antinomy between "the causality of nature" and "the causality of freedom." Kant showed, correctly in Hartmann's opinion, that the freedom demanded by our moral consciousness is not freedom "from" causality of nature, but a different kind of freedom that transcends nature. Hence, for Hartmann, the "causal antinomy" is not an *aporia*, not a crucial problem. But other antinomies arise between the will, which is actual, and the realm of value, which is ideal. How is it possible that moral law binds the will without determining it? Evidently, in virtue of an "ought." But the "ought" in man's will must either be the same as that in the law, or different; if the former, there is no freedom; if the latter, no determination. In discussing this "ought-antinomy" Hartmann distinguished six root-difficulties (*aporiae*) to be clarified. The data of the problem (the consciousness of self-determination, moral accountability and responsibility, the consciousness of guilt) make it clear that the will is not determined purely by moral law, but that ethical life presupposes a partial identity between the two. The term "ought," therefore, includes an equivocation—when applied to moral principles it means "ought to be"; when applied to the will, it means "ought to do." In this light, the moral will appears as a third principle operating on a different plane from the physical, but also on a different plane from the ideal. Hartmann made no claim to have proved the freedom of the will. The skeptical objection, that our consciousness of self-determination and responsibility is merely illusory, is a legitimate one. But Hartmann held that the burden of proof is on the skeptic, and that it is an intolerable burden because it deserts the phenomena. In all theoretical reasoning, according to

Hartmann, there is a gap which can never be filled up from reasoning itself; science can go behind some data and find further facts, but there is always a limit. The moral will must be allowed as marking such a boundary beyond which our desire for explanation cannot go.

So much for Hartmann's theoretical ethics. If we return for a moment to the practical problem, and remind ourselves of the concern which Nietzsche raised in Hartmann's breast, we are now in a position to observe the direction which he felt man must take. It was his opinion that in our day ethics can become truly normative, not by telling man what he must do, but by providing him with regulative principles by means of which he can judge between competing goods. Thus it can realize the Platonic "ideal of ruling and moulding mankind spiritually through the power of philosophical perception, through the vision of Ideas." Although he denied divine providence, Hartmann gave a positive sense to the Protagorean saying, "Man is the measure of all things." In virtue of the fact of consciousness, man not only mirrors the outer world but participates in his own being, and is himself both providence and predestination. These are ambiguous powers: there is a danger point beyond which both foresight and purposive efficacy become intolerable burdens. Man has no choice but to live with them. And Hartmann noted the demonic tendency which these gifts arouse in man. "It happens that the gift, the more he is conscious of the power which is in his hands, leads him astray, lures him to ever higher stakes. But in this frenzy he does not become aware of the limits of his strength, until after he has overstepped them and the game is lost for him."

Still, one should not get the impression that Hartmann was a pessimist. Happily, it is not the task of the philosopher to forecast the world's future. His it is to cultivate wisdom, a word which Hartmann identifies from its Latin root (*sapientia*, from *sapere* "to taste") with "moral taste." It is not to be confused with knowledge or insight in the intellectual sense—these may well breed pessimism—for it signifies "appreciation of everything and an affirming, evaluating, attitude toward whatever is of value." The wise man is conscious of his own narrowness and at the same time of the boundless resources which surround him. "He sees himself as one who is too rich, who is overwhelmed, and whose power to receive is not equal to the gifts bestowed. His cup is already overflowing, his capacity is exceeded by his possessions. And in that he in this way exercises unintentionally an influence as an example, he is a true educator of men in inner spiritual freedom and in the one true happiness."—*J.F.*

PERTINENT LITERATURE
Findlay, J. N. *Axiological Ethics*. New York: St. Martin's Press, 1970.

In his *Axiological Ethics* J. N. Findlay examines the main philosophical writings in axiology, the field of moral philosophy concerned with the study of what is ultimately or intrinsically worth having or doing. Axiology, or value theory, has generally been neglected by moral philosophers in the English-speaking world. Anglo-American philosophers, Findlay notes, have been concerned primarily with obligation and duty (the moral "ought") and metaethics—especially the study of the meaning of the word "good." Although a study of value has implications for the understanding of moral obligation, it deserves attention in its own right.

Findlay is interested in Nicolai Hartmann's *Ethics* for the contributions to axiology which Hartmann makes in the first two of the three volumes. In these two volumes Hartmann classifies and interrelates values and perceptively discusses many individual values. Hartmann is systematic and thorough, Findlay observes; he shows a breadth of vision usually absent in contemporary Anglo-American philosophy. Findlay does not discuss the third volume of the *Ethics*, which is concerned with freedom rather than axiology. He describes this volume as being full of obscurities and inconsistencies.

Findlay discusses and commends Hartmann's insight that it is important for philosophers fully to appreciate that morality has both a negative and a positive face. The negative face of morality lies in its prohibitions, condemnations, and commandments. Murder, adultery, and stealing, for example, concern morality mainly in a negative way. Strong prohibitions and condemnations are connected with doing these acts; avoiding these acts normally brings little praise or commendation. The positive face of morality is seen in ideals which we are encouraged but not obligated to seek. Great heroism, bravery, nobility, and wisdom win our admiration; a lack of these qualities normally brings little condemnation. One who interprets morality solely in terms of prohibitions and duty distorts morality. Philosophers too often concentrate on one of the faces of morality to the exclusion of the other, Findlay notes.

An important thesis of Hartmann's is that values are timeless and unchanging and that they exist in an ideal world independently of human emotion and cognition. Given this view, he needs to explain the existence of the many variations in what people in different eras and even people in different sectors of the same society value. Findlay finds Hartmann's explanation of these variations interesting and persuasive. Hartmann argues that although values are unchanging, what differs at different times and places is the awareness of values. The differences result from a narrowness in man's focus of attention. For most people under most circumstances it is not psychologically possible to give serious attention to all areas within the realm of value during one period. In consequence, some values engage one's attention more than others. When valuable objects that were previously unappreciated or undiscovered move into central focus of attention, objects that had been valued often are pushed out from central focus and forgotten. When much attention is given to a newly recognized value, little attention remains for objects previously valued. It is not that some object has come to have value and another ceased to have value. No value is created or destroyed. Rather, a value, itself eternally existent, is discovered or forgotten.

Although Hartmann maintains that value in an object is not contingent upon human emotional response to the object, he does, Findlay observes, assign feeling and emotion a surprisingly intimate role in value-perception. Our everyday perception of value is normally mediated by emotion, Hartmann says. The emotional effect which a valuable object has on someone *reveals* to him the value in the object. In feeling love or hate, for example, we feel that there is good or bad in an object. In Hartmann's thinking, an emotion of guilt, a feeling of conscience, or a feeling of responsibility, although a noncognitive phenomenon, is a nearly infallible indicator of value.

Findlay's response to this is that in giving personal emotion so much authority in perceiving value Hartmann's thinking at this point is more suited to emotivism, the view that moral pronouncements merely express emotions without asserting facts or judgments about the world, than to Hartmann's own view that values exist in their own objective, timeless realm independently of any emotional response or consciousness.

An important fault Findlay sees in Hartmann's study—a fault he also sees in axiological discussions of other philosophers—is the presentation of many insights about values in the form of unargued-for, undefended *intuitions*. Although Findlay agrees with much of what Hartmann says about values, he believes that more argument or proof is needed. The insights in Hartmann's observations stimulate an appetite for knowing *why* these claims are true. A more developed, more adequate *a priori* ontology of values is needed as a ground or foundation for these analyses, Findlay argues. This *a priori* grounding of values Findlay has tried to provide in some of his own ethical writings.

Findlay is unhappy with the ontological views to which Hartmann commits himself. Hartmann thinks of values as existing in a Platonic world "out there." Within Hartmann's thinking it is only a contingent fact that values have any influence on human feeling and action. It is a contingent fact that the good is liked and the bad disliked. Findlay considers this position unacceptable. Values are related analytically to human feeling, Findlay argues. Although Findlay agrees that values are objective in some important way, he believes that one must derive this objectivity from the emotion and feeling which are at the root of all value.

Hook, Sidney. "A Critique of Ethical Realism," in *Pragmatism and the Tragic Sense of Life*. New York: Basic Books, 1974.

Sidney Hook describes Nicolai Hartmann's *Ethics* as "the most comprehensive treatise on ethics ever published." Hook considers Hartmann's discussion one of the best defenses of Ethical Realism ever presented. Ethical

Realism is the view that values and moral principles exist prior to, and independently of, human consciousness. Hook is an Ethical Naturalist. He believes that values and morals originate from contingent facts about human nature and society. Moral principles ultimately derive their authority from the fact that people happen to like or take interest in some things rather than others. While explaining and illuminating many of Hartmann's varied insights into morals and values, Hook critically evaluates Hartmann's Ethical Realism and argues for the superiority of Ethical Naturalism.

Both Hook and Hartmann agree that Ethical Realism faces an important challenge in the historical relativity of ethical codes, the fact that different societies have esteemed different values and moral principles. How can these variations be explained within a framework where it is claimed that values are unchanging and absolute? Hook examines Hartmann's account. Hartmann likens changes in what people consider valuable to changes in those scientific views which people consider true. That Aristotle's view of the heavens was considered true at one time and Galileo's at another does not entail that the nature of the heavens is contingent upon man's judgments about the heavens. Similarly, that some people consider it bad personally to avenge a murder while others think it good does not entail that the moral character of an act is contingent upon people's judgments about the act.

A Realist, Hook notes, may assign variations in what is valued to varying applications of the same ethical principles or to different judgments, perhaps because of the presence of different circumstances, concerning what is instrumental to some mutually accepted end. Although one society praises while another condemns the act of personally avenging a murder, both societies would acknowledge that wrongful killing morally warrants just punishment. The difference between the societies is in the implementation of this principle and not in the value ascribed to the principle itself.

An assumption which Hook interprets as central to Hartmann's account of historical relativity in moral codes is that moral principles have the same ontological status as mathematical or logical truths. This assumption, Hook argues, is false, Logical truths derive their special ontological standing from the fact that denials of logical truths are self-contradictions. But moral principles are not like this; their denials are not self-contradictory. To deny that it is evil to take pleasure in the undeserved troubles of others is not to state a self-contradiction. There is no moral principle, Hook writes, whose denial is unintelligible or senseless.

A second important problem which Hook sees in Ethical Realism is in accounting for the psychological factor that is present when values are discovered. If value is not contingent upon interest being taken in an object, then what accounts for this interest always being present whenever value is discovered? The explanation which Hook thinks is suggested by Hartmann's discussion is that although awareness and interest accompany the recognition of value, awareness and interest are involved in recognizing anything. The psychological factor is attributable to the act of *recognizing* and not to the existence of that which is recognized.

When discussing whether values are relative to persons, Hartmann acknowledges that there is one respect in which values are relative to people. A person's honor, knowledge, or pleasure is a good *for him* and in being so the value exists in a certain relationship to that person. The value is relative to the person's *existence*, although not to the person's perception of that value, Hartmann explains. Although Hartmann admits that value is relative in this way, he emphasizes that value cannot be created or given to something by a person, nor can value to disposed of by a person. Although a person may try to get rid of the unhappiness or cowardice which he suffers, it is not in his power to get rid of the fact that the unhappiness and cowardice are bad. Thus the badness of unhappiness and cowardice are "objective" in this way and independent of one's own responses to them.

Hook criticizes this explanation of the "objectivity" of values. Hartmann's claim that it is not within one's power to create or destroy the value which something has for a person does not itself show value to be "objective" in any important sense. A parallel claim can be made even for something so subjective and personal as taste. A person is not able to change the taste which a food has for him. We can prepare food in different ways or add different ingredients or spices but cannot determine how a food with certain ingredients and prepared in certain ways will taste to us. From the above account of the objectivity of values it does not follow that values exist in some realm distinct from human consciousness or that they have some eternal, unchanging existence.

Sympathy with Ethical Realism, Hook determines, arises from the fear that if moral principles are tied to contingent facts about people's desires and interests, morality will lose its binding force and become uncertain. However, Hook replies, morality by nature is uncertain. The security which is sought would elude one even if Hartmann's Ethical Realism were adopted. Within the theoretical framework which Hartmann presents, ethical judgments ultimately are unsupportable intuitions, Hook argues. No infallible standard is provided with which a person may distinguish spurious from genuine insights. The only appeal available to support a value judgment is some further intuition. Indeed, Hook adds, when moral absolutism like that which Hartmann defends is accepted in practice as well as in theory there can be dangerous consequences. People who feel confident that their value judgments represent eternal, absolute truths tend to be dogmatic and intolerant of the values and moral judgments of others. Self-serving moral pronouncements are readily presented as absolute moral truths.—*I. G.*

ADDITIONAL RECOMMENDED READING

Garnett, A. Campbell. "Phenomenological Ethics and Self-Realization," in *Ethics*. LIII, no. 3, (April, 1943), pp. 159-172. Garnett argues that many of Hartmann's value insights may be profitably applied to a theory where moral action is interpreted as self-realization.

Hill, Thomas English. *Contemporary Ethical Theories*. New York: Macmillan Publishing Company, 1950. Chapter XVIII presents a clear exposition of Hartmann's ethical ideas within a perspective in which Hartmann's theory is viewed in relation to other recent moral philosophies.

Jensen, O. C. "Nicolai Hartmann's Theory of Virtue," in *Ethics*. LII, no. 4 (July, 1942), pp 463-479. An examination of the way in which Hartmann relates the morality of an act to the motive and consequences of the act.

Stern, Alfred. "The Current Crisis in the Realm of Values," in *The Personalist*. XXXI, no. 3 (Summer, 1950), pp. 245-259. An interesting attempt to show that Hartmann's ethical absolutism provided philosophical support for Hitler's political absolutism.

Werkmeister, W. H. *Theories of Ethics: A Study in Moral Obligation*. Lincoln, Nebraska: Johnsen Publishing Company, 1961. Chapter VII contains a detailed examination of Hartmann's *Ethics*, in which the author defends a naturalistic analysis of values over Hartmann's account.

GENERAL THEORY OF VALUE

Author: Ralph Barton Perry (1876-1957)
Type of work: Ethics
First published: 1926

PRINCIPAL IDEAS ADVANCED

Any object acquires value when any interest, whatever it be, is taken in it.

If some objects are more valuable than others, it is only because some interests are stronger than others.

Man is distinguished from the other animals in being able to plan ahead in accordance with his interests.

There are various kinds of values corresponding to various kinds of interests: values are inherited or acquired, positive or negative, recurrent or progressive, real or playful, aggressive or submissive, subjective or objective.

The highest good is an ideal—a harmonious society of benevolent persons; but the ideal depends upon an interest in working out conflicts cooperatively.

Ralph Barton Perry's theory of value in terms of interest remains one of the most detailed and carefully defended statements of empirical value theory to be found in the history of philosophy. Its very matter-of-fact air and its careful progression from point to point are characteristic of American thought when it is both plain and respectable. There is nothing exciting or revolutionary about Perry's ideas; but what he brings about by his analysis is a new temper of philosophic thought, one in which attention to the facts of the matter takes precedence over recourse to the eternal and elusive realm of ideas. Later philosophers on the subject—such as Charles Leslie Stevenson in his *Ethics and Language* (1944)—may lay stress on the emotive functions of value language, and they may look with forbearance on studies which center their attention on value itself, not on language; but for all that, no significant rebuttal of Perry's theory has been forthcoming or is likely. No rebuttal is likely because the theory that "Any object, whatever it be, acquires value when any interest, whatever it be, is taken in it," is so general, so plausible, so continuously verifiable, that any quarrel about it is likely to be petulant (involving some plaintive appeal to "intuition of the indefinable") or pedantic (reducing itself to quibbles about phrasing or method).

This is high praise for a work of twentieth century philosophy, but the work is worthy of it. It was no easy task for modern thinkers to turn their minds from conceptions, essences, and presumably eternal, immutable, and unanalyzable truths, to those parts of the world of experience that give substance and sense to human discourse. But Perry, together with other empirical and analytic philosophers, has not only pioneered philosophically, but has done so with such diligence and skill that the results of his investigations are worth considering long after we have ceased to be enchanted by the skillful amendments which later philosophers have advanced.

Perhaps it should be made clear that Perry's general theory of value is significant in philosophy not because of its novelty, but because of the novelty of its genesis. The "age of analysis," as Morton White has termed the age of twentieth century philosophy, is distinguished from earlier philosophic periods by its central concern with analysis of some sort as opposed to synthesis, or system-building. Of course, there are living philosophers whose trust is in what is claimed to be the philosopher's peculiar and nonanalytic insight, his intuition, who reject the attempt to explain or dissect value and who prefer to call attention to value as something unique, ultimate, and beyond the possibility of analysis. England's Sir David Ross in his influential *The Right and the Good* (1930) has shown himself to be one of these "old-fashioned" philosophers—"old-fashioned" in the literal sense of holding to the fashion of thinkers in ages prior to our own. But Perry quite aptly terms himself one who tries "to bridge the gap between common sense and science" and who believes that "philosophy must face the facts of life and nature, taking them as both the point of departure and the touchstone of truth."

Perry's theory is a *general* theory in that it attempts to explain value quite without regard to any question as to whose value is under consideration or as to what kind of value it is. Perry is well aware of the fact—which anyone in his right mind acknowledges, some quite seriously—that *what* is valued differs from place to place and person to person, and that what is valued may be valued in different ways, even by the same person. But what he is concerned, in his theory of value, to explain is precisely what is involved in a situation in which something (it does not matter what) is of value (it does not matter of what kind, or for what reason) to someone (it does not matter who).

Perry is not blind to the relevance of a study of the use of language for one who would identify the subject of his philosophical discourse. "The task of the theory of value . . . may be regarded as the study of the act of *valuing*, or as the study of the predicate *valuable*," he writes. Nor is Perry naïve enough to suppose that by turning to the word "value" all ambiguities are resolved and all data given: "The fact is that the word 'value' instead of having a clear denotation like the word 'house' . . . refers us to a region whose nominal boundaries have yet to be agreed upon." A nice distinction is drawn between the empirical aspect of philosophical inquiry—which involves a "topographical survey" of all to which attention has been called by the use of the term "value"—and the legislative act of deciding to limit the denotation of the term to a certain part of the area surveyed. It is just that distinction, among others, which Wittgenstein was concerned to make and illustrate in his *Philosophical Investigations* (1953).

Before developing and defending at some length the proposal that any object of any interest is valuable, Perry examines and discards the opposed ideas that value is irrelevant to interest, that value is the qualified object of interest, and that value is the object of qualified interest.

In considering value as irrelevant to interest, Perry considers the idea that value is immediately perceived, as G. E. Moore claimed in *Principia Ethica* (1903). Objecting to the view that value is an indefinable characteristic inherent in objects and empirically discoverable there, Perry calls attention to the close relationship between value and the interest in agreeable feelings. He suggests that it is only on the assumption that value is an empirical property that the analogies between value and other properties, such as color properties, have any persuasive force. The claim that value is an indefinable property, present for all to witness, is weakened by consideration of the fact that it is always relevant, in determining the value of an object, to go from one judge to another; the verdicts vary because men vary, as do their interests with their differences. Finally, Perry rejects the identification of value with some such property as fitness or self-realization. He argues that fitness and self-realization, as well an organic unity, are understandable only by reference to interest.

The distinction between the idea that value is the *qualified object* of interest and the idea that value is the object of *qualified interest* is not as subtle as it might at first seem.

According to the first view, "certain objects are preeminently qualified to evoke interest. . . ." Perry reviews the most prominent ideas of this sort: the idea that only those objects which are purposive are truly worthy of interest, the idea that the good is the desirable when "desirable" means that which actually evokes desire, the idea that the valuable objects are those which are *capable* of evoking desire (as distinguished from actually evoking it), and finally the idea that the object which has value is the object which ought-to-be. The errors resident in these various ideas, according to Perry, are either instances of supposing that objects actually have the properties of responses human beings make to objects, or of limiting the area of value to whatever most concerns the philosopher in question.

According to the second view—the view that value is the object of qualified interest—only those objects are valuable which become the objects of an interest in some way distinguishable from other interests that might be taken in objects. For example, it might be held that only an interest or desire which is harmonious with nature or with the will of God is a "real" interest, a value-determining desire. Or it might be maintained that only a rational will can determine value, that an object is valuable only if it *would be* desired, *were* the reason in control of desire. Several other ideas, variants of these, are considered by Perry. He concludes that the various kinds of interests which various philosophers have put forward as authoritative and value-determining are none of them paramount and preeminently value-creative; but they do determine various *kinds* of value.

Having shown what is unsatisfactory in the claim that value is the qualified object of interest and in the claim that value is the object of qualified interest, Perry then put forth his preferred generic theory of value: the theory that value is *any* object of *any* interest—that whatever the interest, desire, concern for or in an object, the fact of that interest's having been taken determines the object as an object of value. "That which is an object of interest is *eo ipso* invested with value," he writes.

After noting that the idea is not entirely novel—since it may be found in the works of Spinoza, Santayana, and Prall—Perry mused: "It may appear surprising that a doctrine so familiar, if not banal, as that just stated, should have received so little authoritative support." The unpopularity of the idea among professional philosophers is attributed to philosophical interest in some specific value to the neglect of generic value; and Perry attributes the interest in specific values to the interest in forcing value theory to support some religious or metaphysical notions which would otherwise collapse.

The obvious weakness in the theory is in its very breadth. If an object is made valuable by an act of interest, how could anyone be disappointed? How could some desires be unworthy of virtuous men? It might seem that Perry's theory involves a truly vicious—since indiscriminate—relativism. But Perry does not evade this criticism; he meets it by declaring that a generic theory of value naturally does not account for organizations of value which result in giving preference to certain interests over others. He does not deny that, relative to a certain interest, another interest might be wrong; but what he insists upon is the revelatory character of his principal thesis: that, *generically* considered, an object has value if some interest has been taken in it. A truly vicious relativism, he declares, is one which fails to recognize the relation of interest between subjects and objects.

This is a point well worth emphasizing. To say, as Perry does, that an object has value if someone takes an interest in it, is not to say that there is no such thing as value, or that value is *not worthy* of consideration (an ironic claim) because, after all, it is merely a function of interest. To realize that there is a sense in which interest confers value on objects is to be liberated from the old, constrictive notion that either values are inherent in objects—in which case we should all agree on value considerations—or all discourse about value is meaningless—in which case all value disputes are senseless. And Perry merits serious attention for his view that emphasis on any one kind of interest, with a subsequent upgrading of some particular species of value, is itself an expression of interest, a dogmatic conferring of value on one attitude to the exclusion of other concerns.

In his analysis of interest Perry refused to limit himself to an examination of introspective data. He preferred to "look for interest in the open—upon the plane and in the context of physical nature." Writing in 1926, Perry hailed the advance of psychology as a result of its behavioristic direction and contended that a thorough study of value involves taking advantage of methods which have proved so useful. Consequently, a chapter is devoted to the biological approach to interest, and another to the psychological definition of interest.

The capacity to act in accordance with one's expectations, the ability to plan ahead and to form plans in the service of present inclinations is what distinguishes man, although not sharply but by degree, from other animals. Having claimed this, Perry offers a definition of interest which fits in with the biological and psychological study of man: "An act is interested in so far as its occurrence is due to the agreement between its accompanying expectation and the unfulfilled phases of a governing propensity." In other words, if someone wants something (a house) and acts (by assembling wood, nails, and other materials) because of his expectation that by following a certain procedure (as outlined in the house plans) he can achieve what he wants—then he is *interested* as he acts. This account of interest in general is carefully elaborated by Perry, and it fulfills his intention of explaining interest without having to assume scientifically inexplicable phenomena or capacities in the human being.

In reading Perry one is reminded not only of Spinoza—whom Perry quotes with favor because of Spinoza's claim that things are good because we like them—but also of Montaigne, who, realizing that the worth of things is more dependent on our attitudes than on the nature of things, urged the good sense of changing our attitudes whenever we are dissatisfied with things. Behind Perry's systematic and pedagogical style one discerns the active and practical interest in using value theory as an instrument of human freedom. In pointing out that adaptability is peculiar to men, he is in effect urging that men use their ability to plan ahead in order to satisfy their interests. Nothing could be farther from the old idea of making life fit patterns of conduct derived deductively from presumed revelations of divine will.

In support of his thesis that there are various kinds of interest and, consequently, various species of value, Perry devotes several chapters to what he calls "modes of interest." His survey encompasses the relations between reflex, habit, and instinct; an account of positive and negative interests in terms of approach and withdrawal; clarification of the distinction between recurrent interest (interest which succeeds itself in relation to objects present in the immediate future) and progressive interest (interest which arises with the coming into existence of a certain object of interest); a study of the difference between "real" interest and play interest; a comparison of aggressive with submissive interest; and, finally, a discussion of those modes of interest involving pleasure, pain, and emotion. Perry concludes that values, like interests—because they are functions of interest—can be categorized as "inherited or acquired, positive or negative, recurrent or progressive, real or playful, aggressive or submissive, subjective or objective."

Perhaps the most helpful part of Perry's defense of his theory is his account of value judgments. Perry shows that although interest can be distinguished from cognition, the two are "intimately interdependent." Interest affects cognition, and cognition affects interest; our interest in moving ourselves results in our acquiring knowledge, and our knowledge of objects has its effect on our interests. It is not surprising, then, that Perry decides that judgments of value are similar to other kinds of judgments; judgments of value "have their indices, their predicates and their objects; they are true or false. . . ." It is this claim—that judgments of value are true or false—which proponents of the theory that value judgments are merely expressions of emotion find so disturbing. But Perry underscores his point by definition and example: "To be valuable is to be object of interest," he writes. "To be judged valuable . . . is to be judged to be object of interest." For example, ". . . the judgment 'peace is good' is true when there is an interest such that peace is its objective. It is not necessary that peace should exist, or that the question of its existence should be raised."

Perry's analysis does not neglect the problems which arise because of the conflicts of interest within an individual or between individuals. He regards apologetic reasoning as the effort to find a common ground for harmonious action. Society is not a person and cannot be treated as a person; it is a "composition or interrelation of men," a composition in which individual men, by their actions, affect and modify each other. According to Perry, interests may be integrated through common objects, or by becoming objects for one another, or through mediating one another. The hope of achieving the constructive integration of the various interests of men in society depends upon benevolent cooperation, a kind of general willingness to utilize the various modes of social integration.

How is a critique of values possible for one who regards value as a function of interest? Perry answers that an illuminating answer depends upon recognizing the possibility that one interest may become dominant, and relative to that interest an act or object of another interest may come to be rejected. To take a homely example (not the author's): A cake may be a good cake, the very best available; but that means only that as an object of interest in cake, this cake takes precedence over other cakes. But the interest in remaining slim may take precedence over the interest in eating cake, and consequently, relative to that latter interest, eating cake is bad.

If Perry seems to depart at all from his cautious and fruitful value relativism, it is in his concluding chapter, "The Highest Good." Perry endorses an ideal, realizable by men, as the highest good; it is an ideal which presupposes a harmonious society of benevolent persons. But is harmony a value to the man who lives by conflict, who finds satisfaction only in struggle and in the hope and realization of victory? According to Perry's own theory, if conflict is an object of interest, then it is a value. How, then, account for this concluding endorsement of harmony and benevolence?

Without having to win his point by an awkward calculation of comparative worths, Perry argues that *if* all would concur in working out a resolution of conflicts cooperatively, the resultant situation *would* be better for all; and *if* the resolution of conflicts were such that no greater interest would be elicited by some other resolution, such a state of affairs would be the ideal, the greatest good relative to the interest of each. The highest good, then, is such "as judged by, and only as judged by, the standard of inclusiveness hypothetically applied." Because the value is, in a sense, conditional, no violence is done to Perry's relativism.

As a critically articulated empirical philosophy of value, as an examination of the role of interest in that broad area to which the word "value" in its most general use calls attention, Ralph Barton Perry's *General Theory of Value* remains a provocative statement to be reckoned with by anyone who supposes that value terms are meaningless or that value is an ultimate and unanalyzable aspect of reality.—*I.P.M.*

PERTINENT LITERATURE

Dubs, Homer H. "Value as Interest—A Criticism," in *Ethics*. XL, no. 4 (July, 1930), pp. 474-489.

Homer H. Dubs regards Ralph Barton Perry's theory as fundamentally flawed in its central thesis that value "in the generic sense" is attached to any object of any interest. A value theory, Dubs says, should first be self-consistent, so that its logical implications do not contradict one another. Second, it must agree basically with man's value experience, or else explain how man's misconceptions may have arisen. Finally, it must explain pertinent phenomena, such as the widely divergent valuations people actually make. Dubs faults Perry's theory on all three counts.

The first of five objections entangles Perry in self-contradiction. Albertine, a psychasthenic patient, has no affective responses accompanying her sensations and cognitions. This came about because she failed to consummate her interests, and now (Perry says) she lives in a valueless world. According to Perry's theory, Dubs asserts, Albertine's world should remain as filled with value as ever, despite her failures.

Granted, Perry could rectify the contradiction by adjusting his language. More importantly, the example shows that the theory implies a consequence conflicting with everyday valuations: namely, that failure is just as important as success, for the interest, not its satisfaction, constitutes the value. Suppose, suggests Dubs, that a completely untalented person passionately resolves to become a sculptor. How should we advise him? The value of the anticipated career would depend solely on his desire for it, and failure would make such a career no less valuable. Common wisdom, however, holding that valuation should be a reliable guide to action, would turn the person away from his plan.

Perry mistakenly identifies the desired with the desirable. This entails the second defect: the theory strips away the normative nature of valuation, leaving ethics and aesthetics strictly descriptive sciences which cannot supply standards for human activity. This, however, conflicts with man's view of what value study should do for him.

Since Perry affirms that only interests actually engaging behavior confer value, there could be no ideal values, if Perry's theory were true. More startling yet, there could be no erroneous judgments of value. No one can correct my valuation, for an interest I actually take is simply a fact. Even a mistaken interest confers value. God is valuable if I am interested in God, even if there were no God.

Third, all value must continually recede into the future, since all interest is a striving for what has not yet been attained. If the defense were offered that some interest is taken in keeping good things we have in fact attained, it would entail an odd interpretation of a world in which we guard our goods against thieves—that there will be less value in the world, once it is rid of thieves.

Fourth, Perry's theory cannot account for the value of unanticipated goods, simply stumbled upon rather than sought. Interest in them actually is a consequence of their value, not the prerequisite to it.

Finally, Perry's fundamental thesis provides no real way to explain comparative valuations, despite his adducing the principles of intensity, preference, and inclusiveness. Some ordering, indeed, takes place as more intense interests shoulder others aside; but intensity supplies no norm and no explanation of why some interests become more aroused than others. Neither does Perry supply an explanation of the ordering of preferences. Inclusiveness asserts that the greater number of persons taking an interest in x, the more valuable x is. If six people like symphonies and not Shakespeare, and six others like Shakespeare but not symphonies, while all twelve like crossword puzzles, then crossword puzzles are more valuable than symphonies or Shakespeare. Inclusiveness implies this sort of comparative judgment, unsupported by common valuation, yet cannot explain why common valuative practice arrives at a different result. Thus it fails to meet Dubs's second and third criteria.

Hall, Everett W. *What Is Value?: An Essay in Philosophical Analysis*. New York: Humanities Press, 1952, pp. 67-80.

Everett W. Hall examines Ralph Barton Perry's value theory from the viewpoint of linguistic analysis under the heading, "Is value the referent of a semantical predicate?" Perry essays to treat value, objects, and interests within a behavioristic framework. However, when Perry calls value "a problematic object," since an interest actually anticipates something not yet existing, he concedes that his value theory cannot be expressed solely in behavioristic terms, for behavior cannot exhibit natural relations to objects that do not as yet—and may never—exist. One could of course get around this difficulty by treating value as the referent of a semantical predicate belonging to a problematic object, and Perry appears to fall back upon such means of expressing his full theory where behavioristic language will not do so.

Hall is interested in "translating" Perry's language about the behavior of organisms into a "semantical" language—about names and sentences, thus showing relationships between what people do and how they talk about what they do. If such a translation calls for conspicuous divergence from normal usage in people's talk about what they do, that casts suspicion upon the account of what they do. By this test Hall ferrets out some objectionable features of Perry's theory.

Hall suggests that interest might be the referent of a kind of *sentence* describing an object somewhat as an ordinary empirical judgment describes a fact, and that the difference between interest-expressions and empirical judgments relates to the distinction between value and fact. Perry's "value" would be the referent object of the interest-sentence, as the fact is of the descriptive sentence. Now a fact cannot be referred to by a name, but must be asserted by an appropriate sentence. On such a hypothesis, a value too could not be referred to by a name but would also require an appropriate sentence. The interest-sentence, however, would have to be susceptible to some sort of falsity or invalidity—otherwise it could not be considered a sentence, but merely a name; and for Perry, interests are never false. The odd consequence is that interest-utterances are not actually sentences, but rather *names*. Not only that: since such names contain words to express what is evaluated, they are *names containing sentences*. These "most unfortunate" descriptions of value utterances turn ordinary semantic and syntactical relationships upside down—and are totally inconsistent with ordinary usage.

Further, "interest" includes both seeking and avoiding, which Perry calls positive and negative interests. The duality of positive and negative interests, however, is unlike the duality of positive *versus* negative assertions, or true *versus* false sentences. When a *for*-interest is valid, the corresponding *against*-interest is not necessarily invalid but may be equally valid. The names designating *against*-interests are undifferentiated from those of *for*-interests, whereas in everyday speech we keep clear distinctions between the two.

Finally, if we insist that interest-utterances *are* sentences, the translation test reveals an objectionable relativism. Some sentences can be so cast that their truth depends simply upon the meaning-structure of the sentence, not upon anything in the external world (for example, "Either my tie is black or my tie is not black"). Thus, since value utterances are not falsifiable by reference to the world, they are like these self-certifying sentences, known merely upon someone's asserting them, "true" simply relative to their meaning.

Since taking Perry's "value" as wholly behavioral leads to difficulties, Hall believes it rather more justified than not to question whether Perry's "interest" is the referent of a semantic predicate. In fact, the possibility that such a thorough critic as Hall may be left in doubt of the justness of an interpretation is itself a criticism of the theory in question.

Pepper, Stephen C. "The Goal and the Problem of Terminal Value," in *The Sources of Value*. Berkeley: University of California Press, 1958, pp. 167-199.

In this notable theory of value, Stephen C. Pepper acknowledges that his starting point is Ralph Barton Perry's *General Theory of Value*. Fully sympathizing with Perry's purposes and approach, Pepper endeavors to give value theory a firmer psychological foundation. Pepper devotes one chapter largely to systematic criticism of Perry's value theory. Its defects are not obvious, Pepper affirms, but are found only after searching analysis.

Pepper notes that Perry does not place value in a *satisfaction* but in an "object." Pepper himself describes a goal as compound, consisting of a "goal object"—for example, an apple—and a "quiescence pattern," the cessation of one's hunger drive upon one's eating the apple. A strong argument that quiescence is an essential element of the whole of a value is that everything else in a behavior sequence is subject to modification, as errors are corrected or attempts fall short, until quiescence is attained. Hence it must be both the final goal and the ultimate locus of value for a purposive act. Perry has made a basic error in looking only as far as the goal object, rather than tracing the behavior pattern out to its final resolution.

When behavior begins, Pepper finds, together with Perry's "anticipatory set," a drive or impulse. Some drives are complex and highly mental; others are basic, simple, and fundamentally biological; but behavior arising out of either is purposive, valuative behavior. What Perry does not recognize is that a purposive act can be initiated by a drive without an anticipatory set. A full, unbiased description of purposive value must take drives into account. In his treatment of hunger as a negative interest, an avoidance pattern, Perry not only departs far from the facts, but what is worse, he uses this ill-founded argument as a pattern to explain other impulses, in what amounts to an attempt to get rid of all drives. Thus Perry leaves out two things Pepper finds essential: an impulse pattern to account for the motivation of activity and a quiescence pattern to account for its termination.

Ostensibly, Perry holds an ideomotor theory of judgment, whereby a cognition and an interest are united in one. A judgment valuing an object is automatically a desire for it. Perry's two chapters analyzing cognition, however, are at variance with the ideomotor theory. To extricate himself from trouble that perhaps he only dimly senses, Perry erects a second theory of cognition alongside his first. It admits a "governing propensity," mentioned in one of his systematic definitions of interest, as an independent dynamic factor but having no goal of its own. Thus Perry now has two sorts of purposive activity, one ideomotor, the other motivated by a separate "propensity," making it possible for a cognitive activity to conflict with an interest. By absorbing the motive factor into the acts of judgment themselves, Perry conceals from himself the fact that cognition itself is a purposive activity. When the ideomotor theory alone operates, however, there is no conflict since the only motive factor is within its cognitive activity.

Perry's first inconsistency results from including these two kinds of purposive activity, one of which, not instituting a value, is not an interest. This inconsistency leads to a second, that of introducing a motive force in ideomotor cognition yet denying that cognitive processes have a dynamic factor—leading in turn to a third inconsistency: admitting that incompatibility is possible between the lately introduced "governing propensity" and the anticipatory set or expectation, while making such an incompatibility impossible by giving the two the same goal.—*J.T.G.*

ADDITIONAL RECOMMENDED READING

Frankena, William K. "Ethical Theory," in Roderick Chisholm's *Philosophy*. Englewood Cliffs, New Jersey: Prentice-Hall, 1964, pp. 345-363. In his Section 2, Frankena places Perry with other American naturalists at work between 1930 and 1960; excellent eight-page bibliography on American ethical work of this period.

Frondizi, Risieri. *What Is Value? An Introduction to Axiology*. La Salle, Illinois: Open Court, 1971, pp. 51-59. Criticizes the interest theory as a subjectivist doctrine, leaving entirely aside the qualities of the object and giving no aid in resolving moral conflicts.

Handy, Rollo. *The Measurement of Values*. St. Louis, Missouri: Warren H. Green, 1970, pp. 142-154. The author, strongly behavioristic, finds Perry's theory deficient as a basis for measuring values, partly because of a tendency to make certain inner aspects of behavior the ultimate determinants of value.

Parker, De Witt H. "Value as Any Object of Any Interest," in *Ethics*. XL, no. 4 (July, 1930), pp. 465-473. Parker insists that value is in the satisfaction, not in the interest itself.

Perry, Charner M. "Some Difficulties in Current Value Theory," in *The Journal of Philosophy*. XXV, no. 11 (May 24, 1928), pp. 281-287. Succinctly criticizes Warner Fite, John Dewey, and Perry.

_____ . "Value as Any Object of Any Interest," in *Ethics*. XL, no. 4 (July, 1930), pp. 490-495. Examines four possible interpretations of Perry's definition of value.

Reck, Andrew J. "The New Realism of Ralph Barton Perry," in *Recent American Philosophy*. New York: Pantheon Books, 1964, pp. 3-41. Purely expository rather than critical coverage giving an overall view of Perry's work, using copious quotation.

Urban, W. M. Review of Ralph Barton Perry's *General Theory of Value*, in *The Journal of Philosophy*. XXIV, no. 4 (February 17, 1927), pp. 104-110. Points covered are broad, selected to serve philosophers of a wide spectrum of interests.

THE LOGIC OF MODERN PHYSICS

Author: Percy Williams Bridgman (1882-1963)
Type of work: Philosophy of science
First published: 1927

PRINCIPAL IDEAS ADVANCED

The concepts of physics should be flexible in order not to restrict the possibilities of future experience.

To provide flexibility, concepts should be defined operationally; the concept is synonymous with the operations by which one determines whether the concept applies, or what the measure of something is.

There is no absolute time; time is measured by reference to clocks of some sort.

Such concepts as causality, identity, force, energy, temperature, and light become useful and meaningful as they are defined by reference to physical phenomena and operations of measurement.

Since the turn of the century increased attention has been devoted to critical examination of the concepts and presuppositions of the sciences. In the case of physics this shift of emphasis from content to methods was largely the result of such revolutionary discoveries as the relativity theory and quantum mechanics. These not only revealed new and unexpected truths which had to be assimilated, but also showed that the old methods of studying the world had proved inadequate. Bridgman's contribution to this problem lay in his formulation and development of the *operational method.* While this method was not new and had been more or less unconsciously employed by physicists for some time, Bridgman argued that a much clearer conception of what is really involved was essential if physics was to avoid some of the difficulties through which it had passed in the preceding half century.

Fundamental to this approach, as far as Bridgman is concerned, is a new emphasis on the empirical character of physics. There must be no *a priori* principles which restrict the possibilities of future experience. Experience is determined only be experience. Since this is the case, concepts must be flexible in order to allow for their modification when experiment is pushed into new domains—smaller particles, higher velocities, greater distances, greater pressures, higher temperatures—where discontinuities may appear and the world may change character in unexpected ways. Indeed, we even find that concepts sometimes disappear entirely, as in the case of temperature when applied to a single molecule. We cannot therefore predict that nature will ultimately be embraced in a single formula. While such may actually be the case, we should not approach experience with this expectation, for we shall then try to force nature into a preestablished form and the result may well be that certain of our accepted concepts will become meaningless if we try to use them to interpret the new areas of experience.

The best way to provide for the required flexibility, Bridgman argues, is to define concepts operationally. Let us examine the concept of *length*. Suppose we are trying to determine the length of a house. We apply a measuring rod according to accepted rules and come up with a certain number, say forty-two feet, which we say is the length of the house. Now let us attempt to determine the length of a moving street car. Here we cannot proceed as we did before, for the car is moving and we are at rest. We shall have to stop the car, get on it, start it, measure it, stop it, and get off. Since we have used different measurement techniques we are not really entitled to say that by the *length* of the moving street car we mean the same thing as we do in the case of the *length* of the house. For higher velocities, such as that of the stars, this method will obviously not work and another must be devised. This fact will give us a new meaning of *length*. Or suppose we wish to determine the length of a large piece of land. We shall probably establish this by means of trigonometry and a surveyor's transit. If we extend this method to stellar distances, on the one hand, and to the distances separating molecules, on the other, the measuring techniques will once more be changed.

What conclusion can we draw? There is no *one* meaning of length, but as many meanings as there are ways of measuring lengths. We cannot say what *the* length of anything is. Apart from some operation for measuring length, the concept is meaningless; *the concept is synonymous with the corresponding operations*. If we have more than one set of operations, then, in the interest of precision and in the interest of tying our concept down to the area to which it properly applies, we ought to have a separate concept for each set.

The need for the operational approach is illustrated by the prerelativity attempts to define *time*. Newton believed that "Absolute, True and Mathematical Time, of itself, and from its own nature, flows equably without regard to anything external." But Bridgman points out that we can have no assurance that there exists anything in nature which has such properties. Indeed, we cannot even assure ourselves that the concept of absolute time has any meaning. Certainly if we were to *measure* time, we should have to employ some sort of clock, and we could have no way of knowing whether the clock "flows equably." All time, then, is relative, and dependent upon measurement. We cannot base physics on any concept of time which excludes this flexibility from its meaning; hence we must abandon absolute time.

Bridgman indicates several consequences of this operational method. In the first place, when we approach a new area where previous operations cannot be performed, we must devise a new set of operations, thus redefining our concept. It may be *convenient* to retain the old concept, but we may have to purchase this convenience at the cost of precision in our language. We must recognize these "joints" in our conceptual structure if we are to simplify the tasks of the unborn Einsteins. In the second place, we may often find that as we extend knowledge into new domains, concepts fuse together, as in the case of length and electric field vector when applied to an electron. In the third place, as seen above, *all* knowledge becomes relative. This does not mean that we can never know nature, for the statement that the length of an object can be ascertained by applying a measuring stick to it is a very important and fundamental truth about nature. Furthermore, a thing may be said to have an absolute property if the numerical magnitudes obtained by all observers who measure the object are the same. Finally, if we accept the operational approach, we readily discover how easy it is to reformulate questions which are meaningless when (as in the case of the question about the flow of absolute time) there are no operations by which they can be answered. Some such meaningless questions are: Was there ever a time when matter did not exist? May time have a beginning or an end? May space be bounded? Are there parts of nature forever beyond our detection? May there be missing integers in the series of natural numbers as we know them? Is the sensation which I call blue real the *same* as that which my neighbor calls blue?

The operational approach involves far-reaching change in our habits of thought. While thinking becomes simpler, since fewer sweeping generalizations become possible, much of traditional philosophy becomes unreadable. One looks continually for operational meanings where there seems to be none. Thinking becomes harder in the sense that the demand for operational concepts is often difficult to meet. Finally operational thinking proves to be an unsocial virtue, for a person finds that he is continually antagonizing his friends by insisting in the simplest conversation that all concepts be operationally defined before they are used.

By "experiment" in physics Bridgman means, from the operational point of view, simply reducing a situation to its elements; that is, discovering familiar correlations between phenomena. He claims that an explanatory sequence extending into new areas may be terminated in three ways: (1) By disentangling complexities. This involves nothing new. The best illustration is found in the explanation of the thermal properties of gas by the kinetic theory. (2) By coming up against situations involving such genuinely novel elements that we are at a complete loss as to how to explain them. Quantum phenomena and relativity exemplify these situations, and they present a real crisis in physics. (3) By devising new elements beyond the range of present experiment, or radically modifying old elements, in the attempt to make them fit the novel area into which we have penetrated. Because of the lack of justification for the belief that as we penetrate deeper and deeper into nature we shall find the elements of experience repeated, this method is opposed to the operational approach. It may be used, however, if we recognize its dangers. The new elements must be considered to be simply mental constructs and their utility to lie merely in the fact that they are working hypotheses which may suggest new experimental truths.

Some of the results of Bridgman's application of the operational method to certain physical concepts are as follows: *Space* as used in physics becomes an empirical concept and is meaningless if separated from physical objects and measuring rods. Geometry, therefore, is not an abstract logical system built up from postulates, but a physical framework made up of bodies in relations to one another. We cannot measure the distance between two points in empty space. *Time*, when restricted to "local" time, can be operationally defined by the use of simple clocks; but when extended to include the remote past, or when extended to the process of synchronizing clocks at distant places, it must be defined through the use of various kinds of records and by means of light signals. *Causality* can be defined only by recognizing that it is relative and involves the whole system in which the causally related events take place. The animistic element, originally associated with the concept, is eliminated as far as possible, and the system in which causal action takes place is assumed to be capable of isolation from disturbing forces, so that repeated experiments can be performed on it. *Identity*, as exhibited by ordinary physical objects, can be detected by continuous observation of those objects and noting the absence of change in properties. But this method does not enable us to determine whether an electron jumping about in an atom preserves its identity. *Force*, exhibited by objects at rest, has its locus in muscular sensations, but when extended to objects in motion must be redefined in terms of mass and acceleration. But mass must be capable of measurement independently of force—something which can be done in the ordinary range of experiments with low velocities. However, in the domain of celestial mechanics, where the only thing we can observe about the heavenly bodies is their positions, the concepts of force and mass lose their definiteness and become partially fused. This is characteristic of concepts of the fringe of the experimentally attainable.

Energy is a certain complicated property of a material system, but because of the absence of specifiable operations by which it may be measured, Bridgman believes that it is probably not entitled to the fundamental position that physical thought has been inclined to give it. *Temperature*, basically a physiological concept, is extended by being connected with the physical phenomenon of thermal equilibrium. *Electrical concepts* are defined first in connection with large scale static phenomena. Then they are extended, with proper changes in operations, to high velocities and to very small scales of magnitude. *Light* gets its direct meaning in terms of "things lighted." By experimenting with sources and sinks, with screens placed between a light and an illuminated object, and with rectilinear propagation, we readily conclude that light is a "thing which travels" and has properties analogous to those of all material things which travel. But there is one important difference. We can have evidence of a ball, for example, at intermediate points in its movement, because we can see it or possibly hear it. But the situation is different with regard to light; we can know of its intermediate existence only by interposing a screen of some kind, and this operation destroys the very beam itself; the light cannot continue to travel beyond that point. Thus the concept of light becomes operationally meaningless when we try to speak of it in an empty space between the initial and terminal phenomena. *Relativity concepts* suffer from the fact that there is still a wide gap between the theory and its physical applications; we have no way of relating our physical measures of *time* to the *t* in our formulas. *Quantum concepts* border on the meaningless because they seem to require that space and time be essentially discontinuous at the microscopic level, and this cannot be reconciled with the way in which length and duration were originally defined.

Bridgman suggests that in our study of nature we must try to avoid the unconscious intrusion of hypotheses which might restrain possible future experiences. One *general* hypothesis we cannot avoid; namely, that our minds will continue to function in the future as they have in the past. This certainly does not restrict us too seriously. On the other hand, there are three *special* hypotheses whose roles must be examined—the simplicity of nature, the finiteness of nature as we go to smaller and smaller dimensions, and the causal determination of the future by the present. Bridgman examines each of these.

The hypothesis of simplicity claims that nature is completely describable in terms of a few principles of great breadth and simplicity, such as the inverse square law. This hypothesis does not seem to be borne out in our experience. The *time* of relativity is proving to be much more complex than the *time* of Newtonian physics. We have not been able to extend gravitational laws to small-scale bodies, and we have not yet been able to extend electrical laws to large-scale bodies. Thus we seem to be continually discovering new *kinds* of phenomena where the established concepts will not work.

A second hypothesis is that as we analyze nature into smaller and smaller particles we find that the world is constituted by a smaller number of *kinds* of elements; two molecules may differ from each other though they may consist of atoms which are alike. Nature is simple because everything is made up, perhaps, of only two different constituents—positive and negative electric charges. But present experience in physics does not seem to support this hypothesis either. New experiments show that the universe at any given level is becoming increasingly complex and that simplicity is receding. It is very probable that there are structures beyond the electron and the quantum. Indeed, there is no reason to believe that the analytic process will ever be terminated: a drop of water may be infinite.

As a result of this fact the third hypothesis—that of determinism—is considerably weakened. For if even a small part of the universe had an infinite structure, we could never give a complete description of it and consequently we could never know all of the causal factors that would enter into the determination of the future; to predict anything we must know its *complete* cause. The future would therefore fall into a penumbra of uncertainty—this uncertainty increasing as we pass to finer details of structure. Our belief in causation originates in our experience with mechanical systems, and there is no reason to believe that these systems will still apply when we deal with phenomena of radiation. There is, however, more and more reason for believing that nature is deterministic as far as large-scale phenomena are concerned.

There is still another sense in which the physicist may have a predisposition toward simplicity in the world: he may feel that the universe can ultimately be explained in terms of analysis. This is the thesis that we should start with small-scale things and then proceed to explain large-scale things in terms of these. According to this point of view, the large can be constructed out of the small since the properties of the large are obtained by merely adding the properties of the small. For example, the mass of a very large object is the sum of the masses of its parts. But although a system in which this is true would be one which is easy to handle, we have no assurance that all systems are of this kind. We do not know whether the kinetic energy of a number of electrons making up an electric current is the sum of the kinetic energies of the individual electrons, or whether it is described by means of some non-additive property. Nor do we know whether the mass of an electron is the sum of the masses of its elements.

In conclusion, Bridgman suggests that if we try to look ahead we can see what we shall require of our methodology in the future. We must make a more self-conscious and detailed analysis of all of our physical concepts with a view to clarifying their operational meanings. We shall probably find that as we penetrate deeper the number of concepts will become smaller. Finally, we must examine our mental constructs in the effort to determine which of them are embodied in reality and which of them are pure inventions. A good construct is one which possesses a unique correspondence with the data in terms of which it is defined, which is uniquely connected with other physical phenomena different from those which entered into its definition, and which is useful in suggesting new experiments.—*A.C.B.*

PERTINENT LITERATURE

Russell, L. J. Review of Percy Williams Bridgman's *The Logic of Modern Physics*, in *Mind*. XXXVII, no. 47 (July, 1928), pp. 355-361.

L. J. Russell's critical notice of *The Logic of Modern Physics* provides both a summary and a critique of Percy Williams Bridgman's major arguments. According to Russell, Bridgman's basic claim is that concepts in the physical sciences can be defined in one of two ways: either by reference to properties of objects, where these properties may or may not be encountered directly in our experience, or in terms of the operations by which the numerical values of the concepts can be determined. Bridgman's view is that the former way of defining and establishing concepts leads investigators to depend on preconceptions which may or may not be borne out in experience, while the latter, or "operational" definition, ensures that our concepts are tied directly to experience and experiment.

Bridgman argued that Albert Einstein's restricted (or special) Theory of Relativity emerged as a consequence of his insistence that the concepts of simultaneity, space, and time be defined operationally. Russell is prepared to concede that the Einsteinian revolution may have been a consequence of a careful scrutiny of the operations by which spatiotemporal measurements are made, but Russell argues that it is a mistake to insist that physical concepts cannot, or should not, mean more than a specified set of operations.

Bridgman recognized that in practice physicists behave as though several different kinds of operations can measure the same variable; for example, there are several distinct ways of measuring what we call length, and they are generally taken to be different ways of measuring the same feature, not different features. Bridgman suggests that several operations can be treated as constituting identical concepts if, and only if, the various operations, in similar contexts, generate identical magnitudes for the variables in question. But Russell's response is to argue that if the identity of numerical values is grounds for assuming conceptual identity, then this indicates that concepts are not identical with the operations by which they are measured.

Russell suggests that Bridgman shows that his strict operationalist view is untenable by not sticking to it. If concepts were identical with the operations with which their magnitudes are determined, then it would not make sense to claim, as Bridgman and all scientists do, that empirically determined magnitudes are only approximate. If they are approximate, there must be something over and above the actual operational results to which they approximate. Russell is fully in favor of ensuring that physical concepts are kept in touch with experience and operations; but, he argues, to try to identify concepts with these operations is both absurd and inconsistent with much of Bridgman's own argumentation. Bridgman, after all, recognizes that H. A. Lorentz extended J. C. Maxwell's ideas beyond their operational scope, and that he consequently generated important scientific discoveries which, moreover, were inaccessible to Joseph Larmor, whose ideas were more cautious and more strictly operationalist than those of Lorentz. Russell's claim is that science makes progress precisely because its concepts are not tied solely to operational definitions. According to him, Bridgman wants to avoid the necessity of science undergoing the kind of revolutionary discontinuity it experienced with Einstein and to proceed by a steady accumulation of operationally acquired data. Russell argues that operationalist restrictions would inhibit scientific progress altogether.

Lindsay, R. B. "A Critique of Operationalism in Physics," in *Philosophy of Science*. IV, no. 4 (October, 1937), pp. 456-470.

R. B. Lindsay emphasizes the normative character of Percy Williams Bridgman's proposition that concepts be tied to operations; it is not necessary or inevitable that concepts be operationally defined, but if they are, science will be the better for it. Nevertheless, even with this qualification Bridgman's operationalist thesis is unacceptable to Lindsay. Lindsay argues that operational and experimental results do not mean anything except for the meaning we give to them by locating them in particular theoretical contexts. Lindsay's position is that theoretical presuppositions cannot be eliminated from the description of experimental results. As he says, in the equation used to describe the motion of a freely falling body—namely, $s = \frac{1}{2}gt^2$ (using the usual notation) the quantity g gains its meaning not by direct measurement but solely by virtue of its appearance in the formula.

Lindsay also introduces the argument which L. J. Russell employed: that operationalism implies a proliferation of concepts, while in fact science tries to provide a simple and economical description of the world using as few concepts as possible. For example, he argues that the concept of temperature was initially introduced to refer to a numerical magnitude obtained from the operational employment of a particular thermometer. Subsequently it was found that under apparently identical conditions different thermometers would yield different results. Eventually physicists produced the absolute scale of temperature which is independent of any particular thermometric substance, or set of measuring operations, and against which all thermometers could be calibrated.

Lindsay's position is not that physical concepts should be wholly unrelated to operational determinations, or that theory should be free from experimental tests, but that to reduce theoretical concepts to operational procedures would destroy their utility. Lindsay argues at length that Bridgman cannot account for the possibility, or role and value, of scientific models. Their value is precisely that they do take us beyond existing operations and results to new and unexpected results, even though we cannot be certain in advance that the suggestions deriving from models are correct.

Furthermore, Lindsay argues that operationalism cannot account for some of the most important uses of statistical methods in physics. If one adopts an operationalist perspective there is no possibility of assigning a probability to a single event, and so the idea would be meaningless, whereas he claims that in practice physicists are willing and able to quantify such probabilities. Despite Lindsay's basic sympathy with an empiricist perspective, he believes that Bridgman's formulation of it is far too strict; he believes that it would entail the complete abandonment of ". . . the well-recognized methodology of physics."

Frank, P. G., ed. "The Present State of Operationalism," in *The Validation of Scientific Theories*. New York: Collier Books, 1961.

In 1953 a symposium was held under the auspices of the American Association for the Advancement of Science and the National Science Foundation, and the major papers were published under the title *The Validation of Scientific Theories*. Henry Margenau's contribution to the symposium is brief but direct. He insists that operationalism is not a philosophy, but merely a theory of the meaning of scientific terms. Margenau's view is that operationalism as a complete account of the meaning of scientific terms cannot be successfully defended. Every attempt to do so inevitably defines operationalism in a way which is either trivial or too restrictive. While it may be possible to define operationally the charge, mass, or spin of an electron, the same cannot be said for the concept of the electron itself. Nevertheless, he argues that operationalism has a small, but important, part to play in establishing the meanings of scientific terms.

Margenau claims that for theoretical scientific concepts there are always two sets of requirements to be met: metaphysical and empirical. A concept satisfies the metaphysical requirement if it can be understood as an integral part of a coherent theoretical structure, for this shows that it can provide a possible description of some aspect of the physical world. A concept satisfies an empirical requirement when its empirical validity can be established, and this is possible only in terms of ". . . performed or imagined laboratory procedures." Operational procedures are required to select, among possible theoretical concepts, those which actually apply to this world. For Margenau, therefore, purely operational definitions are necessarily incomplete. A valid concept must belong to a coherent and intelligible theory and must be linked to observations through operations. Consequently, Margenau's view is that without an operational element to concept-definition, science would be sterile speculation, whereas strict adherence to operational definitions and the neglect of metaphysical requirements would reduce science to a narrow and blind form of empiricism which would be completely remote from ". . . the power and beauty of modern physical science."

Gustav Bergmann reinforces several of Margenau's arguments. Bergmann characterizes operationalism as merely a ". . . footnote, though an important one, which has received much attention." Bergmann is prepared to accept that operationalism did, as Percy Williams Bridgman originally claimed, arise from physics as a response to Albert Einstein's analysis of nonlocal spontaneity. Bergmann argues, however, that subsequently operationalism has not had any significant impact in physics; nor has it been missed. Nevertheless, he recognizes (and emphasizes) the enormous impact which operationalist thinking has had upon the discipline of psychology. In particular, Bergmann argues, it facilitated the transition from Watsonianism to modern behavior theory; furthermore, this can readily be understood, since when applied to psychological concepts operationalism becomes methodological behaviorism.

The most challenging and critical contribution to the symposium is provided by Adolf Grünbaum. He challenges Bridgman's claim (which had previously been accepted by all commentators) that Einstein's Theory of Relativity was a product of an operationalist approach. Grünbaum argues that the relativistic account of the temporal order of nature was not generated by a consideration of our actual or possible signaling operations; nor do relativistic ideas derive their meanings from such operations. As Grünbaum says, "It is because no relations of simultaneity *exist* to be measured that *our* measurements cannot disclose them: it is *not* the mere failure of *our* measurements to disclose them that constitutes their non-existence, much as that failure is *evidence* for their non-existence."

According to Grünbaum, what Einstein's analysis shows is not that the concepts of science refer to operations rather than to properties or relationships of physical objects, but that the properties and relationships of physical objects and events are different in some important respects from those assumed within Newtonian science. Furthermore, Bridgman himself recognizes that his operationalist account of meaning, when coupled to a sense-data account of the logical privacy of human experience, generates a view which is fundamentally incompatible with the basic idea of the Theory of Relativity: namely, the invariance of observation with respect to different frames of reference. Grünbaum recognizes that Bridgman wanted to modify physical ideas such that the revolution in the concepts of physics such as that produced by Einstein could never happen again; such discontinuous transitions would be unnecessary and impossible.

Grünbaum, however, suggests that these kinds of conceptual transformations in science are both necessary and desirable, and any attempt to eliminate them would stifle science completely. Although if seventeenth century scientists had employed unique operational definitions of distance and time, their procedure would have precluded their acceptance of Sir Isaac Newton's concepts of space and time, it would have been at the substantial cost of depriving us of Newton's Law of Gravitation, as well as his Second and Third Laws of Motion, along with the system of classical celestial mechanics based on these laws. Similarly, scientists proceeding operationally in the nineteenth century would not have been surprised that the Michaelson-Morley experiment yielded a null result, but only if they had previously impoverished and emasculated classical optics.

Even though Grünbaum is prepared to concede that an operationalist frame of mind may have contributed to the abandonment of H. A. Lorentz's conception of the aether, he insists that this could have been accomplished just as easily in other ways. Grünbaum claims, therefore, that the Theory of Relativity was not a product of an operationalist approach, and that operationalist demands would have smothered physics long before Einstein had an opportunity to make his crucial contribution to physical theory.—*E. M.*

ADDITIONAL RECOMMENDED READING

Benjamin, A. C. *Operationism*. Springfield, Illinois: Charles C. Thomas, 1955. A sustained critique of operationism in the work of Bridgman and others, followed by an attempt to establish a formidable generalized operationist theory. This volume also has a comprehensive bibliography on the subject.

Boring, E. G., *et al.* "Symposium on Operationism," in *The Psychological Review*. LII, no. 5 (September, 1945), pp. 241-294. A careful discussion of the applicability of an operationalist approach in psychology.

Pap, Arthur. "Are Physical Magnitudes Operationally Definable?," in *Measurement: Definitions and Theories*. Edited by C. W. Churchman and P. Ratoosh. New York: John Wiley & Sons, 1959, pp. 177-191. Pap attempts to refine and limit a precise conception of operationalism in physics.

BEING AND TIME

Author: Martin Heidegger (1889-1976)
Type of work: Existential metaphysics
First published: 1927

PRINCIPAL IDEAS ADVANCED

The world, existentially and phenomenologically understood, is a region of human concern; man is a being-in-the-world, in that by participation and involvement the world becomes constitutive of man's being.

Man has being in an environment; and his world is a world he shares with others.

Man is a creature of concerns; in relation to environment, his concerns are practical; in relation to the communal world, his concerns are personal.

The three fundamental features of man are factuality (he is already involved in the world), existentiality (he is a project and a possibility, that which has been, but also that which can become), and fallenness (he has the tendency to become a mere presence in the world, failing to make the most of his possibilities because of gossip, curiosity, and ambiguity).

Through anxiety man encounters nothingness and becomes aware of his finitude and the necessity of death; but through resolution man, who moves in time from past to future through the present, appraises himself, chooses with the whole of his being, and thereby achieves authentic existence.

The primary philosophical problem for Heidegger is the problem of Being. His major philosophical treatise, *Being and Time* constitutes an attempt at a formulation of the basic questions and forms of analysis which are to lead to a clarification of the meaning and structures of Being. The form of analysis which peculiarly characterizes *Being and Time* is what Heidegger calls *Daseinsanalytik* (analysis of human being). This form of analysis is adopted because it is believed that man is the portal to the deeper levels of reality, and that only through a disciplined analysis and description of human being can the path be opened for an apprehension of Being itself.

Heidegger, in his analysis and description of human being or presence (*Dasein*), makes use of the phenomenological method. Philosophy thus becomes "phenomenological ontology." The ontological content of philosophy is Being, and the method which is used to clarify and explicate the meaning of Being is phenomenology. Heidegger was a student of Husserl, and at least in part took over Husserl's transcendental phenomenology and its program of a return "to the data themselves." Adherence to this formula, argues Heidegger, will preclude abstract constructions and formulations, sterile concepts, and the adoption of pseudoquestions which tend to conceal the phenomena or the data rather than reveal them. In the use of the phenomenological method Heidegger seeks to get back to the data of immediate experience, and describe these data as they "show themselves" in their primitive disclosure. The word "phenomenon" has a Greek etymological root φαινόηευου (*phainomenon*), derived from the Greek verb φαινεόδαι (*phainesthai*), which means: that which shows itself or that which reveals itself. The original Greek meaning of λογος (*logos*), the second constitutive etymological element in the word "phenomenology," is discourse, which "opens to sight" or "lets something be seen." Thus, phenomenology, properly understood as the *logos of the phenomenon*, is the disciplined attempt to open to sight that which shows itself, and to let it be seen as it is. In using the phenomenological method, one must therefore discard all preconceived logical and epistemological constructions and seek to examine and describe the phenomena as they show themselves.

The application of the phenomenological method in the analysis of human being or *Dasein* discloses first of all the foundational experience of "being-in-the-world." Man emerges in a world of going concerns and initially discovers himself in his engagement and involvement in practical and personal projects. Heidegger's phenomenological and existentialist concept of the world should not be confused with any objective conceptualization of the world as a substance or an abstract continuum of points. It is Heidegger's persistent argument that Descartes' conceptualization of the world as a *res extensa* entailed a phenomenological falsification of the world as a datum of immediate experience. The world is not an extended substance or an objective spatial container into which man is placed. The world, existentially understood, is a field or region of human concern which is never disclosed independent of this concern. There is no world without man. Thus, to say that man's being is a "being-in-the-world" is to describe human reality in terms of a self-world correlation which underlies all concrete participation and engagement. Man is *in* the world in the sense of being *in* a profession, being *in* the army, being *in* politics, being *in* love, and the like. The relationship between man and the world is not that of a coinherence of substances or objects, but rather the relationship of existential participation and involvement. *Dasein* is in the world in the sense of "being preoccupied, producing, ordering, fostering, applying, sacrificing, undertaking, following through, inquiring, questioning, observing, talking over, or agreeing." The phenomenon of "being-in" denotes the intimacy and familiarity of "being-with" as distinct from the objective spatial proximity of "being-besides."

As the phenomenon of world is falsified when understood as a substance or objectivized entity, so also human being or *Dasein* is distorted when interpreted as a substantial self or a self-identical subject. Again, the error of Descartes' isolation of the thinking substance (*res cogitans*) is disclosed, and the spurious character of the epistemological quandaries which such a view entails is made apparent. Man is not an isolated epistemological subject who first apprehends his own existence and then seeks proof for an objective external world. In his primordial experience man already has his world given in his immediate concerns and preoccupations. The world is constitutive of his being. It is in this way that Heidegger's phenomenology undercuts the subject-object dichotomy, bequeathed by the Cartesian tradition to contemporary epistemological theory, and liberates the self from its lonely, worldless isolation.

A phenomenological description of man's being-in-the-world shows that the world is structurally differentiated into various regions or existential modalities. There is the region of the *Umwelt* (environment), initially disclosed through the utensils which *Dasein* uses in his practical concerns. My world is disclosed in one of its modifications as an instrumental world in which utensils are accessible for the realization of my various undertakings. The German word *Zuhandensein*, which can be translated as "at-handness," designates this accessibility of utensils which constitutes an integral part of my world. Utensils are "at-hand" for one's use and application. But my *Umwelt* is also disclosed in the mode of *Vorhandensein* ("on-handness"). This modality lacks the existential proximity of "at-handness," and is epistemologically secondary and derivative. Heidegger's favorite illustration of these two modifications of the *Umwelt* or environment is his example of the hammer and the act of hammering. In man's primitive experience of his world the hammer is an instrument with which he hammers. The hammer is revealed as a utensil or instrument through the act of hammering. On this level of experience, knowledge and action, or understanding and doing, are in an inseparable unity. Action is already a form of knowledge, and knowledge involves action. One can, however, objectivize one's environmental world and view one's hammer as a physical object in abstraction from its instrumental value. When a hammer becomes a mere object or thing we can speak of it only as being "on-hand" as contrasted with being "at-hand." The hammer in the mode of "on-handness" becomes the object of a theoretical, scientific construction, and is defined in terms of the qualities of weight, composition, size, and shape which constitute it as a material substance. When we say that the hammer *as utensil* is heavy, we mean that it will render more difficult the act of hammering. When we say the hammer *as object* is heavy, we mean that it has such and such a scientifically determined weight. The mode of "at-handness" is thus man's existentially primitive mode—the mode through which *Dasein* first encounters his world in his practical concerns. The world as "on-hand" is a later construction.

Man's "being-in-the-world" thus includes a relatedness to an environmental region—either in the mode of "at-handness" or "on-handness." But man's environment does not exhaust his world. Coupled with his relatedness to an environmental region is his relatedness to a communal region. The *Dasein*-world correlation encompasses a *Mitwelt* as well as an *Umwelt*. Man's world is a world which he shares with others. Human being is essentially communal (*"Dasein ist wesenhaft Mitsein"*). The communality of human being is a pervasive phenomenon which shows itself in man's experience of aloneness as assuredly as in his experience of being-with-others. Aloneness is itself a deficient mode of being-with. Man experiences aloneness only as a privation of an original communal relatedness. Thus *Dasein* possesses an indelible communal character. In society and in solitude man is structurally a communal creature. Now for the most part man exists in the unauthentic communal mode of the "anonymous one." To exist in the mode of the "anonymous one" is to exist in one's communal world in such a way that man's unique selfness is depersonalized and reduced to the status of an "on-hand" being. In short, man transforms himself and another self into an object or a thing, thus depriving both of their unique existential freedom which alone makes authentic communication possible.

The movements of the *Mitwelt* are conceptualized in terms of the categories and relations which obtain in the *Umwelt*, and man becomes a tool or utensil which can be used by another, or a mere object or thing. The "anonymous one," thus depersonalized, moves in the realm of the customs, habits, and conventions of everyday life. He succumbs to what Heidegger calls the everydayness of existence. He simply takes on the mechanical habits, the established customs, and the accepted conventions of everyday life. The "anonymous one" is further characterized by an "averageness" in which the average becomes the measure of his potentialities and the final standard for his creativity. He lives by a spurious "golden mean" in which social behavior is calculated on the basis of socially binding "laws of averages." This leads to a leveling process in which all superiority is flattened and all originality trivialized. Publicity is another existential quality of the "anonymous one." He "opens" himself to the public, conforms to its demands and opinions, accepts its standards, and thus retreats from personal commitment and responsible decision. *Das Man* designates that leveled and reduced self which thinks what the public thinks, feels what the public feels, and does what the public does.

In the various projects of his "being-in-the-world" *Dasein* is disclosed to himself as a creature of care or concern. His existential relation to his environmental world is a relation of practical concern, and his relation to his communal world is one of personal concern. Man's engagement or involvement in his practical and personal projects discloses *Dasein* as that being whose movements are peculiarly characterized by the existential quality of concern. Concern is the ground determinant of the being of *Dasein*. Concern permeates every modality of his "being-in-the-world." Heidegger finds it to be significant that this existential self-understanding of human being as concern was already expressed in an old Latin myth attributed to Hyginus, the compiler of Greek mythology:

As Concern was going across a river she saw some clay. Thoughtfully she took a piece of it and began to form it. As she was contemplating that which she had made, Jupiter appeared. Concern begged Jupiter to bestow spirit upon that which she had formed. This wish Jupiter happily granted her. But when Concern wished to give her name to that which she had made, Jupiter protested and demanded that his name be used. While Concern and Jupiter were disputing over the name, Earth arose and demanded that her name be used as it was she who had offered a piece of her body. The disputing parties sought out Saturn as judge, and he submitted the following decision: "You, Jupiter, as you have given the spirit, shall take the spirit at death. You, Earth, as you have given the body, you shall then again receive the body. But Concern, since she has first formed this creature, may possess it as long as it lives. And as there is a dispute concerning the name, so let it be called 'homo' as it has been made out of earth (humus)."

The fable clearly expresses the point that man has his source in concern, and concern will permeate his being as long as he lives. Man's being-in-the-world has the indelible stamp of concern. Also, the fable is explicit in showing that it is Saturn (time) who submits the final decision relative to the nature of man, making it clear that temporality provides the ontological ground and inner meaning of this creature that has been formed by concern.

The peculiar task of Heidegger's phenomenological ontology is that of a delineation of the constitutive features of *Dasein*, who has been defined as Concern. The three foundational features of *Dasein*, all of which have attached to them a temporal significance, are factuality, existentiality, and fallenness.

The factuality of *Dasein* characterizes man's naked "thereness"—his abandonment or "throwness." As he discloses himself in the various concerns of his being-in-the-world, man finds that he has been thrown into a world without consultation and abandoned to the chance factors which have already constituted him. He discovers himself as already brought into being, a fact among facts, part of a going concern, involved in situations which he has not created and in which he must remain as long as he is. In Heidegger's analysis of factuality we can anticipate the significance of temporality as the final ontological meaning of concern. Factuality expresses primarily the directionality of pastness. *Dasein* reveals himself as *already* being-in-the-world. He is already begun and has a past through which he has been defined and shaped. His factuality is his destiny.

The second constitutive structure of *Dasein* is existentiality. This structure points to man's disclosure of himself as a project and a possibility. Man is that which he has been, but he also is that which he can become. Man finds himself thrown into the world, but he also experiences freedom and responsibility to transform his world and redefine himself in his concerns with it. This involves an apprehension of human being in terms of possibilities. *Dasein* as possibility is projected into the future. Thus, existentiality is temporally rooted in futurity as factuality is rooted in the past. In a sense existentiality and factuality are polar elements of human being. By virtue of his factuality man is always already thrown into a situation; by virtue of his existentiality he exists as possiblity and understands himself as moving into a future.

The third structural element in the ontological constitution of *Dasein* is *fallenness*. Fallenness points to the universal tendency of man to lose himself in his present preoccupations and concerns, alienating himself from his unique and personal future possibilities. Fallen man exists as mere presence, retreating from his genuine self which always involves his past and his future. He thus becomes a reduced self. The fallenness of human being receives its most trenchant expression in the movements of gossip, curiosity, and ambiguity. Gossip is an unauthentic modification of speech which simply repeats the accepted, everyday, conventional, and shallow interpretations of the public. No decisive content is communicated, because gossip is concerned only with a reiteration of the clichés which reflect the present and restricted world horizons of the "anonymous one." Curiosity, which is always allied with gossip, indicates man's insatiable desire to explore everything in his present environment simply for the sake of discovering novelty—not for the purpose of authentic understanding, but simply to engage in pursuits which will provide momentary distraction. Ambiguity is the lack of comprehension and singleness of purpose which results when the self has forfeited its unique possibilities in its preoccupation with the present. Thus, factuality, existentiality, and fallenness constitute the three basic ontological structures of human being. These structures are correspondingly rooted in the three modes of temporality—past, future, and present. Factuality qualifies *Dasein* as already-in-the-world, having arrived from a past; existentiality qualifies him as purposive or as existing in-advance-of-himself; and fallenness qualifies him as present with the world in his everyday concerns.

A phenomenological description which seeks to penetrate to the immediate experience of being-in-the-world will need to give disciplined attention to the phenomenon of anxiety. Anxiety is described by Heidegger as a ground-determinant of the human situation. Anxiety is the basic mood which discloses the threatening character of the world by confronting man with his irremovable finitude. Anxiety, first of all, should not be confused with fear. Fear has a definite object which can be specified either within the region of the environmental world or the communal world. A utensil, an object, or a person constitutes the source of fear. But the source of anxiety remains indeterminate. That which threatens cannot be localized or specified. It remains indefinable. The source of anxiety is nothingness. Through anxiety man encounters the nothingness which is constitutive of his finitude. Anxiety, properly understood, is an intentional disclosure. It is an instance of pretheoretical intentionality, pointing to and revealing a most vital aspect of one's being-in-the-world. The theoretical intentionality of pure thought can never disclose nothingness because thought is always directed to an object, but nothingness can never be objectivized or conceptualized. It can be experienced only on a pretheoretical and preobjective level. The interior of human being remains opaque to purely theoretical analysis. It can be penetrated only through preobjective elucidation and description. This accounts for Heidegger's emphasis on the phenomenological importance of man's "preconceptual understanding of Being." The nothingness, preobjectively disclosed through anxiety, brings *Dasein* face to face with his radical finitude. The accentuation of the principle of finitude is a theme which runs throughout the whole of Heidegger's philosophy. His *Daseinsanalytik* is in its central intention a philosophy of human finitude. In this disclosure of nothingness and finitude anxiety also reveals the contingency of human existence and the threat of meaninglessness. Anxiety breaks down the superficial, surface realities which conceal man's true predicament and reveals the world as something strange and uncanny. The trusted world of everyday and mediocre concerns collapses. What was previously a refuge of security and contentment now becomes strange and puzzling. The world has nothing more to offer. Its former significance is reduced to insignificance. All protections and supports vanish. Nothing remains.

As anxiety discloses man's finitude, so also it discloses his indelible transitoriness—his "being-unto-death." The death which is examined in Heidegger's phenomenological analysis is not the death of the "death-bed," or death understood as the biological termination of empirical reality. Such a view of death is an objectivized view which can be understood only by the one observing, never by the one who has to die. The "being-unto-death" of which Heidegger speaks is an experience of death which interpenetrates one's subjectivity. It is a death which one understands and appropriates in one's existential concerns. It is a mode of existence which *Dasein* takes over as soon as he is. Death is a phenomenon which embraces the whole of life and entails a responsiblity for life. In anticipating his final and irrevocable limit of being-in-the-world, *Dasein* appraises himself in light of the finite possibilities which precede his end, shoulders his reponsiblity for these possibilities, and authentically chooses himself as a whole. As had already been taught by Kierkegaard, death makes a difference for life. The anticipation of death infuses every choice with existential urgency. Man's possibilities are limited by his final end—which is always imminent. As soon as man is born he is old enough to die. Thus, he must seek to take over his death by affirming himself with the whole of his being in every decisive moment. But for the most part man engages in a retreat or flight from his having to die. He loses himself in an unauthentic being-unto-death, whereby death is objectivized and externalized as an "on-hand" factuality which befalls man in general but no one in particular. This is the death of the "anonymous one." An authentic being-unto-death, on the other hand, is an awareness of death as a unique possibility which I, and I alone, will have to face. Numerous responsibilities are transferable and can be carried out by proxy. But no such transferability is possible

for the task of dying. There is no dying by proxy. Every *Dasein* must die his
own death.

Conscience and guilt play a dominant role in Heidegger's *Daseinsanalytik*.
Conscience is defined as the "call of concern" which summons man to an
awareness of his existential guilt. Man as such is guilty. Guilt is an inevitable
and irreducible determinant of human being. The guilt which is under discussion in *Being and Time* is quite clearly not a moral quality which man may
or may not possess. It is a determinant of his finite existence as such. The
concept of guilt in Heidegger's analysis is a transmoral concept. The moral
view of guilt is rooted in an ontology of "on-handness," wherein guilt is
externalized and defined as a "thing" or an "on-hand" reality. The common
expression of such an unauthentic, external view of guilt is the court scene
representation in which man is pronounced guilty by an external judge. The
transmoral concept of guilt understands guilt as a structural implication of
finitude and nothingness. *Dasein* as a field of concern is basically a structure
of finite possibilities, which he is free to actualize in his concrete choices.
These possibilities are primarily rooted in the future. However, the past also
holds possibilities which can be repeated. Thus, in his temporal existence
Dasein is ever projected into one or another of his possibilities, choosing one
and excluding another. Choice involves an inevitable sacrifice or exclusion of
possibilities. In every choice *Dasein* is "cutting off" possible alternatives which
might have been but are not. These nonchosen possibilities remain structurally
a part of his being and constitute one expression of the nothingness of his
existence. "The nothingness which we have in mind belongs to *Dasein*'s being-
free for his existential possibilities. This freedom *is* only in the choice of one,
which means not-having-chosen and not-being-able-to-choose the other."
Conscience calls me to my possibilities, but I must always sacrifice some of
these possibilities in choosing others. In actualizing one I am not actualizing
another, and thereby becoming guilty. Every action implies guilt, but it is
impossible to exist without acting. Thus, guilt is an irremovable quality of
human being.

One would not be too far amiss in saying that the crowning phenomenological concept in Heidegger's *Daseinsanalytik* is resolution. Anxiety has disclosed nothingness and finitude, and has revealed a world without supports.
The exisential reality of death has made man aware of his ephemeral or
transitory being. Conscience has summoned *Dasein* to an acknowledgment
of his inevitable guilt. But man must drive beyond these discontinuities of
existence and affirm his being. He does this through resolution. Resolution
thus becomes a *sine qua non* for authentic existence. This resolution is given
its final meaning in Heidegger's seminal interpretation of the character of
human time. Heidegger's analysis of time is in a real sense the focal point of
the whole discussion in *Being and Time*. Central to Heidegger's analysis is his
distinction between the quantitative, objective, and scientifically measured

clock time, and the qualitative, subjective time of human concern. Quantitative time is understood as an endless, passing, irreversible succession of discrete, objectivized nows. Nows are conceptualized as "on-hand" entities, thus betraying the restriction of this view of time to the region of "*Vorhandensein.*" In "clock time" present moments are viewed as discrete entities. Some moments have gone by and we call them the past. They are no longer real. Some moments are yet to come and we call them the future. They are not yet real. Only the present is real. Qualitative or existential time, as contrasted with "clock time," understands time as an ecstatic unity. The past, future, and present are inseparable phases of the care-structure of human existence. "Temporality temporalizes itself fully in each ecstasy, *i.e.*, in the ecstatic unity of the complete temporalizing of temporality there is grounded the wholeness of the structural complex of existentiality, factuality, and fallenness, which comprises the unity of the care-structure." In existential time the past is *still* real and the future is *already* real. Whereas quantitative time gives priority to the present, existential time gives priority to the future. Man's concerns are primarily oriented to the future. However, the past retains its significance in an existential view of time. The past is never existentially finished. It holds possibilities which can be repeated. Thus, we find Heidegger insisting on the importance of the notion of repetition—a notion which was introduced into modern philosophy by Kierkegaard.

Existential time provides the ontological horizon for man's self-understanding of his historicity. *Dasein* exists historically, which means that he is always arriving from a past, moving into a future, and deciding in the present what he is to become. The authentic self faces the future in resolution. Man achieves integrity when he apprehends himself in his temporal and historical movements, acknowledges his past and future possibilities, appraises himself in light of his final possibility (death), and chooses in the moment with the *whole* of his being. Such a self is unified or authentic. Authenticity and unauthenticity thus receive their final clarification in Heidegger's discussion of time and history. The unauthentic self of the "anonymous one" is a reduced self—a self which has lost itself by virtue of its fall into the mode of "on-handness" and its consequent sacrifice to the present. The "anonymous one" exists in a depersonalized and objectivized mode, in which he has dispersed himself in present concerns to the neglect of both future and past. The time which becomes normative for the "anonymous one" is the quantitative time of the clock and the calendar. But this time applies only to the mode of "on-handness." The final meaning of unauthenticity is thus found in the tendency of man to reduce himself and other selves to "on-hand" reality—to a thing or an object—which has no temporal significance beyond its simple presence as a discrete now. The authentic time of human existence is a unique, qualitative time in which past and future are always copresent. *Dasein* exists authentically when he acknowledges the unique qualitative time of his personal being, and seeks to unify the three ecstasies which are structurally a part of his being as long as he is. These ecstasies are unified in resolute choice. The resolute *Dasein* thus achieves or wins his authenticity when he takes over his unique past, anticipates his unique future, and chooses in such a manner that his past and future are integrated. The past is held in memory, the future is courageously faced, and the moment is creatively affirmed as the "opportune time" for decisive action.—*C.O.S.*

PERTINENT LITERATURE

Macquarrie, John. *Martin Heidegger*. Richmond, Virginia: John Knox Press, 1968.

This brief survey of Martin Heidegger's thought through approximately 1960 by one of the cotranslators of *Sein und Zeit* provides one of the most lucid clarifications of key concepts in *Being and Time* that is available. John Macquarrie asserts, to begin with, that the quest for Being provides the unity that holds all of Heidegger's work together and that those who insist that there is little relationship between the earlier and the later work have become so bogged down in details that they do not perceive Heidegger's philosophy as pervaded by the grand strategy of the dialectic between existence and Being. The structure of this dialectic was traced out in the opening pages of *Being and Time* itself in the discussion of the "hermeneutical circle." Not to be confused with the kind of circular reasoning that consists in begging the question, the hermeneutical circular way of thinking involves a continual interpretation and reinterpretation in which understanding of Being that is already given with human existencce itself is rounded out and corrected while, correspondingly, human existence itself becomes progressively understood in the light of Being.

Macquarrie's exposition of Heidegger's existential analytic proceeds along a way that nicely delineates phases of this progression. First he shows how the threefold structure of care constitutes the Being of everyday *Dasein*. *Dasein* is disclosed as ahead-of-itself in its possibility, in its projecting, and in its understanding. It is pictured as already-in-a world in its facticity, its thrownness, and its affective states. Finally it is seen as close-to-its-world, or absorbed in its world, in its falling, in its immersion in the "they," and in its scattering of its possibilities. Macquarrie stresses that up to this point Heidegger sees the analytic as confirmed by the way men generally—particularly poets—have perennially seen care to be that which is distinctively human. Yet any such delineation considers man only on the level of his routine, everyday existing, in his fragmentariness and inauthenticity. The analytic is extended beyond itself and these limits are broken through, Macquarrie points out, when Heidegger turns his attention to the phenomena of death and conscience. For it is death which allows the *Dasein* to be grasped as a whole, and it is conscience which discloses to *Dasein* the possibility of authenticity in the sense of being its own, something that it has itself expressly chosen.

Macquarrie considers Heidegger's subtle discussion of death and dying to be among the most interesting in *Being and Time*. He maintains that Heidegger does not encourage meditative brooding on death. Rather, his concern is to show that if no thought is given to death and the future stretches out indefinitely, any sense of urgency or responsiblity in life is gone. *Dasein* is being-toward-death, and in recognizing this fact rather than fleeing from it *Dasein* turns toward an authentic existence, an "eschatological" existence, as Macquarrie terms it. Macquarrie considers that for Heidegger death is to be thought of as a kind of "perspective." As the organization of a picture is found in the convergence of perspectives toward a vanishing point, so for *Dasein*, death is that unifying point that organizes all life's possibilities.

Conscience as the authentic self's calling itself back from lostness in the "they" is the opposite of the voice of society or Sigmund Freud's superego, which only dominates and stifles the individual. It is the awareness of how it is with oneself.

Neither death nor conscience, although it isolates *Dasein* from the mass in allowing the self to confront the true self, isolates *Dasein* from community. Macquarrie repeatedly emphasizes that since Being-with is one of the fundamental existentalia of *Dasein*, community for Heidegger must be an indispensable dimension of authentic existence. And, more importantly, he shows that for Heidegger the resoluteness of a whole and authentic life opens out on the history of peoples as the focus of the relationship between man and Being.

Under the heading "Temporality and History," Macquarrie shows Heidegger in *Being and Time* penetrating still further into the structure of existence as he replaces the substantial soul with temporality, thereby providing a more appropriate model for understanding the complex and dynamic character of human life. Man is not, as is the thing, simply *in* time. Only as deteriorated or fallen does man appear as scattered among his immediate concerns, hopping along from one now point to the next. Authentic *Dasein* exhibits "the unity of a future which makes present in the process of having been." Macquarrie goes so far as to say that although Heidegger's is certainly a secular philosophy, nevertheless, inasmuch as *Dasein* transcends the "now" and thus can attain to genuine selfhood, Heideggerian man realizes a kind of "eternal life" within time—yet not in isolation. It is man's temporality that unites him with the historical community. Here the hermeneutical circle again comes into view. It is only because we are historical—oriented to the future, grounded in possibility rather than in fact—that we can take up the study and interpretation of history. History as the life of peoples is what reveals to us "the authentic repeatable possibilities of *Dasein*."

Thus in all of Heidegger's later writings that deal with the past—particularly in his studies of the philosophers that compose the destruction of ontology, originally intended for the last volume of *Being and Time*—Macquarrie sees Heidegger fetching back the possibility that the past contains to make it present in our existence now. This going back through the history of philosophy permits Heidegger to find those places where the forgetting of Being has taken place so that the genuine insights of the beginning may be recovered and made creative for our time.

Biemel, Walter. *Martin Heidegger: An Illustrated Study*. Translated by J. L. Mehta. New York: Harcourt Brace Jovanovich, 1976.

Walter Biemel's book is probably the best brief study in English of Martin Heidegger's work as a whole. Its translator, J. L. Mehta, has himself written an excellent book on Heidegger. Biemel begins his chapter on *Being and Time* by stating that this is not a difficult book to read. It becomes difficult, however, when we attempt to understand it in the light of its fundamental intention, which is to inquire about the meaning of Being. Although *Dasein* is at the center of Heidegger's attention in *Being and Time*, he treats human existence not as subject or consciousness merely, but as the being that has a peculiar relationship to Being. This relationship is secured, oddly, through Being's having a relationship to itself. For unlike other entities man not only *is*; he *has* to be, in that his being is imposed upon him as a task. *Dasein* cannot be defined in its essence by citing "what" it is. Its essence lies in the fact that it always "has its being to be." Its being is always at issue for it.

Since the analysis of *Dasein* is intended by Heidegger as a preparation for the development of the question about the meaning of Being, it is not surprising that after pursuing a provocative account of the basic structures of human existence delineated in *Being and Time*, Biemel brings that account to culmination in a discussion of Heidegger's inquiry into the connection between Being and truth. *Being and Time*, quite properly, is shown to contain only the earliest stages of an inquiry which is elaborated and made more profound in Heidegger's later writings.

Biemel is at pains to show how, in his characteristic way, Heidegger starts with the ordinary understanding of truth which has hardened and come to appear definite, and then moves back to the primordial phenomenon as it was prior to the hardening that has covered it up. The definition of truth that was first propounded in the Middle Ages on the basis of a misinterpretation of Aristotle and that remained current well beyond Immanuel Kant is *adequatio intellectus et rei*, the correspondence of the intellect to the thing. But, Heidegger asserts, intellect and thing are in no way similar. How, then, can they correspond? Or even more baffling, since this definition of truth implies on the one side of the correspondence the act of real judging and on the other side the ideal content referred to in the act of judging, when we consider that this ideal content itself often refers in turn to something real or concrete, is it not obvious that knowing and judging often are severed into two disparate ways or "levels" of being which never can be seen capable of being united? As an interpretation of our actual experience of knowing, is this not a ridiculous distortion?

Heidegger's search for a more adequate interpretation begins with a simple phenomenological analysis of the act of coming to know that something is true. When we attempt to verify a statement such as "the picture on the wall is hanging askew," we are not concerned with a psychical event or a process of representation: We are concerned with the thing itself. The proof of such a statement lies in perceiving. Through the latter the entity in question is "dis-covered." It becomes accessible in its being. It is this disclosure that our statement sets forth. Thus Heidegger can say that "to be true is to-be-discovering." The stress is on the *laying open* of a thing and not on the conformity of mental processes with an ideal content which is then believed to inhere in something real.

Building on what he claims to be the genuinely Greek view of truth, Heidegger regards being-true (*aletheuein*) as a mode of being of *Dasein*. It is *Dasein* that acts in a "discovering" manner. The true in the most primal sense is the action of letting something become accessible and without cover, and only secondarily the thing that becomes uncovered. Thus Heidegger's well-known words "*Dasein* is in the truth" do not mean that *Dasein* possesses all truth. That would be absurd. Rather it means that *Dasein* is in a position to "disclose." It is able to-be-discovering only because it stands in a peculiar relation to itself as the being that is alert and open, directing itself toward possibility and, as being-in-the-world, actively encountering and showing to itself whatever comes into its ken. This is not to revert to subjectivism and to say simply that consciousness is self-consciousness, Biemel insists. It is crucial to remember that for Heidegger the fundamental structure of *Dasein* is being-in-the-world. Being-in-the-world includes the existentalia which are caught up in care and grounded in the temporalization of *Dasein*. *Dasein* projects itself forward onto its possibilities, opening up a world, and finds itself ever in a particular world which presupposes the temporalization of its "has-been." In projecting, *Dasein* may understand itself either authentically in terms of its ownmost possibilities or inauthentically in terms of the world to which it has forfeited itself. The latter mode of self-comprehension is no less definitive than is the former. The openness of *Dasein* is its primordial truth, but *Dasein* is "equioriginally in both truth and untruth."

Heidegger names the prefix in *aletheia* (truth) the "alpha-privitive." For entities are forever being snatched out of concealment, so that discoveredness or unconcealedness is a kind of robbery. Discoveredness must constantly be wrested from illusion and guarded, lest it fall back into dissimulation.

In closing his chapter, Biemel rejoins the theme with which he began. That

Dasein exists in the mode of being open is not only what distinguishes it from all other beings, but it is also what makes possible *Dasein's* understanding of Being. For *Dasein* finds its closest relation to Being in finding itself in or in returning to its inmost selfhood in resoluteness, which is being-toward-death—the foremost mode of being true.

Macomber, W. B. *The Anatomy of Disillusion: Martin Heidegger's Notion of Truth*. Evanston, Illinois: Northwestern University Press, 1967.

This very provocative and informative book throws light on the entire range of Martin Heidegger's philosophy through elevating a simple illustration that Heidegger uses in *Being and Time* to an absolutely key position. The analogy of the broken hammer confronts us in some way on nearly every one of its pages. W. B. Macomber is indeed right in maintaining that a unitive vision informs the development of Heidegger's thought from beginning to end, but it is somewhat doubtful that the hammer analogy is adequate to bear the weight of his demonstration of his view.

Macomber stresses that for Heidegger all things, whether natural or man-made, first appear to us as instruments. Always we are engaged in *using* the beings in our world prior to *knowing* them. For invariably they "mani-fest" themselves to the careful hand before they come into view for the speculative eye. In fact, readers of the later Heidegger are admonished not to lose sight of the fact that, as shown in *Being and Time*, *Dasein* first lets a being be by using it within the context of its specified project. For Heidegger, "mani-pulating" is originally a necessary complement to "letting-be" (*Sein lassen*).

And yet, when a thing serves a useful function it is essentially inconspicuous. For *Dasein's* ordinary encounter with the instrumental complex or "all-em-bracing workshop" that comprises its world is not a conscious encounter in which beings manifest their real presence. Although open to its world through a kind of practical vision which Heidegger calls "Umsicht" (a word Macomber translates as "prudence" or "pro-vision"), *Dasein* is primordially so preoc-cupied with the work to be done that it takes no notice of the instrument that it is using. The true being of a particular thing remains hidden behind its function.

Only when *Dasein* confronts an impasse and can no longer proceed with its work—when the hammer breaks or the typewriter ribbon wears out—is it called back out of preoccupation with the future-oriented project to specific awareness of the present. *Dasein* recognizes now what the individual instru-ment is, what end its function serves, and what its relationship is to the other instruments within the work complex. And for the first time *Dasein* becomes specifically aware of its workshop as opening out upon the environment and the world. What was previously implicit becomes explicit. Even *Dasein's* own selfhood is revealed to it in the question that it is forced to ask itself: What do I do now?

Macomber emphasizes the fleetingness of this Heideggerian moment of revelation. For the deficient tool is immediately taken up into a new human project as *Dasein* sets out to repair, process, or discard it. The instrument withdraws again from human awareness. Yet *Dasein*, in experiencing a gap in the referential structure of its world and so stumbling upon the void, encounters the primordial Nothingness from out of which all truth (*aletheia*) arises. It is in their very vanishing as usable objects that things become transciently and mysteriously present to us in their truth.

Macomber points out that only in one other realm, namely, in the revelatory sphere of the work of art, does Heidegger find truth emerging so forcefully and inescapably. But he doubts whether art, although accorded this special-role, is, after all, decisively different from the practical world where instruments hold a central place. It is not surprising, Macomber thinks, that many modern artists from the Dada movement onward have regarded their art as a broken instrument. In every other realm of human endeavor, he believes, Heidegger himself clearly finds the model of the broken instrument to be applicable. The sequence of activity, breakdown, and awareness is omnipresent in experience. To illustrate the fact, Macomber expands upon Heidegger's claim that the status of a science must be judged according to its capacity to experience crisis in its fundamental concepts, crisis originating not in cognitive difficulties or in a breakdown in thinking, as both Plato and Aristotle supposed, but grounded in a breakdown in *Dasein*'s very being-in-the-world, from out of which all thinking emerges.

Even Heidegger's own philosophy, Macomber is quick to point out, is founded on an understanding of man's relation to Being that lay beyond the grasp of previous thinkers so long as the traditional definition of man was functioning adequately. With the breakdown of the conception of man in the second quarter of the twentieth century, Heidegger has been able to glimpse man in his more fundamental dimensions. One can only say "glimpse"—and what an effervescent glimpsing it would be!—for according to Macomber's view the implication is clear that just as the instrument withdraws again when it is given a function within a new project, so the true being of man must constantly be lost sight of in Heidegger's ongoing project of elaborating a new philosophy.—*C.W.L.*

ADDITIONAL RECOMMENDED READING

Fell, Joseph P. *Heidegger and Sartre: An Essay on Being and Place.* New York: Columbia University Press, 1979. The first five chapters of this impressive book throw much light on the ontology of *Being and Time* by contrasting it with that of Jean-Paul Sartre's *Being and Nothingness.*

King, Magda. *Heidegger's Philosophy: A Guide to His Basic Thought.* New York: Macmillan Publishing Company, 1964. This book provides easy ac-

cess to *Being and Time* for the beginner. It is clear and accurate while still
doing justice to the profundity and complexity of Heidegger's thinking.

Kockelmans, Joseph. *Martin Heidegger: A First Introduction to His Philosophy*. Pittsburgh: Duquesne University Press, 1965. This is a systematic
and very readable treatment of *Being and Time* with some attempt, in the
last chapters, to relate its themes to Heidegger's later works.

Langan, Thomas. *The Meaning of Heidegger: A Critical Study of an Existentialist Phenomenology*. New York: Columbia University Press, 1959. Langan restricts himself in his highly articulate analysis of *Being and Time* to
an existentialist view of its principal themes. Since he regards Heidegger's
later writings as substitutes for the unpublished sections of *Being and Time*,
he imposes an existentialist interpretation on them also.

Marx, Werner. *Heidegger and the Tradition*. Translated by Theodore Kisiel
and Murray Greene. Evanston, Illinois: Northwestern University Press,
1971. One of the best works on Heidegger in any language, Marx's book
contains in Chapter II an excellent account of the way *Dasein* in *Being and
Time* replaces the traditional notions of substance and subject.

Richardson, William J., S. J. *Heidegger: Through Phenomenology to Thought*.
The Hague, The Netherlands: Martinus Nijhoff, 1963. The single aim of
this monumental work is to reach an understanding of what Heidegger
means by thought. Its eighty-page analysis of *Being and Time* is remarkably
well rounded in view of its appearance as one stage along the way to that
goal.

Schmitt, Richard. *Martin Heidegger on Being Human: An Introduction to
Sein und Zeit*. New York: Random House, 1969. Despite its very un-Hei-
deggerian argumentative style and its serious neglect of the theme of time,
this is a good introduction to a number of concepts in *Being and Time* for
the American-trained philosophy student; it contains a wealth of illustrations.

REALMS OF BEING

Author: George Santayana (1863-1952)
Type of work: Metaphysics
First published: 1927-1940 (*The Realm of Essence*, 1927; *The Realm of Matter*, 1930; *The Realm of Truth*, 1938; *The Realm of Spirit*, 1940)

PRINCIPAL IDEAS ADVANCED

There is no logical escape from skepticism; all of our philosophical beliefs are expressions of animal faith in something that makes sense out of experience.

Since essences are merely characteristics considered in abstraction from things, the leap from a consideration of essence to a belief in matter is a leap of animal faith.

Truth is that part of the realm of essence which is realized in the material universe.

Spirit, or conscious intelligence, by going beyond the limits of the present in its operations makes possible a life of reason in which action is ordered for the satisfaction of animal impulse.

Santayana considered *Realms of Being* his magnum opus. It is his most comprehensive work, and may fairly be said to contain his distinctive "system" of philosophy. Here the technical details of his thought are worked out with great virtuosity. But the work was not conceived primarily as a contribution to academic philosophy. Santayana liked to think of himself as representing "human orthodoxy" in an age that was eager to pursue novelties. He was writing not for the professional philosopher so much as for reflective persons in every walk of life. His teachings were intended to be founded on common sense and upon principles which any mind can discover within itself.

It is characteristic of Santayana, however, that he combines the realism of common sense with a strong dose of transcendentalism. His thought may be said to have two focuses: it originates in questioning and doubt, and in an unmistakable predilection for poetry and imagination; but it is never able to escape the tug of impulse and desire. They bind it to the world and keep skepticism from hardening into dogma. Santayana's writings are a constant dialogue between these two interests or aspects of his thought. By questioning at each stage what they have affirmed, the writings arrive at a view which is neither skeptical nor naïve but combines something of both. His position is accurately indicated when he is classified as a *realist*; that is, as a *critical realist*.

The philosophical implications of this dual starting-point are clearly expounded in *Scepticism and Animal Faith* (1923) which is actually an introduction to the work under discussion. A vast abyss is seen to separate the mind, with its ideas, from the existing world of things. We are reminded of

Descartes by the systematic effort which Santayana makes to doubt all existence. But whereas the father of modern rationalism believed that he found in the extremity of doubt a passage from ideas to reality, Santayana freely admits to being unable to span the gulf. Logically there is no escape from skepticism; but logic is not the whole story. Every idea contemplated by the human mind is bound up with bodily impulses; there are some matters which, as animals, we *must* believe. This intentional aspect of experience, which Santayana calls "animal faith," is the basis for our convictions concerning existence. The abyss, however, remains, nor may it be lost sight of. Plato lost sight of it, ascribing reality to ideas; Descartes lost sight of it, affirming rationality of the material world; Hegel lost sight of it, ascribing existence to logic. These errors, which result from confusing the two aspects of experience, are the source of what Santayana calls "metaphysics." Since *Realms of Being* is an attempt to avoid them and their consequences, we are warned not to speak of his system as "metaphysical." (However, as a term of classification, the word fits better than any other; perhaps we can call Santayana's philosophy a *critical* metaphysics.)

When we turn from these methodological considerations to formulate a world view, two divisions are inadequate to the complexities which unfold. In pure skepticism one is confronted with *essences* which do not exist; but there exists even then something by which they are confronted: mind or *spirit*. And the commerce which we have through animal faith with the flux of things and events demands not merely that we acknowledge the existence of *matter*, but that we make a place in the realm of essence for a special province to be known as *truth*—namely, actualized essence.

Essence, matter, truth, and spirit: these are Santayana's four "realms of being." "Being," for Santayana, is pure essence, and does not, as in popular speech, mean existence. The "realms" of being are, therefore, not four regions within the total order of things, each with a status corresponding to its peculiar kind of reality. Strictly speaking, the realms are not real at all: they are "summary categories of logic, meant to describe a single natural dynamic process, and to dismiss from organized reflection all unnecessary objects of faith."

The Realm of Essence: Santayana relates that an early hint of his "essences" came to him when he heard William James criticizing Spencer for saying that a thing passes from indefinite to definite. "Nothing," said James, "can be indefinite. Make a blot of ink at random on a piece of paper. The spot is not indefinite: it has precisely the outline that it has." This kind of determination, whether of an inkblot or a copybook letter, is what "essence" means in modern philosophy. The essence of the color which is before your eyes is precisely *that* kind of color, of the melody which sounds in your ears, *that* kind of melody. Take away from the image every association with its material support or with the mind which attends it: essences are the "characters" which things assume, or which minds contemplate. But, besides these, there are an innumerable multitude of essences which are never actualized either in matter or in thought. Each is individual, concrete, and absolutely and eternally what it is.

The reader, searching for historical analogies, must not think of medieval realists with their Platonizing metaphysics, but of the nominalists and particularly of Berkeley. According to Santayana, each essence is absolutely independent of every other: essences are not subordinated under one another as species and genus. Thus, the "realm of essence" is not to be thought of as a hierarchy of ideas, as an eternal Logos, in which essences are rationally connected and necessarily follow from each other. There is no eternal Reason in heaven or in the earth.

It is true that Santayana stresses with emphasis dialectic and the connections between ideas; but these connections (with the exception of purely analytical ones) are grounded not in the ideas themselves but in the bias of the mind which entertains them. All rational processes have organic roots, are expressions of the same animal intent which affords us our belief in the material world. Thus, the rational processes do not trace eternal truths but human interests. The *a priori* elements of our thought are preformations of the psyche, mental habits which result when an intention becomes settled in the mind. Our efforts after logical cogency are a healthy endeavor after consistency, which is to say, mental harmony and peace. A finished system is a monument to the spirit which composes it. But since systems of ideas are influenced by traditions of various sorts, different systems have become classic and orthodox. But of these orthodoxies, no one is right against another, for there is no external standard by which they may be judged: the only measure of a system is its overall adequacy.

But just as there is no necessary order in the realm of essence, so things on the plane of existence have no rational connection with each other. They are in flux, and temporarily embody first one essence then another: but between the essence which comes before and that which comes after there is no dialectical relation. Causality is not in the order of logic. Neither is the hierarchy of goods. Every instance of essence in nature perfectly realizes its own essence; if we judge one thing to be more nearly perfect than another, it is again by reference to our interests.

The Realm of Matter: Matter represents the opposite pole to essence. We do not, according to Santayana, have any clear knowledge of what matter is, and when we talk about it we must be careful to distinguish between matter and some conventional idea of it—whether Aristotle's or Democritus' or Descartes' or the modern physicist's. As Santayana conceives it, matter is the "flux of existence." It has no characteristic form, but it is that which is constantly assuming first one essence and then another. We do not know it directly or even by inference, but by a kind of "transcendental reflection" analogous to that used by Kant. That is, in order to make our experience intelligible to us, we must postulate this substance which gives actuality to certain essences and provides a field for our bodily action. Following these hints, we go on to postulate concerning matter that it persists, that its quantity remains the same, that each phase of matter is determined by what goes before. But these are idols of the mind, as is indeed our whole concept of an orderly nature.

Matter, then, is the host of essences. It is in flux, perpetually leaving one essence and taking another. But patterns and rhythms are observable within the change. We distinguish as a "natural moment" the interval during which a given essence is realized, and observe several moments forming configurations that we call "events." The essence which is realized by the total complex event we may call a "trope." Examples of tropes are the vibrations within a molecule, the pulse of a heart, the combination of sounds that make up a spoken word, the life cycle of an organism, a historical epoch such as the Renaissance. Santayana does not think of tropes as perspectives, relative to an observer: they are actual structures realized in the flux.

One kind of trope has particular interest in a comprehensive work such as the present one: it is the human psyche, which, according to Santayana, is a complex of tropes, partly in conflict, partly in harmony with one another. This is not supposed to be astonishing, as if inert matter spontaneously gives rise to something as alien as life and spirit. On the contrary, we know nothing about pure matter, and must understand it as a very fertile kind of stuff which does all sorts of unpredictable things. The "laws" which we observe in nature are not to be thought of as binding. Whenever chance produces a trope sufficiently harmonious with itself and with its environment, it tends to survive. In this way complex organisms and even conscious beings have established themselves. The soul or psyche is the sum of vital tendencies which govern the animal. In man, as in the humbler creatures, the soul's activities are almost entirely unconscious and automatic. This is not to deny that man's higher consciousness makes a difference—that it opens up to him vast new possibilities of modifying his behavior and controlling his environment. But always behavior is determined by psyche, a trope in the realm of matter. And this is no less true of intelligent and purposive acts than of instinctive and habitual ones. Consciousness may enlighten our motives, but the motives are rooted in bodily needs, and their execution depends upon adjustments and skills that have already become automatic.

The Realm of Truth: As matter clothes itself in this essence and that, it gives rise to a new realm of being, namely "truth." Truth does not belong to the material world, and it is not to be confused with events or tropes. It belongs to the realm of essence, of which it is a segment—that special segment which comes to have the special dignity of being actualized in matter. In fact, when Santayana began thinking about *Realms of Being* (as early as 1911), there were only three realms—no separate realm of truth. But the distinction between the logical determinations of essence and their material determination is a basic one for an opponent of rationalism. If it is established on the categorical level, many confusions are avoided. Hence, the decision to make truth a separate realm.

The view of truth here held to is, according to Santayana, the view of common sense—presupposed not merely in our pursuit of knowledge but in all our animal striving. The facts of the world are independent of our opinions. The essence which is realized in fact is "truth." The realm of truth is absolute and eternal, comprehending each detail of the world and relating every event to every other.

Truth, then, is not an idea or an opinion, although these share in truth insofar as they correspond to reality. When literal correspondence is out of the question, an idea may be judged true if it rewards the psyche with success in its practical enterprises. However, utility presupposes truth, and therefore must not be regarded as synonymous with it. The notion that truth is a property of ideas and judgments is one of the aberrations of idealism which, because it denies the existence of matter, can think of ideas as being related only to other ideas.

Since truth is bound up with existence, there is no purely logical truth. Mathematics, for example, which concerns only the relationship between essences, is formally cogent, but not true. Only when mathematics is applied to the world of existence is it brought into this new dimension. We have seen that the formal relation that may be traced between essences does not bind the behavior of things in which the essences are embodied. Nevertheless, mathematics has proved a useful fiction in describing the basic rhythms and tropes of the natural world. In this context, its theorems share in the truth. By the same token, the more dramatic images of poetry and myth can sometimes establish the claim to be true: for we must think humanly, and the truth for man often takes on a dramatic quality. Statistics and pointer-readings are inadequate to express the moral reality with which he is always concerned.

And so we come to an important consideration about *knowledge*, which must be carefully distinguished from truth. The latter is comprehensive, impartial, and free from any vagueness or uncertainty. Knowledge, on the other hand, is always limited, biased, and subject to error and doubt. Knowledge, because it aims at truth, makes claims about existence; but, as we have seen, every existential assertion rests at last on animal faith. Faith, therefore, is implicit in knowledge, which, on this account, can never have that certainty, self-evidence, and immutability which Plato and Descartes claimed for it. These high attributes are proper enough to dialectic and intuition, which deal only with essences; but knowledge is the pursuit of truth.

The Realm of Spirit: In introducing the consideration of knowledge and intuition, we have already entered upon the precincts of "spirit," which is Santayana's name for thought or consciousness. As we have seen, psyche is a trope within the realm of matter. It regulates the bodily behavior of the organism according to principles best understood in mechanical terms. Actually, it is a system of tropes which not infrequently are in conflict with each other and at odds with circumstances. These tensions, it would seem, are what generate awareness in the higher animals—pain being the prime example. In man this inner sensibility achieves sufficient steadiness to enter upon a life of its own.

Spirit's attachment to psyche insures that in the first instance it will bring to consciousness the urges, satisfactions, and disappointments of the body. But its spontaneity enables it to go beyond the limits of actual experience, to entertain ideas that are not present, and to invent new ones. Thus, there may grow up between spirit, with its ideals, and the actual world, a conflict which leads to melancholy. When this happens too often, spirit turns out to be a liability to psyche's health. But if the spirit submits to the measure of truth, it can become psyche's truest friend, bringing new scope and perspective into man's activity, revealing to him the limits of possible achievement, and prescribing a regimen for his impulses which will lead to harmony and satisfaction. This is what Santayana describes as the "life of reason." Its use is to bring about the best adjustment between the human body and its environment.

But although the spirit renders a service to the organism, it has motives of its own. Even the most harmonious animal existence falls far short of its ideal, and if spirit is to escape from sorrow and discouragement, it must do so by fixing on other goals than those which make up the will of the particular psyche to which it is attached. If we can think of a will running through all existence, we may say that spirit finds its freedom and peace by resigning so far as possible the unique prerogatives which its own will claims, and uniting itself with the will of every struggling thing. Santayana designates this moment of spirit's coming of age by the word *metanoia* ("conversion") and the new frame of mind as *charity*.

The task of delineating this liberation and fulfillment of spirit takes up the greater part of the fourth volume, involving an extended critique of the greatest religions and philosophies of life. Salvation is not to be gained by repudiating consciousness and sinking into an organic stupor, as some mystics recommend; but neither does it consist in a purely intellectual vision of the truth. While spirit must be loyal to its own affinities, which lie in the realm of essence, it cannot repudiate the existing world of which it is a part. Thus, it cannot deny matter and, in particular, the wills of living things. Naturalism and humanism seek to remedy this indifference: but merely bowing down before reality, with Spinoza and the Stoics, involves the denial of will and alienation from the good; while pledging as one's ideal a merely human good, after the manner of Socrates, involves disloyalty to Truth, since the universe is not governed for man. The ideal to which we most suitably give our allegiance is a comprehensive one, embracing in sympathy and pity the goals of every natural thing. This is what Santayana understands by charity. It is suitably represented in the Christian story of the incarnation of God, where Spirit's scope is as wide as its own life is narrow. Knowing itself as the first-born of all creatures, it does not condemn its brethren for falling short of the ideal but cherishes their good and laments their defeat. This high calling is not beyond the reach of man; for though, on Santayana's accounting, there is no God in the usual sense, and spirit is but an accident in the world, yet the fact remains that a remarkable set of harmonies within the flux of things has preceded its emergence. As nature's highest product, it may in its best moments embrace the universe's whole vast endeavor. In no lesser ideal can it find healing and rest.

The chief characteristic of this work is its catholicity, its faithfulness to the many interests which have a claim upon it. It is humanist, but not at the expense of being uncritical and unnaturalistic; it is otherworldly without ceasing to be this-worldly as well.

The peculiarity of spirit and its good is that, unlike psyche, spirit is not a power. It is not responsible for the world, but merely a guest there; neither can it do anything, only offer suggestions which psyche may or may not be persuaded to adopt.

Santayana never ceased to be interested in the possibilities of bringing intelligence to bear upon moral and political matters. But as a philosopher and contemplative he did not share the enthusiasm of most reformers, both because he held that nonrational factors (passion, tradition, habit) actually direct behavior, and because he knew that as a conscious animal man has problems that can never be resolved on a merely animal level. In other words, he affirmed his naturalism and materialism and accepted their deterministic implications, but he did not allow this to rob the spirit of independence or the immediacy of its own good, which is love without either anxiety or desire.—*J.F.*

PERTINENT LITERATURE

Sprigge, Timothy L. S. *Santayana, an Examination of His Philosophy*. London: Routledge & Kegan Paul, 1974.

Published in the new series "The Arguments of the Philosophers," this volume, which concentrates primarily on George Santayana's epistemology, ontology, and—to a lesser extent—moral philosophy, is designed to represent his thought in technically more precise language than his own style favored, in order to make him more accessible to contemporary British and American philosophers who have been schooled in analysis. Thus Timothy L. S. Sprigge ferrets out from Santayana's flowing prose exact theses, articulates arguments for and against them, and critically evaluates the result.

Concerning the doctrine of essence, Sprigge makes the following points. Whereas, although Santayana's methodological skepticism had uncovered essences as the immediate objects of consciousness and had denied their existence as given to consciousness, he nevertheless described these essences as eternal universal forms, each singularly what it is, it may seem plausible to contend that these objects of consciousness, instead of being essences, in Santayana's sense, are in fact particulars, such as sense impressions and images. Santayana, however, separates particularity from the immediate objects of consciousness and attributes it to the mental acts—intuition—by which essences are apprehended. Sprigge prefers Santayana's theory on the grounds that it preserves as essences the characteristics which, although grasped in different intuitions, remain identical. He finds equally defensible Santayana's thesis that every existing thing actualizes essences, since each thing must have definite characteristics of some sort. But he concedes that whether the essence which is intuited as the immediate object of consciousness is identical with any essence actually possessed by an external object believed to exist is problematic.

Concerning the doctrine of matter, Sprigge stresses that, despite Santayana's delineation of the properties of matter and his explications of space, time, and causality, certain knowledge of the real essences of matter is impossible. The knowledge we have in this regard rests on animal faith; it is symbolic rather than literal. Although Santayana inclined, moreover, to interpret matter in substantialist terms, Sprigge shows, by means of an analysis of Santayana's own description of matter as an existential flux, or unceasing change, that his ontology is indeed similar to the process metaphysics of Alfred North Whitehead, but without the panpsychism and the panentheism. Corollary to Santayana's materialism is his epiphenomenalism. Holding that states of mind (or consciousness) are effects produced causally by the motions of material substances, epiphenomenalism denies that mind (or consciousness) has any causal power of its own, so that it is incapable of affecting either material objects or subsequent mental states. As Sprigge remarks, Santayana's epiphenomenalism is of special interest today, particularly in light of the results of neurophysiology and other scientific investigations into the nature and role of the brain in regard to consciousness.

Concerning the doctrine of truth, Sprigge examines Santayana's distinction between discourse about relations between essences and statements about existent facts. Only the latter can be true or false, according to Santayana. Sprigge finds this thesis defensible and in line with contemporary discussions, but he considers Santayana's position in this regard extremely complicated by virtue of the ontology. For the realm of truth, on the one hand, must pertain to existence, and, on the other hand, is a subpart of the realm of essence, so that essences subtended by truth in consequence of their actualization in existence are also related to the infinite set of essences within the realm of essence proper. Another problem Sprigge probes stems from Santayana's paradoxical thesis that truth is both eternal and contingent: eternal because it consists of essences which are eternal, contingent because it consists of essences selected by the existential flux of matter, which is contingent. The paradox is aggravated by the added reflection that, as eternal, truth embraces all the essences pertinent to past, present, and future events, so that in a fundamental sense the contingency of existence, caught in the logical grip of the eternal, fades into necessity.

Concerning the doctrine of spirit, Sprigge observes that Santayana is unique. Despite his materialism and naturalism, Santayana is a loyal adherent of spirituality as the highest human ideal. Unlike those critics who charge Santayana with self-contradiction, Sprigge recommends him as a significant thinker who, while professing materialism, yet argues that spirit, although arising from matter which is its ground, yet points in the direction where man's highest good is to be found.

In sum, according to Sprigge, on the ontology of each realm of being as well as on the relations between the four realms, Santayana is the most serious and systematic thinker to write in English in the present century, excepting perhaps Whitehead. Sprigge judges that while Whitehead has the merit of a mastery of modern science and mathematical logic, Santayana has the edge in general levelheadedness.

Butler, Richard, O. P. *The Mind of Santayana*. Chicago: Henry Regnery Company, 1955.

This book grew out of the doctoral dissertation which the author, a Roman Catholic priest, prepared at the Angelicum in Rome where he was able to visit and confer with George Santayana during the philosopher's final years. Richard Butler's basic thesis is that Santayana's philosophy is intensely personal. Accordingly, Santayana did not propose objective answers to common questions in the philosophical tradition; rather he strove to resolve personal problems. Further, his philosophy stemmed from his early choice of disillusionment in place of religious faith, a choice influenced by his free-thinking and alienated mother and father, but rendered difficult by the piety of his favorite sister. Nevertheless, Santayana's choice of disillusionment inspired his philosophy of epistemological skepticism and metaphysical materialism, and it initiated him into his ultimate personal religion of detachment from existence. Butler has embellished this theme in his more popular biographical volume, *The Life and World of George Santayana* (Chicago: Henry Regnery Company, 1960). In the professedly technical volume under review, the theme, which in fact underlies the argument, is introduced in Part I and reiterated in the dialogue.

Part II of *The Mind of Santayana* is mainly devoted to an exposition of

Santayana's epistemology and ontology, although as a matter of course, criticism creeps in. Butler concentrates on Santayana's concept of essence, which he regards as the foundation stone of Santayana's whole system of philosophy. In recent philosophy the concept of essence has emerged within the context of the Anglo-American philosophical movement which Butler dubs "critical neo-realism." Essence was introduced to designate those contents or immediate objects of mental acts which function as representatives of externally existing objects. While Butler explores Santayana's various approaches to essence, he focuses on the epistemological approach by means of skepticism. For Santayana the skeptical questioning of all states and beliefs in consciousness terminates in the presence of the indubitab given which, as given, cannot be alleged to exist; this immediate given is essence. Butler scrutinizes this conception of essence, which entails a radical separation from existence; he compares and contrasts it with rival conceptions, such as Aristotle's, St. Thomas Aquinas', and others cherished in the medieval scholastic tradition. In addition to the role of essence in cognition, Butler also examines the relation of essence to the realm of truth, which Santayana described as that realm of being consisting of a subset of essences which are applicable to the existences that make up the realm of matter. When at last spirit appears as the fourth realm of being, it serves Santayana's personal purpose; it culminates in a moral yet aesthetic way of life devoted to the contemplation of essences for its own sake.

Part III is a severe criticism of Santayana's philosophy. Although Butler avows that he is interested only in demonstrating the internal inconsistency or incoherence of Santayana's thought, it is apparent that strictures from external considerations, informed by the priest's allegiance to Thomism, intrude. Thus it is alleged that Santayana's transcendental method misled him into a skepticism from which he could not escape except by blind animal faith. In other words, essences as the immediate objects of consciousness which do not exist function as symbolic of externally existing objects only insofar as there is "animal faith." Santayana's predicament is tantamount to a radical skepticism which is remedied solely by a rationally unjustifiable belief in materialism. In addition to the moral and emotional confusions in Santayana's life which account for this predicament at the psychological level, there is the fundamental ontological error of defining essence as a form of being which is devoid of existence. Consequently, essences fail to perform those functions which Santayana assigned to them, whether to explain the change and multiplicity that characterize the existential flux of matter or to serve as symbols for the knowledge of existence. However, essences successfully function as the pure moral and aesthetic objects of contemplation. Butler charges that this spiritual function of essence is idiosyncratic, however, suitable for a solitary thinker like Santayana who feels himself imprisoned by nothing but illusions and who seeks deliverance by contemplating the elements or essences of these illusions.

Munson, Thomas N., S. J. *The Essential Wisdom of George Santayana.* New York: Columbia University Press, 1962.

This book is designed to offer just what its title says—the essential, even "secret," doctrine of George Santayana. According to Thomas N. Munson, whose book originated in a doctoral dissertation which itself grew out of an M.A. thesis, the run-of-the-mill philosophical commentators and critics, who have scrutinized Santayana's writings for standard philosophical theses and justifying arguments and who have been repelled by the extraordinary style, have misunderstood the philosopher. He uncovers the secret wisdom of Santayana at two levels for analysis. The most basic level is fundamentally religious. Here Munson shares the approach of his fellow priest, Richard Butler. Santayana is portrayed as a lapsed Catholic who elected the disillusionment of materialism instead of the faith of his fathers, which he decried as mythological, but who invested belief in materialism, crowned with a precarious spirituality absorbed in the contemplation of essence, with religious feeling and conviction.

It is at the second level of analysis that Munson breaks new ground. He contends that Santayana, in consequence of his unique religious naturalism, stated his perspective in a form which seems to be akin to traditional philosophy, but which is actually criticism. For Santayana's prose depends upon a theory of language which emphasizes symbolism and which recognizes, besides the denotative and descriptive functions of symbols, their exclusively expressive functions. Conspicuous in poetry but manifest also in Santayana's prose, statements couched in expressive language are neither true nor false, but express the feelings, attitudes, and values of their author. By equating Santayana's philosophy with criticism, Munson affirms that it is neither true nor false but expressive. It is justified by the values it represents, so that it is improper to attempt, as Butler and Timothy L. S. Sprigge do, to extract arguments from Santayana's texts for the purpose of evaluating or rebutting them.

While Munson grazes over the entire range of Santayana's writings, *Realms of Being* comes into focus from time to time. In Chapter III, "The Formulation of a Philosophy," he ascribes Santayana's articulation of a system of categories of being to his felt need for an explicit intellectual foundation for the criticism in which he had already indulged in such earlier works as *The Life of Reason*; and also to his perception of the opportunity afforded by the epistemological developments in new and critical realisms.

Santayana plunged into the arena of epistemology. Employing the skeptical method, he discovered essences at its terminus. According to Munson's interpretation, Santayana regarded essences as names—that is, as symbols for external, existing realities. The doctrine of essence opens into a theory of language; at the same time it confirms Santayana's transcendentalism, epitomized by his preoccupation with spirituality. On the one hand, essences are intuited, and intuitions are the activities of spirit, viewed as the ethereal aura of the corporeal psyche. On the other hand, Munson holds, essences themselves are purely subjective effects within the psyche.

Because it is, according to Santayana's theory, impossible to intuit the real essences of existing things, all of which are represented symbolically and known by means of animal faith, the belief that objective existence is matter rests on faith. Hence Santayana's materialism is ultimately a faith. It is negative in that it denies teleology and theology; yet it serves Santayana exceedingly well. It confirms the relativism of values which allows him to cling to his own preferences and, in their terms, estimate all other values. It is, therefore, a buttress of criticism.

Still the old faith of supernatural religion held Santayana, the materialistic agnostic, fast in its grip. For, as Munson relates, the mystical doctrine of the Holy Trinity is translated analogically by Santayana into the ontological terms of the realms of being. The Father Almighty, creator of heaven and earth, is identified with the realm of matter. Jesus Christ, his only begotten Son, the Logos, is equated with the realm of truth—that part of the realm of essence instantiated existentially in the realm of matter. The Holy Spirit is consciousness, begotten from matter, but transcending it to attain the highest level of liberated Spirit.

Munson, whose perspective is profoundly shaped by his religious faith, condemns Santayana's philosophy as untenable. At the same time he gives Santayana credit for having reaffirmed the precious standpoint of the subject within the framework of naturalism.—*A.J.R.*

ADDITIONAL RECOMMENDED READING

Bowman, Archibald. *A Sacramental Universe, Being a Study in the Metaphysics of Experience*. Princeton, New Jersey: Princeton University Press, 1939. A penetrating metaphysical analysis by a Scottish idealist who sought to establish the primary reality of Spirit.

Cory, Daniel. "Some Notes on the Deliberate Philosophy of Santayana," in *The Journal of Philosophy*. XLVII, no. 5 (March 2, 1950), pp. 113-124. An overview of Santayana's system by his literary secretary.

Hartshorne, Charles. "Santayana's Philosophy of Essence," in *The Philosophy of George Santayana* (The Library of Living Philosophers). Edited by Paul A. Schilpp. La Salle, Illinois: Open Court, 1940, pp. 137-182. Sustained criticism which charges Santayana with neglecting the alternative of process metaphysics and theology.

Reck, Andrew J. *Speculative Philosophy*. Albuquerque: University of New

Mexico Press, 1972, pp. 89-94. Discussion of Santayana's philosophy as a form of realism.

Russell, Bertrand. "The Philosophy of George Santayana," in *The Philosophy of George Santayana* (The Library of Living Philosophers). Edited by Paul A. Schilpp. La Salle, Illinois: Open Court, 1940, pp. 451-474. A critical essay by the famous English logician-philosopher who conceded the correctness of Santayana's ontology if the subject-predicate logic were the exclusively valid logic.

Williams, Donald C. "Of Essence and Existence and Santayana," in *The Journal of Philosophy*. LI, no. 1 (January 7, 1954), pp. 31-42. A sober, well-written appreciation of Santayana's theory.

ETHICS

Author: Frank Chapman Sharp (1866-1943)
Type of work: Ethics
First published: 1928

Principal Ideas Advanced

A volition is right if a reflective, benevolent person would desire it to control the actions of men; right action aims at the general welfare.

Morality is a reflective, rational affair; it involves an interplay between what we take to be right at the time and what we learn to be right.

Good will and ill will conflict in moral consideration; men have both selfish and unselfish inclinations, and ethics must take this fact into account.

Objectivity in morality can be gained by relating rightness to values; the formalists are mistaken in supposing that rightness is a function of universally applicable rules of conduct.

The good is the desirable, and the desirable is what would be desired were one judging reflectively on the basis of relevant information.

Pleasure is always good-in-itself, worth having for its own sake; right action aims at the general happiness.

Frank Chapman Sharp's *Ethics* expresses the results of a long and careful investigation of morality. It belongs to the empirical, utilitarian tradition exemplified by Hume, though it seeks to supplement Hume by developing the objective import of moral judgments. In texture, it is both descriptive and normative.

As a philosophical discipline, ethics concerns itself with the attempt to find well-founded principles for morality, principles which can be justified and applied intelligently. Terms must be clarified and defined and as much unity as possible introduced. Ethics is an old subject which goes back at least to Socrates in the Western world and to Confucius in China. It found development in the writings of Plato and Aristotle, the Stoics, and the Epicureans. As Professor Sharp points out, the egoistic utilitarianism of Thomas Hobbes started a revival of ethical theory largely for the purpose of refuting his assumptions. Rationalism and intuitionism were developed as a base for the establishment of objective rules. In contrast, a more universalistic utilitarianism was also worked out. Something of this interplay still operates. It is well to have a book which develops so carefully and in a concrete way the utilitarian perspective. In a small posthumous book, *Good Will and Ill-Will* (1950), we find Sharp's final reply to intuitionism. It is, he argues, meaningless to talk about moral intuition when there is no universal agreement about moral matters.

The primary aim of ethics is theoretical, as in pure science, but this fact does not preclude interest in practice. As a matter of fact, practice feeds into theory and helps to illuminate it. One must, of course, keep the proper balance between them. Few ethicists have made more careful empirical investigations into morality than has Sharp.

It is a little difficult to classify Sharp's outlook in terms of recent controversy. He is certainly not an *emotivist*, for he puts stress on moral judgment. And he cannot be called a deontologist, for the right and duty have, for him, a foundation in values. Yet the larger part of his book is concerned with what is objectively right. It is apparent that G. E. Moore's famous "naturalistic fallacy" had little meaning for Sharp. He was careful to define the meanings of the terms "right" and "good" and to locate them in morality as a human affair. There is much emphasis these days on the logic of moral discourse and on the language of morals, but although Professor Sharp had a keen ear for usage, his approach was more psychological.

As a utilitarian, Sharp's approach stressed values as terminal. Right, duty, and obligation have to do with the reasonable maximizing of values for those concerned. In point of fact, Sharp intimates that, unlike the ancients, modern philosophers have reflected too little upon human values.

An important chapter in the second part of the book deals with "The Best Things in Life," such as knowledge and beauty. We should not be surprised, therefore, to find Sharp saying that his argument is of the nature of a running criticism of formalism in ethics. The center of the stage is, for him, occupied by volitions, with their motives and anticipated consequences. Volitions are natural human acts, not reducible to something else. The job is to get benevolence, or good will, free from diversions in favor of selfishness and short-sightedness. Morality in its normative aspect stands for the broad, searchlight outlook. It is easy to neglect relevant interests from lack of imagination. There are psychological stimulants and depressants which must be recognized.

Sharp agrees with Aristotle in pointing out the need for moral education. Consequently, he refers to a scientific conscience which must be activated as well as a moral conscience. Conscientiousness involves care. In a broad sense, then, Sharp was a cognitivist rather than an emotivist. His concern was with enlightened judgment working with good will. The authentic is the reasonable in the context of benevolence.

One of the contributions of Sharp was his frank recognition of malevolence or ill will in human affairs. There are dysdemonic volitions as well as eudemonic ones. Desire for revenge operates in punishment. There are sadism and also cruelty. Sharp lived long enough to see these at work during the rise of Communism and national socialism. As normative, morality expresses the demands of the better side of human nature.

Sharp's forte rests on the broadness of his base. There is detailed knowledge of actual moral judgments gained by the use of the questionnaire method, supplemented by careful, personal interviews. His intention was not so much statistical as a matter of exploring moral tendencies. Professor Max Otto aided Sharp in some of this work. His competence in introspective psychology of the James-Stout variety was also important. His treatment of the self illustrates this method. Desires are intrinsic to the self which, in some sense, is more enduring and of larger scope. The contrast between the desired and the desirable has point here. The element of reflection has entered. It is quite wrong to think of the self as knocked about by desires as separate forces.

Ethics was Sharp's primary interest and he knew the history of the subject thoroughly. One has the impression, in reading this book, that every topic has been mulled over. The collection of notes at the end of the book represents a return to key issues in an attempt to make the author's stand as definite as possible.

Sharp's *Ethics* goes with Dewey's and with Tuft's works as one of the solid American contributions to the subject. Of course, it reflects the period in which it was written. A book written now would probably put more stress on the results of psychiatry and on social ethics in relation to the social sciences. Sharp was a liberal and not a radical, so that what stands out is a strong ingredient of common sense. He refused to be either a pragmatist or an idealist.

Sharp discusses numerous topics of major interest in ethical theory, such as the meaning of *right*, the meaning of *good*, the sources of moral approval and disapproval, the operation of standards or ideals, the role of benevolence and of malevolence, the parts played by eogism and altruism, and the status of pleasure. The consideration of these topics will furnish a base from which to judge subjectivism, rationalism, intuitionism, aestheticism, and Sharp's own universalistic utilitarianism. After that, one can consider with him the relation of responsibility to the traditional alternatives of determinism and indeterminism. Here Sharp stresses causality and causal laws and the importance of character.

Sharp was quite aware of the need to define the term *right*. And he wanted to avoid such a tautology as would result from defining it in terms of some outer result, what the intuitionists would call a "natural property." Thus, to say that right *means* "procuring the greatest happiness for the greatest number" would merely result in repetition: actions procuring the greatest happiness for the greatest number procure the greatest happiness. No—according to Sharp, one must be more concerned with the springs of action, with character and will. The correct approach is to recognize agency and the object of moral judgment. *Right* is a term which applies to volitions that necessarily involve motives and consequences. The inner cannot be separated from the outer or, in the last analysis, the outer from the inner. To call a volition *right* means that I believe it to be such that I, in virtue of my benevolence, desire it to control the actions of men under the given conditions. Note the element of objectivity and universalization. I am thinking in a social way. To call a volition wrong is to assert that I believe it to be in conflict with the demands of good will. Of course, I may be guided largely by the acceptance of sanctioned rules. But when these are questioned, Sharp believed, the next step is an appeal to consequences in the way of general welfare. There is here the recognition of tendencies. It is doubtful that Professor Sharp believed in the Benthamite calculus except as an indication of some kind of summation of factors at work. There is meaning to quantity, fecundity, and intensity of pleasure experiences and their contrary, unpleasantness. One must work with psychologists in this area of ethics.

As has been noted, Sharp recognized the working of malevolence or ill will in human nature. These lead to dysdemonic judgments; that is, judgments deviating from welfare. Tribal morality puts the alien, in large measure, outside the group. Cultural development has meant the enlargement of the range of moral attitudes. It seems to be a historical fact that something of the nature of such an extension took place in the ancient world. It has been called an axial period and has been associated with the rise of ethical religions.

It appears that Sharp tried to avoid sentimentality about human nature by acknowledging the struggle between ill will and good will. Morality is an affair of the dominant motivation of benevolence and the sense of the community and its life, as a larger whole. It is in this fashion that Sharp qualified individualism. His discussion of "natural rights" is guided by the ideal of a balance. Rights are inseparable from duties.

Though in many ways a follower of Hume, Sharp wanted to develop the objective import of moral judgment. A right volition is one that one is ready to universalize in an impartial way. Its validity has about it something of the nature of true and false in cognition. Ideals and standards are developed and operate in moral judgments. Here, of course, is the domain of normative ethics as against merely descriptive ethics. And norms must be backed up by adequate motivation. Character enters here as it is recognized that volitions reflect a continuing source. It is from this angle that character gets its own kind of intrinsic value. An aesthetic quality is usually added as connected with moral admiration, but aesthetic theories of morality overemphasize this quality.

On the descriptive side, Sharp argued, it must be recognized that contradictory moral judgments exist. These are due to the spotlight effects of such factors as the striking good, the good of the nearer, or of what is regarded as the more excellent. These factors introduce bias. The moral job is to see the whole situation in a searchlight way, to keep the general welfare impartially before one's eyes. Apparently, Sharp believed that there are social and personal forces supporting this objectivity and impartiality. These factors work for objectivity and reasonableness. There is the increasing awareness that that volition is right which aims at the general welfare. This standard, in Sharp's opinion, corresponds to the actual working of the moral consciousness of the ordinary mind. In interviews, the searchlight outlook can replace the spotlight distortions.

It is interesting to note that Sharp contends that the sense of the welfare of the group operates in the primitive mind, though unreflectively. One would need to analyze the idea of social pressure rather carefully here. Social anthropologists are doing careful work in this field. There is stress on social pathology as well as on social health. Perhaps the feeling is increasing that mere cultural "relativity" is not the correct answer.

If morality is normative, Sharp continues, subjective valuations with their partiality must be controlled. It is easy to care most of all for what is near and known. That is one of the dangers of the exaltation of nationalism which took place in the nineteenth century and which is still continuing, mingled with ideological fervors. Moral judgment develops best in the cool hour. The Golden Rule is fundamentally correct: one must place oneself in the position of others. However, one must not ignore the just demands of the self in the total picture. It is evident that Sharp thought of the ethical imagination as having a social context. There are leaders in what Bergson has called open morality. Hume pointed in this way, for he had a historical sense in his criticism of rationalism. But he was inclined to be conservative. One could consider Sharp a Humian working in another period.

What, then, is a volition for Sharp? It would seem to be a higher level desire which takes into account both *pro* and *con* factors. Morality has learned to stress the importance of what is ignored in motivation as well as of what is dominant. We blame people for what they disregard and seek to call their attention to it. A motorist who drives with great speed through a village is endangering the lives of children. Morality is a reflective, rational affair. It involves an interplay between what we take to be right at the time and what we learn to be right. These do not necessarily coincide. (There are, of course, linguistic difficulties in all this. Words have so many uses.)

Next comes Sharp's discussion of egoism, altruism, and love. Recent social psychology and psychiatry have thrown additional light on these terms. Selfishness is not something innate; it reflects the plasticity of child psychology and the anxieties of adults. Culture has much to do with it. Sharp thought that our American culture is probably too competitive in its texture. He argued for the existence of altruism as a fact. There is more "ready for service" altruism than is often admitted.

Involved in these general principles are supplementary problems. Is there a duty to the self? Sharp argues that there is as regards the future and in a given situation. What we ought not to do is pretty well established. And there is a fair amount of agreement concerning what ought to be done. Praiseworthy conduct and the conduct of the "saint" go beyond ordinary moral expectations.

There is an ambiguity between subjective rightness, which is the sincere volition of a moral agent, and objective rightness, which involves standards and criteria connected with the general welfare. Another ambiguity is that between inner and outer rightness. Inner rightness refers to the will to produce certain results, while outer rightness is a name for the results which a man ought to produce.

As Sharp saw it, there are operative in historical ethical theories varying ideas of the standard of rightness and of the *source* whence comes the standard in the human mind. In modern times, the chief conflict has been between utilitarianism and intuitionism. As in the case of Henry Sidgwick, these can be mixed.

Intuitionism, rationalism, and deontology are closely connected, Sharp believed. He calls them *anaxiotic*; that is, they seek to deny that the rightness of an action has any necessary connection with values. The two central weaknesses in intuitionism are reflected by its failure to account for moral motivation and to explain the lack of agreement on moral matters. But one cannot do justice to this position until one notes that its aim was to supplant egoism and subjectivism. The intuitionists took a shortcut from the demand for objectivity to a belief that reason is a faculty for recognizing moral truths directly—in a manner analogous to the recognition of mathematical axioms. But what Sharp wanted was another foundation for objectivity. It is his contention that objectivity can be gained by linking rightness to values. But one must have a satisfactory value theory in order to defend a value-centered ethics.

Sharp's treatment of the aesthetic approach to morals in Aristotle and the Stoics should be noted. Virtues are attractive and awaken admiration. Sharp agrees that the ideal of the Stoics of self-sufficiency had its appeal, and that Aristotle portrayed the mean between extremes sympathetically. But neither traced out the foundation for the rightness of actions.

Universalistic utilitarianism has a long history. We find something of the kind in Confucius and Mo Ti in China. Richard Cumberland, Francis Hutcheson, and Hume explored its foundations in opposition to rationalism and intuitionism in the debate which followed on Hobbes. As we have noted, Sharp undertook to complete Hume.

Since Sharp's ethics is axiological—value-centered—rather than intuitionistic, it is of interest to examine his conception of the meaning of good, standards of goodness, and the sources of goodness. Sharp's opinion was that we all use the terms "right" and "good," but that their definition requires clarification. Hedonism now comes into the picture. What can we do with what Freud called the pleasure principle?

Early hedonism, Sharp maintained, did not sufficiently recognize the fact that many of our desires are not directed toward pleasure. These are called "anhedonic" desires. Yet it seems to be Sharp's conclusion, from numerous instances, that if pleasure does not finally accompany the attainment of what is desired, desire will wither. We will not then take pleasure even in anticipation. This is the familiar distinction between the idea of pleasure and pleasure in an idea.

We come now to the controversial question of the meaning of the term "good," when what is meant is intrinsic goodness and not instrumental value. One position is that the more we think of intrinsic goodness and pleasure, the more we tend to identify them. This means that the words acquire the same meaning, become synonymous. Thus, satisfaction is intrinsic value.

Consider the distinction between what is desired and the desirable. The good is the desirable and the desirable is what is reflectively judged to be worthy of desire and, of course, is also desired. Pleasure is intrinsically good, no matter whose pleasure it is. This position is called ethical hedonism and it is to be contrasted with psychological hedonism, which holds that pleasure is the sole object of desire. Since Sharp accepted anhedonic desires, he rejected psychological hedonism.

Like most ethical hedonists, Sharp denied qualitative differences in pleasure as such. Much of the belief in higher and lower pleasures comes from aesthetic attitudes and confusion between pleasure as such and our attitude towards the conditions of its occurrence. We are disturbed when a wicked man derives pleasure from his deeds. But it must be remembered that right has to do with volitions and voluntary actions in the light of motives and consequences. Morality tries to hold dysdemonic desires in check both in primary action and in punishment. Professor Sharp stressed deterrence and reform.

There are incidental issues in the *Ethics*. Sharp was opposed to indeterminism in the classical sense as rejecting causality. Probably he would have been favorable to ideas of levels of causality and some measure of self-direction. He suggests that we can improve our own character. And it should be pointed out that Sharp appeals to the role of the brain. But he rejects materialism on two grounds: (1) Berkeley's argument and (2) the irreducibility of consciousness. Any modern notion of materialism must, certainly, deal with these objections.—*R.W.S.*

PERTINENT LITERATURE

Lamont, W. D. Review of Frank Chapman Sharp's *Ethics*, in *Mind*. XXXIX, no. 155 (July, 1930), pp. 354-360.

W. D. Lamont's lengthy review of Frank Chapman Sharp's *Ethics* points out many of the merits and demerits of the book, but his overall appraisal is positive. He begins his review by stating that all moralists who read Sharp's book "will feel under a great obligation to him"; and he closes his review with the remark that if he has played devil's advocate in finding fault, it is only against the claims that Sharp is "a strong candidate for canonisation." Lamont approves of Sharp's attempt to secure data in the form of moral judgments from persons not likely to be prejudiced in favor of any particular ethical (philosophical) theory; but he is less optimistic than Sharp about the possibility of finding such subjects. In any case, Sharp's ethical views are not dependent for their formation or defense on the results of any empirical inquiry.

Sharp is classified as a utilitarian by Lamont. The reviewer mentions Sharp's philosophical starting point: the relatedness and at the same time the distinctiveness of the ideas of the "good" and the "right." Book I of Sharp's *Ethics* deals with the "right" and, accordingly, with the judgment of actions; Book II is a discussion of "good" and the good. Sharp offers as the standard of right action on action's bringing into existence the greatest amount of good possible under the circumstances. The provisional definition of "right," Lamont reports, is that a right action is "that which would be desired when . . . looked at from an impersonal point of view."

As to the good, Sharp held that the only thing good on its own account, "ultimately and really good," is pleasure. But Lamont argues that Sharp is hardly consistent: at one point he appears to maintain that pleasure is the *content* of the good; at another, that pleasure is the *standard* of the good; and at still another, that pleasure is the "harmonizing principle. . . ." Lamont cites Sharp's definition of the term "good": "Good . . . can only mean what is desired when reflection has led me to reduce the original chaos of desired objects to a self-consistent or harmonious system." (Here it would appear, however, that Sharp was considering the *moral* good, not simply the semantical question as to the definition of the term "good.")

According to Lamont, Sharp regarded a judgment of the rightness of an act to involve two judgments: (1) the judgment that a certain state of attainable affairs is good, and (2) the judgment that no alternative state of affairs would be better; that is, more valuable for the agent or for others concerned. When the ideas of the good and the right are combined by Sharp, the result, Lamont reports, is the standard of right (or what one might call Sharp's basic moral principle or law): An *act* is *right* if it produces the greatest possible amount of pleasure; the aim (the moral intention) to produce such a state of affairs is right "in the proper and moral sense of the term."

Lamont then attempts to spell out the distinction that Sharp makes between the *definition* of "right" and the *standard* of rightness. Sharp argues that one can hardly take the standard of right action to be the defining criterion of the term "right." If, for example, Aristotle asserts that the right act is a mean between extremes, he is not asserting that the term "right" *means* "mean between extremes." If to say that the right act is the act productive of the greatest happiness (standard) entailed claiming that the term "right" *means* productive of the greatest happiness, then saying that an act is right if and only if it is productive of the greatest happiness would *mean* that an act is productive of the greatest happiness if and only if it is productive of the greatest happiness—a hardly disputable point. (The criticism ventured by

Sharp is reminiscent of G. E. Moore's argument directed against what Moore called the "naturalistic fallacy.")

Lamont dissents, however; he fails to see that there is any difference between the standard of right action and the definition of "right." He argues that any definition must be capable of being expressed in the form, "'Right' (conducive to the greatest happiness of the greatest number) *means* 'conducive to the greatest happiness of the greatest number (right).'" (The point here appears to be that when one substitutes a definiens for a definiendum *in the statement of a definition*—a pointless enterprise!—the resultant statement, even if the definition is correct, has this kind of circularity. But Sharp's point seems to be that a definition of "right" by reference to the mean or even to happiness does not account for the use and consequent meaning of the term as used by moralists opposed to Aristotelian or utilitarian ethics.)

Lamont also appears to be skeptical about the possibility of reconciling a rejection of psychological hedonism with the advocacy of (altruistic) ethical hedonism. But he contends that Sharp's altruistic hedonism is required by his utilitarian ethics (unlike John Stuart Mill, whose utilitarianism was a kind of mutual "non-interference" view, Lamont maintains, while Sharp's position is one that requires actually promoting the happiness of others in cases in which it is likely that more good will thereby be secured).

Lovejoy, Arthur O. Review of Frank Chapman Sharp's *Ethics*, in *The Philosophical Review*. XXXIX, no. 6 (November, 1930), pp. 613-622.

The distinguished American philosopher and intellectual historian Arthur O. Lovejoy (1873-1962), author of *The Revolt Against Dualism* (1930) and *The Great Chain of Being* (1936), reviewed Frank Chapman Sharp's *Ethics* for *The Philosophical Review* in November, 1930.

Lovejoy characterizes Sharp's book—written in part as a textbook—as "an original treatise, one of the most substantial of American contributions to systematic ethical theory." (Sharp's work in ethics is not often alluded to in the latter half of the twentieth century, perhaps partly because utilitarianism is out of fashion and partly because the academic turn in ethics has been toward a careful examination of the *uses*—rather than the *meanings*—of moral terms, and toward, in some quarters at least, a resurgence of formalism. But Sharp received the critical attention and respect of some of the best minds of his time, and in many ways he anticipated the later work of those who emphasize the critical roles of interest and commitment in the making of moral judgments.)

Lovejoy describes Sharp's defense of universalistic utilitarianism as "fresh and forceful" and as "distinguished by its radical separation of the problem of 'the good' from that of 'the right.'" The problem of the good is, in part at least, the problem of the nature of value; it is also the problem of identifying whatever it is that is worthwhile on its own account. The problem of the right involves the question of who has the strongest claim for possessing the good (although Lovejoy points out that Sharp does not always adhere to this definition). Although in *Ethics* Sharp first of all discusses the "right" (and devotes more than two-thirds of his book to the subject), in Lovejoy's opinion the reverse order is more logical: first the good, then the right. The review proceeds accordingly: first Lovejoy discusses Sharp's ideas concerning the good, then the ideas concerning the right.

Lovejoy contends that Sharp's treatment of the problem of the nature and content of the good preaches "the simple gospel of 'back to Bentham.'" Sharp argues that it is pleasure and pleasure alone that gives the good its content; that the greater the pleasure, the greater the good; that pleasures differ only in quantity, not quality; and that the only standard for deciding on the value of a state of consciousness is the pleasure standard.

At this point Lovejoy calls Sharp's basic proposition into question. Lovejoy does not deny that pleasure is good—that is, that a pleasant feeling, considered as a feeling, is a good feeling. But he finds no case made in support of the claim that pleasure is the *only* good. Although Sharp rejects psychological hedonism (the view that we are all so constituted as to have as our sole objective the attainment of pleasure), he does argue that only pleasure can be the object of "reflective desire." (The good is what, upon reflection and as informed, we *would* desire, not simply what, as a matter of fact, we happen to desire—and Sharp finds that only pleasure, among various candidates for status as final or intrinsic goods, passes the test of reflective desire.) Lovejoy contends that most persons, Sharp included, prefer—or at least regard it as preferable—to develop the "higher" faculties of intelligence and feeling. Lovejoy writes: "And if Professor Sharp were given the power to create either a world inhabited exclusively by constantly and intensely pleased pigs or one occupied by a number of frequently and painfully dissatisfied Socrates, it is, I am sure, the latter that he would unhesitatingly call into being."

Lovejoy argues that a consistent quantitative hedonism has more radical implications in almost every sphere of life than Sharp appears to realize. Quantitative hedonism, Lovejoy contends, leads to a kind of moral primitivism, a rejection of intellectual and moral plesures (of the kind, no doubt, that Sharp preferred), and the pursuit of quick and easy gratification.

In his discussion of right action Sharp maintains that surveys of persons untutored in philosophy show that in the making of moral judgments people are much more inclined to be reflective and to judge teleologically by reference to consequences than the sociologists and anthropologists have supposed (who argue that moral judgments simply reflect prevailing mores). Lovejoy suggests that surveys of the kind Sharp undertook are unnecessary and that if one surveys instead the kinds of reasons thinking people give for regarding acts as right one finds that the reasons relate to the *effects* of conduct. Not all moral judgments reflect convention, but certainly many of them do. What is important in Sharp's account, Lovejoy concludes, is not his criticism of the social-pressure theory of ethics but his own defense of consequential reasoning.

Lovejoy calls attention to Sharp's switch from a relativistic theory of moral judgment—the theory holding that acts are "right" relative to a judge if they lead to the sort of consequences the judge prefers—to a theory which makes the "impersonal point of view" essential to right judgment. But, Lovejoy argues, if judgment is relative to the impersonal point of view, then it is not relative to the good and the bad except insofar as one presumes the impersonal point of view to involve desires that determine the good. Sharp apparently came to realize that the desires of a judge are irrelevant, Lovejoy reports. What matters are the claims of competing interests; the objective judgment weighs such claims and decides for the course of action most likely to result in the greatest satisfaction of the interests involved.

There remains the problem of moral motivation. Sharp identifies right action with reasonable action, and he urges that "objective" judgment—judgment that takes all concerned into account and works for the greatest happiness—be regarded as eminently "reasonable" by virtue of its impartiality. Lovejoy points out, however, that if reasonableness is not itself a kind of ultimate good to each agent, how can the unreasonable person be brought to the point of being willing to be reasonable? Lovejoy suggests that had Sharp so modified his theories of the good and the right as to "bring the two ultimate categories of morals into a genuine synthesis," his ethics would have been satisfactorily concluded. In any event, Lovejoy concludes, it is a merit of Sharp's *Ethics* that the good and the right have not been confused.—*I.P.M.*

ADDITIONAL RECOMMENDED READING

Sharp, Frank Chapman. *Good Will and Ill Will: A Study of Moral Judgments*. Chicago: University of Chicago Press, 1950. Proceeding from another empirical study of moral judgments, Sharp concentrates on the relations of benevolence and malevolence to moral judgment. A thoughtful development of ideas first defended in *Ethics*.

See also the following classics discussed elsewhere in this work:

Bentham, Jeremy. *An Introduction to the Principles of Morals and Legislation*. A major defense of utilitarianism.

Bradley, Francis Herbert. *Ethical Studies*. Self-realization theory. Contains criticism of Mill.

Mill, John Stuart. *Utilitarianism*. The classic statement.

Sidgwick, Henry. *The Methods of Ethics*. A penetrating study of utilitarianism, as well as of intuitionism and egoism. Sidgwick attempts a synthesis of the three "methods," but he has difficulty reconciling egoism with utilitarianism.

THE QUEST FOR CERTAINTY

Author: John Dewey (1859-1952)
Type of work: Philosophy of philosophy; pragmatism
First published: 1929

PRINCIPAL IDEAS ADVANCED

In the past the quest for certainty, to be achieved by the discovery of eternal truths and ultimate reality, led to the misleading distinction between theory and practice.

Science and philosophy, by becoming experimental and operational, have shown that idea and practice work together as instruments: ideas relate experiences and make predictions possible, and by experience ideas are tested.

Statements about present enjoyments are factual, while value judgments indicate attitudes to be assumed; such judgments are instrumental and corrigible.

The Quest for Certainty, considered against the background of traditional philosophies, is a revolutionary work. In his book Dewey does not claim originality for all of its ideas, but he justifiably asserts that were its program enacted, a revolution comparable to the Copernican would be effected not only in philosophy but also in the moral, social, and economic dimensions of daily life. That this claim is a valid one is partially verified by the pervasive influence of Dewey's teachings on many phases of American culture, especially on education. That Dewey's works should have such an influence is especially appropriate in view of his constantly recurring emphasis upon the importance of an intimate, reciprocal relationship between theory and practice. Whether the reader finds all of Dewey's methods and conclusions acceptable or not, it is undeniable that the author's searching criticism of older theories combined with constructive suggestions of remedial and progressive measures have profound practical import.

The quest about which Dewey writes is an ancient one, originating as a need for security from the perils of primitive life, security sought first, perhaps, by prayers and rites performed in an attitude proper to the holy, or on the other hand, by magical manipulations of fortunate or lucky tangible objects. Mystery and glamour attended the former, while the latter were regarded as more amenable to practical control. Gradually this distinction was generalized and abstracted into that between the spiritual and intellectual on the one hand and the material and practical on the other; the distinction was also between superior and inferior respectively, and resulted in an isolation of theory and knowledge from practice which has hampered human progress ever since. Action is notoriously subject to failure or at least unforeseen results; material objects are only partially amenable to man's control. Consequently, man was led to seek certainty in an eternal, immaterial realm of thought not subject to the risks of action. This was conceived as the realm of true Being or ultimate reality, unchanging, thoroughly rational, and governed by the laws of logic, and hence alone the object of genuine science. The mundane world, on the contrary, was regarded as infected with non-being, unreality, and change; it was irrational and the object only of belief or opinion, not genuine knowledge. Moreover, the Good was identified with the real so that value was attainable only by knowledge, and both were dissociated from action.

The developments of these distinctions have had ramifications into almost every traditional philosophical theory, Dewey argues; the ideals of certainty in knowledge, various metaphysical views, theories about mind and how it knows—all of these, even when formulated by strongly opposing schools, have stemmed from the jealously guarded barrier between theory and practice erected in the quest for certainty. Since modern philosophy has accepted the conclusions of natural science while retaining doctrines about mind, knowledge and values formulated in prescientific ages, it has found itself increasingly isolated from the actual problems and values of contemporary life. Consequently, the basic problem for philosophy today is the integration of our beliefs about existence and those about values, especially since this gap has been widened by misinterpretations of certain developments of modern science.

Greek science, says Dewey, was basically aesthetic in character; its explanatory and descriptive categories, such as harmony, symmetry, and proportion, were used to organize logically the qualitative characteristics of experienced objects into kinds of species. Thus nature, considered only an inferior kind of reality patterned after the eternal forms, was known—insofar as it was an object of knowledge at all rather than of opinion or belief—by reason rather than by experience. Greek natural philosophy was also teleological, holding that things and events tended toward their own proper ends or goods and thus toward the highest and best. This outlook, lasting through the Middle Ages, fostered an attitude of acceptance rather than an art of control such as that made possible by modern science.

Galileo and other founders of the new science effected a revolution by eliminating the qualitative and purposive and by substituting the quantitative interpretation of scientific objects. Rather than classifying things into species defined by and tending toward eternal forms, the new science saw them as reducible, for its purposes, to a few basic categories of space, time, mass, and motion. Phenomena such as heat, light, mechanical motion, and electricity could be converted or translated into one another; homogeneity replaced the heterogeneity basic to the Greek view, and "All that counted for science became mechanical properties formulated in mathematical terms. . . ." The revolution was not completed at once, however. Though Newton ostensibly subscribed to the empirical approach, remnants of the old metaphysics were obvious in his belief that change occurred only in the external relations between particles of permanently fixed natures. This postulate of permanence was really evidence of the longstanding quest for certainty rather than a hypothesis experimentally verified. Even the most avowedly empiricist school showed this same bias; for them, knowledge was founded on sensory impressions given by an antecedent reality unaffected by knowing. Later, objective idealists held that reflective thought merely reproduces the rational structure of a universe constituted by an Absolute Reason. Even now realism holds that valid inquiry apprehends prior existence—it does not modify it. All these views presuppose that inference and judgment are not originative.

As the new science became truly experimental, however, this premise was abandoned; science now "*substitutes data for objects.*" This means that science, instead of taking qualitative objects such as stars and trees as finalities waiting only for logical classification, takes them as problematic, inviting further interpretation and investigation. The latter is undertaken in response to problems and unresolved difficulties which are never wholly theoretical but are always ultimately rooted in need for practical security; these problematic situations determine the lines of inquiry and the criteria of successful solution. Experimental knowledge, inference, or judgment then becomes originative in a very real sense; its "procedure is one that installs doing as the heart of knowing. . . ." Change, once regarded as evidence of the inferiority of the experienced world to the ideal and eternal, now becomes useful: "*The* method of physical inquiry is to introduce some change in order to see what other change ensues; the correlation between these changes, when measured by a series of operations, constitutes the definite and desired object of knowledge." The objects of scientific knowledge are not qualitative entities, but *events*, mathematically formulated relations between changes undergone by experienced objects, and most important for our present purposes, *consequences*.

Dewey takes physical science as a model for experimental philosophy because on the whole the former yields the best authenticated and reliable knowledge we enjoy at present, while at the same time its conclusions are corrigible and its hypotheses subject to revision in the light of future evidence and problems. Besides, in its technological applications it is as a matter of fact already the dominant feature of modern life. Philosophy can learn from it, Dewey believes, how to approach the basic modern problem of reintegrating beliefs about existence with those about values, as well as how to avoid some of the more technical philosophical problems to which traditional theories inevitably led.

Dewey cites with approval Bridgman's statement in *The Logic of Modern Physics* (1927): ". . . we mean by any concept nothing more than a set of operations; *the concept is synonymous with the corresponding set of operations.*" The philosophical implications of such an experimental empiricism (as distinguished from traditional sensational empiricism), understood at the time by only a few thinkers such as William James and Charles Sanders Peirce, are so far-reaching as to make it "one of three or four outstanding feats of intellectual history." It shows that neither sensational empiricism nor *a priori* rationalism was wholly right or wholly wrong: ideas are empirical in origin, but sensory qualities, to be significant, must be related by ideas; the new method's concepts of scientific objects are neither *a priori* nor reducible to sensation. The object of knowledge is "eventual; that is, it is an outcome of directed experimental operations, instead of something in sufficient existence before the act of knowing." Thus the sensory and rational elements of knowledge do not compete but cooperate; the latter are used to organize and direct, the former to test and verify or correct. Conclusions, not the previously given, are *truly known*; but conclusions of former investigations become in turn instrumental to the achievement of new solutions.

The operational method makes mind a participant rather than a mere spectator in the knowing situation. As is illustrated by the Heisenberg principle of indeterminacy, the act of observation is itself an essential ingredient in what is known. From this point of view, then, nature is neither rational nor irrational as it has been described traditionally, but is, rather, intelligible; it is *to be* known through intelligence. This approach also yields new definitions of intelligence, thought, and mind. Merely mechanical and animal responses to uncertain and perilous situations are reactions or direct actions, but "response to the doubtful as such" is definitive of mind and thinking, and when responses "have a directed tendency to change the precarious and problematic into the secure and resolved, they are *intellectual* as well as mental." Misinterpretations of Newtonian science, by emphasizing the difference between ordinary perceptual experience and the scientific formulation of nature, had reinforced the metaphysical distinction between mind and body, but in Dewey's view, "There is no separate 'mind' gifted in and of itself with a faculty of thought; such a conception of thought ends in postulating the mystery of a power outside of nature and yet able to intervene within it." As defined above, thinking is observable behavior, whereas traditional theories on the contrary tried to explain the more by the less obvious. Now with our greater understanding of the relation between sensory organs and perception we are able to conceive the same relation as holding between the brain and thought.

One stronghold of the rationalistic and mentalistic schools, however, and one not adequately accounted for by traditional empiricism, was the structure of mathematics. Because mathematics seemed to rest on self-evident axioms known intuitively, and because of the universality, immutability, ideality, and logical necessity of mathematics, it was thought to demonstrate the subsistence of a realm of eternal essences and a nonphysical reality; the applicability of mathematics to the physical world, moreover, seemed to show a rational element even therein. Does the operational theory of ideas, together with its implications concerning the nature of mind and thought, break down here?

Dewey thinks not. We must distinguish between overt and symbolical operations, operations to be enacted and those merely possible but without actual consequences. Just as the concepts of space, time, and motion were finally seen to be ways of correlating observations rather than as reflecting properties of Being, and their worth was found in the former function, so logical and mathematical principles and relationships may be interpreted. They may have arisen from practical needs for manipulation and organization of physical things, later to be developed more fully and independently of immediately instrumental purposes. Men then become interested in such operations as operations which, when symbolized, can be performed without any direct reference to existence. That this is the case seems most clearly illustrated by the history of geometry, which originated in the need for measurement of utilitarian objects. The formal order and internal relations such systems show are analogous to the self-consistent structure of a machine designed for a certain purpose. The means-consequence relation as exemplified in the operation of a machine may be *thought* abstractly as an operation to which the imperfections of actual machines are irrelevant; so conceived, the function has the ideality, immutability, internal necessity, and universality which characterizes the realm of essence supposedly encountered in logic and mathematics.

The worth of a machine is judged by the efficacy with which it performs the function for which it was designed, and the more abstractly this function is conceived—the more it is idealized—the more clearly it can be understood. But in the conception of function ideas for improvement are germinated. Thus, the operational or experimental method is capable of projecting new goals and values and of instituting its own standards. It is imperative that this lesson learned from science be applied in the moral, social, and political life, where it is not yet fully operative. The apparent value-sterility of quantitative and operational science can now be regarded as illusory, the illusion being rooted in the notion that science discloses reality as it is in itself. The experimental method is an effective way of thinking of things, but since it is not the only way to think of them, it is not actually inimical to qualitative experience, and it can make positive contributions to the qualitative aspects of human life by affording means of making values more available and secure. We recall that, according to Dewey, the main problem for modern philosophy is to reintegrate beliefs about existence and those about values. It is obvious now that his purpose in tracing the development of operationalism and instrumentalism is to show their significance for what he calls, typically, the "*construction*" of good, suggesting thereby that values, like objects of knowledge, are not so much given as achieved.

By "value" Dewey means "whatever is taken to have rightful authority in the direction of conduct." But there are still rival theories about the status of values comparable to the traditional epistemological opposites, empiricism and rationalism. Some writers would equate goods with actual enjoyments, while others see them as eternal, universal, absolute. Dewey favors the empirical and subjective theories to the extent that they relate "the theory of values with concrete experiences of desire and satisfaction," but the operational approach again makes a significant emendation: values are not antecedently given, but are enjoyments attained as *consequences*. Previous goods and present enjoyments are problematic, as are immediately experienced qualitative objects in relation to knowledge. The crucial differences here are indicated in the very suffixes of terms such as "the enjoyed and the enjoyable, the desired and the desirable, the satis*fying* and the satis*factory*." This is in no sense to derogate immediate enjoyments and likings, but mere feelings have no claim over us as ideals and future goods, any more than objects as immediately experienced are adequate as scientific objects. Whereas propositions about present enjoyments are factual and may be of instrumental worth, value judgments and appraisals indicate attitudes *to be* assumed and hence do make claims on us. Dewey summarizes this view in what he describes as his main proposition: "*Judgments about values are judgments about the conditions and the results of experienced objects; judgments about that which should regulate the formation of our desires, affections and enjoyments.*"

Value judgments, then, like their counterparts in science, are relational in nature. They, too, are instrumental and never final, and are thus corrigible. There are criteria of goods—for example, genuine goods are not later regretted; in achieving goods concern is centered on the valuable object rather than on the mere feeling of satisfaction—but such criteria are never absolute and fixed. It is thus impossible to set up a detailed catalog of values in hierarchical order. Dewey's approach "would place *method and means* upon the level of importance that has, in the past, been imputed exclusively to ends," for as long as ends alone are considered ideal and of true worth, while means are scorned as merely practical, ends fail to be realized. While failure to achieve the good has been attributed to perversity of will, the real obstacle has been lack of adequate knowledge of means. Hence the traditional elevation of spirit over matter is similarly mistaken, for the material serves as means.

The traditional separation of ends and means, another reflection of that of theory and practice, has left action without the guidance afforded only by knowledge. Consequently, some means, such as material wealth, have been overvalued as ends in the absence of any adequate philosophy of values appropriate to contemporary problems. The technological applications of science have been used selfishly and irresponsibly. Nowhere is the failure properly to relate ends and means more evident than in industrial life, and the resulting tragedy is that enjoyment of the highest social and cultural values, the truly human goods, is dependent on economic conditions ignored by many ethical philosophers. Our economy tends therefore to evade moral guidance as irrelevant and to be frankly materialistic, but the remedy is not to treat economics as beneath the notice of ethics; it is rather to apply here the instrumentalist approach.

Whereas mechanistic philosophy rejected the concept of purpose as explanatory of natural events, the developments of modern science have made clear the role of the observer in knowledge; and Dewey holds that in a significant sense purpose has been restored to nature, since "distinctively human conduct can be interpreted and understood only in terms of purpose." By removing the artificial barriers between knowledge and practice, science and values, and the consequent false problems such as those of the relationships between mind and body, spirit and matter, nature can be regarded as the ultimate source of all ideals and goods. To remove such obstacles, to free men's minds and hearts from slavery to the past, to turn them from the quest for an illusory certainty to discoverable paths to enjoyable goods, is the task of contemporary philosophy. No longer in competition with science through claims to sole superior knowledge of reality, philosophy takes up the task of exploring the richly various ways of putting science to truly human use.–*M.E.*

PERTINENT LITERATURE

Ratner, Joseph, ed. *Intelligence in the Modern World: John Dewey's Philosophy*. New York: Random House, 1939.

Joseph Ratner's "Introduction" to *Intelligence in the Modern World* is more than an introduction to the philosophy of John Dewey. It is also an example of philosophy done under the influence of Dewey's thought. Ratner is critical of Dewey's work; he recognizes that Dewey is not always consistent and that on many occasions he is not clear in his thinking. On these matters Ratner tries to improve Dewey's philosophy; but there is no doubt in Ratner's mind that Dewey's basic position—that philosophy must be scientific, that it must be experimental and self-correcting—is absolutely correct.

Intelligence in the Modern World is a selected anthology of Dewey's writings. Organized under headings such as "The Meaning of Philosophy," "Philosophy and Science," "Intelligence in Social Action," "Science and the Philosophy of Education," "Perception, Language and Mind," and "The Artistic-Esthetic in Experience," Ratner includes selections from Dewey's *Philosophy and Civilization* (1931), *The Quest for Certainty*, *Ethics*, *Experience and Education* (1938), *Experience and Nature* (1925), and *Art as Experience* (1934). In his Introduction Ratner seeks to introduce all of Dewey's major works by developing what he considers to be Dewey's central position. According to Ratner, all of Dewey's thought has its roots in his criticism of idealized philosophies—philosophies which concern themselves with some eternal and immutable reality. Dewey maintains that such philosophies are, at best, vacuous, and at worst, harmful. The proper domain of philosophy is the temporal, mutable reality that is the world in which people live.

Ratner gives a brief summary of Dewey's analysis of the history of Western philosophy from the time of the ancient Greeks through modern times. In Dewey's mind it was the Greek philosophers who initiated the "quest for certainty," the attempt to find security from the hazards of the temporal world, by going beyond this world. Ratner applies this critique of Western philosophy to the philosophies of two of Dewey's contemporaries: Bertrand Russell and Alfred North Whitehead. In Ratner's estimation both Russell and Whitehead have continued the Western tradition of going beyond the temporal, mutable world. By contrasting Dewey with two contemporary examples of "idealized" philosophy, Ratner intends to demonstrate the uniqueness of Dewey's thought.

While Ratner's interpretation of Russell's philosophy, and more specifically of Russell's philosophy in *The Analysis of Matter*, is sound, his interpretation of Whitehead's philosophy is highly questionable. Ratner's contention that Whitehead's "quest for certainty" takes him outside the world of experience would be disputed by virtually all of Whitehead's interpreters. The fact that one cannot rely on Ratner's understanding of Whitehead is regrettable, but it does not seriously damage his introduction to Dewey's thought. Dewey believed that the data with which philosophers ought to begin should come from ordinary life experience and that the test of a philosophy is whether or not its conclusions render these experiences more significant and our dealings with them more fruitful. Philosophies which begin with some idealized or refined experience and which never check their conclusions against ordinary experience are useless. Ratner may not understand Whitehead's philosophy, but he understands Dewey's thought very well.

Feldman, W. T. *The Philosophy of John Dewey: A Critical Analysis*. Westport, Connecticut: Greenwood Press, 1968.

W. T. Feldman's book *The Philosophy of John Dewey: A Critical Analysis*, first published in 1934, deals with John Dewey's thought from his first publication through *Experience and Nature* and *The Quest for Certainty*. Although cognizant of the tremendous influence of Dewey's work and genuinely respectful of Dewey's intellectual prowess, Feldman is convinced that there are serious problems with Dewey's philosophy which make it impossible to accept his thought as a whole. In his excellent book, Feldman aims to illuminate the ambiguities, the equivocations, and the contradictions which he detects in Dewey's work.

According to Feldman, there are three distinct meanings of "experience" in Dewey's philosophy, a fact which obfuscates Dewey's commitment to empiricism. The first meaning of "experience" presupposes an idealism similar to that of George Berkeley. Experience is the ground of being; to exist is to exist in conscious experience. The second meaning of "experience" is the "interaction of an organism with its environment." Unlike the first meaning, which presupposes a philosophical idealism, the second meaning presupposes a type of naturalism; experience is a coping with one's surroundings. The third meaning of experience, and the meaning most often employed in *The Quest for Certainty*, is immediate, self-enclosed awareness. This third meaning does not deny that experience is somehow dependent upon external events, but it does deny that these events are revealed in experience. In Feldman's estimation, Dewey's empiricism is confounded by his equivocation between experience as the interaction of an organism with its surroundings and experience as immediate, self-enclosed awareness.

Feldman also finds fault with Dewey's implicit concept of continuity and his inconsistent statements regarding value and objectivity. According to Feldman, Dewey employs a concept of continuity as a basis for criticizing most of Western philosophy without ever explicitly defining what he means by "continuity." Moreover, Dewey opposes the separation of minds and bodies, ideas and objects, and values and experiences, and yet fails to develop a concept of continuity which is capable of holding these things together. (The matter is further complicated by Dewey's doctrine of emergent intelligence. In his essay in *Creative Intelligence*, 1917, and in *Experience and Nature*, Dewey adopts the position that intelligence characterizes a level of existence separate from the organic realm out of which it evolved. This doctrine appears to introduce a dualism into Dewey's thought and thereby to undermine his commitment to continuity.)

Another aspect of Dewey's thought that Feldman finds problematic is his position concerning value and objectivity. In *The Quest for Certainty* and elsewhere, Dewey maintains that the dichotomy between objective knowledge and moral concerns is a false dichotomy. All thought is marked by a moral bias and concern. According to Dewey, it is both impossible and undesirable to construct a world view that is something other than a projection of how one believes reality ought to be. Yet Dewey also contends just the opposite: that objective knowledge is possible and that it ought to be sought. One can and should, he contends, keep one's self out of the data.

Despite Feldman's critical evaluation of many aspects of Dewey's thought, his book is a good introduction to Dewey's philosophy. His focus on the major concepts underlying Dewey's philosophy and the complexities involved in each of them is most illuminating.

Flower, Elizabeth and Murray G. Murphey. *A History of Philosophy in America*. Vol. II. New York: Capricorn Books, 1977.

Elizabeth Flower's and Murray G. Murphey's *A History of Philosophy in America* is the most complete study of philosophy in America to date. It

combines a very adequate account of the careers of America's best philosophers from the Puritans to C. I. Lewis with a lucid exposition and careful
analysis of their philosophies.

Critical of scholars who have tried to "encapsulate" John Dewey's philosophy, Flower and Murphey seek to illuminate the organic structure of Dewey's
thought by emphasizing the centrality of his psychology to the rest of his
work. The uniqueness of Dewey's thought, in their estimation, lies in his
belief that a naturalistic psychology dissolves the distinction between fact and
value. Since knowing and action are inseparable, and since action is always
purposive and valuing, fact and value do not exist in separate spheres. To
view fact and value as inhabiting distinct realms is, in Dewey's estimation,
to misunderstand both.

Flower and Murphey divide their discussion of Dewey's thought into five
sections: (1) Absolutism and Experimentalism; (2) A Naturalistic Psychology,
Individual and Social; (3) Theory of Inquiry; (4) Ethics and Valuation; and
(5) Social Philosophy.

In the first section Flower and Murphey discuss Dewey's life, particularly
its intellectual and professional aspects, and they present a broad analysis of
his shift from Hegelianism to a biologically oriented functionalism.

In the second section they discuss what they understand to be the core of
Dewey's philosophy—his naturalistic psychology. In his early articles, which
were devoted to psychology, and in his *Syllabus*, in which he applies psychology to moral judgments, Dewey lays the foundation for all of his later
work. According to Flower and Murphey, Dewey's central concern in the
articles on psychology is to show that the experiencing individual imports
unrecognized biases into his or her experience. A related concern is to erad-
icate biases of philosophers and psychologists which have created artificial
problems that follow from the compartmentalizing of experience. Experience
for Dewey is unified; it is not divisable into acting and thinking, sensation
and reflection, private and public.

The third section is devoted to a discussion of Dewey's logic. Dewey's logic
deals with understanding in general; it is an inquiry into inquiries. Scientific
inquiries, commonsense inquiries, and value inquiries are all of a piece for
Dewey; they are all ways of adjusting to or interacting with one's environment.
Dewey's investigations into the origins and boundaries of logic are, according
to Flower and Murphey, a study of the dynamic interrelationship which exists
between the individual and the world.

Valuation, a specific aspect of the interaction between an individual and
the world, is the focus of section four, in which Flower and Murphey discuss
The Quest for Certainty. The great significance of Dewey's ethical thought,
of which *The Quest for Certainty* is one element, is its emphasis upon the
developmental nature of valuation. Dewey is opposed to the notion that
values are somehow permanent and unchanging. His position is that, just as

scientific knowledge is "being made," values are "being made"; and just as absolutes are out of place in science, so are they out of place in ethics.

The final section is concerned with Dewey's social philosophy. By "social philosophy" Flower and Murphey mean his political philosophy, his philosophy of culture, his philosophy of law, and his philosophy of education. In addition to commenting briefly on Dewey's social philosophy, Flower and Murphey note the relation between his social philosophy and his social psychology. What is important to note, they maintain, is that Dewey's thought leads inevitably to social philosophy. Dewey did not engage in social philosophy as an afterthought; rather, his philosphy is inherently social by virtue of his naturalistic psychology.

Flower's and Murphey's thesis that Dewey's naturalistic psychology is the foundation for the rest of his work deserves careful consideration. Their book serves to unify and to illuminate Dewey's life and thought.—*M.F.*

ADDITIONAL RECOMMENDED READING

Bernstein, Richard J. *John Dewey*. New York: Washington Square Press, 1966. A sympathetic and comprehensive statement of Dewey's thought; a very good statement and analysis of Dewey's philosophy and its development.

Boydston, Jo Ann and Kathleen Poulos. *Checklist of Writings About John Dewey*. Carbondale: Southern Illinois University Press, 1978. This book should be very useful to the student interested in Dewey's philosophy. It contains a complete listing of all published and unpublished works about Dewey and lists of reviews of Dewey's books, as well as reviews of works about Dewey.

Geiger, George R. *John Dewey in Perspective*. New York: Oxford University Press, 1958. Geiger emphasizes Dewey's understanding of aesthetic experience as the key to understanding Dewey's thought as a whole.

Gouinlock, James. *John Dewey's Philosophy of Value*. New York: Humanities Press, 1972. Dewey's moral philosophy, according to Gouinlock, is integral to Dewey's understanding of nature. By developing this thesis Gouinlock seeks to clarify Dewey's moral philosophy.

Hook, Sidney. *John Dewey: An Intellectual Portrait*. Westport, Connecticut: Greenwood Press, 1971. This republication of the 1939 edition shows how Dewey the philosopher and Dewey the man and social reformer fit together. Generally regarded as the definitive delineation of Dewey.

Schilpp, Paul A., ed. *The Philosophy of John Dewey*. New York: Tudor Publishing Company, 1951. Contains a biography of Dewey written by his daughters, a collection of seventeen essays on Dewey's philosophy, Dewey's responses to these essays, and a bibliography of Dewey's writings from 1885 to 1950. The essays are of very high quality.

THE PHILOSOPHY OF ART

Author: Curt John Ducasse (1881-1969)
Type of work: Philosophy of art
First published: 1929

PRINCIPAL IDEAS ADVANCED

Art is a human activity consisting of the expression of feeling through objectification: art is the language of feelings.

Feeling is objectified when an object created by the artist is capable of yielding to the artist the feeling it was intended to yield.

A work of art is intended to yield feeling when aesthetically contemplated; aesthetic contemplation is an attending to something for the sake of its feeling import.

Works of art need not be beautiful; the artist aims at the expression of feeling, whether or not the resultant work is beautiful.

Aesthetic feelings are endlessly various; only a few have proper names.

Judgments passed on works of art and other aesthetic objects involve standards of criticism, but standards are not universal or provable; they are functions of the particular constitutions of critics.

Curt John Ducasse of Brown University, whose *Nature, Mind, and Death* is a distinguished work covering a wide range of topics in the fields of philosophy, metaphysics, and epistemology, was also a distinguished and provocative philosopher of art. His most thorough and technical treatment of problems in aesthetics is his *The Philosophy of Art*, but his eminently clear and responsibly simplified statement, *Art, the Critics, and You* (1944), is also well worth the attention of any serious student of aesthetics.

In the Introduction to his work on the philosophy of art, Ducasse first of all states in no uncertain terms his conviction that for the understanding of problems of aesthetics one must turn to the philosopher, not the artist. The artist's task is something quite different from the task of dealing with the theoretical questions that prompt philosophical reflection and resolution—questions such as "What is art?", "What is beauty?", "Is art a form of play?", and "What, if any, are the proper standards of art criticism?"

Ducasse then briefly sketches his ideas concerning the nature of philosophical inquiry. He argues that philosophy is, in a certain broad sense of the term, a "science," in that philosophy is a systematic, knowledge-yielding enterprise. The subject matter of philosophy is "facts of the sort called *valuations*," and the task of the philosopher is not to pass value judgments but to clarify and criticize statements *about* value judgments. What this amounts to is the effort to understand what such terms as "right," "wrong," "true," "false," "good," "bad," "beautiful," and "ugly" are used to communicate, and to identify, if possible, the kinds of procedures by which it is determined whether, in any given case, one of these value terms applies. Accordingly, Ducasse offers as a summary definition of philosophy the following: "Philosophy is general theory of criticism."

The philosophy of art, then, is "the general theory of the criticism of art and aesthetic objects." Later in his book Ducasse makes it clear that the class of aesthetic objects—of matters that may be contemplated for the sake of the experience of contemplation alone—is much broader than the class of works of art: one can contemplate sunsets, mountains, and other human beings aesthetically, as well as works of art.

Also in the Introduction one finds a statement of Ducasse's theme concerning art criticism—that art criticism usually tells us more about the critic than it does about works of art. The point is that value judgments are functions of standards as applied to the subjects of criticism, and there are no universal standards. Relative to a specified standard, however, a value judgment can be true and informative.

Ducasse begins the body of his work by claiming that art is not a quality of things but a human activity—the kind of activity (yet to be defined) that yields works of art. What one finds in art museums are not instances of art but of works of art; the paintings, works of sculpture, and other constructions that one finds there do not possess some elusive quality that makes them "art," for they are "art" only in the sense that they are the products of the art activity.

Ducasse next claims that many works of art are ugly (he invites the reader to find his own examples), and accordingly he contends that art, as a distinctive human activity, cannot be understood to aim at the creation of beauty. (By an "ugly" work of art, Ducasse does not mean a work of art portraying something ugly; he means a work of art that in contemplation is displeasing.)

What the artist does aim at, according to Ducasse, is objective self-expression. The artist seeks through the use of some material to make an object that will embody feeling or emotion; if the attempt is successful, the object created is a work of art whether or not it is beautiful. Since some beautiful objects are not works of art and some works of art are not beautiful (they may, indeed, be ugly), there is no essential connection between art and beauty, Ducasse concludes.

Before elaborating and clarifying his basic contention that art is the language of the feelings and that a work of art is an objectification of feeling, Ducasse considers the somewhat similar theories proposed by Eugène Véron and Leo Tolstoy. Véron contended (in *L'Esthétique*, Paris, 1882) that art is essentially language, that expressions of the feelings (such as pain and joy) are natural to human beings as well as to other animals. Human beings have the ability to elaborate their modes of expression, and they pass from spontaneous cries and gestures to imitative language, pictorial language, and finally to the use of symbols that are arbitrary, in the sense that the symbols do not resemble what they signify. The signs used by the artist as elements of his language become more and more varied, including not only verbal signs (of the kind used by the poet) but also forms, colors, lines, sounds—whatever can be employed for expressive purposes. Although all art is expressive, a distinction can be made, according to Véron, between *decorative* art, which expresses pleasure and hence aims at beauty, and *expressive* (narrower sense) art, which aims at the external expression of "sentiments . . . virtues and vices. . . ." Finally, Véron contends that art should be evaluated by reference to the sincerity of the artist and to the worth of his ideas and sentiments.

Tolstoy's philosophy of art is much like Véron's, Ducasse suggests, and it is likely that Véron's basic ideas were important influences in Tolstoy's thinking in aesthetics. Like Véron, Tolstoy contends that art is the language of feeling, that the value of a work of art is a function of the moral worth of the artist (although Tolstoy went on to suggest that Christian feelings are of greatest worth and, accordingly, that Christian art is the best), and that art is a way of communicating from person to person. What distinguishes Tolstoy's ideas from Véron's, Ducasse points out, is that Véron describes art as the *expression* of feeling, while Tolstoy contends that art necessarily involves the *transmission* of feelings from one person to another.

John Dewey's contention that language requires "a context of mutual assistance and direction," that it is not fundamentally expressive but communicative, and that communication involves conscious cooperation, is rejected by Ducasse as too limiting a definition. Not all signs are signals, he points out, and not all signaling requires cooperation; to signal, Ducasse suggests, is to "operate" on another, and only reciprocal signaling involves cooperation.

Ducasse insists that language is the intentional expression of an inner state: it is not communication, although it may be used to communicate. By an "inner state" Ducasse means "a belief, doubt, volition, emotion." If art is the language of feeling, then, it is the expression, not the communication, of feeling.

Ducasse criticizes Benedetto Croce's *Aesthetic* (and especially the translation of the work) as a confusing work because of the idiosyncratic use of terms that, in English, mean something quite different from what Croce intends them to mean. Croce writes as if he were explaining the meanings of terms in common use, but what he actually does, Ducasse contends, is to prescribe meanings to suit his needs. In any case, Croce defines art as "expression," by which he means a "spiritual aesthetic synthesis" (apparently something quite different from what Ducasse means by "expression"), and then equates the meaning of the term "expression" with the term "intuition." By expression in art Croce means not the use of words, lines, colors, sounds, and the like, but *images* of such matters. Accordingly, Croce regards the physical work of art as only a copy of the real work of art—which is an image, the product of the imagination.

Ducasse finds fault with Croce's account of the psychology of art, with his thesis concerning the physical work of art, and with his view of beauty. Croce's faults stem (according to Ducasse) from his insistence on giving priority in the account of art to "spiritual activity," at the expense of coming to understand how the artist in fact proceeds through the use of material to create a physical work that expresses feeling. That Croce's view is couched in misleading language only compounds the difficulty.

DeWitt H. Parker's theory (as presented in *The Analysis of Art*, 1927) is that art is the imaginative expression of a wish. Ducasse objects to Parker's idea on several counts. For one thing, Ducasse argues, art need not remain within the imagination (as Parker contends); nor need art simulate reality; nor need art satisfy through representation something wished for (indeed, usually it *cannot*); and, finally, despite Parker's claim to the contrary, art *can* clarify an emotive state through the objective expression of it.

Ducasse objects to Aristotle's claim that art springs from "the instinct for imitation and the instinct for harmony and rhythm." According to Ducasse, even when to some degree an artist makes a likeness, he is not so much imitating his subject as "editing" it. In any case, the imitation theory fails to account for nonrepresentative art, and the account of the impulses that lead to art is not in accord with the introspective reports of artists.

Nor can art be understood by reference to its evolutionary utility, as Charles Darwin maintained. Darwin erred in supposing that art aims at attraction through beauty, and he errs further in supposing that the gaudy display by an animal is artistically contrived or aesthetically appreciated: the fact is, there is a display, and there is a reaction—and this has nothing to do with art.

Ducasse proceeds to a criticism of the instrumentalist theory of art as proposed by Dewey. He quotes Dewey's claim that "Any activity that is productive of objects whose perception is an immediate good, and whose operation is a continual source of enjoyable perception of other events, exhibits fineness of art" (from *Experience and Nature*, 1925). After spelling out what he describes as the "strangeness" of the instrumentalist life-ideal ("a life of toolmaking"), Ducasse rejects one by one the fundamental features of Dewey's claim (as expressed above and elsewhere). For one thing, Ducasse writes, neither artistic production nor aesthetic perception need involve meaning—yet Dewey argues that all intelligent activity involves the attempt to achieve meaning. Nor is it the case that—as Dewey argues—all emotions are responses to objective situations; Dewey confuses the question of *what* emotion is with the question of the circumstances under which it occurs. Ducasse insists that art is the objective expression of emotion, whether or not the emotion arises in a problematic life situation.

Finally, before giving the details of his own theory, Ducasse considers the proposal that art is play. He mentions F. C. S. Schiller's idea that art is a kind of aesthetic play subjected to formal control, and he cites Herbert Spencer as claiming that art is a kind of disinterested play by which surplus energy is discharged. Ducasse defines play as "the systematic pursuit of an end set up or accepted expressly for the purpose." In play a goal is established in order to make the effort to secure it possible; enjoyment comes, if it does, from the pursuit.

Ducasse objects to the claim that art is play on the ground that art has an end—namely, the creation of an object expressive of feeling—and the end is not set up simply to provide something to pursue. Whether play be imitation, recreation, or the satisfaction of the instinct to prepare for one's life activities (the latter being the theory of Karl Groos), it is clear that art is not play; nor is it work, if by "work" is meant an activity in which the specific character of the end is known; for the character of the work of art emerges in the art process and is not known, at least in its entirety, at the outset. Furthermore, the obligation to attain an end is "external" in work, "internal" in art: "The obligation in art is a categorical imperative, uttered, as it were, to ourselves by ourselves. It is the obligation imposed by the laws of one's inward being, to give birth to that which one bears darkly in oneself." Thus, according to Ducasse, art stands on its own as art; it is neither essentially work nor essentially play.

Ducasse, having rejected various opposing views of the nature of art, finally develops his own theory. Art is skilled activity, neither work nor play but self-objectification; it is aesthetic objectification—namely, the creation of an object to be contemplated for the sake of its feeling impact, designed to yield the feeling that gave rise to the effort to express it. (Note that Ducasse uses the term "aesthetic" to mean "having to do with perception," *not* "beautiful.")

In contending that art is the *objective expression of feeling*, Ducasse means that the artist creates an object he can contemplate with the intention that it yield back to him the feeling which in that way he attempts to express. Art thus requires critical judgment: unless the artist judges the work to be an objective expression of his feeling, it is not a work of art.

Ducasse distinguishes between the receptive, effective, and judgmental attitudes. Art is "practical," Ducasse writes, in that it is effective; that is, the art activity makes differences, has effects on material. Hence, art creation is effective; but art involves judgment along the way: the artist considers whether what he has done to the material is what he wants—hence, art is judgmental. The consideration of the work, however, involves taking a contemplative attitude towards it: the artist (like the art consumer) must be receptive.

Aesthetic contemplation is described by Ducasse as a "listening" for feelings, a throwing oneself open to feeling, an "attitude of *directed but contentless receptiveness*. . . ." One looks (or listens, or reads, or touches, or whatever) for the sake of the feelings consequent upon doing so. One attends *to* an object *for* its feeling import. The contemplation is undertaken in order that in the course of contemplation one will feel; the feeling (emotion) is the end of the activity of aesthetic contemplation.

After a brief discussion of empathy and ecpathy (the former a mode of perception involving interpreting an object as a dramatic agent, the latter the mode of attention proper to the contemplation of aesthetic objects), Ducasse turns to a discussion of the aesthetic feelings. They may be of any sort, and only a few have proper names. They are not to be confused with sensations; they are whatever happens in the way of feeling as one contemplates aesthetically.

Ducasse regards beauty and ugliness as positive and negative aesthetic value. An object is beautiful if, when contemplated aesthetically, it yields pleasure; ugly, if it yields displeasure. There is also a narrow sense of the term "beautiful" such that an object is beautiful if it approaches (or meets) an ideal of positive aesthetic value. (Ducasse also discusses the pretty, the graceful, the sublime, the tragic, and the comic.)

Criticism is judgment of worth, Ducasse writes; the value of an object may be mediate (good for something) or immediate (the object is pleasant as such). A judgment of worth involves reference to a standard, he continues, but the standard chosen will be a function of the interest of the critic. A work of art may be criticized as art, as an aesthetic object, as a communication, as having a moral or immoral effect, as being beautiful or ugly, or as being practically beneficial or harmful; and within each of these categories, the standard employed will depend on the interests of the judge (critic). Hence, in a sense, a judgment may tell us more about the judge than about the matter judged.

Ducasse concludes his detailed examination of art and of matters related to art by a profession of aesthetic liberalism. The aesthetic liberal contends that judgments of value are capable of proof only when they are judgments of *mediate* value (it can be shown whether something will in fact lead to what is desired); judgments of *immediate* value are beyond proof, without objective validity, indicative only of the particular constitution of the critic. People may agree in their judgments and standards, but there is no way of showing that they ought to agree. Just as one cannot refute another's judgment of immediate value, however, so the other cannot refute one's own judgment. There is no reason why one should not hold to one's opinion of value as strongly as one pleases. "That our own opinion must in the nature of such matters be dogmatic," Ducasse concludes, "is no reason why it should not be honest, vigorous, and unashamed."—*I.P.M.*

PERTINENT LITERATURE

Tomas, Vincent. "Pictures and Maps," in *Current Philosophical Issues: Essays in Honor of Curt John Ducasse*. Compiled and edited by Frederick

C. Dommeyer. Springfield, Illinois: Charles C. Thomas, 1966.

Fourteen philosophers—some, former students of Curt John Ducasse; others, friends and associates—contributed insightful essays on subjects of their own choosing but related to Ducasse's work to this volume in his honor. Vincent Tomas' essay, "Pictures and Maps," is concerned directly with one of Ducasse's central propositions in his philosophy of art, but essays by Marvin Farber and Morris Lazerowitz bear on Ducasse's philosophy of philosophy, a position briefly developed in his *The Philosophy of Art* (1929) and extensively treated in his *Philosophy as a Science: Its Matter and Its Method* (1941). (Tomas refers to the original edition of Ducasse's *The Philosophy of Art*, published in New York by Dial Press in 1929. The revised edition, published in New York by Dover Publications, in 1966, includes as additions an essay entitled "Some Questions in Aesthetics," from *The Monist*, January, 1932— a reply to critical comments on the original version of the book—a new index, and selections from a discussion originally published in *Philosophy and Phenomenological Research*, June, 1961.)

Tomas begins his essay by referring to Ducasse's observation that for most representational paintings, three typical modes of interpretation may be distinguished: (1) one abstracts a flat design of colors, lines, and shapes; (2) the colors, lines, and shapes are taken as representing the relations of volumes in three-dimensional space; (3) one attends to the subject-matter; the volumes in three-dimensional space are interpreted as dramatic entities.

When paintings are interpreted as designs and not dramatically, a well-painted turnip is as good as a well-painted Madonna, but from the dramatic standpoint there is such a significant difference between, say, a turnip and a Madonna, that a painting dealing with the one subject matter has a radically different aesthetic import from that of a painting, taken dramatically, dealing with the other. Tomas quotes Ducasse's views to this effect, and he then calls attention to Ducasse's effort to counter the *avant-garde* tendency (of 1929) to regard dramatic entities as irrelevant to the aesthetic value of works of art.

Tomas refers to the view advocated by José Ortega y Gasset in his *The Dehumanization of Art* (1925) that evinces the attitude of rejection with regard to subject matter; and he quotes Ortega's comment that "preoccupation with the human content of a work of art is in principle incompatible with aesthetic enjoyment proper."

One of the most effective arguments in support of the view that in art subject matter is aesthetically irrelevant, Tomas reports, is the argument that the emotive concerns provoked by the third mode of interpretation, that of taking subject matter dramatically, interfere with and, in fact, exclude the taking of the aesthetic attitude toward a work of art so interpreted. The contention is that in dealing with subject matter dramatically—that is, in recognizing a painting as in some sense representing three-dimensional objects of recognizable kinds—one looks *through* the painting, not *at* it. Therefore, it is argued, since aesthetic attention requires that one look "at" a painting, not "through it," art cannot properly be attended to by way of the third mode of interpretation.

Tomas reports Ducasse's retort that if a painting is taken as an illustration in the sense of something to satisfy curiosity regarding what something looks like, then it is indeed not being taken aesthetically; but it is possible to regard the subject matter in another way—namely, by way of aesthetic contemplation: one contemplates the dramatic entity as presented; one does not concern oneself with the question of whether it happens to show what something outside the painting looks like.

Tomas distinguishes between what he calls "categorical" representation and "conditional" representation. In attending to Velasquez's "Pope Innocent X," Tomas writes, one may simply attend to the "firm-willed man" depicted (without regarding the painting as an illustration—that is, without taking the portrait to be the portrait of a historical figure) or one may take the dramatic entity *in* the picture (when the picture is interpreted in the third mode) as representative of a flesh-and-blood figure *outside* the painting. To follow the first procedure is to take the representation as "categorical"; to follow the alternative procedure is to take it as "conditional."

The view that representation is artistically irrelevant has seemed plausible, Tomas maintains, only because this distinction—between categorical and conditional representation—has not been recognized; in effect, the critics of the view that representational art is possible have presumed all representative art to be subject only to conditional interpretation. Tomas points out that when a painting is representative, the dramatic entity (fixed by paint on canvas) remains the same whether it is taken categorically or conditionally—but, he argues, if it is taken conditionally the dramatic entity fails to be artistically relevant, while if it is taken categorically, that is, aesthetically and not as illustration, it is artistically relevant. Tomas defends his thesis—which he regards as supportive of Ducasse's position—by reference to differences between pictures and maps and to differences in how maps and pictures are used.

A map of an actual region is usually used as a source of information; such a map is illustrative. A map of an imaginary (not in the public domain) region, however, cannot be inaccurate because it does not purport to represent an actual region the features of which could be misrepresented by the map; such a map is likely to be taken categorically. (One could, of course, take an illustrative map aesthetically, as simply a picture of a region, without presuming that there is such a region; and one could take a fanciful map conditionally, as an illustration: it would be futile, however, to attempt to journey by reference to it.) To take a representation as a map is to take it conditionally; to take it as a picture is to take it categorically (in the latter case, one deals with what is presented, the dramatic entity as presented, without concerning oneself with the question of whether the representation is illustrative).

Tomas' conclusion is that only categorical representation can be aesthetically and artistically interesting and relevant. Critics who have argued that representation is artistically irrelevant have failed to take representation in any way other than conditionally (as if every representative painting were a map); such critics have been looking "through" paintings, and they have failed to realize, as Ducasse has shown, that it is possible to look "at" a painting aesthetically by, as Tomas puts it, looking at it as a categorical representation.

Ducasse, Curt John. "Appendix II: Some Questions in Aesthetics," in his *The Philosophy of Art*. New York: Dover Publications, 1966.

Curt John Ducasse's essay "Some Questions in Aesthetics" does not appear in the 1929 edition of his *The Philosophy of Art*, and it deserves special attention because not only does it provide references to critical comments on the book as it originally appeared but it also sets forth Ducasse's responses to criticism, thereby filling out the ideas central to the book.

Ducasse first of all considers objections that have been made to his thesis that there is no necessary connection between fine art and beauty. He points out that beautiful things that are not works of art abound: "Flowers, rainbows, landscapes. . . ." He concedes, however, that it is not so easy to win acceptance of the claim that there are ugly works of art; many persons argue that if a painting, drawing, or sculpture is ugly, it is thereby *not* a work of art— or, insofar as such a work is ugly, it is just to that degree and on that account not a work of art.

Ducasse rejects the implicit definition of "art" as meaning "the human activity the products of which are beautiful things," on two grounds: (1) such a definition would require that we describe as "art" the production of beautiful things even when such production is mechanical or accidental, and (2) such a definition would make the descriptive term "art" a function of a subjective factor; namely, the kind of interest that is satisfied by the contemplation of a certain kind of thing. (To say "That object is beautiful," Ducasse argues, is to express a *subjective evaluation* of the subject.)

Ducasse reviews his accounts of beauty and art. Art, he claims, is the "critically controlled, objective expression by the artist of a feeling." (An expression is "objective," he writes, when its product is such that when contemplated aesthetically—for the sake of the experience of contemplation— it "induces back in him the feeling which he intended to express." And an object is beautiful if it gives pleasure to someone in aesthetic contemplation.

Lawrence W. Beals's criticism consists in the claim that if the artist is successful, what he produces is a work of art; and since success is pleasing, the work of art is beautiful.

Ducasse rejects Beals's criticism on the ground that the pleasure of success is one thing; pleasure occasioned by an object as contemplated aesthetically is another. Hence, it has not been shown that works of art are necessarily beautiful.

Beals also proposes another point of criticism: if art is not beautiful, then, according to Ducasse, it tends to discourage aesthetic contemplation; but if a work is such that it is not contemplated aesthetically, then, according to Ducasse's account, it is not a work of art. Hence, art must be beautiful. Ducasse replies that all that is necessary if a work is to be a work of art is that it objectify the artist's feelings; whether others choose to contemplate it and whether they find in it what he intended to express makes no difference.

D. W. Gotshalk's criticism is similar to Beals's: art is skill, and skill is pleasant. (Beals relates success to pleasure; Gotshalk relates skill to pleasure—but since skill is the ability to be successful, there is a connection of views here.)

Ducasse replies that contemplators may be pleased (or displeased) by an object because of its character as perceived in aesthetic contemplation without knowing or even being able to know whether the object is the product of skilled activity; that is, of activity skillful in the respect of producing an objective expression of the artist's feelings. A contemplator may regard a work of art as a sign of skill because it is beautiful, but the reverse is not the case: the object's being beautiful is not contingent upon its being recognized as the product of skilled activity.

Israel Knox argues that all art is beautiful because all art involves perfection of form, and perfection of form is aesthetically pleasing. DeWitt Parker argues along similar lines: a work of art must be beautiful because it aims at the creation of value through the use of design. Ducasse responds that whatever form or value may be involved in a work of art, it need not be of the sort that is beautiful or that consists in beauty: the form may be ugly, the value may be negative.

Ducasse also considers briefly the criticism of his claim that art need not involve communication; it is enough if art is objectively expressive. He maintains that although many artists decide to communicate, they need not do so.

Finally, Ducasse considers the claim that if his theory of judgment and of art is true, art criticism is impossible; if only the artist knows whether he has done what he intended, and if value judgments are based on subjective factors, then, it is maintained, art criticism is impossible. Ducasse replies that judgment is related to criteria that may have nothing to do with the artist's success; and although one's judgment may be entirely a matter of personal interest and irrelevant to the interests of others, there is no reason why the critic's interest cannot be an objectively verifiable feature of the work of art and, hence, of some possible interest to others.—*I.P.M.*

ADDITIONAL RECOMMENDED READING

Ducasse, Curt John. *Art, the Critics, and You.* New York: Oskar Piest, 1944. A brief yet clear and adequate account of Ducasse's theory of art and art criticism. Suitable for the general reader.

_____ .*Philosophy as a Science: Its Matter and Its Method.* New York: Oskar Piest, 1941. Ducasse's approach to problems of aesthetics and his theory of aesthetic judgment both illustrate and support his account of philosophical method and of the nature of philosophy. The basic idea is that philosophy is the attempt to clarify value terms and matters relating to value judgments.

Duffield, Holley Gene and Manuel Bilsky, eds. *Tolstoy and the Critics: Literature and Aesthetics.* Chicago: Scott, Foresman and Company, 1965. Ducasse, who does not agree with Tolstoy's contention that art necessarily involves the communication of emotion, here concerns himself with the question, "What Has Beauty to Do With Art?" (The volume also contains a number of relevant essays on aesthetics by other contributors.)

Hospers, John, ed. *Artistic Expression.* New York: Appleton-Century-Crofts, 1971. An excellent collection of fifteen articles on art as expression. Includes an essay by C. J. Ducasse and a number of references to his views in essays by other philosophers. Vincent Tomas' contribution to a selection involving parts by Douglas Morgan and Monroe Beardsley is especially relevant.

McGreal, Ian Philip. "Is Beauty Aesthetic Value?," in *The Journal of Philosophy.* XLVI, no. 17 (August 18, 1949), pp. 553-557. McGreal criticizes Ducasse's identification of aesthetic pleasantness with positive aesthetic value.

MIND AND THE WORLD-ORDER

Author: Clarence Irving Lewis (1883-1964)
Type of work: Epistemology
First published: 1929

PRINCIPAL IDEAS ADVANCED

A priori *truths are definitive in nature; they specify the real because of antecedently determined criteria of what is to be called "real."*

Empirical truth is never more than probable because descriptions of matters of fact are hypothetical propositions, pragmatic in character.

Knowledge is the result of interpreting the sensuously given by means of a priori *concepts; thus, there is no contradiction between the relativity of knowledge (to the concepts) and the independence of the object (understood in terms of the given).*

To know is to have reason to expect that were we to act in certain ways, our experience would present the character we expect.

The a priori *has its origin in mind, but its applicability is a function of the world order; a world which would not, relative to some interpretative act of mind, exhibit order is practically inconceivable.*

Pragmatism, sometimes called the characteristically American philosophy, is usually considered to have been best exemplified in the writings of William James, C. S. Peirce, and John Dewey. The position is sometimes called "humanism" (for example, the point of view developed by the English philosopher, F. C. S. Schiller) and sometimes called "instrumentalism." Although there were many variations in the specific philosophies of these individuals, they shared a belief in the relativity of truth to the concrete verification processes and to the practical role which man plays in the world. In general they were in agreement also in being more or less hostile towards metaphysics, at least of an absolutistic sort, and feeling that a view of the universe which "made no difference" to the common man, either in the sense that it could not be confirmed or disproved by observable phenomena, or in the sense that it did not help him to live a better life, was really meaningless, and that indulgence in speculation of this kind was a waste of time.

Except for Peirce, none of this group had any great familiarity either with epistemology or with modern logic and its problems. They approached philosophy largely from the "human" point of view—through ethics, social and political philosophy, religion, education. C. I. Lewis has had many of the same interests that Peirce did, and, like Peirce, he has made important contributions to the fields of the philosophy of science and symbolic logic. Lewis' *Survey of Symbolic Logic* (1918) is one of the standard works in this area. In *Mind and the World-Order*, this broad knowledge of the nature of deductive systems and of the difference between *a priori* and *a posteriori* cognition is used to develop a position which Lewis chose to call "conceptualistic pragmatism." It has much in common with the views of the earlier pragmatists, and Lewis frankly acknowledges his indebtedness to these philosophers; but it also has certain distinctive aspects. For this reason it deserves careful consideration as an important contemporary philosophical position. Posterity will undoubtedly credit Lewis with having modified pragmatism in such a way as to make it compatible with the methodologies of the mathematical and natural sciences.

Lewis attempts to reduce his point of view to three principles: (1) *A priori* truths are not forms of intuition or categories which determine the content of experience; they are, rather, definitive in nature and limit reality only in the sense that whatever is called "real" is selected from experience by means of criteria which are antecedently determined. (2) The application of any *a priori* concepts to a particular experience is hypothetical because it is instrumental or pragmatic; consequently, empirical truth is never more than probable. (3) No belief in the conformity of experience to the mind or its categories is required, for a complete nonconformity of these two aspects of knowledge is inconceivable.

To explain these principles Lewis begins with an analysis of the philosophical method. Philosophy is not "another science," nor is it a substitute for science. It is the critical and reflective application of the mind to experience. It deals with what is already familiar to us, but it analyzes this familiarity into the clear ideas which constitute it. Philosophy begins with the experiences of reality, goodness, and validity, which we all have, and attempts to clarify these notions by critical consideration of what is implicitly in them and therefore does not transcend experience. (A person with no sense of reality will not acquire one by the study of metaphysics.) More specifically, this analysis of experience involves the discovery of *categories*—the formulation of the criteria of reality. Experience does not determine its own categories; *mind* provides these criteria and they are imposed upon the given by our active attitude. Philosophy is not empirical if this claim means that it takes what is merely given to the mind as the totality of experience; nor is it analytic in the sense that it accepts a ready-made experience. Philosophy is not rationalistic if this claim means that it forces reality into a Procrustean bed; but it is rationalistic in the sense that it is particularly concerned with that aspect of experience which the mind contributes by its interpretive act.

Analysis of knowledge reveals two elements: the concept and the sensuously given. The former is the product of thought; the latter is merely presented, and involves no such activity. The conceptual element is *a priori*, and philosophy can be defined as the study of the *a priori* in the sense that it undertakes to define, or explicate, such concepts as the *good*, the *right*, the *valid*, and the *real*. The pure concept and the sensuously given do not limit each other; they are mutually independent. Knowledge is the result of interpreting the given by means of concepts. Consequently there is no knowledge in the mere awareness of the given. Furthermore, all empirical knowledge is only probable because it is based on the application of a temporally extended pattern of actual and possible experiences to something which is immediately given, and this pattern may have to be revised in view of what future experiences disclose. However, the independence of the conceptual and the given in no way prevents us from having valid knowledge. Nor does it in any way restrict the possibility of finding concepts under which any conceivable experience can be subsumed.

There are two theories of experience, Lewis argues, which do not accept the partition of experience into the given and the conceptual. One of these eliminates the conceptual entirely and reduces experience to the given. This theory is exemplified by Bergson and the mystics. Its inadequacy can be clearly seen in its inability to handle the fact of error. If mind is pure receptivity, that with which it coincides in knowledge must always have the same objectivity, and we can never make mistakes. The other theory eliminates the given and reduces knowledge to the conceptual. This is the position of the idealists. Its inadequacy lies in its failure to recognize in knowledge an element which we do not create by thinking, one which we cannot, in general, displace or alter. This element is always ineffable; for if it is describable, concepts must have been brought in. And it is an abstraction, for it never exists in isolation in any experience or state of consciousness. It is given *in*, not *before*, experience. It is made up of "qualia," which are repeatable and recognizable, but have no names. They are fundamentally different from the universals of logic. They may be characterized by such terms as "the given," "the data of sense," "the sensuous," and "the given in its feeling character," provided one does not in the use of this terminology give the qualia merely a psychological status.

The conceptual element of experience, on the other hand, is quite different from the given. It is the construction, or interpretation, which is put upon the given. It is not to be understood in terms of any imagery or any psychological state of an individual mind. On the contrary, it is defined as "that meaning which must be common to two minds when they understand each other by the use of a substantive or its equivalent." Verifying the commonness of meaning in the case of any concept takes one of two routes: exhibiting the denotation by a behavioral act, or employing a definition. The former is unsatisfactory because it does not enable us to determine *uniquely* the meaning of the concept. The latter specifies the meaning directly in terms of a pattern of other concepts: A is defined in terms of B and C, and these are defined by other concepts. This is obviously a process which is never completed, but it does enable us to ascertain a genuine identity of meaning in two minds. It should not be interpreted as an analysis of meaning in the sense of a repeated dissection of a meaning into other meanings until one is reached which is no longer relational; *every* concept is a pattern of other concepts. To argue this definition of concepts on the grounds (a) that when we use a concept we "seldom have in mind" such a pattern of concepts, and (b) that we may have a meaning which we cannot state in terms of such a pattern without further thought, is to overlook the fact that concepts play a role in knowledge which is primarily practical; meanings may be exhibited implicitly in the consistency of behavior, as well as explicitly in the statement of definitions.

Having indicated that experience consists of two elements, the given and the conceptual, Lewis proceeds to ask what is involved in our perceptual knowledge of objects. His first task is to show that there is no knowledge by mere acquaintance; that is, knowledge *always* transcends the immediately given. This view requires him to distinguish, on the one hand, between qualia and our immediate awareness of them, and, on the other, between objects and our knowledge of them.

Qualia are subjective and have no names in normal language; they can be indicated by such phrases as "looks like" or "appears to be." Since they are immediately given they have no need of verification and we cannot possibly be mistaken about them. But if we take the simplest concepts, for example, "blue" or "round," we can see that what they embrace are not qualia but patterns of relations. This is shown by the steps which we would take in order to confirm our judgment that a given penny, say, is round: we might walk around it or view it from a different angle, we might pick it up and turn it in our fingers, we might move toward it or away from it. In each case we are attempting to confirm certain predictions which are involved in the supposition that it really *is* round. If these do not turn out as anticipated, we withdraw our judgment. The objective reality of the property consists in what would verify it and in what would disprove it. Thus the existence of an objective property is not constituted by the presentation of a given quale, but by the presentation of a given quale *plus* the concept of an ordered relation of different qualia tied up with certain conditions of behavior. The concept *means* this pattern of qualia. It therefore extends temporally beyond the given quale, permitting the pattern to be confirmed or disproved as an interpretation of the given, and it always prescribes possible ways of acting toward the presented object. *Without* such a pattern we could never identify an object. But—unfortunately, perhaps—even with such a pattern we cannot surely identify an object because the pattern always contains unrealized future experiences and because a certain pattern may serve to identify different qualia; also, different patterns may be applicable to the same quale. Our perceptual knowledge of an object is consequently more than mere acquaintance with a quale; when we ascribe objectivity to a presentation, the "acquaintance with" changes into "knowledge about" and we have a conceptual interpretation of what is presented. Knowledge consists of that part of the flux of experience which we ascribe to ourselves and which we change by our activities, and of that part which is objective and which we cannot predicate of ourselves. The world is bigger than the content of our direct experience only because we are active beings, only because we can say to what is revealed in our experience, "If we should do this, then we should experience that," and we find that the carrying out of these actions often reveals new truths about the world.

In further elaboration of this theory of knowledge Lewis shows that the examination of the problem of how we know has been guided since Descartes by an erroneous belief in the incompatibility of three alternatives: knowledge is not relative to the mind; the content of knowledge is not the real; and the real is dependent on mind. He proceeds, first, to show that there is no contradiction between the relativity of knowledge and the independence of the object. Indeed, relativity *requires* an independent character in what is thus relative. The fact, for example, that the weight of an object can be determined only relatively to a standard, such as a pound or a gram, does not imply that weight "in itself" has no meaning and that the object is therefore outside the category of weight. The concept of weight is an interpretation which *transcends* this relativity because it is a relational pattern exhibited by the independently real object. Furthermore, one should not, on the grounds that mind cannot be known, argue from the dependence of knowledge on mind to the conclusion that such knowledge cannot be of the real.

For I do know my mind, Lewis argues, though I learn it only in its commerce with real objects. In other words, I can learn the relation between mind and object by varying the object and noting the variation in its appearances and subjective manifestations, and by varying the mind and noting the resulting variations in the object. Finally, the fact that mind may have unrecognized limitations in its capacity to know the real does not imply either that knowledge is deceitful or that we must forever remain ignorant of the real.

Having shown that there is no knowledge without interpretation, Lewis examines the consequences of this fact. One of these is that there must be at least *some* knowledge which is *a priori*. The reasons for this are easy to see. Interpretation represents an activity of the mind and is always subject to test by future experience. The mere fact that interpretation reflects the character of past experience is not sufficient; there must be an assumed orderliness in experience which will entitle us to *expect* a certain kind of future on the basis of what the past has disclosed. This knowledge that nature is orderly must be *necessarily* true and independent of the particular character of experience. Knowledge of this kind is *a priori*.

After proving that certain historical conceptions of the *a priori*, which identify it with that which is psychologically undeniable, that which is self-evident, or that whose denial implies its affirmation, are erroneous, Lewis turns to an explanation of the *a priori*. The *a priori* has nothing to do with anything which is inescapable; it always permits of alternatives. It has its origin in an act of mind, thus exhibiting mind's creativity and not its dependence on anything inside or outside itself. Mind is, of course, limited in the sense that our perceptual organs are restricted to a certain range of stimuli; dogs can smell things which we cannot smell, and eagles can see things which we cannot see. But these things are not beyond the range of our *conception*, though they are beyond the range of our *perception*. Could there be anything, then, which *is* beyond the range of our conception? Obviously not, for in saying that an object is conceivable we are really saying something whose opposite makes no sense; the alternative to what can be experienced could not even be phrased. But although the range of the *conceivable* cannot be determined by any act of mind, the range of the *real* might be so determined. Science, in fact, does precisely this. It prescribes the character which reality must possess. Consequently, when we say that we experience dream objects, or fairies, or mermaids, science tells us that these kinds of "objects" cannot possibly be real.

A priori principles are required to limit reality; they are not required to limit experience. An interpretation is *a priori* only in the sense that it prescribes for a particular case and is thus not subject to recall even if the particular should fail to conform to the prescription. On the other hand, an interpretation is *a posteriori* if it is abandoned when the case does not fit. Let us suppose, for example, that we set up the categorial interpretation of scientific reality as "the realm in which every event has a cause." Now let us further assume that we come upon what is presumably a genuine miracle. We have two alternatives: we can say that the miracle did not really happen, or we can say that real events can happen without any natural causes. If real events must always have natural causes, then the miracle could not have been real; but if real events generally have causes (but might not), then the particular case could constitute an exception to the generalization. In the former case our interpretation is *a priori*; it can be maintained in the face of all experience, *no matter what*. In the latter case our interpretation is empirical and subject to disconfirmation in terms of experience. Lewis illustrates his point by the story of the man who boastfully made out a list of the names of all the men whom he could whip. When one burly man, whose name appeared on the list, approached him belligerently and insisted that *he* could not be whipped, the maker of the list said, "All right; then I'll just rub your name off." His original boast had no *a priori* character.

The apparent problem, of course, is how to get the empirical and the *a priori* together. But the real problem, according to Lewis, is not to "get them together" but to discover their co-presence in all cases of knowledge. The analysis of knowledge reveals the following five phases: (1) the immediate awareness of the given, exemplified by "This looks round"; (2) judgments about presented objects exemplified in "This object *is* round"; (3) the *a priori* development of abstract conceptual schemes, exemplified in such mathematical judgments as "In a Euclidean triangle the sum of the angles equals 180 degrees"; (4) the categorial knowledge implied in our interpretation of reality, exemplified in the judgment, "If this is a round object, then if I change my position in a certain way, it will appear elliptical"; and (5) empirical generalizations, such as "All swans are white."

Misunderstanding is sure to arise if we fail to distinguish phase (1) from phase (2). Merely to be aware of an appearance (a quale) is, as we have seen, not knowledge. But to judge that an object *is* round, rather than *appears* round, is knowledge. What makes it knowledge is the fact that it rests for its corroboration on a judgment of the kind indicated in phase (4): "If this object is round, then I can expect certain other appearances to reveal themselves." In fact, when I say that it is round, I assert implicitly *everything the failure of which would falsify the statement.* This is *a priori* and regulative in character, for it commits me to saying, "If I find that the presented object does *not* confirm my predictions of its other appearances, I shall deny that it is round." An *a priori* proposition always has this characteristic. For example, the statement "All swans are birds" is *a priori* because if any creature originally designated as a swan were discovered not to be a bird, the designation "swan" would be withdrawn. On the other hand, an empirical generalization, such as "All swans are white," might be contradicted if we found a black swan. Thus, an *a priori* proposition does not assert any limitation of experience; it asserts merely that we are tentatively trying out a certain categorial system which is so compactly organized that if one of its concepts does not fit reality, its other concepts will also not fit, and we should therefore abandon it and try another. Only if we have such a rigid scheme can we have knowledge of reality at all. For if an object is to be identifiable in terms of a certain concept, we must be provided with a criterion by means of which we can decide whether the object exemplifies the concept. If we were to change our criterion whenever an object failed to exemplify it, we could never have any criteria and we could never have knowledge. It *does* follow, of course, that our knowledge of objects can be probable only, never certain, for no matter how many predictions concerning the expected appearances of the object have been confirmed, there is always the possibility that the next one will not be; all verification is partial and a matter of degree. If we demand, therefore, something more than this, and require that in order to save us from skepticism empirical knowledge must be *certain*, we are doomed to disappointment.

Lewis concludes with a chapter entitled "Experience and Order." If all knowledge is in terms of concepts and concepts are of the mind, the application of concepts to experience demands a certain orderliness in the world. The givenness of certain qualia must be a clue to certain expected sequences, and the occurrence of these sequences in the past must be a valid ground for our belief in their occurrence in the future. This is commonly called the "assumption of the uniformity of nature."

Lewis tries to show just what is involved in this necessary "uniformity." It can be expressed in three principles. *Principle A* says that "it must be false that every identifiable entity in experience is equally associated with every other." This assumes merely that there are *some* recurrent sequences in nature; that is, there are things of such nature that concepts can be applied to them. *Principle B* states that whenever we have cases where *Principle A* does not apply (namely, where the sequences seem to be "random"), we can extend these situations through certain identifiable entities in such a way as to make them satisfy *Principle A*. For example, if we can find no order among events, we can pass to simpler elements by deeper analysis, or to a larger whole containing the original constituents, or to a higher level of abstraction by disregarding irrelevant aspects. In each case we will find order where there had previously appeared to be none. *Principle C* affirms that "the statistical prediction of the future from the past cannot be generally invalid, because whatever is future to any given past, is in turn past for some future." This states simply that the person who uses as a basis for prediction a statistical generalization which is continually revised in terms of actual observations cannot fail to make more successful predictions than one who does not. A world which exhibits these principles is certainly not an inconceivable one. Indeed, since all we want to assure ourselves of is the *probability* of our apprehensions and our generalizations, not their *certainty*, we can hardly imagine a world which would *not* provide a basis for such knowledge. For certain modes of cognition and irreducible variety in the world would be completely irrelevant. Moreover, our demand for uniqueness in the individual thing seems to require a world of unlimited variety. But in most modes of understanding the uniformity is not *discovered* in the world, but *imposed on the world* by our own categorial procedure. What we are really saying, therefore, when we assert that the world is orderly is merely that there must be apprehensible things and objective facts—and to this conclusion there seems to be no conceivable alternative except the nonexistence of everything.
—*A.C.B.*

PERTINENT LITERATURE

Firth, Roderick. "Lewis on the Given," in *The Philosophy of C. I. Lewis* (The Library of Living Philosophers). Edited by Paul A. Schilpp. La Salle, Illinois: Open Court, 1968, pp. 329-350.

In *Mind and the World-Order*, C. I. Lewis holds the doctrine that our knowledge of the external world can be justified, ultimately, only by indubitable apprehensions of the immediate data of sense. Empirical knowledge has two aspects or phases: the presentation of something given, and the conceptual interpretation we put upon it. When we see a piece of white paper, for example, we apprehend something given—namely, a certain complex of sensa or qualia describable in expressive language by the use of adjectives of color, shape, size, and so forth—then by the application of concepts we render that complex *meaningful*. Our apprehensions of the given are characterized by certainty, Lewis claims, and without such certainties there could be no perceptual or empirical knowledge at all. In a penetrating analysis of Lewis' notion of the "given" in empirical knowledge, Roderick Firth defends Lewis against three potentially damaging criticisms.

What Firth calls the ontological objection stems from Lewis' use of so-called sense-datum terminology when referring to what is sensibly given in perception. The idioms (sensum, sense-datum, datum of sense, presentation) that Lewis customarily employs when speaking about sense experience appear as nouns which purportedly designate particular nonmaterial entities. The traditional problem with sense-data theories is explaining how such entities are related epistemologically to other kinds of things or events such as material objects, shadows, mirror images, and hallucinations. Firth demonstrates that Lewis' theory of knowledge is entirely independent of the use of any one particular terminology for describing sense experience. More importantly, Lewis never falls into the mistake of viewing the given as an *object* of perception, although it surely is a necessary condition of perception.

A possible "phenomenological objection" arises from the fact that in describing sense experience Lewis seems to be offering a "sensory core" theory of perception. He gives the impression, for example, that if we analyze our experience of seeing a penny that is held obliquely to our line of vision, we shall discover that we are ordinarily aware of an elliptical presentation. On such a view, the penny as an object of perception becomes defined as the totality of the actual and/or potential sense-data, and hence can be *discovered* by a careful examination of ordinary perception. Pragmatists, Gestalt psychologists, and phenomenologists have shown, however, that what is given in experience is something which has "constancy" under varying conditions of observation. In the example of the penny, what is given is not an elliptical presentation at all, but a "whole object" with characteristics not restricted to those normally associated with any one specific mode of apprehension. As these philosophers argue, rightly or wrongly, the "phenomenal object" is *created*, not discovered. Firth is quick to point out that, while using different terminology, Lewis is in basic agreement with the phenomenologists. There is a distinction between sensing and perceiving; indeed, only with respect to the latter is it proper to speak of a perceived *object*—an object which by its nature is a meaningful content, a whole, a constancy. Where phenomenologists use the term "phenomenal object," Lewis speaks of our "interpretation" of the given.

The third, or "epistemological," objection is construed as a set of possible arguments against Lewis' idea that our apprehensions of the given exhibit a certainty which, in turn, provides a basis for all empirical knowledge. Critics might argue (1) that no apprehensions are certain, or (2) that apprehensions of the given are not *uniquely* certain, since some judgments about objective reality are equally certain, or (3) that Lewis does not sufficiently define what he means by "apprehension" or "certainty," or (4) that even supposing that apprehensions of the given are certain, it does not follow that they constitute a necessary condition for all empirical knowledge. It is the epistemological objection which Firth considers most important and to which he devotes the most space.

Firth begins by clarifying what Lewis means by "apprehension" and "certain." Although it is the case that by expressive language we may formulate statements *about* the given, Lewis explicitly states that apprehensions of the given are *not* judgments or beliefs. Sense presentations simply are *had* at a momentary point in time: they do not refer beyond present experience, and they do not stand in contrast with some possible kind of error. In tasting what appears to be pineapple juice, the given—the sense presentation—is something being experienced *now*; it is immediate and not subject to error. Error becomes possible if and when a judgment occurs, but that presupposes conceptual interpretation. One might be mistaken that they are tasting pineapple juice, but their apprehension of a set of sense qualia neither requires verification nor is subject to error.

In saying that our apprehensions of the given are certain, Lewis implies that they are beyond mistake, that they are not falsifiable. Contrasted with empirical statements about objective reality, which theoretically are always subject to further testing and verification, no conceivable future experience can ever count against the givenness of our immediate presentations. Firth adds to this the idea that our apprehensions of the given are epistemologically *decisive* in a way in which empirical judgments are not: when asserting the truth of an objective statement, we know that in principle some new evidence in the future may disconfirm it; whereas we know that no future evidence could conceivably disconfirm an immediate presentation. Apprehensions of the given are certain, therefore, in a sense which objective statements are not. On this point, at least, Lewis appears to be justified.

Firth concludes his analysis by suggesting that even though Lewis may be justified in claiming that empirical knowledge, *in fact*, is based on "sense certainties" which are evidentially ultimate, it is a much larger issue whether without such certainties there could *in theory* be no perceptual or empirical knowledge at all—in other words, whether sense certainties constitute a *necessary condition* for the possibility of empirical knowledge. Lewis addresses this issue in the context of his discussion on the nature of evidence and probability.

Rosenthal, Sandra B. *The Pragmatic A Priori: A Study in the Epistemology of C. I. Lewis*. St. Louis, Missouri: Warren H. Green, 1976.

At the heart of C. I. Lewis' theory of knowledge, to which he attaches the label "conceptual pragmatism," is his novel doctrine of the pragmatic *a priori*. Sandra B. Rosenthal's study offers an exceptionally clear, insightful, well-documented exposition of that doctrine and how it fits into Lewis' general epistemology. She traces the logical origins of Lewis' thought, examines his basic theory of meaning, and makes explicit the distinctively pragmatic elements in his philosophy, all with the aim toward clarifying the nature and function of the pragmatic *a priori* in relation to empirical knowledge.

Lewis' fundamental thesis is that all empirical knowledge arises due to the mind's conceptual articulation—or interpretation—of an original field of consciousness, or what he calls the "given" element in experience. A hallmark of traditional philosophy has been the splitting up of knowledge into two aspects, one sensuous and one intellectual, often with a subsequent distinction between these dual elements and the so-called "object" of knowledge. Depending on the focus of emphasis, competing epistemologies arise. Phenomenalism, for example, stems from giving precedence to the element contributed by the senses (sense-data, or phenomena); idealism comes about by attributing primacy to the mind's contribution (concepts, or universals); and Kantian transcendentalism emerges as a sort of hybrid of the two. Of the three examples mentioned, Lewis comes closest to Immanuel Kant.

Nowadays it is commonly accepted that a purely sensuous phase of experience cannot be separated from a purely intellectual phase. As Kant well recognized, sensation and thought go hand in hand. In *Mind and the World-Order*, Lewis maps out a theory of knowledge wherein he tries to take more seriously what he felt many of his contemporaries were giving only lip service to. He attempts to show how indeed the mind and the senses cooperate in the development of human knowledge. The foundation for his theory is his notion of the pragmatic *a priori*.

To speak of the *a priori* is to speak of the purely conceptual. Concepts originate in the mind; they are common, shareable, expressible meanings which signify patterns of relations, logical intentions, and classification schemes. By the use of concepts we are able to identify and discriminate among the particular objects and events we encounter in daily experience. Empirical knowledge is made possible, according to Lewis, by the application of *a priori* concepts to the data of experience—data which in their brute givenness lack form, order, and meaningfulness. In short, *a priori* concepts are regarded as the definitive principles or rules for distinguishing, relating, classifying, and ordering the sensible aspect of experience. Through conceptual interpretation, sequences of possible experiences and patterns of relationships among objectivities are delimited. Not unlike Kant, Lewis wishes to stress that "thoughts without content are empty, sensations without concepts are blind." Knowledge somehow depends upon a fusion of the conceptually *a priori* and the perceptually given.

Although strongly influenced by Kant, Lewis differs from him in at least two significant ways, as Rosenthal early points out. Lewis cannot accept Kant's claim regarding the possibility of synthetic *a priori* propositions. And while Kant argues that the *a priori* categories of the understanding are universal, eternal, logical structures of the mind necessary for the possibility of knowledge, Lewis contends that the mind's *a priori* concepts are not fixed and absolute, but are subject to change over time. Not that the concepts themselves change; rather, over periods of time and because of shifts in man's sociocultural environment, old concepts simply are given up and replaced by new ones. How we conceptually interpret the data of experience at any given point in history depends entirely upon the *a priori* concepts we have adopted and taken up in our lives, whatever their source or explanation.

But upon what basis does the mind adopt and apply its interpretative concepts? Is it an arbitrary process; strictly a matter of conscious choice; something learned through course of habit; or what? It is in addressing this general issue that Lewis' pragmatism becomes most evident. Our concepts, he declares, are a function of our needs and interests. The character of our experience is shaped by the concepts that will best serve our interests, our purposes, our private and social ends. Inasmuch as human interests change, so too will the retention and abandonment of given conceptual schemes. Even the laws of logic operate as modes of conceptual interpretation: we hold to the law of noncontradiction, for example, not because it is a transcendental structure of the rational mind, but because it best serves our interests to conceive the world in terms of logical consistency. All empirical knowledge, according to this view, is relative to an *a priori* element; and the governing *a priori*, in turn, is relative to the pragmatic considerations of human interests.

In the final section of her book, Rosenthal discusses the concept of "world" as it functions in Lewis' epistemology. Lewis distinguishes between "world" and "reality." Whereas the latter can be defined as a continuum of indiscrete givenness, a chaotic much-at-onceness, as William James often describes it, the former indicates a concrete, orderly, self-consistent system of objectivities which have been "fixed" or "carved out" of the aboriginal data of experience by way of conceptual interpretation. "Reality" harbors within itself an infinite set of possibilities and potentialities; our "world" is that particular potentiality as it has been actualized through the pragmatic adoption of particular concepts. In this sense, not only our *knowledge* of the world, but also the *world itself*, is relative to the mind's pragmatic *a priori*.—R.A.S.

ADDITIONAL RECOMMENDED READING

Cornman, James W. "On Acceptability Without Certainty," in *The Journal of Philosophy*. LXXIV, no. 1 (January, 1977), pp. 29-47. At the base of Lewis' theory of knowledge is the Cartesian principle that "if anything is to be probable, then something must be certain." For Lewis, that certainty can be found in the "given" element of experience. After carefully considering possible arguments in support of and against Lewis' position, Cornman ultimately rejects the idea that probability must be grounded in certainty.

Rosenthal, Sandra B. and Patrick L. Bourgeois. "Lewis, Heidegger, and Kant: Schemata and the Structure of Perceptual Experience," in *The Southern Journal of Philosophy*. XVII, no. 2 (Summer, 1979), pp. 239-248. An enlightening, provocative discussion of the Kantianism dominant in Lewis' dispositional theory of meaning. Special attention is given to affinities between pragmatism and existential phenomenology, and how both involve a return to lived experience.

Schilpp, Paul A., ed. *The Philosophy of C. I. Lewis* (The Library of Living Philosophers). Vol. XIII. La Salle, Illinois: Open Court, 1968. Unquestionably the most comprehensive single source of philosophical commentary on the work of Lewis. Contributors include many of Lewis' outstanding disciples and notable critics. In addition to the twenty-four descriptive and critical essays on his philosophy, this volume contains a short autobiography by Lewis, a letter of reply to his critics, and a complete bibliography of his writings.

PROCESS AND REALITY

Author: Alfred North Whitehead (1861-1947)
Type of work: Metaphysics
First published: 1929

PRINCIPAL IDEAS ADVANCED

Only a philosophy of organism can describe a universe in which process, creativity, and interdependence are disclosed in immediate experience.

Philosophy involves generalization from the concrete particulars we know to universals; it aims at a description of the dynamic process which is reality.

A philosophical system should be logically consistent and coherent, and it should be grounded in immediate experience.

The categories of this philosophy of organism are the category of the ultimate (creativity), the categories of existence (actual entities, prehensions, nexūs, subjective forms, eternal objects, propositions, multiplicities, and contrasts), the categories of explanation (twenty-seven in number), and the categories of obligation (nine in number).

Everything but God is an actual entity occasioned by something; but God, although an actual entity, is not an actual occasion.

Every event in the creative, interdependent process is qualified by past, present, and future.

Process in reality is a creative advance in which feelings are integrated, actual occasions grow together toward a final phase of satisfaction, and God is conditioned by, and reciprocally affects, events in the temporal world.

The central aim in Whitehead's chief work, *Process and Reality*, is to replace the traditional philosophy of substance with a philosophy of organism. The thesis of the author is that only a philosophy of organism can provide clarification of a universe in which process, dynamic actualization, interdependence, and creativity are disclosed as the primary data of immediate experience.

Although Whitehead expresses some far-reaching reservations regarding traditional modes of thought, he formulates his philosophy of organism through a dialogue with the great logicians, scientists, metaphysicians, and theologians of the past. He finds the thought of Plato more decisive than that of Kant; he considers Bergson more suggestive than Hegel; he contends that Locke was closer to a philosophy of organism than Descartes; and he is ready to choose Leibniz over Aristotle. Western philosophy is defined by the author as a series of footnotes to Plato. Some of these footnotes he wishes to salvage and reformulate; others he is quite happy to see deleted. Of all the philosophical giants in the Western tradition, Kant is the least cordially received. The author makes it clear that his philosophy of organism constitutes a recurrence to pre-Kantian modes of thought. According to Whitehead, the Copernican revolution of Kant was not as revolutionary as many of his followers maintained it to be. Whitehead's philosophy is a speculative philosophy formulated into a coherent and logical system of general concepts which are intended to provide the categorial interpretation for any and all elements of human experience.

In examining the methodological foundations of Whitehead's system, we find first a procedure of descriptive generalization, and second an epistemology which expresses both a rational and an empirical side. Philosophical method involves generalization, in which there is a movement from the concrete particular to the universal. This generalization is based on description rather than deduction. Whitehead considers it to be a mistake that deduction, the primary method of mathematics, has intermittently become the touchstone for philosophical inquiry. Deduction is for the author an auxiliary mode of verification that should never be given primacy in philosophical methodology. Applied in Whitehead's philosophy of organism, this method of descriptive generalization takes the form of a description of *dynamic process* rather than of static structure. Morphological description is replaced by description of dynamic life processes.

Whitehead's epistemology contains both rational and empirical elements. The rational criterion is coherence and logical consistency; the empirical criterion is applicability and adequacy. A philosophical system must be coherent and logical. No entity can be conceived in abstraction from all other entities, nor can an entity be understood as long as its relation to other entities is not specified according to logical rules. But knowledge demands also an empirical justification. Categories must be applicable and adequate. They are applicable when they describe all related experience as exhibiting the same texture. They are adequate when they include all possible experience in their conceptual vision. Whitehead was deeply concerned to maintain an experiential basis for his philosophy: "The elucidation of immediate experience is the sole justification for any thought." Philosophy should aim at generalization, but it should not overreach its mark and lose itself in abstractions that are not grounded in experience. One of the chief errors in philosophy, contends the author, is the "fallacy of misplaced concreteness." This fallacy results when an abstraction becomes an exemplification of the system and replaces the concrete entity of which it is an abstraction. The success of philosophy, continues the author, is commensurate with the degree to which it avoids this fallacy.

Through the implementation of his method of descriptive generalization Whitehead derives a categorial scheme which sets forth the governing concepts of his philosophy of organism. His categories are classified according to a fourfold schematic division: (1) the category of the ultimate; (2) categories of existence; (3) categories of explanation; and (4) categorial obligations.

The *category of the ultimate* is creativity. Creativity is the universal of universals, the ultimate metaphysical principle which underlies all things without exception. Every fact of the universe is in some way or another an exemplification of creativity. Even God is subordinate to the category of the ultimate. As the ultimate metaphysical principle, creativity is also the principle of *novelty*. It provides the reason for the emergence of the new. In its application to the novel situation, of which it is the origination, creativity expresses itself as the "creative advance."

The *categories of existence* are eight in number: (1) actual entities; (2) prehensions; (3) nexūs (plural of nexus); (4) subjective forms; (5) eternal objects; (6) propositions; (7) multiplicities; and (8) contrasts. *Actual entities*, which replace the traditional concept of particular substances, are the final facts of the universe; they are the real things of which the world is made up. *Prehensions* are the concrete facts of relatedness, exhibiting a "vector character," involving emotion, purpose, valuation, and causation. A *nexus* is a particular fact of togetherness of actual entities. *Subjective form* is the determining or defining quality of private matters of fact. *Eternal objects* are the pure potentials by reason of which facts are defined in their subjective forms. *Propositions* render meaningful the distinction between truth and falsehood; as abstract potentialities they are suggestions about the concrete particularity of actual entities. *Multiplicities* indicate the disjunctions of diverse entities. *Contrasts* indicate the mode of synthesis which occurs in a prehension or a concrete fact of relatedness. Along with these eight categories of existence Whitehead delineates twenty-seven categories of explanation and nine categorial obligations. We shall discuss the explanations and obligations as they become relevant in the development of the author's system.

Actual entities, which constitute Whitehead's first category of existence, are the building blocks of his organismic universe. Here the philosophy of organism inverts Spinoza. For Spinoza actual entities, as particulars, are inferior modes; only the Infinite Substance is ultimately real. In the philosophy of organism actual entities are the ultimate facts. These actual entities are in a process of "perpetual perishing," but as they perish they are somehow taken up in the creative advance, pass into other actual entities through the operation of prehension, and achieve objective immortality. This interpretation of a universe of flux in which actual entities come to be and pass away must be understood, according to the author, as simply an expansion of a sentence in Plato's *Timaeus*: "But that which is conceived by opinion with the help of sensation and without reason is always in the process of becoming and perishing and never really is." The universe, as it is immediately disclosed, is a universe of becoming, flux, and perishing. The category of actual entities has universal applicability. It applies to nonliving matter as well as to all instances of life. It applies to the being of man as well as to the being of God.

A significant implication of this doctrine is that God, for Whitehead, is not

outside the system. He is within the reach and range of the categories. However, God is differentiated from all other actual entities in that he is not
occasioned by anything. Thus, all actual entities other than God are also
occasions. God is an actual entity but not an actual occasion. Every actual
occasion exhibits a dipolar structure consisting of a physical pole and a mental
pole. By reason of its physical pole the actual occasion prehends other actual
occasions; by reason of its mental pole a prehension of eternal objects is made
possible. In this description of the bipolar structure of actual occasions the
author formulates an alternative to the Cartesian dualism of mind and body.
God also exhibits a dipolar structure. He possesses two natures—a primordial
nature and a consequent nature. His primordial nature, which consists of an
envisagement of all the eternal objects and an appetition for their actualization, corresponds to the mental pole of actual occasions. His consequent
nature, which is the consequence of the reaction of the world upon God,
corresponds to the physical pole of actual occasions.

Actual occasions are grouped into societies or nexūs through the operation
of prehension. A prehension, according to the eleventh category of explanation, consists of three factors: (1) the subject which is prehending; (2) the
datum which is prehended; and (3) the subjective form which designates the
manner in which the subject prehends its datum. A nexus, according to the
fourteenth category of explanation, "is a set of actual entities in the unity of
the relatedness constituted by their prehensions of each other." By reason of
their physical poles actual occasions can prehend each other and form societies
or nexūs. There results an organismic coinherence in which every event in
the universe is a factor in every other event. All things ultimately inhere in
each other. There are no isolated events. For Whitehead the universe is an
interdependent universe in which all parts are interrelated. The analogy of
the organism replaces the analogy of the machine. Not only, however, do
actual occasions prehend each other by reason of their physical poles; they
also prehend eternal objects by reason of their mental poles. Eternal objects
are permanent and immutable principles of determination, clearly reminiscent
of the eternal forms or ideas in the philosophy of Plato. An eternal object
is a pure potential which, in itself, remains neutral to any particular fact of
ingression in the temporal order. There are no new eternal objects. They are
fixed in the timeless primordial vision of God. However, each eternal object
is a potentiality in the history of actual occasions. An actual occasion prehends
an eternal object and thus the object becomes realized in time and space.
Ingression refers to the particular mode in which the potentiality of an eternal
object is realized in a particular entity, contributing to the structure and
definition of that actual entity. Eternal objects contribute the necessary structure which keeps the organismic process from dissolving into an indeterminate
and discontinuous succession. Process does not contradict structure in Whitehead's analysis. Process and structure are interdependent concepts.

Actual occasions, and the societies which they form, are in a process of growing together until they reach a final phase which is called "satisfaction." This process of growing together, in which new prehensions constantly take place, is designated by the author as "concrescence." "In a process of concrescence, there is a succession of phases in which new prehensions arise by integration of prehensions in antecedent phases. . . . The process continues until all prehensions are components in the one determinate integral satisfaction." Each actual occasion as it is objectified in the process of concrescence exhibits a claim upon the future. The future is in some sense constitutive of the being of every actual occasion. Whitehead expresses this when he describes an actual occasion as a "subject-superject." Every occasion is at once the subject experiencing and the superject of this experience; it is the present experiential datum, but it is also the future result or the aim of its present experience. This aim or future project is called the "subjective aim," which controls the becoming of the actual occasion and lures it to its final satisfaction. All becoming thus occurs within a spatiotemporal continuum, in which all entities experience the bite of time. Each event in the universe is qualified by the past, present, and future. Although actual occasions perish, they enter into the internal constitution of other actual occasions, in which they become objectified. Every present fact of the universe is thus constituted by all antecedent phases. So also is every present fact constituted by its potentialities for future realization by its subjective aim. An actual entity is that which it can become. "That *how* an actual entity *becomes* constitutes *what* that actual entity *is*; so that the two descriptions of an actual entity are not independent. Its 'being' is constituted by its 'becoming.' This is the 'principle of process.'"

That all things flow is the one ultimate generalization around which Whitehead develops his whole system. This doctrine of a fluent, becoming universe, remarks the author, was already suggested in the unsystematized insights of Hebrew literature (particularly the Psalms), as well as in the early beginnings of Greek philosophy (particularly Heraclitus). Coupled with this doctrine of flux, however, is a competing notion—the permanence of all things. These two notions, contends the author, constitute the complete problem of metaphysics. Whitehead does not intend to reject the doctrine of permanence, but rather seeks to adapt it to his ultimate generalization that all things flow. This adaptation is expressed in two implicatory principles of his system—his doctrine of self-constituting identity and his doctrine of cosmic order. In his nine categorical obligations the author formulates the category of objective identity, which asserts the essential self-identity of every actual entity as an individual constituent in the universe. Each actual entity is a cell with an atomic unity. In the process of concrescence actual entities grow together but they do not sacrifice their atomic unity. They retain their self-identity and thus give expression to a life of their own. Viewing the organismic process from the side of the cellular and atomic units which comprise it, we need to acknowledge a self-constituting individuality which indicates a permanence within the flow of all things. As there is objective self-identity in Whitehead's philosophy of organism, so also is there preestablished harmony or universal cosmic order. The latter aspect of the universe is indicated in the author's seventh category of obligation, the category of subjective harmony. The process of concrescence exhibits a preestablished harmony in which all prehensions are viewed as being contributive to a stable cosmic order, informed by the eternal objects and directed by the subjective aim. Thus does the doctrine of permanence receive another expression in Whitehead's system. His elaboration of the notion of preestablished harmony has some interesting implications for the author's position on the nature of evil. Although he does not formulate an explicit theodicy, he veers in the direction of a Leibnizian resolution to the problem. Novelty is not to be identified with creativity. The emergence of novelty in the organismic process may inhibit and delay the creative advance and thus provide the condition for the rise of evil. Evil constitutes a real fact in Whitehead's universe. Spinoza's attempt to explain away evil as an illusion arising from our finite, modal point of view is thus rejected. Evil is for Whitehead an *ens reale*, and not simply an *ens rationis*. However, when the creative advance attains its final phase or its satisfaction, the universe is the better off for the fact of evil. The satisfaction or the final phase is richer in content by reason of the particular cosmic disharmonies. All inhibiting novelties are somehow contributive to a greater good. In the creative advance of the world, particular evil facts are finally transcended.

Whitehead's philosophy of organism occupies a unique position in the history of philosophy in that it makes the sentient quality of experience decisive. His theory of prehension and his doctrine of the creative advance are governed by a notion of the pervasiveness of feeling. In the final analysis, prehension involves an objectification of feelings, and the creative advance is a process in which these feelings are integrated in an exemplification of harmony. "In the place of the Hegelian hierarchy of categories of thought, the philosophy of organism finds a hierarchy of categories of feeling." This accent on the sentient quality of experience by Whitehead has both epistemological and metaphysical implications. It entails, first of all, a rejection of the subject-object dichotomy as the foundation for knowledge. Most traditional varieties of philosophy, claims the author, give priority to the intellect and the understanding. In such a view the knowing subject is the primary datum and the philosophical task becomes a demonstration of the validity of propositions about the objects encountered by the subject. It was particularly in the Cartesian tradition that this subject-object form of statement became normative.

In Whitehead's philosophy of organism the subject is an emergent datum, rather than the foundational datum. The complex of feelings constitutes the primitive datum. The primitive element is sympathy, or feeling in another and feeling conformally with another. Intellect and consciousness arise only in the higher phases of concrescence. The universe is initially disclosed as a system of "vector feelings." This primacy of feeling is made explicit in Whitehead's doctrine of "presentational immediacy." In its immediate presentment the world is *received* as a complex of feelings. Primitive experience must thus properly be understood in terms of *sense-reception* rather than *sense-perception*. In sense-reception the interconnections of feelings are simultaneously disclosed. There is thus an internal bond between presentational immediacy and causal efficacy. Both Hume and Kant, in giving priority to the conscious subject, were unable to grasp this point. The sense-perception of the subject was for them the primary fact, and any apprehension of causation was somehow to be elicited from this primary fact. In the philosophy of organism, which gives primacy to sentient experience, causal relations are disclosed on the level of feelings. They are directly felt on a pretheoretical or precognitive level of experience. The types of feeling are indefinite, and depend upon the complexity of the data which the feeling integrates. There are, however, three primary types of feeling which are constitutive of all more complex patterns: (1) physical feelings, (2) conceptual feelings, and (3) transmuted feelings. *Physical feelings* arise from the physical pole of the actual entity and have for their initial datum another actual entity. *Conceptual feelings* arise from the mental pole and have for their datum an eternal object. *Transmuted feelings* are akin to physical feelings in that they proceed from the physical pole, but their objective datum is a nexus of actual entities rather than a single entity. The creative advance integrates these various types of feeling in its progression toward satisfaction. This integration proceeds in such a manner that the earlier phases of feelings become components of later and more complex feelings. Thus, in each phase there is an emergence of novelty. This goes on until the final phase is reached, which is the complex satisfaction in which all earlier phases of feelings are taken up as formative constituents of a final and coordinated whole.

The categories of Whitehead's philosophy of organism receive their final exemplification in his metaphysics of theism. The doctrine of God completes Whitehead's system. In formulating his metaphysics of theism he has no intention of submitting rationally demonstrative proofs for the existence of God; rather, he intends to provide a theoretic system which gives clarification to the immediate facts of religious experience. The touchstone of religious experience is love. The author finds the most decisive expression of this religious attitude in the Galilean origin of Christianity. The theism suggested in this Galilean origin must be contrasted, on the one hand, with the theism of Aristotle, in which God is the unmoved mover who exhibits no concern for his creation and, on the other hand, with the theism of medieval theology, which, according to the author, gave to God the attributes which belonged exclusively to Caesar. The author's intention is thus to formulate a theistic view which arises from a religious experience in which love is the governing datum.

In Whitehead's philosophy this God of love is not to be treated as an exception to the categories and the metaphysical principles which they enunciate. God is the chief exemplification of the metaphysical system. In this role of chief exemplar his nature can be viewed from two perspectives—as *primordial* and as *consequent*. As *primordial*, God is unlimited or infinite potentiality. He is a unity and plenum of conceptual feelings, in abstraction from any physical feelings, and hence lacks the fullness of actuality. God as primordial is deficient in actuality. As a unity of conceptual feelings and operations he is a free creative act. He is in no way deflected by the particular occasions which constitute the actual world. The actual world presupposes the primordial nature, but the primordial nature does not presuppose the actual world. All that the primordial nature presupposes is the general and abstract character of creativity, of which it is the chief exemplification. As unlimited potentiality the primordial nature includes the eternal objects and accounts for the order in their relevance to the process of creation. So also God in his primordial nature is the *lure* for feeling or the "object of desire." He provides the condition for each subjective aim and draws the process to its final satisfaction.

Coupled with God's primordial nature is his *consequent* nature. His consequent nature is derivative. It expresses the reaction of the world upon God. The consequent nature is thus, in part, subject to the process of actualization in the actual world. By reason of his consequent nature God can share in the fullness of physical feelings of the actual world as these physical feelings become objectified in God. God shares with every actual occasion and every nexus its actual world. As consequent, God is conditioned by the world. His nature is consequent upon the creative advance of actual occasions in the process of concrescence. The primordial nature is free, complete, eternal, actually deficient, and unconscious. The consequent nature is determined, incomplete, everlasting, fully actual, and conscious. By reason of his consequent nature God establishes a providential relation to the world. His providential love is expressed through a tender care that nothing be lost. He saves everything in the world and preserves it in his own life. God's providence also manifests itself in the workings of divine wisdom. Through his infinite wisdom he puts to use even that which in the temporal world would be considered mere wreckage. The consequent nature thus makes possible a continuing point of contact and a reciprocal relation between God and the world. The events in the temporal world are transformed through God's love and wisdom, and his love and wisdom then pass back into the world. God thus receives his final definition as the great companion—the fellow sufferer who understands.—*C.O.S.*

PERTINENT LITERATURE

Leclerc, Ivor. *Whitehead's Metaphysics: An Introductory Exposition.*
Bloomington: Indiana University Press, 1958.

Widely acclaimed as one of the best introductions to Alfred North Whitehead's thought, Ivor Leclerc's book is a tremendous aid to those who seek
to understand Whitehead's philosophy. Leclerc's book is carefully structured
and well written. It presupposes some familiarity with philosophy, but it does
not assume that one has any knowledge of Whitehead's metaphysics.

There are three reasons why Leclerc is so successful in his effort to explicate
Whitehead's thought: (1) he presents Whitehead's various concepts in a linear
fashion, (2) he relates Whitehead's ideas to the classical issues in Western
philosophy, and (3) he provides quotations from Whitehead's books as a
means of illustration and as a way of bringing together the introductory
exposition and the original texts.

Leclerc abandons Whitehead's holistic approach in favor of the more traditional linear style of exposition. Whitehead viewed his metaphysics as a
unified system in which each aspect of the system is dependent on every other
aspect for its full meaning. Consequently, in his most extended statement of
his metaphysics—*Process and Reality*—he introduces the whole of his system
in Chapter II and then spends the remainder of this rather lengthy book trying
to make his account in Chapter II intelligible. Although one can readily accept
Whitehead's reason for writing *Process and Reality* in the manner in which
he chose to write it, the fact remains that it is virtually impossible for anyone
to read this book with any understanding of its contents. Leclerc, in his effort
to make Whitehead's thought accessible to the inquiring student, limits himself
to introducing only one Whiteheadian concept at a time. The benefits of this
approach are immediately manifest, especially when one considers Whitehead's neologisms. Unfortunately, Whitehead's system is such that every aspect really does depend upon every other aspect for its full meaning. This
limitation is important, but not fatal. Every method of exposition has its
limitations as well as its benefits. The advantages associated with Leclerc's
linear style of expression complement the advantages associated with Whitehead's holistic style. As long as one does not read Leclerc's book instead of,
but rather in addition to, reading Whitehead's own works, one can only profit
from Leclerc's account of Whitehead's metaphysics.

Leclerc's book is useful in another respect: it shows the relationships between Whitehead's thought and the classical issues in Western philosophy.
Leclerc's primary thesis in this book is that Whitehead's later thought is a
response to specific problems in Western philosophy. At various times Whitehead himself indicates which philosophical issues bear on his thought, but all
too often he does not. By systematically noting the philosophical issues un-

derlying Whitehead's metaphysical notions, Leclerc illuminates many facets of Whitehead's thought.

Leclerc's book is also helpful because of his use of quotations. In order to facilitate the transition from secondary material to the texts themselves, Leclerc includes in his book many passages from Whitehead's work. His use of quotations serves an additional function: not only does it help one make the transition from secondary to primary sources, but it also makes one want to read the original works.

Cobb, John B., Jr. *A Christian Natural Theology, Based on the Thought of Alfred North Whitehead*. Philadelphia: Westminster Press, 1965.

The primary purpose of John B. Cobb Jr.'s book *A Christian Natural Theology* is to construct a Christian natural theology on the basis of Alfred North Whitehead's philosophy of organism. The term "natural" is used here in contrast to "supernatural." A natural theology is one in which God exemplifies the same metaphysical principles as every other instance of actuality. Cobb favors a natural theology over a supernatural theology because he opposes a separation of religious beliefs from nonreligious beliefs. Such a split, he contends, is unnecessary and may have disastrous consequences. When persons are unable to integrate their religious beliefs with their other convictions, religious beliefs become isolated and problematic. According to Cobb, religious beliefs—for example, the concept of God and God's activity in the world—ought to be explainable in terms of the same categories which are employed in the understanding of other actualities and their relations. In that Whitehead also held this view, it is hardly surprising that Cobb chooses Whitehead's philosophy of organism as the basis of his Christian natural theology.

Cobb opens his book with an excellent introduction to Whitehead's metaphysics. Beginning with the rationale which underlies Whitehead's thought, Cobb discusses the problems associated with psychophysical dualism and the equally serious problems associated with materialism and idealism. If there are two fundamentally different types of actualities, how are they related, how do they interact? If everything actual is material, how can mentality be explained? Conversely, if everything is finally mental, how can physical things be accounted for? In light of these traditional philosophical issues, and the conceptual problems which confronted physicists at the turn of the twentieth century, Cobb presents Whitehead's understanding of "actual occasions of experience."

What Cobb terms his "introduction" to Whitehead's philosophy is relatively brief. He devotes less than twenty pages to an explanation of "actual occasions," "physical prehensions," "propositional feelings," "corpuscular societies," and other Whiteheadian concepts. These pages are well written and they provide a general guide to Whitehead's thought, but they do not con-

stitute a full introduction to Whitehead's metaphysics. Were this the extent
of Cobb's explication of Whitehead's thought, one would be well advised to
consider a more extended introduction. However, Cobb continues to explicate
Whitehead's philosophy throughout his book. When, for example, Cobb discusses the human psyche, personal identity, and freedom and self-determin-
ism, he does so in terms of Whitehead's metaphysics. Indeed, one of the
major strengths of Cobb's account is his interest in bringing Whitehead's
metaphysics to bear on such topics as anthropology, ethics, and religion. By
focusing on matters such as these, Cobb emphasizes the existential relevance
of Whitehead's thought.

One need not fear that Cobb's Christian beliefs and his interest in con-
structing a Christian natural theology color his understanding of Whitehead's
thought. In those parts of the book where Cobb is using Whitehead's thought
as the basis for a Christian natural theology, he states very clearly that these
are his thoughts and not Whitehead's. In addition to being a major Christian
theologian, Cobb is one of the most respected interpreters of Whitehead's
philosophy; even if one has no interest in Christian theology (natural or
supernatural), one will find Cobb's book extremely useful for illuminating
Whitehead's metaphysics.

Kraus, Elizabeth. *The Metaphysics of Experience: A Companion to Whitehead's* Process and Reality. New York: Fordham University Press, 1979.

Elizabeth Kraus's book is neither a popularization of *Process and Reality*
nor a commentary on it. It is just what it purports to be: a companion volume
intended to illuminate Alfred North Whitehead's great and extremely abstruse
text. Aimed at the advanced student, *The Metaphysics of Experience: A
Companion to Whitehead's* Process and Reality is too difficult to be useful to
most people. Whitehead's philosophy is both complex and uncommon, and
his terminology is absolutely unique. A guide to *Process and Reality*, Kraus
maintains, cannot change these facts. But the difficulties that confront the
reader of *Process and Reality* go beyond those posed by the originality of
Whitehead's metaphysics and his new language—the structure of the book
presents problems of its own. Kraus seeks to obviate those problems, which
are a result of the structure of *Process and Reality*.

Except for two sections preceding the main body of Kraus's book, *The
Metaphysics of Experience* has the same five-part organization as *Process and
Reality*. In the Introduction Kraus presents a compact explanation of Whitehead's thought in general and of its early development. In Chapter 1 she
examines at some length Whitehead's 1925 work, *Science and the Modern
World*. According to Kraus, the philosophical scheme that Whitehead develops in detail in *Process and Reality* is sketched in broad strokes in *Science
and the Modern World*. Her comments on this earlier work are perceptive

and helpful for understanding the technical expression of Whitehead's position in *Process and Reality*.

In Chapters 2, 3, 4, and 5, Kraus presents the most important aspects of Parts I, II, III, and IV of *Process and Reality*. Chapter 2 deals with Whitehead's understanding of speculative philosophy and his "Categoreal Scheme." Chapter 3 deals principally with his concept of societies and his modal theory of perception—perception in the mode of causal efficacy, perception in the mode of presentational immediacy, and perception in the mode of symbolic reference. In Chapter 4 Kraus presents Whitehead's genetic analysis of concrescence, and in Chapter 5 she explains his theory of extension. Whitehead's account of his theory of extension is virtually impenetrable. Most readers dismiss this section of *Process and Reality* as irrelevant. Kraus not only demonstrates the relevance of Whitehead's theory of extension; she also succeeds in shedding a great deal of light on its meaning. Chapter 5 is without question the single most helpful chapter.

Chapter 6 is devoted to Whitehead's concluding remarks concerning the relationship between God and the world. In this chapter Kraus decides to enter into an interpretive debate. The first part of this chapter is given to countering Charles Hartshorne's concept that God is a temporally ordered society of divine occasions and to speculating on the possibility of subjective immortality. Kraus argues that Whitehead's concept of God is similar to the mystical understanding of God and that subjective immortality is a real possibility. One ought to recognize that on these matters Kraus's book is not acting simply as a guide to understanding *Process and Reality*; it is venturing out on its own.

Process and Reality is definitely in need of a guide; without a guide one will almost certainly become lost. Kraus's *The Metaphysics of Experience* is a very able guide, and the advanced student will find it very useful.—*M.F.*

ADDITIONAL RECOMMENDED READING

Christian, William. *An Interpretation of Whitehead's Metaphysics.* New Haven, Connecticut: Yale University Press, 1959. This presentation of Whitehead's philosophy is remarkable for its clarity and for its accuracy. Christian's book is an excellent introduction to Whitehead's advanced thought, especially his concepts of actual occasions, eternal objects, and God.

Hartshorne, Charles. *Whitehead's Philosophy.* Lincoln: University of Nebraska Press, 1972. Charles Hartshorne has been the major Whiteheadian scholar and commentator since 1925. This book is a collection of thirteen essays he has written on Whitehead's philosophy, including "Whitehead's Metaphysics," "The Compound Individual," "Whitehead's Idea of God," and "Whitehead's Theory of Prehension."

Lowe, Victor. *Understanding Whitehead.* Baltimore: The Johns Hopkins

University Press, 1962. This book is a very good introduction to Whitehead's philosophy. Part II, "The Development of Whitehead's Philosophy," traces Whitehead's thought from his early work in mathematics up through *Process and Reality* and *Adventures of Ideas*. Lowe is not, by his own account, a Whiteheadian, but he appreciates Whitehead's genius.

Schilpp, Paul A., ed. *The Philosophy of Alfred North Whitehead* (The Library of Living Philosophers). New York: Tudor Publishing Company, 1951. This book contains a short autobiographical sketch by Whitehead, nineteen essays on Whitehead's thought, a very brief summary of Whitehead's thought, and a bibliography of Whitehead's work. Victor Lowe's essay "The Development of Whitehead's Philosophy" and Charles Hartshorne's "Whitehead's Idea of God" are particularly good.

Sherburne, Donald. *A Whiteheadian Aesthetic*. Foreword by F. S. C. Northrop. New Haven, Connecticut: Yale University Press, 1961. In this volume, Sherburne seeks to construct a theory of aesthetics on the basis of Whitehead's understanding of reality. The first four chapters are devoted to explaining Whitehead's philosophy. His sections on "Creativity," "Eternal Objects," and "God," are especially fine.

THE RIGHT AND THE GOOD

Author: William David Ross (1877-1971)
Type of work: Ethics
First published: 1930

PRINCIPAL IDEAS ADVANCED

Rightness and goodness are simple and unanalyzable properties; they cannot be explained in terms of feelings, nor are they scientifically discoverable.

We cannot discover value or rightness by the use of the senses; such properties are discoverable only by intellectual intuition.

Basic moral truths are invariant; they are not products of various cultures.

The claim that "right" means "productive of the greatest possible good" is mistaken, for some acts—such as keeping a promise—are right regardless of whether they are productive of the greatest possible good.

Moral principles, discoverable by anyone who is intellectually mature, fall into a moral order; but the moral order cannot specifically be stated, for the resolution of conflicts between moral principles must be made in the light of particular circumstances.

Sir William David Ross, one of the most influential of recent philosophers, has played a leading role in the development of contemporary ethics. He is the best-known exponent of a nonnaturalistic deontological ethical theory, a type of theory that has been at the center of philosophic controversy during most of the first half of this century.

Like H. A. Prichard and E. F. Carritt, or in an earlier period, Kant and Richard Price, Ross is a deontologist or formalist insofar as he insists that the concepts of "right," "duty," and "obligation" are fundamental concepts that cannot be explained in terms of, or derived from, other value concepts such as "good." In this respect he differs from utilitarians such as J. S. Mill and, recently, G. E. Moore, who have argued that concepts of moral obligation can be derived from "good," the primary notion. However, like Moore, Ross is a nonnaturalist insofar as he insists that properties such as right and good are not to be explained in terms of the feelings or inner states of the judge, nor are they properties that can be detected by the senses or discovered by any scientific procedure. They are, rather, "nonnatural" properties apprehended by intellectual insight. This doctrine places him in opposition to naturalists such as George Santayana, John Dewey, Ralph Barton Perry, C. I. Lewis (to a certain extent), and to a number of sociologically inclined thinkers such as David Émile Durkheim. It also opposes him to emotivists such as A. J. Ayer and C. L. Stevenson, who deny that the ethical significance of terms is cognitive at all. Ross's views are expressed most elegantly in *The Right and the Good*, a book that has become a modern classic in the literature of ethics. They are expanded somewhat in a later book, *The Foundations of Ethics* (1939), which an interested reader will want to consult.

In this review we shall adopt Ross's order of discussion, starting with right and turning later to good. When he speaks of "right," he has in mind the closely related concepts of "right," "obligation," and "duty" which, he says, with minor qualifications refer to the same thing. He is using the term "right" not in the weaker sense of "not wrong" but in the stonger sense of "wrong not to." The property of rightness, he says, is simple and nonanalyzable, and the concept of "right" is consequently indefinable. Here he is following the pattern laid down by Moore in his *Principia Ethica* (1903), although Moore applied it there to the concept of "good" only. Furthermore, he argues, as Moore did in the case of "good," that in addition to being indefinable, "a word like 'right' . . . does not stand for anything we can point out to one another or apprehend by one of the senses." Rather, it is a property we recognize in certain types of action by an intellectual insight or intuition.

Ross believes that even though "right" is indefinable, most of us will know what it means, for most of us are moral people who constantly make moral judgments quite satisfactorily. If we are not sure, we can always consider particular cases and see that we do distinguish between moral behavior on the one hand and other kinds of behavior on the other. And if we are confused about the relationship between the notion of "right" and value concepts such as "good," once again we can clarify the issue only by attending to, analyzing, and comparing cases. Ultimately each of us must examine his own moral consciousness if he wishes to attain clarity, for, as Ross has already argued, "'right' . . . does not stand for anything we can point out to one another." The moral insight is private in the sense that we cannot look to make sure the other person is apprehending what we apprehend. This does not mean that communication is impossible, for observation and discussion will reveal that on the whole we agree that there is moral behavior and we agree, also, on the kinds of behavior that are moral.

Ross himself discusses and criticizes several prominent philosophical views that deny one or another of the major points of his own position. Thus he argues against thinkers like Durkheim by claiming that moral insight is not to be equated with or explained away in terms of the mores a culture happens to have at some particular time. The insights men have may vary from time to time, as may the codes men lay down, but basic moral truths themselves are invariant. Against Moore's doctrine in *Principia Ethica*, that "right" means "productive of the greatest possible good," he has two arguments. First, he uses Moore's own open question technique against him, for, he says, it surely is an important question whether actions that produce the greatest good are right. This is not the trivial question it would be if the corresponding statement were analytic, and it would be analytic if the alleged definition were correct. Second, he argues that the rightness of certain actions, such as that of promise keeping, does not depend entirely or essentially upon the good produced by such actions. It is to be noted that later on, in *Ethics* (1911), Moore himself changed his mind and agreed with Ross that "right" is indefinable.

Ross also argues against the view that to say an act is right is to say that it is morally good; that is, that it stems from a morally praiseworthy motive. Here, too, he uses two arguments. First, he says that since motives are feelings or desires that cannot be summoned up at a moment's notice, it would be impossible in many cases to do what is surely our duty. Since *ought* implies *can*, it cannot be our duty to act from a good motive. (This is not to deny that it is our duty to develop our character or that we can act from good motives.) Second, it is not our duty to act from a sense of duty but rather our duty simply to do certain things, such as to return the book we have borrowed. The goodness of the act is important if we are concerned with the virtue of the agent, but this goodness must not be confused with another property the act may have, that of being right or obligatory.

Ross then turns from the question of the meaning of ethical terms to another major question: What is the criterion of right and wrong? Here too he is reacting against Moore and other utilitarians, for regardless of whether they think they are giving a definition of right, they all maintain that the goodness produced by an act is the sole criterion of its rightness. Ross replies that this is not the case with respect to a wide variety of actions. We have already mentioned promise keeping. Ross acknowledges that the consequences of keeping a promise must be taken into account when we consider whether or how we should keep it, and he acknowledges that in some cases these consequences are such that we should not keep it, but he points out that in many cases we are obliged to keep a promise even if it should result in less beneficial consequences than some other action, and that in all cases involving a promise there is a moral consideration present which has nothing to do with consequences. In the case of promises, an obligation arises because of a special sort of action in the past rather than because of future consequences, and it arises because in promising, and by promising, we "create a moral claim on us in someone else." The utilitarian ignores the fact that the act of promising is the source of an obligation. Other things being equal, then, we are obliged to keep our promises, and this obligation is not the obligation to produce beneficial consequences. Ross does assert that we are also obliged to act so as to benefit others, but this is another, quite different, obligation.

Ross maintains that there are still other sorts of obligation. First, there are obligations similar to that of keeping promises in that they stem from the particular actions of men. He writes not only of promises and contracts, but also of cases of fidelity such as the "implicit promise" underlying the understanding that we will tell the truth. Also included in the category of "special obligations" are our obligations to compensate others for the wrongs we have done them (the duty of reparation) and to return the services of those who

have helped us (the duty of gratitude). In contrast to these "special obligations" which occur only if one party to the obligation has acted in a particular
way with respect to the other, there are the "general obligations" we have
with respect to all men simply because and insofar as they are men. In addition
to the duty to benefit others, Ross mentions our obligations to distribute
happiness according to merit (justice), to improve ourselves, and to refrain
from injuring others. Ross believes he has given a complete catalogue of
duties, but he is less concerned with defending this contention than he is with
emphasizing that there are many types of obligation quite distinct from the
obligation to maximize the amount of good in the world. The important point
is that not one of these obligations can be explained away in terms of any of
the others. The utilitarian is mistaken when he asserts that there is only one
criterion of what is right, for there are many, each as fundamental and irreducible as the others.

Each of these is a moral principle, each is a moral truth. Together they
express the "moral order" which is "just as much part of the fundamental
nature of the universe . . . as is the spatial or numerical structure expressed
in the axioms of geometry or arithmetic." Men have not always apprehended
these principles, but any who "have reached sufficient mental maturity and
have given sufficient attention" to them should recognize their self-evident
truth.

Since there will be many particular cases where these principles will clash,
it cannot *always* be obligatory to keep a promise, or to rectify wrongs done
to others, or to benefit others, and so on. For this reason, Ross says that
promise keeping and other kinds of acts which are usually obligatory are
prima facie right, meaning by this that if no stronger and contrary moral
consideration is relevant to the case in point, promise keeping, or whatever
it is, is morally obligatory. He draws an analogy with the parallelogram of
forces in physics: the fact that one makes a promise "tends" to make a certain
action right, but the fact that this same act will harm another person "tends"
to make it wrong. If only the first tendency were present, it would determine
the outcome and keeping the promise would be right or obligatory and not
merely *prima facie* right. But since there are two opposing "tendencies" actual
duty will be determined by the stronger of the two. The weaker tendency is
still present, though overcome. It may be wrong to keep the promise in this
situation but even so, keeping it is still *prima facie* right. This is Ross's way
of maintaining the absoluteness of moral principles in the face of the obvious
fact that they clash in particular cases.

Ross does not think these principles can be arranged hierarchically in such
a fashion that when any two clash we know beforehand which must take
precedence over the other, and he does not believe there is any principle that
enables us to resolve such conflicts. He maintains that our moral life is far
more complex than the systematizers of ethics imply it is. We must consider

cases as they come, weigh the relative strengths of the moral considerations as they occur in the individual cases, and reach our decisions accordingly. As a result, we cannot be nearly as certain about the rightness of particular acts as we can be about the truth of the general principles, for while the latter is self-evident, the former can never be known with certainty.

In his discussion of the good, Ross is concerned primarily with "intrinsic" goodness which he, like many others, distinguishes from "instrumental" goodness. Something is intrinsically good if it is good for its own sake, quite apart from any value it might have as a means of attaining some other good. Ross believes that only states of mind or relations between them can have intrinsic value and, therefore, that anything else has value only insofar as it produces such states or relations. Thus, for instance, the physical painting has instrumental value but only the experience it produces in us has intrinsic value. It follows that a world that contained no conscious beings would be a valueless world.

When we examine our states of mind, Ross says, we will find that only four things are intrinsically valuable. The first three, in increasing order of importance, are (1) pleasure, (2) knowledge and right opinion, and (3) morally good states such as virtuous dispositions and morally good motives. Of the third, sense of duty ranks highest followed by feelings such as sympathy and benevolence. He presents "the apportionment of pleasure and pain to the virtuous and the vicious respectively" as the fourth intrinsic good. To support his view he asks us in each case to consider two universes which are equal in all respects except that the state under consideration is present in one and absent in the other, believing that in each case we will agree that the universe containing the state in question is the better one. If anything other than these four things is intrinsically good, it can only be something exhibiting several of them. Thus, for example, the intrinsic goodness of aesthetic enjoyment involves both pleasure and knowledge.

Ross's analysis of the nature of intrinsic goodness is like that of G. E. Moore, to whom he acknowledges his debt. Good is a simple, unanalyzable property of a state of mind, a property it has in virtue of the fact that it has some other property, that of being pleasant, knowing, or virtuous. Good is not to be confused with these other properties. Good is a "consequential" or "dependent" property insofar as the state of mind has goodness only because it also has some other properties, but good is not a "constitutive" property of the state of mind, as the other properties are, for it does not belong to the essential nature of the state of mind. That is, while a statement such as, "A state of knowing is a cognitive state" is an analytic statement, the statement, "A state of knowing is intrinsically valuable" is synthetic.

Good is a simple property and the corresponding concept, "good," is indefinable. Ross defends this claim by arguing that no offered definitions have been able to survive examinations. Some fail because either they exclude actions that are right or include actions that are wrong. And all, even those in which the denotations of the *definiens* and the *definiendum* may coincide, fail because they do not express what we mean by "good." This latter argument is much like Moore's use of the open question technique which we have already mentioned in our discussion of right. Ross does not insist that we can prove that "good" is indefinable, but he does hold that the fact that all proffered definitions have failed is extremely strong evidence, especially when we consider that there is no reason in the first place why we should think that good is a complex property. In brief, Ross ends up as Moore did, by considering good to be a simple, unanalyzable, "nonnatural" property that is present in something because of the presence in it of certain other quite natural properties.

This conception of a nonnatural property and the related notions of intuition and synthetic *a priori* truths lie at the center of Ross's position, and as such have been the targets of most of the criticism directed against him. Nonnatural properties have been especially bothersome. Ross and Moore both maintain that value and moral terms refer to properties of things and actions, and yet both insist that these properties are not sensed and cannot be discovered by scientific means. Consequently, they have the difficult task, which has bothered Moore particularly, of trying to explain what such nonnatural properties are. As Moore's long puzzlement indicates, they have not succeeded even to their own satisfaction. On the other hand, they have refused to abandon the notion because they believe that the consequence would be the destruction of the cognitive significance of moral and value statements, a consequence made all too clear by the work of the later emotivists. The dominating model of significance and truth is that made familiar by empirical propositions: if a statement is cognitively significant, then it must be capable of being true; and if it is capable of being true, then it must refer, correctly or incorrectly, to things and properties. Furthermore, we must be able to observe things and their properties. Applying this model to value statements, we are forced to make a similar series of moves. If the statement "*A* is good" is true, then there must be such a property as good, *A* must possess it, and we must be able to examine *A* and notice that *A* possesses it. We may be puzzled as to exactly what sort of thing the examination reveals, but if we say that *A* is good, it seems that we are forced to admit that we have inspected *A* and have noticed that it has the property we call good.

Very recently writers such as S. Toulmin, P. H. Nowell-Smith, K. Baier, and A. I. Melden have attacked the underlying model of significance, arguing that the concepts of "reasonable," "valid," and "true" have quite legitimate and distinctive uses in moral discourse, uses which vary from the uses of these terms in scientific discourse. Thus, they contend, we can escape the postulation of puzzling nonnatural properties without giving up the contention that moral discourse does differ significantly from scientific discourse, and we can do so without denying that moral statements have cognitive significance. That is, very recent thought has broken out of the bonds indicated by our recent classification of ethical theories as being either naturalistic, nonnaturalistic, or emotivist, a scheme of classification which presupposed the acceptance of the dominant model that has been mentioned.

As for Ross, no matter how severely some of his ideas are being criticized, there is no doubt that he has played a very important role in the development of contemporary ethical theory and that his influence still lives strongly. His insistence that moral and value terms differ from descriptive terms, his insistence on a deontological ethics, and his insistence that morality is far too complex to be contained by any theory which would reduce it to a single principle have been and continue to be very influential. These basic ideas persist even in the views of many who are somewhat unhappy about the epistemological framework within which Ross has expressed them.—*L.M.*

PERTINENT LITERATURE
Pickard-Cambridge, W. A. "Two Problems About Duty," in *Mind.* XLI, nos. 161, 162, 163 (January, April, July, 1932), pp. 72-96, 145-172, 311-340.

W. A. Pickard-Cambridge believes that W. David Ross's view of duty and his criticism of ideal utilitarianism are oversimplified. Since Ross finds duty to consist in the *actual production* of a sought state of affairs, attempting is not enough—one's duty is to *succeed.* The realities of situations, however, reveal fatal flaws in this view. Ross uses "ought" to apply to that which is directly done or ought to be done. However, as simple an action as returning a borrowed book (a Ross example) requires the doing of many acts by persons other than the one responsible—a mail collector, mail handlers, a carrier— yet Ross calls all of it the primary agent's duty; and this is not how we truly understand duty. More properly, Pickard-Cambridge concludes, Ross should say that a person's duty is to *aim at* producing the sought situation by actions that may reasonably be thought *likely* to produce it. In his later work, *The Foundation of Ethics*, Ross indeed comes around to the view that our duty is to "set ourselves" to accomplish a situation or action.

The intuitionist such as Ross argues with two advantages. First, he uses logical standards against his opponent; yet the opponent cannot use them against him, for the intuitionist claims that inspection, not argument, produces his knowledge. Second, if the intuitionist agrees with his opponent on a judgment of what a duty is, he can claim that not the opponent's argument but his own intuition is his basis. The only promising way that Pickard-Cambridge finds to argue with the intuitionist, therefore, is to compare instances of one and the same act, which must always be intuited in the same way, in which the resulting goodness or badness varies. If moral judgments of appropriate observers in these instances vary concomitantly with differences of resulting good or evil, this should be a rebuttal to the intuitionist.

Using this method, Pickard-Cambridge takes up Ross's two kinds of duty, *prima facie* and actual or absolute duty, to show that what actually determines either kind is not intuition, but the amount of good done by the action when carried out. Without defining ideal utilitarianism, he takes its principle to be that our duty is to do the act that leads to the most good, the best subsequent situation. Exhibiting in one imaginary instance after another, with significant variations, what in practice we do judge the duties of the agents to be, he shows that when we take a full range of factors of the actions into account, a utilitarian calculation of the resulting good or evil coincides with the judgments of duty. Thus, ideal utilitarianism suffices to explain satisfactorily the determinations of duty, whereas Ross himself admits that intuition has shortcomings.

Ross's examples are oversimplified. The assumption of "other things being equal" is never justified; every case involves many persons, not two only. Results accruing to other persons and to society as a whole must be heeded. So must subjective forms of good as well as objective (sometimes measurable) ones. Pickard-Cambridge's examples examine the effects of considering the abilities of beneficiaries to use the benefits well, the extent to which their desires affect our obligation, the relative moral character of alternative beneficiaries of our actions, and the like. The very fulfillment of an expectation is a good, and must be considered in the calculation.

Pickard-Cambridge finds that the intuitionist theory provides no way for differing judges to find common ground and to come to agreement. The ideal utilitarian method, however, provides a clear and intelligible principle, considerably narrows the margins of inexactness or judgmental differences, encourages us to analyze out different elements of duty, provides for expressing them appropriately for rational deliberation, and promises that we can actually come to know our duty. On the other hand, the method of intuition simply adopts an unchecked personal impression, admitting fallibility. Any moral theory which rules out the possibility of certainly knowing our duty stands condemned.

McCloskey, H. J. "Ross and the Concept of a *Prima Facie* Duty," in *Australasian Journal of Philosophy*. XLI, no. 3 (December, 1963), pp. 336-345.

Nearly all the critical response to W. David Ross has centered on his analysis of right, obligation, or duty, not on his analysis of the good. Many critics have complained that he has not made it clear what *prima facie* duty is and what is its relation to absolute or actual duty. H. J. McCloskey asserts that Ross has made a mistake in attempting to derive *prima facie* duties from actual or absolute duties; instead, he should base the latter on *prima facie* duties.

Ross makes two claims, equally unclear. (1) *Prima facie* duties are not really duties, although it is convenient even if misleading so to term them. (2) They are rather *tendencies* to be duties. Ross, however, does not mean "tendencies" in the usual causal sense, and does not explain in what sense he does intend it. Ross at times accepts the causal model, but at other times comes near to a view that McCloskey outlines and defends.

Contending that *prima facie* duties are actually not duties is the source of Ross's trouble, although he nowhere deliberately rejects the possibility that they may be duties. Most likely Ross intends merely to stress that certain acts that at first appear to be obligatory turn out not to be obligatory. McCloskey asserts that to be subject to a *prima facie* duty is to be in a moral situation and under some obligation to act in a certain way, although not being *absolutely* obligated to act in that way. This is quite different from being subject conditionally to a duty, or to being obligated sometimes or usually (*tending* to be obligated).

The qualities that determine absolute duties to be duties are present in and spring from the *prima facie* duties. There are differences, however. First, since "'ought' implies 'can,'" we are always able to carry out our absolute duties, but are not always able to carry out our *prima facie* duties. Next, although not obligated to do something other than fulfill a duty, we are always under obligation to fulfill the most important *prima facie* duty or duties in the situation. And the obligatoriness that thus binds us is the same obligatoriness that that duty has as a *prima facie* duty; it does not come from somewhere else. A given *prima facie* duty does not change its nature when it is identified as the one that is most important and that therefore is to be fulfilled, to the exclusion of others. Thus Ross errs in using language suggesting that *prima facie* duties are something other than duties, but become duties under certain conditions. It is by virtue of the presence of other things, other *prima facie* duties, that one *prima facie* duty emerges as an absolute or ultimate duty.

The expression "absolute duty," then, is a short way of designating the largest sum of fulfillable *prima facie* duties, including the most important or most morally insistent. It is as the absolute or operative duty that a duty has special qualifications, not as *prima facie*. Thus an analysis of duty should base the absolute, operative duty upon the *prima facie* duties rather than the other way around.

Stocker, Michael. "Intentions and Act Evaluations," in *The Journal of Philosophy*. LXVII, no. 17 (September 3, 1970), pp. 589-602.

In making the larger point that motives play no role in the rightness or wrongness of actions, W. David Ross asserts that no morally good act is ever morally obligatory. To establish this, he appeals to Immanuel Kant's principle that "'ought' implies 'can,'" together with the factual premise that one cannot by choice and at a moment's notice produce in himself a morally good motive.

Examining this "curious" argument, Michael Stocker tries to find what Ross consistently could have meant by it.

That X is my duty implies that I can perform X, for if X were asserted to be my duty but I could not perform it, that would be unjust, and no actual duty is ever unjust. However, "'ought' implies 'can'" cannot imply "action from a morally good motive is never obligatory" unless we can never act from such a motive. In fact we do act at times from morally good motives. So "'ought' implies 'can'" does not make it inconsistent to believe both that we have obligations and (what Ross denies) that our obligations may include acting from a morally good motive. Even if we do not have a *duty* to act from a good motive, we can at least sometimes perform a morally good act from a sense of duty.

All that Ross may conclude from "'ought' implies 'can'" is that we have an obligation to perform a morally good act only when we *can* perform it—which is true of all duties. Ross believes that we have a *prima facie* duty to do whatever morally good actions we can; and such a position should admit doing some of the acts that are done from morally good motives since they are morally good acts. Examining two possible reformulations of Ross's argument, Stocker shows that one proves too much: namely, that we have no obligations at all. The second allows either for performing the obligated act simply, or else for performing it with a good motive. Ross should concede that regarding it obligatory to act with morally good intentions is consistent with "'ought' implies 'can.'"

Ross's argument that motives (good or not) never are commanded by duty cannot be correct. For example, to keep a promise one must do something with the intention of keeping the promise. To do nothing while other events merely happen to bring about the object of the promise, or to keep it by accident or by mistake, does not constitute *keeping* the promise—doing what fulfills the obligation—for the motive of intending to perform is part of what is promised. Other *prima facie* duties also may include a component of motive or intention in the content of the duty. The motive affects our evaluation of these acts.

There are other kinds of cases. Although a person fulfills an obligation from a nonconscientious motive, he might still fulfill it from a moral motive if he had not had his other motive; and if he fulfills it with a conscientious motive, we cannot argue that he does better than if he fulfills it with a lesser motive, for the quality of the motive here is irrelevant so long as the fulfillment is adequate. To perform an obligatory action with a morally good intention is to create a moral good over and above discharging one's obligation. Acting from a bad motive alone may suffice to constitute an action morally bad.

In sum, to act on good or bad intentions affects some, but not all, act evaluations. Good intention appears necessary, and sometimes sufficient, for doing a morally good act. Acting on a bad intention appears sufficient for acting wrongly; but except in the special cases where to have the intention is part of the obligation, the act that fulfills is sufficient to discharge an obligation. It need not have a morally good motive.—*J.T.G.*

ADDITIONAL RECOMMENDED READING

Atwell, John. "Ross and *Prima Facie* Duties," in *Ethics*. LXXXVIII, no. 3 (April, 1978), pp. 240-249. Although various formulations of *prima facie* duty all fail (usually because they are circular), the author attempts formulations of *prima facie* wrongness, finally finding one he maintains is not circular, is sufficiently general, and is consistent with Ross.

Broad, C. D. "Some Reflections on Moral-Sense Theories in Ethics," in *Broad's Critical Essays in Moral Philosophy*. Edited by David R. Cheney. New York: Humanities Press, 1971, pp. 188-222. Starting with ought-sentences, Broad elicits and tests forms of intuitionist theories from a moral-emotivist point of view.

Ewing, A. C. *The Definition of Good*. London, Routledge & Kegan Paul, 1948. Ewing converts to his own use Ross's notion of *prima facie* duty.

—————— . "The Pursuit of the Good," in *Ethics*. New York: Macmillan Publishing Company, 1953. Ewing shows that the position of Ross on *prima facie* duty and the position of the ideal utilitarian on the intrinsic goodness of an act can be brought very close together.

Johnson, Oliver A. *Rightness and Goodness: A Study in Contemporary Ethical Theory*. The Hague, The Netherlands: Martinus Nijhoff, 1959. A study of recent ethical theory to extract the valuable contributions of the intuitionistic deontologists while not embracing their doctrine.

Muirhead, John H. *Rule and End in Morals*. Freeport, New York: Books for Libraries Press, 1969. Historical and critical comment on the revolt against idealistic ethics culminating in Ross; elicits seven principles for a synthesis of the opposing positions.

Rosen, Bernard. "In Defense of W. D. Ross," in *Ethics*. LXXVIII, no. 3 (April, 1968), pp. 237-241. Alleges that Strawson's attack upon Ross (see below) is totally ineffective because Strawson misreads Ross.

Stocker, Michael. "Rightness and Goodness: Is There a Difference?," in *American Philosophical Quarterly*. X, no. 2 (April, 1973), pp. 87-98. Rather than joining the controversy over whether "good" is derived from "right," or the reverse, the author asserts that there is no moral difference, centering his argument against the antiaxiological argument on Ross's statement of it.

Strawson, P. F. "Ethical Intuitionism," in *Readings in Ethical Theory*. Edited by Wilfrid Sellars and John Hospers. Appleton-Century-Crofts, 1952. Succinct criticism of ethical intuitionism cast in the form of dialogue.

PROBLEMS OF ETHICS

Author: Moritz Schlick (1882-1936)
Type of work: Ethics
First published: 1930

PRINCIPAL IDEAS ADVANCED

Ethics is a science in that it is the effort to acquire knowledge about the right and the good.

We use the term "good" to recommend something as desired by society; by discovering what is desired, one is able to define the good.

Human beings choose to perform whatever actions most appeal to them as they consider the possibilities.

Moral valuations are emotional reactions according to normal expectations concerning the pleasant or unpleasant consequences of performing certain acts.

Values and obligations are relative to the desires of persons, and they are objective in the sense that, as a matter of fact, human beings do prefer some things to others.

A free will is not an undetermined will; it is a will which is not compelled.

Schlick's *Problems of Ethics* is one of the earlier ethical works of the school of logical positivism. Readers interested in ethical developments of this general position should consult other works influenced by, but significantly differing from, those of the Vienna Circle, of which Schlick was a founder. Typical of such later works are those of the emotivists, Alfred J. Ayer and Charles L. Stevenson.

Ethics, Schlick holds, is a science in that its object is knowledge. It seeks to understand the right and the good, not to produce them. Contrary to the views of many modern ethicists, its primary task is not to establish a definition of "good," though it must discover the meaning empirically and scientifically. Opposing G. E. Moore's position that "good" is indefinable, Schlick insists that while it cannot be exhaustively defined any more than can the name of a color, it can be defined sufficiently to locate its content accurately, as can any meaningful word. He then describes the formal characteristic of the good as *its being demanded of us*, its "oughtness." But what is the origin of oughtness? This suggests the material characteristic: we use the term "good" to recommend something as desired by society.

By examining approved acts and dispositions we can find and generalize their common characteristics in a rule of the form, X must have properties A, B, C . . . and N in order to be called "good." (Note that the rule concerns not what *is*, but what is *called* "good.") This rule or norm would thus express a fact, and hierarchical arrangement of such norms would ultimately yield a moral principle or definition of "good." Hence, the usual opposition of factual to normative sciences is false. While ethics does justify particular judgments by reference to rules or norms, such justification is relative rather than absolute; as a science, ethics must still investigate the sources of norms. It cannot ultimately justify or establish the highest norms and values, since to justify is to refer to a higher principle. Instead, "Such norms . . . must be derived from human nature and life as facts." Schlick thus rejects the radical distinction commonly made between the "is" and the "ought" or the factual and the normative. The central task of ethics when it arrives at the highest values is then to seek their causal explanation or factual sources; since the causes of conduct in general are more fundamental than those of moral behavior, the method and materials of ethics mmust be psychological.

What, then, are the ultimate relevant causes or motives of conduct? Schlick states the law of motivation thus: ". . . the decision of the will proceeds in the direction of the most pleasant end-in-view, in the following manner: of the ideas which function as motives, that one gains the upper hand which finally possesses the highest degree of pleasant emotional tone, or the least unpleasant tone. . . ." Schlick argues that the law needs little proof, being exemplified constantly, although there are apparent exceptions requiring explanation. In cases of self-sacrifice or martyrdom, it might at first seem that the agent was not motivated by pleasure or the avoidance of pain—a false assumption. Unusual conditions change what is ordinarily pleasant and painful, and the goal of the inspired hero appears so desirable that other motives, such as fear of death, are repressed. It is impossible to desire something absolutely unpleasant, since to desire is to entertain an idea with pleasure; hence, the self-sacrificial decision must be motivated by some dominant pleasure even while accompanied by pain. There is no necessary connection between a pleasant idea of a state and an idea of a pleasant state, and thus martyrs may anticipate with pleasure what is usually painful. But overwhelming confirmation of this law of motivation is the fact that institutions of all kinds—religious, educational, and political—apply it as the sole means of controlling conduct.

But the law is insufficient to distinguish good from evil or the moral from the immoral. Schlick solves this problem indirectly by examining the term "egoism," resignating a chief object of moral censure and thus leading to the discovery of what is meant by "immoral" and "moral." Some philosophers describe egoism as the impulse to personal welfare, to pleasure, or to self-preservation, but in context all these terms prove too vague, broad, or inaccurate. The true meaning of "egoism" is "inconsiderateness"; it designates not so much impulses of the self as the manner in which some personal inclinations are fulfilled to the neglect of the social impulses, and therefore egoism is disapproved by society. This suggests ". . . the following law as a fundamental ethical insight: the moral valuations of modes of behavior and characters are nothing but the emotional reactions with which human society responds to the pleasant and sorrowful consequences that, according to the average experience, proceed from those modes of behavior and characters."

Here the affinities of Schlick's views with the social approval theory, psychological hedonism, and utilitarianism become clear. "Approved" in its moral sense means "desired," and pleasure and pain are the governing factors in desire. Schlick significantly emends the utilitarian concept of what is approved, however: he agrees that what is considered morally good is "what advances the pleasure of society," but whereas utilitarians attempted to say what good *is*, Schlick avoids this difficult problem by claiming only that "In human society, that is *called* good which is *believed* to bring the greatest happiness." Similarly the "demand" character of the good stems only from the desires of society reinforced by sanctions. Thus good and obligation are factual as originating in human nature, but they are relative to it rather than absolute or self-subsistent.

The theory of absolute values is that they are wholly independent of human emotion and knowledge and relate to everyday reality only through man's obligation so to act as to bring about the most valuable results. Schlick's first criticism of this theory alleges the impossibility of determining the meaning and truth of its value judgments. What objective criteria might one use? Not concomitant pleasure since the theory itself rejects that: the good may be pleasant, but pleasure is not the good. Not in such a criterion as contribution to upward evolution, since such terms as "upward" are circular in presupposing a meaning of "value." Indeed, the error of this approach is "in seeking value distinctions in the objective facts themselves, without reference to the acts of preference and selection, through which alone value comes into the world."

Are there then subjective criteria? Some abolutists describe a specific experience or intuition of value, comparable to sensory perception of material objects. But unless one has this experience it is difficult to accept the theory, and value judgments do not show the consistency of sensations. To consider comparing value judgments to logical or mathematical statements, as some absolutists do, is unsatisfactory, for such statements are tautological and do not express factual truth. Were value judgments comparable they would be unverifiable and, worse, irrelevant to life, whereas "Judgments about value ought to tell us just what is most important."

The oughtness of good is likewise incapable of an absolute subsistence, contrary to the teaching of Kant. " 'I ought to do something' never means anything except 'Someone wants me to do it' " and the reward, punishment, or other consequences will attend satisfaction or neglect of the desire. Kant's description of a categorical or absolute imperative, Schlick adds, is contradictory because it defines "oughtness" without reference to one who demands or desires, while such reference is essential to the concept. The only verifiable experience of the ought is the familiar awareness of compulsion: sanctions have feeling tones which dominate those of other ideas and so determine volition. In this way values and moral law affect conduct, but an absolutist theory cannot show any relationship between values and desire or action.

But if not absolute, to what extent are values relative and subjective? Schlick thinks they are relative to the feelings of the subject, but are not capricious; given certain relations of specific objects and subjects with fixed constitutions and dispositions, the feeling reactions or values will also be determined unambiguously. This is an objective fact; neither the relativity nor the objectivity of value is metaphysical. But value relativity is more complicated than has yet been shown; while the view that pleasure is essentially or frequently worthless is largely prejudice, it is true that sorrow is sometimes valuable. Why? "Happiness" and "sorrow" name indefinite, complex states not identical with pleasure and pain—themselves complex and variable. Pain, for example, can have pleasant components and is sometimes associated with pleasure, as when painful labor produces pleasant effects. Many great pleasures follow great pains according to the law of "contrast." Furthermore, we feel that suffering provides a dimension of depth not otherwise attainable, and is sometimes valuable inherently, rather than by association alone. Schlick explains that we feel pleasure in being stirred to the depths of our nature, but this occurs infrequently; thus, when a partially painful experience moves us deeply, as does emotional involvement in dramatic tragedy, we find it pleasant. Suffering and extreme joy are both expressed by tears, which pure pain does not yield. Great art, one notes, is concerned more immediately with sorrow than with pleasure, and it thus provides further evidence of the heterogeneity of feeling tone.

Schlick then turns to a pseudoproblem which, he insists, was solved long ago by Hume and others; it involves misunderstanding of "freedom of the will" and obscures the genuine but simple problem of moral responsibility. Every science presumes the principle of causality, or that every event is under universal law, but it has been and still is argued that such determinism precludes free will and hence responsibility. This conclusion confuses two meanings of "law": (1) compulsory rule and (2) description of events. To describe nature as governed by universal law means merely that events occur uniformly and are predictable, not that they are *compelled* in the sense of "forced against the will." Similarly, psychological laws do not compel decisions but merely describe those we do make. The confusion between determinism, or universal causality, and compulsion breeds related confusion between their opposites, indeterminism and freedom, so that the champions of "free will" proceed to confuse freedom with the opposite of causality. Morality requires both freedom, or "absence of compulsion," and responsibility; the latter involves the possibility of changing motives, and hence implies causality. Advocates of "free will" fail to see that a decision without a cause would be a matter of mere chance and utterly irrational, and that it is quite consistent to admit both freedom and determinism in the senses defined. To act from our own desires is not to act without a cause, and it is ridiculous and unfortunate that these confusions have been perpetrated.

Schlick's concluding chapter returns to the main problem of ethics as he sees it: to discover why man acts morally. To answer this exhaustively would be to show how the joys and valuations of morality arise from the most underivative pleasures, and how the latter occur. But we have insufficient psychological knowledge to do so with precision. Besides, the previous discussion has ignored an essential feature of human inclinations—changeability—which has more practical import than does the original problem. Consequently, Schlick substitutes the more pertinent questions: How are moral dispositions strengthened? How do we attain the valuable? The obvious answer is that we do so by suggestion, punishment, and reward—but less primitive and more permanent means are desirable.

These superior means lie in recognizing the distinction between motive pleasures and realization pleasures, those which determine and those which result from an act. (The distinction shows, incidentally, that it is possible for man to seek something other than happiness.) When discrepancies occur, as when anticipated pleasure materializes in pain, the act tends to be eliminated and replaced by one in which motive and realization feeling tones are similarly pleasant. Thus the key to consistent character and behavior is in encouraging those acts for which this relationship is fairly constant. The effects of external compulsion to morality will be weakened unless moral conduct itself leads to pleasure, and the ultimate justification of moral behavior is simply that it yields happiness to the agent. "It follows from the universally valid law of volition that he can will only such ends as are valuable for him. However, he will then distinguish genuine from spurious values: both are real, but the latter can be destroyed by the assimilative process. Spurious values exist by virtue of the pleasure which belongs to the *idea* of the end alone, and not to the end itself; while genuine values consist in those feelings of pleasure with which the end itself is experienced."

The inclinations which best qualify as genuine are the social impulses, in which the idea of pleasant or unpleasant states of others have similar feeling tones for the self. When these states of others are realized as the ends of our conduct, our perception of others' pleasures is also pleasant for us, and thus the motive and realization pleasures concur, reinforcing altruistic behavior. Again the insight of Bishop Butler is relevant here: concern for the good of others is not contrary to but rather one of our own interests, and its fulfillment contributes to our own good. Thus, fortunately, the chief motives of morality are these social impulses; virtue and happiness have common causes. There are of course values which are more obviously personal, and differences in rank among these; the so-called "lower" pleasures such as those of the body are not evil, but unrestrained gratification diminishes their realization value, whereas the "higher" pleasures make the subject more susceptible to new joys and thus not only multiply but also diversify accessible goods. The social impulses are in the higher group; in fact, one of them, love, provides the highest happiness possible. Such impulses relate individuals rather than an individual to mankind in general; Schlick rejects the utilitarian goal of the greatest happiness of the greatest number as too abstract.

But when happiness is sought directly, paradoxically it most frequently eludes us; consequently the emphasis should be put on the capacity for happiness. Schlick does not claim that virtue guarantees happiness; the best that man can do is to heed the precepts, "At all times be fit for happiness" and "Be ready for happiness," imperatives which come as close as possible to being moral principles. (Schlick appears to forget here that at first he described moral principles as factual propositions, indicative statements reporting generalizations from particular moral approvals.) Since the greatest capacity for happiness is found in the altruistic impulses, which may seem contradictory to the neophyte in virtue, the earlier stages of morality involve renunciation and compulsion; but as the individual progresses and experiences the joys rewarding these social inclinations, the ethics of duty gives way to the ethics of kindness. To the objection that unmitigated kindness is nothing but misguided weakness, Schlick answers that, of course, correction by intelligence and by insight into the consequences of generous impulses is necessary. But he maintains that if we subsume all altruistic impulses under "kindness" and describe the rational harmony of all impulses as "personality," we will have named the two prerequisites of the good life.—*M.E.*

PERTINENT LITERATURE

Rynin, David, ed. "Introduction," in Moritz Schlick's *Problems of Ethics*. Translated by David Rynin. New York: Dover Publications, 1962.

In this interesting article written as an introduction to Moritz Schlick's moral philosophy, David Rynin argues that Schlick's *Problems of Ethics* is an excellent alternative to much of the moral philosophy being done by philosophers in the analytic tradition. Much contemporary Anglo-American moral philosophy, Rynin maintains, is narrow in breadth and oversubtle. Schlick's moral philosophy is broader in perspective; in his compact, concise ethical treatise Schlick discusses and illuminates a wide variety of moral issues.

Analytic philosophers give too much attention to analyzing the meanings of ethical terms and too little attention to the other interesting, enduring problems in moral philosophy, Rynin believes. Schlick does, admittedly, offer some observations concerning the meaning of the word "good" (he thinks that, strictly speaking, the word is indefinable in the way that the word "green" is but that it has the "formal characteristic" of being "that which is demanded or commanded"). Schlick believes that providing a clear definition of ethical terms is one of the moral philosopher's tasks, Rynin observes. However, in Schlick's opinion the task is of little inherent importance, and it gains what value it has primarily from its usefulness as a preparation for studying other ethical issues. Schlick rejects the view, now common, that the *primary* job of the moral philosopher is to analyze the meanings of moral terms. It would be curious, Schlick remarks, if the purpose of a whole field of study were merely the definition of a concept. Who is interested in mere definitions?, he asks. In any case, people are very familiar with the meanings of ethical words. If the meaning of the word "good" were not already well-understood by people, Schlick observes, they would not know that, for example, "good" is the translation of *bonum*.

Rynin praises Schlick's criticism of the doctrine of absolute values, the view that the existence of values is independent of contingent facts about the physical world and of people's emotional reactions to valuable objects. To Nicolai Hartmann's view that value-propositions are objective or absolute in the way that propositions of logic and mathematics are, Schlick objects that propositions of logic and mathematics are empty tautologies, sentences which convey no information whatsoever about what exists or about how things do or should behave. If value propositions were like logical or mathematical truths in this essential respect they too would be tautologous and thus empty. However, Schlick responds, value-propositions are not empty and uninformative in this manner; on the contrary, they tell us what is most important to know. Thus value-propositions differ importantly from logical and mathematical propositions.

Rynin praises Schlick's criticism of intuitionism (the view that moral truths are self-evident—that they are known by direct intuition and not through deduction from other facts), Schlick's original contributions when defending a hedonistic utilitarian morality, and Schlick's analyses of human motivation, egoism, and the problem of free will and determinism.

Ethics can and should be scientific, Schlick maintained. Rynin discusses this idea of Schlick. In Schlick's opinion the central moral question is "What motives may people have for acting morally?" or "Why do people act morally?" Schlick considers this a psychological and thus a scientific question. The explanation of how human desires might be influenced so that they might be directed at the moral good—that which society demands from us—is to be found in a psychological study, a scientific study of human motivation. Much of Schlick's discussion in *Problems of Ethics* ties in with his attempt to answer this question.

Although he was a leading logical positivist, Schlick avoided, Rynin explains, the more sensational faults which are found in the moral thinking of other positivists. Commitment to the positivist principle that a sentence contains factual meaning only if it is empirically verifiable or falsifiable led A. J. Ayer to the striking position that moral assertions are cognitively meaningless—that they are uttered merely with the purpose of expressing or venting emotion. (In Ayer's opinion, by saying 'Joe is wicked' one is not assigning some property of wickedness to Joe. This sentence is not verifiable or falsifiable and thus is not cognitively meaningful. A person who utters this sentence is merely expressing his emotion or negative attitude toward Joe.) Schlick did not consider ethical statements unverifiable or cognitively meaningless. Schlick's view, roughly, was that moral judgments can be determined to be correct or incorrect by comparison to the norms which society in fact accepts, and that these norms themselves arise from purely hedonistic considerations. An act is morally good when it is demanded or desired by the average person in a society; in practice, actions are demanded or desired by society in proportion as they are believed to be advantageous or useful (conducive to pleasure).

Rynin believes that Schlick's ethics could serve as a corrective to the excessively one-sided views on moral discourse of the contemporary philosophers who maintain that the primary use of ethical discourse is not to inform but to express, advise, or commend. By putting so much stress on the *rhetorical* aspects of moral language, these philosophers, Rynin argues, overlook the fact that language is most persuasive and influential when it conveys truths. It is only because ethical discourse has cognitive content that it influences passions and actions. Those who deny that ethical discourse has significant cognitive meaning put themselves in a position where they are unable to allow reason a serious role in ethical discourse and moral life.

Campbell, C. A. "Is 'Freewill' a Pseudo-Problem?," in *Mind*. LX, no. 240 (October, 1951), pp. 441-465.

In *Problems of Ethics* Moritz Schlick argues that the problem of freedom and determinism which has worried philosophers is a pseudoproblem, an issue of no deep or enduring significance. Philosophers have commonly thought that the admission that the actions of men, like other events in the world, are *caused* conflicts with the ordinary presumption that men act through a free will and are morally responsible for their actions. Schlick argues that the appearance of a problem or conflict here arises from a failure properly to understand the meanings of the key terms in the controversy—"causality," "free will," and "moral responsibility." Developing a position first taken by David Hume, Schlick maintains that the view that man's actions are caused or determined is consistent with the view that man acts out of a free will and that man is morally responsible for his actions.

C. A. Campbell is critical of Schlick's solution of the problem. Campbell's aim in his paper is not to show that man is free and not determined, or determined and not free, but simply to show that Schlick has not succeeded in solving the problem. Determinism is not compatible with free will and responsibility, he argues. Campbell's broader aim in this paper is to counter the opinion, common among logical positivists and ordinary language philosophers, that the problems that have perplexed philosophers over the centuries are pseudoproblems arising from misconceptions about language.

Schlick argues that to say that a person's action was *free*, or that the person acted from a free will, is to say that he was not prevented from acting as he naturally wanted to act. A person's action is *unfree*, or compelled, to the extent that he is prevented from acting as he wants. A philosopher who says that people's actions are *caused* or determined is not saying that people are unable to act as they want or that their actions are compelled or forced. Rather, the determinist is claiming that even when we act as we want to act our actions are caused; our desires are among the factors that determine or cause our actions. When determinism and freedom are understood in this way there is no incompatibility in holding both that man's actions are caused and that man acts from a free will.

A person is *morally responsible* for an immoral action, Schlick explains, when he is the person to be punished for the action. *Punishment*, Schlick says, is an instrument of deterrence; it is justified only insofar as it deters a wrongdoer from repeating a wrong action or intimidates others from doing that act. When punishment and moral responsibility are understood in this manner there is no conflict between the view that human actions are caused and the view that people should be held morally responsible and punishable for wrong actions. The claim that a person's actions are caused is not inconsistent with the claim that we might deter him from repeating the act or intimidate others from doing it by punishing him or holding him "morally responsible" in the sense explained.

The view commonly held that punishment is a natural retaliation or moral repayment for some wrong act Schlick rejects as barbarous. The idea that some past wrong action can "be made good again" by inflicting a new evil or sorrow on someone—an idea that seems to originate from a primitive instinct for vengeance—should no longer be defended by civilized people. Punishment inflicted in this manner leaves the world a worse rather than a better place.

Campbell replies that the incompatibility which philosophers have seen between determinism and moral responsibility does not arise simply from equating causality with "compulsion" and being unable to act as one wants. Rather, the claim that an act was caused entails that the person at the time of the act was not able to do otherwise, and this claim entails that it is improper to hold the person morally responsible or to punish the person for the act. If we condemn or hold someone morally responsible for not doing something we imply that he ought to have done it. To say that someone ought to have done something is to imply that it was *possible* for him to have done it. *Ought* implies *can*, Campbell writes. Since punishing someone or holding him morally responsible for a bad act is incompatible with maintaining that the person could not have acted otherwise, it is also incompatible with maintaining that the person's actions were caused. Thus, Campbell argues, moral blame and responsibility are incompatible with determinism. The incompatibility is genuine, not illusory.

Campbell is also critical of Schlick's account of punishment and moral responsibility. Schlick describes punishment and moral responsibility as instruments justified solely by their (deterrent) consequences. In his response, Campbell argues that moral responsibility is not analyzable in terms of punishment in the way that Schlick maintains. There are times when punishment would deter yet where the subject of the punishment is not morally responsible, and times when a subject is morally responsible but cannot be deterred by punishment. The dog who steals food from the family's dinner table no doubt could, by being punished, be deterred from repeating the act, yet the dog is not morally responsible or morally blameworthy for the act. The animal does not know better. Furthermore, we often assign moral responsibility to people no longer living for events in the distant past. In these cases, a decision concerning who is morally responsible cannot be a decision concerning who might be favorably influenced by punishment. The agents in question are not even available for punishment. Thus Schlick's utilitarian, future-oriented analysis of punishment and moral responsibility is inadequate. Missing is the element of desert and "repayment for transgression"; when these elements are introduced, punishment (and moral responsibility) is incompatible with determinism. Although punishing someone for acting wrongly may deter him or others from repeating an act, Campbell points out, the problem is that it does not seem *fair* to punish a person for an act if he could not have acted otherwise. The person does not deserve punishment.—*I.G.*

Additional Recommended Reading

Berman, Martin. "The Empirical Hedonism of Moritz Schlick," in *Studies in Philosophy and the History of Philosophy*. V (1970), pp. 344-350. Berman traces the faults which he sees in Schlick's ethics to Schlick's logical positivist philosophy.

Gass, William H. "Schlick, Moritz," in *Encyclopedia of Morals*. Edited by Vergilius Ferm. New York: Philosophical Library, 1956, pp. 524-529. A clear, detailed description of Schlick's moral philosophy.

Hazelton, Roger. "Law and Norm in Ethics: A Comment on the Ethics of Logical Positivism," in *Ethics*. L, no. 4 (July, 1940), pp. 450-456. Hazelton argues that Schlick is unable to keep his analysis of morals to the non-normative, purely factual plane to which he, as a logical positivist, commits himself.

Margolis, Joseph. "On Value Theory, by Way of the Commonplace," in *Philosophy and Phenomenological Research*. XVII, no. 4 (June, 1957), pp.

504-515. Margolis replies to Schlick's criticisms of the view that values are objective.

Sahakian, William S. *Systems of Ethics and Value Theory*. New York: Philosophical Library, 1963, pp. 401-408. A useful exposition and criticism of Schlick's ethical theory.

THE DESTINY OF MAN

Author: Nikolai Berdyaev (1874-1948)
Type of work: Theology, ethics, epistemology
First published: 1931

PRINCIPAL IDEAS ADVANCED

Ethical knowledge is a way of being; it is different from scientific knowledge in that it is not knowledge about objects or events.

Freedom is necessary to morality; it is the primeval abyss out of which all distinctions arise; it is the condition of being itself.

Without a theodicy—a justification of God in a universe of which evil is a disturbing part—there can be no ethics: the only satisfactory theodicy is one in which God is shown as subject to an uncreated freedom.

Without an adequate theory of man, there can be no ethics: the only satisfactory philosophical anthropology is one in which man is shown as a personality, a being capable of transcending his natural and social world.

There is an element of the demonic in man; to overcome the demonic, to make creativity possible, man must be deified through the presence of God in time.

In *The Destiny of Man* Berdyaev undertakes the formulation of a philosophico-theological ethics. This ethics is defined both as an ethics of creativeness and as a theo-andric ethics. The treatise begins with a delineation of the foundational principles which undergird such an ethics, proceeds to an elaboration of three distinct but interrelated ethical theories (ethics of law, ethics of redemption, and ethics of creativeness), and concludes with a discussion of the significance of eschatology for ethics. The style is heavy and ponderous and the form is consciously systematic. The author is convinced that ethics, ontology, and theology comprise an interdependent complex of considerations, and his pattern of argument is developed in such a manner that it expresses throughout an attempt at a systematic integration of these three areas.

The foundational principles of Berdyaev's ethical system are explicated in Part I of his treatise. The first principle is an epistemological one, having to do specifically with the nature of ethical knowledge. The author's views on epistemology express a marked existentialist influence. Epistemology is subordinated to ontology. Knowledge is a part of being. The knowing subject is at the same time an existing subject, and all of his reflections arise from, and are rooted in, his project of existing. Kant is credited with having disclosed the irremovable limitations of objective knowledge, and thus his services to epistemology are deemed invaluable. It is impossible, says the author, to return to a precritical form of philosophizing. At the same time, however,

Berdyaev is led to reject Kant's transcendental consciousness, because it results in the reflection of an epistemological ego which loses touch with concrete existence. The Kantian epistemology answers the problem of knowledge on the level of abstraction, but has no relation to the concrete man who is the knower. It is for this reason that he chooses the existentialists over Kant. Knowledge, for Pascal, Kierkegaard, and Heidegger is *existentially* determined. It remains a part of concrete life. This existentialist point of departure entails a rejection of the applicability of the subject-object dichotomy to ethical knowledge. Objectivization destroys life and being. The author grants that the subject-object distinction is relevant in natural science, where truth claims are justified through empirical and objective investigations, but least of all can ethical knowledge be objectivized. Scientific knowledge is "*about* something," but not so with ethical knowledge. Ethical knowledge "*is* something"; it is not *about* an object which somehow stands over against it. Ethical knowledge is irreducible and immediate. The objectivization of ethical knowledge leads inevitably to "normative" ethics, and for the author all normative ethics are tyrannical.

The second foundational principle is freedom. Morality presupposes freedom. Any ethics of creativeness demands freedom as a precondition. Freedom as a philosophical category is for the author a broader designation than simply *human* freedom. Freedom has both a cosmic and a precosmic status. It is precosmic and uncreated in that it is the source of being itself. Being springs from freedom, not freedom from being. Freedom indicates the primeval abyss (the author makes use of the notion of the *Ungrund* to express this primeval freedom—a notion which he takes over from Jacob Boehme), out of which all distinctions of being arise. Freedom as uncreated is the nonbeing which remains impenetrable even to the being of God. God as the Creator is all-powerful over being, but he has no power in his function of Creator over nonbeing—the primeval, uncreated freedom. Man is both a child of God and a child of uncreated freedom. The fact of uncreated freedom accounts for the dark side of human nature, out of which arises both creativeness and destructiveness. Freedom provides the condition for a continuing co-creation with God, but it also provides the condition for the rise of evil. Freedom thus accounts for tragedy as an essential element of morality.

Through freedom the distinction between good and evil arises, and thus the problem of theodicy makes its appearance. Without a theodicy, says the author, there can be no ethics. If there is a real distinction between good and evil, then God must be justified, for only in this way can the problem of evil be solved. Berdyaev finds the traditional doctrines of theodicy to be philosophically and theologically impoverished. The traditional theological explanation of evil through a created freedom and a doctrine of the Fall results in a divine comedy in which the only part is a monologue—played by God. Evil cannot be simply explained as being due to the misuse of a freedom with which God endowed his creatures. Hence, the views of both Augustine and Leibniz on theodicy are in the final analysis superficial. The Marcionites, the Gnostics, and the Manichees were more poignantly aware of the tragic character of life, and saw the inadequacy of explaining evil through a freedom which was itself created by God. It is only with a doctrine of precosmic, uncreated freedom that the ways of God can be justified. God himself emerges out of the *Ungrund*, and is subject to a freedom which he has not created. Thus, he cannot be held responsible for the freedom which gives rise to evil.

Such a theodicy leads to a metaphysical dualism, and this conclusion the author is ready to embrace. All monistic systems founder because they are incapable of dealing productively with the problem of evil. A theodicy which is adequately formulated will thus justify God by placing the origin of evil in uncreated freedom. But if God "precedes" the determination of evil, so also he "precedes" the determination of good. It is equally wrong to say that God is bound to will the good. God is "beyond good and evil." The distinction arises only from the side of man in his fallen existence. God is above good as he is above evil. The highest value thus lies beyond good and evil. Nietzsche saw the full force of this insight. Ethics must at the same time provide a basis for morality and point out its falsity. It is significant that Berdyaev has chosen as the epigraph for his book the lines from Gogol's notebook: "It is sad not to see any good in goodness."

The fourth fundamental principle for ethics has to do with an adequate doctrine of man. The distinction between good and evil arises only through man, hence one is always driven back to the basic question, "What is man?" Ethical inquiry cannot proceed without an adequately formulated philosophical anthropology. In the formulation of his philosophical anthropology, Berdyaev draws heavily from the insights of Max Scheler. It was Scheler, argues the author, who grasped the implications of anthropology for ethics more profoundly than any preceding philosopher. The determinant of personality is central for both Scheler and Berdyaev. True anthropology is personalistic. Personality should not be confused with individuality. Individuality is a naturalistic and biological category, personality is a religious and ethical one. Personality denotes the image and likeness of God in man, by virtue of which he is able to rise above the natural life. As personality cannot be reduced to mere individuality, so also it cannot be reduced to a function of society. As a being with personality man is capable of transcending both his natural and his social world. Personality liberates man from the tyranny of society and public opinion, and makes creativity possible. Society is an object of moral valuation, but never its source. Personality determines the self as unique and irreplaceable, possessing an original freedom, through which alone moral actions can occur.

The author sees clearly that an awareness of personality and moral action presuppose an acknowledgement of other persons (an I-Thou relationship, as Martin Buber would say), but he insists on a distinction between sociality and communality (*sobornost*). Sociality has to do with customs and manners which are the result of social sanctions, but remains intentionally neutral to moral facts. Communality is a religiomoral category which expresses a free union of personal selves as they stand in the presence of God. (This distinction between sociality and communality is also expressed by Scheler when he distinguishes *Gesellschaft* from *Gemeinschaft*.) A philosophical anthropology, which remains true to the facts of concrete experience, will need to give due consideration to the element of the demonic in man. Uncreated freedom is the source of man's destructiveness as well as his creativeness. To define man simply as a bearer of a universal reason who strives for order and harmony, is to define man partially. This is to neglect that aspect of human nature which contradicts reason and order. This neglect, according to the author, is the chief weakness in all varieties of idealism. Modern psychopathology has proved to be invaluable for philosophical anthropology by uncovering the demonic tendencies which result from repressed instincts and drives. Psychopathology has shown that man is a creature of unreason as well as reason. This truth, continues Berdyaev, was already part and parcel of the biblical doctrine of man, which disclosed the demonic as a structural implication of the Fall. But the biblical doctrine does not begin, nor does it conclude, with the fallenness of man or the fact of human sin. It begins with man made in the image of God and concludes with God becoming man. Thus the fall must always be understood within the context of Creation and Incarnation. God enters human existence in the person of Christ. The central anthropological idea of Christianity is thus the idea of a divine humanity. The crowning moment in the Christian drama is the deification of humanity. There can be no ethics of creativeness so long as there is a separation between God and man, between the divine and the human. Creativity is made possible only through the presence of eternity in time. It is this which properly defines Berdyaev's ethics as a theo-andric ethics.

In Part II of his treatise the author sets forth a typology of philosophico-theological ethics. Three major types are delineated: ethics of law, ethics of redemption, and ethics of creativeness. The distinguishing mark of the ethics of law is its social character. It legislates for the social rather than the personal conscience, and hence is unable to acknowledge personal freedom, uniqueness, and creativity. It is concerned only with that which is universally binding and thus disregards the element of particularity in moral action. The ethics of law strives for a social homogeneity and cohesiveness, and it can best bring about this end by localizing the source of moral judgment in some centralizing authority—either a clan, tribe, caste, priesthood, or government. Respect for rank becomes the basis for moral action. The head of the clan, the hierarchy of the church, or the ruler of the government legislates the universally binding norms. As respect for rank constitutes the source of law ethics, so fear accounts for its maintenance. An ethics of law inevitably inspires fear. The socially prescribed "oughts" are upheld because of a fear of the consequences which would follow their violation. The tragic implication of an ethics of law is that it degenerates into a herd morality. Personality is dissolved into sociality, the exceptional and the unique are leveled to the average and the standardized, and creativity is curtailed. Quite clearly, Nietzsche, Kierkegaard, and Heidegger are in the background of Berdyaev's critique of law ethics. Reference is made by the author to Heidegger's concept of *das Man*, which indicates the anonymous and depersonalized existence of the individual who has lost himself in the public conventions of a standardized mode of life. An ethics of law reduces everything and everyone to a common denominator and cools the fires of the creative spirit. Yet, Berdyaev's attitude toward an ethics of law is not wholly negative. The ethics of law does provide a positive value. Although it warps personality it still preserves it. In a world into which sin has entered, life itself would be threatened were it not for the protections of social sanctions. Exclusive dependence upon an ethics of grace and an ethics of creativity would endanger the very existence of personality. Man lives in a sinful, fallen world. Hence, the law is needed. The ethics of law must be transcended, but it cannot be abrogated.

The ethics of redemption stands in a paradoxical relationship to the ethics of law. On the one hand redemption presupposes law; on the other hand it implies a liberation from the law. Redemption presupposes law because the world which is redeemed is a sinful world in which relative justice must be safeguarded by legal sanctions—both political and ecclesiastical. Justice is the highest achievement of the ethics of law. The ethics of redemption does not cancel this justice, but transfigures it through love. The highest achievement of the ethics of redemption is love. Thus, on the one hand redemption is continuous with law; but on the other hand redemption expresses a movement through which man is freed from the law. The redeemed man is not subject to universally binding norms. He sees every moral problem as one that demands an individual solution. Christianity, as the supreme expression of the ethics of redemption, knows no universally legislative morality. Christian ethics is lost in that moment that it is transformed into a norm. In its liberation from the ethics of law, the movement of redemption transvalues the moral principles which have become standardized by the legal consciousness. The "wicked," the "rebellious," the "adulterers," the "unbelievers" prove to be more acceptable to God than the "good," the "pious," the "just," and the "faithful." Thus, the ethics of redemption becomes a stumbling block for the ethics of law. It teaches that the first shall be last and the last shall be first. The moral judgments of the rationalized and legalized conscience are ironically disclosed as pharisaical vices. The moral ambiguity of the sinful world, which is the condition for the ethics of law, renders impossible a clear demarcation between the evil and the good. Redemptive ethics is disclosed on the other side of the sinful world, as an answer to it, and thus lies beyond the distinction between good and evil. The ethics of redemption transvalues the interpretive moral categories of the ethics of law.

The ethics of creativeness demands three conditions: (1) a primeval, uncreated freedom; (2) gifts or talents bestowed upon man by God; and (3) the world as the field of man's activity. Every act of human creation thus involves a condition which is supplied by God—the gift of genius; but also there is that condition which resides in the abyss of the self and which does not proceed from God—uncreated freedom. Thus, it is first in the ethics of creativeness that we see man in his superlative grandeur and true nobility. Man becomes a veritable co-creator with God. He creates *ex nihilo*—out of the nothingness which resides in the depths of his self. This creativeness has an inner and an outer aspect. The inner aspect is the primary creative intuition which as such is not concerned with realization. It is the energy or the potentiality which makes realization possible. The outer aspect has to do with the realization process, which terminates in the statue, the painting, the book, or the social institution: the created "object." But in this second aspect there is a cooling down of the creative fire. A created "object," by virtue of the fact that it becomes an object, is inevitably less than the creative intuition from which it took its rise. This is the essential tragedy of human creativity. The ethics of creativeness differs from the ethics of law in that it is personal and creative rather than social and legislative. Creativity can never be confined to universally binding rules. It differs from the ethics of redemption in that its first concern is with values and not with salvation. It presupposes a morality different from that of both law and redemption. The creator engages in a movement of self-transcendence, forgets about himself, and understands all moral progress to be adventitious to the creative vision. No amount of ethical striving for moral edification will enhance his creativity. His creativity has to do with values above man; it strives for the "selfless and disinterested love of God and of the divine life, of truth and perfection and all positive values." It is at this point that the creative and theo-andric aspects of Berdyaev's ethics are harmonized. Creativity, in its final dimension, is a movement expressing a divine humanity.

The third and final part of Berdyaev's philosophico-theological treatise consists of an examination of the relevance of eschatology for ethics. The problems of death and immortality, of hell and paradise are discussed in the light of their ethical significance. The author credits Kierkegaard and Heidegger for having recognized the paramount significance of death for ontological ethics, and his analysis is markedly influenced by the reflections of both the Danish and German existentialists. Death is understood not simply as a biological happening, but as an event which embraces the whole of life. Death penetrates life in every experience of transitoriness and separation. Death is existentialized as a phenomenon experienced in the midst of life.

Immortality provides the answer to the anxiety which is created in the encounter with existential death. But immortality, as defined by the author, is not an objectivized and naturalized life beyond the grave. It too is existentialized as a subjective mode of existence which is attained while still in time.

Berdyaev carefully distinguishes objective immortality, which is a peculiar legacy of Greek rationalism, from subjective immortality, or eternal life, which has its roots in the Judaic-Christian tradition. Eternal life is not a life in a future world, but rather a qualification of the present life of man in the creative moment. Eternal life comes not in the future, but in the "depths of an instant of time." Hell and paradise, as the central eschatological symbols of Christianity, can thus never be understood as objectivized regions of reality. They are symbols of man's spiritual life—of his experience of complete separation from God and his experience of reunion in the creative moment. Hell is the experience of an utter isolation and loneliness, and a final inability to love, in which every instant of time appears as an endless duration. This is the bad infinity of which Hegel had already spoken, and which can properly be thought of as hell. Paradise symbolizes the experience of eternity in time. Eternity becomes present, not in an endless duration, but in the moment of creative inspiration and reuniting love. Berdyaev's theo-andric and creative ethics thus receives its final meaning through eschatology.—*C.O.S.*

PERTINENT LITERATURE

Spinka, Matthew. *Christian Thought from Erasmus to Berdyaev*. Englewood Cliffs, New Jersey: Prentice-Hall, 1962.

Matthew Spinka recounts that Nicholai Berdyaev was born in Kiev. His family was aristocratic, his father being a retired officer in the Cavalier Guard who placed Nicholai in the Pages' Corpus for military training. The youth's interests, however, were in philosophy, and having graduated from military school Berdyaev entered Kiev University. At fourteen he had read Immanuel Kant, Arthur Schopenhauer, and G. W. F. Hegel. During his time at Kiev he became a leader of the student Marxists, was expelled from the University, and spent three years in exile, although in his autobiography *Dream and Reality* he denies he was ever an orthodox Marxist. He rejected determinism and could not go along with "the rejection of the supreme principle of spiritual values independent of the material world." In his later life, the biblical prophets, Job, the Greek tragedies, and the writers Miguel de Cervantes, William Shakespeare, Johann Wolfgang von Goethe, Lord Byron, Charles Dickens, Honoré de Balzac, Henrik Ibsen, Fyodor Dostoevski, Leo Tolstoy, and Fyodor Tyutchev strongly influenced him.

Spinka indicates that Berdyaev agreed with Kant that the human personality is the highest value to be found in the world. He was interested in Marxism because he thought it held that view, and he became disenchanted with Marxism when he discovered that it did not. He then came to accept a basically Christian interpretation of human personality and life. According to Spinka, Berdyaev described himself as more a mystical than a religious man, and was critical of the Orthodox Russian Church. He described himself as searching for meaning and eternity, and found that his search for meaning was his first search for God and that his search for eternity was his first search for salvation. In Spinka's opinion, Berdyaev was a lay Christian who offers too individualistic an interpretation of Christianity for him to be seen as a representative of Russian Orthodox thought.

During World War I, Spinka continues, Berdyaev published an article which denounced the Holy Governing Synod, and as a result he was scheduled to be tried as a blasphemer; punishment for conviction would have been permanent exile to Siberia. But the exigencies of war caused the trial to be postponed, and in fact it was never held. Nevertheless, Spinka reports, Berdyaev was expelled from Russia in 1922, having been twice imprisoned and having written a book condemning both the Russian intelligentsia and the Bolshevik Revolution of 1917. He had been appointed to the chair of philosophy by the faculty of the University of Moscow, but, as Spinka suggests, because of his convictions he could not long retain the post. Upon his exile in 1922, he moved to Berlin, and two years later he went to Paris where he spent the rest of his life.

Spinka asserts that Berdyaev was a religious philosopher, not a theologian. His work is an elaboration of the thesis that human personality has the highest value of anything in the world. He offered a Christian personalism or existentialism intended to provide a knowledge of human existence, and, through that knowledge, a knowledge of the world. He begins not with being as Aristotle and many of the medieval philosophers had done, but with freedom. Thus what is primary in Berdyaev's thought, according to Spinka, is the existent subject, the individual human being.

Spinka notes that Berdyaev records his disbelief in the objective world of nature and history. What is primarily real or existent, he thinks, is the free person whose thinking determines what meaning objects are to have. For Berdyaev, the ultimate sin, intellectual and religious, is objectification—treating a person as a nonperson or object, or, in Kant's terms, treating a person as means and not also as ends, or treating what in fact has dignity as if it had only price.

Spinka reminds us that Berdyaev reports that he accepted Christianity because in it he found the strongest basis for his belief in the value and destiny of the human spirit. A human being, he says, is a unity of two components, a spirit and a body-mind organism. The body-mind organism is the object of study of the natural and social sciences; such study is useful, but by itself superficial. Given only the natural and social sciences, Spinka continues, Berdyaev contends that one can discover no significance or meaning to one's life. Such significance or meaning is, in Berdyaev's view, created by persons. Apart from there being persons, there is no such significance and meaning (and Berdyaev at times seems to infer from this that therefore persons create what meaning or significance there is).

For Berdyaev, Spinka notes, the mind-body organism is "objective." Each person is an individual; so is each diamond or pencil. Spinka adds that Berdyaev holds that the spirit is not merely individual; it is also personal. Personality is attained by an effort of the spirit as it dominates the physical-psychical component of humanity. According to Berdyaev, a human being who possesses brilliant individuality may not possess personality to any extent, and so may live without being a person.

What Berdyaev meant by this is somewhat clarified, Spinka suggests, by his doctrine (echoing Kant) that the items studied in the natural and social sciences exist within a deterministic causal nexus; given a causing event, the effected event cannot but occur. No such item is free. Insofar as a human being is only an object of study of the natural and social sciences, he is an individual and not a person. The component of humanity that Berdyaev calls "spirit" has little or no effect.

Spinka finds Berdyaev contending that to become a person rather than merely an individual is a matter of finding salvation. Living merely as an individual, treating others as objects and being so treated by them, and living as if one were oneself merely an object, is living in a "fallen" condition. Even in this condition, however, human beings retain freedom of choice. Berdyaev holds, Spinka tells us, that in the Incarnation of God in Jesus Christ one finds not only the highest revelation of God, but also an example of what a person may and ought to be. Since God was in Christ, reconciling the world to himself, Berdyaev maintains, those who freely respond favorably to the revelation in Christ become transformed from individuals to full persons. Such a transformation, interpreted along the lines of the individual coming to participate in the sort of nature Christ possesses, involves an encounter between the human spirit and God. This encounter is effected by the Holy Spirit. Since for Berdyaev salvation can only be freely accepted, those who freely reject it inflict suffering and self-destructiveness on themselves. Thus, Spinka concludes, for Berdyaev the end or goal of history involves the end of all objectification and a kingdom of God in which each member is treated, and treats others, as spirits, or as ends and not means only.

Nucho, Fuad. *Berdyaev's Philosophy: The Existential Paradox of Freedom and Necessity*. Garden City, New York: Doubleday & Company, 1966.

According to Fuad Nucho, Nicholai Berdyaev adapted a notion of uncreated freedom from Jacob Boehme and made it fundamental to his philosophical perspective by claiming that this sort of freedom is essential to human nature. Nucho reports that critics have argued that the notion involves a sort of dualism incompatible with Christian doctrine (in particular, with the doctrine of God as a sovereign Creator) and imports into his system an assumption it does not require. It is plausibly suggested, Nucho continues, that Berdyaev's reason for positing an uncreated freedom in human beings rather than saying that God gave human beings freedom is that Berdyaev believes that if God gives one freedom and one misuses it, then God is responsible for that misuse. His critics deny this, Nucho reports, and note that in any case, in Berdyaev's view, God has created the persons who have freedom, uncreated or not, and so God is responsible for what persons do.

Nucho tells us that Berdyaev's response was to deny that his position involved an ontological dualism, or indeed any ontological position at all. His concern, he said, was not with ontology, or being, but with existence. Nucho notes that what this involved concerning uncreated freedom was that, in ascribing uncreated freedom to persons, Berdyaev was merely saying that a person is free only if his or her freedom (specifically, his or her *exercise* of freedom) is "self-determined" or not surreptitiously caused by something other than the agent himself or herself. Another part of Berdyaev's reply, Nucho indicates, is that "uncreated freedom" is a symbol for something which cannot be defined.

Regarding theodicy, Nucho writes, *The Destiny of Man* did say that it should account for the origin of the distinction between good and evil in such a manner as to justify the ways of God to humankind. But this, Nucho contends, is qualified by the claim that revelation shows that God is himself the source of all values, and that the role of theodicy is to defend God against human (that is, nonrevealed) conceptions. Elsewhere, Nucho adds, his message is that "Christ is the only theodicy." So, he concludes the degree to which Berdyaev is interesting in philosophical theodicy is small indeed.

Nucho says that Berdyaev insists that it is existence, not being, which is the proper beginning place for the philosopher. Part of what this means, Nucho explains, is expressed in Wilhelm Dilthey's doctrine that the meaningfulness and the truth of any system depends on its "being referred to some concrete experience." Moreover, Nucho suggests, it is the experience of agents as goal-seeking and as self-conscious which is to be accepted at face value. It is not to be "reduced" to anything that can be given mechanistic or materialistic description. For Berdyaev any such attempt at reduction would be "objectivizing." Personal experience is supplemented by revelation in which God is experienced as free, loving, and sacrificing. It is in this revelation, Nucho reports, that the solution to the problem of theodicy is found for Berdyaev.

Nucho tells us that *The Destiny of Man* identified "the world of love" as "the world of reality" and that this reflects Berdyaev's eschatological confidence. Nucho records that Berdyaev suffered from childhood from a nervous condition that was unpredictable and uncontrollable, causing him embarrassment in public and anxiety in private. He endured permanent exile from his homeland. But he believed that the course of history ultimately will be transformed by the Kingdom of God. He accepted the doctrine of universal salvation, believing that in a mystical way every person participated in Christ's work of salvation.

Part of Berdyaev's view of redemption, Nucho indicates, involves human activity; Berdyaev tends to change the doctrine of the incarnation into a doctrine of cooperation in which human beings are not recipients but co-producers. Further, Nucho notes, to the degree that participation in the salvational work of Christ renders each person's redemption sure, as the doctrine of universal salvation suggests, human freedom is restricted, if not simply nonexistent, in terms of its influence on one's redemption. Perhaps when, but not whether, one is saved is a matter of choice. Thus, Nucho suggests, the doctrine of universal salvation fits ill with Berdyaev's strong emphasis on freedom. Perhaps, Nucho reflects, this illustrates the continued influence of Jacob Boehme on Berdyaev, for Boehme's own doctrine of an uncreated freedom in humankind posits an essential part of human nature which is not created by God, and this introduces a limitation on divine sovereignty. Perhaps, Nucho remarks, this influences Berdyaev when he also restricts the role God has in providing the basis of human redemption. Nucho reminds us that Berdyaev, in his autobiography, did say that he could not in conscience describe himself as a typical "orthodox" of any kind. Nevertheless, Nucho contends, basic to Berdyaev's view of the world is the contention that only in the freedom which Christ, as God Incarnate, offers is there genuine freedom. (Perhaps Berdyaev also illustrates that consistently combining Christianity with a philosophical perspective is not necessarily made any easier if that philosophy starts with "existence" rather than with "being."—*K.E.Y.*

ADDITIONAL RECOMMENDED READING

Blackham, Harold J. *Six Existentialist Thinkers*. London: Routledge & Kegan Paul, 1952. Chapters on six existentialists, including one on Berdyaev. Useful for comparison of Berdyaev with others in the existentialist fold.

Heinemann, F. H. *Existentialism and the Modern Predicament*. New York: Harper and Brothers, 1953. Discussion of Berdyaev's place in the context of modern thought.

Lowrie, Donald A. *Rebellious Prophet: A Life of Nicolai Berdyaev*. New York: Harper and Brothers, 1960. For those who wish to know about Berdyaev himself as well as his philosophy.

Seaver, George. *Nicolas Berdyaev: An Introduction to His Thought*. New York: Harper and Brothers, 1950. An introduction to Berdyaev's philosophy; clear and useful.

Spinka, Matthew. *Nicolas Berdyaev: Captive of Freedom*. Philadelphia: The

Westminster Press, 1950. A sympathetic treatment of Berdyaev by an excellent writer.

Tillich, Paul. "Nicolaus Berdyaev," in *Religion in Life*. VII, no. 3 (Summer, 1938), pp. 407-415. A distinguished liberal Protestant theologian writes in a popular vein about Berdyaev.

THE SPIRIT OF MEDIAEVAL PHILOSOPHY

Author: Étienne Henry Gilson (1884-1978)
Type of work: Ontology, theology
First published: 1931-1932

PRINCIPAL IDEAS ADVANCED

The central idea in medieval philosophy is the idea of Being; in contrast to the Greek conception of being as essentially intelligibility and perfection, the medieval philosophers' conception of being was conditioned by religious belief: God is Being.

According to the medieval philosophy, God is self-sufficient and perfect because he exists.

God created the world ex nihilo *(out of nothing), the medieval philosophers claimed; consequently, man's being is the image of Being Itself.*

The medieval philosophy regarded ethics as an expression of God's will and man's fulfillment as being in the life following resurrection.

History as having a beginning (the creation), a middle (the incarnation), and an end (the Last Judgment) was the invention of medieval Christians.

Étienne Gilson's book, *The Spirit of Mediaeval Philosophy* (The Gifford lectures for 1931 and 1932), is an attempt to show that medieval philosophy was more original and significant than many contemporary critics believe. Much of what Gilson argues for in the book is not as widely questioned today as it was when the lectures were originally given. And Gilson, probably more than any other single figure, has been rsponsible for the great change that has occurred concerning this question. Few historians of philosophy today retain the simple erroneous view (stemming originally from the Renaissance humanists) that the Middle Ages, since their culture consisted merely of a misunderstood remnant of classical culture, can safely be ignored in discussing the history of Western philosophy. Anyone who has read even one of Gilson's books knows that this Renaissance view is simply false. Contemporary philosophers are much in Gilson's debt for pointing out so forcefuly and so clearly that the medieval period included quite an array of thinkers of a high order, and that modern philosophy has in the medieval tradition roots which are just as significant as the roots it has in Greece and in science as inaugurated by Galileo, Kepler, and Newton.

Gilson recognizes that there were differences between the various medieval philosphers, that between Augustine, Anselm, Aquinas, and Duns Scotus there were genuine differences in philosophical orientation and in philosophical conclusions. But he argues that their differences all occur within a wider framework which these philosophers shared without disagreement. This wider framework is made up of two elements: the Greek metaphysical tradition and the Judeo-Christian religious tradition. The medievals questioned neither the intention of the Greek metaphysicians nor the provisional adequacy of the syntheses the Greeks produced. On the other hand, they were committed on religious grounds to the tradition developed in Palestine as it found expression in the Christian Scriptures and in the writings of the Patristic fathers. The task the medieval philosophers set themselves was to make a synthesis of the two traditions, a task which involved elaborating, complementing, and modifying the Greek metaphysical tradition in such a way that the religious insights of Christianity transformed and gave new life to that same metaphysical tradition.

The central idea in medieval philosophy, according to Gilson, is the idea of Being. The concept of being (a capital "B" indicates the medieval idea and a lowercase "b" indicates the Greek concept) was a familiar one to the Greeks, but Gilson argues that the Greek concept of being was radically transformed and reinterpreted in the light of the Christian revelation. In spite of obvious similarities between the Greek concept of being and the medieval idea of Being there are fundamental differences. Gilson's book amounts to an extended treatise on the idea of Being, first contrasting it with the Greek concept of being and then tracing the implications of the medieval doctrine for a variety of philosophical problems.

To the Greek, intelligibility and metaphysical perfection were the essential components in the concept of being; the more intelligibility and perfection (self-sufficiency) a thing had, the more being it had. It is probable that this philosophy found its fullest expression in Plato's doctrine of degrees or reality. As a mind ascends in the Platonic hierarchy from nonbeing through becoming to the realm of being itself, the mind moves from less to greater intelligibility and self-sufficiency. Finally, in the Idea of the Good, the mind reaches the ultimate in intelligibility and self-sufficiency; indeed, the very ground of being itself. Aristotle, too, shared in this interpretation of the concept of being. His unmoved movers were self-sufficient and completely intelligible. They were pure forms and, as such, were preeminently intelligible, and the fact that they were themselves unmoved is equivalent in the Aristotelian scheme to saying that they were self-sufficient. Intelligibility and perfection, then, were the ground of existence in the Greek view of things, so much so, in fact, that even the gods were criticized in the light of this metaphysical persuasion by the philosophers. In Plato's scheme of education as set forth in the *Republic* certain myths and religious poems were outlawed because they were judged inadequate in the light of his metaphysical views.

Things were different for the medieval philosophers. Rather than judging their theological tradition in the light of metaphysical doctrine, they used the theological doctrines to judge the metaphysical tradition. One of Gilson's points illustrates in a very striking fashion the medieval reversal of the Greek attitude toward the interplay of metaphysics and theology and it can serve here to exemplify Gilson's concern, which runs throughout the book, to show that medieval philosophy is something more than just new wine in old bottles. He points out that the Greeks never finally emerged from polytheism in religion. Plato never referred to the Idea of the Good as God, for example, and in spite of the fact that he often uses the singular term "God," he also uses the plural "gods," indicating that he never advanced to full-blown monotheism. Aristotle, too, remained a polytheist. He was uncertain whether, under his first Unmoved Mover, there were forty-nine or fifty-five subordinate Unmoved Movers. By contrast, the Hebrews had no doubts on this score; at the very core of Judaism is Moses' ringing cry: "Hear, O Israel, the Lord our God is one Lord." (Deuteronomy VI:4.) And Christianity is just as monotheistic, as the opening words of the Nicene Creed proclaim: "I believe in one God. . . ." Thus, in this unmistakable manner the matter was settled for the medievals; there is only one God, and all that remains is to see the implications of monotheism for metaphysics. Never again, Gilson reminds us, was there any serious consideration of polytheism in Western civilization. Even in our day, when attitudes toward religion are considerably more heterogeneous than they were in the medieval period, the question for philosophers of religion is whether God exists—not how many gods there are.

Just as the question of how many gods there are was settled for the medievals by their religious faith, so it was that from their religious convictions they derived their conception of God's nature. It was not because God was self-sufficient and intelligible that he existed, but because he existed in the fullest and most complete sense they knew he was self-sufficient and intelligible. What is God? God is Being, for Moses again had recorded the words that settled the matter, this time repeating the very words of God himself. Moses, while tending sheep in Midian, came upon the burning bush out of which God spoke to him, directing him to lead the Children of Israel out of their bondage in Egypt. Moses himself had no doubt about his divine commissioning, but he wondered what the Israelites would think. He asked Jehovah what he should tell the Israelites when they asked him who sent him to lead them out of captivity—what was God's name? God then answered out of the burning bush: "And God said unto Moses, I AM THAT I AM: and he said, Thus shalt thou say unto the children of Israel, I AM hath sent me unto you." (Exodus II:14.) God's very name, "Jehovah," means (in translation) "I AM." Here, then, out of their religious faith, came the content for the medievals' idea of Being. God's nature is *existence*—not mere intelligibility or perfection; God is Being. Religious faith and metaphysical beliefs meet at the apex of each other; what remains for the philosopher is to elaborate the body of philosophical doctrine which is suspended from the idea of Being as it is thus filled out with a content that has been religiously revealed. The medievals used Greek terminology and Greek thought patterns, since the created world had its (derivative) being from Being Itself, and, furthermore, the reason-

ableness the Greeks had discovered and formulated was the intrinsic reasonableness of this derivative being. Nevertheless, the medievals did not hesitate
to transform or to go beyond the insights of the Greeks, provided this step
was necessary to make their philosophy compatible with their religious faith.

From the idea of Being, cast against the background of the Christian Scriptures, Gilson moves on to consider derivative beings. The medieval philosophers differed from the ancients on this question, too. For the Greeks, the
world about us is a metaphysical ultimate, or at least the stuff of that world
is ultimate. There was no doctrine of creation in Greek philosophy. The
nearest approach to a creation doctrine was perhaps Plato's myth in the
Timaeus about the origin of the world. But in this latter myth the Demiurge
(the divine agent) merely forms (or *in*forms) a preexistent matter. The matter
itself is not made; it is an ultimate in the metaphysical picture. Of course, the
Christians could not go along with this Platonic or Greek interpretation, for
they had all read the opening words of Genesis: "In the beginning God created
the heaven and the earth." Just before the beginning—if one overlooks for
the moment St. Augustine's observation that it makes no sense to talk this
way—there was nothing, nothing in the strictest possible sense. Then God
created it all, ordering it both temporally and physically, as is recorded in
Genesis.

Certain other elements from the Genesis account are taken into the medieval metaphysical picture. God not only created the world *ex nihilo*, but
he "saw that it was good." Furthermore, he made the crown of creation, "in
his own image." All this has consequences for metaphysics. In the first place,
the world in which we live has a derivative being, a being that is an effect of
God's, or Being's, creative activity. The rocks, trees, animals, and the rest
have being because they were created by Being. And in a special sense man
also has being since he, too, is created, and therefore Being has communicated
being to him. But man's being bears on its face an additional mark. Man's
being is the image of Being Itself. This idea had an added consequence for
the medieval philosophers; an epistemological doctrine was derived which
parallels the ontological and anthropological doctrines. In knowing himself
man knows an analogue of Being Itself. There is therefore a pathway to
knowledge of the divine. Out of the metaphysical emerges the epistemological. Descartes' well-known remark about the mark of the Craftsman, left
imprinted on his handiwork, is but a later reflection of this medieval doctrine
of the analogy of being and an example of the often overlooked influence of
medieval thought on modern philosophy.

The doctrine of the analogy of being is one example of how the idea of
Being influenced medieval metaphysics. Gilson considers many other examples of this transformation of Greek metaphysics in the light of Christian
belief. Two important areas of medieval philosophical concern which he discusses are ethics and history.

One of the most noticeable differences between the ethical views of classical Greece and Christianity is the presence in the latter of the concept of sin. In Greek ethics and in Greek religion there was no concern with sin in the Christian sense. There were, of course, rules regarding what was proper religious conduct, but they dealt mainly with ritual purity. And in Greek ethics there were general rules of conduct, but they were not interpreted in such a way as to make violations of them sinful acts. The best-known Christian code of conduct, however, the Ten Commandments, was attributed directly to God, and God made it clear that violation of the Commandments was a personal affront to him. ("For I the Lord thy God am a jealous God. . . .") Again, the Christian God was added to the philosophical tradition by the medievals and a new synthesis emerged. The ethical principles of the Greeks were retained, but they were not merely the deliverances of reason (although the medievals did not deny that reason could, and indeed had discovered them). But the ethical rules were also the expression of God's will regarding man's conduct. Just as man's being was an indelible mark indicating the fact that he was a creature made by God, so man's conscience had written on it God's Law. The Greeks had discovered the Natural Law because God had written that Law on the hearts of all men. The Greeks knew the Law, but they had not known that it was another stamp left on man by his Creator.

But there was still more in the medieval ethical position. The Greek believed that the rules of ethics told him how to live his life most satisfactorily here on earth, but there was no transcendent reference. For the Christian, however, conduct was the key not only to satisfactory living here in this life, but it was also the crucial determiner of his eternal destiny. Man's fulfillment, for the medieval, was not in this life, but in the life following the resurrection. This idea, Gilson argues, introduced two considerations that were lacking in the Greek view: a concern for the individual man as a being of eternal worth, and an attitude toward the physical world which again rested on an affirmation of the everlasting worth of the resurrected body. As another example of the shift from the usual perspective which results from Gilson's sympathetic reading of medieval philosophy, we might note here his observation on medieval monastic asceticism. He points out that it does not originate in a Platonic rejection of the body, as is the usual understanding; instead, it reflects an effort to discipline the body in order to make that very body serve more adequately in its proper spiritual vocation.

These observations about the consequences of the doctrine of the resurrection of the body for ethics lead easily into a consideration of the medieval philosophy of history. Surely the speculations of St. Augustine on time in the concluding books of the *Confessions* and his doctrine of the two cities in the *City of God* insure Augustine's eminence in this area of philosophical inquiry. Gilson merely points out that this philosophy of history is another instance of the pervasive influence of the central idea of Being in the thought of the medieval Christians. The Greeks had only a cyclical view of history, they had no feeling at all for history as the tale of the significance of individual human striving. For St. Augustine in particular, and the medievals generally, however, history had an origin, a direction, and a goal, and was made up of the acts of individual human beings, beings with immortal souls and with bodies which would again be active following the Resurrection. History, as told in terms of human personality and as having a beginning (the creation), a middle (the incarnation), and an end (the Last Judgment), was clearly the invention of the medieval Christians. It resulted from speculation that operated against the background of Christian revelation. Such a conception of history was lacking in the Greek world; it originated in the medieval interval, and remains with us today.

In spite of the many excellences of Gilson's book, and his refreshing refusal to view medieval philosophy as a pointless, logic-chopping debate over silly questions, there are certain inadequacies that remain. Some medieval philosophers are barely mentioned, and their views are slighted. Siger of Brabant, whose Averroistic doctrine of separate truths for faith and reason does not fit in well with Gilson's picture, is an example. The tension at Paris during the thirteenth century between, on the one hand, Siger's emphasis on fidelity to Aristotle's own text, even when it conflicted with Scripture and religious tradition, and, on the other hand, the Thomist concern to accommodate Aristotle to religious orthodoxy is not given the discussion it should receive in a book on medieval philosophy. The realism-nominalism controversy, around which so much philosophical debate centered, is another problem which Gilson treats less fully than one might expect. Ockham, a commanding figure in the late medieval period, is given scant notice. Generally speaking, the Thomist synthesis occupies such a dominant position in the book that many of the rich countermelodies of medieval thought do not emerge.

Finally, the sophisticated Protestant reader cannot help feeling that some of Gilson's incidental remarks about Martin Luther reveal less sympathy for the spirit of the Reformation than they do for the spirit of Thomistic philosophy. It is a rare person indeed who can look at both St. Thomas and the impulsive and often horribly mistaken Luther without feeling that one of them was seriously in error, but one suspects that there must have been in the medieval period a tradition that somehow provided a background for the Reformation. The nominalist Ockham and the philosophers who held that will was superior to intellect in God provided parts of this background. Gilson leaves the reader with the feeling that these stresses were almost entirely missing in the medieval intellectual milieu.

But these are errors of omission, not of commission. It would be a mistake to make more of them than merely to mention them. And Gilson himself has shown in other of his writings his awareness of the influences which he here neglects. In spite of its shortcomings, Gilson's book remains an excellent interpretation of what is clearly the main current of medieval thought. It is a book that no historian of philosophy can afford to be without, and it is a book that makes understandable and commendable the current revival of interest in scholastic philosophy generally and in St. Thomas specifically. Neo-Thomists have enriched contemporary philosophy considerably in areas as diverse as philosophy of religion and logic. Professor Gilson's very important role as one of the leaders among this group cannot surprise anyone who reads *The Spirit of Mediaeval Philosophy.—R.E.L.*

PERTINENT LITERATURE

Phelan, Gerald B. "A Christian Philosophy," in *Commonweal.* XXV, no. 13 (January 22, 1937), pp. 366-367.

Prior to the publication of his Gifford Lectures, the name Étienne Gilson was hardly known in this country even to Catholic philosophers. Reviewing these lectures for *Commonweal*, a Catholic publication, Gerald B. Phelan remarked on the fact that this leading authority on medieval thought had to be discovered for English-speaking Catholics by a great secular university.

Gilson's claim on their attention went beyond his qualifications as a historian. On the basis of his historical studies, Gilson had challenged the view generally accepted among Catholic philosophers of that time that medieval philosophy was to be interpreted simply as a continuation of the philosophy of the Greeks. Thus, according to Phelan, the thesis of *The Spirit of Mediaeval Philosophy* is that medieval thinkers, while inheriting a philosophic content from pagan Greeks, transformed that content in the light of the Judeo-Christian revelation in which they believed. This transformation gave rise to Christian philosophy, and these Gifford Lectures constitute an examination of the reality of "Christian philosophy."

At the outset Gilson acknowledges that a Christian biology or a Christian geometry would not make sense. Why, then, a Christian philosophy? Would it not seem somewhat contradictory, since Christianity is a dogmatic creed and philosophy is the product of reason's reflection upon experience? Gilson is sensitive to these objections, especially since the very notion of Christian philosophy has been a controversial notion even among Catholic historians of medieval thought. Thus his complete answer was something he sought to expound in his series of twenty lectures ranging over a number of medieval thinkers and the problems they addressed. Gilson's method, as Phelan observes, was to select leading philosophical problems and show how Christian speculation in each instance went beyond that of the Greek predecessors while preserving their insights and their specifically philosophical discipline. Phelan agrees with Gilson's thesis that Christian philosophy was a transformation of Greek philosophy in which, however, the orders of faith and reason were kept distinct.

Gilson's notion of Christian philosophy is illustrated in many ways throughout the series of lectures, but the prime example has to do with the medieval understanding of the nature of Supreme Being. Where Plato understood the highest entity to be the form of Goodness, and Aristotle spoke of self-thinking thought, and at the top of his hierarchy Plotinus placed the One, medieval theologians and philosophers came to think of God in terms of being, and especially one unique being, the Creator of heaven and earth. Gilson argues that the medieval thinker was guided to focus on the nature of God as existing being by that test of *Exodus* (III:14), wherein God, under the aspect of the voice of the burning bush, when asked who he was, told Moses that I AM THAT I AM. Thus alerted to the significance of existence, medieval philosophers were no less philosophical when they started their reflections by concentrating on the being of things. They were further alerted to the contingency of the world of existing things by reading in *Genesis* that the world was created by God out of nothing. Starting with the dependent existence of the things of their experience, Christian philosophers argued philosophically to the existence of one god whose essence was to *be*—that is, a unique, necessary being in whom essence and existence are identical.

While the Gifford Lectures were delivered in English at Aberdeen, they had first been published in French with extensive notes. Phelan, who praises the translation, complains that, for reasons of space, the translator has given only a "selection" of the notes. Granted that the notes are the most important part of the work, says Phelan, the publishers know their public, and most readers would rather read Gilson's conclusions than undertake to follow him in his long and laborious research.

Cresswell, J. R. Review of Étienne Gilson's *The Spirit of Mediaeval Philosophy*, in *The Philosophical Review*, XLVII, no. 3 (May, 1938), pp. 310-313.

J. R. Cresswell agrees with Gerald B. Phelan that the purpose of Étienne Gilson's lectures is to demonstrate the existence of a Christian philosophy; but he is more inclined than Phelan to qualify, although not to deny, Gilson's achievement. Thus, without being a hostile review, his is one that begs to disagree, or, at least, to modify or suggest another context for Gilson's evidence.

For example, while recognizing that the principal contribution of Judeo-Christian revelation to the heritage from the Greeks was how God is to be considered, Cresswell wonders how it is possible for a modern historian to take seriously the claim of medieval thinkers to find in God's words to Moses anything resembling the doctrine that essence and existence are identical in God and in God alone.

Again, commenting on the claim that for the Christian philosopher the universe is not dependent "on the necessity of a thought thinking itself," as Aristotle held, but that it is "suspended now from a freedom of a will that wills it," Cresswell objects that the conception of "free creative action" makes it misleading to use Aristotelian language in the five cosmological proofs. When, for example, St. Thomas Aquinas speaks of efficient causality, what he really means is "creative causality." This makes one wonder, says Cresswell, whether St. Thomas has really presented us with "proofs" of God's existence.

Cresswell makes a point with which Gilson has agreed in other places, but which he emphasizes less in these Gifford Lectures: that the Christian philosophy of the Middle Ages embraces a variety of philosophies. That of St. Augustine is different from Aquinas'; St. Bonaventure, Peter Abelard, and St. Anselm differ from John Duns Scotus. There is no one Christian philosophy. Gilson has made the same point in the context of his discussion of Scholasticism. There is no one Scholastic philosophy; rather, there are a number of different theologians who have developed somewhat different metaphysical principles to serve their theology. Gilson's original point still stands in that in the development of their metaphysics they were guided to look at a world of contingently existing things, the product of the free creative causality of a being they had been inspired to understand as *Esse Ipsum*.

Writing in the 1930's, when the philosophies of history of Oswald Spengler and Pitirim Sorokin were enjoying more popularity, Cresswell takes up Gilson's chapter entitled "The Middle Ages and History." He comments favorably that the medieval philosophers of history tended to look upon the unfolding of time in a progressive, optimistic way; for they believed in history as the product of an intelligent, providential God. Cresswell suggests that his contemporaries could learn something from the study of this chapter. He concludes his review by proposing that if the affirmation of the intrinsic goodness of the universe seems too dogmatic, "they can always examine the evidence by perusing the works of the great medieval philosophers. This book provides an admirable introduction to them."—*D.J.F.*

ADDITIONAL RECOMMENDED READING

Brezik, Victor B., C. S. B., ed. *One Hundred Years of Thomism, Aeterni Patris and Afterwards, A Symposium*. Houston, Texas: Center for Thomistic Studies, University of St. Thomas, 1981. The encyclical *Aeterni Patris* (1879) of Leo XII was on the "Restoration of Christian Philosophy"; thus Gilson was using a phrase recommended by the highest Church authority. The important collection of papers focuses on reviewing what has happened in the century since this call for the restudy of Christian philosophy was made.

Gilson, Étienne. *The Christian Philosophy of St. Thomas Aquinas*. New York: Random House, 1956. This translation by L. K. Shook of *Le Thomisme* makes available the synthesis of the Christian theologian who, Gilson holds, preeminently represents the ideal of Christian philosophy. Gilson began as a historian of philosophy, studying the background of René Descartes, and only gradually became a Thomist.

_____ . *Elements of Christian Philosophy*. Garden City, New York: Doubleday & Company, 1960. Here is Gilson's effort to provide teachers with a textbook suitable for undergraduate students. It ranges from the metaphysics of God through the problems of philosophical anthropology to moral philosophy, casting the insights of Aquinas into contemporary language.

_____ . *History of Christian Philosophy in the Middle Ages*. New York: Random House, 1955. Here, in a work published some twenty years after the Gifford Lectures, Gilson further documents the special quality of medieval speculation: philosophy guided to look in certain directions through faith.

_____ . *The Philosopher and Theology*. New York: Random House, 1962. This autobiographical study of how his Christian faith influenced his philosophizing is a key to Gilson's special understanding of Christian philosophy. Written in his mid-seventies, it expresses his reflections on what shaped his thinking and researches.

Lynch, Lawrence E. *A Christian Philosophy*. New York: Charles Scribner's Sons, 1968. This book by a student of Gilson was originally a series of talks over CBC Radio. It is an excellent brief introduction to the topic and content of Christian philosophy.

COLLECTED PAPERS

Author: Charles Sanders Peirce (1839-1914)
Type of work: Logic, epistemology, metaphysics
First published: (1931-1958, eight volumes)

PRINCIPAL IDEAS ADVANCED

A belief is a habit of action; different beliefs give rise to different modes of action.

Our idea of anything is our idea of its sensible effects; objects are distinguished according to the difference they make practically.

True ideas are those to which responsible investigators, were they to push their inquiries far enough, would finally give assent; reality is what true ideas represent.

Of the four methods of fixing belief—the method of tenacity, of authority, of a priori *judgments, and the method of science—the scientific is preferable as providing critical tests of procedures.*

By the conceptions of Firstness, Secondness, and Thirdness, a metaphysics of cosmic evolution can be developed; Firstness is the individual quality of a thing, Secondness is the relatedness of a thing to something other than itself, and Thirdness is the tendency to mediate, to contribute to law.

There is chance in the universe (tychism); the universe begins in a chaos of unpersonalized feeling and develops habits or patterns of action (synechism); finally, as laws develop, the universe moves toward a condition of perfect rationality and symmetry (agapasm).

Although it is almost a century since Charles Sanders Peirce—in conversation with William James, Chauncey Wright, Nicholas St. John Green, and Oliver Wendell Holmes at informal meetings of the "metaphysical club" in Cambridge, Massachusetts—developed and brought to clear expression the central ideas which became the core of pragmatism, the pragmatic philosophy continues to prevail as the predominant American philosophy. Of course, if one were to make a survey, it might very well turn out that the majority of American philosophers would deny being pragmatists, although few would deny having been influenced by the ideas of Peirce, James, and John Dewey. But idealism in America is practically dead, despite some isolated champions in its behalf; and the new linguistic empiricism—which represents the emphasis of the Vienna positivists on grounding philosophical claims in experience (and manipulating statements according to an impartial logic), together with the emphasis of the British philosophers on the study of ordinary language in the multiplicity of its uses—comes very close to being a sophisticated, latter-day version of the American pragmatism which Peirce invented and defended.

But Peirce was more than the creator of pragmatism; he was a scientist, mathematician, logician, and teacher—although his career as a professor was limited. He lectured at Harvard and The Johns Hopkins University. Peirce's failure to find, or to be offered, a university position suitable for one of his talents, was a consequence of his independent and undisciplined nature. The result of his being free from academic restrictions was perhaps both fortunate and unfortunate: as an outsider, his creative powers had no formal limits, but his intellect was brilliant, and he knew where to stop in his inventions and speculations; but because he was an ousider, he had neither the security nor the incentive to fashion his essays into any coherent whole. Although he attempted, in later life, to write a great, single work in which his views on logic, nature, science, man, and philosophy would be developed in some mutually illuminating and supporting fashion, his poverty and isolation—together with his iconoclastic stubbornness—combined to frustrate his great ambition.

The most comprehensive collection of Peirce's papers is the *Collected Papers of Charles Sanders Peirce* (eight volumes, 1931-1958), edited by Charles Hartshorne and Paul Weiss, but other selections from his essays are available, including *Chance, Love, and Logic: Philosophical Essays by the Late Charles S. Peirce* (1923), edited by Morris R. Cohen, and *The Philosophy of Peirce* (1940), edited by Justus Buchler.

Although the critical interest in Peirce's writings is as lively now as it has ever been, and the attention given to the papers has intensified since the publication of the *Collected Papers*, so that new discoveries are constantly being made and new enthusiasms are frequently aroused, most editors of Peirce's essays and most commentators on his work are agreed on the importance of certain essays as being particularly characteristic of Peirce at his best. Among the early essays are "The Fixation of Belief," and "How to Make Our Ideas Clear," and among the later, "The Architecture of Theories" and "The Doctrine of Necessity Examined." Since these essays contain some of the most famous and revealing statements of Peirce's basic opinions, an examination of them will serve as an introduction to other significant essays.

Peirce's thought, varied and original as it was, falls naturally into four categories: the pragmatic, the epistemological, the logical, and the metaphysical. The poles are the pragmatic ideas of meaning and truth (ideas which condition the epistemological conceptions), and, at the other extreme of his thinking, the metaphysical ideas. The effort to relate these poles to each other rewards the student of Peirce with a synoptic idea of Peirce's philosophy which illuminates the otherwise confusing variety of essays to be found in the *Collected Papers*.

In the essay "How to Make Our Ideas Clear," which first appeared in the *Popular Science Monthly* for January, 1878, Peirce set out to clarify the unclear conception of clarity to be found in Descartes' writings on method. The first step was to clear up the conception of belief. Peirce began by speaking of doubt as a kind of irritation arising from indecisiveness in regard to action; when a man does not know what to do, he is uneasy, and his uneasiness will not leave him until he settles upon some mode of action. Belief is "a rule for action," and as it is acted upon repeatedly, each time appeasing the irritation of doubt, it becomes a habit of action. Thus, Peirce concluded, "The essence of belief is the establishment of a habit, and different beliefs are distinguished by the different modes of action to which they give rise."

In a previous essay, "The Fixation of Belief," which appeared in the *Popular Science Monthly* for November, 1877, Peirce had written of doubt as a state of dissatisfaction from which we try to free ourselves, and of belief as a satisfactory state. The struggle to remove the irritation of doubt and to attain belief, a rule of action, was described as "inquiry," and the settlement of opinion was set forth as the sole object of inquiry.

It was Peirce's conviction that logic, as the art of reasoning, was needed to make progress in philosophy possible; he anticipated logical positivism in urging that only "a severe course of logic" could clear up "that bad logical quality to which the epithet *metaphysical* is commonly applied. . . ."

Thus, the first step in learning how to make our ideas clear is to come to the realization that belief is a habit of action, the consequence of a process of inquiry undertaken to appease the irritation of indecisiveness. Since the entire purpose of thought, as Peirce conceived it, is to produce habits of action, it follows that the meaning of a thought is the collection of habits involved; or, if the question has to do with the meaning of a "thing," its meaning is clear once we know what difference the thing would make if one were to become actively, or practically, involved with it. Peirce's conclusion was that "there is no distinction of meaning so fine as to consist in anything but a possible difference of practice."

As an example, he referred to the doctrine of transubstantiation and to the Catholic belief that the elements of the Communion, though possessing all of the sense properties of wine and wafers, are literally blood and flesh. To Peirce such an idea could not possibly be clear, for no distinction in practice could be made between wine and wafers, on the one hand, and what *appeared* to be wine and wafers, on the other. He argued that no conception of wine was possible except as the object of the reference, "this, that, or the other, is wine," or as the object of a description by means of which certain properties are attributed to wine. But the properties are conceivable only in terms of the sensible effects of wine; "Our idea of anything *is* our idea of its sensible effects. . . ." Consequently, "to talk of something as having all the sensible characters of wine, yet being in reality blood, is senseless jargon." The rule for attaining clearness of thought, Peirce's famous pragmatic maxim, appears in "How to Make Our Ideas Clear" as follows: "Consider what effects, which might conceivably have practical bearings, we conceive the object of our conception to have. Then, our conception of these effects is the whole of our conception of the object."

Peirce's discussion of his maxim, centering about examples, makes it clear that the rule for the clarification of thought was not designed to support a simple phenomenalism. Although Peirce used sentences such as "Our idea of anything *is* our idea of its sensible effects. . . ," he did not use the expression "sensible effects" to mean sensations merely. By conceiving, through the use of the senses, the effects of the action of a thing, we come to understand the thing; our habit of reaction, forced upon us by the action of the thing, is a conception of it, our belief regarding it. The object is not *identifiable* with its effects—that is not even proper grammar, and Peirce was aware of the relation of linguistic practice to philosophical perplexity—but the object can be conceived as "that which" we conceive only in terms of its effects.

Peirce's pragmatic rule should be distinguished from William James's version of the same principle. James stressed an idea's becoming true; he used the misleading expression "practical cash-value" to refer to the pragmatic meaning of a word, and he sometimes emphasized the *satisfactoriness* of an idea, as constituting its truth, in such a way that no clear line was drawn between sentimental satisfaction and the satisfaction of a scientific investigator.

Peirce, on the other hand, in developing the ideas of truth and reality made careful use of the contrary-to-fact conditional in order to avoid any loose or emotional interpretation of the pragmatic method. He wrote, in "How to Make Our Ideas Clear," that scientific processes of investigation "if only pushed far enough, will give one certain solution to every question to which they can be applied. . . ." Again, in clarifying the idea of reality, Peirce came to the conclusion that "The opinion which is fated to be ultimately agreed to by all who investigate, is what we mean by the truth, and the object represented in this opinion is the real." In other words, those opinions to which systematic, responsible investigators, *would* finally give assent, *were* the matter thoroughly investigated, are true opinions. It was Peirce's dissatisfaction with the tender-minded versions of the pragmatic method that led him finally to give up the name "pragmatism," which he invented, and to use in its place the term "pragmaticism."

Peirce's preference for the scientific method of inquiry is nowhere more clearly expressed and affirmed than in his early essay, "The Fixation of Belief." Regarding the object of reasoning to be the discovery of new facts by a consideration of facts already known, and having argued that a belief is a habit of action which appeases the irritation of doubt or indecisiveness, he went on to examine four methods of fixing belief: the method of tenacity, which is the method of stubbornly holding to a belief while resisting all criticism; the method of authority, which consists of punishing all dissenters; the *a priori* method, which depends on the inclination to believe, whatever the facts of the matter; and, finally, the method of science, which rests on the following assumption: "There are real things, whose characters are entirely independent of our opinions about them; those realities affect our senses according to regular laws, and, though our sensations be as different as our relations to the objects, yet, by taking advantage of the laws of perception, we can ascertain by reasoning how things really are, and any man, if he have sufficient experience and reason enough about it, will be led to the one true conclusion."

Peirce strongly endorsed the scientific method of inquiry. He argued that no other method provided a way of determining the rightness or wrongness of the method of inquiry itself; the test of a procedure undertaken as scientific is an application of the method itself.

In support of the realistic hypothesis on which the method of science is based, Peirce argued that the practice of the method in no way cast doubt on the truth of the hypothesis; furthermore, everyone who approves of one method of fixing belief in preference to others tacitly admits that there are realities the method can uncover; the scientific method is widely used, and it is only ignorance that limits its use; and, finally, the method of science has been so successful that belief in the hypothesis on which it rests has been strengthened proportionately.

These passages should be of particular interest to those who suppose that Peirce, as the founder of pragmatism, was absolutely neutral in regard to commitments ordinarily regarded as metaphysical. He did not claim to know the truth of the realistic hypothesis, but it did seem to him eminently sensible, accounting for the manner in which nature forces experience upon us, and making uniformity of opinion possible. (However, his theory of cosmic evolution, as shall be seen, is a peculiar kind of realism.)

In the essay "The Architecture of Theories," published in *The Monist* in January, 1891, Peirce introduced the critical conceptions of First, Second, and Third, which he described as "principles of Logic," and by reference to which he developed his metaphysics of cosmic evolution. He defined the terms as follows: "First is the conception of being or existing independent of anything else. Second is the conception of being relative to, the conception of reaction with, something else. Third is the conception of mediation, whereby a first and second are brought into relation."

Arguing that philosophical theories should be built architectonically, Peirce offered the conceptions of First, Second, and Third as providing the logical principles of construction. Any adequate theory, he maintained, would order the findings of the various sciences by the use of the principles of First, Second, and Third. Thus, in psychology, "Feeling is First, Sense of reaction Second, General conception Third, or mediation." Significantly, as a general feature of reality, "Chance is First, Law is Second, the tendency to take habits is Third," and, Peirce maintained, "Mind is First, Matter is Second, Evolution is Third."

Peirce went on to sketch out the metaphysics which would be built by the use of these general conceptions. He wrote that his would be a "Cosmogonic Philosophy," and that it would describe a universe which, beginning with irregular and unpersonalized feeling would, by chance ("sporting here and there in pure arbitrariness"), give rise to generalizing tendencies which, continuing, would become "habits" and laws; the universe, such a philosophy would claim, is evolving toward a condition of perfect rationality and symmetry.

Four more papers, all published in Cohen's selection, *Chance, Love, and Logic*, develop the ideas introduced in "The Architecture of Theories." They are "The Doctrine of Necessity Examined," "The Law of Mind," "Man's Glassy Essence," and "Evolutionary Love."

In "The Doctrine of Necessity Examined," Peirce argued for the presence of chance in the universe. But Peirce's conception of chance was not the usual conception of the entirely uncaused and irregular, acting without cause or reason. He wrote of chance as "the form of a spontaneity which is to some degree regular," and he was careful to point out that he was not using the conception of chance as a principle of explanation but as an element in the description of a universe in which there is the tendency to form habits and to produce regularities. The doctrine of absolute chance was named "tychism," and the doctrine of continuity was named "synechism." The essay "The Law of Mind" develops the latter doctrine.

In "The Law of Mind," Peirce argued that there is but one law of mind, that ideas spread, affect other ideas, lose intensity, but gain generality and "become welded with other ideas." In the course of the article Peirce developed the notion of an "idea" as an event in an individual consciousness; he argued that consciousness must take time and be in time, and that, consequently, "we are immediately conscious through an infinitesimal interval of time." Ideas are continuous, Peirce claimed, and there must be a "continuity of intrinsic qualities of feeling" so that particular feelings are present out of a continuum of other possibilities. Ideas affect one another: but to understand this, one must distinguish three elements within an idea (Firstness, Secondness, and Thirdness make their appearance again); the three elements are, First, the intrinsic quality of the idea as a feeling, its *quale*; Second, the energy with the idea affects other ideas (its capacity to relate); and, Third, the tendency of an idea to become generalized (its tendency to be productive of law). Habits are established by induction; general ideas are followed by the kind of reaction which followed the particular sensations that gave rise to the general idea. Mental phenomena come to be governed by law in the sense that some living idea, "a conscious continuum of feeling," pervades the phenomena and affects other ideas.

Peirce concluded "The Law of Mind" with the striking claim that matter is not dead, but it is mind "hidebound with habits."

In the essay "Man's Glassy Essence" Peirce argued that mind and matter are different aspects of a single feeling process; if something is considered in terms of its relations and reactions, it is regarded as matter, but if it is understood as feeling, it appears as consciousness. (This is a more sophisticated philosophy than James's radical empiricism, which resembles Peirce's hypothesis in some respects.) A person is a particular kind of general idea.

If it seems intolerable to suppose that matter is, in some sense, feeling or idea, one must at least consider that for Peirce an idea must be considered not only in its Firstness, but in its Secondness and Thirdness as well. In other words, an idea or feeling, for Peirce, is not *simply* a feeling as such; that is, a feeling is more than its quality, its Firstness. A feeling is also that which has the tendency to relate to other feelings with which it comes in spatial and temporal contact, and it works with other feelings toward a regularity of development which can be known as law. It does not seem likely that Peirce can be properly interpreted so as to delight a physical realist who maintains that matter is in no way feeling or mind; but his philosophy is much more acceptable, to one concerned with the multiplicity of physical phenomena, than an idealism which regards ideas as static individuals existing only in their Firstness (merely as feelings).

In "Evolutionary Love," Peirce maintained that his synechism calls for a principle of evolution that will account for creative growth. How is it that out of chaos so irregular that it seems inappropriate to say that anything exists, a universe of habit and law can emerge? Chance relations develop, the relations become habits, the habits become laws; *tychism* emphasizes the presence of chance, *synechism* emphasizes the development of relations through the continuity of ideas, and *agapasm* (Peirce's term) emphasizes the evolutionary tendency in the universe. Thus, we discover how the logical (ordering) principles of Firstness, Secondness, and Thirdness make intelligible not only the idea (with its *quale*, its relatedness, and its tendency to contribute to the development of law), but also the person (who is a general idea), matter (which is mind hidebound with habits), and the character of the universe. The logical principles become metaphysical.

Peirce is important in contemporary thought primarily because of his pragmatic, logical, and epistemological views. There is a great deal of material in the *Collected Papers* that remains to be explored, and those who would picture Peirce as the forerunner of linguistic and empirical philosophy can find much to support their claims in his essays. His metaphysics is regarded as interesting, though as pragmatically insignificant; but this is partly a matter of current taste. When interest in metaphysics revives, and there is no methodological reason why it cannot revive and be respectable, the metaphysics of Charles Sanders Peirce, his theory of cosmic evolution or agapasm, will certainly be reconsidered.—*I. P. M.*

PERTINENT LITERATURE
Barnes, Winston H. F. "Peirce on 'How to Make Our Ideas Clear,'" in *Studies in the Philosophy of Charles Sanders Peirce*. Edited by Philip P. Wiener and Frederic H. Young. Cambridge, Massachusetts: Harvard University Press, 1952, pp. 53-60.

At the heart of Charles Sanders Peirce's philosophy is his principle of clarification, or, as it is sometimes referred to, his pragmatic principle, which was first enunciated in an early essay from his *Collected Papers* entitled "How to Make Our Ideas Clear" as follows: "Consider what effects, that might conceivably have practical bearings, we conceive the object of our conception to have. Then, our conception of these effects is the whole of our conception of the object." Winston H. F. Barnes seeks to clarify this principle of clarification.

Peirce recognizes three grades of clearness of apprehension. The first grade of clarity is familiarity with a concept, the second grade comes from the definition of a concept, and the third grade implies the possible concrete utilization of a concept of actual affairs. Peirce's principle is a rule for attaining clarity of the third (and highest) degree.

Barnes quickly dismisses two common misinterpretations of Peirce's principle. The first suggests that the meaning of a concept is to be equated with the volitions or actions to which it gives rise. Barnes explains that although the spirit of the maxim is that clarity of apprehension manifests itself in purposeful action, Peirce does not mean that acts constitute the meaning or purport of any given word (as a linguistic symbol). A second misinterpretation proposes that the meaning of a concept consists solely in its effects upon the senses. Peirce himself repudiates this interpretation by his emphatic statement that concepts cannot be explained by anything but concepts. In other words, ideas are not clarified by percepts, images, or any effects on the senses.

Shifting only slightly from the paths laid by the above two misinterpretations, Barnes demarcates two much more plausible translations, what he terms the *Conceptual Pragmatic* view and the *Conceptual Experiential* view. In the former view, the meaning of a concept becomes clarified in terms of *conceiving* the volitions or actions to which it gives rise, whereas in the latter, clarification is in terms of *conceiving* possible effects on the senses. Both of these accounts have certain strengths. Although Barnes does not totally commit himself to one or the other, he confesses that the experiential account has somewhat greater plausibility.

Peirce tells that to clarify our conception of an object we must substitute our conception of those sensible effects that under certain conditions of practical importance an object would have. Stated in this way, there seems to be a close parallel to the logical positivist principle that the meaning of a proposition is its method of verification. The meaning of "chlorine," then, would consist of our conception of the sensible effects chlorine would produce in us—namely, its color, odor, and the like, along with the sensible effects resulting from contact with other materials (turning clothes white, creating hydrochloric acid when mixed with hydrogen, and so forth). While this is on the right track, Barnes claims that Peirce intends something more.

On the Conceptual Pragmatic Interpretation the meaning of a concept is linked with a conceived conditional disposition. To have a concept is to have a particular belief regarding what sensible effects would arise should a certain type of action be performed. To clarify the concept is to clarify the belief and to bring that belief into consciousness as a *conceived* conditional disposition. Hence the concept of chlorine becomes understood as a conceived belief that "if I should wish to bleach clothes, then I should use a certain yellowish-green liquid, irritating to the nose, and capable of turning clothes white." The occasion for using the chlorine may never arise, and we may never use chlorine, but the concept is essentially tied to possible action.

The Conceptual Experiental Interpretation casts the rule for clarifying concepts in terms of a conceived conditional *expectation*, instead of a *disposition*. Again using the example of chlorine, the concept is to be understood by conceiving *what I would expect* to happen "if I should take this yellowish-green liquid, which is irritating to the nose, and capable of turning clothes white, and add it to the water when washing my clothes." Instead of being tied to a conceived disposition to act in a certain way, as on the Conceptual Pragmatic Interpretation, the meaning of chlorine is exhibited by a conceived expectation.

Using Barnes's example, the difference between the two plausible views can be illustrated in the following ways. Given a singular belief such as "These are coals," and assuming that combustibility is a part of the meaning of the concept of coal, then (1) according to the experiential theory "These are coals" is clarified by a conceived conditional expectation: for example, "If these were in contact with flame, they would burn. (2) According to the pragmatic theory, the same meaning is clarified by a conceived conditional disposition: for example "If I wished to obtain heat, I would bring these into contact with flame." Whichever interpretation may be correct, Barnes concludes, the principle of clarification stands as one of the most provocative and foundational aspects of Peirce's philosophy.

Davis, William H. *Peirce's Epistemology*. The Hague, The Netherlands: Martinus Nijhoff, 1972.

The question of skepticism stands as one of the major issues in the history of Western philosophy. Is knowledge of reality possible and if so, how? Throughout his career, Charles Sanders Peirce was forced again and again to wrestle with the intractable problem of knowledge. In a penetrating analysis of Peirce's epistemology, William H. Davis brings into focus a set of ideas which he believes can serve as a key to uncovering the nature of human knowledge. Davis' work is more than simply an exposition of Peirce's philosophy; it is itself a commendable essay in epistemology.

In his *Collected Papers*, Peirce attacks the traditional "intuitionist" theory of knowledge that has its paradigm in René Descartes. Descartes sought to base all knowledge on primitive intuitions, what he called "clear and distinct ideas." Peirce's alternative is that knowledge is a process of flowing inferences. By "inference" he does not mean merely conscious abstract, logical thought; he means any cognitive activity whatever, including perceptual cognition and even subconscious thought processes. The inferential process whence derives all knowledge he terms "synthetic thinking," which implies a continuous activity of comparing, connecting, and putting together thoughts and perceptions. Knowing simply cannot be immediate and intuitive, he argues, for if nothing else it is a temporal process occurring over a period of time. No experience whatever is an instantaneous affair. Supposing that Peirce is correct, the question then becomes: What can be said about synthetic thinking?

Peirce recognizes three kinds of reasoning processes: deduction, induction, and abduction, the latter being original with him. He holds a generally orthodox view of deduction and induction. He agrees that deduction is analytic in essence and therefore yields no new knowledge. New knowledge comes from synthetic thinking, which he divides into two categories, inductive and abductive. Abduction is understood basically as a creative hypothesis-building process. The main difference between induction and abduction is that in the former "we generalize from a number of cases of which something is true and infer that the same thing is true of a whole class," whereas in the latter "we find some curious circumstance which would be explained by the supposition that it was a case of a certain general rule, and thereupon adopt that supposition." Davis pursues this distinction by showing that actually every induction involves an abduction, that in a sense induction is best viewed as a form of abduction. Such being the case, it follows that all new knowledge arises by way of abduction. Because of the importance Peirce attaches to abduction, Davis spends a great deal of time examining that notion and relating it to Peirce's pragmatism.

Davis' study probably more than any other has demonstrated the truly revolutionary significance of Peirce's doctrine of abduction and the implications and consequences it has for philosophy in general and epistemology in particular. The book is divided into five chapters: I. Inference: The Essence of All Thought; II. Hypothesis or Abduction: The Originative Phase of Reasoning; III. Fallibilism: The Self-corrective Feature of Thought; IV. Concrete Reasonableness: Cooperation Between Reason and Instinct; and V. The Cartesian Circle: A Final Look at Scepticism.

Murphee, Idus. "The Theme of Positivism in Peirce's Pragmatism," in *Studies in the Philosophy of Charles Sanders Peirce, Second Series*. Edited by Edward C. Moore and Richard S. Robin. Amherst: University of Massachusetts Press, 1964, pp. 226-241.

What is the connection between Charles Sanders Peirce's pragmatism and his professed positivism? Depending on how Peirce's *Collected Papers* are interpreted, there will be different answers to this important question. It might be thought, for example, that pragmatism and positivism are at odds with each other. Whereas the language of pragmatism emphasizes belief, action, and practical effects, the language of positivism stresses the accumulation of positive evidence, experimentation, and scientific verification. Idus Murphee takes the position that the basic concepts underlying Peirce's pragmatism do not blunt in any way his strong commitment to experimentalism, but in fact serve to emphasize and reinforce that commitment.

Peirce's idea of belief is that of conviction which is fixed by perceptual evidence. All belief is "expectative" in the sense that the meaning of a belief comes down ultimately to the practical effects which can be expected or anticipated in such case that the belief is acted upon. Hence meaningfulness, on the pragmatic formula, is a function of practical considerations. At the same time, Murphee points out, what any concept or proposition claims must be translated in terms of positive evidence. By this Peirce implies that beliefs are in essence forms of scientific hypotheses, whereupon their meaning embodies laboratory methods of verification; to believe such and such is to assert that if a given experiment were carried out, an experience of a given description would result. Furthermore, since belief implies conviction, or assent, the belief itself hinges upon the evidence which has proven sufficient to insure the requisite commitment to action. In this way Peirce's pragmatism fundamentally intertwines with his positivism.

Murphee goes into much detail to show that when Peirce speaks of the evidence for belief he means phenomena or observations which in theory are open to the public. Commitment to action is not enough to qualify a conviction as a belief. While Peirce acknowledges that beliefs may be mistaken, and that erroneous beliefs may really be believed, he observes that every belief is at least thought to be true by the person holding it. Given Peirce's definition of truth—namely, that to which a community of investigators would give assent, based upon the results of their cooperative inquiry—it clearly follows that, in Murphee's words, "a claim to truth is a public claim which only a public can verify." The evidence for any such claim, therefore, and the basis for the correlative conviction to action, must of necessity lie in the public domain, open to scrutiny by a community of inquirers. Private nuance, introspection, and the like are insufficient for "fixing" belief and creating meaning.

In sum, there is no contradiction for Peirce, in phrasing pragmatism in the language of positivism. Pragmatic meaning is preliminary to verification, and the conditions under which truth and falsity may be asserted (in specific terms, the conditions for scientific inquiry, experimentation, and verification) are precisely those which Peirce intends the pragmatic formula to specify.— *R.A.S.*

ADDITIONAL RECOMMENDED READING

Buchler, Justus. *Charles Peirce's Empiricism.* London: Kegan Paul, Trench, Trubner & Company, 1939. Justus Buchler is recognized as a leading authority on the philosophy of Peirce. The present study organizes and clarifies those ideas in Peirce which serve as a foundation for the empiricism he espoused. Exposition is limited to the methodological side of Peirce's thought, focusing on his commonsensism, his pragmatism, and his theory of the formal sciences.

Feibleman, James K. *An Introduction to the Philosophy of Charles S. Peirce.* Cambridge, Massachusetts: M. I. T. Press, 1970. The most comprehensive introduction to Peirce's philosophy available. Part of the aim of this book is to exhibit the system which the author finds inherent in the seemingly disordered collection of Peirce's philosophical writings. This is a revision of an earlier work on Peirce published in 1946.

Moore, Edward C. and Richard S. Robin, eds. *Studies in the Philosophy of Charles Sanders Peirce, Second Series.* Amherst: University of Massachusetts Press, 1964. This second volume of Peirce studies updates the previous series (Wiener and Young, 1952) by bringing into focus the heightened interest in Peirce's scientific contributions. Themes discussed include logic, probability and induction, perception and belief, Peirce's evolutionism, and his scientific metaphysics.

Scheffler, Israel. *Four Pragmatists: A Critical Introduction to Peirce, James, Mead, and Dewey.* New York: Humanities Press, 1974. A competent discussion of those ideas in Peirce most crucial to his pragmatism, including his cosmology, his theory of inquiry, and his so-called "pragmatic maxim."

Thompson, Manley. *The Pragmatic Philosophy of C. S. Peirce.* Chicago: University of Chicago Press, 1953. An impressive commentary aimed toward a systematic construction of Peirce's philosophy. Peirce's disparate writings are organized and interpreted in relation to the chronological development of his pragmatism.

Wiener, Philip P. and Frederic H. Young, eds. *Studies in the Philosophy of Charles Sanders Peirce.* Cambridge, Massachusetts: Harvard University Press, 1952. One of the early major achievements of the Charles S. Peirce Society, this book is a collection of twenty-four fine essays which expound, elaborate, and critically assess important aspects of Peirce's philosophy.

THE TWO SOURCES OF MORALITY AND RELIGION

Author: Henri Bergson (1859-1941)
Type of work: Ethics, philosophy of religion
First published: 1932

PRINCIPAL IDEAS ADVANCED

There are two kinds of morality: compulsive morality and ideal morality.

There are two kinds of religion: popular religion and dynamic religion.

Corresponding to the two kinds of morality and the two kinds of religion are two kinds of societies, the closed and the open, and two kinds of souls, the enslaved and the free.

The two sources of morality and religion are the practical needs of men and societies and the idealistic impulse.

Men rise above the static patterns of compulsive moralities and popular religions, achieving freedom in open societies, when they recapture, through mystical intuition, their original vital impetus.

In no sense was Bergson's philosophy a mere compilation of the scientific findings of his time. Nevertheless, his kind of empiricism required him to investigate on his own principles the subject matter of various sciences. His early works may be viewed as studies in psychology. In *Creative Evolution* (1906) he turned to biology. His last great work, *The Two Sources of Morality and Religion*, took him into the fields of sociology and cultural anthropology. Here he made "vital impulse" the key to understanding morality, religion, and history. The work is admittedly more speculative than its predecessors. Whereas in *Creative Evolution* he had tried to "keep as close as possible to facts," in this later work he permitted himself to argue from "probabilities," on the grounds that "philosophical certainty admits of degrees." Whenever possible, philosophic intuition should be "backed up by science"; but where science falls short, Bergson maintained, it is legitimate to appeal to the testimony of great prophetic and mystical teachers. The author regarded this work as a valuable confirmation of the thesis presented in *Creative Evolution*. Others have found it rewarding for the fresh perspectives it has brought to social studies.

As the title indicates, the author's approach was a genetic one. Understanding of the phenomena under investigation meant seeing how they were necessitated by the evolutionary impulse. Bergson's contribution was to suggest that morality and religion cannot be understood in terms of one kind of explanation only. Followers of Comte, Spencer, and Marx had tried to explain all morality and religion as arising out of the needs of society. Bergson went a long way with them; but he insisted that since some morality and religion are, in the usual sense, antisocial, they must be traced to another source;

namely, the spiritual vision of exceptional men. In fact, according to Bergson, all historical systems of morality and religion are blends, combining idealistic with pragmatic elements. This amalgamation takes place because man's life is so largely dominated by intelligence, which moderates the seemingly extravagant claims of mystical insight even as it relaxes the hold of tradition and habit. Bergson denied that it is possible to explain either moral obligation or religious belief on intellectual grounds: reason is emphatically not one of the two sources from which morality and religion arise. Nonetheless, its presence is felt.

To make his thesis plain, Bergson discussed morality and religion under separate chapters. His argument is that there are two kinds of morality and two kinds of religion. Corresponding to these there are two kinds of souls and two kinds of societies.

The first kind of morality is a *common, compulsive morality* demanded by society for its protection. Bergson regarded social life as a device of the life impulse for increasing its mastery over matter and enhancing its freedom. Social life is an evolutionary advance, for the true individual is found only in society. But there are grades of social life. Insects have purchased their efficient organization only at the expense of adaptability. But it was the gift of intelligence which enabled man to break out of the hard and fast regulations imposed by instinct. The problem for man is that of preserving the social organism. Bergson imagines, as an example, that an ant momentarily endowed with sufficient intelligence asks herself whether it is in her interests to perform the onerous tasks imposed upon her by the group. He concludes that were she to consider long enough, she might at last arrive at the conclusion reached in the history of human thought by John Stuart Mill, and resume her labors, happy in the belief that her interests are identical with those of the group. Meanwhile, however, she will perish unless instinct draws her back with the imperative, "You must because you must." Such, according to Bergson, is the sense of obligation which lies at the basis of common morality. Closely connected with habit, it is a weakened form of instinct. Intellect, far from providing a basis for moral obligation, is what obligation was designed to overcome. Moral obligation operates impersonally in a compulsive manner, and has its analogies in somnambulistic behavior. But moral compulsion is not natural in the sense that animal instincts are. Bergson denied that acquired characteristics—such as moral compulsions—are inherited. Moral patterns must be learned by each generation from its predecessor and may be modified in the process. Thus, the moralities of civilized nations differ radically from those of primitive peoples. But obligation as such is the same in all societies and everywhere exercises identical control.

Contrasted with morality of this compulsive kind is that which works under the attraction of an *ideal*. For example, an ordinary man feels obliged to render what he thinks of as justice to his friends, such as returning a favor, and to his enemies, such as exacting vengeance. But rare individuals have caught a glimpse of a higher kind of justice, what we call "social justice," that makes no distinction between friends and enemies and treats all men as equals. It is impossible, according to Bergson, to explain the origins of the latter as a development or modification of the former. Customary morality speaks for an existing order which demands to be perpetuated; the higher morality speaks for a vision which inspires in sensitive people a demand that the existing order be changed. It does not ordinarily require great effort either to learn or to practice common morality; but an ideal morality requires constant propaganda even to keep it alive and is practiced only at the expense of personal discipline and self-denial. Accordingly, we have to look not to the mass of men for its origins but to exceptional persons who have had a vision of reality in its unity and striving. Prophets through their preaching and mystics through their example call upon mankind to enter a truer way. And their teaching, not subject to the vicissitudes of history and tradition, is a perennial source of insight and motivation to lesser men.

Analogous to the first kind of morality is *popular religion*, which Bergson calls *static*. Like conscience, by which nature secures the individual's submission to the welfare of the group, religious belief is a protective device, invented by vital impulse to overcome the hazards which attend the use of intelligence in the "human experiment." Instinctive acts are performed without thinking and without any doubt as to whether they will be effective, but intelligent acts are complex; and deliberations concerning means and ends would paralyze human activity altogether if nature did not come to the rescue and teach man to invent necessities where none exist. This is what lies at the bottom of myth. A myth is a kindly hallucination which fills up the gaps left by our understanding, permitting man to act with assurance and ease.

The hunter, facing a beast at bay, needs to believe that his arrow is directed after it leaves his hand; and the farmer is comforted by the belief that there are powers which preside over the seed which he has planted in the earth. Somewhat in the same way, man needs assurance in the face of death, which has never threatened the nonreflective animal as it does man. The belief in an afterlife neutralizes doubt and fear, and provides man with the sense of self-mastery. In these ways provident nature preserves her favorite, man, making it possible for him to benefit by intelligence without being destroyed by it.

In Bergson's view, myth and magic pass over into religion in the same proportion that men accustom themselves to think of environing powers in personal terms. The *mana*, which anthropologists claim is the basis of the religious response, Bergson took to be an expression of purposive activity. In magical practices, man supposes that he employs this mysterious power himself; in religious acts, he seeks the cooperation of unseen beings who, he believes, have even greater *mana* at their disposal. For Bergson, religion is not primarily a matter of knowledge, nor is it based on poetic imagination. It has its origins in practical needs, and it provides a scaffolding for human activity.

Opposed to this static religion, which has no cognitive worth, is the *dynamic religion* which has its source in mysticism. Bergson was sparing in his use of the ambiguous term "mysticism"; like William James, he regarded mystical insight as a definite kind of experience which most of us never directly share. The visions of mystics bypass the constructions of myth and imagination as well as those of rational argument, and yield immediate experience of reality in its character as a whole. Bergson held that the Greeks, because of their intellectualism, never attained to a full-blown mysticism. In India, it developed further, but frequently it was blighted by a speculative tendency or perverted into hypnotic trance. The prophets of ancient Israel contributed the vision of a God as just as he was powerful: but his transcendence above the world and the particularism of his purpose were residues of static belief. Only the Christ of the Gospels—to whom we owe the truth that God is love— was completely open to divine reality. The great mystics of the Church are "the imitators, and orginal but incomplete continuators, of what the Christ of the Gospels was completely." Christ's influence is also seen, according to to Bergson, in the mystics of Islam, and such modern Hindus as Ramakrishna and Vivekananda. (Bergson, it may be noted, was a Jew, although in his latter years he showed sympathy for Roman Catholicism.)

According to Bergson, genuine mysticism is not pessimistic, nor antisocial, nor quietistic. The vision of God as love generates in the beholder charity toward all of God's creatures, stirring in him the desire to lead all men into the higher form of life which has been disclosed to him. Furthermore, it releases energies in him and opens his eyes to possibilities that are sealed off from ordinary men. God works through him. He becomes the agent of the evolutionary impulse in its purpose to transcend the present stage of human life. But, as always, divine freedom must adjust its steps to material conditions. In order to draw men upward to higher freedom, the mystic accommodates his teaching to the capacity of his hearers. To get a portion of the truth accepted, the mystic has to compromise. For humanity understands the new only as it is incorporated into the old.

Dynamic religion is the result of this compromise. It does not come into being through a natural development of the static, but by the deliberate adaptation of old forms to new ends. Like the higher ethics, dynamic religion requires a constant effort to keep it from lapsing completely into familiar static forms. Indeed, a constant tension exists between the "civic" and "universal" functions which all of the higher religions seek to perform.

The whole problem is illuminated by Bergson's distinction between "closed" and "open" societies, and the types of souls which correspond to them. Natural societies are *closed societies*: examples are families, clans, city-states, and sovereign nations. They exist to serve the interests of their own members and take no responsibility for the rest of man. "Self-centeredness, cohesion, hierarchy, absolute authority of the chief"—such are the features of the closed society. The *open society*, by contrast, is largely an ideal existing in the minds of chosen souls. In principle it embraces all humanity. But in practice the most that ever is achieved is an enlarging here and there of closed societies. Such enlargement, according to Bergson, never takes place of itself but only as a result of propaganda carried on by dedicated men, who may effect more or less far-reaching transformations of the existing order. "But after each occasion the circle that has momentarily opened closes again. Part of the new has flowed into the mould of the old; individual aspiration has become social pressure; and obligation covers the whole." Bergson regarded modern democracy as in principle an "open society," founded as it is on the ideals of liberty, equality, and brotherhood of all men. Thus, it rests on foundations quite different from those of Athenian democracy. Nevertheless, the tensions between the demands of nation-states and the service of mankind remain; in fact, our Western democracies, too, are "closed societies."

In a final chapter entitled "Mechanism and Mysticism," Bergson explains the bearing of these investigations on the thesis set forth in *Creative Evolution*: that in man the divine impulse toward freedom is destined to realize itself. Does the history of the human race support this thesis? Bergson's answer was affirmative. But, as we have seen, he had to depart from the simplicities that characterize most theories of cultural evolution. They assume that through intelligence man has progressed thus far toward liberty and justice. Bergson maintained that intelligence was not a sufficient explanation and that had it not been supplemented by a halo of "intuition," it would have proved fatal to man. What enables man to rise above the static, ingrown patterns of natural societies is the capacity, never entirely lost to him, of recapturing in his own self, through the mystic vision, the original vital impetus, and moving forward with it toward higher unity and greater freedom.

Viewing the situation in our times, Bergson lamented the fact that man seems to have fallen slave to the machine. But he was unwilling to subscribe to any kind of economic determinism. Industry, which came into existence to satisfy real needs, has taken a different direction and fostered artificial ones. But this can be corrected, and by simplifying his way of life man can make machines a benefit. "The initiative can come from humanity alone, for it is humanity and not the alleged force of circumstances, still less a fatality inherent to the machine, which has started the spirit of invention along a certain track." Bergson thought that a new mysticism, with an attendant ascetic discipline, might well be in the offing, which would renew in man a sense of his high calling. In view of the breakdown of popular religion, psychical research seemed to him also to bear some promise, by restoring to the masses belief that life is more than meat and the body more than raiment.

"Mankind lies groaning," he concludes, "half crushed beneath the weight of its own progress. Men do not sufficiently realize that their future is in their own hands. Theirs is the task of determining first of all whether they want to go on living or not. Theirs the responsibility, then, for deciding if they want merely to live, or intend to make just the extra effort required for fulfilling, even on their refractory planet, the essential function of the universe, which is a machine for the making of gods."—*J.F.*

PERTINENT LITERATURE

Copleston, Frederick C., S. J. "Bergson on Morality," in *Proceedings of the British Academy*. XLI (1955), pp. 247-266.

Frederick C. Copleston begins his discussion of Henri Bergson by noting that in *The Two Sources of Morality and Religion* Bergson relied on data provided by such sociologists as Lucien Levy-Bruhl and Émile Durkheim. He wished to answer the question "What is the source of morality?" What exactly this question means, Copleston notes, depends in part on what is meant by "source"; the meaning Bergson had in mind is something we have to infer from his procedure. Copleston indicates that two sorts of data provide Bergson with his starting place—data concerning codes of conduct and particular societies, and data concerning moral insight. Bergson then endeavors to explain the two sets of data—to offer an account of their cause. The explanation, Copleston notes, is in turn intended to yield a moral philosophy.

Codes of conduct and human societies, Copleston remarks, are obviously related; a particular society will accept a particular code of conduct, and persons who come to maturity in that society will likely develop their own values in accord with their society's code. Bergson, Copleston continues, notes that different societies often have different codes, and people do not always naturally act in accord with their society's code. They do, however, feel social pressure to act so. This pressure to social conformity is the source of an individual person's sense of obligation. The code of one's society appears to one as an impersonal imperative which one is free to disobey, but only at the price of going against the pressure to conform—to conform to the code of conduct of one's society, as well as to the pattern of conduct of most of one's peers.

Copleston's exposition of Bergson can be put in these terms: consider some person—say, Sandra Stone. Sandra's sense of obligation (say, to tell the truth to Sam), according to Bergson, has an efficient, or productive, cause: social pressure to conform to the code of Sandra's society, which sanctions truth-telling. It also, according to Bergson, has a final, or justificatory, cause: the preservation of Sandra's society, which requires that the code be respected.

Now, Copleston contends, before one can effectively ask whether this explanation is correct, one must know what the theory says. This seems clear, but according to Copleston is not. "Society," as it appears in the explanation, refers to some particular "closed society," and each closed society has a "closed morality." A "closed society" is a particular group of persons who regard themselves as distinct from all other groups and who accept a common moral code which functions to preserve the identity of their group. Such a code will be a "closed morality" in the sense that its principles will apply to the members of the group in a way in which they do not apply to nonmembers. Only its members will benefit by its rules being followed. Reading "society" as "closed society," Copleston notes, it is easy to give clear empirical content to the notion of social pressure.

Copleston reminds us of Bergson's statement that social pressure is felt by the individual as a sense of obligation. This statement Copleston regards as ambiguous in that it may express a theory about the nature of obligation: obligation is simply social pressure, and a feeling of obligation is a feeling of social pressure; or it may be a causal statement concerning the origin of a sense of obligation: a sense of obligation is elicited by social pressure, although the pressure is one thing and the sense of obligation something else. For Copleston, Bergson seems not always clear which he means, but it would appear that he is offering a theory about the nature of obligation.

Copleston finds that, unfortunately, Bergson uses the term "obligation" in a variety of senses: as referring to a particular, specific duty; or meaning the natural necessity to form habits in accord with the requirements of one's society; or as identical in meaning to "sense of obligation." This considerably complicates the task of interpretation. Still, Copleston indicates, the gist of Bergson's view is that the ultimate cause of obligation is a natural impulse to form habits of obedience to social rules—an impulse obviously not brought about by intelligence, but simply one present in human nature. So the origins of obligation, Copleston points out, are, in Bergson's view, nonrational. This is so even when we add the view that intelligence, not instinct, selects the particular social rules which, in any given case, satisfy the natural necessity that there be rules.

Copleston suggests that one problem with Bergson's view is that one can consistently accept his account of how persons come to have a sense of obligation while denying that having a sense of obligation to do something is the same as being obligated to do it. Furthermore, he indicates, one can add that reason has a signficant role, beyond any that Bergson allows it, in determining what the content of our obligations are. Another problem that Copleston raises with Bergson's view is that it allows the distinction between moral rules and social conventions to collapse; or, one might say, it never arises. But while social pressure is brought to bear, both against an announced intent to murder and an announced intent not to wear a tie at dinner, it by no means follows that both are matters of morality. Indeed, from the fact that social pressure is brought to bear in favor of (or against) doing some particular thing, nothing whatever follows about the morality of so acting.

Copleston does not doubt that Bergson was aware that the Sermon on the Mount does not express a closed morality. He suggests that one way to deal with this—and with Antigone's appeal (in Sophocles' play) against the king's commands to the unwritten laws of heaven, or Immanuel Kant's categorical imperative—would be to revise Bergson's theory of obligation. Instead, Copleston tells us, Bergson postulates a radically different sort of morality of love of all mankind. The origin of this "open morality" is mystical experience in which, in contact with God, persons feel deep love for all of humankind and adopt an ideal in which rules are to be constructed with everyone's welfare in mind. This origin is conceived as supraintellectual, just as the origin of closed morality was conceived as infraintellectual. Attachment to open morality spreads as persons freely respond to its attractiveness as seen in the persons and lives of those (for example, the mystics) who have already adopted it. Copleston reminds us that, given this difference in origin and content, in Bergson's view there can be no process of transition from closed to open morality. Still, as both sorts of morality are "refracted" through reason, actual moralities arise which are a mixture of elements of closed with elements of open morality. Were there to be but one world society, this would remove the "closedness" of closed society and transform the nature of obligation.

Without supposing Bergson to be completely mistaken, Copleston explains that we can note another difficulty with Bergson's theory of obligation for which particular obligations have reference to particular rules of a particular society. He raises this difficulty as follows: If performing a human sacrifice today is what custom requires of me, it is obligatory on me to do it; and if you appeal to a higher ideal in trying to dissuade me, it would be morally wrong of me to follow that higher ideal. If one presses the claim that higher ideals, when offered by the mystics, whom Bergson praises, really *are* higher, then, Copleston argues, one abandons the apparent relativism entailed by identifying obligations—and Bergson uses "obligation" in a *moral* sense—with social pressures. But, Copleston continues, if one presses the claim that social pressures produce genuine obligations, then the "higher" ideal will not be higher after all.

Copleston concludes that the view of morality in *The Two Sources of Morality and Religion* is itself part of a larger view which includes the doctrines of *Creative Evolution*, and it assumes the context of that later view: for example, in the roles assigned (and denied) to intelligence, in the conception of evolution used, in the teleology which seems presupposed, and in other ways. So, Copleston says, it cannot be assessed entirely on its own; and he adds that impressionistic nature of Bergson's philosophy gives his views the status of vague, if sometimes brilliant, hypotheses.

Gallagher, Idella J. *Morality in Evolution: The Moral Philosophy of Henri Bergson*. The Hague, The Netherlands: Martinus Nijhoff, 1970.

Idella J. Gallagher reports that, according to Henri Bergson, we discover two distinct forces affecting our moral lives: a pressure that each society exerts on its members, and an attraction exercised by a few on the many. If we reflect on this, Bergson thinks, we can make the further discovery that there are two moralities, each quite distinct from the other. There is *open* morality, and there is *closed* morality.

Gallagher continues his exposition by noting that, according to Bergson, each society, through education, fosters in its members a set of habits which reflect the basic needs of the society. Introspective data include our memories of being impelled by our parents to conform; historical data include the automatic tendency of the individual to identify with the group in primitive society and the training that is made necessary by the phenomenon of division of labor and its corresponding social complexity. The common thread, Gallagher notes, is pressure to accept behavior patterns which will serve the needs of one society. Our sense of being urged, even forced, to adopt and act in accord with these habits, plus a feeling that we can go against the grain, provide the explanation of a feeling of obligation.

Gallagher reports Bergson's contention that while the individuals within a society are free agents, we tend to speak of social life in terms which are applicable to the natural order. Society's laws are imperatives and laws of nature are descriptive; but, Bergson says, we tend to reverse this and treat social laws as things we cannot disobey and laws of nature as spelling out obligations. When we contemplate rebellion against our society, this confusion of social and natural order is strengthened, for we feel an enormous pressure against what we contemplate. For Bergson, Gallagher indicates, what necessity is to nature, habit is to society, and ordinarily we act in accord with our habits (and so with our obligations) as naturally as water flows downhill. Only occasionally does a sense of conflict arise between our inclination and our obligation, for it is our nature to conform to habit. What gravity is to the body, moral obligation is to the soul.

Gallagher indicates that in the *élan vital* from which Bergson believes we evolved, two forms of consciousness were present, according to Bergson: instinct and intelligence. These forms of consciousness, Bergson says, ultimately flowed into different courses, represented by insects, who possess instinct, and human beings, who possess intelligence. Physical structure determines an insect's activities; not so for human beings. Still, Gallagher continues, for Bergson every society is an organization and every organization survives only if it follows some appropriate body of laws.

Gallagher explains to what degree intelligence, in Bergson's view, has freedom. What these laws shall be in a particular society, intelligence decides.

That there be laws, or rules, which serve the basic needs of a society is imbedded in the structure of human nature. In this manner, freedom of action is reconciled with habit. While *The Two Sources of Morality and Religion* does not formally discuss human freedom, it is clearly presumed there that persons are free. For example, Bergson says that only beings who are free and intelligent experience a sense of obligation.

For Bergson, Gallagher emphasizes, free action presupposes radical creativity—not choice between alternatives, but creation of something unforeseen and unforeseeable. Further, Bergson believes there is a deep-seated self, which grows through a series of unforeseeable qualitative changes and comprises true personality, and a superficial self, which is the projection of the deep-seated self, "refracted through intelligence." It is the deep-seated self that is free, and since that self, according to Bergson, is impenetrable to the intellect, freedom cannot be explained; nor can one effectively argue for its presence. One can know its presence only in its exercise.

In Bergson's terms, Gallagher reminds us, a small society which is self-sufficient and self-engrossed, focused on self-protection and ready for war, is a closed society. The rules of a closed society are constructed for the benefit of its members. So far as protection or aid goes, its rules pertain only to its members. Bergson calls it not a "human" but a "social" morality.

A morality concerned with all of humanity, with love of all humankind as its goal, is, for Bergson, quite distinct from closed morality, which Bergson identifies with the morality of obligation. Further, it must have a different source, and this Bergson finds in the personal appeal of special persons who communicate new, more elevated moral goals to the rest of the race.

Gallagher records Bergson's opinion that the closed morality is natural to human beings; open morality must be acquired. Acquisition is possible because open morality has emotional appeal; thus emotion is the source of moral progress. The emotion which leads to acceptance of open morality arises form mystical experience. The goal of mysticism is to establish contact with "the creative effort which life itself manifests." This effort is caused by God, says Bergson, if it is not itself God. A great mystic is able to transcend nature and continue the evolutionary effort. Evolution comes to a static end in the closed society with its closed morality; it moves on in an open society with an open morality. Gallagher finds that Bergson's intent in *The Two Sources of Morality and Religion* is to use the fact that mystical experience occurs as one element in an empirical explanation of open morality.

Gallagher notes that, according to Bergson, the mystic, in achieving contact with the "creative effort" or *élan* of evolution, discovers that its essence is love—a love which includes all persons within its scope. Bergson holds that the emotional strength of this love is sufficient to make the mystic able to communicate it to others. Thus another kind of obligation is experienced, although Bergson tends to use "obligation" comfortably only in connection with closed morality. In any case, Gallagher continues, there is a difference in kind for Bergson between open and closed morality. Gallagher explains this distinction as follows: closed morality comprises the rules of one or another closed society—the society is static and self-centered, the rules geared to guaranteeing the welfare of the society to which they belong. The moral community the rules create is at best a fraction of humanity. The obligations they generate derive from social pressure. Open morality finds its source in an emotion—love—and includes all humanity within its scope. It is possible only because it is possible to transcend the necessities of natural order. In mystical experience, a few experience the emotion; their example attracts others, though not all, also to adopt an open morality. Gallagher concludes by emphasizing that Bergson places all of this within a general evolutionary framework, although whether it is best described as an evolutionary perspective containing religious themes or as a religious perspective containing evolutionary themes is unclear.—*K.E.Y.*

ADDITIONAL RECOMMENDED READING

Carr, Herbert Wildon. *The Philosophy of Change: A Study of the Fundamental Principle of the Philosophy of Bergson.* London: Macmillan and Company, 1914. A study of Bergson's philosophy by the author of the standard work on G. W. Leibniz.

Collins, James. *A History of Modern European Philosophy.* Milwaukee: Bruce Publishing Company, 1954. A discussion of modern philosophy by one of its best historians, with a chapter on Bergson and his place in modern philosophy.

Cunningham, G. Watts. *A Study in the Philosophy of Bergson.* New York: Longmans, Green and Company, 1954. A study of Bergson's philosophy by the author of a standard work on the philosophy of George Berkeley.

Hocking, William E. *Types of Philosophy.* New York: Charles Scribner's Sons, 1929. A distinguished philosopher here compares the Bergsonian type of philosophy to contrasting kinds of views.

Lindsay, Alexander D. *The Philosophy of Bergson.* London: J. M. Dent, 1911. A Kantian examines Bergson.

Maritain, Jacques. *Bergsonian Philosophy and Thomism.* New York: Philosophical Library, 1955. An early work of Maritain's, in which Bergson's philosophy is compared to Thomism.

DEGREES OF KNOWLEDGE

Author: Jacques Maritain (1882-1973)
Type of work: Metaphysics of knowledge
First published: 1932

Principal Ideas Advanced

Several kinds of knowledge are granted to man, each with its own merit and dignity.

Sensation, reason, revelation, and mystical union all make their contributions.

Apparent conflicts between their respective claims can be adjusted if we rightly distinguish between physics and natural philosophy, metaphysics and theology, reason and the suprarational.

A leading member of the neo-Thomist school, Maritain owes his philosophical outlook to St. Thomas Aquinas, whom he follows closely in the first half of his book, entitled "The Degrees of Rational Knowledge." But in the second half, entitled "The Degrees of Suprarational Knowledge," he goes beyond St. Thomas, and takes as his guide the sixteenth century Spanish mystic, St. John of the Cross.

Maritain calls his philosophy "critical realism," without wishing to be identified with the group usually known by that name. Its claim to be called "realism" follows from its commonsense starting point: with the plain man, Maritain holds that what the mind knows is identical with what exists in the world of things. But it is "critical realism" in that it subjects knowledge to scrutiny, and in so doing avoids the naïve view that the mind literally and materially copies nature. Maritain follows Aristotle in holding that essences can exist both materially in things and immaterially in minds. When the mind knows a thing, it becomes, after its own mode, the thing known—not in every respect, but in respect of the properties apprehended.

Maritain's realism puts him in a strong position with regard to modern physical science, which, he argues, can never be satisfied with the irrationalist and nominalist foundations supplied for it by modern disciples of Hume and Kant. According to these latter, whether positivists, logicists, or pragmatists, universal notions and intelligible necessities are creations of the mind and have no foundation in the world of sensible experience. But science, even in its most sophisticated expression, can never get away from the fundamental intuitions of Euclidean space, of real time, and of causal determination. Following Aristotle, Maritain maintains that science is necessary knowledge, and that those investigations of nature which rise to the level of necessary knowledge presuppose a structural aspect in the world which, though not directly observable, is nevertheless the ontological ground for the stable relations which we discern there.

In this connection, Maritain introduces the scholastic distinction between essences which exist only in the mind (*entia rationis*) and essences which exist in things as well (*entia realia*). The former, which we may call mental fictions, play an important role in all sciences, especially in the earlier inductive phases. Their function is to help the investigator translate observations into manageable form. Notions such as ether and gravity, mass and energy, belong to this order, together with imaginary and irrational numbers and non-Euclidean spaces. They are mere "beings of reason," though insofar as they enter helpfully into scientific theory they presuppose and are founded upon "real beings." Deductive sciences, such as mathematical physics, on the other hand, often attain to the "real being" of things. Real dimensions, real space, real time, real causality, the structure of molecules, and patterns of crystallization are mentioned by Maritain as examples of scientific concepts which are true determinations in nature. In his view, positivists and pragmatists, who treat all scientific concepts as "beings of reason" or fictions, are guilty of overlooking an important distinction which scientists do not overlook.

Maritain does not wish to see natural science handed back to the philosophers. He cheerfully admits that the ancients were asking the wrong questions so far as experimental knowledge was concerned. Physics was on the wrong track when it supposed that bodies have natural places toward which they ascend or descend, and biology had to give up its preoccupation with teleology and eternal species. Modern science, from the time of Galileo and Harvey, has fully vindicated itself in throwing off these Aristotelian notions. The ancients failed, in many instances, to distinguish between philosophy of nature and the special sciences. And now that the distinction is clear, both stand to gain.

For the remarkable progress of the special sciences does not, according to Maritain, do away with the need for philosophy of nature and for metaphysics. The special sciences are never completely intelligible taken by themselves. Not only are their categories and principles in need of clarification, as positivists insist; they need to be fitted into a larger vision if their significance and proportion are not to be lost from view. And here, Maritain argues, the ancients still have much to teach us. The collapse of "hylomorphism" (Aristotle's famous doctrine that things must be understood in terms of their matters and their forms) as a principle of natural science does not destroy its value for philosophy of nature. Thus, Aristotle's *Physics*, which interprets motion in terms of potentiality and actuality, is no match for Galilean mechanics as a principle of celestial or terrestrial dynamics; but it is not without value for understanding nature in its more general aspects.

Natural philosophy, for Maritain, is a speculative science standing between natural sciences and metaphysics. Natural sciences are closely bound to sense perception; metaphysics is based on pure intellectual intuition. It is essential to the sciences that they concern themselves with special characters of material being, whereas metaphysics deals with being as such, whether material or immaterial, temporal or eternal. Natural philosophy is more specific than metaphysics—it deals only with "nature"; that is to say, with being which is material, spatial, and temporal. It must begin with sense knowledge, but it goes beyond experimental truth to lay hold on the deeper intelligibility of natural processes. In Maritain's terms, mechanistic determinism, vitalism, and emergent evolutionism are attempts at natural philosophy. Working scientists implicitly employ some natural philosophy or other, often without being aware of what they are doing. It is Maritain's purpose to replace lazy, uncritical notions about natural process with true notions which the mind can achieve if it makes natural processes in general the object of inquiry.

Metaphysics, for Thomists, is not a hypothetical extension of our knowledge beyond the limits of empirical verification, but an intuitive apprehension by the intellect of the essential characters of being. Instead of reasoning by logical inference, as do scientists and natural philosophers—who deal with universals abstracted from sense experience—the metaphysician must reason by analogy because he is dealing with different orders of being—corporeal, spiritual, and divine. Consider the category, *substance*: one can speak of corporeal substance or of spiritual substance, of created substance or of uncreated substance; but inferences cannot be made directly from one to the other. Nevertheless, the intellect discerns certain relations. One can say that spiritual substance is to spiritual being what material substance is to material being. In this way, Thomists believe, it is possible to avoid such dogmatic impasses as Cartesians and Hegelians have encountered, while continuing to affirm that being is always and everywhere rational.

Of special interest to Thomists is the part of metaphysics which concerns divine being, often called natural theology. Thus, true to tradition, Maritain takes a moderate position between those who (like St. Anselm) believe that man's reason can fathom the depths of God's being, and those who (like William of Ockham) believe it can fathom nothing. The attributes under which we represent God to ourselves (the "divine names") do, according to Maritain, tell us something about his nature. When we say that God is One or Good or True, we are not, to be sure, using these words in the same sense they have when we apply them to creatures; but neither are we using them in a completely different sense. We use them "analogically," understanding that Unity or Goodness or Truth in the divine modality is comparable to unity or goodness or truth in the human. Analogies, according to Maritain, are more than metaphors. The latter are based on extrinsic and accidental resemblances, but the former are based on inherent characters of being and thus form an essential bond between the different modes.

Metaphysics, which is sometimes called speculative wisdom, was thought by Aristotle to be the highest form of knowledge. And Thomists agree that this is true so far as man's natural knowledge is concerned. As Christians, however, they hold that man's capacities are not fully realized on the natural plane. Man's proper end, for which he was created, is the intellectual vision of God in eternity when, according to the Bible, the faithful shall "be like him" and shall "see him face to face." Because of sin, man has lost the vision; but the grace and revelation of God are medicaments for its restoration. Thus there is a higher wisdom, which the pagan Aristotle did not know. Actually, according to Maritain, this higher wisdom is divided into two parts—*theological wisdom* and *mystical theology*.

Theological wisdom is based upon the truth of revelation. It is conceptual knowledge, like metaphysics. But whereas metaphysics knows God from the outside, as it were, viewing him as Perfect Being, theology knows him from within, sharing the mysteries of his Deity. This latter, of course, is possible only to the extent that God has spelled out his secrets in terms suitable to our understanding. For example, the doctrine of the Trinity reveals that there are three Persons in the unity of the Divine Being, and that these are Father, Son, and Holy Spirit. In making known his mysteries, God has employed analogy so that the truth may be suited to our understanding. The metaphysician would never be able to understand divine analogies by his unaided reason. Nevertheless, according to Maritain, they have their basis in the fundamental unity of being which permits divine secrets to be traced out in human lineaments. Maritain speaks of these analogies as "parabolic" analogies, with reference to the use which Christ made of parables. Like the analogies used by metaphysics, they are "proper proportionalities," and express truths in a precise and determinate degree; but they are more fruitful than those of metaphysics, in that they seem to overflow with meaning, and express more than they literally say.

Higher than theological wisdom, however, and the very acme of human knowledge is the beatific vision—assured to all the faithful in heaven, but permitted to a select number while yet on earth. The unitive experience by which God is known is knowledge in the perfect degree, for the mind becomes that which it knows without the mediation of concepts, which are essential on all lower planes. Such experience is, therefore, intimately personal, and involves the infusion of the soul with the special ministrations of the Three Persons of the Trinity. By the same token, it is essentially incommunicable: only indirectly, by metaphors and poetic figures, can the mystic express what he has beheld. Nevertheless, there is a *mystical theology*, a practical discipline, wherein the masters of a wisdom which is itself incommunicable set down counsels and rules for the guidance of others. With St. John of the Cross, whom Maritain takes for his example, mystical wisdom is through and through a practical science, the counterpart on the suprarational level of the "practical reason" of rational philosophy. (See Aristotle's *Ethics*, Book VI.) Maritain stresses emphatically the practical issues of mystical knowledge, agreeing in this respect with the teaching of Bergson in *Two Sources of Morality and Religion* (1932). Mystical knowledge, according to Maritain, renders man ever more perfectly spiritual and, as it does so, enables him to see all creatures in the light of faith and in turn to love all things with divine charity.

Maritain's discussion of mysticism is completely orthodox. He has no use for the "comparative religionist" approach to the subject, which takes a naturalistic view of all such phenomena. Holding fast to the distinction between natural and supernatural knowledge, he will tolerate no account of mysticism which seeks to make it something less than a special manifestation of the Holy Trinity in the heart of man. This view raises a question as to the validity of the mysticism of the non-Christian East. Is one bound to deny that non-Christians have experienced union with God because they are outside the Church and without the means of divine grace? According to Maritain, we would be bound to deny it, if we were sure that they had not received God's grace. He appeals, however, to the Church's doctrine of "spiritual baptism," according to which teaching there are persons outside the pale of the visible Church who, though they have never heard the gospel or received the sacraments, nevertheless have been visited by the grace of God. Authentic mystical experiences among non-Christians are, in his opinion, to be understood in this way. In place of the usual comparative phenomenalist mysticism, he would like to see a comparative theological mysticism, which would bring some norms to bear upon the confusion that now prevails in the field.—*J.F.*

PERTINENT LITERATURE

Henle, Robert J., S. J. "Maritain's Metaphysics," in *Selected Papers from Conference-Seminar on Jacques Maritain's* Degrees of Knowledge (American Maritain Association). St. Louis: Christian Board of Publication, 1981.

The *Degrees of Knowledge* is a formidable book. Written in the Aristotelian-Thomistic tradition yet taking into account the natural sciences (in their 1930's state of development), Jacques Maritain's reflections on knowledge range from the relationship between the philosophy of nature and the experimental sciences through mathematics to metaphysics, and beyond the natural wisdom of metaphysics to the supernatural wisdom of the mystical experience of God especially as presented in the writings of Saint John of the Cross. The full title: *The Degrees of Knowledge or Distinguish in Order to Unite* suggests that the object of analysis is to bring order into the multiplicity of human knowledges. Maritain agrees with the view expressed in Étienne Gilson's *The Unity of Philosophical Experience*—that a mistake repeatedly made by modern philosophers since René Descartes' time has been to try to order human knowledge according to the standard of a particular science. The movement of logical positivism, especially dynamic when this book was first published, was then only the most recent example of that mistake.

In his contribution to the 1980 Conference on the *Degrees of Knowledge*, Robert J. Henle, S. J., undertakes to summarize Maritain's metaphysics. Noting that Maritain divided metaphysics into three parts—critique of knowledge, ontology, and natural theology—Henle points out that for Maritain the modern distinction between epistemology and metaphysics does not obtain. On the contrary, metaphysics, since it is highest wisdom, includes epistemology and criteriology, reflecting as it does not only on its own principles but also on the modes of knowledge which are formal to all other disciplines: "It belongs to the wise man to order all knowledge."

As a consequence, Maritain's philosophy is a thoroughgoing realism in which things as they present themselves to us are the source and measure of all knowledge. That Maritain chose to call his epistemology "critical realism" has, however, given rise to some controversy, owing to the fact that Gilson, with whom Maritain was in basic agreement (both following the inspiration of Saint Thomas Aquinas), repudiated the notion of any suggestion of a Kantlike critique of preceding metaphysics. Maritain insisted, however, that since his realism was an examined and not a naïve realism he had every right to call himself a critical realist.

Maritain further agreed with Gilson that some of the Louvain neo-Thomists who tried to discover within the Thomistic tradition a sort of Cartesian doubt and then a "cogito" were on the wrong track. Thus, instead of a discovery of "I think" at the beginning of our knowledge, for Maritain there is the basic *scio aliquid esse*: "I know something to be." In this initial understanding of being, says Henle, all the primordial intelligibles of being are implicitly grasped, including the principles of identity, sufficient reason, finality, and causality. In this initial understanding, apprehension and judgment are not two separate acts. As Maritain was to put it in a later book, *Existence and the Existent*, intellect apprehends and judges at the same time, forming its first idea (being) while making its first judgment (exists).

While our experience is of sensible things, we rise, as it were, to a knowledge of transsensible being by way of our search for the cause of being. At this stage of metaphysical analysis we undertake to establish the existence of God as the cause of being. We are in the realm of analogical knowledge (or, as Maritain called it, "ananoetic" knowledge), approaching a knowledge of God through understanding the being of his creatures. By means of analogies drawn from what we do know, we rise to knowledge of objects which are otherwise unthinkable and unknown. Accordingly, for Maritain and other Thomists, the only knowledge which man is able to have of God, apart from revelation, is by the application of analogies drawn from the sensible world to a mode of being of which we have no direct apprehension.

At the beginning of the *Degrees of Knowledge* Maritain had written of the grandeur and misery of metaphysics. Henle agrees that although metaphysics aims at understanding God, metaphysics proceeds blindly while God remains hidden. Thus, metaphysics would appear to be a tragic failure. But Maritain argues that metaphysics is a natural wisdom and that beyond metaphysics are two supernatural wisdoms, that of theology and that of mystical contemplation. Thus, the second half of the *Degrees of Knowledge* is devoted to the study of the wisdoms beyond metaphysics.

Simon, Yves R. "Maritain's Philosophy of the Sciences," in *The Thomist.* V (January, 1943), pp. 85-102.

While in this century metaphysics as a science has been controversial, philosophy of nature as a science, distinct from both metaphysics and the empirical sciences, has been virtually unknown outside of the circle of contemporary Thomism. Yet within the Aristotelian-Thomistic tradition, this science of nature, having changing material reality for its subject matter (*ens mobile seu sensible*), has been most important. In fact, philosophy of man or philosophical anthropology is the highest part of this philosophy of nature, and in the study of the immortality of the human soul, the philosophy of man edges into metaphysics.

When Jacques Maritain wrote the *Degrees of Knowledge* in the early 1930's, he took into account what might be considered the imperialism of the natural sciences, the claim on the part of some positivistic philosophers of science to the exclusive right to study physical reality. This challenge was, perhaps, what most threatened the existence of Thomism in the contemporary academic world. There were historical reasons. The so-called rise of modern science in the seventeenth century had entailed the simultaneous repudiation of Aristotle's physics with its fourfold causes and its principles such as potentiality and actuality, substance and accidents, and the hylomorphic, matter/form composition, of natural substances. One objective of the *Degrees of Knowledge* was to clarify the complementary approaches possible in the study of the natural world.

To understand Yves R. Simon's remarks, it should be recalled that, following Aristotle and Saint Thomas Aquinas, Maritain affirms essences or natures in natural things as the source of their characteristic activities or properties. Again following Aquinas, Maritain locates the philosophy of nature and the empirical sciences on the level of the first degree of abstraction, in which attention is paid to the commonsensible properties of things while the peculiar individuating characteristics of a thing are ignored. Thus man is studied in all his physical behavior, but whether a particular subject is brown-eyed or blue-eyed is regarded as irrelevant. Both the philosopher of nature and the empirical scientist are studying *ens mobile seu sensible* but the emphasis differs; the philosopher focuses on the *ens*, the being of the physical thing, and the scientist on those regularities of operation in the physical thing.

Here it is important to keep in mind two kinds of intellectual activity, one of which is suited to the first degree of abstraction and one of which is not.

The kind of thinking which penetrates to the essence of an object and perceives its definition, Maritain designates *dianoetical* (from *dia*, meaning "through," and *noein*, meaning "to think"). But according to Maritain—and this is typical of Aristotelians as opposed to Platonists and Augustinians—dianoetical intellection is not fully operative on the level of sensible things. Thus, unable to know the nature or essence of physical objects, we settle for what we can know: namely, a detailed description of their properties.

This second kind of thinking, which terminates in perceived regularities, Maritain called *perinoetical* intellection (from *peri*, meaning "around"). It is the method of knowing proper to the empirical sciences, and while it does not penetrate to the essence, it approximates it.

The term *empiriological* is used to refer to the method of the natural sciences: observation, the formation of a hypothesis to account for the regularity observed, and then the further empirical testing of the implications of the hypothesis. Since the seventeenth century work of Galileo and René Descartes, much of the observation has involved measurement, the quantification of the phenomena, and thus has given rise to the physicomathematical sciences and molecular biology. While Aristotle was unaware of these sciences, he anticipated their category by his recognition of music, optics, and astronomy as physical sciences entailing measurement.

The practical point, as Simon points out, is that the philosopher of nature and the natural scientist often find themselves talking at cross purposes because they use the same term to refer to different things—the one having in mind the being of a thing, the other its measurable properties. Simon analyzes the different significances of the term "determinism" as used in physics and in the philosophy of man: an empiriometrical determinism versus an ontological determinism.

Simon congratulates Maritain for successfully distinguishing between the direction of the natural sciences and the philosophy of nature, a task hardly undertaken by contemporary scholastics before the pioneer landmark of the *Degrees of Knowledge.*—D.J.F.

ADDITIONAL RECOMMENDED READING

Evans, Joseph W., ed. *Jacques Maritain: The Man and His Achievement.* New York: Sheed & Ward, 1965. Another *festschrift* on the occasion of his eightieth birthday in 1962 by the then-head of the Jacques Maritain Center at Notre Dame University. Contains an essay on Maritain's growth as a Christian philosopher by his most famous student, the late professor Yves Simon.

Maritain, Jacques. *Challenges and Renewals.* Edited by Joseph W. Evans and Leo R. Ward. Notre Dame, Indiana: University of Notre Dame Press, 1966. These selected writings from a number of works introduce the reader to Maritain on ethics, aesthetics, politics, and philosophy of history, as well as metaphysics and epistemology.

_____ . *Existence and the Existent*. New York: Vintage Books, 1966. A translation of *Court Traité de l'existence et de l'existant*, written in Rome in 1947 when Maritain was France's Ambassador to the Vatican. In it Maritain took up, some fifteen years after the *Degrees of Knowledge*, issues such as our grasp of being and developed them against the background of existentialism which was then making a great impact on popular consciousness.

_____ . *A Preface to Metaphysics*. New York: Sheed & Ward, 1939. A translation of *Sept Leçons sur l'être et les premiers principes de la raison spéculative*, published in 1934, not long after the *Degrees of Knowledge*. In this work Maritain gives a fully detailed account of our coming to know such principles as those of identity and causality.

The Maritain Volume of the Thomist. Vol. V. Washington D.C.: *The Thomist*, January, 1943. This was a special edition of *The Thomist*, put together by a number of Maritain's friends and students on the occasion of his sixtieth birthday. It includes studies of various aspects of his philosophy, as well as a bibliography of his writings up to 1942.